Models for Practice With Immigrants and Refugees

To the people who inspire me:

My parents, my husband, my sister, my best friends Debbie and Janie, and the refugees who trusted me with their stories and became my teachers.

And to my daughter, Maya, who I hope to inspire.

—Aimee Hilado

To the students who have shared their personal histories and committed to dreams for the future, and to every client whose courage and resilience has moved them beyond the worst of despair, this volume honors you.

—Marta Lundy

Sara Miller McCune founded SAGE Publishing in 1965 to support the dissemination of usable knowledge and educate a global community. SAGE publishes more than 1000 journals and over 800 new books each year, spanning a wide range of subject areas. Our growing selection of library products includes archives, data, case studies and video. SAGE remains majority owned by our founder and after her lifetime will become owned by a charitable trust that secures the company's continued independence.

Los Angeles | London | New Delhi | Singapore | Washington DC | Melbourne

Models for Practice With Immigrants and Refugees

Collaboration, Cultural Awareness, and Integrative Theory

Edited by

Aimee Hilado
Northeastern Illinois University

Marta Lundy
Loyola University Chicago

Los Angeles | London | New Delhi
Singapore | Washington DC | Melbourne

FOR INFORMATION:

SAGE Publications, Inc.
2455 Teller Road
Thousand Oaks, California 91320
E-mail: order@sagepub.com

SAGE Publications Ltd.
1 Oliver's Yard
55 City Road
London, EC1Y 1SP
United Kingdom

SAGE Publications India Pvt. Ltd.
B 1/I 1 Mohan Cooperative Industrial Area
Mathura Road, New Delhi 110 044
India

SAGE Publications Asia-Pacific Pte. Ltd.
3 Church Street
#10–04 Samsung Hub
Singapore 049483

Acquisitions Editor: Nathan Davidson
Editorial Assistant: Alissa Nance
Production Editor: Andrew Olson
Copy Editor: Karin Rathert
Typesetter: Hurix Systems Pvt. Ltd.
Proofreader: Victoria Reed-Castro
Indexer: Mary Mortensen
Cover Designer: Scott Van Atta
Marketing Manager: Katherine Hepburn

Library of Congress Cataloging-in-Publication Data

Names: Hilado, Aimee, editor. | Lundy, Marta, editor.

Title: Models for practice with immigrants and refugees : collaboration, cultural awareness and integrative theory / [edited by] Marta Lundy, Loyola University Chicago, Aimee Hilado, Northeastern Illinois University, Chicago.

Description: Los Angeles : SAGE, [2018] | Includes bibliographical references and index.

Identifiers: LCCN 2016045550 | ISBN 9781483377148 (pbk. : alk. paper)

Subjects: LCSH: Social work with immigrants—United States. | Immigrants—Services for—United States. | Refugees—Services for—United States.

Classification: LCC HV4010 .M63 2018 | DDC 362.89/912530973—dc23
LC record available at https://lccn.loc.gov/2016045550

17 18 19 20 21 10 9 8 7 6 5 4 3 2 1

CONTENTS

PREFACE

OVERVIEW

The purpose of our edited book is to establish a foundational framework for mental health and community practitioners and other providers wanting insight into best practices and considerations when working with vulnerable and trauma-exposed immigrants and refugees. The framework is grounded in critical thinking, solidly lodged in a collaborative and empowering relationship that strives for client self-determination, and is strengthened by the ecological systems perspective that facilitates a thorough, culturally mandated and openly reflective questioning of the needs and wishes of the often trauma-exposed, transnational populations. The possible utility, adaptation, and application of Western theory and practice strategies are discussed in relation to culturally relevant and population-specific norms throughout the text. The text provides a number of case examples and conceptual/applied frameworks that employ integrative strategies to inform and empower immigrants and refugees. The book also includes broad discussions related to ethical best practices across international settings and when working with families and children, indigenous communities, organizations, and vulnerable and trauma-exposed immigrants and refugees across diverse service settings. In doing so, our goal is to define transnational practice (i.e., direct services and therapeutic interventions with culturally and linguistically diverse immigrant and refugee populations across global settings) using an integrative approach to applying theory and interventions with vulnerable and/or trauma-experienced populations. We believe this type of transnational work requires a collaborative approach that honors the self-determination of the client system (individual, couple, family, or community) at all times, with careful judgment of a respective country's laws, policies, and regulations that could impact that client system. And in this process, the professionals working with transnational groups should improve their skills in critical thinking, advocacy, and cultural competence in addressing the unique and diverse needs of new immigrant arrivals.

ORGANIZATION OF THE BOOK

The book is intended to guide readers through relevant practice theories with transnational populations by providing examples of integrative models in practice with case examples (when applicable) for working with individuals, communities, and within organization settings. We begin with three chapters in Unit I: "Defining Immigrant and Refugee Populations" to introduce the terminology related to working with immigrants and refugees (Chapter 1: "Defining the Immigrant and Refugee Populations," Chang-Muy).

This is followed by an examination of the stages of migration—for example, the pre-migration, migration, and post-migration experiences that directly influence immigrant and refugee adjustment and well-being upon arriving in a destination or host country (Chapter 2: "The Context of Migration: Pre-Arrival, Migration, and Resettlement Experiences," Allweiss & Hilado). Stabilizing health and mental health are important to the adjustment process for new immigrants; thus one chapter (Chapter 3: "Physical and Mental Health Stabilization: The Importance of Well-Being to the Adjustment of New Immigrants," Hilado & Allweiss) is dedicated to discussing the physical and mental health needs of immigrants and refugees and the resources available to stabilize overall well-being.

Unit II: "Theoretical Orientations and Reorientation" provides a foundation for understanding the role and utility of Western theory when working with transnational groups. This unit begins with a definition of what we mean by transnational practice and the necessary integration of Western theory and cultural beliefs to ensure work with immigrants and refugees is respectful and culturally sensitive (Chapter 4: "Transnational Practice as the Client's Process: Reorienting Practice With an Integrative Theoretical Approach to Practice With Immigrants and Refugees," Lundy & Hilado). An in-depth discussion of the construct of transnational practice sets the foundation for our examination of integrative theoretical frameworks and approaches to practice, which are provided in the book. The unit also provides a discussion of everyday discrimination that affects immigrant and refugee lives (Chapter 5: "The Perception and Experience of Everyday Discrimination Among U.S. Immigrants," C. Brettell) and specific perspectives to support effective engagement with non-Western populations (Chapter 6: "Postcolonial Feminist Social Work Perspective: Additional Considerations for Immigrant and Refugee Populations," Deepak). Together, this section explores the potential misuse of Western theory when working with non-Western individuals and communities, while providing a framework and examples of using Western theory in a manner that is collaborative, culturally sensitive, and flexible to the needs of the respective client system and circumstance.

Unit III: "Intervention Modalities Using an Integrative Approach" introduces the reader to specific models and approaches that, as the title suggests, embody an integrative approach to practice. There are six levels of client systems that examine integrative approaches used in interventions in each respective to system level. Chapter 7 explores practice with individuals ("Practice With Individuals," Hilado), Chapter 8 explores practice with couples and families ("Practice With Families," Lundy), Chapter 9 explores practice with groups ("Support and Psychoeducational Groups for Immigrant Women," Lundy, Rodgers, Sánchez, Egan, & Simon), and Chapter 10 explores community-based interventions ("Community Practice," Goodman, Letiecq, Vesely, Marquez, & Leyva). Organizational structures are also discussed in Chapter 11, with the introduction of a practice model embedding mental health interventions within an organizational context ("Organizational Practice," Hilado). Finally, this unit ends with a chapter dedicated to efforts to train a local workforce and volunteers to build interventions for trauma-exposed immigrants and refugees in international settings (Chapter 12: "Preparing a Local and Volunteer Workforce," Sokhem et al.). These six chapters provide examples and frameworks—both conceptual and applied—that are used to illustrate the value and usefulness of an integrative framework for practice.

Unit IV: "Practice Applications With Vulnerable and Trauma-Exposed Immigrants and Refugees," turns our attention to some of the most cruel realities of the immigrant and refugee experience by defining trauma and the complex nature of its effects on transnational individuals and communities. This section builds on the theoretical orientations and models in the preceding sections and goes one step further in preparing professionals to work with transnational populations. This section examines direct application of an integrative framework with trauma-exposed immigrants and refugees. The chapters are organized into specific target groups, starting with a focused discussion of practice with trauma-exposed immigrants and survivors of torture (Chapter 13: "Defining Trauma: Practice Applications With Vulnerable and Trauma-Exposed Immigrant Population and Survivors of Torture," Smith). This is followed by practice applications with violence-exposed women (Chapter 14: "Practice Applications With Women," Fong et al.), applications with LGBTQ identifying immigrants (Chapter 15: "Practice Applications With LGBTQ Immigrants and Refugees," Ramirez), and finally transnational practice with immigrant and refugee youth (Chapter 16: "Practice Applications With Immigrant and Refugee Youth," Benson, Abdi, & Ford-Paz). For each chapter, the authors provide definitions used for their target group followed by case scenarios, reflective questions, and discussion that highlight the need for an integrative approach to intervention and the benefits and challenges specific to each group.

The final component of the book is appropriately titled Unit V: "Consolidation." This section discusses the connection between theory, practice, and the future in global social work with transnational populations. The coeditors contribute the first chapter in this section, discussing the common denominators needed in working with all transnational populations irrespective of setting—specifically, the need to maintain critical consciousness and cultural humility in order to be most effective in the field (Chapter 17: "Maintaining Critical Consciousness, Collaborative Accompaniment, and Cultural Humility: The Common Denominators of Transnational Practice," Hilado & Lundy). The text ends with a chapter on the future of global social work and the implications for transnational practice and international social justice (Chapter 18: "Social Justice and Implications for the Field," Lundy & van Wormer).

Collectively, this text provides a foundation for thinking about what is involved in working with immigrants and refugees. In recognition of the potential disconnect between Western theoretical frameworks for practice when used with non-Western client populations, we offer a way of thinking and conceptualizing need using an integrative theoretical framework, defining this term and its application in the field. We introduce ways of conceptualizing practice with different client systems and direct applications with specific needs among subgroups of the immigrant and refugee population worldwide. And we provide suggestions for the future of practice with immigrants and refugees, particularly those who are vulnerable and trauma experienced, and areas of learning and study that are still required in the field of transnational service delivery. In addition, we provide an extensive glossary for clarification of terms and concepts and appendices of interesting and valuable handouts, national and international documents, and potential online resources. As such, this book offers a starting point for discussing transnational practice, knowing that our knowledge will need to expand and adapt with the changing populations that migrate across the globe daily.

PEDAGOGICAL APPROACH

The organization of five units and the chapters themselves flows from conceptual to concrete application. Each chapter is structured to provide elements of theory along with practice applications that we hope will stimulate critical thinking and self-reflection. For this to happen, each chapter begins with key terms and highlights within the chapter, followed by content and reflective questions related to the material presented. Some chapters also include critical thinking exercises that can be completed independently or as a group, case studies to further extend the dialogue, summative points, and a glossary (when applicable) to help connect the ideas to action. Our intention is to introduce critical concepts alongside case examples (when available), so that readers can better conceptualize innovative approaches to working with transnational populations and develop concrete skills for direct practice in the field.

APPLYING A SOCIAL WORK ORIENTATION ACROSS DISCIPLINE AND PRACTICE ENVIRONMENTS

The social work profession was founded in the era of immigrant-serving settlement houses, popularized by Jane Addams and the Hull House of Chicago in 1889. Historically, the focus of social work practice has been on service, activism, and social justice for the most vulnerable, underserved, and marginalized members of society. The social work profession is guided by a document titled the *Code of Ethics of the National Association of Social Workers* that outlines the values and mission of social workers in the field. Its preamble states

> The primary mission of the social work profession is to enhance human well-being and help meet the basic human needs of all people, with particular attention to the needs and empowerment of people who are vulnerable, oppressed, and living in poverty. A historic and defining feature of social work is the profession's focus on individual well-being in a social context and the well-being of society. Fundamental to social work is attention to the environmental forces that create, contribute to, and address problems in living. (*Code of Ethics of the National Association of Social Workers*, revised in 2008, socialworkers.org, n.d.)

Moreover, the mission of the social work profession is rooted in a core set of values that have guided social workers throughout the profession's history: service, social justice, dignity and worth of the person, importance of human relationships, integrity, and competence. These values are brought to life in the different activities social workers have used to engage people, communities, research, and policy development in the service of creating a more just society. Likewise, social workers have historically employed strength-based approaches that draw on natural abilities and capacity for growth to move individuals and societies forward.

The efforts of our first social workers were to aid European immigrants arriving in the United State during the early 19th century by entering their communities as "friendly home visitors." Social workers built relationships in the homes, using that natural context to deliver information and services in a culturally appropriate and responsive manner. Decades later, we see a multitude of helping professions and human service disciplines—medicine, public health, counseling, and so forth—recognizing the importance of cultural context and tailoring efforts to meet clients where they are—that is, understanding their circumstances, their belief systems/worldview, and their understanding of their own problems or needs. We see volunteers and stakeholders in the general populations embodying social work values, such as the promotion of social justice and valuing the dignity and worth of the person. Through individual and collective efforts, we see movements to create awareness and action in the campaigns to end human trafficking, to end discrimination based on sexual orientation or disability, to enhance women's rights in reproductive health areas, and the call to end female genital mutilation practices globally, to name a few. Moreover, we see individuals, families, and community members worldwide already playing the role of a social worker (albeit without that title or training), serving their communities through accessing resources and information, distributing goods to those in need, and advocating for systemic change to policies and practices that negatively impact others.

The efforts to enhance the well-being of all human beings does not and has never fallen solely on the shoulders of social workers; many diverse professions and invested people have made incredible contributions to address social problems (local and global) in their own respective settings. Some of the language and discussions in this book are intended for social workers—however, helping professionals across disciplines can glean from the same dialogue around best practices and important considerations for working with immigrant and refugee populations worldwide. In the same vein, some of the content is geared toward mental health and community health professionals, yet the understanding of mental health and its connectedness to all other areas of a person's ability to thrive and excel are equally valuable to non-mental health and community health providers. We believe there are lessons to be gained for all who intend to work with this focal population; professionals, paraprofessionals, volunteers, and invested members of our global society alike. And so we suggest the use of this text as a guide to culturally responsive transnational practice but call for professional discretion and critical thinking in the application of the concepts within diverse service settings.

SUMMARY

Our text highlights the intersections of theory, practice, and culture when working with transnational populations. It is intended to be useful across professional credentials at all levels, from the generalist entry-level professional to those with advanced clinical certifications or degrees. The text can also supplement other courses or trainings focused on immigrant and refugee populations or those specific to migrant mental health. Irrespective of one's professional role, there is a critical need to examine supportive interventions that are based in sound theoretical frameworks and are research informed. Our text recognizes the value of adapted and revised Western theory when working with transnational populations, while also realizing its limitations. At the same time, the text challenges professionals to apply critical thinking when applying theories to practice with ethnically diverse groups. We emphasize the importance of cultural relevance and integrative approaches that utilize the most effective and relevant theoretical elements to promote client self-determination, and establish a collaborative and empowering relationship where providers "walk with" their clients toward positive outcomes. Theory application cannot be conceptual alone, thus the practice models and case examples in the text are included to help solidify learning and professional development. In sum, our book hopes to revisit critical theories, introduce overarching collaborative approaches to theory application with transnational groups, and provide concrete strategies for sensitive and culturally relevant engagement.

ACKNOWLEDGMENTS

It is estimated that one in every 122 individuals in the world is a refugee, internally displaced, or seeking asylum. (UN High Commissioner for Refugees, 2015)

The editors want to acknowledge and gratefully thank every author who contributed chapters to this edition and the students who contributed behind the scenes in organizing the materials. Our contributors are in practice settings and academic programs across the country, and our student supports have been undergraduate and graduate social work students at Northeastern Illinois University and Loyola University Chicago, School of Social Work. We appreciate all your contributions to this book and your efforts to support forcibly displaced populations worldwide.

PUBLISHER'S ACKNOWLEDGMENTS

SAGE gratefully acknowledges the contributions of the following reviewers:

Ann Alvarez, Wayne State University

David Androff, Arizona State University

Susan D. Barnes, Western New Mexico University

Jayshree S. Jani, University of Maryland, Baltimore County

Njeri Kagotho, Ohio State University

Ericka Kimball, Augsburg College

Maura Nsonwu, North Carolina Agricultural and Technical State University

Hadidja Nyiransekuye, University of North Texas

Cathryne L. Schmitz, University of North Carolina Greensboro

Uma Segal, University of Missouri—St. Louis

Holly C. Sienkiewicz, Center for New North Carolinians at the University of North Carolina at Greensboro

Holly Sienkiewicz, University of North Carolina at Greensboro

Jennifer Simmelink McCleary, Tulane University School of Social Work

Patti West-Okiri, Western New Mexico University

ABOUT THE EDITORS

Aimee Hilado, PhD, LCSW, is an assistant professor of social work at Northeastern Illinois University, where she serves as the curriculum specialist for the human behavior and the social environment (HBSE) curriculum in the bachelor's program. In this role, she oversees the HBSE two-course sequence and its instructors to ensure students obtain a foundational understanding of direct practice theories and the bi-directional relationship between person and environment, while infusing content on integrative theory, cultural humility, and trauma-informed approaches to understanding human behavior and motivation. She also teaches the entry-level and advanced courses on Social Work Practice with Immigrants and Refugees, preparing generalist social workers to work with diverse immigrant and refugee populations in the field.

Dr. Hilado is also the founding manager of RefugeeOne's Wellness Program, a mental health program for immigrant and refugee children and adults in one of the largest refugee resettlement agencies in Illinois. Dr. Hilado designed and implemented the program, including implementation of the *cultural mergence model*, a practice framework she created to guide mental health service delivery in the program. The program opened its doors for service in June 2011, and in five years of service, the Wellness Program has provided therapy services to over 450 youth and adult clients, screened over 1,500 refugee adult arrivals for mental health needs, and provided over 80 education workshops on health and mental health topics. She continues to oversee operations and conducts ongoing program evaluations to inform best practices in the area of refugee mental health, while coordinating other immigrant and refugee mental health providers through her work as a co-founder of the Illinois Refugee Mental Health Task Force.

Additionally, Dr. Hilado has been recognized at national and statewide conferences, including ZERO TO THREE and the Council on Social Work Education, for her practice and research efforts around refugee mental health and early intervention with vulnerable immigrant children and their families. She also remains active in a number of professional associations and advocacy groups as a founding member of the North American Society of Refugee Health Care Providers (NASRHCP) and a member of the Council on Social Work Education (CSWE), the National Association for Social Workers (NASW), the Illinois Association for Infant Mental Health (ILAIMH), the Illinois Children's Trauma Coalition (ICTC), and the Illinois Infant Practice Roundtable, advocating for supportive services to immigrant and refugee populations. Moreover, Dr. Hilado continues to serve as an expert consultant on state criminal cases and consults in national and state forums on areas related to trauma and refugee mental health.

She is a licensed clinical social worker with a Doctor of Philosophy degree in Social Work, with Distinction, and a master of social work degree from Loyola University Chicago. She also obtained a master of science degree in applied child development, specializing in infant studies, from Erikson Institute. Together, her teaching, research, and practice interests continue to be informed by the lessons she learns in the classroom and in the field working with trauma-exposed new immigrants over the past ten years. Dr. Hilado lives in Chicago, Illinois, with her husband and their rambunctious toddler.

Marta Lundy, PhD, LCSW, professor, at the School of Social Work, Loyola University Chicago. Dr. Lundy initially began her academic career at Jane Addams College of Social Work, University of Illinois, Chicago, from 1987 through 1994, and came to Loyola in July 1994, where she has been a teacher, researcher, and clinician for over 20 years. Dr. Lundy teaches in both the masters and doctoral programs, in the areas of clinical practice, HBSE, and teaching in the academy.

Dr. Lundy's research interests parallel and inform her teaching—that is, she has conducted research in domestic and interpersonal violence while she also developed and taught the course in Social Work Practice with Family Violence. Dr. Lundy is one of two faculty who have developed and teach in the Migration Sub-Specialization Program, a unique program at Loyola University and in social work education. Five different courses are offered in conjunction with the specialization, although only three are required to achieve the certificate. Dr. Lundy teaches the Social Work Practice with Immigrants & Refugees, as well as Social Work Practice with Families: Focus on the Mexican Family. The family course is taught every summer for two weeks in Mexico City, as part of a two-course, co-taught immersion course for students with her colleague in the Migration Sub-Specialization. Dr. Lundy also co-teaches the HBSE course on diversity, in Nogales, Sonora, Mexico, and Nogales, Arizona, every year over spring break, as part of an immersion course for students to experience the United States Mexico border. Dr. Lundy is a strong advocate for an integrative model of social work practice with immigrants and refugees. She has written and teaches the relevance of self-awareness of privilege, clarity of focus and client self-determination, and flexibility, solidarity, and humility when using Western theory with individuals, families, and groups from different cultures and areas of the world.

Dr. Lundy also conducts research with support/self-help groups for Latina women immigrants. New groups are offered every semester, with Dr. Lundy as the supervisor for the students who facilitate the groups. The facilitators are fluent in Spanish—that is, Spanish is their native language—and knowledgeable about the stages of migration, group work in general, and women's groups specifically. Dr. Lundy has been lead author in the revised and translated version of the *Manual for Women's Emotional Health*. Based on the original work written and conducted in Mexico City, with Jesuit Migrant Services, the original has been used extensively in Mexico with Mexican women. The revised and adapted instructional text for psychoeducational self-help is now being used with Mexican women immigrants in a host country, primarily in the Chicago area. Preliminary results are available in the chapter in the text and in an article, in press.

Dr. Lundy is a licensed clinical social worker and has maintained her own practice in the Chicago area since 1987, where she works with survivors of trauma and other vulnerable groups.

CONTRIBUTING AUTHORS

Saidi M. Abdi, LCSW, is a Licensed Clinical Social Worker and a PhD Candidate at Boston University. She holds another Masters degree in Communications. She has extensive experience working with refugee and immigrant populations. She specializes in providing trauma informed care to refugee and immigrant youth and families. She has specific expertise in patient/community engagement, cultural humility and the use of interpreters and cultural brokers to reduce health disparities and enhance refugee access to mental health services. Ms. Abdi is fluent in multiple languages. As of member of the leadership team at the Boston Children's Hospital Refugee Trauma and Resilience Center (BCHRTRC), Ms. Abdi has co-developed a manual for school-based groups focusing on acculturative stress experienced by young refugees, worked with team members to develop the Refugee Services Toolkit, implemented Trauma Systems Therapy for Refugees in Boston Public Schools, and provided training and consultation to providers in multiple sites in the US and abroad. She has supported sites nationwide that have adapted and implemented Trauma Systems Therapy for Refugees and participated in numerous refugee research and evaluation projects. Ms. Abdi is currently an investigator in the largest longitudinal research project undertaken to understand the experiences of Somali refugee youth in North America. In addition, in her current role as the Associate Director for Community Relations, Ms. Abdi takes a leadership role in the Refugee Trauma and Resilience Center's work with partners around community engagement and integration of cultural and clinical methods to enhance community resilience and system responsiveness to the needs of vulnerable populations.

Samantha Allweiss, AM, LSW, is a social worker/therapist at RefugeeOne, the largest refugee resettlement agency in Chicago. She graduated from The University of Chicago's School of Social Service and Administration, with an emphasis on international social work in a clinical setting, after receiving her undergraduate degree in Social Welfare and Gender and Women's Studies from the University of Wisconsin, Madison. Samantha provides individual and group therapy services to trauma-exposed populations and assists with the daily administrative tasks for the mental health program. She has worked internationally, studying and interning at the Tata School of Social Sciences in Mumbai, India, and participating in community empowerment programs through Amigos De Las Americas in Michoacán, Mexico. Her area of focus is culturally sensitive clinical work with refugee and immigrant populations, and she is dedicated to utilizing an integrative approach based on best-practice strategies in the field.

Molly A. Benson, PhD, is a licensed clinical psychologist, an instructor of psychology at Harvard Medical School (HMS), a staff psychologist and assistant in psychology in the Department of Psychiatry at Boston Children's Hospital (BCH), and the associate director of refugee treatment and services at the Refugee Trauma and Resilience Center (RTRC) at BCH. Dr. Benson has worked in the field of child and adolescent refugee mental health for over a decade. She has extensive training and experience in providing evidence-based treatment to children and adolescents and applying these interventions in real-world settings. Her specific expertise is in adapting interventions for refugee children and families. In her current role, she provides oversight and supervision to projects focused on the implementation and dissemination of Trauma Systems Therapy for Refugees (TST-R) and the development of refugee-focused resources for the National Child Traumatic Network. She frequently provides training and consultation to providers on topics related to intervention with refugee children and families and trauma-informed care. She was a member of the *APA Task Force on the Psychosocial Effects of War on Children and Families Who Are Refugees from Armed Conflict Living in the United States* and a contributor to the Refugee Health Technical Assistance Center (RHTAC). For several years, she provided clinical services and supervision through the Psychosocial Treatment Program at BCH and helped refugees and youth seeking asylum. She currently maintains a small private practice. Dr. Benson completed her PhD in clinical psychology (child specialty) at the University of Vermont, completed her clinical internship at BCH, and completed a postdoctoral fellowship at Boston Medical Center/Boston Consortium.

Caroline Brettell, PhD, is University Distinguished Professor of Anthropology and Ruth Collins Altshuler Director of the Dedman College Interdisciplinary Institute at Southern Methodist University. She has a BA degree from Yale University and a PhD degree from Brown University. She has spent her career studying the immigrant populations in Europe, Canada, and the United States (most recently in the DFW area). Her particular and most current interests are in the gendered aspects of migration, issues of identity and citizenship, and the relationship between immigrants and cities. In addition to numerous journal articles and book chapters she is the author, co-author, or editor/coeditor of 17 books. Her most recent books are *Anthropological Conversations: Talking Culture Across Disciplines* (2015); *Following Father Chiniquy: Immigration, Religious Schism and Social Change in Nineteenth Century Illinois* (2015); and *Civic Engagements: The Citizenship Practices of Indian and Vietnamese Immigrants* (co-authored with Deborah Reed-Danahay, 2012). With political scientist James F. Hollifield she has coedited a book that is now in third edition titled *Migration Theory: Talking Across Disciplines*. At SMU, Brettell has served as director of the Women and Gender Studies Program (1989–1994); chair of the Department of Anthropology at SMU (1994–2004); dean-ad-interim of Dedman College (2006–2008); and as president of the faculty senate (2001–2002). Nationally she has served as president of the Society for the Anthropology of Europe (1996–1998) and president of the Social Science History Association (2000–2001).

Kristin Buller, LCSW, received her masters in social work from University of Chicago School of Social Service Administration, with a concentration in clinical social work focused on trauma and international social work. She co-chaired the International Social Welfare group and received a human rights award to go Cambodia. After her initial internship at the Cambodian Women's Crisis Center, Kristin worked as a social work advisor for Social Services of Cambodia, a program evaluation and research consultant for a number of local and international organizations, and as a trainer for local organizational staff around issues of social work skills, self-care, and gender issues. After four years in Cambodia, Kristin returned to Chicago, where she works at a community counseling center as well as her private practice, where she provides individual and couples therapy and specializes in veterinary social work support to pet owners and veterinary and training professionals. E-mail: kristinbuller.lcsw@gmail.com

Fernando Chang-Muy, JD, is the Thomas O'Boyle Lecturer at the University of Pennsylvania School of Law where he teaches refugee law. He also teaches courses on nonprofit management and immigration for social workers at Penn's Graduate School of Social Policy and Practice. In addition to teaching, he combines his experience in academia and operations, as principal and founder of Solutions International, providing independent management consulting, facilitation and training to philanthropic institutions, nonprofit organizations, and government entities. His areas of expertise include designing and facilitating large group, task-focused strategic planning, board governance, staff internal communications and performance, and resource development. He has served as legal officer with both the Office of the UN High Commissioner for Refugees (UNHCR) and the UN World Health Organization (WHO), AIDS Program. Before joining the UN, he was a staff attorney at Community Legal Services in Philadelphia serving as director of the Southeast Asian Refugee Project, providing free legal aid to low-income people in Philadelphia. He is also past founding director of the Liberty Center for Survivors of Torture, a project of Lutheran Children and Family Services, established to serve newcomers fleeing human rights violations. He serves on the boards of local public interest organizations, government, and foundations, including the board of the Wells Fargo Regional Foundation. In 2008, Philadelphia Mayor Nutter appointed him as a commissioner to the Philadelphia Commission on Human Relations. He is former board member of the Delaware Valley Grantmakers, The Philadelphia Award, and the Southeast Asian Mutual Assistance Coalition. He is author of numerous articles on diverse topics dealing with immigration and refugees, public health and management, and is coeditor of the text *Social Work with Immigrants and Refugees* (NY: Springer Publication, 2008). He is a graduate of Loyola, Georgetown, Antioch, and Harvard Law School's Program on Negotiation. He is a 2011 recipient of the Penn Law Public Interest Supervisor/Advisor of the Year Award honoring outstanding project supervisors and advisors.

Prak Chankroesna is a graduate of the Royal University of Phnom Penh, majoring in Psychology and is a senior social worker and trainer at First Step Cambodia (FSC), a local NGO that provides services to children and families affected by sexual violence and abuse. Chankroesna is a passionate advocate for children and also leads FSC's strategy relating to disability and child protection mainstreaming. In 2015, she presented a keynote workshop at the South-South Institute on sexual violence against men and boys, the very first conference in South East Asia to focus on this area of need.

Yung Chanthao is a senior social worker–trainer at First Step Cambodia, where he has worked for five years. He graduated in sociology at The Royal University of Phnom Penh in 1998. He has worked for a number of NGOs in Cambodia, including Hagar International, as a counselor for children and women; Pour un Sourire d'Enfant

(PSE), as a social worker; and The Children's Fund, as a trainer. In the last five years, he has worked at FSC with boys, young men, caregivers, and families affected by sexual abuse and with problematic and harmful sexual behaviors. Chanthao is a passionate advocate for social justice.

Anne C. Deepak, PhD, LMSW, is an associate professor at Monmouth University School of Social Work. She teaches in the International and Community Development concentration and advanced core courses in human rights and social justice. She has been an appointed member of the Council on Social Work Education's Council on the Role and Status on Women in Social Work Education since 2013. Her scholarship and research examines globalization and international partnerships, the application of postcolonial feminist theory to global social problems, the impact of Islamophobia on social work practice, and the use of popular culture and technology in the delivery of antiracism content in social work education. In 2011, she was awarded Feminist Scholarship Award by the Council on the Role and Status of Women in Social Work Education for her paper, "Sustainability and Population Growth in the Context of Globalization: A Postcolonial Feminist Social Work Perspective." In 2015, she was awarded the *Journal of Social Work Education's* Best Qualitative Manuscript Vol. 50, for an article she co-authored with Mary Tijerina titled "Mexican American Social Workers' Perceptions of Doctoral Education and Academia."

Andrew Egan, MSW, is a recent graduate of Loyola University Chicago, where he received his master of social work degree, specializing in children and families and sub-specializing in immigration and international social work. Egan also holds a bachelor's degree of political science and a bachelor's degree in public administration. Egan is a former AmeriCorps VISTA volunteer and Peace Corps volunteer, where he served in Panama. Egan previously interned for the United States Senate and House of Representatives as an undergrad and interned with youth at-risk in both Chicago and in Chiapas, Mexico, as a graduate student. Egan is especially interested in looking at community interventions for youth at-risk to help integrate them into the formal economy.

Rowena Fong, EdD, MSW, the Ruby Lee Piester Centennial Professor in Services to Children and Families in the School of Social Work at the University of Texas at Austin, is a fellow of the American Academy of Social Work and Social Welfare (AASWSW) and founding co-chair of the Grand Challenges for Social Work Initiative (GCSWI). She has served nationally as a past president of the Society for Social Work and Research (2009–2013) and is an inaugural fellow of SSWR. Dr. Fong received her BA in Chinese studies and psychology from Wellesley College, her MSW in children and families from UC Berkeley, and her EdD in human development from Harvard University. Dr. Fong's areas of research are international adoptions from China, victims of human trafficking, racial disproportionality in public child welfare, and immigrant and refugee children and families.

She has over 100 publications, including 10 books: Dettlaff, A., & Fong, R. (Eds.). (2016). *Immigrant and refugee children and families: Culturally responsive practice.* New York: Columbia University Press; Fong, R., & McRoy, R. (Eds.). (2016).

Transracial and intercountry adoption practices and policies: A resource for educators and clinicians. New York: Columbia University Press; Fong, R., Dettlaff, J. J., & Rodriguez, C. (2015). *Eliminating racial disproportionality and disparities: Multi systems culturally competent approaches.* New York: Columbia University Press; Dettlaff, A., & Fong, R. (Eds.). (2012). *Child welfare practice with immigrant children and families.* New York: Taylor & Francis Books; Franklin, C., & Fong, R. (2011). *The church leader's counseling resource book: A guide to mental health and social problems.* New York: Oxford University Press; Fong, R., McRoy, R., & Ortiz Hendricks, C. (Eds.). (2006). *Intersecting child welfare, substance abuse, and family violence: Culturally competent approaches.* Washington, DC: Council on Social Work Education; Fong, R. (Ed.). (2004). *Culturally competent practice with immigrant and refugee children and families.* New York: Guilford Press; Smith, M., & Fong, R. (2004). *Children of neglect: When no one cares.* New York: Brunner-Routledge Press; Fong, R., & Furuto, S. (Eds.). (2001). *Culturally competent social work practice: Skills, interventions and evaluation.* Boston, MA: Allyn & Bacon; and Freeman, E., Franklin, C., Fong, R., Shaffer, G., & Timberlake, E. (Eds.). (1998). *Multisystem skills and interventions in school social work practice.* Washington, DC: NASW Press.

Rebecca E. Ford-Paz, PhD, is an assistant professor at Northwestern University Feinberg School of Medicine, Department of Psychiatry and Behavioral Sciences, the coordinating psychologist of the Mood & Anxiety Program, and a child clinical psychologist in the Child Center for Childhood Resilience at the Ann & Robert H. Lurie Children's Hospital of Chicago. She has long-standing clinical and research interests in the reduction of mental health disparities for underserved, ethnic minority youth and culturally responsive implementation of evidence-based treatments in real-world settings. As a bilingual (Spanish-speaking) clinician, she has experience conducting trauma evaluations for detained unaccompanied minors from Central America and providing a variety of evidence-based trauma interventions for refugee and immigrant youth, including trauma systems therapy, cognitive processing therapy, and trauma-focused cognitive behavioral therapy. She is a founding co-chair of the Illinois Childhood Trauma Coalition's Ad-Hoc Committee on Refugee and Immigrant Children and Trauma. She also is the academic co-chair of the Alliance for Research in Chicagoland Communities, a program at Northwestern University that supports community-based participatory research. Dr. Ford-Paz received her PhD in clinical psychology (child subspecialty) from DePaul University, completed her clinical internship at the Boston Consortium (Boston Medical Center & Boston VA), and completed her clinical research postdoctoral fellowship in child psychopathology at Brown Medical School.

Rachael D. Goodman, PhD, LPC, is an associate professor in the Counseling and Development Program at George Mason University. Dr. Goodman's scholarship focuses on trauma counseling from an ecosystemic, social justice-focused lens. She is interested in the ways in which marginalized individuals, families, and communities are impacted by ecosystemic traumas, such as discrimination, institutionalized oppression, and intergenerational trauma. Her work focuses on understanding the unique ways in which marginalized communities persist within difficult and unjust conditions and how practitioners can develop interventions that create resilience-fostering environments. Along with her university and community partners, Dr. Goodman utilizes community based participatory research (CBPR) methods to critically co-investigate the needs of underserved communities, while also developing collaborative, culturally responsive interventions. Her recent projects focus on immigrant women and families, including undocumented Central American immigrants and refugees/asylees in the D.C.-area. Dr. Goodman's previous community-engaged work has included leading counseling outreach projects for communities experiencing acute and/or ongoing traumas and social injustice, including the Pine Ridge Indian Reservation, post-Katrina New Orleans, and South Africa. She served as the editor for a special issue on trauma counseling and interventions for the *Journal of Mental Health Counseling* and was the coeditor and author of the book *Decolonizing "Multicultural" Counseling Through Social Justice* (Springer, 2014). She also conducts research on how mindfulness practices may be used for trauma counseling as well as counselor training that can facilitate the development of empathy and reduction in prejudice and bias.

Laurie Cook Heffron, PhD, MSW, is an assistant professor of social work in the School of Behavioral and Social Sciences at St. Edward's University in Austin, Texas. She has interest and expertise in the areas of forced migration, domestic and sexual violence, and human trafficking, and her research explores the experiences of and relationships between violence against women and migration.

As former associate director for research at the University of Texas at Austin's Institute on Domestic Violence and Sexual Assault (IDVSA), she has contributed to multiple research projects since 2001, including a program evaluation for services to victims of human trafficking, a statewide domestic violence prevalence study, program evaluation of Texas' Non-Report Sexual Assault Forensic Exam Program, and a national pilot program to develop professional and organizational resiliency among child welfare workers. Laurie also worked with IDVSA in completing a study of resettlement experiences among Congolese refugee women and a statewide evaluation on human trafficking and existing laws and social services in collaboration with community organizations and governmental agencies.

Laurie has both direct social work practice and research experience with a variety of immigrant communities, including refugees, survivors of human trafficking, and asylees. Previously, she served as program coordinator for Green Leaf Refugee Services, providing intensive health and emotional health case management services to refugees, victims of trafficking, asylees, and other immigrants in Central Texas. Currently, she provides assessments and serves as an expert witness in immigration cases of women and children seeking T visas, U visas, and asylum based on domestic violence.

Laurie earned a BS in linguistics at Georgetown University and a master of social work (MSW) from The University of Texas at Austin. As a Donald D. Harrington Fellow at The University of Texas at Austin, Dr. Cook Heffron completed her doctoral degree in August 2015. Her dissertation research was titled, "*Salía de uno y me metí en otro:*" *A Grounded Theory Approach to Understanding the Violence-Migration Nexus Among Central American Women in the United States.*

Alstair Hilton, originally from the United Kingdom, has lived and worked in Cambodia since 2005. He has a background in social and community work for over

30 years, most of which has been related to working with children, young people, and adults affected by sexual abuse and violence. He was a founder member of First Step (Leicester, UK) in 1997 and in 2007 led a team of local researchers that carried out and published the very first in-depth study of the sexual abuse of boys and men in Cambodia, *I Thought It Could Never Happen to Boys*, which ultimately led to the launch of First Step Cambodia in 2010. Alastair is a passionate advocate and activist and in 2013, alongside the Refugee Law Project (Uganda) and MSSAT (New Zealand), co-founded and took part in the very first South-South Institute on Sexual Violence Against Men and Boys (SSI) in Kampala and co-hosted the SSI in Phnom Penh, Cambodia, in May 2015.

Bethany Letiecq, PhD, is an associate professor and the director of the Human Development and Family Science program—a joint academic program of the College of Education and Human Development and the College of Humanities and Social Sciences. She received her PhD in health education/family studies and her MS in family and community development from the University of Maryland, College Park. Dr. Letiecq employs community-based, participatory, and action research approaches to conduct research in partnership with families to promote culturally responsive and strengths-based interventions. She is keenly interested in how social policies facilitate or hinder family functioning and health across all families. Currently, she is working with immigrant, refugee, and asylee women to delineate pathways to resilience and well-being. Previously, she worked in partnership with Mexican migrants settling in new, nontraditional receiving sites in the Rocky Mountain West to build *Salud y Comunidad—Latinos en Montana*, a community-based organization focused on researching and promoting migrant family health, well-being, and justice. With her community partners, she also co-founded the Montana Immigrant Justice Alliance (MIJA.org), a statewide nonprofit working for immigrant rights. Dr. Letiecq teaches courses on family law and public policy; race, class, gender, and family diversity; and relationships and family systems. She serves as an associate editor for the *Journal of Family Issues*, is a member of the *Family Relations* editorial board, and has published her research in such professional outlets as *Family Relations, Fathering, Journal of Family Issues, Journal of Intergenerational Relationships, Journal of Immigrant and Minority Health*, and *Health Education and Behavior*. She is affiliated with the National Council on Family Relations (currently serving as chair of the Family Policy Section), the American Sociological Association, and the American Public Health Association.

Krishna J. Leyva was born and raised in San Juan, Puerto Rico. She completed a bachelor degree in criminal justice at the Interamerican University of Puerto Rico and a master in social work at the University of Southern California. Krishna has worked over 15 years with low-income immigrant youth and families in Northern Virginia. She was the founding and award-winning director of an "exemplary" tutoring and mentoring program for immigrant high school students. She is currently working as the Family and Community Engagement Manager for Alexandria City Public Schools. Krishna was appointed to the Board of Psychology and served as a citizen's member for five years. In addition to her work with immigrant families, she is an avid community advocate and has served as an advisory member of many boards and committees. Her passion is to engage families in their children's education and to improve the lives of immigrant families. Her work focus is advocacy, family engagement, and equality.

Colleen Lundy, MSW, PhD, is a social work Professor Emeritus at Carleton University, Ottawa, Canada. She is the North American representative on the IFSW Human Rights Commission. She is a co-author (with Therese Jennissen) of *One Hundred Years of Social Work: A History of the Profession in English Canada 1900–2000* (Waterloo: Wilfrid Laurier Press, 2011), the first complete history of social work in Canada. The book is based on extensive archival work and secondary literature and is informed by feminist theory and political economy. A second edition of her authored book, *Social Work, Human Rights and Social Justice: A Structural Approach to Practice* (Toronto: University of Toronto Press, 2011) makes an important contribution to the understanding of structural social work and a social justice/human rights perspective.

She has published on the impact of economic transformation on women in Cuba and Russia and was a component leader on a five-year funded partnership between Carleton University and the University of Havana.

Marlene Marquez completed her bachelor degree in social work in 2015 from George Mason University. She has worked as community organizer and research assistant on community-based participatory research with undocumented immigrant families in the DC-metro region. She is currently working with The Child and Family Network Centers as a family support worker. Her work and interests focus on immigrant families and children. In particular, she has a great interest in family reunification, since she experienced this herself. In the future, she would like to work with immigrant families on the issue of reunification and help to address the many ways in which separation and reunification affect children and parents. She is an incoming student in the master program in Social Work at GMU.

Milka Ramirez, PhD, MSW, received her PhD in philosophy of social work from the University of Illinois, Chicago-Jane Addams College of social work. Her areas of research include social work practice and lesbian, gay, bisexual, transgender, and queer communities. Dr. Ramirez is an assistant professor at Northeastern Illinois University, Chicago, where she teaches in the social work program, women and gender studies program, and Latino and Latin American studies program. Dr. Ramirez has conducted research exploring homophobia and school social work practice; sexual victimization of older lesbian, gay, and bisexual women of color; and intimate partner violence among LGBTQ populations and has over 10 years of practice experience with diverse populations and settings.

Patrick Rodgers, MSW, earned his master of social work from Loyola University Chicago, focusing on mental health and migration studies. He grew up in the Chicagoland area but has traveled extensively. He spent a year living abroad in Guadalajara, Mexico, teaching English, where he gained an excellent command of the Spanish language. His first field placement was in Chiapas, Mexico, in 2014 at K'inal Antsetik and Natik, two organizations that work directly with indigenous youth and women. At these two sites, he co-facilitated with the women a women's self-help group, using concepts of solidarity, accompaniment, empowerment, and affirmation as the principle philosophy for the group model. The model included 19 themes on empowering women's self-esteem and sense of self. This group was highly successful, with the co-facilitators continuing the groups after Patrick left his field sites. Patrick's second field placement was at Catholic Charities Employee Assistance program, where he worked directly with immigrant populations. He is currently working at Chicago House Social Services Agency, as he continues his advocacy work with immigrant and LGBTQ communities, utilizing his experience learning about migration from the perspectives of Mexicans and other Latinos in both countries.

Celeste N. Sánchez, MSW, relocated to the United States after several years of direct service work with children and adolescents in Central America. She graduated with an MSW at Loyola University Chicago with a sub-specialization in migration studies. In her second year of studies, she received the highly prestigious President's Medallion for distinction as a student. Her work abroad and with unaccompanied minors in the U.S. has prompted her interests in resiliency and migration. After completing her degree she hopes to continue working with underserved populations in Latin America.

Shirley R. Simon, ACSW, LCSW, is Associate Professor, School of Social Work, Loyola University Chicago. She has been a social work educator for over thirty-five years, has published on group work education, practice and history, and has facilitated over one hundred fifty student and alumni presentations at professional association conferences. She serves as book review editor for North America for the international journal, *Groupwork*, and is active in the International Association for Social Work with Groups (IASWG), both locally and internationally. She has provided group work training for social work agency staff and field instructors. Research and scholarship interests include group work education in MSW programs, hybrid-online group work instruction, curricular strategies for connecting students and professional associations, and social work dissertations on group work. Professor Simon can be contacted at ssimon@luc.edu.

Hawthorne E. Smith, PhD, is a licensed psychologist and clinical director of the Bellevue/NYU Program for Survivors of Torture. He is also an assistant clinical professor at the NYU School of Medicine in the Department of Psychiatry. Dr. Smith received his doctorate in counseling psychology (with distinction) from Teachers College, Columbia University. Dr. Smith had previously earned a bachelor of science in foreign service from the Georgetown University School of Foreign Service, an advanced certificate in African studies from Cheikh Anta Diop University in Dakar, Senegal, as well as a masters in international affairs from the Columbia University School of International and Public Affairs. Among his clinical duties, Dr. Smith has facilitated a support group for French-speaking African survivors of torture for the past 18 years. He also speaks extensively at professional conferences and seminars on providing clinical services for survivors of sociopolitical violence and enhancing cross-cultural clinical skills among therapeutic service providers. Dr. Smith has been recognized for his work with such awards as the Robin Hood Foundation's Hero Award; the Frantz Fanon Award from the Postgraduate Center for Mental Health; the

W.E.B. DuBois Award from the International Youth Leadership Institute; the Distinguished Alumni—Early Career Award from Teachers College; the Man of Distinction Award from the National Association of Health Service Executives; the Union Square Award for Community Advocacy from the Fund for the City of New York; and a Humanitarian Award from the Consulate General of the Republic of Haiti. Dr. Smith is also a professional musician (saxophonist and vocalist) with national and international experience.

Nong Socheat currently works for First Step Cambodia as senior social worker and trainer. Following her graduation with a degree in psychology from the Royal University of Phnom Penh in 2006, she worked for several organizations in Cambodia providing psychosocial services and carrying out research. Socheat was also a member of the team that carried out the very first in-depth research to explore the sexual abuse of boys and young men in Cambodia, *I Thought It Could Never Happen to Boys*, published in 2008. During her eleven years as a practitioner she has worked with young people and their families, people affected by HIV & AIDS, drug users, street living children and families, children with harmful sexual behaviors, and with boys and young men who have experienced abuse. Socheat is currently leading FSC's 'Children First' Project, which is focused on developing support for children with harmful sexual behaviors.

Kong Sokhem survived the genocidal Khmer Rouge regime of the 1970s and after studying in Vietnam and Bulgaria, supported the reconstruction of Cambodia by working in the Department of Social Affairs. She has subsequently worked for a number of local NGOs for almost twenty years, providing services for victims of trauma and abuse and their families as well as developing and providing innovative training for government and NGO staff. Sokhem was also a member of the team that carried out the first ever study to focus on the sexual abuse and exploitation of boys in Cambodia—*I Thought It Could Never Happen to Boys* (2008)—and is now the social work manager of First Step Cambodia, a unique NGO providing specialist services to boys and young men affected by sexual violence and abuse.

Im Sreytha is a senior social worker and trainer at First Step Cambodia and a psychology graduate from the Royal University of Phnom Penh. Sreytha has worked for a number of NGOs in Cambodia, including Social Services of Cambodia (SSC), and also as a researcher for Domrei Research Consultancy. She has worked with women and girls experiencing sexual and domestic violence and for the last five years, with boys and young men at FSC. Sreytha is also the co-author of the "Some Boys Say" information, assessment, and advocacy tool kit, the very first Khmer language resource of its kind.

Katherine van Wormer, MSSW, PhD, is professor of social work at the University of Northern Iowa. She has a PhD in sociology from the University of Georgia and has taught and practiced social work in Northern Ireland and Norway. She is the author or co-author of over 20 books, including most recently two volumes of *Human Behavior and the Social Environment*, Micro and Macro Levels (3rd ed., in press, Oxford University Press), *Addiction Treatment: A Strengths Perspective* (3rd ed., 2012, Cengage), *Restorative Justice Today* (SAGE, 2013), and *Women and the Criminal Justice System*

(4th ed., 2014, Pearson). The following 2012 book from LSU Press has recently been reissued in paperback: *The Maid Narratives: Black Domestics and White Families in the Jim Crow South*.

Colleen Vesely, PhD, is an assistant professor of early childhood education and human development and family science in the College of Education and Human Development at George Mason University in Fairfax, Virginia. Her work focuses on the experiences of diverse, marginalized young children and their families. Dr. Vesely's most recent work utilizes a community-based participatory research (CBPR) approach to understand low-income immigrant and refugee families' experiences of trauma and resilience and how these experiences shape families' navigation and negotiation of parenthood, including experiences with the child care system, in the United States. A second area of work, funded by the Center for the Advancement of Well-being at George Mason University, is focused on early childhood education teachers' ecosystemic well-being and how this shapes teachers' interactions with young children. Dr. Vesely's work is published in *Early Childhood Research Quarterly*, *Early Education & Development*, *Educational Psychology Review*, *Journal of Family and Economic Issues*, *Journal of Counseling and Development*, *Journal of Children and Poverty*, and the *Hispanic Journal of Behavioral Sciences*. Her work has been funded by the Office for Child Care in the U.S. Department of Health and Human Services as a child care scholar as well as the Bruhn Morris Family Foundation and the Bernard van Leer Foundation. Dr. Vesely teaches graduate courses focused on family engagement in early childhood care and education and undergraduate courses focused on family processes and dynamics. Dr. Vesely received her PhD in family science from the University of Maryland, College Park, in 2011.

Karin Wachter is a doctoral student in the School of Social Work at The University of Texas at Austin and a project director at the Institute on Domestic Violence & Sexual Assault. Before moving to Austin, Karin spent 10 years working with the International Rescue Committee as a humanitarian aid worker responding to violence against women and girls in conflict affected contexts, primarily in Africa. Her expertise includes intervention design, logic models, and program evaluation. The focus of Karin's research is currently on women's social support mechanisms in forced migration. She teaches research methods and forced migration and social work practice at UT Austin.

DEFINING IMMIGRANT AND REFUGEE POPULATIONS

"It is this constant flow of immigrants that helped to make America what it is. . . . To this day America reaps incredible economic rewards because we remain a magnet for the best and brightest from around the globe. In an increasingly interconnected world, . . . being an American is not a matter of blood or birth. It's a matter of faith. . . . 'E pluribus unum.' Out of many, one. That is what has drawn the persecuted and impoverished to our shores. That's what led the innovators and risk-takers from around the world to take a chance here in the land of opportunity. That's what has led people to endure untold hardships to reach this place called America."

~ President Obama's Immigration Address, July 1, 2010, at American University

Learning Objectives

Review common terminology and policies related to immigrant and refugee populations.

Explore relevant pre-migration, migration, and post-migration factors that impact immigrant and refugee adjustment to life in a new country.

Examine the role of physical and mental health among new immigrants and the importance of health stabilization to support positive adjustment outcomes.

INTRODUCTION

Unit I: "Defining Immigrant and Refugee Populations" introduces the definitions and common terminology used throughout the book (Chapter 1). There is a discussion of the context of migration, examining the pre-migration, migration, and post-migration/resettlement experiences that impact adjustment of new immigrants to life in a destination country, the degree of integration and acculturation, and overall well-being (Chapter 2). As part of the adjustment process, a discussion of the importance of health and well-being is included (Chapter 3), as it is a salient part of the immigrant experience. At the completion of Unit I, readers should understand basic terminology related to transnational populations and have a general sense of the immigrant or refugee experience.

Before diving into the core terms of this book, it is important to examine the general content of global migration, salient migration terms, and policies that shape the experiences of individuals and families moving across borders in numbers not seen in recent times.

GLOBAL MIGRATION TRENDS

There is a long history of global migration patterns that reflect the critical circumstances of the time, be they regional conflicts, famine, adverse affects of climate change, unstable governments, and limited opportunities that have served as a catalyst for migration. In more recent decades, these same factors have only increased with intensity, placing people in dire circumstances that force mass movement toward safety and opportunity. The United Nations High Commissioner for Refugees (UNHCR) is a prominent global agency that is mandated by the United Nations to ensure respect for the rights of people fleeing war and persecution and to find lasting solutions to their plight (unhcr.org, 2015a). Annually, the UNHCR disseminates *Global Trends Reports* outlining global migration patterns, with the most recent report reflecting population movement by the end of 2014. According to the 2014 UNHCR *Global Trends* report (see UNHCR, 2015a), there was a reported 59.5 million forcibly displaced persons worldwide (19.5 million refugees, 38.2 million internally displaced persons [IDPs], and 1.8 million asylum seekers). These totals together could make up the 24th largest nation in the world, and projections for 2015 suggest even higher numbers given the escalating crisis in Syria and throughout Central and East Africa. More than half of the refugees worldwide in 2014 (53%) came from three countries: Syrian Arab Republic (3.88 million), Afghanistan (2.59 million), and Somalia (1.11 million). Additionally, the countries hosting refugees have changed, as Turkey became the largest refugee-hosting country worldwide for the first time, with 1.59 million refugees residing in its border. Turkey was followed by Pakistan (1.51 million refugees), Lebanon (1.15 million refugees), Islamic Republic of Iran (982,000 refugees), Ethiopia (659,000 refugees), and Jordan (654,100 refugees). Of the total number of registered refugees, 51% were below the age of 18; the highest figure in more than a decade. These are astounding numbers of displaced persons

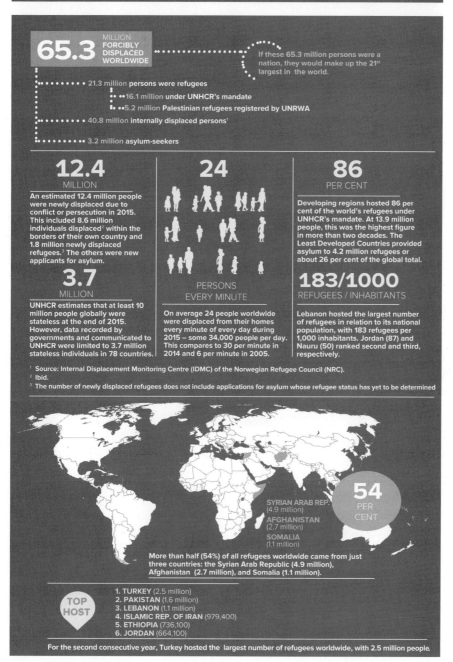

Figure 0.1 Current Trends and the International Staffing to Help Address Migrant Populations

65.3 MILLION FORCIBLY DISPLACED WORLDWIDE

If these 65.3 million persons were a nation, they would make up the 21st largest in the world.

21.3 million **persons were refugees**
16.1 million **under UNHCR's mandate**
5.2 million **Palestinian refugees registered by UNRWA**
40.8 million **internally displaced persons**[1]
3.2 million **asylum-seekers**

12.4 MILLION

An estimated 12.4 million people were newly displaced due to conflict or persecution in 2015. This included 8.6 million individuals displaced[2] within the borders of their own country and 1.8 million newly displaced refugees.[3] The others were new applicants for asylum.

24

PERSONS EVERY MINUTE

On average 24 people worldwide were displaced from their homes every minute of every day during 2015 – some 34,000 people per day. This compares to 30 per minute in 2014 and 6 per minute in 2005.

86 PER CENT

Developing regions hosted 86 per cent of the world's refugees under UNHCR's mandate. At 13.9 million people, this was the highest figure in more than two decades. The Least Developed Countries provided asylum to 4.2 million refugees or about 26 per cent of the global total.

3.7 MILLION

UNHCR estimates that at least 10 million people globally were stateless at the end of 2015. However, data recorded by governments and communicated to UNHCR were limited to 3.7 million stateless individuals in 78 countries.

183/1000 REFUGEES / INHABITANTS

Lebanon hosted the largest number of refugees in relation to its national population, with 183 refugees per 1,000 inhabitants. Jordan (87) and Nauru (50) ranked second and third, respectively.

[1] Source: Internal Displacement Monitoring Centre (IDMC) of the Norwegian Refugee Council (NRC).
[2] Ibid.
[3] The number of newly displaced refugees does not include applications for asylum whose refugee status has yet to be determined

54 PER CENT

SYRIAN ARAB REP. (4.9 million)
AFGHANISTAN (2.7 million)
SOMALIA (1.1 million)

More than half (54%) of all refugees worldwide came from just three countries: the Syrian Arab Republic (4.9 million), Afghanistan (2.7 million), and Somalia (1.1 million).

TOP HOST
1. **TURKEY** (2.5 million)
2. **PAKISTAN** (1.6 million)
3. **LEBANON** (1.1 million)
4. **ISLAMIC REP. OF IRAN** (979,400)
5. **ETHIOPIA** (736,100)
6. **JORDAN** (664,100)

For the second consecutive year, Turkey hosted the largest number of refugees worldwide, with 2.5 million people.

Source: United Nations High Comissioner for Refugees, *Global Trends: Forced Displacement in 2015* (Geneva: UNHCR, 2015), 2–3.

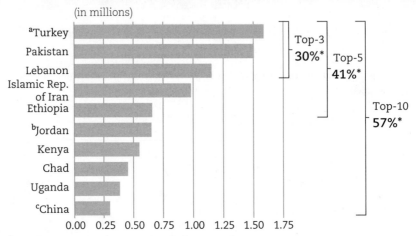

Figure 0.2a Major Refugee-Hosting Countries (mid-2014)

(in millions)

[Bar chart showing refugee-hosting countries:]
- [a]Turkey
- Pakistan
- Lebanon
- Islamic Rep. of Iran
- Ethiopia
- [b]Jordan
- Kenya
- Chad
- Uganda
- [c]China

[X-axis: 0.00 0.25 0.50 0.75 1.00 1.25 1.50 1.75]

Top-3 **30%***
Top-5 **41%***
Top-10 **57%***

*Reflects proportion out of global number of refugees at end 2014.
[a]Refugee figure for Syrians in Turkey is a Government estimate.
[b]Includes 29,300 Iraqi refugees registered with UNHCR in Jordan. The Government estimates the number of Iraqis at 400,000 individuals at the end of March 2015. This includes refugees and other categories of Iraqis.
[c]The 300,000 Vietnamese refugees are well integrated and in practice receive protection from the Government of China.

Source: United Nations High Comissioner for Refugees, *UNHCR Mid-Year Trends 2015* (Geneva: UNHCR, 2015), 8.

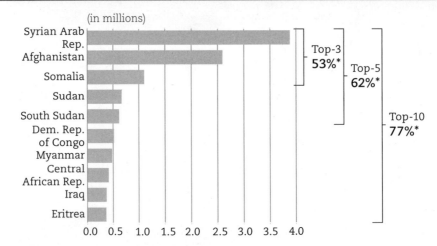

Figure 0.2b Where Do the World's Refugees Come From? (mid-2014)

(in millions)

[Bar chart showing countries of origin:]
- Syrian Arab Rep.
- Afghanistan
- Somalia
- Sudan
- South Sudan
- Dem. Rep. of Congo
- Myanmar
- Central African Rep.
- Iraq
- Eritrea

[X-axis: 0.0 0.5 1.0 1.5 2.0 2.5 3.0 3.5 4.0]

Top-3 **53%***
Top-5 **62%***
Top-10 **77%***

*Reflects proportion out of global number of refugees at end 2014.
Source: United Nations High Comissioner for Refugees, *UNHCR Mid-Year Trends 2015* (Geneva: UNHCR, 2015), 8.

who have limited opportunity based on their filing status (refugee, asylum seeker, undocumented IDP). And of all global partners in the world, only 26 countries admitted the 105,200 refugees who applied and were approved for third country resettlement in 2014. The United States admitted the highest number that year, admitting 73,000 refugees, but it is a minuscule number in comparison to the 59.5 million displaced persons worldwide seeking a solution. The UNHCR graphic in Figure 0.1 on page 3 prepared in June of 2015 provides a visual of the current trends and the international staffing to help address migrant populations (accessed at http://www.unhcr.org/en-us/figures-at-a-glance.html).

The numbers only continue to increase with each passing month. According to the former UN High Commissioner Antonio Guterres, "We are witnessing a paradigm change, an unchecked slide into an era in which the scale of global forced displacement as well as the response required is now clearly dwarfing anything seen before" (UNHCR, 2015a). To illustrate the growing need, Figures 0.2a and b on the facing page are from the *UNHCR Mid-Year Trends 2015* report (UNHCR, 2016, pp. 6–7) (http://www.unhcr.org/56701b969.html), highlighting the rise in numbers between the end of 2014 reports and six months into 2015.

The most recent map from the *UNHCR Mid-Year 2015* report, Map 2 (http://www .unhcr.org/56701b969.html, p. 5), illustrates the concentration of current refugee populations globally, in which we see displacement increasing both by numbers and the regions impacted.

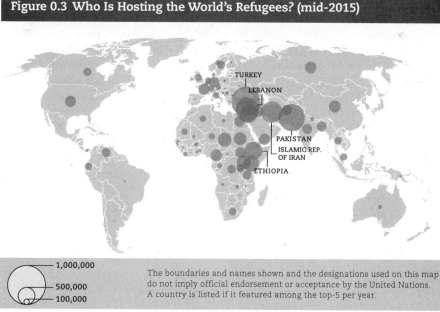

Figure 0.3 Who Is Hosting the World's Refugees? (mid-2015)

The boundaries and names shown and the designations used on this map do not imply official endorsement or acceptance by the United Nations. A country is listed if it featured among the top-5 per year.

Source: United Nations High Comissioner for Refugees, UNHCR *Mid-Year Trends 2015* (Geneva: UNHCR, 2015), 5.

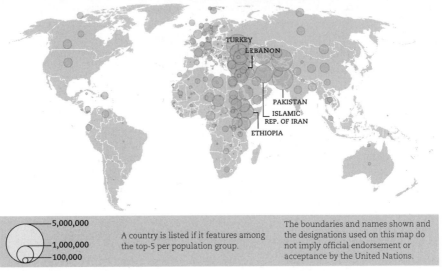

Figure 0.4 Refugees, Including Persons in a Refugee-Like Situation (end 2014)

5,000,000
1,000,000
100,000

A country is listed if it features among the top-5 per population group.

The boundaries and names shown and the designations used on this map do not imply official endorsement or acceptance by the United Nations.

Source: United Nations High Comissioner for Refugees, *UNHCR Mid-Year Trends 2015* (Geneva: UNHCR, 2015), 5.

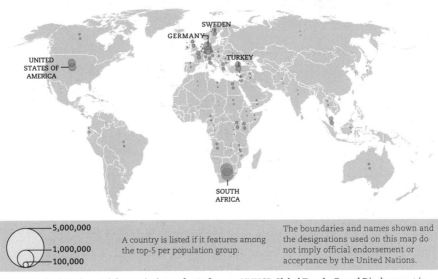

Figure 0.5 Asylum-Seekers (pending cases) (end 2014)

5,000,000
1,000,000
100,000

A country is listed if it features among the top-5 per population group.

The boundaries and names shown and the designations used on this map do not imply official endorsement or acceptance by the United Nations.

Source: United Nations High Comissioner for Refugees, *UNHCR Global Trends: Forced Displacement in 2014* (Geneva: UNHCR, 2015), 6–7.

Figure 0.6 IDPs Protected/Assisted by UNHCR, Including Persons in an IDP-Like Situation (end 2014)

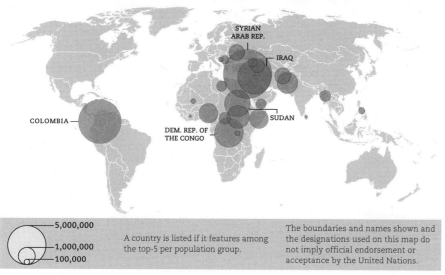

SYRIAN
ARAB REP.
IRAQ
COLOMBIA
SUDAN
DEM. REP. OF
THE CONGO
5,000,000
1,000,000
100,000
A country is listed if it features among the top-5 per population group.
The boundaries and names shown and the designations used on this map do not imply official endorsement or acceptance by the United Nations.

Source: United Nations High Comissioner for Refugees, *UNHCR Global Trends: Forced Displacement in 2014* (Geneva: UNHCR, 2015), 6–7.

Figure 0.7 Returned Refugees, Returned IDPs (end 2014)

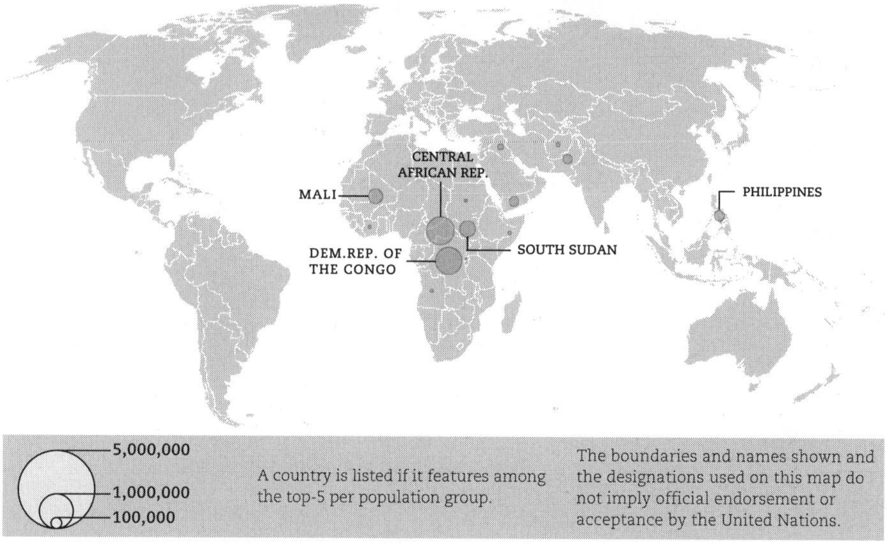

CENTRAL
AFRICAN REP.
MALI
PHILIPPINES
DEM.REP. OF
THE CONGO
SOUTH SUDAN
5,000,000
1,000,000
100,000
A country is listed if it features among the top-5 per population group.
The boundaries and names shown and the designations used on this map do not imply official endorsement or acceptance by the United Nations.

Source: United Nations High Comissioner for Refugees, *UNHCR Global Trends: Forced Displacement in 2014* (Geneva: UNHCR, 2015), 6–7.

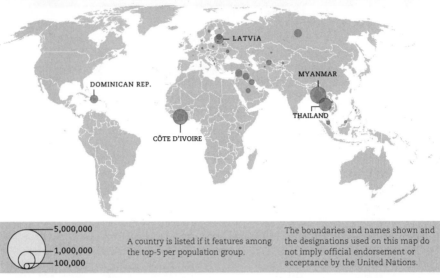

Figure 0.8 Persons Under UNHCR's Statelessness Mandate

A country is listed if it features among the top-5 per population group.

The boundaries and names shown and the designations used on this map do not imply official endorsement or acceptance by the United Nations.

Source: United Nations High Comissioner for Refugees, *UNHCR Global Trends: Forced Displacement in 2014* (Geneva: UNHCR, 2015), 6–7.

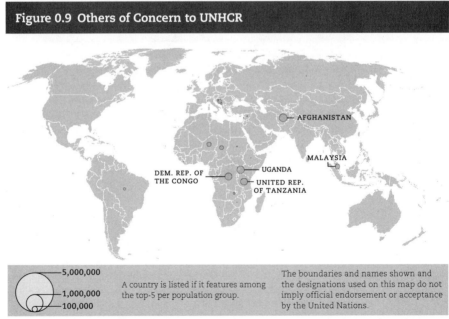

Figure 0.9 Others of Concern to UNHCR

A country is listed if it features among the top-5 per population group.

The boundaries and names shown and the designations used on this map do not imply official endorsement or acceptance by the United Nations.

Source: United Nations High Comissioner for Refugees, *UNHCR Global Trends: Forced Displacement in 2014* (Geneva: UNHCR, 2015), 6–7.

Compounding these numbers are "populations of concern to UNHCR," who are not identical or synonymous with the 59.5 million forcibly displaced persons noted. There are additional persons (in the millions) who are returnees or those who found a durable solution and returned home and at least 10 million stateless persons who were not forcibly moved but have no legitimacy within their current residing country. Make no mistake that these latter categories are equally at risk: Their situations are tenuous and could ultimately result with these populations fleeing their current country of residence if circumstances change again for the worse. The preceding graphics provide a great depiction of all populations of concern by the end of 2014, and it should be noted that numbers in each region have only increased with the passing year. The *UNHCR Global Trends 2014* report, Map 1 (http://www.unhcr.org/en-us/statistics/country/556725e69/unhcr-global-trends-2014.html), further highlighted the location of different populations of concern that are reflected in the maps in Figures 0.4–0.9.

There has also been a striking increase in the number of asylum seekers globally. According to the *UNHCR Mid-Year Trends 2015* report (UNHCR, 2016), countries are seeing the highest number of new applications logged, a number that does not reflect all the cases that are filed but pending; thus the total number of applications may actually be higher than what has been reported. Germany has the highest number of new asylum applications, with 159,900 recorded, with Syrian applications more than doubling from 12,100 applications in the first half of 2014 to 32,500 at the same period in 2015. The Russian Federation had the second highest number, with 100,000 logged applications, followed by the United States, at 78,200 asylum claims (and the most new claims for 2015). U.S. claims from Honduras, El Salvador, Guatemala, Mexico, and China increased the most in this reporting period and are only expected to increase.

An additional group that needs attention are the current numbers of undocumented immigrants and unaccompanied minors who are entering the United States from Central America—mainly, El Salvador, Guatemala, Honduras, and Mexico—fleeing

Figure 0.10 Apprehensions of Children and Their Families Exceed Those of Unaccompanied Children in 2016		
	Unaccompanied children	Children and their families
2014	28,579	19,830
2015	15,616	13,913
2016	27,754	32,117

Note: Apprehension numbers for children and their families include both the children and adults traveling with them. Data refer to the number of apprehensions, not the number of unique individuals apprehended.

Source: Adapted from Krofstad, Jens Manuel. "U.S. Border Apprehensions of Families and Unaccompanied Children Jump Dramatically." *Pew Research Center.* May 4, 2016. http://www.pewresearch.org/fact-tank/2016/05/04/u-s-border-apprehensions-of-families-and-unaccompanied-children-jump-dramatically/

the gang violence and poverty that plague these respective countries. Some apply for asylum, while others arrive and simply fall under the radar of the immigration authorities. Figures 0.10 and 0.11 from Krogstad (2016) at the Pew Research Center

Figure 0.11 Surge in Apprehensions of Children and Their Families Driven by Honduras, Guatemala, and El Salvador		
	2015	2016
El Salvador	3,313	11,093
Guatemala	4,537	9,720
Honduras	3,418	8,065
Mexico	2,193	1,644

Source: Adapted from Krofstad, Jens Manuel. "U.S. Border Apprehensions of Families and Unaccompanied Children Jump Dramatically." *Pew Research Center*. May 4, 2016. http://www.pewresearch.org/fact-tank/2016/05/04/u-s-border-apprehensions-of-families-and-unaccompanied-children-jump-dramatically/

Notes: Apprehension numbers for children and their families include both the children and adults traveling with them. Apprehensions data refer to the number of apprehensions and not to the number of unique individuals apprehended. Family apprehensions from other countries and unaccompanied child apprehensions are not shown.

Figure 0.12 Foreign-Born Population and as Percent of Total Population

Long-term trends

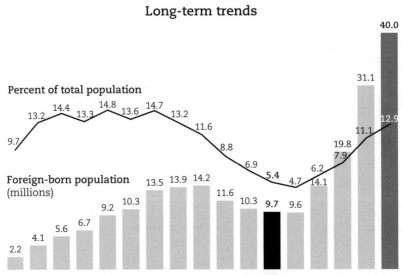

Source: U.S. Census Bureau, 1850—2000 Decennial Census; 2010 American Community Survey.

highlight the dramatic increase in apprehensions of families and unaccompanied minors in 2016, showing that situations abroad are becoming more desperate and people are more willing to risk a great deal—exploitation, injury, and death—to flee to another country.

The United States is equally subject to these migration trends, and thus we have seen a steady increase in foreign-born populations that have changed the face and fabric of U.S. society (see Figure 0.12 for the U.S. Census Bureau Chart from 1850–2010). The arriving populations are coming from different regions throughout the world and resettling across the country. For example, immigrants from Europe during the 1960s were resettling in the Northeast and Midwest regions of the country, whereas today's immigrant populations are mostly arriving from Latin America and Asia and settling in the South and West. Current reports from the 2010 census show the foreign population at approximately 40 million (12.9% of the total population). These numbers reflect the different categories of displaced populations described (refugees, asylum seekers, etc.) and are at the source of the heated immigration debates raging in the country.

Ultimately, there is a reality for persons who are forcibly displaced from their home country and who seek solace and refuge in foreign lands. As the daily news reports unfold, there are people who risk their lives by sea, air, and foot in search of new opportunities, a life away from the threat of constant violence and hunger and a chance to attain the basic human rights of an education and freedom from persecution. Those without status and with no place of statehood or residence are at added risk. Sadly, we are seeing a generation of children and young adults who belong to no country, have no access to education or basic healthcare, are unauthorized to work, and must face the harsh life of unregulated work, victimization, and in some cases trafficking, prostitution, and other inhumane means of survival.

MIGRATION FORCES

Conversations about migration trends must include a discussion of the underlying reasons why people leave their home country in the first place. Frequently, the terms *forced migration*, *survival migration*, and *push-pull factors* are used to describe the circumstances leading to internal movement within a country or outmigration. **Forced (or involuntary) migration** can include a number of legal or political categories under the definition promoted by the International Association for the Study of Forced Migration (IASFM), including conflict-induced displacement, development-induced displacement, and disaster-induced displacement (forcedmigration.org, n.d.). Evident in the name, conflict-induced displacement refers to those who are forced to flee their homes because of armed conflict—such as civil war, generalized community violence, or threat and persecution based on personhood (nationality, race, religion, political opinion, social group, sexual orientation). Development-induced displacement refers to people who are moved as a result of projects that are intended to "develop" a region—such as mining or deforestation projects, building of infrastructure such as roads and ports, or conservation efforts. Finally, disaster-induced displacement refers to natural disasters (floods, earthquakes, landslides, global warming) and human-made disasters (industrial accidents) that compel people to leave their home (forcedmigration.org, n.d.). As a result, there are multiple types of migrants who will be discussed to varying degrees in this book: refugees recognized by the United Nations High Commissioner for Refugees (UNHCR), asylum seekers, internally displaced persons (who are outside of their community but within the same country), development displacees (tied to development-induced displacement), environmental and disaster displacees (tied to disaster-induced displacement), smuggled migrations moved for a profit, and trafficked peopled who are moved by deception/coercion for the purpose of exploitation (forcedmigration.org, n.d.). In each category, there is a clear evidence of risk to one's safety and survival that serves as a catalyst for movement within and across national borders.

Similarly, **survival migration** is a term that has emerged to reflect migration patterns that are outside of the original framework for displaced persons or "refugees[1]" broadly. Survival migration refers to people who have left their country for the same reasons outlined under the forced migration definition, but the added distinction is that there is no domestic remedy that would allow them to remain or return to their country of origin (Betts, 2010). Some may argue it is semantics, that those who are forced to migrate are in similar circumstances of not being able to return home and that they, too, are in survival mode. That being said, however, the term survival migration provides a construct that further defines and allows us to understand migration experiences. Each term shapes the personal narratives of affected populations, who make migration decisions because they have no choice but to move, if they want to remain safe and alive.

Broadly, the term **displacement** has been used to reflect the endemic phenomenon of populations being uprooted for social, political, developmental, and environmental reasons. And the movement evokes new processes including "labeling, identity management, boundary creation and maintenance, management of reciprocity, manipulation of myth, . . . forms of social control . . . and [the creation of] new diasporas with their own political interests" that shape people and communities (Colson, 2003, p. 1). This "shaping" can manifest in how people and communities understand and adapt to their circumstances and their individual and collective outlook for the future.

Push and pull factors have also applied to the discussion of migration patterns. Simply put, push factors involve forces that drive people away from their home, while pull factors involve forces that draw people to a new place. The same reasoning presented under the forced and survival migration terms can apply as factors that either push or pull people to any one country. In more recent times, the application of the push-pull factors construct has expanded to include why people move based on education opportunities (Li & Bray, 2007; Mazzarol & Soutar, 2002), financial opportunities (Fratzscher, 2012; Kirkwood, 2009), employment opportunities (Kline, 2003), retirement plans (Shultz, Morton, & Weckerle, 1998), and even travel (Kim, Lee, &

---

[1] As noted by Castles (2004), popular speech tends to use the term "refugee" to all those who flee their homes and seek refuge elsewhere, but the reality is that the term refugee is a very narrow legal category. In this instance, the term refugee is used to broadly reflect persons who flee for their safety and security and not under the strict definitions outlined by the UNHCR.

Klenosky, 2003). Nonetheless, the concepts apply to current discussions of migration patterns, especially as the number of migrants worldwide continues to outpace rates seen even a decade ago.

Together, these terms are valuable for organizations and professionals working with persons for which these migration terms apply and who have endured a variety of stressors (push-pull factors) that resulted in the movement away from their country of origin. The meanings behind these terms are equally valuable for governing bodies (global, national, and local) for developing policies and procedures to address the migration trends and deficits that are the basis for the widespread level of movement we see today. The terms are particularly helpful in understanding the needs of new immigrants who arrive in a host or destination country. The context surrounding the immigrant's story can directly inform what health, mental health, and adjustment needs (housing, employment, family reunification, etc.) will be necessary for that person to thrive in a new country.

SOCIOCULTURAL AND SOCIOPOLITICAL FORCES: ARE FORCIBLY DISPLACED PERSONS[2] TRULY WELCOMED?

The rhetoric around immigration and the policies used to regulate migration flows globally impact existing immigrant and refugee communities worldwide and in very direct ways. Sociocultural forces (combining social and cultural factors) and sociopolitical forces (combining social and political factors) have jointly shaped how we understand immigration and its effects on the receiving society in both positive and negative ways. Discrimination of new arriving ethnic groups is not novel to any one society, but we are now in a time when the heated rhetoric and use of "public safety" justifies the grounds for targeting, oppressing, marginalizing, and denying due process under the law for people and communities considered dangerous to the United States and global interests. The September 11, 2001, terrorist attacks in the United States by the Islamic terrorist group Al-Qaida profoundly shaped immigration policy and perceptions of the Arab world into the foreseeable future. The response to the deadly attacks on the World Trade Center and the Pentagon was swift, with the United States enacting security measures and building up military forces in the Middle East to ensure the perpetrators of one of the greatest tragedies on U.S. soil would be brought to justice and the U.S. public would remain safe from future attacks.

Terror groups, however, did not disappear but evolved into new factions that continue to bring fear and destruction to countries worldwide. The reports of terror and persecution have escalated since 2001, including the kidnapping of 276 Chibok school girls by Boko Haram, an extremist group tied to the Islamic State in Nigeria in April 2014; the systematic kidnapping, murder, and rape of Yazedi women during the Iraq insurgency by the Islamic State of Iraq and the Levant (ISIL) since early

---

[2] In this context, a forcibly displaced person can refer to an immigrant (documented or undocumented), refugee, internally displaced person, or asylum seeker.

2014; the suicide bombings that killed 138 people in Paris, coordinated by ISIL, in November 2015; suicide bombings in Brussels killing 32 people and injuring 300 by ISIL in March 2016; the attack on foreigners at a hotel in Burkina Faso by the Al-Qaeda affiliate, Al-Qaeda in the Islamic Maghreb (AQIM), which took the lives of 29 people in January 2016; and the most recent alleged ISIL-affiliated attack in Florida that claimed the life of 49 people at a gay night club in June 2016, the single most deadly mass shooting on U.S. soil to date. Global intelligence and networks have increased collaboration to ward off the threats of mass violence, yet while global leaders are coming together with a united front to fight terrorism and extremism, there remains confusion in the general population. Uninformed communities worldwide are blending assumptions about culture, religion, and warped religious extremism used to justify terrorism into one category, and the effects are damning.

Hate crimes against Arab populations have increased dramatically post-9/11 (Disha, Cavendish, & King, 2011; Hendricks, Ortiz, Sugie, & Miller, 2007). This has included increased harassment of people perceived of Arab descent, damage to churches and mosques, and in some cases physical assaults—including attacks, shootings, and murders (Hendricks et al., 2007). The same hate crimes and fear of the unknown has also applied to undocumented immigrants and unaccompanied minors coming from Central and South America. Violence along the borders between the United States and Mexico has been well-documented over the last two decades. According to Stacey, Carbone-Lopez, and Rosenfeld (2011), "Hispanic immigration to the United States has become a politically charged public issue, with significant consequences for immigration policies, communities, individual immigrants, and the U.S. residents who resemble them in language, customs, and appearance" (p. 278), and as a result, a positive correlation with increased hate crimes against new immigrants. As the fear of difference continues to spread, there is potential for targeting of other marginalized or under-represented groups based on ethnicity, gender, sexual orientation, religion, and political opinion.

Hate crimes and hate speech are only further normalized and accepted when the rhetoric of political leaders, television and sports personalities, and other perceived experts use media platforms like the nightly news, Facebook, and Twitter to disseminate misinformation and fear. The powerful intersection of ignorance and technology have created an environment that is harmful to new immigrants and native-born citizens of immigrants who must exist in a space where there is increasing intolerance, fear of what is different, and constant discussion around building walls and excluding people based on country of origin. Unfortunately, major immigration policies globally are being informed by the wealth of misinformation and fear around terrorist groups, impacting those immigrants who are neither seeking opportunities to harm others nor those who would take advantage of the resources of a country. Many are simply wanting an opportunity to better themselves and their families while becoming productive, contributing members in their receiving country. This backdrop of fear mongering and hate has and will continue to have a long-lasting impact on the lives of native-born children of immigrants and new immigrants for decades to come.

SUPPORTING FORCIBLY
DISPLACED PERSONS GLOBALLY

As mentioned previously and in the *UNHCR Global Trends 2014* report, there were 59.5 million forcibly displaced persons worldwide—a number including refugees, internally displaced persons, and asylum seekers—by the end of 2014 (UNHCR, 2015a). Estimates for forcibly displaced persons by the end of 2015 project numbers closer to 70 million but potentially higher. This is because of the difficulty in tracking movement across borders, given the numbers have increased at such a rapid rate in a short period of time, which makes efforts to document arrivals in real time nearly impossible. Again, these ever-increasing numbers also do not reflect the number of undocumented migrants who do not have any formal registered status within the countries they reside.

For displaced people worldwide, citizenship status matters. It affords a level of legitimacy in a country, protections under the law, and access to financial and social resources that are critical for integrating into a new country. Citizenship status also contributes to a sense of identity and belonging (Tsuda, 2006), which may influence the levels of acculturation, but there is no one immigration policy that guides status determinations across countries. Each country has its own procedures for processing displaced persons—immigrants, refugees, asylum seekers, and undocumented migrants—fleeing their country and the immigrant integration policies that apply once these persons arrive in a destination country. According to Schlueter, Meuleman, and Davidov (2013), it has been hypothesized that many of the immigration policies are decided on by majority members, some of whom may have anti-immigrant sentiments. An examination in cross-national studies has found that the perception of threat or fear toward immigrant groups directly influenced the expansiveness of immigrant integration policies—specifically, countries with more permissive immigrant policies were those countries with a lower perception of immigrants being of imminent threat (Schlueter et al., 2013). A related finding suggests that when immigrant integration policies are conducted in a way that supports new immigrant adjustment into a new society, the attitudes of key policy-makers can also be influenced to be less critical of immigration. This discussion is vital to the preservation of comprehensive and compassionate immigration policies globally that are not driven by hate speech and fear of extremists. Against the backdrop of many countries curtailing their entry quotas and the backlash of native-born citizens who are misinformed of who these displaced persons are, there is a need for rational and collaborative policies in modern immigrant-receiving societies that must address the global migrant crisis that is of epic proportions.

Much of U.S. history has been built on the shoulders of immigrants and refugees who have contributed in vast ways to make the country the superpower it is today. Often immigration has been understood in terms of its impact on the labor market (Fix, Passel, Enchautegui, & Zimmermann, 1994; Scheve & Slaughter, 2001), the economic benefits to individuals and country (Borjas, 2011), and finally, the role of immigration and its relation to the U.S. welfare state (Borjas, 2011; Zolberg & Zolberg, 2009). As

Figure 0.13 U.S. Refugee Screening Process

THE SCREENING PROCESS

FOR REFUGEE ENTRY
INTO THE UNITED STATES

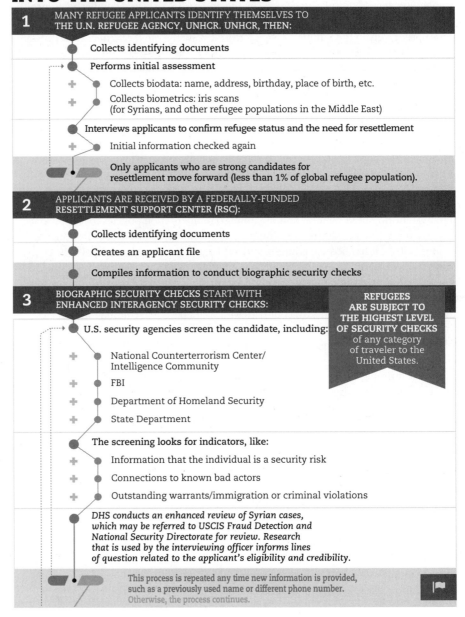

1 MANY REFUGEE APPLICANTS IDENTIFY THEMSELVES TO THE U.N. REFUGEE AGENCY, UNHCR. UNHCR, THEN:

- Collects identifying documents
- Performs initial assessment
  - Collects biodata: name, address, birthday, place of birth, etc.
  - Collects biometrics: iris scans (for Syrians, and other refugee populations in the Middle East)
- Interviews applicants to confirm refugee status and the need for resettlement
  - Initial information checked again
- Only applicants who are strong candidates for resettlement move forward (less than 1% of global refugee population).

2 APPLICANTS ARE RECEIVED BY A FEDERALLY-FUNDED RESETTLEMENT SUPPORT CENTER (RSC):

- Collects identifying documents
- Creates an applicant file
- Compiles information to conduct biographic security checks

3 BIOGRAPHIC SECURITY CHECKS START WITH ENHANCED INTERAGENCY SECURITY CHECKS:

REFUGEES ARE SUBJECT TO THE HIGHEST LEVEL OF SECURITY CHECKS of any category of traveler to the United States.

- U.S. security agencies screen the candidate, including:
  - National Counterterrorism Center/ Intelligence Community
  - FBI
  - Department of Homeland Security
  - State Department
- The screening looks for indicators, like:
  - Information that the individual is a security risk
  - Connections to known bad actors
  - Outstanding warrants/immigration or criminal violations
- DHS conducts an enhanced review of Syrian cases, which may be referred to USCIS Fraud Detection and National Security Directorate for review. Research that is used by the interviewing officer informs lines of question related to the applicant's eligibility and credibility.
- This process is repeated any time new information is provided, such as a previously used name or different phone number. Otherwise, the process continues.

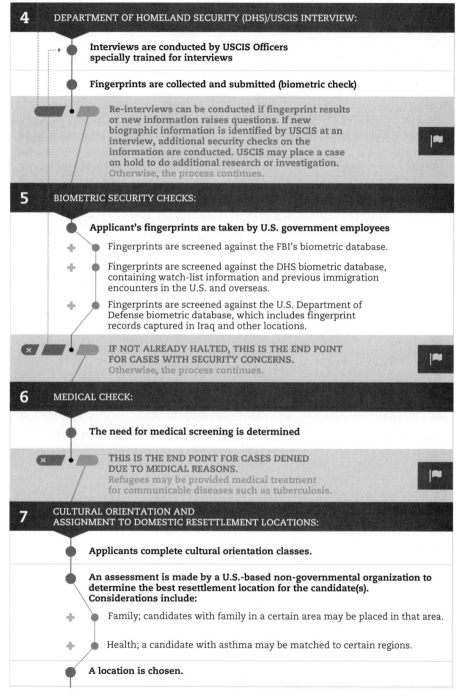

4 DEPARTMENT OF HOMELAND SECURITY (DHS)/USCIS INTERVIEW:

Interviews are conducted by USCIS Officers specially trained for interviews

Fingerprints are collected and submitted (biometric check)

Re-interviews can be conducted if fingerprint results or new information raises questions. If new biographic information is identified by USCIS at an interview, additional security checks on the information are conducted. USCIS may place a case on hold to do additional research or investigation. Otherwise, the process continues.

5 BIOMETRIC SECURITY CHECKS:

Applicant's fingerprints are taken by U.S. government employees

Fingerprints are screened against the FBI's biometric database.

Fingerprints are screened against the DHS biometric database, containing watch-list information and previous immigration encounters in the U.S. and overseas.

Fingerprints are screened against the U.S. Department of Defense biometric database, which includes fingerprint records captured in Iraq and other locations.

IF NOT ALREADY HALTED, THIS IS THE END POINT FOR CASES WITH SECURITY CONCERNS. Otherwise, the process continues.

6 MEDICAL CHECK:

The need for medical screening is determined

THIS IS THE END POINT FOR CASES DENIED DUE TO MEDICAL REASONS. Refugees may be provided medical treatment for communicable diseases such as tuberculosis.

7 CULTURAL ORIENTATION AND ASSIGNMENT TO DOMESTIC RESETTLEMENT LOCATIONS:

Applicants complete cultural orientation classes.

An assessment is made by a U.S.-based non-governmental organization to determine the best resettlement location for the candidate(s). Considerations include:

Family; candidates with family in a certain area may be placed in that area.

Health; a candidate with asthma may be matched to certain regions.

A location is chosen.

(Continued)

(Continued)

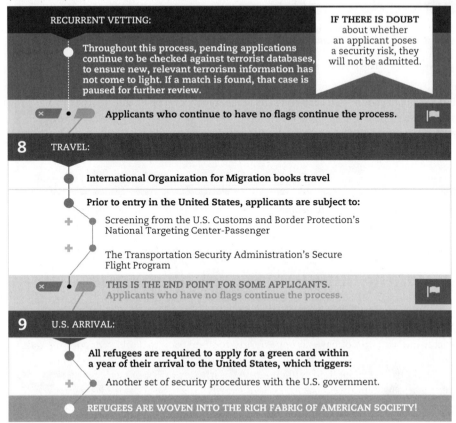

RECURRENT VETTING:

Throughout this process, pending applications continue to be checked against terrorist databases, to ensure new, relevant terrorism information has not come to light. If a match is found, that case is paused for further review.

IF THERE IS DOUBT about whether an applicant poses a security risk, they will not be admitted.

Applicants who continue to have no flags continue the process.

8 TRAVEL:

International Organization for Migration books travel

Prior to entry in the United States, applicants are subject to:

✛ Screening from the U.S. Customs and Border Protection's National Targeting Center-Passenger

✛ The Transportation Security Administration's Secure Flight Program

THIS IS THE END POINT FOR SOME APPLICANTS. Applicants who have no flags continue the process.

9 U.S. ARRIVAL:

All refugees are required to apply for a green card within a year of their arrival to the United States, which triggers:

✛ Another set of security procedures with the U.S. government.

REFUGEES ARE WOVEN INTO THE RICH FABRIC OF AMERICAN SOCIETY!

Source: Pope, Amy. "Infographic: The Screening Process for Refugee Entry into the United States." *The White House: President Barack Obama*. Nov. 20, 2015, https://www.whitehouse.gov/blog/2015/11/20/info graphic-screening-process-refugee-entry-united-states

such, "[U.S.] immigration policy not only emerged as a major instrument of American nation-building, but also fostered the notion that the nation could be designed, stimulated the elevation of that belief into an article of national faith" (Zolberg & Zolberg, 2009, p.2). And with that belief came dialogue and decisions around who should be allowed to enter the country and how many; a dialogue that continues into present and is shaped by misperceptions, assumptions, and fears of the multicultural populations that seek entry and refuge in the United States.

U.S. immigration policies, blending both pro- and anti-immigrant sentiments, are enacted through detailed processing systems with extensive rules and regulations (sometimes redundant) that slow down family reunification and granting status to eligible applicants. Despite fears of fast-tracked immigration processes that allow would-be terrorists to enter as immigrants or refugees, the immigration processes in place are deliberately slow, comprehensive, and intense. The extensive checks by the U.S. Department of State, U.S. Homeland Security, and in some cases the Federal Bureau of Investigation are able to thwart entry efforts of dangerous persons into the United States and provide intelligence to inform other global partners of possible terror suspects who are seeking entry into other countries. The U.S. Refugee Resettlement Program, overseen by the U.S. Department of State and in collaboration with the UNHCR, is the most controlled and rigorous of all immigration programs in the country. There are extensive background checks and waiting times to allow each agency sufficient time to review each case. For this reason, many refugees wait an average of four to five years for entry. In some cases, refugees wait on average fifteen to seventeen years for approval to be resettled in the United States. To illustrate the extensive nature of refugee screening, Figure 0.13 outlines the screening process that begins oversees for refugees registered with the UNHCR (see whitehouse.gov, Infographic: The Screening Process for Refugee Entry Into the United States, 2015).

Refugees have the most rigorous vetting process prior to being granted entry into the United States, and this is in part to ensure that terror suspects do not enter the country via the Refugee Resettlement program. Applications for immigrant visas based on family petitions or for other approved circumstances (e.g., student visas, business professional visas, migrant visas, etc.) undergo a level of scrutiny but not to the same degree. Furthermore, we must recognize that there are millions of people worldwide who do not have an opportunity to immigrate to a different country and remain displaced internally in their country of origin (internally displaced persons) or remain undocumented in other countries without protections or a pathway to citizenship. Immigration policies do not directly affect these latter groups, but attention is necessary nonetheless. As adverse circumstances continue to push or pull people to new borders, the policies need to reflect the need for countries to provide safe entry and a solution for populations that have no choice but to move for survival purposes.

We recognize that not all countries have the resources or the capacity to welcome the millions seeking refuge. For those who do have resources, however, we believe the borders should be opened and welcome immigrants in a logical and controlled manner, with timely processing and resources to help new arrivals integrate into the host society. Countries including the United States, Canada, Germany, the United Kingdom, and other European Union nations have a history of welcoming refugees, asylum seekers, and immigrants, but their criteria for entry varies. In all instances, however, countries can help the adjustment of new arrivals with an infrastructure of resettlement programs, social services, and financial resources that are necessary at arrival to aid in integration. Alongside these resources, communities of welcome must be present; people who embrace and are good neighbors to new immigrants, who combat discrimination against ethnic and culturally diverse populations, and who advocate for humane immigration policies that impact entire societies.

CONTRIBUTING NEW MEMBERS OF SOCIETY

New immigrant arrivals seek opportunities to give back to their receiving society, contributing to advancing economies (Eraydin, Tasan-Kok, & Vranken, 2010), innovation, and entrepreneurship (Saxenian, 2002). Despite the ambiguous feelings toward immigrants as either contributors or a social burden (Coates, 2006), the growing research finds that new immigrants (documented and undocumented) are making major contributions to society, and this is particularly true in the United States. From 1995 through 2005, it was reported that 25.3% of all engineering and technology companies in the United States had at least one key immigrant founder and that these immigrant-founded companies amassed more than $52 billion in sales and created almost 450,000 jobs as of the end of 2005 (Wadhwa, Saxenian, Rissing, & Gereffi, 2007). In many ways, immigrants have been seen as a driving force in new business and intellectual property development, which is projected to increase into the future (Kloosterman & Rath, 2001) as well as aid growth in the agricultural sector (Pena, 2010). Immigrant contributions can also be understood in other ways. Immigrant children are "active agents in supporting and sustaining their families, households, and schools" (Orellana, 2001, p. 366) through their roles as cultural and linguistic brokers and being able to access education and jobs that support entire families. Even older adults in immigrant families make contributions that impact entire societies. They are able to provide care to other kin, keep families intact, and preserve culture, which can be critical to immigrant adjustment in a new country (Treas & Mazumdar, 2004).

Immigration ultimately can generate unambiguous gains for the native population (Kemnitz, 2003), and while no policy can be perfect, immigration policies must be responsive to global migration trends and supportive of integration practices that will benefit societies as a whole. Policies intended to discriminate, persecute, and block movement to already marginalized and vulnerable displaced populations are both morally wrong and only serve as a catalyst for more violence and dire situations where people will make decisions and act out of sheer desperation to survive. We see this in the rising death tolls of Syrian and African people attempting to enter Europe by sea or the injuries and deaths of those from Central and South America who traverse the dangerous rocky terrain and heat by foot to enter the United States. Thousands of lives, including infants, die in these attempts to reach countries for refuge, and the time has come for all countries to recognize the migrant crisis that exists today.

OUR CALL TO ACTION: REBUILDING LIVES THROUGH ADVOCACY AND SERVICE

Despite the heated dialogue around immigration policies worldwide and what it means for countries to open their borders to the vulnerable that are seeking an opportunity to rebuild their lives, we as members of this global society have a responsibility to advocate for compassionate immigration policies that respect the dignity and worth of *every* human being. We must give access and opportunities to the basic human rights—freedom from fear and persecution, liberty, health, and an education. Our book seeks to uphold the belief that every immigrant and refugee has a right to live a productive and fulfilling life. We believe that health service professionals from diverse disciplines play a role in helping rebuild lives after traumatic migration experiences. Mental health providers in particular have an opportunity to provide culturally sensitive and compassionate services and resources to those who are most deserving and in need. Through the lens of trauma, mental health, and well-being, this book provides entrée to a discussion of multilevel, dynamic approaches to serving immigrants and refugees through an integration of Western theories of intervention with cultural understanding relevant to the populations resettling in countries across the globe. We have an opportunity to support communities of immigrants that have served as the bedrock for societies across the world, and this book is just one tool in achieving this goal.

GLOSSARY

Displacement. The phenomenon of populations being uprooted for social, political, developmental, and environmental reasons.

Forced (or involuntary) migration. Forcible movement of people because of conflict, development, or disaster.

Push and pull factors. Terms to describe the forces that drive people away from their home (push factors) and forces that draw people to a new place (pull factors).

Survival migration. Refers to people who have left their country because of conflict, development, or natural disasters (see definition for *forced migration*), when there is no domestic remedy that would allow them to remain or return to their country of origin.

REFERENCES

Betts, A. (2010). Survival migration: A new protection framework. *Global Governance: A Review of Multilateralism and International Organizations, International Migration, 16*(3), 361–382.

Borjas, G. J. (2011). *Heaven's door: Immigration policy and the American economy*. Princeton, NJ: Princeton University Press.

Castles, S. (2004). Why migration policies fail. *Ethnic and Racial Studies, 27*(2), 205–227. http://dx.doi.org/10.1080/0141987042000177306

Coates, P. (2006). *American perceptions of immigrant and invasive species: Strangers on the land*. Oakland: University of California Press.

Colson, E. (2003). Forced migration and the anthropological response. *Journal of Refugee Studies, 16*(1), 1–18. doi: 10.1093/jrs/16.1.1

Disha, I., Cavendish, J. C., & King, R. D. (2011). Historical events and spaces of hate: Hate crimes against Arabs and Muslims in post-9/11 America. *Social Problems, 58*(1), 21–46. doi: 10.1525/sp.2011.58.1.21

Eraydin, A., Tasan-Kok, T., & Vranken, J. (2010). Diversity matters: Immigrant entrepreneurship and contribution of different forms of social integration in economic performance of cities. *European Planning Studies, 18*(4), 521–543. doi: 10.1080/09654311003593556

Fix, M., Passel, J. S., Enchautegui, M. E., & Zimmermann, W. (1994). *Immigration and immigrants: Setting the record straight.* Washington, DC: Urban Institute.

Forcedmigration.org. (n.d.). *What is forced migration?* http://www.forcedmigration.org/about/whatisfm

Fratzscher, M. (2012). Capital flows, push versus pull factors and the global financial crisis. *Journal of International Economics, 88*(2), 341–356. doi: 10.1016/j.jinteco.2012.05.003

Hendricks, N. J., Ortiz, C. W., Sugie, N., & Miller, J. (2007). Beyond the numbers: Hate crimes and cultural trauma within Arab American immigrant communities. *International Review of Victimology, 14*(1), 95–113. doi: 10.1177/026975800701400106

Kemnitz, A. (2003). Immigration, unemployment and pensions. *The Scandinavian Journal of Economics, 105*(1), 31–48.

Kim, S. S., Lee, C., & Klenosky, D. B. (2003). The influence of push and pull factors at Korean national parks. *Tourism Management, 24*(2), 169–180. doi: 10.1016/S0261-5177(02)00059-6

Kirkwood, J. (2009). Motivational factors in a push-pull theory of entrepreneurship. *Gender in Management: An International Journal, 24*(5), 346–364. http://dx.doi.org/10.1108/17542410910968805

Kline, D. S. (2003). Push and pull factors in international nurse migration. *Journal of Nursing Scholarship, 35*(2), 107–111. doi: 10.1111/j.1547-5069.2003.00107.x

Kloosterman, R., & Rath, J. (2001). Immigrant entrepreneurs in advanced economies: Mixed embeddedness further explored. *Journal of Ethnic and Migration Studies, 27*(2), 189–201.

Krogstad, J. M. (2016). U.S. border apprehensions of families and unaccompanied children jump dramatically. Pew Research Center website. Accessed at http://www.pewresearch.org/fact-tank/2016/05/04/u-s-border-apprehensions-of-families-and-unaccompanied-children-jump-dramatically/.

Li, M., & Bray, M. (2007). Cross-border flows of students for higher education: Push–pull factors and motivations of mainland Chinese students in Hong Kong and Macau. *Higher Education, 53*(6), 791–818.

Mazzarol, T., & Soutar, G. N. (2002). "Push-pull" factors influencing international student destination choice. *International Journal of Educational Management, 16*(2), 82–90. http://dx.doi.org/10.1108/09513540210418403

Orellana, M. F. (2001). The work kids do: Mexican and Central American immigrant children's contributions to households and schools in California. *Harvard Educational Review, 71*(3), 366–390.

Pena, A. A. (2010). Legalization and immigrants in US agriculture. *The BE Journal of Economic Analysis & Policy, 10*(1). doi: 10.2202/1935-1682.2250

Saxenian, A. (2002). Silicon Valley's new immigrant high-growth entrepreneurs. *Economic Development Quarterly*, *16*(1), 20–31.

Scheve, K. F., & Slaughter, M. J. (2001). Labor market competition and individual preferences over immigration policy. *Review of Economics and Statistics*, *83*(1), 133–145.

Schlueter, E., Meuleman, B., & Davidov, E. (2013). Immigrant Integration policies and perceived group threat: A multilevel study of 27 Western and Eastern European Countries. *Social Science Research*, 42(3), 670–682. doi: 10.1016/j.ssresearch.2012.12.001

Shultz, K. S., Morton, K. R., & Weckerle, J. R. (1998). The influence of push and pull factors on voluntary and involuntary early retirees' retirement decision and adjustment. *Journal of Vocational Behavior*, *53*(1), 45–57. doi: 10.1006/jvbe.1997.1610

Stacey, M., Carbone-Lopez, K., & Rosenfeld, R. (2011). Demographic change and ethnically motivated crime: The impact of immigration on anti-Hispanic hate crime in the United States. *Journal of Contemporary Criminal Justice*, 27(3), 278–298. doi: 10.1177/1043986211412560

Treas, J., & Mazumdar, S. (2004). Kinkeeping and caregiving: Contributions of older people in immigrant families. *Journal of Comparative Family Studies*, pp. 105–122.

Tsuda, T. (2006). Localities and the struggle for immigrant rights: The significance of local citizenship in recent countries of immigration. *Local Citizenship in Recent Countries of Immigration: Japan in Comparative Perspective*, pp. 3–36.

UNHCR. (2015a). *UNHCR global trends report for 2014*. Accessed at http://www.unhcr.org/en-us/statistics/country/556725e69/unhcr-global-trends-2014.html

UNHCR. (2015b). *UNHCR statistical yearbook for 2014*. Accessed at http://www.unhcr.org/56655f4b19.html

UNHCR. (2016). *UNHCR mid-year trends 2015*. Accessed at http://www.unhcr.org/56701b969.html

Wadhwa, V., Saxenian, A., Rissing, B. A., & Gereffi, G. (2007). *America's new immigrant entrepreneurs: Part I.* (Duke Science, Technology & Innovation Paper, 23).

Zolberg, A. R., & Zolberg, A. R. (2009). *A nation by design: Immigration policy in the fashioning of America*. Cambridge, MA: Harvard University Press.

Chapter 1

DEFINING THE IMMIGRANT AND REFUGEE POPULATIONS

FERNANDO CHANG-MUY

KEY TERMS

nonimmigrants, immigrants, refugees, asylees, deportation, citizenship

---

CHAPTER HIGHLIGHTS

- Differences between immigrants, refugees, and asylees
- Reasons for deportation/removal
- Obtaining citizenship

Given current economic, social, and environmental trends, more and more people move across borders to escape persecution, find better employment, find better education for themselves or their children, or to join families already abroad. Once in the new country, social service providers may be providing housing, health, mental health, education supports, or other services. An understanding of legal policies and procedures and knowledge of key terms may help social workers, mental health practitioners, and other human service providers to ensure effective and culturally competent service.

This chapter will provide an understanding of differences between immigrants, refugees, and citizens but will focus on refugees as a particular vulnerable but resilient population. Throughout, the chapter will explore the role that social workers, mental health practitioners, and other providers can play along the way to ensure strong and resilient immigrant and refugee communities.

KEY TERMS

U.S. Immigration law defines individuals who live outside and come into the United States as "aliens." This chapter will use the word *newcomer*, although the word is also not quite accurate. Some individuals have been in the United States for a long time and therefore are not quite "new." Immigrant, as a legal term of art, refers to individuals who have lawfully immigrated to the United States and are now **lawful, permanent** residents or have their "green cards."

NONIMMIGRANT AND IMMIGRANT. Some individuals may have originally entered for a short term (e.g., to study, to work, to visit). They are called nonimmigrants.[1] There are over 22 categories of nonimmigrants, but reasons individuals typically enter the United States temporarily as nonimmigrants include to visit, to study, or to work temporarily. If later, the nonimmigrant wants to remain in the United States, there are two main avenues for permanent residency. The first is to be sponsored by a family member, and in this way she or he can then become a lawful permanent resident.[2] If an employer sponsors the individual, this too is an avenue toward a lawful permanent residency.[3] Absent family or employment sponsorship, individuals can sponsor themselves, if they can show that they deserve protection from persecution and should not be returned home.[4]

Given the dangerous situation of refugees if returned to the country of origin and the need for health and mental health supports in the new host country, this chapter will focus on this population of people who seek protection from persecution and ask that they not be deported.

REFUGEE AND ASYLEE. The definition of a refugee, as found in the UN Refugee treaty[5] and as mirrored by the U.S. government in the US Refugee Act[6] defines a refugee as a person who

> Owing to well-founded fear of persecution for reasons of race, religion, nationality, membership of a particular social group or political opinion, is outside the country of his nationality and is unable or, owing to such fear, is unwilling to avail himself of the protection of that country.

If the person is OUTSIDE of the United States trying to come in and succeeds, the person enters with the legal designation "refugee." For example, an Iraqi crosses the border into Jordan and is interviewed by the U.S. authorities in a refugee camp or at the U.S. embassy in Amman, Jordan, applies for protection, meets all of the elements of the refugee definition above, and enters/is resettled to the United States as a "refugee."

---

[1] Immigration and Nationality Act (INA); 8USC 1101 lays out the 22 various categories of non-immigrants—from students to visitors to temporary workers as examples
[2] INA Section 203(e)
[3] Ibid.
[4] Immigration and Nationality Act, The Immigration and Nationality Act of 1952 (Pub. L. 82–414, 66 Stat. 163); Title 8 of the United States Code (8 U.S.C. ch. 12).
[5] UN 1951 Convention relating to the Status of Refugees, adopted by the United Nations General, Resolution 429(V) of 14 December 1950; amended by the 1967 Protocol relating to the Status of Refugees, Resolution 2198 on December 16, 1966
[6] United States Refugee Act of 1980, Pub. L. 96-212; 8 U.S.C. Ch. 12, Sub Ch. I § 1101 et seq.

If the person entered the United States as a nonimmigrant—for example, as a visitor, student, temporary worker—or entered with documents and the documents expired, or entered without documents, the person can apply for protection as well. If the individual is already INSIDE the United States and applies for protection and meets all of the elements of the refugee definition above, the applicant gets the legal designation of "asylee." For example, an Iraqi might enter the United States as a visitor or to study (without having gone through a second country like Jordan, as in the example above), then applies for protection in the United States, is recognized as a refugee, and gets asylum. In both cases, whether applying for protection outside the United States or already inside the United States, the standard is the same: The applicant has to prove "a well-founded fear of persecution on account of race, religion, nationality, or political opinion." (See Footnote 6.)

In sum, refugee status is given to an individual *before* entering the United States. Asylum status is granted *after* someone enters the United States and formally applies for asylum. Many potential asylum seekers enter the United States on visas that do not show that they are fleeing persecution (e.g., short-term visitor visas or student visas) or with no documents at all. These individuals can apply for asylum upon entering the United States. However, as immigrant populations are often viewed with suspicion in the United States, asylum seekers remain at risk of being detained and/or threatened with deportation.

The service provider's role in supporting an individual applying for asylum can greatly enhance the chances of obtaining asylum. Regardless of the stage in the asylum process— assessing eligibility stage, the application stage (telling the story), and after the interview or hearing—the social worker or mental health provider can make a meaningful difference.

ASSESSMENT/ELIGIBILITY STAGE

Since newcomer individuals might have more contact with service providers than with lawyers (whether public interest or private attorneys), providers can help individuals engage in a first-level "self screening" to see if they are eligible for asylum and then refer to a legal expert. If after discussion the applicant feels she or he might be eligible, the service provider may then help with identifying and referring to attorneys with specialization in immigration and/or refugee law.[7]

As described above, both international and U.S. law requires that all asylum seekers prove each of the following criteria in order to obtain protection and get asylum:

- Have a well-founded fear of persecution on account of race, religion, national origin, political opinion, or membership in a particular social group

---

[7] Immigration Advocates maintains a list of nonprofits around the United States that can assist a person in immigration matters. Search by state link: http://www.immigrationadvocates.org/probono/volunteer/

- Must apply for asylum within one year of most recent arrival to the United States. If the applicant is applying AFTER the one-year deadline, service providers can help with applying for a waiver of the failure to meet the deadline (grounds for possible exemptions or waivers will be described below)

The applicant's narrative, laying out the fear of persecution and on which ground(s) the fear is based is laid out on an immigration form, "Application for Asylum."[8] This section will dissect each of the elements, so that service providers can help the individual assess whether they are even eligible to apply for asylum.

FEAR. The first element of the refugee definition that applicants must meet is "fear." The element of fear is both subjective and objective. *Subjective fear* refers to the *individual's* own fear of persecution. This can be established through the applicant's candid, sincere, and truthful testimony. The service provider can help the applicant talk and later write about what happened to him- or herself, or to relatives (shootings, torture, disappearances), such that she fears that what happened to them might also happen to her. *Objective fear* refers to whether this fear is based on events happening in the country of origin. The UN published a handbook to help government authorities and advocates determine who is a refugee. This *UN Handbook on Procedures and Criteria for Determining Refugee Status*[9] states:

> The applicant's statements cannot, however, be considered in the abstract, and must be viewed in the context of the relevant background situation. A knowledge of conditions in the applicant's country of origin—while not a primary objective—is an important element in assessing the applicant's credibility. In general, the applicant's fear should be considered well-founded if he can establish, to a reasonable degree, that his continued stay in his country of origin has become intolerable to him for the reasons stated in the definition, or would for the same reasons be intolerable if he returned there.[10]

Applicants do not need to prove that they will definitely be persecuted if they return home. They need to demonstrate a "reasonable" fear of this occurring.

PERSECUTION. In addition to proving fear, both subjectively and objectively, as described above, asylum seekers must prove that they fear persecution if returned home. Providers can also help applicants to first **identify** the type of persecution (imprisonment, torture, or even death) and then help the applicant gather **evidence** of the persecution (expert witnesses, newspaper clippings, journal articles, etc.). Applicants for asylum who can testify as to past or future harm, and in addition, present evidence that backs up the past persecution or fear of future persecution—through articles, witnesses, affidavits—can increase their chances of obtaining asylum.

---

[8] Form I-589, available at http://www.uscis.gov/sites/default/files/files/form/i-589.pdf
[9] The *UN Handbook on Procedures and Criteria for Determining Refugee Status*, HCR/IP/4/Eng/REV.1 Reedited, Geneva, January 1992, UNHCR 1979
[10] Ibid, para. 42.

Individuals who have not been previously persecuted are still eligible to apply but may have a more difficult time proving their fear of future persecution. In this case, it is especially useful to explain current conditions in one's home country and submit materials to support the claim. Providers, especially mental health providers, can help applicants articulate and write about the persecution they suffered or may suffer and do so in a nurturing, thoughtful way that minimizes the trauma the individual may face in retelling the story. In an application for asylum, the individual may have to tell the story a minimum of three times: to the lawyer, to the service provider (who may be helping put the testimony together and gather evidence and find expert witnesses as described above), to the lawyer again in a mock interview or hearing through various client prep sessions, and finally to the government authority who will make the final decision. The applicant may have to tell their story an additional time to a higher-level government authority, if there is an appeal from a denial of a first decision.

"ON ACCOUNT OF RACE, RELIGION, NATIONAL ORIGIN, POLITICAL OPINION, OR MEMBERSHIP IN A PARTICULAR SOCIAL GROUP" (see Footnote 6). Finally asylum seekers must link the fear of persecution to one or *any* or the grounds of persecution: race, religion, national origin, political opinion, or membership in a particular social group. If applicants do not fit into the first four categories, the "social group" category is sometimes used as a catch-all to try to win asylum. Again, service providers can help applicants to develop the grounds for fear of persecution. Applicants must first prove that they are a member of this group, for example, the LGBT community. In this example, it may be difficult if U.S. immigration officers assigned to the case have ideas about LGBT identity that are based on U.S. norms and stereotypes. Government officers' expectations do not always match an applicant's expression of their personal sexuality and/or gender identity. The applicant's own testimony, plus documents proving membership in an LGBTQ organization, evidence of engagement in same-sex relationships, or expert witness testimony as to persecution of LBGT individuals in that country may all increase the likelihood of winning asylum based on membership in a particular social group.

Next, applicants must prove that they fear persecution specifically because of their social group. The applicant must prove that the government commits the persecution or that the persecution is perpetrated by nongovernment forces (e.g., gangs, paramilitary, grandmothers performing female genital mutilation on their granddaughters), which the government is unable or unwilling to control. There are several immigrant-serving nonprofits that can provide detailed information on country of origin information to support the application, and there are nonprofit direct legal services providers who can effectively provide service.[11]

APPLY WITHIN ONE YEAR OF ARRIVAL. In addition to proving fear and persecution—based on a ground(s), the final prong an applicant may have to prove, depending on

---

[11] As an example, the LGBT Freedom and Asylum Network page offers details on the application process at http://www.lgbt-fan.org/application-process/

the application venue—the asylum seeker must file the request within one year (365 days) of the last arrival in the United States. The one year filing deadline is measured from the applicant's most recent arrival, so earlier trips to the United States should not affect applications unless the applicant was previously deported. Applicants who are approaching one year in the United States can submit a "skeleton case" of Form I-589 before the deadline and later add supporting information and documents to strengthen their case.

Applicants who have been in the country for more than one year *may* be able to claim an exemption from the one-year filing requirement, *if* they can argue one of the following exemptions:

1. *Changed Circumstances*: An asylum applicant can argue that a change in circumstances after the deadline prompted them to apply. For example, they may not have "come out," or they may not have realized that they identify as LGBT until they entered the United States. They may have maintained a lawful immigration status (i.e., a visa sponsored by an employer) since arriving to the United States, which abruptly ended. Perhaps their home country introduced new laws criminalizing LGBT identity while the applicant was in the United States.

2. *Extraordinary Circumstances*: An asylum applicant can argue that he or she was *unable* to apply by the deadline. For example, they may have been misled by their lawyer, suffered significant mental health concerns or mental health depression upon entering the United States, or been otherwise prevented from submitting their claim.

With the latter reason for filing late (after the 365 day deadline), providers can be helpful in drafting affidavits to support the applicant's reasons as to why he failed to meet the deadline. Reasons can be depression (if well-documented by the provider), which may have been caused by trauma in the home country, trauma caused in the flight, or trauma experienced in the new host country. The resulting depression, an applicant might argue, is an "extraordinary circumstance," which may have barred the individual from filing within the one-year deadline. A provider's affidavit explaining services provided and root cause of the trauma and depression may buttress the applicant's claim of mental health issues, which may then result in the application being allowed to move forward.[12]

POST-DECISION ASSISTANCE

If the applicant loses the application for asylum, depending on a number of grounds, there may be a possibility of appeal. Again the provider may be able to refer the individual to a legal services organization with expertise in immigration matters.[13]

---

[12] The USCIS training to their immigration officers contains a "lesson plan" on issues related to the one-year deadline http://www.uscis.gov/sites/default/files/USCIS/Humanitarian/Refugees%20%26%20 Asylum/Asylum/AOBTC%20Lesson%20Plans/One-Year-Filing-Deadline-31aug10.pdf

[13] Immigration advocates maintain a list of nonprofits around the United States that can assist a person in immigration matters. Search by state link: http://www.immigrationadvocates.org/probono/volunteer/

DEPORTATION. An applicant may lose his or her application for asylum because the government determines that

- the applicant did not meet all of the criteria for asylum—fear, persecution, nor any of the grounds—or

- the applicant falls within one of the grounds of deportation.

U.S. immigration policies set out various reasons for deporting individuals.[14] They are the following:

- The person was inadmissible at the time of entry into the United States. This includes many inadmissibility grounds, such as convicted of a crime, false representation of being a U.S. citizen, insufficient passport expiration date, and invalid visa.

- Criminal offenses.

  - If the person is convicted of a crime involving moral turpitude and the crime was committed within five years of admission and the sentence for the crime the applicant was convicted of is one year or longer.

  - An alien or lawful permanent residence is deportable if, after admission, the person is convicted of two crimes involving moral turpitude and the two crimes arose not from one single scheme of criminal conduct.

- An alien or lawful permanent residence is deportable if he or she commits aggravated felonies at any time after admission, plus failure to register and falsification of documents. A person is deportable if he or she either (a) commits document fraud, (b) fails to notify the USCIS in writing of an address change as required by law, or (c) claims false U.S. citizenship.

- Security and related grounds. A person who has engaged, is engaged, or at any time after admission engages in espionage or sabotage or violates or evades any law prohibiting the export from the United States of goods, technology, or sensitive information; activity, which endangers public safety or national security or any activity a purpose of which is the opposition to or the control or overthrow of the government of the United States by force, violence, or other unlawful means.

- The person becomes a public charge. A person may be subject to deportation if the U.S. Attorney General opines that he or she has become a public charge within five years of entry from causes not shown at the time of entry.

- Unlawful voting. A person who votes in violation of any federal, state, or local government law is deportable.

---

[14] INA Section 237

CITIZENSHIP

If the applicant wins the asylum case, providers can continue to provide other needed support—housing, health, mental health, job training, and referrals to educational institutions such as community colleges. In addition, if the applicant wins asylum, a year later, she can apply to "convert" the asylum status to lawful resident status and obtain her "green card." To become a U.S. citizen and naturalize, the law states that applicants must have been a lawful permanent resident from three to five years (depending on how they became lawful permanent residents), and must take a test on the following:

- English

- Civics (U.S. history and government)

After winning asylum, providers can help lawful permanent residents apply to become naturalized U.S. citizens by preparing them or referring them to agencies that can help them to prepare for the English and civics portion of the naturalization test.[15] In this way, individuals can participate in the full fabric of U.S. society—voting, working, and supporting their children so that they can be equally resilient and contributing members of society.

---

[15] The US government provides resources to help prepare. For more information on the Naturalization Test http://www.uscis.gov/us-citizenship/naturalization-test. For civics study Citizenship Resource Center http://www.uscis.gov/citizenship.

REFLECTION QUESTIONS

1. For macro students: If you were in charge of policy, what recommendations would you have for policy changes at the local, state, and/or federal level to strengthen immigrant and refugee communities?

2. For clinical practice students: If you were providing services to immigrants and refugees, what would be the top five steps your organization could take to ensure access to services to the community?

CASE STUDY

Mauricio, a young man from Honduras, fled eight years ago and is now in your office. He claims he refused to join a youth gang and did not want to become involved in its violent and criminal activities. He is now asking you for advice on how he can stay in the United States.

1. What are some questions you might want to ask to ascertain if he is eligible for asylum?

    a. What might be his grounds for asylum?

    b. What might be the biggest challenge in meeting the eligibility criteria?

2. What are some nonlegal questions you might ask to assess his health, mental health, and other needs?

3. In your region, where might you refer him for further assistance?

Chapter 2

THE CONTEXT OF MIGRATION
Pre-Arrival, Migration, and Resettlement Experiences
SAMANTHA ALLWEISS AND AIMEE HILADO

KEY TERMS

acculturation, pre-migration, migration, resettlement, U-curve of adjustment, self-sufficiency

---

CHAPTER HIGHLIGHTS

- Examination of migration experience from pre-arrival to resettlement
- Introduction to acculturation theories and the adjustment process for new arrivals
- Discussion of critical resources and supports that enhance positive acculturation outcomes
- Implications for organizations, professionals, and paraprofessionals serving trauma-exposed immigrant populations

---

INTRODUCTION

Each migration story is unique. There are those who leave their countries of origin by choice and with resources to aid in their adjustment to a new country. There are those, however, who flee their country because of a fear of persecution, natural disasters, failing economies, or lack of access to basic services and resources to survive. Individuals and families worldwide continue to cross borders, with documentation or without, seeking opportunities to change or rebuild their lives in a new community and society. While we recognize the uniqueness of each migration story and recognize the resilience necessary to thrive before, during, and after one immigrates to a new place, this chapter focuses on the migration experiences of one specific group: trauma-exposed immigrants and refugees and their respective experiences and needs when adjusting to life in a new country.

Unfortunately, displaced immigrants and refugees are a growing population worldwide who are in dire circumstances: persons who flee their homes after enduring threats to their safety and well-being, who have witnessed horrific violence in their communities, who have survived human rights violations, and who present with complex health and mental health needs as a result of their time displaced in urban and rural settings. To better prepare professionals working with this population, our chapter provides the context for understanding the realities of immigration and the negotiations that are made as new immigrants adjust to life in a new country, information we believe is critical for building a connection with culturally diverse, trauma-exposed new immigrants. It is the breadth of experiences combined that shape how new immigrants and refugees come to understand themselves, the blending of old and new cultures, and their place in a new society. Sadly, the circumstances of forcibly displaced persons often correlate with increased health and mental health needs. Thus, an understanding of migration context, the terminology used to categorize immigrants and the subsequent benefits attached to status, and the health and mental health characteristics of current populations moving globally can develop a more informed workforce.

To begin, we provide operational definitions and supporting literature to discuss the three elements of the migration experience: *Pre-arrival experiences* in the country of origin, *migration* experiences while in transit to the resettlement country, and *resettlement experiences* (post-arrival) in the new host country. As mentioned, we discuss the diversity of labels used to describe different categories of forcibly displaced persons and the citizenship or status rights associated with these labels. We also include a discussion of acculturation theory (Berry, 1997; Phillimore, 2011) and the U-curve of adjustment (Lysgaard, 1955) to provide a framework for understanding the process of adjustment. Finally, we provide a discussion around unique needs presented among trauma-exposed populations and common services and resources that promote positive adjustment in new countries. Given that the majority of immigrants and refugee arrivals seek opportunities to improve their own life conditions and contribute to their new societies, this chapter provides the foundation for understanding how professionals can better support new arrivals in reaching this goal.

THE MIGRATION PROCESS

The process of immigrating begins with making the decision to leave one's country, continues through the experience of traveling, and ends with the adjustment of the individual to the new social-political circumstances of the new country (Foster, 2007). Migrants undergo transitions within three primary aspects of their lives: These include altering social supports and connections, transitioning to a new socioeconomic system, and adjusting to new cultural norms (Kirmayer et al., 2011) Before diving into the different phases of migration, it is important to highlight the common thread of trauma, which is defined as a deeply distressing or disturbing event or series of events. At each stage of the journey, trauma can be experienced and this is particularly unfortunate for persons who have already experienced a series of traumatic events that often are the catalyst for them leaving their home country. Perez-Foster (2005) recognizes the possibility of *peri-migration trauma*, which means there is a risk for trauma to occur at multiple different points in the journey. For example, the initial events leading to migration (e.g., war or poverty), events that occur during migration (e.g., rape, theft, exploitation, or hunger), issues with obtaining legal status (such as asylum) and associated stress after entering a country, and the struggles of surviving as a new immigrant because of xenophobia, limited employment opportunities, and poor living conditions can all be experienced as traumatic events. This is shared to underscore the complex nature of immigration, compounded with trauma, which ultimately influences the degree to which new arrivals are able to adjust and integrate into a new society. In an effort to support new immigrants as they heal from past experiences and learn to thrive in a new environment, professionals must be keenly aware of the complex and overlapping nature of trauma that interweaves through each migrant story.

Pre-Migration Experiences

The catalyst for migration is diverse yet rooted in the migrants' experiences within their country of origin. Lack of access to resources that meet basic needs is reason enough for people to migrate. Others leave their home countries because of overt threats to their safety and well-being; this includes acts of genocide, ethnic or political persecution, widespread crime, civil war, and civil unrest. Still more flee because of environmental issues that cause draught, famine, disease, or loss of home and livelihood during natural disasters. These events are known as push factors, meaning people are driven out of their homes because of issues within their country of origin. Conversely, pull factors are appealing aspects of another country, such as political stability or increased economic opportunities, which motivate individuals to leave their country. Migration can take many forms, including being internally displaced within one's country or crossing an international border with or without documents to have legal protections in the temporary host country. We recognize the broad spectrum of migration experiences and the vast implications they have on individuals during transit.

CATALYSTS FOR MOVEMENT. The decision to leave one's country may be a thought-out process or may happen suddenly because of serious safety concerns. While some migration is controlled with extensive applications (i.e., refugee processing), some migration patterns are uncontrolled and unregulated, driven by fear and a need for safety. Unaccompanied minors are defined by the United Nations Committee on the Rights of the Child as any child under the age of 18 "who has been separated from both parents and other relatives and are not being cared for by an adult who, by law or custom, is responsible for doing so" (www.ohchr.org, n.d.). These youth are predominantly from El Salvador, Guatemala, Honduras, and Mexico; they are driven out of their home by lack of economic opportunities and high homicide and crime rates and immigrate without their guardian to countries like the United States in desperate hope for safety. U.S. Customs and Border Protection reported 68,541 unaccompanied minors were detained while trying to enter the border from October of 2013 to September of 2014. During the journey, the minors face many dangers associated with unsafe travel, such as illness or death as well as increased vulnerability to sexual or financial exploitation (Rosenblum, 2015). The case of unaccompanied minors highlights both push and pull factors, as the youth are driven out of the home because of violence but have hopes of increased safety and economic opportunities.

Applicable to the experiences of unaccompanied minors, the journey for immigrants often means leaving family, relatives, and friends behind and taking the journey, perhaps with some family members or completely alone. In addition to the loss of social supports, many immigrants and refugees also leave behind material possessions that they will never return to. Upon making the decision to leave, migrants may travel on foot, bus, boat, or plane. If an individual is granted a visa, there may not be special considerations for entering a country, but those traveling undocumented often take perilous journeys in order to avoid detection while entering. Recent news highlighted the potential for an immigrant's journey to end in tragedy when an image surfaced of a small Syrian boy, Alan Kurdi, washed up on shore after drowning on September 2, 2015, while trying to flee with his family by boat from Syria. This heartbreaking picture brought international attention to the largest refugee crisis in recent history and cast refugee issues into the forefront of global politics.

The International Organization of Migration estimated that in 2015 alone, 3,700 migrants perished while trying to reach Europe, which brings the death toll average to approximately 10 people each day. Syrians have been the largest group displaced population in recent times, emigrating from their native country because of a civil war beginning in 2011 that has since displaced half of the total Syrian population and killed at least 300,000 citizens. Millions have fled to surrounding countries, such as Lebanon, Jordan, and Turkey, but refugee camps in neighboring nations are now facing overcrowding and limited resources, such as food and shelter. Many Syrians are making the decision to migrate to neighboring countries in Europe in hopes of finding improved conditions. They are typically traveling by foot, vehicle, or by boat, either in overcrowded rafts on the Mediterranean, journeying on land through perilous paths in the Balkins, or riding in inhospitable conditions in the back of cars or trucks. Four million people continue to flow out of Syria, and as some decide that survival means making the journey to European countries, the death toll will likely continue to rise in the future, and we will see the implications of mass forced migration play out in real time. These examples—the unaccompanied minors of Central America and the displaced Syrian populations—highlight the sad reality of migration trends and shed light on the relevance of this topic and the importance of obtaining a better understanding of specific migration experiences that should directly influence how we serve these populations in the field.

THE IMPORTANCE OF LABELS. There has been much debate in the literature and media regarding the interchangeability of the terms *immigrant* and *refugee*. Many advocates for immigrants' rights argue that outdated guidelines determine which populations meet the classification of refugees, and this often excludes millions of people who are suffering from the deprivation of basic human rights that directly threaten their safety and well-being. However, the UNHCR argues that immigrants are people who choose to leave their home in hopes of improving their life, regardless of prior circumstances, and they face no danger should they choose to return to their country of origin (Edwards, 2016). The 2015 through 2016 migration crisis in Europe has highlighted the problematic usage of the term migrant, as some governments attempted to avail themselves of responsibility for the wave of Syrians who entered the European Union by arguing that the mass migration was because of economic factors. Millions more from countries such as Zimbawe, Haiti, and Libya are fleeing because of the failure of local government; they seek financial gains as the only means of survival and cannot return home without facing the same dire circumstances (Betts et al., 2014). It is problematic to conflate the terms immigrant and refugees, as refugee status has massive legal implications and the immigrant experience encapsulates those leaving to gain greater financial stability versus those seeking resources to survive. However, it is essential to recognize immigrants could face greater challenges because of the lack of legal protections if they are undocumented when they enter another country.

For the purpose of this chapter, we want to delineate the experiences of three vulnerable groups who are likely to migrate or are already considered immigrants: *Internally displaced persons, stateless citizens,* and *refugees* (broadly defined here as persons who cross an international border because of a well-founded fear of persecution). We acknowledge that unaccompanied minors and asylum seekers are also in a position of being forcibly displaced, however, for the purpose of illustrating adjustment needs, we will focus on specific immigration status. Despite that delineation, the information around migration experiences and service considerations can apply across all categories of displaced persons. In each case, the experiences abroad directly impact adjustment outcomes once they are resettled in a new country. And despite the label given to each individual, there is the common thread that connects people moving from one place to another: the hope for a better future.

INTERNALLY DISPLACED PERSONS.   There are those who remain within the borders of their country of origin; such individuals are labeled as **internally displaced persons** or IDPs. An individual may become displaced for three reasons: natural disaster, armed conflict or civil unrest within the country, or interstate conflict (Walter, 2008). Those displaced because of internal conflict are often considered the largest vulnerable population in the world, and one of the most urgent humanitarian issues of this age, as these people often flee their homes only to remain within the legal jurisdiction of a government that caused their flight (Hampton, 2014). Across the world, rates of morbidity, malnutrition, and mortality are higher for this population compared to nondisplaced citizens (Guerrier et al., 2009; Nielson, Prudhon, & de Radigues, 2011; Toole & Waldman, 1997). All too often, access to basic medical care and critical resources are purposely limited by those in power, putting these individuals at increased risk for morbidity and mortality (Leus, Wallace, & Loretti, 2001). As of 2014, the Internal Displacement Monitoring Centre calculated a total of 38 million IDPs because of political disaster alone and 19.3 million displaced by geophysical and weather-related disasters. Relief aid is often provided for emergency situations, but all too often, those who are displaced for long periods of time find themselves without adequate resources or humanitarian support (Agier, 2008). The hopeful outcome for these individuals is stabilization within their country and a return to their homes and livelihoods, but too frequently political IDPs are forced to seek another resolution by fleeing across borders in order to survive. At this point, IDPs will become classified as immigrants (documented or undocumented) or refugees.

STATELESS CITIZENS. **Stateless citizens** are people who, because of corrupt or broken political systems, are denied nationality in any country. The UNHCR estimates more than 10 million individuals across the world are stateless, but it has proven difficult to track this population because of their precarious legal status and understandable desire to remain invisible (UNHCR, 2012). As of 2013, the UNHCR identified Myanmar (also known as Burma), Ivory Coast, Thailand, and Latvia as countries that have created the largest number of stateless citizens; either because of the dissolution of political structures, redrawing of borders, or targeted political efforts aimed at ethnic cleansing. Discussions of statelessness bring up questions regarding citizenship and basic human rights—what French anthropologist Michael Agier (2008) identified as the inherent "right to have rights" (p. 189). There are efforts underway to resolve the issue of statelessness, as stateless individuals are often denied basic rights and are particularly vulnerable to police brutality and discrimination, with no method for recourse. Stateless citizens are denied access to financial systems, such as banks, and are often unable to access public education systems. Additionally, they face of life of poverty and exploitation, since they are not legally allowed to work in any country. They are forced to live life on the fringes of society, often fearing what the future holds. As with IDPs, their only hope may be fleeing their country of origin in hopes of a better life.

REFUGEES. The United Nations High Commissioner for Refugees (1951) currently defines a **refugee** as a person, "who owing to a well-founded fear of persecution for reasons of race, religion, nationality, membership of a particular social group or political opinion, is outside of the country of his nationality and is unable to, or owing to such fear, is unwilling to avail himself to the protection of the country." As mentioned previously, we recognize that the classification of refugee can be exclusionary and by no means includes all those facing human rights violations. The UNHCR estimated there were 19.5 million refugees around the world at the end of 2014. These are individuals and families who cannot trust that their governing bodies or their countrymen will act in their best interests. In some instances, gross human rights violations are perpetuated at the hands of authority figures and neighbors alike—thus, a refugee is displaced from his or her home and must cross an international border to seek refuge and safety in a neighboring country. Oftentimes, the trek across the border can be perilous in itself, and these individuals can be vulnerable to continued acts of violence while in transit. If individuals safely cross an international border, they must then reach a United Nations-designated processing center within an organized refugee camp or at a designated location within an urban city. At that time, an application for refugee status can be filed, and the UNHCR must find a solution for each person, if their situation qualifies them for refugee status. At this time, there are only three solutions: voluntary repatriation into one's country of origin, host country integration, or third country resettlement.

Voluntary repatriation is the solution for the majority of registered refugees. This involves returning to the country of origin after the conflict has been resolved. The responsibility to ensure citizens' safety rests primarily on the country of origin, but international parties remain involved to oversee the reintegration process. *Host country integration* means that the individual is absorbed by the country where they originally sought asylum. Oftentimes, this will be a country that borders their country of origin, and the country recognizes that individuals cannot return home because of prolonged conflict or indefinite fear of persecution upon return. According to the UNHCR, approximately 1.1 million refugees have been granted citizenship status in the country where they originally sought protection.

Third country resettlement is the last and least likely outcome for a refugee. This means that a refugee is granted a path to citizenship by an outside country. These refugees leave the country that granted them asylum and move to another country to rebuild their lives. For many, third country resettlement is the only option, as continued conflicts lead to unstable situations in entire regions, and many surrounding countries are unable to absorb or adequately serve the large numbers that flee during crises (UNHCR, 2012). However, the likelihood of being granted this opportunity would be the equivalent of winning a global lottery. As of 2015, there were 59.6 million refugee applications filed throughout the world. This number doesn't account for the IDPs who have yet to file for refugee status but are equally endangered and unable to return to their homes. Of that number of identified refugees, less than 1% will become eligible to be resettled in a third country. In FY2015, the United States Refugee Resettlement Program led the world in serving as a humanitarian model, receiving approximately 70,000 of the 150,000 refugees globally who had been approved for thirdcountry resettlement. With that said, refugees approved for resettlement understand the gravity of that opportunity. While many do not know the details of what life in a new country will be like, they understand that third country resettlement will be the closing of a chapter in their life abroad. And with that may come joy and excitement as well as grief and guilt; joy for the opportunity to start life anew but grief and guilt for leaving so many behind with no certainty for the future.

Overseas processing requirements vary by country but typically involve a series of interviews, health, and background checks. The interviews are conducted to both justify the application for refugee status and determine the level of need and risk. Women and children are typically seen as most at-risk in displacement and given priority over others, although the rules are not concrete. Health evaluations are required to ensure refugee applicants do not have a communicable disease that could compromise the health of the larger community upon resettlement. And background checks are instituted to ensure safety of the host country's citizens, with specific requirements defined by the receiving country. For the United States, background checks are extensive and completed by the U.S. Department of Homeland Security to ensure members of any terrorist organization cannot infiltrate U.S. borders through this pathway. Interviews by field agents through the U.S. Department of State are also conducted and once approved, refugees sign a travel loan (meaning they are expected to repay the government) to obtain an airline ticket and are escorted by a representative from the International Organization for Migration (IOM) to their point of entry state in the United States.

EXPERIENCES IN TRANSIT
BASED ON IMMIGRATION STATUS

The process of displacement and resettlement is physically and emotionally stressful for those who leave their country with either undocumented or documented status—including those with immigrant, refugee, or stateless status; asylum seekers; and unaccompanied minors (internally displaced persons are excluded for the purpose of this discussion of resettlement). There is fear and uncertainty for the future, grief for the loss of loved ones and country, and the cumulative impact to health and mental health when there is no consistent access to food, adequate medical care, education, or employment opportunities throughout the process. For asylum seekers and refugees, the application process narrates a story fraught with pain and recounting horrific memories in an effort to justify being "worthy" of eligibility for rights and status in a new country. There is distrust in the system and a fear of disappointment that has been felt throughout the journey. Specific to those with refugee status, when approval is received to travel, there is still hesitation and disbelief. Oftentimes, these feelings start with the departure from the refugee's country, through transit, and during those first three critical months of adjustment in a new country. And since refugees make the decision to leave their country out of fear for their safety, third country resettlement can bring forth the realization that they will likely never return to their country of origin.

The experiences in transit from one country to another can be directly influenced by the travel documentation that is available prior to departure and upon entry in a host country or temporary destination. In certain cases when the political situation is dire with no hope of resolution, citizens can be processed within their country of origin, and this is the case for those seeking refugee status in designated countries including Iraq, the former Soviet Union, and Vietnam or those with parolee status in the case of Cuba. For all others, the issue of documentation and immigration status in a receiving country directly influences the level of stress during transit and the ease of adjustment upon arrival (Pérez & Fortuna, 2005; Sullivan & Rehm, 2005), because immigrant status affords specific legal rights, assurances, and access to public resources. While we discuss specific immigration statuses—documented and undocumented immigrants—we also recognize that the UNHCR tracks other displaced groups and populations of concern, including returned refugees, returned IDPs, stateless persons, and populations under the UNHCR category of other concerns. Although not included in the main discussions, portions of our discussion can equally apply to these groups and are worth considering.

Figure 2.1 provides a decade-long look at the trends for refugees and asylum seekers and internally displaced persons around the world who seek status in other countries. This image shows both the enormity of the issue as well as the almost consistently increasing numbers throughout those years with the end-of-year 2014 number surpassing any year prior (The UNHCR *Global Trends 2015* report—see introduction chapter for full citation). This image highlights the relevance of the topics discussed in this book and demonstrates the likelihood that the refugee crisis will remain an international issue in the foreseeable future.

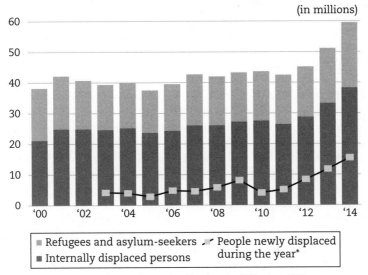

Figure 2.1 Displacement in the 21st Century, 2000–2014

(in millions)

Legend:
- Refugees and asylum-seekers
- Internally displaced persons
- People newly displaced during the year*

* Displaced internally and across international borders. Available since 2003.

Source: United Nations High Comissioner for Refugees. *Global Trends: Forced Displacement in 2015* (Geneva: UNHCR, 2015), 6.

IMMIGRANT STATUS. Immigrants arrive to their host country with a basic set of legal protections and documentation stating their right to stay, but there are often country-specific limitations regarding the resources immigrants are allowed to access before being granted permanent citizenship. There are different types of visas that allow for legal travel into a different country, including visas for students, businessmen, leisure travel, and professional presentations (see travel.state.gov for visa categories in the United States). When compared to refugees, those granted immigrant status are more likely to be highly educated and have access to financial resources, which points to the selectivity of the immigration process (World Migration in Figures, 2013). The process for applying for immigration status can be costly and lengthy and often means the immigrant needs financial supports and social capital that allow them to navigate the system. Those without such means will not likely be able to complete the process and will have to seek alternative options should they wish to leave their home country.

UNDOCUMENTED IMMIGRANT STATUS. Individuals who immigrate to a country without legal status face a number of challenges, including the real and constant threat of deportation. Additionally, undocumented individuals face barriers to accessing safety nets and resources, particularly financial and medical supports. In 2011, 71% of undocumented immigrants in the United States did not have any form of medical insurance, which meant they only accessed medical care during emergency situations (Capps, Fix, Van Hook, & Bachmeier, 2013). Undocumented individuals also were at greater risk for negative mental health outcomes, such as poor self-esteem and feelings of shame, fear, guilt, and the lack of security. They have limited legal rights, which could make them vulnerable to exploitations in the workplace or from landlords. Undocumented immigrants in the United States report high rates of acculturative stress connected to financial concerns, which is likely tied to limited employment opportunities and the exclusion from receiving public benefits (Cavazos-Rehg, Zayas, & Spitznagel, 2007). Although this is far from an exhaustive list of implications, these outcomes illuminate the reality that documentation has a cumulative effect on health, mental health, and adjustment outcomes.

REFUGEE STATUS (ADULTS AND MINORS). All individuals seeking refugee status must cross into a bordering country prior to beginning their paperwork. Regardless of whether an individual has a visa or is without documentation, those seeking refugee or asylum status still need to follow the appropriate steps to register for status. After crossing international borders, they are first required to register with the UNHCR and undergo an interview to determine if the case will be categorized under refugee status. In order to better understand the steps for processing, it can be helpful to provide a case study on a specific country, while recognizing there are unique rules and regulations for each country. The next steps are particular to the United States but exemplify the complexity of processing. Within the United States (U.S.) there are three different levels of processing priorities, and a refugee must qualify for one of these before they are granted an interview with a U.S. Citizenship and Immigration Services (USCIS) officer. Priority one (P1) is reserved for those that are recognized by the UNHCR, the U.S. embassy, or particular NGOs working within the region. Priority two (P2) are those recognized by the U.S. program for refugees as needing humanitarian aid. Finally, Priority three (P3) is reserved for individuals who have certain family members living legally with the United States. This includes spouses, parents, and single children below the age of 21 who have a family member accepted to the United States as either a refugee or an asylum seeker.

Once this status is obtained, the refugee must undergo a series of health and security checks, a process that takes an average of 18 months for the United States according to the U.S. Department of State, but can take as little as four months for other countries. Refugees often site issues with processing, such as trouble accessing the processing offices or obtaining necessary paperwork for security checks. There are often substantial administrative delays, and thousands of refugees are currently in a holding pattern, waiting to come to the United States after completing all aspects of their processing.[1]

Although some refugees are processed within one to two years (omidadvocates.org, 2011), some refugees are relegated to "temporary" camps while waiting for processing. These settlements are often established as short-term solutions to provide safety when a crisis occurs, but the average time spent in camps is now 17 years (National Public Radio, 2014). In 2012, there were approximately 6.4 million people living for five or more years in the country where they sought asylum, with no resolution or move toward permanent resettlement (UNHCR, 2012). The prolonged stay in camps results

---

[1] (http://www.npr.org/2015/09/04/437596917/hias-president-u-s-europe-treating-migrant-crisis-like-business-as-usual).

from hopes that the continued political instability within their country of origin will subside, but human rights activists argue these protracted encampments violate basic rights outlined in the 1951 UN Refugee Convention (www.unhcr.org). For example, while in camps, most refugees face restricted movement and are unable to earn wages through work; this relegates them to a life of poverty within camps originally designed to be temporary establishments. Additionally, refugees often do not have access to adequate healthcare, leading to increased rates of diseases. A meta-analysis comparing the prevalence of mental health issues for refugee versus nonrefugee populations found refugees held in camps had poorer mental health outcomes (Porter & Haslam, 2005). Experiences vary; however, it is acknowledged that refugees in camps or urban settings are vulnerable and face a life of waiting and hoping for a better outcome and permanent resettlement.

POST-MIGRATION RESETTLEMENT: THE REFUGEE EXPERIENCE

The nature of adjusting to life in a new country will be directly influenced by one's social capital, sense of resilience, and overall health (Pahud et al., 2009; Schweitzer, Greenslade, & Kagee, 2007). As we have suggested, there is no typical migration experience, but there are common experiences shared among migrants irrespective of formal citizenship status, method of transportation, and shared experiences of fear and persecution. At the same time, social service organizations serving those with refugee status—although varied by country—tend to be the most comprehensive and holistic in their approach to help refugees integrate into a new society. For this reason, we focus our discussion on the resettlement experiences of individuals with *refugee* status. Although this is a very specific category of immigrants, national or state programs supporting documented and undocumented immigrants may benefit from the information on service infrastructures designed for refugee arrivals.

Once a refugee is granted access to a destination country and given a plane ticket to travel, a refugee begins the journey to their new home. The resettlement period refers to when an immigrant or refugee arrives in a new country (sometimes referred to as a "host" country) and begins the formation and integration of a new social identity that aligns with his or her new environment (Berry, 1997; Bhatia & Ram, 2009). As mentioned, irrespective of immigration status (documented or undocumented) or intention to migrate (planned or unplanned), adjustment to a new country impacts all parties to varying degrees. The first 90 days post-arrival is a particularly critical period for all newly arrived immigrants. Lysgaard's **U-curve of adjustment** (1955) illustrates the ways in which newly arrived immigrants transition through several phases of adjustment, starting with the honeymoon period. This is the time immediately following arrival when the individual is happy to have arrived and excited to experience all aspects of their new culture. However, following this is often a period known as culture shock, when the individual feels overwhelmed by the reality of their new situation and often faces setbacks that cause them to feel challenged within their new environment. As the individual begins to familiarize themselves with aspects of this new environment and adapt to cultural norms and expectations, they enter a period known as adjustment. The final stage is mastery, which is often achieved within approximately two years of resettlement and involves a return to full functioning and comfort.

Resettlement experiences are further impacted by the ease with which an individual is able to enter the adjustment phase. Refugees face the unique challenge of rebuilding their lives after being forcibly displaced during traumatic situations and often arrive to their new country with few social or financial resources. They must rely on social supports established within their host country, and these systems vary across the world. Refugees range from highly educated to illiterate even within their native language (Nezer, 2014). They may also be able-bodied and of working age or elderly with severe mental or physical challenges. Common challenges include lack of access to adequate housing or employment, which can perpetuate a refugee's feelings of exclusion and trauma even within their new country. Refugees may find themselves in a country they know little about and that they did not desire to immigrate to, and therefore adjustment can be a prolonged and arduous process.

Within the refugee experience, there is a continuum of need, so it is important to understand the systems that aid in resettlement and assist those seeking support during their adjustment period. Specific to the United States, refugees are offered resettlement and adjustment services through **resettlement agencies**. The agencies provide support in each critical area of resettlement: housing, case management, employment, English language training, mental health services, citizenship applications, family reunification, and youth services. They also receive cash benefits and food assistance from the government on a time-limited basis. Given that the needs of refugees can be complex, other support organizations, known as **mutual aid associations**, assist refugees after they have phased out of services at the resettlement agency. Mutual aid associations (also known as ethnic community-based organizations) are agencies started by previously resettled populations from specific ethnic groups to aid in the resettlement of refugees from their country or region of origin. These agencies are started through grassroots efforts and community organizing around the needs of the population and are created by refugees and for refugees; they offer many services, including case management and immigration and interpretation support, while also fostering a shared sense of community. Moreover, religious organizations and social service organizations also play a vital role in supporting the refugees with services extending beyond resettlement needs.

RECOVERY/ADJUSTMENT. The overall adjustment to a new society can be further understood in terms of acculturation levels. Berry (2005) defined **acculturation** as "a process of cultural and psychological changes that involve various forms of mutual accommodation" (p. 699), ultimately transforming aspects of both populations involved. There is great variability regarding the strategies individuals or groups deploy to achieve acculturation, but Berry denounces earlier assertions that immigrant populations must assimilate, meaning adapt to the dominant culture by adopting the prevailing cultural and linguistic practices and relinquishing aspects of their native identity.

The extent to which migration is voluntary is an important contextual factor when examining the process of acculturation (Phillimore, 2011). Additionally, certain sociopolitical factors within the country of resettlement are also important; dominant ideologies range from cultural pluralism to monoculturalism, and this determines how accepting a society will be of newcomers and whether legal and social forces will allow for acculturation versus assimilation. Based upon these factors, there are four identified acculturation strategies: assimilation, separation, incorporation, and marginalization (Berry, 1997). **Assimilation** is the full emergence of the newly arrived populations into the dominant culture. Conversely, separation is defined as the desire of nondominant groups to preserve their unique cultural identity by avoiding contact with those not from their culture. Incorporation is when both groups interact regularly but also maintain important aspects of their own culture. This has been identified as a "transcultural identity" and is seen as the most adaptive strategy for successful adjustment (Suarez-Orezco & Qin-Hilliard, 2004). However, marginalization occurs when cultural groups are excluded from interactions with others but do not have a strong association with their culture of origin because of pressures imposed upon them by the dominant groups.

Critics of Berry's model feel that acculturation does not happen linearly but is a dynamic, fluid process that accounts for historical context and the ongoing interactions between both parties (Bhatia & Ram, 2009), and we would agree. It is argued refugees should be seen as active participants in the adjustment process, negotiating between cultures and not simply accepting of the host-country's norms (Kamali, 1999). In addition to sociopolitical factors, there are a number of variables that mediate each person's experience of acculturation. For this reason, it is imperative not to make sweeping generalizations about refugee populations that are resettled within a particular area without noting the varied ways each person may internalize and cope with the experience (Lopez et al., 2011; Zagelbam & Carlson, 2011). However, it is essential to note trends within the refugee population, so practitioners have an understanding of the possible needs and are proactive in assessing when working with individuals.

The common thread noted throughout literature is the prevalent exposure to trauma among refugees. Many refugees arrive to their host country after experiencing trauma, such as torture, forced imprisonment, death of loved ones, and starvation (Murray, Davidson, & Schweitzer, 2010; Palic & Elklit, 2010). Although exact numbers are unknown, it is estimated that up to 91% of refugees experience post-traumatic stress disorder (or PTSD) as a result of their traumatic history (Johnson & Thompson, 2006). Although trauma is the largest reported mental health issue, refugees are as diverse in their mental health needs as any other population, and there is no universal experience; 2011 through 2014 trends from one of the largest refugee resettlement agencies in Chicago revealed that 30% of individuals resettled received mental health services for adjustment-based needs, while 28% suffer from anxiety (including trauma symptoms) and 22% from mood-based disorders. Although the exact rates of intimate partner violence (IPV) in newly arrived refugee communities is unknown, reports of the humanitarian crisis in Syria project the rates of IPV and gender-based violence (such as child marriage) is on the rise because of the stress of migration, the lack of government oversight, and increased financial pressures (Anani, 2013).

Since stress is positively correlated to increases in IPV, refugee populations undergoing trauma and corresponding resettlement stress will likely have higher rates of domestic violence. Additionally, women are particularly vulnerable. At least one in five displaced women in humanitarian emergency situations experience sexual assault, and they often arrive to their host country with the physical or psychological ramifications of the trauma (Vu et al., 2014). Research further suggests that the challenges refugees face post-arrival, such as difficulty accessing employment or ELT-based supports, are connected to the progression and continuation of trauma symptoms (Carlsson, Mortensen, & Kastrup, 2005; Kinzie, 2006). Many refugees face continued stress and secondary trauma because their loved ones remain in camps or warzones (Murray et al., 2010). The process of resettlement in a new country often causes psychological distress, which is connected to higher rates of poor mental and physical health outcomes (Agbényiga et al., 2012; Berry, 1997). Most refugees arrive to their host country with a limited understanding of the new culture, sometimes only learning where they will be resettled days prior to the flight. Refugees from specific ethnic backgrounds can face discrimination in housing, employment, and education sectors and can feel excluded and isolated from the dominant society.

In the role of professional and community member, the hope is that we are able to validate and respect the culture and unique identity of each new immigrant while integrating an understanding of the rules and norms of their resettlement/destination country during this recovery/adjustment phase. This is no simple feat. New immigrants offer a great deal of resources to their resettlement country, including a strong work ethic, a desire to improve their lives and their community, and an aspiration to become contributing citizens of their new society. At the same time, they face formidable challenges in their adjustment and journey toward becoming self-sufficient (i.e., economically stable and able to navigate the new society independently). Language barriers; nontransferable skills; lack of understanding of the various education, healthcare, and financial systems in the United States; and the cumulative impact of trauma on health and mental health functioning can inhibit reaching self-sufficiency goals. There are key resources and factors, however, that support positive adjustment and acculturation in a resettlement country. These factors will be discussed in the next section.

KEY ELEMENTS OF ADJUSTMENT

For the purpose of our discussion on social services and resources to support adjustment, we will be focusing on those supports given specifically to refugees. The services provided to those with refugee status versus other immigrant statuses (undocumented, student/employment, asylum seeker, etc.) is often vastly different across countries, as international law mandates specific protections and support to refugee populations but does not necessarily have strict guidelines or mechanisms for protecting the rights of immigrants. Each country determines the rights and privileges of immigrants based on eligibility and immigrant status. The Refugee Resettlement Program in the United States is overseen by the U.S. Department of

State, which has specific mandates for the services that must be made available to those entering the country with refugee status. Many of the core services discussed in this section are available only to refugees, despite the apparent need for increased services for immigrants. That being said, we offer the discussion to demonstrate the breadth of services that can and do help with adjustment for new immigrant arrivals irrespective of legal status in the country. Any agency serving immigrants (documented or undocumented) or refugees can enhance integration and positive adjustment when using holistic and integrated services that typically exist for newly arrived refugees. These services include supports to addresses the financial, emotional, and educational needs of each refugee arrival. Based on the literature and what we understand in practice, there are several important components that support positive adjustment to a resettlement country, and those components are as follows: housing, access to community, access to English- or native-language training, family and social support, financial and employment resources, and adequate health and mental health supports.

HOUSING. Resettlement agencies are responsible for identifying affordable housing that will serve as the refugee's first home upon arrival. This is particularly critical for refugees who do not have established familial connections when arriving to their destination country. Shelter is a basic human need that assists with feelings of safety and security, and stable housing is connected to reduced stress and better adjustment outcomes (Lindencrona, Ekblad, & Hauff, 2008). At the same time, many housing management companies would be reluctant to rent an apartment to a new refugee arrival who has no income and no credit history or employment at move-in. Organizations play a critical role in advocating for new arrivals and vouching that language and employment services will be provided to help refugees get on their feet quickly, secure a job, and be able to pay for rent on their own. In the United States, three months of housing funds are allocated to offset initial costs, yet more supports are necessary. These include information on how to live in apartments—including use of the utilities, how to deal with common household pests, and the rules and regulations set forth in the lease enumerating allowed activities in rented spaces. The organization teaches clients how and when to pay rent, who to speak to when maintenance is required, and other critical skills that foster mutually beneficial relationships between tenants and landlords. Resettlement organizations can also build diverse ethnic communities by resettling new arrivals from diverse cultures in specific neighborhoods as a natural social support in adjustment. Moreover, thoughtful consideration of where housing is located—as it relates to public transportation, school systems, groceries, religious communities, proximity to vital social and health services, and so forth—will be critical to integration for new immigrants.

ACCESS TO A COMMUNITY (INCLUDES LANGUAGE, FOOD, RELIGIOUS ORGANIZATIONS, TRADITIONS). Refugees come with a complex social history and thriving cultural and religious backgrounds. Although acculturation involves integrating aspects of the host-country's culture, individuals also benefit from community resources that celebrate important aspects of their native culture. Thoughtful housing that builds ethnic communities is one opportunity to cultivate supportive cultural communities, but resettlement organizations can also do more to support the importance of continued connection to meaningful aspects of a person's culture, as noted in current acculturation literature. Celebration and validation of religious practices and cultural events is valuable to new arrivals. This can include adjusting training programs (language, employment, etc.) to account for cultural holidays and making accommodations so refugees can practice their culture in a meaningful way. Ensuring that new arrivals know where to buy foods native to their home country and accessing established ethnic or religious communities already in the area is also critical. Part of this is education on how to navigate new cities, but it also requires thoughtful placement of new arrivals into communities that maintain their connection to important aspects of their culture.

ACCESS TO ENGLISH-LANGUAGE TRAINING OR NATIVE LANGUAGE TRAINING. Language is vital for adjustment; it allows newcomers to navigate unfamiliar legal and social systems and fosters financial stability through increased workforce participation. Language skills are correlated with mental health outcomes; those with lower levels are more likely to experience mental health concerns upon arrival to their host country (Hilado & Kim, n.d.). Unfortunately, many refugees do not possess language skills upon arrival to the destination country, and refugees arrive with widely varying levels of education. The United States not only accepts the largest number of refugees per year but has the least stringent language and education requirements for resettlement, accepting any vulnerable individual without stipulations on English language skills, employment, or education history. For this reason, intensive English-Language Training (ELT) programs are an essential aspect of refugee resettlement programs in the United States. These services may be offered within resettlement agencies, local colleges, or religious organizations and are available to refugee populations at no cost. Oftentimes, these programs incorporate language used in the workplace and language to foster daily living skills, including navigation of local community resources (health services, groceries, schools, financial institutions, public transportation, etc.). As such, language training is essential to helping new refugee arrivals navigate a new country and its diverse service systems while becoming self-sufficient and independent of the resettlement organization.

FAMILY AND SOCIAL SUPPORT. Social supports are defined as positive interactions with family, friends, or professionals that promote coping by providing tangible resources or emotional guidance (Stewart & Lagille, 2000). These supports become critical during transitions, such as when moving to a new country. Those working with refugees cited that "having social support helps newcomers by fostering a sense of empowerment, community and social integration, building networks, sharing experiences and problems, reducing stress, and contributing to physical and mental health (Simich et al., 2005, p. 263). Social supports provide the platform on which the newcomers can rebuild their lives. Refugee processing recognizes the benefits of familial support and often prioritizes family reunification when considering where to resettle an individual. For example, if a refugee has family in Germany they were separated from during flight, they will likely be resettled within the city their family is located. Family reunification is a priority in the United States Refugee Resettlement Program under the same premise that families and communities thrive when connected. For those without familial or social networks upon arrival, resettlement organizations must make an extra effort to increase a refugee's connection to others through connecting him with similar cultures in the community, mentorship programs, or partnerships with ethnic-specific partner agencies.

FINANCIAL AND EMPLOYMENT RESOURCES. Many refugees arrive to their destination country with few economic resources. Even those who were wealthy within their country of origin often lose most assets while fleeing or by paying smugglers to facilitate their escape. For this reason, financial supports become critical for most refugees upon arrival to their host country (Hilado & Kim, n.d.). Each country resettling refugees allocates a specific amount to aid arrivals during the initial adjustment period. The total financial amount and the length of time refugees can access financial support varies by country. In the United States, newly arrived refugees are allocated a housing stipend to aid with housing for the first three months, access to medical insurance for low-income residents, and access to food stamps. However, once the financial resources run out (i.e., housing resources), refugees can find themselves in a precarious financial situation. Although policies within the United States and many other countries emphasize self-sufficiency through employment as a primary and immediate goal for resettlement (Capps & Fix, 2015), the trauma-history and challenges of adjusting to a new society can be difficult to realize within the first year post-arrival. As such, refugee resettlement organizations place great effort into securing viable employment to help refugees reach self-sufficiency as quickly as possible. This often includes partnering with companies, educating them about who refugees are and the skill sets they can provide, and serving as a liaison when there are cultural misunderstandings or additional training required in the workplace. Simultaneously, other refugee adjustment programs like language training and health services are accessed to ensure refugees can enter the workforce ready to perform the necessary tasks on the job.

A good fit between refugee skills and available jobs is also a consideration for both the resettlement agency and newly arrived refugees. Labor markets within many developed nations have shifted; thus newly arrived refugees find themselves with decreased economic opportunities and a greater likelihood of remaining within or slightly above the poverty line (Portes & Zhou, 1993). Some have been required to accept labor-intensive jobs within factories, restaurants, hotels, or ethnic groceries in which language capacity and work history are not critical factors in getting employed. Highly educated professionals may find themselves in countries that do not recognize their previous training or work history, thus requiring a reapplication process to become recertified or entering completely different (often less skilled) sectors to access employment.

Many refugees are able to integrate into the workforce and become self-sufficient (i.e., able to pay one's basic expenses and thrive independently of the resettlement agency and without over-relying on public benefits) within one year of arrival. Naturally, it may take longer for those without transferrable skills that allow them to find a job readily or those who have health or mental health problems that inhibit their ability to function readily in a new society. In those cases, there are social safety nets available in the United States, but they are by no means sufficient as a long-term solution. As such, refugee resettlement organizations focus on creative partnerships with employers in the community and develop training programs to ensure refugees have the necessary skills and opportunities to become financially viable. The ability to support oneself and one's family is both important to society but also a new arrival's sense of self-worth, which contributes to her overall adjustment as well.

ADEQUATE HEALTH AND MENTAL HEALTH SUPPORTS. Health and mental health services can offer critical support and a platform for processing and healing (physical and psychological) from prior experiences that may impede adjustment to life in a new country. Observations from a Chicago-based refugee resettlement agency revealed that many refugees arrive with complex physical health needs that are not adequately treated prior to arrival. These health needs may be chronic, such as hypertension or diabetes, or a curable illness, such as tuberculosis or Hepatitis C. For this reason, clients should be immediately connected with a family doctor that can assess all physical health needs and connect clients to specialists as needed. Case managers at resettlement organizations often serve as liaisons between doctors' offices and clients, and they may be in charge of follow-up on referrals or obtain the results of testing.

In addition to physical health, mental health should be addressed upon arrival. Exposure to trauma is virtually a universal aspect of the refugee experience, but the prolonged response of the individual depends on the length and the severity of the trauma and on individual factors, such as resilience and social support. Exposure for this population tends to be prolonged, instead of single-episode events, which is correlated to higher rates of PTSD comparatively (Carlson & Rosser-Hogan, 1991; Silove, 1999). Adequate mental health services are essential, because studies show refugees are more likely than the general population to experience poor mental health symptoms (Porter & Haslam, 2005). The resettlement process is also a source of stress, as individuals face an uncertain future. Recent studies show that the process of resettlement can lead to negative mental health outcomes, so it is important to locate the source of distress when assessing a client's needs (Kirmayer et al., 2011).

Clients experiencing mental health issues may not be able to attend ELT or employment courses until stabilized, so providers should assess their functioning and advocate for proper treatment prior to engaging in additional services when appropriate. Mental health professionals serving trauma-exposed refugees must provide strengths-based services that focus on the resiliency of the individual and natural resources found within the community (Murray et al., 2010; Papadopoulos, 2007). For mental health services to be effective, providers should be culturally responsive, utilize best practice strategies appropriate for the populations served, and practice a trauma-informed approach. Therapists should use formally trained interpreters in order to prevent misunderstandings and remove linguistic barriers to care. Mental health services embedded within refugee resettlement agencies can be particularly effective, as they are easily accessible and located within the office refugees often travel to for employment, housing, and ELT services.

As it comes to health conditions, it is imperative to address health concerns that are often ignored or undertreated during flight and processing. There are higher rates of chronic and acute health issues for this population, so medical services become critical for many immediately upon arrival (Morris et al., 2009). These services include ensuring clients have access to medical insurance, connecting clients to linguistically responsive health care providers, providing psycho-education on health issues and medication managements, and overseeing medical care to ensure services are coordinated. Stabilization of health and mental health needs will only further prepare refugees (and any new immigrant) to actively engage in their new home country.

IMPLICATIONS FOR THE FIELD

The process of resettlement and adjustment for any new immigrant is complex and challenging yet full of opportunity when the proper resources and supports are provided to new arrivals. Each new immigrant arrives with a unique story, unique skill sets, and a spirit of resilience that can directly influence the ease (or struggle) in which he or she adjusts to life in a new country. And there are resources—housing support, language training, employment services and health services, to name a few—that can support positive adjustment when made available to new arrivals. The critical resources that must be received upon arrival are also important variables that can directly impact the immediate adjustment experiences upon arrival. Thus, countries need to be prepared with the knowledge that adjustment resources can influence the degree to which new immigrants successfully integrate into a new society and become contributing, productive members.

This chapter sought to highlight the importance and relevance of experience prior to arrival, experiences in transit, and post-arrival experiences that shape the adjustment process for any newly arrived immigrant. Attention to both the concrete needs of a new immigrant (e.g., housing, financial resources, community) and overall well-being (e.g., health and mental health) is necessary to ensure new immigrants—particularly trauma-exposed immigrants and refugees—have a solid foundation for starting a new life in a new country that is rooted in the dignity and self-worth of each new member of society.

REFLECTIVE QUESTIONS

1. Direct practice: If you are a case manager working with this family, what would you identify as the major priorities that must be addressed with the family as a whole and for each individual member?

2. Macro practice: How can the community support trauma-exposed immigrants like

Fatimah and her family? What policy, research, and advocacy efforts could help make the transition for individuals like Fatimah easier as they adjust to life in a new country?

CASE STUDY

Fatimah is a 45-year-old woman who was forced to leave her home suddenly after witnessing her husband's murder. She fled with her five children (ages 4–19) from Iraq to Jordan, where they spent nine months in a refugee camp. Fatimah describes being treated poorly by Jordanians, as they felt threatened and overwhelmed by the sudden influx of refugees from surrounding countries. Fatimah was focused on the survival of her family during the time and turned to her eldest brother, Mohammad, for support. Since they had familial ties, Fatimah and her children were resettled with Mohammad and his wife in Chicago. Upon arrival, staff at the refugee resettlement agency quickly noted a number of potential obstacles for self-sufficiency. Fatimah and Mohammad both displayed symptoms of severe post-traumatic stress after prolonged exposure to violence, and Fatimah's two youngest children began displaying behavioral issues in school. There was constant stress within the home, particularly between the eldest son and Mohammad, and finances were a continuous issue for the family. Out of nine people, only the two eldest children were able to work; they could only find low-wage jobs and were unable to support the basic needs of the family.

SUMMATIVE POINTS

- The term *refugee* has political connotations and is determined by the United Nations High Commissioner for Refugees. Those who face political crisis or discrimination are separated into three categories, with corresponding legal implications: internally displaced, stateless citizens, or refugees.

- A refugee's acculturation is determined by group dynamics and context as well as individual characteristics.

- There are important resources that should be provided for all refugees—including housing, access to community, access to ELT resources, family and social supports, financial supports, and adequate mental health services.

GLOSSARY

acculturation. A process of cultural and psychological changes that impacts both the population immigrating and the receiving country.

assimilation. The full emergence of the newly arrived populations into the dominant culture.

internally displaced person (IDP). Individuals who remain within the borders of their country of origin but are displaced from their home because of a natural disaster, armed conflict/civil unrest within the country, or interstate conflict.

mutual aid association (MAAs). Also known as ethnic community-based organizations, MAAs are agencies started by previously resettled populations from specific ethnic groups to aid in the resettlement of currently resettled refugees from their country or region of origin.

refugee. The United Nations High Commissioner for Refugees (1951) currently defines a refugee as a person, "who owing to a well-founded fear of persecution for reasons of race, religion, nationality, membership of a particular social group or political opinion, is outside of the country of his nationality and is unable to, or owing to such fear, is unwilling to avail himself to the protection of the country."

resettlement agency. Local agencies funded through government contracts provide support in each critical area of resettlement: housing, case management, employment, English language training, mental health services, citizenship applications, family reunification, and youth services.

stateless citizen. People who are denied nationality or legal rights in any country because of corrupt or broken political systems.

U-curve of adjustment. A framework that illustrates the ways in which a newly arrived immigrant transitions through several phases of adjustment, starting with the honeymoon period, transitioning to culture shock, and ending with mastery.

REFERENCES

Agbényiga, D. F., Barrie, S., Djelaj, V., & Nawyn, S. (2012). Expanding our community: Independent and interdependent factors impacting refugees' successful community resettlement. *Advances in Social Work, 13*(2), 306–324.

Agier, M. (2008). *On the margins of the world.* Malden, MA: Polity Press.

Anani, G. (2013). Dimension of gender-based violence against Syrian refugees in Lebanon. Syria Crisis. http://www.fmreview.org/sites/fmr/files/FMRdownloads/en/ detention/anani.pdf

Berry, J. W. (1997). Immigration, acculturation, and adaptation. *Applied Psychology, 46*, 5–34.

Berry, J. W. (2005). Acculturation: Living successfully in two cultures. *International Journal of Intercultural Relations, 29*, 697–712.

Betts, A., Bloom, L., Kaplan, J., & Omata, N. (2014). *Refugee economies: Rethinking popular assumptions.* Report from Humanitarian Innovation Project, University of Oxford.

Bhatia, S., & Ram, A. (2009). Theorizing identity in transnational and diaspora cultures: A critical approach to acculturation. *International Journal of Intercultural Relations, 33*(2), 140–149.

Capps, R., & Fix, M. (2015). *Ten facts about US refugee resettlement.* Washington, DC: Migration Policy Institute.

Capps, R., Fix, M., Van Hook, J., & Bachmeier, J. D. (2013). *A demographic, socioeconomic, and health coverage profile of unauthorized immigrants in the United States.* Washington, DC: Migration Policy Institute.

Carlson, E. B., & Rosser-Hogan, R. (1991). Trauma experiences, posttraumatic stress, dissociation, and depression in Cambodian refugees. *American Journal of Psychiatry, 148*, 1548–1551.

Carlsson, J., Mortensen, E., & Kastrup, M. (2005). A follow-up study of mental health and health-related quality of life in tortured refugees in multidisciplinary treatment. *Journal of Nervous and Mental Disease, 193*(10), 651–657.

Cavazos-Rehg, P. A., Zayas, L. H., & Spitznagel, E. L. (2007). Legal status, emotional well-being and subjective health status of Latino immigrants. *Journal of the National Medical Association*, *99*, 1126–1131.

Edwards, A. (2016). *UNHCR viewpoint: "Refugee" or "migrant": Which is right?* http://www.unhcr.org/en-us/news/latest/2016/7/55df0e556/unhcr-viewpoint-refugee-migrant-right.html

Foster, M. (2007). *International refugee law and socio-economic rights: Refuge from deprivation*. New York, NY: Cambridge University Press.

Guerrier, G., Zounoun, M., Delarose, O., Defourny, I., Lacharite, M., & Brown, V. (2009). Malnutrition and mortality patterns among internally displaced and non-displaced population living in a camp, a village or a town in Eastern Chad. *PLoS ONE*, *4*(11), e8077. doi: 10.1371/journal.pone.0008077

Hampton, J. (2014). *Internally displaced people: A global survey* (2nd ed.). New York: Taylor and Francis.

Hilado, A., & Kim, C. (n.d.). *Ethnicity, gender and experience: Examining refugee mental health trends by demographic characteristics and resettlement experiences*. Unpublished manuscript.

Johnson, H., & Thompson, A. (2006). The development and maintenance of post-traumatic stress disorder (PTSD) in civilian adult survivors of war trauma and torture: A review. *Clinical Psychology Review*, *23*(1), 36–47.

Kamali, M. (1999). Distorted integration: Problems of monolithic order. *Innovations: The European Journal of Social Sciences*, *22*(1).

Kinzie, J. D. (2006). Immigrants and refugees: The psychiatric perspective. *Transcult Psychiatry*, *43*(4), 577–591.

Kirmayer, L. J., Narasiah, L., Munoz, M., Rashid, M., Ryder, A. G., Guzder, J., . . . Pottie, K. (2011). Common mental health problems in immigrants and refugees: General approach in primary care. *CMAJ : Canadian Medical Association Journal*, *183*(12), E959–E967. http://doi.org/10.1503/cmaj.090292

Leus, X., Wallace, J., & Loretti, A. (2001). Internally displaced persons. *Prehospital and Disaster Medicine*, *16*(3), 116–123.

Lindencrona, F., Ekblad, S., & Hauff, E. (2008). Mental health of recently resettled refugees from the Middle East in Sweden: The impact of pre-resettlement trauma, resettlement stress and capacity to handle stress. *Social Psychiatry & Psychiatric Epidemiology*, *43*(2), 121–131. doi: 10.1007/s00127-007-0280-2

Lopez, I., Escoto, E. R., Monford-Dent, T., & Prado-Steiman, P. (2011). Theories of acculturation and cultural identity. In J. Carlson & A. Zagelbaum (Eds.), *Working with immigrant families: A practical guide for counselors*. New York: Taylor and Francis Group.

Lysgaard, S. (1955). Adjustment in a foreign society: Norwegian Fulbright grantees visiting the United States. *International Social Science Bulletin*, *7*, 45–51.

Morris, M. D., Popper, S. T., Rodwell, T. C., Stephanie, B. K., & Brouwer, K. C. (2009). Healthcare barriers of refugees post-resettlement. *Journal of Community Health*, *34*, 529.

Murray, K. E., Davidson, G. R., & Schweitzer, R. D. (2010). Review of refugee mental health interventions following resettlement: Best practices and recommendations. *American Journal of Orthopsychiatry, 80*(4), 576–585. doi: 10.1111/j.1939-0025.2010.01062.x

National Public Radio. (2014, Sept 4). HIAS president: U.S., Europe treating migrant crisis like "Business-as-usual" (Radio broadcast episode). *All Things Considered.* Washington, DC: National Public Radio.

Nezer, M. (2014). An overview of pending asylum and refugee legislation in the US congress. *Journal on Migration and Human Security, 2*(2), 121.

Nielson, J., Prudhon, C., & de Radigues, X. (2011). Trends in malnutrition and mortality in Darfur, Sudan, between 2004 and 2008: A meta-analysis of publicly available surveys. *International Journal of Epidemiology, 0*(4), 971–984.

Omidadvocates.org. (2011). *The process of becoming a refugee.* http://www.omidadvocates.org/uploads/2/4/8/2/2482398/the_process_of_becoming_a_refugee_english.pdf

Pahud, M., Kirk, R., Gage, J. D., & Hornblow, A. R. (2009). The coping processes of adult refugees resettled in New Zealand. *The UN refugee agency: Policy development and evaluation service.* Retrieved from http://www.unhcr.org/4b167d769.pdf

Palic, S., & Elklit, A. (2010). Psychosocial treatment of posttraumatic stress disorder in adult refugees: A systematic review of prospective treatment outcome studies and a critique. *Journal of Affective Disorders, 131*(1), 8–23.

Papadopoulos, R. K. (2007). Refugees, trauma and adversity-activated development. *European Journal of Psychotherapy and Counselling, 9,* 301–312.

Pérez, M. C., & Fortuna, L. (2005). Psychosocial stressors, psychiatric diagnoses, and utilization of mental health services among undocumented immigrant Latinos. *Journal of Immigrant and Refugee Services, 3,*107–123.

Perez-Foster, R. M. (2005). The new faces of childhood perimigration trauma in the United States. *Journal of Infant, Child, and Adolescent Psychotherapy, 4*(1), 21–41.

Phillimore, J. (2011). Refugees, acculturation, strategies, stress and integration. *Journal of Social Policy, 40*(3), 575–593.

Porter, M., & Haslam, N. (2005). Predisplacement and postdisplacement factors associated with mental health of refugees and internally displaced persons: A meta-analysis. *The Journal of the American Medical Association, 294*(5), 602–612.

Portes, A., & Zhou, M. (1993). The new second generation: Segmented assimilation and its variants. *The Annals of the American Academy of Political and Social Science, 530,* 74–96. Retrieved from http://www.jstor.org/stable/1047678

Rosenblum, R. (2015). *Unaccompanied child migration in the United States: The tension between protection and prevention.* Transatlantic Council on Migration.

Schweitzer, R., Greenslade, J., & Kagee, A. (2007). Coping and resilience in refugees from the Sudan: A narrative account. *Australian and New Zealand Journal of Psychiatry, 41*(3), 282–288.

Silove, D. (1999). The psychosocial effects of torture, mass human rights violations and refugees trauma: Toward an integrated conceptual framework. *The Journal of Nervous and Mental Disease, 187*, 200–207.

Simich, L., Beiser, M., Stewart, M., & Mwakarimba, E. (2005). Providing social support for immigrants and refugees in Canada: Challenges and directions. *Journal of Immigrant Health, 7*(4), 259–268. doi: http://dx.doi.org/10.1007/s10903-005-5123-1

Stewart, M. J., & Lagille, L. (2000). A framework for social support assessment and intervention in the context of chronic conditions and caregiving. In M. J. Stewart (Ed.), *Chronic conditions and caregiving in Canada: Social support strategies* (pp. 3–28). Toronto, Canada: University of Toronto Press.

Suarez-Orezco, M., & Qin-Hilliard, D. (2004). *Globalization: Culture and education in the new millennium*. Berkeley: University of California Press.

Sullivan, M. M., & Rehm, R. (2005). Mental health of undocumented Mexican immigrants: A review of the literature. *Advances in Nursing Sciences, 28*, 240–251.

Toole, M. J., & Waldman, R. J. (1997). The public health aspects of complex emergencies and refugee situations. *Annual Review of Public Health, 18*, 283–312. Retrieved from http://search.proquest.com.ezproxy.library.wisc.edu/docview/235222907?accountid=465

UNHCR. (1951). Original articles. http://www.unhcr.org/en-us/1951-refugee-convention.html

UNHCR. (2011). *The process of becoming a refugee*. Retrieved from http://www.omidadvocates.org/uploads/2/4/8/2/2482398/the_process_of_becoming_a_refugee_english.pdf

UNHCR. (2012). Displacement: The new 21st century challenge. *UNHCR: Global Trends 2012*. Retrieved from http://fas.org/irp/agency/dhs/fema/displace.pdf

United Nations Human Rights Committee on the Rights of the Child. (2016). *Monitoring children's rights*. Retrieved October 29, 2016, from http://www.ohchr.org/EN/HRBodies/CRC/Pages/CRCIntro.aspx

U.S. State Department: Bureau of Population, Refugees, and Migration. (2004). United States refugee assistance and resettlement programs fact sheet. Retrieved from http://www.state.gov/j/prm/releases/factsheets/2015/244056.htm

Vu, A., Adam A., Wirtz, A., Pham, K., Rubenstein, L., Glass, N., Beyrer, C., & Singh, S. (2014). The prevalence of sexual violence among female refugees in complex humanitarian emergencies: A systematic review and metanalysis. *PLoS Currents*.

Walter, K. (2008). *Strengthening the rights of internally displaced persons*. Brookings website. Retrieved from https://www.brookings.edu/opinions/strengthening-the-rights-of-internally-displaced-persons/

World Migration in Figures. (2013). *United Nations high level dialogue on migration and development and OECD*. Retrieved from https://www.oecd.org/els/mig/World-Migration-in-Figures.pdf

Zagelbam, A., & Carlson, J. (2011). Orientation to working with immigrant families. In A. Zagelbam & J. Carlson (Eds.), *Working with immigrants and families: A practical guide for counselors*. New York: Taylor and Francis Group.

Chapter 3

PHYSICAL AND MENTAL HEALTH STABILIZATION
The Importance of Well-Being to the Adjustment of New Immigrants

AIMEE HILADO AND SAMANTHA ALLWEISS

KEY TERMS

health stabilization, healthcare utilization and barriers, mental health service providers

---

CHAPTER HIGHLIGHTS

- Examine common health and mental health trends among immigrant and refugee populations
- Review of common health considerations and barriers to healthcare utilization
- Review of common mental health considerations and barriers to mental health service utilization
- Discussion of the importance of health stabilization as it relates to adjustment in a destination country

---

UNDERSTANDING THE IMPORTANCE OF HEALTH STABILIZATION

The health status of immigrant and refugee arrivals is a key influence on adjustment and long-term health outcomes in their destination country, and it directly contributes to the population health overall. By its very nature, many immigrants and refugees who are forced to migrate for diverse reasons—threats to their safety, violence/conflict in the region, or the search for better opportunities—experience a degree of social, psychological, and physical vulnerability that is often associated with the journey. The consequences of traumatic events, be it war or assimilation to new cultures, can lead to long-term health problems well documented in the literature (Cunningham & Cunningham, 1997; Handelman & Yeo, 1996; Hollifield et al., 2002; Mirza et al., 2014; Mollica et al., 1993; Piwowarczyk, 2007). Appropriately, the prevalence of chronic health problems (physical and mental health) directly influences the quality of adjustment to life in a new country (Barry, 2000; Lara, Gamboa, Kahramanian, Morales, & Hayes Bautista, 2005; Lora et al., 2011; Suinn, 2010). Consideration must therefore be given to the specific health needs of immigrants and refugees, the dimensions that impact utilization of healthcare and mental health services, and strategies to engage this population in stabilizing and maintaining good health.

Newly arrived immigrants and refugees access a variety of health services and interface with professionals across disciplines, as they adjust to their new community. Primary health care is generally the first entry point for immigrants and refugees accessing the health care system (Bellamy, Ostini, Martini, & Kairuz, 2015) and has historically been a critical starting point for identifying and stabilizing health needs among new immigrants. To maintain good health, however, involves other factors—language capacity among providers, cultural appropriateness of services, adequate insurance coverage, and even knowledge of preventative procedures to maintain good health— that are not always readily available or given to immigrant and refugee arrivals. Health needs also change over time, thus problems not evident during initial health visits may not get the attention necessary when needs are present later. Thus, we examine the literature on health and mental health considerations that are necessary to stabilize one's overall well-being, a significant adjustment factor for new arrivals.

HEALTH CONSIDERATIONS

Defining Physical Health and Current Needs

The health[1] needs of immigrants and refugees globally vary by country and the circumstances of individuals and communities without that country. Depending on the region and the resources, access to quality health services and medications vary despite the universal needs present (Bhatta, Shakya, Assad, & Zullo, 2015; Wagner et al., 2015). For refugees, it has been reported that chronic diseases, such as diabetes and hypertension, have been undiagnosed or unmanaged prior to resettlement in their destination country (Eckstein, 2011; Wagner et al., 2015). There are also increased rates of heart disease and obesity (Bhatta et al., 2015) related to lack of knowledge around nutrition (Rondinelli et al., 2011) and physical inactivity (Wieland et al., 2012). Others suffer from cancer (Bhatta et al., 2015) and infectious diseases, such as HIV and Hepatitis (B and C) (Redditt, Janakiram, Graziano, & Rashid, 2015). In other countries, refugees show higher rates of malnutrition and complications because of

---

[1] Reference to *health* in this chapter can be applied to physical health symptoms as well as one's general sense of well-being. A separate discussion of mental health implications is also provided, recognizing health encompasses both physical and mental health (body and mind) connections generally understood in both Western and non-Western communities.

sexual violence (UNHCR.org, n.d.). As evident, the health problems vary by region and the sociopolitical environment within that region.

Additionally and according to the United Nations High Commissioner for Refugees (UNHCR), the following trends have been documented worldwide: High rates of morbidity and mortality have been attributed to "overcrowding, harsh climatic conditions with poor shelter and lack of adequate facility to treat severe cases, and delayed case finding because of poor treatment seeking behaviour" (UNHCR, 2014, p. 20). The leading causes of death recorded from 2008 through 2012 were acute upper and lower respiratory infections (URTI and LRTI) and malaria. The most successful preventative measures to communicable diseases are vaccinations, but administration of refugee populations is difficult, because they are often in high conflict zones, in transit, or in over-populated refugee camps.

For refugees arriving in the United States, the Center for Disease Control (CDC) has noted the following trends among arrivals: (a) Bhutanese refugees are disproportionately impacted by anemia, vitamin B12 deficiency, and mental health concerns, (b) Iraqi refugees have higher rates of diabetes, hypertension, and malnutrition, (c) Burmese refugees are more likely to be diagnosed with Hepatitis B and intestinal parasites, and (d) Congolese refugees are more likely to suffer from parasitic infections, malaria, mental health concerns, and health conditions from sexual and gender-based violence (Lee et al., 2013). Additionally, a 2009 CDC study of 104, 954 newly arrived refugees and immigrants in the United States found that 18.4% of immigrants and 27% of refugees polled had health problems, and the most common health concern was latent tuberculosis (Lee et al., 2013). The UNHCR also reports that noncommunicable diseases (NCDs), such as those found in the cardiovascular, digestive, respiratory, and musculoskeletal systems, are increasing in frequency and are more frequently impacting women.

Table 3.1 illustrates some of the health trends we are seeing globally. Around the world, the CDC confirmed that NCDs account for over 75% of all deaths, making this the primary focus for many global health organizations. These numbers suggest growing health problems that exist among immigrant and refugee communities, with refugees being more likely to have recorded health concerns because of screenings prior to arrival. Much of this is because of the conditions in the home country or host country (applicable to displaced persons who seek refuge in other countries). By extension, there are implications of poor health outcomes on a new immigrant's ability to adjust to a new culture and to live an active, productive life.

Factors Impacting Healthcare Utilization

It is generally understood that health disparities in the population can be directly related to access to health services that affect health outcomes (Beal, 2011). Healthcare access and utilization have been a prominent topic of discussion in the research and medical fields: When groups of refugees and new immigrants are unable to access basic health care as needed, the public health system as a whole may be impacted adversely (Bellamy et al., 2015); a productive and economically vibrant society needs healthy

Table 3.1 Trends in Overall Morbidity Patterns, 2008, 2010, and 2012

2008		2010		2012		N	%
1	URTI	1	URTI	1	URTI	640, 678	21%
2	LRTI	2	Malaria	2	Malaria	441,144	14%
3	Malaria	3	LRTI	3	LRTI	342,248	11%
4	Watery diarrhea	4	Watery diarrhea	4	Intestinal worms	194,901	6%
5	Skin disease	5	Intestinal worms	5	Watery diarrhea	194,597	6%
6	Intestinal worms	6	Skin disease	6	Skin disease	187,334	6%
7	Eye disease	7	Eye disease	7	Eye disease	102,884	3%
8	Injuries	8	Injuries	8	Injuries	73,303	2%
9	Chronic disease	9	Chronic disease	9	Chronic disease	59,839	2%
	Other		Other		Other	859,215	28%

Source: UNHCR Health Information System

citizens to contribute. The concepts of access and utilization, however, are complicated, with numerous contributing factors informing how and why consumers use healthcare resources. We provide a discussion of the eight factors that are most relevant to immigrant and refugee populations.

CULTURE

Culture encompasses the traditions, belief systems, and values of one's country of origin. For immigrants and refugees, culture defines how they understand themselves and provides a framework for how and why they make decisions, especially in the area of health; all varied and unique to one's cultural heritage. For example, a study of Bosnian and Soviet refugees showed that adults would neglect their own healthcare needs so that they could focus on the healthcare needs of their children (Lipson, Weinstein, Gladstone, & Sarnoff, 2003). Latino parents with chronic kidney disease often normalize the symptoms or lack information, because of language barriers, which can influence health behaviors within the family structure (Lora et al., 2011). Somali refugees cited cultural values that impressed the importance of self-reliance and handling health problems alone, thus they were less likely to seek any healthcare advice or services (Ellis et al., 2010). Kosovar refugee women cited the patriarch in the family as the major influence in accessing/seeking health care services (Redwood-Campbell et al., 2008). In other cases, spiritual healing from a religious leader and prayer took the place of seeking medical attention (Carroll et al., 2007), or cultural and religious beliefs affected the acceptability of treatment (Smith et al., 2013). For others, receiving care from Western-trained medical professionals was avoided, because of the differing views of an illness based on culture (Bellamy et al., 2015; Englund & Rydstrom, 2012) and a desire to use traditional medicines native to one's country (Bellamy et al., 2015). Each example illustrates the influence of culture on help-seeking behaviors when it comes to health needs, and in some cases, to the detriment of the individual, family, and community, when avoidant behaviors are suggested and spread. Without a knowledge of symptoms and the cultural barriers to seeking services, health conditions can worsen globally without intervention, thereby impacting physical, psychological, and social-emotional functioning; not simply adjustment to a new country.

LANGUAGE BARRIERS AND INTERPRETATION

Language has proven to be a formidable barrier in accessing healthcare services. While many major hospitals and clinics have access to interpreters by phone, access to qualified and culturally sensitive interpreters and even the lack of available qualified interpreters can be a deterrent to clients seeking or returning for medical procedures (Bellamy et al., 2015; Mirza et al., 2014). Others who did not use interpreters but also didn't have confidence in their limited English reported feeling they were not understood or that they did not understand what was being communicated (Cristancho, Garces, Peters, & Mueller, 2008; McKeary & Newbold, 2010). Other consumers were concerned with the written instructions for follow-up care or did not understand the legal consent forms they were required to sign, thus avoided services all together (Morris et al., 2009). In other cases, there was a distrust and lack of confidence in the interpreter's ability to aid in the medical evaluation or treatment (Herrel et al., 2004). For many new immigrants and refugees arriving in a new country, language competence is a reality that can greatly define the ease with which they will navigate all areas of their new home, including the healthcare system.

INADEQUATE HEALTH INSURANCE

Health insurance policies vary by country, yet there are multilevel barriers related to adequate health insurance coverage that directly impacts service utilization. Mirza et al. (2014) cited three levels of barriers related to public health insurance that impact healthcare access—system-level, provider-level, and individual-level barriers. Grounding the discussion in the experience of refugee arrivals in the United States, where refugees have access to public health insurance under the Affordable Care Act (ACA), the challenges are formidable. At the system-level, the policies for refugee health insurance coverage are limited to Medicaid (medical insurance for low-income families in the United States), with specific medical interventions that are covered (Mirza et al., 2014). For those who are unable to work but do not fit the category of medically disabled, they are at risk of not having access to important health and financial benefits by virtue of the policies in place. At the provider-level and given the nature of Medicaid, there is difficulty securing specialists who take this specific insurance type, and for those that do, there are long waiting lists that further compromise health outcomes (Mirza et al., 2014). And then there are the individual-barriers, as new arrivals cited difficulty learning a new and complex medical insurance system with specific rules and regulations about how to request and verify coverage (Mirza et al., 2014).

According to Pace, Al-Obaydi, Nourian, and Kamimura (2015), "not all refugees who are eligible for the ACA would actually obtain health insurance" (p. 64), and to illustrate, there were reports in 2014 wherein one fourth of Iraqi refugees were reported as not having health insurance (Taylor et al., 2014). Obtaining insurance coverage, accessing health care services, and costs are all barriers that remained despite eligibility for ACA healthcare coverage (Sommers, Maylone, Nguyen, Blendon, & Epstein, 2015). Moreover, some insurance consumers (as in the case of refugees) require expanded health insurance coverage, given the burden of chronic conditions (Yun, Fuentes-Afflick, & Desai, 2012), yet despite insurance access, may remain at risk of being uninsured or under-insured (Pace et al., 2015).

KNOWLEDGE OF THE MEDICAL SERVICE SYSTEM AND MEDICATION

Bellamy et al. (2015) and Mirza et al. (2014) discuss medical service systems as a maze of different providers, policies, and regulations that make it difficult for new immigrants to decipher how and where to access healthcare services. In some countries, new immigrants and refugees have difficulty even accessing community pharmacies and medication, because of limited exposure to pharmacists in their home country, language barriers, and pharmacy staff being ill-equipped with cross-cultural communication skills to answer questions (Bellamy et al., 2015). Providers have also cited the challenges of having patients who are unfamiliar with Western healthcare systems, which has resulted in missed appointments, noncompliance with taking medication, and attending to referrals (Johnson, Ziersch, & Burgess, 2008). Managed care health systems have become complicated, with automated phone systems to answer billing and service questions, providers being restricted to serving only those in a specific insurance plan, and complicated service policies. Unsurprising, the complexity of the medical service system has been a barrier to service utilization for immigrants and native-born citizens alike. The limited accessibility and availability within a complicated system only lower utilization rates further (Edward & Hines-Martin, 2015).

TRANSPORTATION

Transportation and finding the location of providers has become a documented barrier to healthcare access for immigrants and refugees. Kosovar refugee women cited difficulty in finding the clinic as a deterrent to addressing health needs (Redwood-Campbell et al., 2008). The lack of knowledge around using public transportation was also an issue (Lawrence & Kearns, 2005), as was the fact that some providers are outside of the community, thus making the commute more difficult (Palmer, 2006; Willging, 2008). And even issues with scheduling appointments (Asgary & Segar, 2011), arriving at appointments on time (Lawrence & Kearns, 2005), and understanding the provider referral process (Redwood-Campbell et al., 2008) were sufficient reasons to deter people from seeking medical assistance. Embedded in these barriers is the need for cultural learning around Western models of medical practice, with appointment times and the medical insurance system. Additional learning also comes with adjusting to a new community and learning how to navigate the resources in that community. As such, immigrant serving organizations and other health care providers should create opportunities to provide education so that transportation and lack of knowledge of the healthcare system won't be a sustained issue lowering healthcare usage.

OTHER CONSIDERATIONS

There are also subtle cross-cultural considerations that need attention when discussing the motivation for seeking (and avoiding) healthcare services. According to Shannon, O'Dougherty, and Mehta (2012), refugees were less likely to initiate conversations about trauma histories with their physicians because of cultural norms that require deference to the professional's authority. In some cases, immigrant and refugee clients feel that they cannot ask questions of authority figures, or there is the perception that the doctors will not take the time to adequately hear the patient's needs. The appropriateness of gender-related exams, such as Pap smears and breast exams, or discussing reproductive health are topics that require extra cultural sensitivity (Johnson et al., 2008), as oftentimes these topics are not discussed outside the family context, thus resulting in avoidance of these necessary procedures. The perceptions of certain health and mental health conditions also require thoughtful consideration, as there may be stigma attached that can impact both the individual and the community if disclosed. This includes fear of isolation in the community for those diagnosed with HIV/AIDS (Othieno, 2007) or those diagnosed and treated for a mental illness (de Anstiss & Ziaian, 2010; Palmer, 2006). Additionally and relevant for new immigrants, there are persistent fears of deportation if certain mental health diagnoses are given (Asgary & Segar, 2011) and even fear of discrimination based on one's ethnic clothing in medical settings (Omeri et al., 2006). While these considerations are subtle, the fears and concerns about cultural appropriateness can be formidable deterrents to consistently accessing care. And these problematic belief systems can be shared and perpetuated, thereby deterring others from seeking health services as needed.

Implications and Resources

Professionals working with immigrants and refugees must be aware of the health concerns that impact different communities based on region and conditions in that region. As discussed, access to healthcare services is based on what is available in the region, and the quality of care and population needs varied greatly worldwide. Upon arrival to one's destination country, health stabilization becomes critical to overall adjustment and the long-term health outcomes for that person. To support efforts to address health needs among new immigrants and refugees, different organizations and resources are available.

GLOBAL COORDINATION AND INFORMATION-SHARING EFFORTS. The United Nations High Commissioner for Refugees (www.unhcr.org) and the International Rescue Committee (www.irc.org) have extensive platforms for dissemination of health and general information on vulnerable migrant populations globally. The UNHCR also has collaborations with sister organizations, including the World Food Programme (WFP), the UN Children's Fund (UNICEF), the World Health Organization (WHO), the UN Development Programme (UNDP), the Office for the Coordination of Humanitarian Affairs (OCHA), the UN High Commissioner for Human Rights (OHCHR), and the Joint UN Programme on HIV/AIDS (UNAIDS), to further study the needs in the field and initiate activities and projects to specific vulnerable regions and populations. To coordinate efforts, the Office for the Coordination of Humanitarian Affairs (www.unocha.org) was established in 1991 as an entity within the United Nations Secretariat. The Office for the Coordination of Humanitarian Affairs (OCHA) supports mobilization, funding, and coordination of humanitarian action in response to complex emergencies and natural disasters. Beyond OCHA, each respective group is actively engaged in supporting displaced persons throughout the world, providing information on impacted communities with clearly defined areas of services, advocacy efforts, research, and mechanisms for getting involved. Across all of these intentional organizations, efforts to address health disparities and to address health crises are a cornerstone of the initiatives implemented by the respective groups in depressed, vulnerable communities globally.

NATIONAL PROFESSIONAL ASSOCIATIONS. There are hundreds of local, state, and national health professional associations in the United States and abroad that coordinate knowledge and the workforce to address the health needs in the community (see Appendix for the full list). National associations may focus on specific areas of the population, including community health (www.nachc.com) or home care and hospice (www.nahc.org) as well as more associations with a more general focus on connecting providers (www.nahpusa.com; www.naahp.org; www.ahca.org) or getting professional development materials into the hands of direct service professionals (www.nahq.org). Some disciplines have specific resources to support professionals by field of discipline, including the National Association of Social Workers (www.nasw.org), the American Counseling Association (www.counseling.org), and the Association for Psychological Science (http://www.psychologicalscience.org). Additionally, there is a network of refugee health coordinators across U.S. states resettling refugees to coordinate health access and information sharing to promote health outcomes.

LOCAL PROGRAMMING. Immigrant and refugee-serving organizations have developed different medical case management service models to complement other services that support adjustment to a new country. Stabilizing health needs is a common first priority in many settings. Several refugee-receiving states in the United States are developing medical case management protocols for evaluating the complex health cases outlining detailed service plans that include increasing knowledge of navigating medical systems, managing health problems, and securing the appropriate providers (see Appendix for sample protocols from Minnesota and Illinois). Frontline staff and health providers also coordinate within the community, forming health task forces and volunteer groups to communicate professional development opportunities and health trends among new immigrant and refugee arrivals. To illustrate, the Illinois Refugee Health Task Force has been in existence for over a decade, in an effort to coordinate health education and health responses to refugee needs in Illinois.

Generally, efforts to support health stabilization and healthcare access/utilization require a multilevel perspective that looks at healthcare policies, providers, and individual usage. The barriers to stabilizing health are varied based on the unique experiences of each immigrant and refugee; however, those barriers can be addressed with culturally responsive health services and coordinate health professionals who are able to deliver care in the appropriate language of the healthcare consumer. Thoughtful acknowledgment of the barriers and attention to the subtle factors that affect usage can be impactful in increasing help-seeking behaviors that may have lifelong benefits for new immigrants and refugees.

MENTAL HEALTH CONDITIONS

Defining Mental Health and Well-Being

According to the WHO, mental health is defined as "a state of well-being in which every individual realizes his or her own potential, can cope with the normal stresses of life, can work productively and fruitfully, and is able to make a contribution to her or his community" (WHO, 2016). Mental health is just one dimension of what it means to be a healthy person as defined by the WHO, which states, "health is a state of complete physical, mental and social well-being and not merely the absence of disease or infirmity" (WHO, 2016). These definitions remain misunderstood, despite the clear presentation that mental health is important for **all** individuals and is not synonymous with mental illness. Although the research suggests a correlation between mental health problems and mental illness, with the cultural changes associated with migration (Mann & Fazil, 2006; Procter, 2005), here remain prominent barriers to accessing and utilizing mental health services among immigrant and refugee populations. Consequently, new immigrants and refugees have lower utilization rates than the general population (Cristancho et al., 2008; Hassett & George, 2002).

Current Needs Among Immigrants and Refugees

The migration process is stressful for any immigrant or refugee, as it heralds the need to acculturate to a new culture, a new language (in some cases), and a degree of social isolation (Yako & Biswas, 2014). Any previous trauma compounds the stress of these resettlement experiences in a way that can exacerbate mental health problems that impede adjustment to a new country. Depression, generalized anxiety, and post-traumatic stress disorder (PTSD) are common mental health symptoms among refugees (Slewa-Younan, Uribe Guajardo, Heriseanu, & Hasan, 2015). PTSD symptoms often apply to those with prolonged exposure to trauma and survivors of torture (Gjini et al., 2013), which we see in higher frequency among immigrants and refugees who are forced to flee their country for survival reasons. Evidence is available showing elevated incidences of psychotic disorders after migration as well (Cantor-Graae, 2007; Coid et al., 2008; Jarvis, 2007). Others exhibited adverse mental health symptoms associated with a prolonged series of traumatic experiences, starting from their time in their home country, to experiences during transit to a destination country and the adjustment experiences upon arrival in the resettlement country (Kirmayer et al., 2011). Still others reported somatic symptoms as indicators of psychological distress, often in the form of chronic headaches, radiating pain throughout the body, and odd sensations that could not be explained despite a battery of tests (Aragona et al., 2005). Focus on such physical complaints has led to under-identifying mental health problems and referrals to the appropriate treatments (Kirmayer, 2001), which is problematic when working to stabilize health quickly. All things considered, it should be understood that the nature of the migration experience increases the likelihood of immigrants and refugees experiencing adverse mental health symptoms that impact all areas of life, including acculturation levels, social relationships, and overall functioning. That being said, utilization of mental health interventions can directly improve adjustment and health outcomes, yet they remain underutilized within this population.

Dimensions Impacting Mental Health Service Utilization

Within immigrant and refugee communities, the challenges in addressing mental health needs are apparent but difficult to address directly. Similar to services addressing health problems and healthcare utilization, comparable barriers exist when accessing mental health services. Transportation, the desire to deal with one's own problems, and concerns of not being understood were salient themes in the underutilization of mental health services among immigrant and refugee groups (Nadeem et al., 2007; Whitley, Kirmayer, & Groleau, 2006; Wong et al., 2006). Inadequate insurance coverage or understanding of coverage for mental health services remain equally salient (Pace et al., 2015). Moreover, the idea of mental health services has been deeply stigmatized in many cultures, as it has been associated often with custodial or hospital treatments for the most severely ill or psychotic in developing countries (Kirmayer et al., 2011). Building on this, there are three particular areas related to mental health service utilization that are worth further examination.

Language Barriers and Interpretation

Language barriers are problematic and stand out as a major barrier to mental health service utilization. For new immigrants, there are concerns that practitioners would not understand their mental health needs (Chen, Kazanjian, & Wong, 2009) or the impediments in communication will only make already sensitive topics even more difficult (Cristancho et al., 2008; Sadavoy et al., 2004). Without understanding of services, immigrants and refugees have perceived mental health facilities to be hostile environments that do not understand the new arrivals' belief systems (Palmer, 2006). And while family members have been used as interpreters in health services, it can create issues of miscommunication and an assumption that the family member is a caregiver with full knowledge of the person's symptoms, and this may not be the case (Rosenber, Leanza, & Seller, 2007). For many reasons, mental health providers should also learn how to work with interpreters to build relationships with non-English-speaking clients and ways to navigate cultural and linguistic barriers that arise (see Chapter 7 for more content on the role of the interpreter). Research suggests that the use of professional interpreters improves communication substantially, as opposed to using relatives or children (Flores, 2005; Karliner et al., 2007), yet in the event this level of interpretation is unavailable, steps to ensure understanding, confidentiality, and responsiveness can and should be implemented. Language barriers can also be addressed to assure immigrants and refugees through disseminating information in the language of the person and education efforts in the community in an effort to explain the nature of mental health interventions and the availability of such services that support overall health and adjustment.

Culture

Culture plays a particularly important role in shaping the perceptions of mental health. In some cultures, mental health is either inherited or a product of personal transgressions or that of one's parents or ancestors (Bhugra, 2004), and such stigma can directly prevent new immigrants from seeking mental health services (van der Velde, Williamson, & Ogilvie, 2009). The loss of natural support systems (Bhugra, 2004) and the culturally appropriate ways of seeking help via family networks or community leaders (Hassett & George, 2002; Sadavoy, Meier, & Ong, 2004) make mental health services even more important, yet there is reluctance to seek mainstream services given cultural traditions for seeking help. Complementary and alternative treatments—that is, mind-body medicine, biologically based practices, manipulative and body-based practices, and energy medicine (MacDuff, Grodin, & Gardiner, 2011), the integration of spirituality and integrating the idea of the balance between physical, spiritual, and moral dimensions of self—is often missing in Western medicine, leading to a conflict with cultural beliefs (Sadavoy et al., 2004). Given this content, culture remains a salient undercurrent that shapes how and why people decide to seek mental health advice outside of their family and community, and it is a topic you will see throughout the book. Cultural beliefs must be addressed in any service, and it is equally appropriate to integrate the client's perspectives into the treatment plan. Equally relevant is involving relevant religious leaders or family members into the sessions as a means of honoring cultural beliefs while still addressing mental health problems in a culturally sensitive manner (discussed in greater detail in Unit 3).

Understanding the Different Mental Health Providers

Current mental health providers cross various disciplines, which can be confusing for new arrivals who are unfamiliar with Western medicine models or mental health services generally. Providers can include psychiatrists (M.D.), licensed social workers (LSW) and/or licensed clinical social workers (LCSW), licensed professional counselors (LPC) and/or licensed clinical professional counselors (LCPC), marriage-family therapists (MFT), and psychologists (PsyD, PhD), and insurance coverage varies based on the client's insurance plan. The providers listed have licenses that represent appropriate professional training and orientations to practice and make them eligible for liability insurance prior to delivering mental health services; this is important for reducing risk to the client and maintaining best ethical practices. Professional training programs vary in length of time and specific orientation to practice, but all generally have specialized courses with a mental health focus while preparing the workforce to provide individual, group, family, couples, and community-based interventions. The practice settings are also varied, as you will find mental health service providers in outpatient medical settings, community-based programs, private practice, and in for-profit or not-for-profit organizations—equally confusing to populations trying to access mental health services for the first time. Many cultures have people in the community who play the role of a mental health provider or health expert who may not fall under any of these titles, only adding confusion when mental health-like services are sought in the new country.

There are obvious challenges in the available mental health workforce as well. While different professional disciplines work with refugee populations, the vast majority do not have explicit training in immigrant/refugee mental health, given the lack of training programs on multicultural practice currently available (Kuo & Arcuri, 2014). Given the barriers in access and utilizations, compounded with the unique needs of immigrants and refugees, mental health professionals working with refugees should be knowledgeable of the unique migration experiences and resettlement needs in addition to refugees' mental health symptoms. Specifically, mental health professionals should seek training in trauma-informed and culturally responsive practice, as trauma experiences can continue during the adjustment period in a new country. Oftentimes, professionals will need to work on addressing basic adjustment needs before most individuals can process past trauma; a reality that is often missing in training programs for mental health providers. Effective mental health providers must also recognize that the role they have in this country may not even exist in the client's home culture, and so education on the role of the provider will be necessary, even before mental health services can begin.

Implications and Resources

Supporting mental health is critical to supporting overall health and well-being, and the barriers to mental health service access and utilization parallel that which we reviewed among immigrants and refugees needing primary and specialized healthcare services. And there are resources that exist at multiple-systems levels (global, national, local) to help coordinate mental health professionals, disseminate best practices research, and provide professional development opportunities. These efforts will prepare mental health providers to adapt to changing populations that arrive as a result of ever-changing migration patterns because of war/conflict, famine, and the desire for a better future. The need to reorient mental health treatment modalities will only continue in order to remain relevant and culturally sensitive to the changing ethnic groups in need of mental health services.

Global organizations like the UNHCR and leaders across countries have put great effort toward reducing mental health stigma through awareness campaigns and education (see previous *Health* section and Appendix for global organizations and NGOs). Each country also has its own structures to dissemination information on mental health trends and providers. In the United States, the U.S. Department of Health and Human Services (www.HHS.gov) and the Substance Abuse and Mental Health Services Administration (www.SAMHSA.gov) are both government entities that disseminate information and conduct research on mental health needs in the population. Under HHS, there is also a site called MentalHealth.gov (www.mentalhealth.gov) providing extensive resources to address a range of mental health problems and connect people with providers in their respective state/county. Additionally, there are national associations, such as the National Institute for Mental Health (www.nimh.nih.gov), the National Council for Behavioral Health (www.thenationalcouncil.org), and the National Alliance on Mental Illness (www.nami.org) to coordinate providers and training. There are also age-specific mental health associations, including the World Association on Infant Mental Health (www.waimh.org) and local affiliates; in Illinois, we have the Illinois Association for Infant Mental Health (www.ilaimh.org). Local networks (formal and informal) have also developed in response to the need to coordinate mental health information; in some cases, specific to addressing needs in immigrant and refugee communities. To illustrate, Illinois established the Illinois Refugee Mental Health Task Force (www.ilrmh.org) in 2015 to ensure collaboration and coordination of mental health service efforts within Chicago and the surrounding suburbs in response to surges in Iraqi, Syrian, and Congolese refugee arrivals to the area.

Conclusion

Health needs—both physical and mental health—among newly arrived immigrants and refugees are significant factors that have short- and long-term implications for adjustment, productivity, and overall well-being. Individuals, families, and communities are affected when members of the community cannot access necessary health services that can improve quality of life or allow them to actively participate in society. As discussed in this chapter, the barriers to access and utilization of health services outline the unique circumstances of immigrant and refugee populations adjusting to new systems, new cultures, and new approaches to maintaining health in a new country. The complex health systems of any country can be daunting, especially for new arrivals who do not speak the language and who have extensive trauma histories that impair their ability to concentrate, communicate, or problem-solve without assistance. The literature provides evidence of effective strategies to increase engagement and usage through consideration of cultural context and adjustment needs. And there is a wealth of information about health trends, treatments, and providers worldwide (global organizations, national associations, local networks) that can further inform all parties—providers and healthcare consumers—on the importance of maintaining good health and the strategies to secure the necessary services to achieve it. This wealth of information, if used appropriate to change system- and personal-level barriers, may influence access and usage of healthcare services to those who need comprehensive health services most.

REFLECTIVE QUESTIONS

1. Micro practice: How can chronic health problems impact mental health? What role can the mental health provider play in stabilizing overall health?

2. Macro practice: We understand that physical and mental health directly influence one another and impact how well immigrants and refugees adjust to life in a new country. How can policies better reflect this relationship to provide more holistic services, specifically to immigrants and refugees?

CASE STUDY

Wisam is a 72-year old refugee from Iraq who arrived in Chicago after separating from his wife and two children, who remained in Iraq. Wisam planned to petition once he was settled and financially stable, and he was optimistic he could find a job, as he was a highly skilled individual, serving as an interpreter for the U.S. army after managing an American-owned company in Iraq for many years. Wisam had been diagnosed with heart failure prior to coming to Chicago and was immediately hospitalized upon arrival. Doctors quickly discovered Wisam needed heart bypass surgery to increase blood flow to his heart. Wisam also suffered from chronic hypertension, high cholesterol, and asthma, which all required regular medical attention.

In addition to his physical health concerns, Wisam is suffering from severe trauma symptoms as a result of his time in combat with the U.S. military. He witnessed many deaths, and his life was at risk several times when enemy forces located his unit and rapid gunfire and bombs were directed at it. His primary symptoms are flashbacks, nightmares, hypervigilance, and insomnia. In addition, Wisam is experiencing extreme anxiety about his health as well as social isolation and feelings of depression because of the lack of social supports in the community. Because of his heart condition, he is unable to work, which leaves him feeling unproductive and unable to be the true provider for his family. Wisam fears for the future of his family, while he is also coping with the realization that he is unemployable at this time and will be unable to support his wife and children if they were to come to Chicago.

CRITICAL THINKING EXERCISES (BASED ON CASE STUDY)

1. What are Wisam's personal strengths and experiences that can help him access health and mental health services?

2. What could be major barriers to Wisam accessing health and mental health services?

3. What resources and supports are necessary to ensure Wisam is able to maintain good health in his new home country?

SUMMATIVE POINTS

• Healthcare and mental health service access and utilization is less common among immigrant and refugee populations, yet the chronic health and mental health problems rates are higher than the general population.

- Barriers, such as culture, language, inadequate insurance, inadequate knowledge of the medical care systems/policies, and logistical concerns are all barriers to immigrant and refugee use of health and mental health services.

- Health and mental health providers have to be knowledgeable of the unique circumstances of immigrants and refugees—including trauma histories, migration experiences, and resettlement experiences—that can directly influence the degree to which they will seek services or remain compliant in treatment.

- There are numerous resources to inform providers of general immigrant and refugee health needs, best practices, and connecting with other service providers.

- All providers working with immigrants and refugees, irrespective of discipline or purpose, can gain insight into the factors that influence help-seeking behaviors and behaviors to maintain good health.

REFERENCES

Aragona, M., Tarsitani, L., Colosimo, F., Marinelli, B., Raad, H., Maisano, B., & Geraci, S. (2005). Somatization in primary care: A comparative survey of immigrants from various ethnic groups in Rome, Italy. *International Journal of Psychiatry Medicine, 35*(3), 241–248. doi: 10.2190/2G8N-MNNE-PGGP-PJJQ

Asgary, R., & Segar, N. (2011). Barriers to health care access among refugee asylum seekers. *Journal of Health Care for the Poor & Underserved, 22*(2), 506–522.

Barry, D. T. (2000). East Asians in America: Relationships between ethnic identity, self-construal, mental health, and acculturation patterns in East Asian immigrants in the United States. *Dissertation Abstracts International: Section B: The Sciences and Engineering, 61*(6-B), 3269.

Beal, A. C. (2011). At the intersection of health, health care, and policy. *Health Affairs, 30*(1), 1868–18713. doi: 10.1377/hlthaff.2011.0976

Bellamy, K., Ostini, R., Martini, M., & Kairuz, T. (2015). Access to medication and pharmacy services for resettled refugees: A systematic review. *Australian Journal of Primary Health, 21*, 273–278. doi: 10.1071/PY14121

Bhatta, M. P., Shakya, S., Assad, L., & Zullo, M. D. (2015). Chronic disease burden among Bhutanese refugee women aged 18-65 years resettled in Northeast Ohio, United States, 2008–2011. *Journal of Immigrant and Minority Health, 17*(4), 1169–1176. doi: 10.1007/s10903-014-0040-9

Bhugra, D. (2004). Migration and mental health. *Acta Psychiatrica Scandanavica, 109*, 243–248.

Cantor-Graae, E. (2007). Ethnic minority groups, particularly African-Caribbean and Black African groups, are at increased risk of psychosis in the UK. *Evidence Based Mental Health, 10*, 95.

Carroll, J., Epstein, R., Fiscella, K., Volpe, E., Diaz, K., & Omar, S. (2007). Knowledge and beliefs about health promotion and preventative health care among Somali women in the United States. *Health Care for Women International, 28*(4), 360–380.

Chen, A. W., Kazanjian, A., & Wong, H. (2009). Why do Chinese Canadians not consult mental health services: Health status, language, or culture? *Transcultural Psychiatry, 46*, 623–641.

Coid, J. W., Kirkbride, J. B., Barker, D., Cowden, F., Stanps, R., Yang, M., & Jones, P. B. (2008). Raised incidence rates of all psychosis among migrant groups: Findings from the East London first episode psychosis study. *Archeological General Psychiatry, 65*, 1250–1258.

Cristancho, S., Garces, D. M., Peters, K. E., & Mueller, B. C. (2008, May). Listening to rural Hispanic immigrants in the Midwest: A community-based participatory assessment of major barriers to health care access and use. *Qualitative Health Research, 18*(5), 633–646.

Cunningham, M., & Cunningham, J. D. (1997). Patterns of symptomatology and patterns of torture and trauma experiences in resettled refugees. *Australia New Zealand Journal of Psychiatry, 31*, 555–565.

De Anstiss, H., & Ziaian, T. (2010). Mental health help-seeking and refugee adolescents: Qualitative findings from a mixed-methods investigation. *Australian Psychologist, 45*(1), 29–37. doi: 10.1080/00050060903262387

Eckstein, B. (2011). Primary care for refugees. *American Family Physician, 83*(4), 429–436.

Edward, J., & Hines-Martin, V. (2015). Exploring the providers perspective of health and social service availability for immigrants and refugees in a southern urban community. *Journal of Immigrant and Minority Health, 17*(4), 1185–1191. doi: 10.1007/s10903-014-0048-1

Ellis, B. H., Licoln, A. K., Charney, M. E., Ford-Paz, R., Benson, M., & Strunin, L. (2010). Mental health service utilization of Somali adolescents: Religion, community, and school as gateways to healing. *Transcultural Psychiatry, 47*(5), 789–811. doi: 10.1177/1363461510379933

Englund, A. D., & Rydstrom, I. (2012). I have to turn myself inside out: Caring for immigrant families of children with asthma. *Clinical Nursing Research, 21*(2), 224–242.

Flores, G. (2005). The impact of medical interpreter services on the quality of health care: A systematic review. *Medical Care Review, 62*, 255–299.

Gjini, K., Boutros, N. N., Haddad, L., Aikins, D., Javanbakht, A., Amirsadri, A., & Tancer, M. E. (2013). Evoked potential correlates of post-traumatic stress disorder in refugees with history of exposure to torture. *Journal of Psychiatric Research, 47*(10), 1492–1498. doi: 10.1016/j.jpsychires.2013.06.007

Handelman, L., & Yeo, G. (1996). Using explanatory models to understand chronic symptoms of Cambodian refugees. *Family Medicine, 28*(4), 271–276.

Hassett, A., & George, K. (2002). Access to a community aged psychiatry service by elderly from non-English-speaking backgrounds. *International Journal of Geriatric Psychiatry, 17*, 623–628.

Herrel, N., Olevitch, L., DuBois, D. K., Terry, P., Thorp, D., Kind, E., & Said, A. (2004). Somali refugee women speak out about their needs for care during pregnancy and delivery. *Journal of Midwifery & Women's Health, 49*(4), 345–349.

Hollifield, M., Warner, T. D., Lian, N., Krakow, B., Jenkins, J. H., Kesler, J., . . . Westermeyer, J. (2002). Measuring trauma and health status in refugees: A critical review. *JAMA, 288*(5), 611–621.

Jarvis, G. W. (2007). The social causes of psychosis in North American psychiatry: A review of the disappearing literature. *Canadian Journal of Psychiatry, 53*, 287–294.

Johnson, D. R., Ziersch, A. M., & Burgess, T. (2008). I don't think general practice should be the front line: Experiences of general practitioners working with refugees in South Australia. *Australia and New Zealand Health Policy*, *5*, 1–11. doi: 10.1186=1743-8462-5-20

Karliner, L. S., Jacobs, E. A., Chen, A. H., & Mutha, S. (2007). Do professional interpreters improve clinical care for patients with limited English proficiency? A systematic review of the literature. *Health Services Research*, *42*, 727–754.

Kirmayer, L. J. (2001). Cultural variations in the clinical presentation of depression and anxiety: Implications for diagnosis and treatment. *Journal of Clinical Psychiatry*, *62*(Supple13), 22–28.

Kirmayer, L. J., Narasiah, L., Munoz, M., Rashid, M., Ryder, A. G., Guzder, J., Hassan, G., . . . Pottie, K. (2011). Common mental health problems in immigrants and refugees: General approach in primary care. *Canadian Medical Association Journal*, *183*(12), E959–E967. doi: 10.1503/cmaj.090292

Kuo, B. C. H., & Arcuri, A. (2014). Multicultural therapy practicum involving refugees: Description and illustration of a training model. *The Counseling Psychologist*, *42*(7), 1021–1052. doi: 10.1177/0011000013491610

Lara, M., Gamboa, C., Kahramanian, M. I., Morales, L. S., & Hayes Bautista, D. E. (2005). Acculturation and Latino Health in the United States: A review of the literature and its sociopolitical context. *Annual Review of Public Health*, 26, 367–397. doi: 10.1146/annurev.publhealth.26.021304.144615

Lawrence, J., & Kearns, R. (2005). Exploring the "fit" between people and providers: Refugee health needs and health care services in Mt. Roskill, Auckland, New Zealand. *Health & Social Care in the Community*, *13*(5), 451–461.

Lee, D., Philen, R., Wang, Z., McSpadden, P., Posey, D. L., Ortega, L. S., . . . Painter, J. A. (2013). Disease surveillance among newly arriving refugee and immigrants. *CDC Morbidity and Mortality Weekly Report*, *62*(SS07), 1–20.

Lipson, J. G., Weinstein, H. M., Gladstone, E. A., & Sarnoff, R. H. (2003). Bosnian and Soviet refugee's experiences with health care. *Western Journal of Nursing Research*, *25*(7), 854–871.

Lora, C. M., Gordon, E. J., Sharp, L. K., Fischer, M. J., Gerber, B. S., & Lash, J. P. (2011). Progression of CKD in Hispanics: Potential roles of health literacy, acculturation, and social support. *American Journal of Kidney Diseases*, *58*(2), 282–290. doi: 10.1053/j.ajkd.2011.05.004

MacDuff, S., Grodin, M. A., & Gardiner, P. (2011). The use of complementary and alternative medicine among refugees: A systematic review. *Journal of Immigrant and Minority Health*, *13*(3), 585–599.

Mann, C. M., & Fazil, Q. (2006). Mental illness in asylum seekers and refugees. *Primary Care Mental Health*, *4*, 57–66.

McKeary, M., & Newbold, B. (2010). Barriers to care: The challenges for Canadian refugees and their health care providers. *Journal of Refugee Studies*, *23*(4), 523–545. doi: 10.1093/jrs/feq038

Mirza, M., Luna, R., Mathews, B., Hasnain, R., Hebert, E., Niebauer, A., & Mishra, U. D. (2014). Barriers to health care access among refugees with disabilities and chronic health conditions resettled in the U.S. Midwest. *Journal of Immigrant Minority Health*, *16*, 773–742. doi: 10.1007/s10903-013-9906-5

Mollica, R. F., Donelan, K., Tor, S., Lavelle, J., Elias, C., Frankel, M., & Blendon, R. J. (1993). The effect of trauma and confinement on functional health and mental health status of Cambodians living in Thailand-Cambodia border camps. *Journal of the American Medical Association, 270*, 580–586.

Morris, M. D., Popper, S. T., Rodwell, T. C., Brodine, S. K., & Brower, K., C. (2009). Healthcare barriers of refugees post-resettlement. *Journal of Community Health, 34*(6), 529–538.

Nadeem, E., Lange, J. M., Edge, D., Fongwa, M., Belin, T., & Miranda, J. (2007). Does stigma keep poor young immigrant and US-born black and Latina women from seeking mental health care? *Psychiatric Services*.

Omeri, A., Lennings, C., & Raymond, L. (2006). Beyond asylum: Implications for nursing and health care delivery for Afghan refugees in Australia. *Journal of Transcultural Nursing, 17*(1), 30–39.

Othieno, J. (2007). Understanding how contextual realities affect African born immigrants and refugees living with HIV in accessing care in the Twin Cities. *Journal of Health Care for the Poor and Underserved, 18*(3), 170–188.

Pace, M., Al-Obaydi, S., Nourian, M. M., & Kamimura, A. (2015). Health services for refugees in the United States: Policies and recommendations. *Public Policy and Administration Research, 5*(8), 63–69.

Palmer, D. (2006). Imperfect prescription: Mental health perceptions, experiences and challenges faced by the Somali community in the London borough of Camden and service responses to them. *Primary Care Mental Health, 4*, 45–56.

Piwowarczyk, L. (2007). Asylum seekers seeking mental health services in the United States: Clinical and legal implications. *Journal of Nervous Mental Disorders, 195*(9), 715–722.

Procter, N. G. (2005). "They first killed his heart (then) he took his own life." Part 1: A review of the context and literature on mental health issues for refugees and asylum seekers. *International Journal of Nursing Practice, 11*(6), 286–291.

Redditt, V. J., Janakiram, P., Graziano, D., & Rashid, M. (2015). Health status of newly arrived refugees in Toronto, Ont: Part 1: Infectious diseases. *Canadian Family Physician, 61*(7), e303–309.

Redwood-Campbell, L., Thind, H., Howard, M., Koteles, J., Fowler, N., & Kaczorowski, J. (2008). Understanding the health of refugee women in host countries: Lessons from the Kosovar resettlement in Canada. *Prehospital & Disaster Medicine, 23*(4), 322–327.

Rondinelli, A. J., Morris, M. D., Rodwell, T. C., Moser, K. S., Paida, P., Popper, S. T., & Brouwer, K. C. (2011). Under- and over-nutrition among refugees in San Diego County, California. *Journal of Immigrant and Minority Health, 13*(1), 161–168. doi: 10.1007/s10903-010-9353-5

Rosenber, E., Leanza, Y., & Seller, R. (2007). Doctor–patient communication in primary care with an interpreter: Physician perceptions of professional and family interpreters. *Patient Education and Counseling, 67*(3), 286–292. doi: 10.1016/j.pec.2007.03.011

Sadavoy, J., Meier, R., & Ong, A. Y. M. (2004). Barriers to access to mental health services for ethnic seniors: The Toronto study. *Canadian Journal of Psychiatry, 49*(3), 192–199.

Shannon, P., O'Dougherty, M., & Mehta, E. (2012). Refugees' perspectives on barriers to communication about trauma histories in primary care. *Mental Health in Family Medicine, 9*, 47–55.

Slewa-Younan, S., Uribe Guajardo, M. G., Heriseanu, A., & Hasan, T. (2015). A systematic review of post-traumatic stress disorder and depression amongst Iraqi refugees located in Western countries. *Journal of Immigrant and Minority Health, 17*(4), 1231–1239. doi: 10.1007/s10903-014-0046-3

Smith, M., Low, W., & Bindra, J. (2013). Prescribing for refugees. *Australian Prescriber, 36*, 146–147.

Sommers, B. D., Maylone, B., Nguyen, K. H., Blendon, R. J., & Epstein, A. M. (2015). The impact of state policies on ACA applications and enrollment among low-income adults in Arkansas, Kentucky, and Texas. *Health Affairs, 34*(6), 1010–1018. doi: 10.1377/hlthaff.2015.0215

Suinn, R. M. (2010). Reviewing acculturation and Asian Americans: How acculturation affects health, adjustment, school achievement, and counseling. *Asian American Journal of Psychology, 1*(1), 5–17. doi: 10.1037/a0018798

Taylor, E. M., Yanni, E. A., Pezzi, C., Guterbock, M., Rothney, E., Harton, E., . . . Burke, H. (2014). Physical and mental health status of Iraqi refugees resettled in the United States. *Journal of Immigrant and Minority Health, 16*(6), 1130–1137. doi: 10.1007/s10903-013-9893-6

UNHCR. (n.d.). Public health tab. Retrieved from http://www.unhcr.org/en-us/public-health.html

UNHCR. (2014). *Global strategy for public health*. Washington, DC: Author.

van der Velde, J., Williamson, D. L., & Ogilvie, L. D. (2009). Participatory action research: Practical strategies for actively engaging and maintaining participation in immigrant and refugee communities. *Qualitative Health Research, 19*(9), 1293–1302. doi: 10.1177/1049732309344207

Wagner, J., Berthold, S. M., Buckley, T., Kong, S., Kuoch, T., & Scully, M. (2015). Diabetes among refugee populations: What newly arriving refugees can learn from resettled Cambodians. *Current Diabetes Reports, 15*(8), 618. doi: 10.1007/s11892-015-0618-1

Whitley, R., Kirmayer, L. J., & Groleau, D. (2006). Understanding immigrants' reluctance to use mental health services: A qualitative study from Montreal. *Canadian Journal of Psychiatry, 51*, 205–209.

Wieland, M. L., Weis, J. A., Palmer, T., Goodson, M., Loth, S., Omer, F., . . . Sia, I. G. (2012). Physical activity and nutrition among immigrant and refugee women: A community-based participatory research approach. *Women's Health Issues, 22*(2), E225–E232. doi: 10.1016/j.whi.2011.10.002

Willging, C. E. (2008). Medicaid managed care for mental health services: The survival of safety net institutions in rural settings. *Qualitative Health Research, 18*, 1231–1246.

Wong, E. C., Marshall, G. N., Schell, T. L., Elliot, M. N., Hambarsoomians, K., Chun, C. A., & Berthold, S. M. (2006). Barriers to mental health care utilization for U.S. Cambodian refugees. *Journal of Consultation Clinical Psychology, 74*, 1116–1120.

World Health Organization. (2016). *Mental health*. http://www.who.int/topics/mental_health/en/

Yako, R. M., & Biswas, B. (2014). "We came to this country for the future of our children. We have no future": Acculturative stress among Iraqi refugees in the United States. *International Journal of Intercultural Relations, 38*, 133–141. doi: 10.1016/j.ijintrel.2013.08.003

Yun, K., Fuentes-Afflick, E., & Desai, M. M. (2012). Prevalence of chronic disease and insurance coverage among refugees in the United States. *Journal of Immigrant and Minority Health, 14*(6), 933–940. doi: 10.1007/s10903-012-9618-2

THEORETICAL ORIENTATIONS AND REORIENTATION

> **"We think of immigration as a Western issue but, of course, it isn't."**
>
> **~ Kiran Desai**

INTRODUCTION

Unit II Theoretical Orientations and Reorientation provides a foundation for understanding the role and utility of Western theory when working with transnational groups (Chapter 4: "Transnational Practice as the Client's Process," Lundy & Hidalgo). Before we discuss theory, however, the text provides working definitions for the terms *transnational population*, *transnational practice*, *solidarity*, and what we mean by *reorienting practice*, along with the implications of these terms. This chapter also introduces broad topics related to how we understand the immigrant and refugee experience and the frameworks used to inform our approach to practice. With working definitions in place, the authors discuss the construct of transnational practice and how professionals are charged with reorienting their approaches—commonly informed by Western theory—to ensure cultural-sensitivity, self-awareness, and flexibility as priorities in their practice. A discussion of the components of an integrative theoretical approach is introduced, in which the editors identify relevant Western theories used in practice today and constructs to ensure cultural appropriateness, awareness of a state of privilege of the practitioner, and opportunities for blending Western models with non-Western cultural practices as a more appropriate method of engaging multicultural populations.

Learning Objectives

Examine the limitations of current Western theories used in direct practice with immigrants and refugees.

Introduce an integrative theoretical framework that incorporates Western theory with important considerations for serving transnational populations, e.g., become a collaborator in solidarity with clients, emphasize client self-determination and cultural relevance, and consider adaptation of theory.

Discuss general and common problems as well as resilience, identifying strengths when working with immigrant and refugee populations.

Directly related to a discussion of a reoriented model of practice based on the circumstances of the population are two additional chapters that are equally charged with the perspective of the client. For example, there is a discussion of discrimination (Chapter 5: "The Perception and Experience of Everyday Discrimination Among U.S. Immigrants," Brettell) and feminist empowerment frameworks (Chapter 6: "Postcolonial Feminist Social Work Perspective," Deepak). Together, these chapters provide the theoretical basis that can and should inform practice with immigrants and refugees. Specifically, this unit proposes the value of integrative processes when applying theory, awareness of the sociocultural and sociopolitical environments welcoming immigrants, as well as alternative frameworks for understanding need. Finally, important considerations when working with transnational populations are provided by authors who look at the effects of globalization, power, and discrimination on the local and global stage. This content will support one's conceptualization of practice when moving into the next section of the book that looks at modalities of practice.

At the completion of Unit II, readers should understand basic terminology related to transnational populations and common Western theories used to work with these groups. The content prepares readers to have a working conceptual model of integrative theoretical methods for providing culturally sensitive interventions with immigrants and refugees in diverse settings.

Chapter 4

TRANSNATIONAL PRACTICE AS THE CLIENT'S PROCESS

Reorienting Practice With an Integrative Theoretical Approach to Practice With Immigrants and Refugees

MARTA LUNDY AND AIMEE HILADO

KEY TERMS

integrative theoretical framework, transnational practice, solidarity, solidarity movements, pre-and post-colonial perspectives, intersectionality

---

CHAPTER HIGHLIGHTS

- Definition of an integrative transnational practice, including solidarity, intersectionality, and post-colonial perspectives
- Description of benefits and challenges of relevant Western theories as they apply to working with immigrants and refugees
- Description of the perspectives and tasks of providers

INTRODUCTION

The purpose of this chapter is to define transnational practice as it applies to professionals working with new immigrant populations across the globe; specific attention is given to clinical professionals who provide mental health services. The term *transnational* reflects the expansive populations that traverse countries in the pursuit of new opportunities and a better life. With this movement comes diversity across the dimensions of ethnicities, cultures, and experiences that shape communities and individuals worldwide. By centering the text on the understanding that communities across the world are made of people and cultures whose lives and values are diverse, complex, and intricately interwoven together by local and global social forces, any intervention to aid those who are new to a country requires careful attention to the complexity of the individual and her community, informed by her beliefs and experiences prior to arrival. This chapter begins the discussion of a transnational practice framework for working with immigrants and refugees and how we can apply such an approach to working with immigrant populations in diverse settings across countries. Integration and critical application and adaptation of Western theories to address the needs of non-Western clients is also presented in this chapter to set the foundation for integrative transnational practice, which is discussed in the remaining sections of the book.

DEFINING TRANSNATIONAL PRACTICE

The term *transnational practice* is one that encompasses a variety of generalist and clinical approaches that can and have been used to support the diverse needs of ethnically, culturally, religiously, and linguistically diverse individuals and communities. We use the term transnational, as opposed to *international practice*, because of the multidirectional nature of connections we have with communities throughout the world. Globalization and vibrant migration patterns have contributed to the need for a framework of practice that reflects the patterns of movement and relationships that exist today. As such, the "practice" that is derived from a transnational orientation requires professionals to honor the culture of our clients, acknowledge and validate the pre- and post-migration experiences that define clients' sense of reality, and the integration of culture of origin and the culture of the receiving country.

For the purpose of this book, transnational practice is defined as the following:

- Transnational practice includes at its core a commitment to client self-determination, a belief in social justice, and a readiness to adapt Western theory to fully respond to the needs of the immigrant and/or refugee client system.

- A transnational integrative theoretical framework honors the experiences and perspectives of different cultures, migration patterns, and experiences, based in a culturally sensitive, collaborative, affirming, and mutually respectful relationship.

- A transnational theoretical orientation upholds cultural imperatives to bridge, maintain, and connect intergenerational and relocated family systems as desired by the immigrant and/or refugee while facilitating the resettlement of the current client system.

- Transnational practice also is aligned with social change and is cognizant of the reality that providing relevant, culturally sensitive services will likely include an active commitment to social change (Salas, Sen, & Segal, 2010).

RELEVANCE OF A TRANSNATIONAL PERSPECTIVE FOR DIRECT PRACTICE

The broader and deeper inclusion of individual and familial issues in relation to migration and resettlement requires a wide range of clinical theories to choose from in order to adequately respond to the complexity of issues that may require attention from various providers for health and mental health. In addition, it requires the ability to assess overlapping identities and resultant influences.

With few exceptions, immigrants and refugees migrate as family units, although more often as partial family units, and strive to bring other family members along with them as soon as possible. Collective societies generally are comprised of closely aligned and linked family systems across generations, including extended family. These are systems that provide organization, support, and resources, even when they themselves have little. These family systems also carry family traditions and responsibilities and often are the interpreters and arbiters of family history and purpose. In some cases, it may be that only the elders in the family can provide the balm of forgiveness and the approved sanction that will allow the immigrant to successfully emotionally leave their home country and the tragedies experienced there and move on with resettlement. Although providers may collaborate with individuals, the acknowledgment and incorporation of the family system is extremely relevant when working with immigrants and refugees. The transnational model includes a family systems perspective in addition to relevant individual practice theories, all of which may be integrated to adequately respond to individual and family difficulties. The transnational perspective develops and reinforces the need for a both/and approach to physical and mental health practices, including nuanced and subtle as well as sharply defined complex problems, and incorporating shamans, curanderos, doctors, counseling, community leaders and healers, clinical mental health providers, and others who may be needed to fully respond to the needs of the client systems.

The concept of intersectionality speaks directly to the complexities of the lives of immigrants and refugees. Intersectionality provides a lens that identifies the individual (gender, race, culture, disability, sexual orientation, age, ethnicity, religion, etc.), familial (collective and/or individualistic), and sociopolitical position (power, oppression, discrimination, marginalization, voice, poverty, etc.), of each immigrant, emphasizing the multiplicative effects on the functioning of the individual (Kelly, 2011, p. E44). The approach is not only instructive but also facilitative in understanding the complex lived experiences of human beings (Lockhart & Danis, 2010) and as such, greatly contributes to the knowledge and understanding of a transnational integrative perspective. Shields (2008) and Stirratt, Meyer, Ouellette, and Gara (2008) describe intersectionality as a method for understanding the construction of mutual relationships based on different forms of oppression and privilege, which share perspectives and consequences. In addition, intersectionality directs service providers to identify the "intersection of multiple identities and experiences of exclusion and subordination" (Davis, 2008, p. 67). As an example, some

Asian Indian women arrive in the United States with a high degree of education, exceptional marketable skills, but a dark skin tone and therefore a lifetime of marginalization and subordination. In the United States, an Asian Indian woman may be discriminated against for her migration status and marginalized in her own family because of colorism but because of her education, be successfully employed in a career of her choice with the benefits that are derived from that position. Therefore, she experiences and is aware of marginalization and also privilege. It is these intersections that when fully examined help us to better understand the complexities of the lived experiences of immigrants and refugees, making the concept of intersectionality a critical component for our understanding.

The relevance of overlapping identities and intersectionality must be integrated into the framework for delivering culturally sensitive mental health services to transnational populations. Its inclusion emphasizes client-centered practice in a manner that honors the role of culture and the individual's experiences. At the same time, such an approach promotes cultural sensitivity and cultural awareness in the context of a helping, collaborative relationship—a major tenet of what we understand as necessary in culturally responsive transnational practice.

HISTORICAL PERSPECTIVE: A LOOK BACK AT PERSPECTIVES APPLIED TO IMMIGRANTS

The foundation to this idea of transnational practice is not a new phenomenon. There is a history of generalist and clinical practice approaches that have been used with immigrant populations, although not as clearly defined and studied as they are today. The following sections examine several movements that have contributed to how we understand transnational practice in today's modern world.

PRE- AND POST-COLONIAL PERSPECTIVES. The United States has transitioned from an agrarian society, during the time of our founding, to an industrial revolution, which forever changed society, and more currently to a global player in an electronic, post-industrial era in which destructive changes in the environment are challenging every nation of the world. Throughout that time, immigrants and refugees have resettled in the United States in large numbers and for similar reasons—that is, for greater security, more economic opportunity, and to build a safe and secure life for their families. Immigrants and refugees have come from the impoverished and war-torn countries of Europe, the conflicted and exploited Middle East, the oppressed societies in Africa, and the economically insecure Mexico and Central America and South America. And in response, social work began as a profession. "Social work is a profession that began its life as a call to help the poor, the destitute and the disenfranchised of a rapidly changing social order. It continues today still pursuing that quest, perhaps with some occasional deviations of direction from the original spirit" (McNutt, 2013, p. 1). Social work started in response to the needs and economic plight of the poor, expanded and changed to include the psychosocial needs of the troubled and educated, and is struggling to this day to derive one clear message as the primary purpose: social justice or clinical social work. One of the contributions of this text is the inclusion of both, as each is relevant to the needs of immigrants and refugees, and together they provide a full complement of services from which to draw and expand.

SOLIDARITY MOVEMENTS. There have been many historic and critically important solidarity movements—for example, the union workers solidarity movement in Poland (1980s), which sparked the beginning of a democratic society in Poland; the peoples movement in Czechoslovakia (1950s); the teachers protests in Oaxaca, Mexico (2016); and the student revolution in Egypt, backed by the International Campaign of Solidarity (Tadamon) with Students (2012–2013), (International Union Network of Solidarity and Struggles http://www.encrointernacional.com; Mena International Solidarity www.mensolidaritynetwork.com). However, currently we seem to find ourselves in a crisis, with fewer people and countries willing and/or afraid to take a positive stand on the issue of migration. The current situation is summarized by Ki-moon, secretary general of the United Nations:

> More than 60 million people—half of them children—have fled violence or persecution and are now refugees and internally displaced persons. An additional 225 million are migrants who have left their countries in search of better opportunities or simply for survival. But this is not a crisis of numbers; it is a crisis of solidarity. Almost 90 percent of the world's refugees are hosted in developing countries. Eight countries host more than half the world's refugees. Just ten countries provide 75 percent of the UN's budget to ease and resolve their plight. (Ki-moon, 2016)

With the realization of the massive global needs of immigrants, refugees, and asylees, as providers we must become more aware of, recognize, and acknowledge the common humanity of all of us and then speak up. We must realize the contribution that these diverse populations will make to our society, both with their rich cultural heritage and their social and economic achievement. In addition, we need to advocate better methods to assist immigrants and refugees. We must stand up against discrimination and intolerance and hold responsible those who force displacement. And until the situation changes and the world is a safer place for all to live, we must contribute to and enlarge systems that are globally responsible for the care and support of immigrants and refugees (Ki-Moon, 2016).

As immigrants and refugees come to the United States, it is incumbent upon us to be prepared for the stories of their migration journey and the events surrounding their arrival and be open to facilitating their resettlement. We can achieve this by using a nonlinear, transnational, integrative approach that provides great flexibility for offering assistance, while at the same time, the provider is walking in solidarity with newly arrived immigrants and refugees—that is, joining and believing in their process, a perspective that is congruent with successful resettlement and mental health. According to Ki-moon, "Movements of people are a quintessentially global phenomenon that demands a global sharing of responsibility" (2016, p. 3).

CURRENT UNDERSTANDINGS. There is now worldwide recognition of the migration crisis that is impacting countries. The threat of terrorism and ever-changing immigration policies that integrate both pro- and anti-immigrant sentiment are shaping the nature of supports (financial resources and social supports) given to displaced populations globally. Global leaders and leaders in diverse faith communities are calling for unity in addressing the migration crisis but not in uniformed ways, with fear and the threat of unpredictable, violent attacks on citizens as the key informant on immigration policy. As discussed in the introduction

> According to Schlueter, Meuleman, and Davidov (2013), it has been hypothesized that many of the immigration policies are decided on by majority members, some of whom may have anti-immigrant sentiments. An examination in cross-national studies has found that the perception of threat or fear toward immigrant groups directly influenced the expansiveness of immigrant integration policies—specifically, countries with more permissive immigrant policies were those countries with a lower perception of immigrants being of imminent threat. (Schlueter et al., 2013; see also Hilado & Lundy, Unit I: Introduction)

As such, there is no global unified plan to address the millions of immigrants, refugees, and asylees seeking safety in new countries despite the unified agreement that immigration is a global issue. This leaves vulnerable displaced persons in precarious situations, risking their lives by boat and foot to cross borders in the hope of refuge outside of their home country with no guarantee of help or survival. And for those who are migrating as a result of forced or survival reasons—those who often have been in protracted, uncertain circumstances with exposure to extreme violence and threats to their personhood—the relevance of trauma on health and mental health is both an individual and global health problem. This is of particular importance as we consider the needs of those trauma-experienced persons who seek to integrate and acculturate into new societies.

DEFINING TRANSNATIONAL PRACTICE AS THE CLIENT'S PROCESS

Given this context, transnational practice is seen as an approach to working with new immigrant populations in a manner that recognizes the interconnectedness between country, culture, and individual experience that goes beyond the boundaries of one's country of origin. It is a method of practice that recognizes the impact of globalization on the mindset and perspectives of global citizens who are exposed to more than their own cultural practices. Finally, transnational practice builds on the historical trends and approaches that inform current practice methods but with a greater emphasis on cultural humility and mutual learning and collaboration, given the diversity of populations we now encounter in our practice settings, and with an openness to the potential need for adaptation and integration of theories in order to more thoroughly respond to the needs of a diverse population.

TRANSNATIONAL PRACTICE AS THE CLIENT'S PROCESS. Building upon this definition, we then need to consider the role of the client (individual and/or community) and the client process. As we examine the stages of migration and resettlement, we begin to unwrap the variables and factors that shape the identity and worldview of arriving immigrants. Many arrive with few assets or resources, although some arrive with a referral or an idea of whom to call and where to look for housing. Almost everything is new and unfamiliar, and the necessity of locating secure housing, employment, and food and water can be overwhelming. If not immediately, a bit later most begin to grieve their family, friends, and the familiarity of home, even as they gratefully realize that they are now safe. Commonly, immigrants and refugees need to mourn what they have left behind, and the process of either embracing or denying that will create its own difficulties with adjustment to a new country.

Additionally, immigrants and refugees will need to process their experiences of the migration journey. As described in previous chapters, the five stages of migration include pre-, in transit, detention and/or refugee camp, post-, and resettlement. The push to resettle and become functioning parts of the U.S. economic life often results in a misplacement of the experiences of migration, but it is incumbent on providers to realize the needs for processing this experience and to suggest attention to it. By utilizing the transnational integrative framework, the various aspects of their decision, migration, and resettlement will have been discussed at the very beginning and can be returned to for clarification and discussion. The process of initially joining with the immigrant provides the opportunity to plan for future work and consider items to be discussed in the future after settling in, and it is after settling in that these topics might be addressed and explored.

For those immigrants, refugees, and asylees who have been trauma exposed, there is a need to return to those events and determine a course of action. The impact of trauma does not quietly go away without attention. Indeed, it has a tendency to increase without further attention, erupting in the moments we least expect it, and often derailing the progress of the process of resettlement. The nonlinear, transnational, integrative model provides methods for addressing trauma, responding to it in as brief a manner as possible or with more time to narrate one's personal experiences, and examine the impact. The flexibility of the model increases the providers' ability to respond to the specific needs of the client; the nonlinear construction of the model enables the provider to be open to the possibilities from assessment and for clinical responses derived from the model, while the bond that has been deliberately and diligently formed facilitates the likelihood that this process can provide relief for the client. And this relief can translate to better adjustment to life—social, financial, emotional—in a new country.

WESTERN THEORETICAL APPROACHES: CURRENT FOUNDATIONS FOR PRACTICE

The use of a transnational practice approach to supporting adjustment to life in a new country, while addressing mental health problems that may serve as a barrier to achieving overall well-being, requires consideration of the current theoretical frameworks that have been used in the field. The use of Western approaches to address psychosocial problems is well documented and present with both benefits and challenges to its participants. The following section gives a brief account of relevant theories (adapted from Barker, 2003 and other cited authors), while Table 4.1 provides an overview of the benefits and challenges of each when applied to newly arrived immigrant and refugee populations.

- **Ecological perspectives/life model**: An orientation in social work and other professions that emphasizes understanding people and their environment and the nature of their transactions. Important concepts include adaptation, transactions, goodness of fit between people and their environments, reciprocity, and mutuality. In professional interventions, the unit of attention is considered to be the interface between the individuals (or group, family, or community) and the relevant environment (Barker, 2003, p. 136). The life model (Germain & Gitterman, 1980) integrates this ecological perspective using an integrated approach to practice, with individuals and groups to "release potential capacities, reduce environmental stressors, and restore growth-promoting transactions" (Barker, 2003, p. 250).

- **Family systems theory**: Family systems theories comprise intergenerational, structural, solution-focused, and narrative family theories, all of which focus on intergenerational and interpersonal relationship patterns, behaviors, and communication styles. Each theory utilizes specific constructs to identify family patterns and problems and works toward resolving family problems. The application of systems theories applies—that is, the reciprocal relationships, patterns, principles, and influence between individual elements that constitute a whole system and vice versa (von Bertalanffy, 1968)—and this case systems theory is applied to family units. This approach recognizes that, within each family system, members play distinct roles and there are boundaries that shape relationships (Kaslow, Dausch, & Celano, 2003) and there are collective and individual effects when the family unit is impacted by internal factors (biopsychosocial factors that impact individual family members) and external factors (biopsychosocial factors that come for the larger social environment).

- **Psychosocial approaches**: Psychosocial approaches examine biological predispositions, development in the early years, and psychological processes similar to psychoanalysis (Freud) but also expand the scope of theory to include other factors, such as developmental stages past adolescence, accounting changes through older adulthood, and influences from the larger social environment. The work of Erik Erikson (1902–1994) is most famous within this theoretical umbrella, with the goal of strengthening interpersonal skills, mobilizing resources, addressing mental health needs, and enhancing the goodness-of-fit between the person and his/her environment.

- **Psychodynamic approaches**: An approach to understanding human behavior and motivation that examines unconscious and conscious processes that are the product of biological underpinnings, past and present experiences, learned and conditioned patterns of thinking and behaviors, and culture.

- **Cognitive-behavioral approaches** (including mindfulness): A psychotherapeutic approach that addresses dysfunctional emotions, maladaptive behaviors, and cognitive processes and contents through a number of short-term, goal-oriented, explicit systematic procedures that focus on the present. This approach includes selected concepts and techniques from behavior theory, social learning theory, cognitive theory, and task-centered treatment (Barker, 2003).

- **Trauma-focused cognitive-behavioral therapy** (TF-CBT): An evidence-based treatment for children and adolescents impacted by trauma and their parents or caregivers. Research shows that TF-CBT successfully resolves a broad array of emotional and behavioral difficulties associated with single, multiple, and complex trauma experiences (tfcbt.org, n.d.).

- **Empowerment approaches to therapy**: An approach to practice that focuses on increasing personal, interpersonal, socioeconomic, political, and other related strengths to help improve ones circumstances and ability to thrive across different social systems, including families, groups, communities, and organizations.

- **Narrative therapy**: A psychotherapeutic approach that emphasizes the client's narrative or life story that is captured through written and verbal accounts of one's life, thought processes, and understanding of self and the world.

- **Narrative exposure therapy**: An effective, short-term, culturally universal intervention for trauma victims—including the latest insights and new treatments for dissociation and social pain. The approach focuses on telling the trauma narrative until the story no longer elicits anxiety (Schauer, Neuner, & Elbert, 2011).

- **Solutions-focused problem-based theory**: An approach to direct practice, examining how strengths and progress rather than deficits and problems impact a person's ability to fulfill life roles. The focus is on exceptionality and identifying skills and thought processes that allowed a person to succeed in similar circumstances and then applying those skills/perspectives to current issues.

Examination of Methods for Adapting Practice Methods to Focus on Transnational Processes

Transnational practice—and its focus on the client process—requires a thoughtful reorientation or adaptation of Western theories of practice to be culturally and linguistically sensitive to the needs and beliefs of non-Western participants. Effective practice requires professionals to cultivate critical thinking skills as it relates to the applicability of Western theoretical approaches to the needs of non-Western clients

Table 4.1 Benefits and Challenges of Western Concepts and Theories

Theory	Benefits	Challenges
Ecological perspectives/ life model theories	Contextualizes the wide range of both positive and negative circumstances Identifies the various systems that influence, enhance, and/or impede functioning Clearly identifies in detail the current situation of the client system	Identifies many different systems and environmental influences Can be overwhelming to hear multilevel, multisystem approaches, potentially creating additional stressors and problems
Family systems theory	Collective societies identify the family as the core-orienting unit of life The family is the primary resource—that is, the family sets expectations, assigns goals, offers support, and provides sanction and solace, which may align with non-Western communities Addresses family interaction patterns, historical messages, communication styles, and so forth Emphasizes strengths and empowerment Builds resources of family system within existing environment	The loss of the family system can create havoc, loss of stability, and emotional vulnerability as well as loss of direction Maintaining and/or reestablishing connections among family systems of transnational families requires professional commitment and creativity
Psychosocial framework	Derived from Freudian theory and based in person in situation Central foci include assessment, relationship, respect, and empowerment; encourages existing strengths, resources, and abilities; works to increase functioning Widely applicable	Not a brief form of therapeutic relationship Facilitated through the power of the relationship May be challenging for those who do not desire and are not familiar/comfortable with this type of problem solution

Theory	Benefits	Challenges
Psychodynamic approaches	Derived from Freud's psychoanalytic theory but not focused on the id and ego Focus is on attachment theory and conscious and unconscious forces that influence behavior and emotion Change is achieved by working through and gaining understanding of the meaning of feelings and events for the client	May be unfamiliar form of relationship-building for the client and therefore initially uncomfortable The concepts around unconscious and intrapsychic processes may conflict with how other cultures define health and mental health
Cognitive-behavioral approaches	Structured, time-limited, and highly collaborative Thoroughly researched and effective Provides a method for examining and refocusing thoughts and beliefs about events and relationships and what they mean Learn methods for gaining a different perspective on the meaning of events, freeing the client from derogatory and self-blaming thought processes that determine negative and undermine behaviors Many different forms and variations in what to do and how to use it Requires a relaxed state of being but with attentiveness May attend to a problem area or situation Engages person in examination of inner self in relation to environment May be empowering as client collaborates and/or instructs provider	Requires committed and thoughtful attention Energy and resources of the client system may not always be sufficient to respond Requires a relaxed state May feel intrusive to some clients Extremely challenging to accomplish when in high anxiety state of resettlement in United States

(Continued)

(Continued)

Theory	Benefits	Challenges
Mindfulness practice (related CBT approach)	Engages client in reflecting on the present focusing attention on the issues to which people have control Creates a deeper connection between thought patterns and physical sensations of stress and anxiety, using the process of quieting the mind to calm both mind and body Allows clients to develop the skills of focusing one's attention and actively adjusting thought patterns that do not serve the client	Requires a relaxed state Requires time and consistent practice to fully develop mindfulness skills This method may feel foreign to those who have not integrated mindful medication and relaxation techniques in the past
Trauma-focused cognitive-behavioral therapy	Focused on amelioration of trauma using wide range of theories and therapeutic constructs Flexible utilization of theory, methods, and focus as well as time frame Focus is on children and families in environment Widely researched and effective	Intended to be as efficient and effective as possible Demands attention and commitment, which may be difficult when families have competing priorities of employment, resettlement issues, and so forth Participants may not be accustomed to the techniques involved and the interactive/intense approach to symptom reduction, potentially reducing treatment compliance
Empowerment approaches to therapy	Encourages awareness of individual and family strengths and resilience as well as skills and abilities Affirms capacities often forgotten by immigrants and refugees in the strains of daily living	Works to identify strengths when the hardships have continued for so long that adaptive behaviors to disappointment and failure have been developed

Theory	Benefits	Challenges
Narrative therapy	Every person has a life story, as he or she understands it, and that story often guides the interpretation of all past and future events without reconsideration, often from a negative, self-blaming and derogatory perspective Narrative theory provides guidelines to facilitate client's re-examination and interpretation of life events from a less punitive, more contextual and positive perspective Respective and non-blaming Persons are considered the experts in their lives, and practitioners should honor that knowledge	Changing and/or giving up one's lifelong understanding and/or beliefs about personal events may be frightening and difficult Requires a description of life story and explanation of meanings and events, which may be extremely challenging for some
Narrative exposure therapy	Immigrants, refugees, and asylees tell their stories as victims of war, armed conflict, and long-term, spontaneous violence Specifically relevant for victims of war, violence, and conflict that has occurred over long periods of time Effective in current level of research trials Effective with refugees and asylees Brief treatment	May need to develop a relationship and/or a certain level of trust prior to initiating this model, however, not included in the discussions as necessary component
Solution-focused problem-based theory	Cognitive approach Focus is on identifying the times when problems do not occur Directs the client system to utilize those times as a method to resolve problems	Often clients want to talk about and receive help with the problems, and examining when problems don't occur may not be easily managed

(Continued)

(Continued)

Theory	Benefits	Challenges
Other Relevant Concepts		
Intersectionality	Examines the intersection of experiences of marginalization and discrimination in relation to privilege and success, in order to better understand the complexities and ultimate decisions of people's lives	The examination of areas of oppression, discrimination, and marginalization requires sensitivity and mutual rapport as well as significant trust Relationships may not be able to achieve this degree of closeness
Culture and identity	Defined as "customs, habits, skills, technology, art, values, ideology, science, and religious and political behavior of a group of people in a specific time period..." (Barker, 2003, p. 105, in Denby & Bowner, 2013, p. 1) Understood through gender, race, ethnicity, class and economics, religion, sexual orientation, and age Evolves with each new generation Culture and identity shape meaning and behaviors	Complex and extensive sets of information to identify, assess, and understand Seek greater understanding and clarity from the immigrants or refugee Focus on issues of social justice, using concepts of social justice to facilitate an understanding of the experiences of immigrants, refugees, and asylees, and to work toward greater inclusion (Danso, 2015)

Source: Adapted from the *Social Work Encyclopedia* (2013), Rasheed, Rasheed, and Marley (2011), and Barker (2003).

and conceptualizing theory in a manner that is more sensitive to nuanced beliefs and needs among new immigrants. To achieve this, the provider is required to

- First and foremost, establish a collaborative, affirming, and respectful working relationship

- Integrate the concept of collaborative accompaniment

- Conceptualize transnational practice as relationship based and nonlinear. Cultivate a relationship that builds trust and guides the adaptation process by deeply learning about the client, the client's culture and experiences, and the client's process

- Become a person in solidarity with your client

- Examine strategies for cultivating critical thinking skills

- Examine methods for adapting, adjusting, and applying appropriate theories to non-Western populations

- Apply relevant concepts from popular education methods—for example, Freire

- Focus on the complex layers of identity of each survivor, exploring intersectionality in relation to how providers might respond with a relevant flexible theoretical framework for services

Figure 4.1 Transnational Integrative Process

Client introduction & presentation: Develop and build a relationship

- *Addressing concrete needs for safety*: Housing and food security.
- *Relationship-building*: Build trust and mutual respect through solidarity, collaboration, cultural awareness/sensitivity, and accompaniment. In turn, efforts support the development of client self-determination and self-efficacy.
- *Integrative theoretical approaches*: Ecological systems theory, narrative therapy, and psychosocial approaches.

Early theoretical orientation

- *Assessment*: Affirmative person-in-context assessment; use elements of assessment as change agent for the client system.
- *Managing power dynamics*: Understand and employ social justice and collaborative accompaniment to manage balance of power.
- *Integrative theoretical approaches*: Empowerment approaches to identify and confirm goals; ecological systems theory to understand needs with respect to sociocultural context and the larger environment; cognitive approaches to identify mental health needs.

Middle and ending theoretical orientation

- *Assessment*: Ongoing trauma assessment.
- *Integrative theoretical approaches*: The following theories may be integrated to reach treatment goals—family systems theory, behavior theory, cognitive behavioral theory (including TF-CBT), psychodynamic theory, narrative theory, solutions-focused problem-solving therapy, focus groups.

The reflective process is nonlinear, recognizing that progress and client engagement must be evaluated and re-evaluated throughout the helping process. As issues arise in the goodness-of-fit between client needs and the approaches used to guide practice, adjustments should readily be made to maintain the relationships. Validation of culture and client experiences must also remain constant throughout the practice to ensure clients remain empowered in the process of addressing issues that impact their ability to thrive in a new setting. And in the process, transnational practice remains client centered, culturally relevant, and theoretically aligned to promote the gains for the client.

To illustrate the application of nonlinear transnational integrative practice, the preceding flowchart applies. At each stage of the engagement with transnational populations, different theories and considerations may apply based on the client need, the client's pre- and post-migration experiences, and the goodness-of-fit of the selected theories with the client's circumstances.

IMPLICATIONS FOR PROFESSIONALS

Reorienting theory within a transnational integrative practice framework requires a great deal from the professional. In working with immigrants and refugees, the professional is the provider, trainer, facilitator, and coordinator of services. The provider will often be in the situation of simultaneously learning about the circumstances of the client while affirming the various experiences. At the same time, the provider must be mindful of her own demeanor, as she considers theoretical frameworks and their possible adaptation in order to facilitate her client's process and progress through a maze of often life-threatening and traumatic events and certainly continuous, difficult, and demanding circumstances while adjusting to a new society. The ability of the provider to be aware of and to fulfill these tasks at the same time, often while working with an interpreter, and to facilitate the process with immigrants and refugees who have to begin to organize and make sense of their lives immediately is primary to collaboratively facilitating the goals of the immigrant and/or refugee.

The transnational integrative framework requires a full commitment to learning clinical theory, staying abreast with current clinical research, having an awareness and sensitivity to different cultural backgrounds and a self-reflective knowledge of one's own history, embracing the need to stretch and reach out to different cultural groups, a willingness to learn history as it relates to the populations currently migrating to the United States, and to stay informed on the U.S. as well as local policies and laws governing immigrants and refugees. Indeed, there is a need for research that clarifies the utility and potential flaws of this model, and providers need to be exploring methods for conducting research, seeking outcomes for their work.

However, a transnational integrative theoretical approach also provides the flexibility to fully respond to the needs of the client systems. It provides a great sense of purpose and a very extensive repertoire of resources. The theoretical framework allows the provider to assess and then explore the integrative set that will most comprehensively and fully respond to the stated circumstances and needs of the immigrant and/or refugee system. Ever alert to the cultural influences and the history of the stages of migration, the transnational integrative approach offers above all the flexibility for change and adaptation. It is extremely gratifying to have the capacity to extend oneself with confidence and determination and with the knowledge that if indeed one theoretical construct does not resonate with the client, there may be another that will better address their needs.

REFLECTIVE QUESTIONS

1. Micro practice: What theories would be a guide for the role of the clinical provider when establishing a new relationship with an immigrant or refugee?

2. Micro practice: As a practitioner, how would you describe the lens of intersectionality as it relates to clinical mental health practice?

3. Macro practice: How might agency policy influence the clinical work required when using an integrative transnational practice with immigrants and refugees?

CRITICAL THINKING EXERCISES

1. How would you describe methods for staying critically self-aware while also fulfilling the role of establishing a culturally sensitive, clinically responsive, and collaborative provider?

2. How would you envision and describe the learning process for gaining a transnational

integrative perspective for working with immigrants and refugees?

3. Based on the following case study, how can transnational perspective and integrative theoretical approaches be used to support the mental health and adjustment needs of each family member in the "Abdalla" family?

CASE STUDY

This excerpt is about the Abdalla family, a new immigrant Ethiopian family living in Chicago. In Ethiopian culture, men are typically the breadwinners and lead the household, while the wife is responsible for taking care of the home. Children must respect adults and follow family rules. Each family member has different needs that must be addressed.

(Father) Yussuf, Age 45, unemployed

(Mother) Rabiya, Age 40, full-time employment

(Son) Hajo, Age 16, high school student

(Daughter) Halfiya, Age 10, elementary school student

The Abdalla family moved to Chicago from Ethiopia in 2002. In Ethiopia, Yussuf was a carpenter, while his wife stayed at home and cared for their children. After arriving in the United States, Yussuf had a back injury and could no longer work. Because of rising expenses, Yussuf's wife, Rabiya, accepted a full-time position as a cleaning lady in a hospital. She began working 15-hour night shifts, six days a week, leaving Yussuf to care for the home and the children.

During this time, Yussuf became very depressed and began drinking alcohol heavily. When drunk, Yussuf is physically and verbally violent to the other family members; Rabiya is his main target. When confronted with his drinking issues, Yussuf becomes angry and states it is the family's fault for always irritating him. Rabiya's long shifts at work provide some safety for her, but she worries about the safety of her children. Rabiya often feels guilt for going to work, but she knows she must maintain a job to support the family. To help in the care of the family, Rabiya relies heavily on Hajo to care for the household and the youngest, Halfiya.

Hajo took over the family responsibilities, since his father could not, and his relationship with Yussuf has deteriorated; they no longer speak to each other except when fighting. Hajo prepares the family meals and is the primary caretaker for his younger sister, Halfiya. Hajo makes sure that his sister finishes her homework, acts as the family contact in school, and protects Halfiya whenever Yussuf gets drunk and/or violent. In school and in the community, Hajo is a model teen. He maintains good grades in school and volunteers in after-school programs with children who are exposed to domestic violence in their homes. Hajo remains very close with his mother and they phone each other daily.

Halfiya is in elementary school and struggles to do well socially and academically. On days when Halfiya witnesses violence in the home, she often gets into fights with her peers and becomes disruptive in the classroom. Halfiya is unable to connect closely with Rabiya, since her mother is always at work, but she has a close relationship with her brother. When alone in the house with her father, she locks herself in her room and plays aggressively with her toys. When scared, Halfiya will wet her bed at night and often sleeps with Hajo because of nightmares. She often says she is ugly and that no one likes her, and Hajo works hard to tell her otherwise.

The needs of the family are complex. Yussuf is not included in any decision-making for the family, but the other members are closely involved. Rabiya is considering leaving Yussuf if he doesn't stop abusing the family and if he doesn't address his drinking problems. The children are in agreement and supportive of their mother's position. Ultimately, the family wants an opportunity to thrive in their new home, yet attention is needed on both the individual and family system's needs simultaneously.

SUMMATIVE POINTS

- Establishing a mutually respectful, affirming, culturally sensitive, and collaborative relationship that supports and informs the interests and plans of the client system is the critically most important factor in providing services and working with immigrants, refugees, and asylees.

- The work of a clinical mental health provider must respond to the verbal and nonverbal needs of the client system. In that capacity, the provider requires a wide range of knowledge about various theories that will respond to and provide for the needs of the client, thus requiring a transnational integrative theoretical framework from which to draw.

- There are both benefits and challenges in applying an integrative approach in direct practice with transnational populations; however, the effort ensures practice efforts remain relevant to the client's culture, identity, and issues of intersectionality that directly influences the presentation of need.

REFERENCES

Barker, R. L. (2003). *The social work dictionary* (5th ed.). Washington, DC: NASW.

Danso, R. (2015). An integrated framework of critical cultural competence and anti-oppressive practice for social justice social work research. *Qualitative Social Work, 14*(4), 572–588.

Davis, K. (2008). Intersectionality as buzzword. *Feminist Theory, 9*(1), 67–85.

Denby, R. W., & Bowmer, A. (2013). Culture and identity in generic social work. In *Encyclopedia of social work*. doi: 10.1093/acrefore/9780199975839.013.890

Germain, C. B., & Gitterman, A. (1980). *The life model of social work process: Advances in theory and practice* (3rd ed.). New York: Columbia University Press.

Graham, J. R., & Barter, K. (1999, January–February). Collaboration: A social work practice method. *Families in Society*, 6–13.

Kaslow, N. J., Dausch, B. M., & Celano, M. (2003). Family therapies. In A. S. Gurman & S. B. Messer (Eds.), *Essential psychotherapies: Theory and practice* (2nd ed.). New York: Guilford.

Kelly, U. A. (2011). Theories of intimate partner violence: From blaming the victim to acting against injustice: Intersectionality as an analytic framework. *Advances in Nursing Science, 34*(3), E29–E51.

Ki-moon, B. (2016, May 10). *Refugees and migrants: A crisis of solidarity.* HuffPost. www.huffpost.com

Lockhart, L. L., & Danis, F. S. (Eds.). (2010). *Domestic violence: Intersectionality and culturally competent practice.* New York, NY: Columbia University.

Lundy, M. (2008). An integrative model for social work practice: A multi-systemic, multi-theoretical approach. *Families in Society, 89*(3), 394–406.

McNutt, J .G. (2013). The history of social work practice: History and evolution. *Encyclopedia of Social Work.* Alexandria, VA: National Association of Social Work and Oxford University.

Rasheed, M. N., Rasheed, J. M., & Marley, J. A. (2011). *Family therapy: Models and techniques.* Thousand Oaks, CA: Sage.

Robjant, K., & Fazel, M. (2010). The emerging evidence for narrative exposure therapy: A review. *Clinical Psychology Review, 30*(8), 1030–1039.

Salas, L. M., Sen, S., & Segal, E. A. (2010). Critical theory: Pathway from dichotomous to integrated social work practice. *Families in Society, 91*(1), 91–96.

Schauer, M., Neuner, F., & Elbert, T. (2011). *Narrative exposure therapy: A short-term treatment for traumatic stress disorders*. Boston, MA: Hogrefe.

Schlueter, E., Meuleman, B., & Davidov, E. (2013). Immigrant integration policies and perceived group threat: A multilevel study of 27 Western and Eastern European countries. *Social Science Research*, *42*(3), 670–682. doi: 10.1016/j.ssresearch.2012.12.001

Shields, S. A. (2008). Gender: An intersectionality perspective. *Sex Roles*, 59, 301–311.

Stirratt, M. J., Meyer, I. H., Ouellette, S. C., & Gara, M. A. (2008). Measuring identity multiplicity and intersectionality: Hierarchical classes analysis (HICLAS) of sexual, racial, and gender identities. *Self and Identity*, 7(1), 89–111.

tfcbt.org. (n.d.). Trauma-focused cognitive behavioral theory: National Therapist Certification Program. Retrieved from https://tfcbt.org.

von Bertalanffy, L. (1968). *General systems theory*. New York: George Braziller.

Chapter 5

THE PERCEPTION AND EXPERIENCE OF EVERYDAY DISCRIMINATION AMONG U.S. IMMIGRANTS

CAROLINE B. BRETTELL

KEY TERMS

perceived discrimination; group versus personal discrimination; context of discrimination, forbearance or confrontation

---

CHAPTER HIGHLIGHTS

- Introduces the concept of perceived discrimination
- Compares experiences of discrimination across different immigrant populations
- Emphasizes coping strategies deployed to deal with discrimination
- Focuses on differences according to context
- Distinguishes between group and personal discrimination

What is the impact of discrimination and discriminatory practices on immigrants in the United States? How do new immigrants negotiate the U.S. racial hierarchy as well as the racialization of their own identities? How do they subjectively experience and respond to job discrimination and housing market segregation? Social scientists have formulated the concept of "perceived discrimination" to better understand how unequal treatment is experienced by immigrants as well as the impact it may have both on mental health and incorporation into a receiving society (Dion, 2001, 2002; Finch, Bohdan, & William, 2000; Liebkind & Jasinskaja-Lahti, 2000; Moradi & Risco, 2006; Moradi & Talal Hasan, 2004; Noh, Beiser, Kaspar, Hou, & Rummens, 1999). Rates of perceived discrimination have been shown to vary across ethno-racial groups and are related to racial self-identification. Thus, Asians who self-identify ethnically as Asian but racially as white have a perceived discrimination rate of 45%, compared with a rate of 13% for Asians who ethnically and racially identify as Asian (Jackson, Williams, & Torres, 1997). A sense of ethnic pride, being involved in ethnic practices, having a strong commitment to a racial or ethnic group, and strong social support networks have all been found to alleviate the stress of discrimination (Jasinskaya-Lahti et al., 2006; Mossakowski, 2003). Alternatively, however, Finch et al. (2000) have argued that foreign-born Mexicans are more likely "to perceive discrimination as their level of English usage and acculturation increases" (p. 309). They work to belong, but the barriers to belonging never fully disappear.

It is important to differentiate between perceptions of discrimination against a group and perceptions or experiences of personal discrimination. The former is generally reported at higher rates than the latter (Taylor et al., 1990) but there is variation from one immigrant population to the next (Dion, 2001; Dion & Kerry, 1996). There is equally variation in how individual members of minority or immigrant populations respond to the experience of discrimination and what this means for physical and/or emotional well-being. Does confrontation mitigate the impact of perceived discrimination, because it may lead to change and reduce a sense of victimization or alternatively, does confrontation enhance distress (Noh et al., 1999)? Is forbearance—that is, passively accepting the experience or not reacting to it because conflict is avoided—a better option? Noh et al. (1999) observe that confrontational versus forbearance responses may vary by cultural group (see also Kuo, 1995) and argue, based on their research among Southeast Asian refugees, that forbearance is effective in limiting depression outcomes, especially among those with strong ethnic identification. Other scholars have argued that context or situation is more important than culture in influencing the kind of response—confrontation or forbearance—that is chosen (Mattlin, Wethington, & Kessler, 1990).

This brief essay explores how immigrants of five different national origins (Mexican, Salvadoran, Indian, Vietnamese, and Nigerian) understand and deal with experiences of discrimination. Data were collected as part of a broader baseline project on new immigration into Dallas-Fort Worth (DFW).[1] The interview[2] schedule deployed in the research included questions about discrimination as well as real and potential engagements with law enforcement. Respondents were also asked a series of questions about hypothetical scenarios and how they would handle them. Among these hypothetical scenarios were the following: If you witnessed a serious crime (for example,

---

[1] The project was supported by the Cultural Anthropology Program of the National Science Foundation (NSF/BCS 0003938). Other investigators involved in the project were James F. Hollifield, Dennis Cordell, and Manuel Garcia y Griego. The data was collected between 2002 and 2005. Any opinions, findings, and conclusions or recommendations expressed in this paper are those of the author and do not necessarily reflect the views of the National Science Foundation. The project involved multiple research instruments and both quantitative and qualitative methods and face-to-face semi-structured interviews with slightly more than 600 immigrants across the five groups. For further discussion of the methods deployed in this project, see Brettell (2011). For further discussion of recent immigration to DFW, see Brettell (2008a, 2008b). In this essay, I do not differentiate strongly between immigrants and refugees, because the Vietnamese, the only refugee-origin population in the sample, had generally been in the United States for some time and were asked to evaluate their experiences in the United States, not those they had years earlier as they left their country.

[2] Quotes from the interviews collected in the NSF/BCS 0003938 study are included in the chapter to further illustrate the experiences of discrimination among new immigrants included in the project.

a person gets shot), what would you do? If your car were stolen, what would you do? If someone owed you a large sum of money (say $2000), and you could not get that person to pay, what would you do? If a minor child of yours was taken away from you by the government (i.e., Child Protective Services), what would you do? If you applied for a job, and you suspected that you were not hired because of your race, national background, or religious affiliation, what would you do? If you worked extra hours and your employer refused to pay you more than the usual number of hours, what would you do? And, if you tried to rent an apartment, and you were told that none were available, but you suspected that you were being turned away because of your race, national background, or religious affiliation, what would you do? While initially formulated to grasp how immigrants understand their political, social, and civil rights, several of these hypothetical questions also yielded qualitative data on how newcomers to the United States perceive and think about discrimination. Based on an analysis of these data, it is argued here that from the perspective of immigrants themselves, discrimination is not just about phenotypical racial characteristics but also about language abilities, class and educational differences, and immigration status. Understanding these variations may help us to better assist immigrants in coping with the multiple forms of discrimination and exclusion and hence with their everyday well-being.

GROUP VERSUS PERSONAL DISCRIMINATION

When asked if they thought that members of their nationality group faced serious problems of ethnic or racial discrimination in the United States, more than 80% of Mexican research participants, both male and female, responded "yes," higher than the rate among Nigerian men (64%), although 80% of Nigerian women responded "yes." Eighty-six of the Mexicans interviewed for this project were unauthorized at the time of the interview, and 80% of these responded that their group faced discrimination. Of the 40 Mexicans interviewed who had green cards, 90% answered "yes," and of the 44 who were naturalized citizens, 98% answered "yes." Mexicans in the DFW area believe that ethnic or racial discrimination is an issue for their nationality group no matter what their immigration or citizenship status, and among those whom one might consider to "most belong"—that is, the naturalized citizens—the proportion is very close to 100%.

Fewer Salvadorans than Mexicans, among both men (56%) and women (70%), thought that members of their nationality group faced serious problems of discrimination in the United States. Of the 15 Salvadorans who were unauthorized at the time of the interview, 47% responded "yes," while 59% of those with green cards (29 in total) said "yes," and 77% of those who were naturalized citizens (22 in total) responded "yes." Twenty-five respondents were under temporary protected status at the time of the interview, and of these, 64% said their group faced discrimination.[3] These proportions by immigration status are all lower than those among Mexicans, but quite interestingly

[3] Temporary Protected Status is extended to foreign nationals when conditions in a home country (armed conflict, environmental disaster, other extraordinary events) prevent them from returning there safely or when the country is not able to adequately handle their return. TPS does not by itself result in a green card, but someone in this status may immigrate permanently under other legal provisions. See www.uscis.gov.

and again like the Mexican-origin population, the more secure their immigration status, the more discrimination Salvadorans perceive. One might expect that the unauthorized in both these populations would express a greater sense of discrimination than those in various forms of authorized status, particularly in the context of vehement and vocal national opposition to and criminalization of so-called "illegals" that has characterized the immigration debate in the United States during the first decade and a half of the 21st century. However, these data suggest that the unauthorized choose to keep a lower profile, even in relation to the articulation of or complaints about discrimination, while those who are authorized or citizens are more aware of their rights and may be more willing to articulate any infringement of them. Worthy of further exploration are the differences between these two "Hispanic" populations—are Mexican immigrants more sensitive to discrimination, because they are the more visible Latino population and the population most associated with being in the country illegally and hence designated as unwelcome.

The opinions of Indian men and women are quite distinct from those of Mexicans and Salvadorans. Almost 80% of men and 71% of women claimed that their group *did not* face discrimination. Interviews with Indian immigrants as well as the broader ethnographic literature (for example, Bhatia 2007) suggest that first-generation Indians in the United States downplay a racial identity and concomitantly promote a class identity, based on high levels of education, professional status, and income, as a basis for belonging. While the color divide in the United States is acknowledged by some, it is often linked to the barriers in claiming an American identity. One adult male research participant who held some political ambition observed that he needed to self-identify as American, but his name and physical features marked him as Indian. "Whether I want it or not it is with me."

Forty-two percent of Vietnamese men and 37% of Vietnamese women indicated that their group was discriminated against. It is important to note that 85% of the Vietnamese respondents in this study were naturalized citizens (an additional 11% were legal permanent residents) compared with 45% of Indians who were naturalized citizens (and 25% legal permanent residents). Explanations for these nuanced differences will become more apparent as the analysis proceeds. Individuals from different nationality backgrounds identify different sources and contexts for discrimination.

Respondents were also asked if they had personally encountered prejudice or discrimination in U.S. society from any group. Perhaps not surprisingly, the Nigerians, both men and women, showed the highest proportion of "yes" answers to this question (70% in each case), followed by Vietnamese men (42%). The figures for Salvadoran, Indian, and Mexican men respectively were 38, 38 and 39% and for women 48, 19, and 45%. Clearly these responses indicate, in accordance with the broader literature, that individuals distinguish discrimination against a group from their own personal experience with it. However, it is also evident that there are important differences in perceived discrimination (group versus personal) across national origin groups. While Indians are less likely to claim that their group has experienced discrimination, more will acknowledge that they have personally experienced it. The balance is tipped the same way for Nigerians, although not unexpectedly, more claim to have personally experienced discrimination, not only in relation to color but also in relation to language. For these two populations, class status and educational level may impact the absence of a perception of group discrimination, while phenotypical factors may impact the presence of experiences of individual discrimination.

By contrast, more Mexicans claimed that they as a group are discriminated against than claimed to have experienced it personally. One Mexican respondent summed it up this way: "They don't pay us what is right; we cannot live in areas where we want to live; we don't have jobs that are adequate and accessible; we don't have access to health services and someone who looks like a mestizo will not get attention in a hospital." Mexican immigrants are well aware of the broader societal hostility directed toward them and particularly toward their unauthorized status. The Vietnamese fall in the middle, and the proportions are quite similar, suggesting that of all these groups, it is the Vietnamese who translate their personal experiences into a group experience. This may have to do with the shared experience of the Vietnamese as refugees who have fled the communist regime. More than half of the participants in this study entered the United States prior to 1980 and more than two-thirds prior to 1990.

CONTEXTS OF EVERYDAY DISCRIMINATION: THE WORKPLACE

Across all five groups, our research participants acknowledge subtle workplace discrimination that has influenced both raises and promotions, but differences in education and English language abilities nuance the experience of everyday workplace discrimination.

Sunil Bhatia (2007) has observed that many Indian professionals have clearly articulated that they did not reach the highest positions in their company because they were Indian. Many of the Indian participants in our study articulated similar concerns about "glass ceiling" discrimination in the workplace. One male respondent, for example, recalled trying to find work in the computer industry when he first arrived in the United States, "I had a lot against me. I had an accent, I am brown, and I was over forty" (Bhatia, 2007, p. 158). Another respondent said he had watched less competent individuals who were white Americans advance faster than he had. A third simply described feeling out of place. He described being the only Indian at his company, and when everyone started discussing football, he had nothing to say or share—a cultural bias that also enhances difference and challenges some people's sense of and right to belong. A fourth Indian respondent focused more on citizenship than on race or ethnicity. He claimed that, if he were a U.S. citizen, he might have a hundred people working under him at this point in his career. "There is a barrier; it's a slow thing. You don't get the raises at the same pace. . . . I have to apply for visas if I change jobs and I can't get two times the money at Boeing or Lockheed, because of the required security clearance." This individual clearly thought that full rights come with citizenship, including the right to contest any form of workplace discrimination.

The strongest comments on workplace discrimination came from Nigerians, who suggested that sometimes it was their blackness and sometimes it was their Nigerian-ness that led to workplace discrimination. One respondent, who was applying to become a police officer, claimed he made the seventh highest score on the exam but was not hired. When he applied to another jurisdiction in the DFW area, he recalled that the white interviewer kept saying that he could not understand him. Another Nigerian who had worked for Oracle claimed that the Indians and Africans were given the programming jobs, while the whites landed the jobs in management. All these concerns were best summed up by one individual who stated: "I have never experienced racial discrimination in terms of getting a job, [but] I have been passed over for promotions because of race. I trained people who were later promoted over me. However, I did not go to court in order to protect my family."

Mexican respondents described workplace discrimination in two ways—that directed toward employees and that directed toward Hispanic customers at their respective places of employment. In the first case, the references are to not being paid equally, not being paid at all, or to discrimination that emerges in association with their inability to speak English well—an issue also of concern to the Vietnamese and Salvadoran research participants. One Mexican research participant, José, told a story of being hired by an "Anglo man," who picked him up at a day laborer center, was demanding in the work he asked for, and then pretended not to understand when he asked about his pay. While driving José back to the spot where he had been picked up, the man stopped for gas. He drove off while José was in the men's room. José was never paid for his day's work. A second Mexican research participant reported that her mother was constantly demeaned at her place of work because she does not speak English, even though she has the skills for the job. A third raised another form of discrimination in the workplace. When there are work accidents, he observed, the Americans receive help but the Hispanics do not—"they say, how great, it was a Mexican, it will be cheap." Others described workplace hierarchies where the heavy work is left to Mexicans. These hierarchies, research participants observed, are equally manifested in the treatment of Hispanic customers who are given the smallest portion possible at a restaurant or who are told at a store that they can receive credit but not cash for a returned item, while an Anglo customer can walk away with the cash. These observations about broader discrimination directed toward Hispanics that are witnessed in workplace contexts further reinforce the importance of understanding the distinction between group and personal perceptions of or experiences with discrimination. A sense that your group is broadly demeaned or treated differently can have as much impact on well-being as can a personal encounter with discrimination.

CONTEXTS OF EVERYDAY DISCRIMINATION: NEIGHBORHOODS AND COMMUNITIES

Within neighborhoods and communities, racial profiling (couched as unwarranted encounters with the police) and residential segregation are the most commonly identified sources of discrimination. Vietnamese, Salvadoran, and Mexican research participants described incidents of harassment with area police. One Vietnamese respondent described being pulled over and arrested when he was leaving for a fishing trip with friends early in the morning. "The cop said someone called and complained that there were some kids toilet-papering their house. We all knew the cop pulled us over because our car was a low rider and the fact that we look Asian with spiky hair." A Mexican respondent offered a different perspective on local police who do not respond to calls from Hispanics as rapidly. "There is no equality. There is a lot of discrimination in the application of justice. They do not punish the same crime in the same way for a black or a white as they do for Mexicans."

But even a few Indian research participants described encounters with police, particularly in the early years after 9/11. A turbaned Sikh man described being at a McDonald's restaurant with a group of friends. They were discussing business and had some papers out on the table. The next thing they knew there were a group of police asking them who they were and what they were doing. They called the chief, and he knew they were Sikhs and let them go. He said that his lawyer has recommended that he always have his passport and visa on him, because it has become dangerous in the United States.

Mexicans described forms of community discrimination most extensively. They talked about being ignored in banks, hospitals, and restaurants or noticing that better service was given to those of other races or those who were better dressed. Some Mexican parents complained that their children or Hispanic children more generally were not given as much attention in schools or were treated unfairly. One female respondent held on to a long-ago memory of being in a high school biology class. The teacher asked if anyone had questions. Although she raised her hand, the teacher never recognized her. Another told a story about being in a private school where the majority of the students were "Anglos" and had money. "I was the opposite and they did not accept me; they viewed me as a minority who did not really belong in that school." For many Mexicans, discrimination is voiced as someone being treated as invisible, a lesser person, a nonperson, an insignificant person. It is about not being accorded respect.

Invisibility, an idea rarely discussed in the literature on discrimination, was also mentioned by Nigerians. One research participant described applying for a license to open a business. "I walked into the office and the lady just sat there and didn't acknowledge me. Then a white man came in and she immediately attended to him and when I told her that I was there first she said that he had called." Another, recalling a time when he was in a restaurant with some white friends, said that when his friends ordered their food the waitress took the orders with no problem. When he tried to order, she ignored him and would not look him in the eye. Although he was served food along with his friends, "the waitress continued not to speak or make eye contact with me during the whole meal. She would not speak to me because I was Nigerian."

Indians described subtle forms of stereotyping within neighborhoods where they settled. One female research participant recalled walking in her neighborhood (where there are no other Indian families) and someone new to the neighborhood stopped her to ask if she knew another cleaning lady who wanted to work. She said she responded that she would ask her cleaning lady. She also reported answering the door of her home and being asked for the "lady of the house." These behaviors, she concluded, stem from ignorance. One Indian research participant, for example, described buying a house a year earlier, and before they moved in, someone in the neighborhood came to ask if they had purchased the house. "When we said yes, he muttered, 'there goes the neighbourhood.'" This respondent went on to report that this neighbor does not acknowledge them to this day. But reflecting on it, he claimed that while this incident blemished their experience, it did not diminish how they thought about America. People like this man, he stated, exist all over the world.

COPING WITH DISCRIMINATION: FORBEARANCE OR CONFRONTATION?

Sociologist Joe Feagin (1991) has described the various ways in which African Americans respond to discrimination in public places, ranging from withdrawal, to resigned acceptance, to verbal or physical confrontation, to legal action. What is the range of responses that characterizes first-generation immigrants? Do they simply ignore and rise above situations of discrimination—a response captured by the concept of forbearance (Noh et al., 1999)—or do they choose to pursue some sort of action and redress—that is, confront discrimination head on.

In this research, participants were asked how they might respond to several hypothetical situations of discrimination.[4] The first hypothetical asked research participants what they would do if they applied for a job and suspected that they were not hired because of their race, national background, or religious affiliation. Across all five groups, the highest proportion (40% or more) of research participants said they would just forget about it and look for another job. Further, the reasoning for this was similar across all five groups. Individuals indicated that filing a complaint was not worth the time, effort, money, or trouble. Across all five populations, research participants indicated that they preferred not to work for an employer who discriminates, and that there were other jobs to be had. "It is better to stay away from places where you know you are not welcome," said one Vietnamese respondent. "There are other jobs to find that will want you, so if they don't like you for your race—then forget about them," said another. However, one Vietnamese respondent who suggested that he might take some action described his own learning process: "This happened to me years ago, and I just forgot about it. Now I understand the system and know what my rights are." An Indian respondent said he would do nothing because he is pragmatic and it would not be worth it. But, offering a strategy of quiet resistance, he quickly added: "I would tell all my friends that it was a lousy company and that they should not apply there for a job."

---

[4] While the questions were posed initially to elicit an open-ended response (and recorded as such), the responses were also immediately coded by the interviewer into predetermined broader categories to which they most closely conformed. If the answer did not closely conform to one of the predetermined categories, it was coded as "other." It is important to note that some respondents had difficulty relating to a hypothetical. Interviewers also probed for why people responded as they did.

Several Nigerians also indicated that it was not worth it to file a complaint. The following response reflected that of several others who understood the challenges of a lawsuit for job discrimination: "I'll do nothing, it's part of life. You can't do anything unless you have good evidence of discrimination and you're already on the job. If you are applying for the job there's nothing you can do." Nigerians and Indians were the most vocal about how difficult it is to prove discrimination at the time of employment. "I feel that this kind of discrimination is difficult to prove in most of the cases, because everyone knows discrimination is bad," said one Indian respondent. "Therefore, if it happens, it will most likely be in a situation where someone has said no to me, but I do not know whether the qualifications of the hired employee are better or worse than mine. It is difficult to prove what is going on in someone's head." A Nigerian said that he would want to make sure that he was being treated unfairly, because otherwise the dispute would be dismissed for insufficient evidence. Another said: "You cannot prove discrimination. Taking action would 'red flag' your next job search." A female Indian respondent suggested that there are 1000 reasons why one does not get a job. She then went on to add that her own personal encounter with discrimination was based not on her color or national background but because she is female. In some areas of engineering, she said, "people think women cannot do the work. They think it requires people with physical strength." To work in computer maintenance, she suggested, "you are supposed to be on call and they do not think women can be on call 24 hours a day." But, she continued, "there is not much you can do about it. It is not my right, it is their right to give or not give me the job."

Several Mexicans said they were without documents and therefore did not have much choice in this matter. They had to lay low. As one respondent declared, "those who hire you are those who command. If you don't have papers you cannot insist." Those who said they would not fight it often indicated, like those of other immigrant groups included in the research, that they did not want to work where they were not wanted; but others indicated that the lack of time or money would deter them from filing a complaint or fighting it. Others said they would look for another job. At the time, there was a sense that jobs were more plentiful than people might think today. While some respondents said they would seek out an organization for help, such as LULAC or one of the local regional associations (Casa Chihuahua, Casa Guanajuato), in general, Mexicans and Salvadorans were the least willing to file complaints, precisely because doing so would bring them in contact with government bureaucracy and potentially expose their immigration status or jeopardize their potential to legalize their status. For the few who indicated that they might complain, the idea that everyone has a right to work, including the undocumented, was an important principle. Some suggested that fighting discrimination is a way to educate people about its unacceptability. As one Mexican respondent put it, "if you ask that they treat you with respect, they will do it. But you have to demand it."

A second hypothetical question asked respondents what they would do if they tried to rent an apartment and were told that none were available, but they suspected that they had been turned away because of their race, national background, or religion. Again the highest proportion across all groups (40% or more) would forget about it, although the Nigerians demonstrated more reluctance than others. Most respondents just thought that there were many places to live so why bother. As one Vietnamese respondent put it, "if they don't want my money, that's their problem." Another observed: "I would just forget about it and look for another apartment. You can't change them; they will still discriminate against you and treat you badly if you fight and move in. That's too much trouble." More metaphorically, a Salvadoran women commented that "if no one answers at one door, one should knock at another," while a male compatriot stated that he would not want to live where he is not wanted and went on to suggest that if this happened to his children he would expect them to fight it, because they were born in the United States.

But there were research participants across all groups who were indignant about housing discrimination and stated that this would lead them to file a complaint—from 18% of Salvadorans up to almost half of the Nigerians—or hire a lawyer to help them. One Vietnamese respondent said that he would talk to the owner and ask for proof that no apartments were available. If he was not satisfied with the answer, he said he would try to expose the injustice, "perhaps by contacting the press." Another Vietnamese participant reported actually experiencing housing discrimination. He described trying to buy a house as an investment, "but when the owner, who was an American veteran of the war in Vietnam, found out that I was Vietnamese, he backed out of the deal. When I went to talk to him about this in his office, he screamed at me to get out of his office and out of his country."

One Indian research participant, who had responded to the job question by saying that he would forget about it and look for another job but responded to the housing question by saying that he would fight it, offered the following explanation for the different actions. On the job, he said, you would have to interact with the people who were racist and that would not be worth it. But, he continued, we all have a right to equal housing and you do not have to interact with your neighbors—so it is less tied to others and that is why he said he would complain. Housing should be for all; employment depends on social ties. A Nigerian who claimed he would challenge housing discrimination, reported that in one place where he had lived "the landlords put all Africans in one wing of the apartment complex and the whites in another." A Mexican respondent observed that there are many places to live but that if he was set on a place, he would find the appropriate authority to complain to. "Discrimination is legally punishable here," he observed, "but at least the laws work." Across all groups, there seemed to be a faith in the law on this matter and a belief that housing discrimination was easier to prove than job discrimination.

To summarize, this hypothetical exercise yielded nuanced reasoning behind the responses that individuals across all five groups suggested they might make to discriminatory acts. Forbearance appears to be a characteristic response across all five populations but for different reasons, and there are certainly individuals across all groups who were developing a sense of their rights such that they discussed possible modes of confrontation, particularly in relation to housing discrimination. What is most striking is that many of these research participants are fully aware of the fact that acts of discrimination are often subtle and hence that mustering the evidence to prove one's case may not be a challenge worth pursuing.

CONCLUSION

This chapter has compared experiences with and attitudes toward everyday forms of discrimination among first generation immigrants to the United States from five different national origins. Individuals from all five groups have encountered both subtle and not so subtle discrimination since arriving in the United States. The subtle forms are manifested in not being acknowledged or recognized in public places—that is, being treated as if one is invisible and does not exist. This is discrimination against personhood and was articulated most clearly by Mexican and Nigerian research participants. Indian and Vietnamese research participants hold on more strongly to the notion that merit trumps discrimination and were more willing to acknowledge that, while the subtle slights are there, they are not serious. One Vietnamese offered a conservative perspective when noting, "If you are really good, you can overcome any handicaps associated with your race or ethnicity. If you are not very good at your job, then you may want to claim discrimination—it is a good excuse for failure. Of course whether there is something to this claim depends on the circumstances, on the context." The idea of merit trumping color may extend beyond the Indian immigrant community, but nevertheless members of both these immigrant populations have occasionally confronted barriers to success, promotion, and full acceptance.

Even Nigerians, who acknowledge the phenotypical foundations of racism most directly, sometimes observed that discrimination is a product of history and one has to adapt to its pervasiveness. One noted, "whites in a shop won't wait for very long, some barbers still won't cut black hair; others won't cut white hair. ProCut is a white product, Supercut is a black product." A Vietnamese informant observed that "all people are racist at some level. Everyone discriminates because they want to be with their own kind. We must accept this natural fact and live with it. . . . We (as immigrants) often have to work for less money. This is the price you pay for being an immigrant—a foreigner. Younger people have less (sic) problems than older people because the young can speak English and they understand the system." This individual's comment about language is important. Across all five groups, research participants noted the low tolerance in the United States for those who do not speak English, do not speak it well, or speak it with an accent. This low tolerance can result in anything from subtle discrimination to racist epithets. It is a stigmatization of the foreign born in a country that is ambivalent about itself as a "nation of immigrants."

Other dimensions of human capital also influence the everyday experience of discrimination. Well-educated Nigerian and Indian immigrants identify discrimination in relation to their professional advancement, while low-skilled or unskilled Mexican immigrants emphasize their vulnerability in the labor market, something that is further affected by their immigration status (legal or undocumented). However, when confronted with hypothetical scenarios about job and housing discrimination, a significant number across all five groups, for one reason or another, said they would choose to ignore (forbear) the discrimination rather than confront it or seek legal action. Feagin (1991) has observed with regard to African Americans' coping strategies in the face of discrimination "in many situations, resigned acceptance is the only realistic response" (p. 103). This is a strategy shared by first generation immigrants, many of whom do not feel they have the resources (including linguistic ability and legal status) to pursue a more confrontational response. But rather than label these responses as resigned, it is more appropriate to view them as well-reasoned and strategic. That more of the research respondents were willing to react against housing discrimination than against job discrimination supports this emphasis on considered, strategic behavior. Over the course of time, it appears that immigrants, even those who are not yet citizens of the United States, begin to learn about their rights and hence evaluate when to exercise them.

While most theories of prejudice and discrimination focus on the sources of discriminatory behavior—in fear and scapegoating, economic competition, ethnocentrism, group boundary construction, socialization—this chapter has focused more on how these behaviors are perceived and processed by first generation immigrants themselves. While there are important variations across the five populations included in this research, some of it associated with dimensions of human and financial capital, there are also many similarities in how skilled, semi-skilled, and unskilled immigrants think about and cope with everyday forms of discrimination. Particularly revealing for example are the stronger perceptions of group discrimination articulated by Mexican immigrants by contrast with Indian immigrants. This difference suggests that the intersection of class and "race/ethnicity" is worthy of further investigation in research on discrimination against immigrant newcomers.

REFLECTIVE QUESTIONS

1. What is the difference between real and perceived discrimination?

2. What are the various ways in which immigrants cope with perceived discrimination?

3. What are the variations that can be found in attitudes toward discrimination from one immigrant population to the next, and how can these be explained?

4. What would you do if confronted with job or housing discrimination, and how would your actions make you feel?

5. While this essay does not differentiate strongly between immigrants and refugees, can you imagine any situations where refugee status might matter in relation to perceived discrimination?

CASE STUDY

Manuel, a Mexican immigrant, reported confronting prejudice when he arrived in the United States at the age of nine. He discovered that he was the only Hispanic child in a white neighborhood in West Houston. He heard words like "spic" and "wetback" directed toward him by other students at his school. "They asked me what stroke I used to swim across the river" and whether I "lived in a cardboard shack." Because he was Hispanic, he said, he was automatically labeled an alien. "It was horrible. I was beat up and spat upon. I started denouncing my ethnicity. I told people I was from Spain. Everyone was okay with that. For years I went like that. I never heard a positive word about Mexicans. 'Stinking Mexicans, f__ Mexicans, dirty Mexicans.' It was impossible to clean it up." Eventually Manuel went to college, and there he met others who had faced similar experiences. But he also started to understand how the media shaped people's attitudes, and it made him angry. By studying about Mexico in college, he regained his pride in his ancestry.

SUMMATIVE POINTS

- Discrimination is encountered and experienced differently by immigrants from various national backgrounds.

- Discriminatory acts occur not just in relation to phenotypical racial differences and English-language deficiencies, but also in relation to class position, immigration status, foreignness, and personhood.

- Immigrants exercise agency in decisions they make about whether to confront or forebear acts of discrimination. There are variations in these choices depending on national origin and immigration status.

REFERENCES

Bhatia, S. (2007). *American karma: Race, culture and identity in the Indian diaspora*. New York: New York University Press.

Brettell, C. B. (2008a). Big d: Incorporating new immigrants in a sunbelt metropolis. In A. Singer, S. Hardwick, & C. B. Brettell (Eds.), *Twenty-first century gateways: Immigrant incorporation in suburban America* (pp. 53–86). Washington, DC: The Brookings Institution.

Brettell, C. B. (2008b). Immigrants in a sunbelt metropolis: The transformation of an urban place and the construction of community. In L. M. Hanley, B. A. Ruble, & A. M. Garland (Eds.), *Immigration & integration in urban communities: Renegotiating the city* (pp. 143–175). Washington, DC and Baltimore: Woodrow Wilson Center Press and Johns Hopkins University Press.

Brettell, C. B. (2011). Experiencing everyday discrimination: A comparison across five immigrant populations. *Race and Social Problems, 3*(4), 266–279.

Brettell, C. B., Hollifield, J. F., Cordell, D., & Garcia y Griego, M. (n.d.). Experiencing everyday discrimination: A comparison across five immigrant populations (2002–2005) funded by the Cultural Anthropology Program of the National Science Foundation (NSF/BCS 0003938).

Dion, K. L. (2001). Immigrants' perception of housing discrimination in Toronto: The Housing New Canadians Project. *Journal of Social Issues, 57*(3), 523–539.

Dion, K. L. (2002). The social psychology of perceived prejudice and discrimination. *Canadian Psychology, 43*(1), 1–10.

Dion, K. L., & Kerry, K. (1996). Ethnicity and perceived discrimination in Toronto: Another look at the person/group discrimination discrepancy. *Canadian Journal of Behavioral Science, 28*(3), 203–213.

Feagin, J. R. (1991). The continuing significance of race: Anti-black discrimination in public places. *American Sociological Review, 56*(1), 101–116.

Finch, B. K., Bohdan, K., & William, V. (2000). Perceived discrimination and depression among Mexican-origin adults in California. *Journal of Health and Social Behavior, 41*, 295–313.

Jackson, J. S., Williams, D. R., & Torres, M. (1997). Perceptions of discrimination, health and mental health: The social stress process. In A. Maney & J. Ramos (Eds.), *Socioeconomic conditions, stress and mental disorders: Toward a new synthesis of research and public policy* (Chapter 8). Washington, DC: National Institute of Mental Health.

Jasinskaja-Lahti, I., Liebkind, I., Jaakkola, M., & Reuter, A. (2006). Perceived discrimination, social support networks and psychological well-being among three immigrant groups. *Journal of Cross-Cultural Psychology, 37*(3), 293–311.

Kuo, W. H. (1995). Coping with racial discrimination: The case of Asian Americans. *Ethnic and Racial Studies, 18*, 109–127.

Liebkind, K., & Jasinskaja-Lahti, I. (2000). The influence of experiences of discrimination on psychological stress: A comparison of seven immigrant groups. *Journal of Community and Applied Social Psychology, 10*(1), 1–16.

Mattlin, J., Wethington, E., & Kessler, R. C. (1990). Situational determinants of coping and coping effectiveness. *Journal of Health and Social Behavior, 31*, 103–122.

Moradi, B., & Risco, C. (2006). Perceived discrimination experiences and mental health of Latina/o American persons. *Journal of Counseling Psychology, 53*(4), 411–421.

Moradi, B., & Talal Hasan, N. (2004). Arab American persons' reported experiences of discrimination and mental health: The mediating role of personal control. *Journal of Counseling Psychology, 51*(4), 418–428.

Mossakowski, K. N. (2003). Coping with perceived discrimination: Does ethnic identity protect migrant health. *Journal of Health and Social Behavior, 44*(3), 318–331.

Noh, S., Beiser, M., Kaspar, V., Hou, G., & Rummens, J. (1999). Perceived racial discrimination, depression and coping: A study of Southeast Asian refugees in Canada. *Journal of Health and Social Behavior, 40*, 193–207.

Taylor, D. M., Wright, S. C., Moghaddam, F. M., & Lalonde, R. M. (1990). The personal/group discrepancy: Perceiving my group, but not myself, to be a target of discrimination. *Personality and Social Psychology Bulletin, 16*, 254–262.

Chapter 6

POSTCOLONIAL FEMINIST SOCIAL WORK PERSPECTIVE

Additional Considerations for Immigrant and Refugee Populations

ANNE C. DEEPAK

KEY TERMS

asylee, immigrants, refugees, immigration policies, collective empowerment

---

CHAPTER HIGHLIGHTS

- Introduction to postcolonial feminist social work perspective and its application to immigrant and refugee mental health
- Analysis of risk factors for poor mental health outcomes embedded in U.S. immigration policies of family detention and deportation and patriarchal global economic oppression
- Overview mental health promotion as collective resistance and empowerment
- Strategies mental health providers can use to become stronger allies

---

The experiences of refugees and immigrants are shaped by a transnational landscape of social, cultural, historical, and structural factors that can promote or compromise mental health. In this chapter, a postcolonial feminist social work perspective will be introduced to understand this macro context. This perspective centers the gendered dynamics of globalization, power, and resistance and the social work values of self-determination and social justice (Deepak, 2014). In exploring the experiences of refugees and immigrants, it will be used to explore risk factors for poor mental health outcomes, mental health promotion through collective resistance and empowerment, and the role of social workers and mental health providers as allies. Within this discussion, the terms *immigrants* and *refugees* include asylum seekers and undocumented immigrants.

A POSTCOLONIAL FEMINIST
SOCIAL WORK PERSPECTIVE

A postcolonial feminist social work perspective is a theoretical lens that integrates postcolonial feminist theory with the social work values of social justice and self-determination (Deepak, 2014). The perspective foregrounds the gendered impact of global inequality as it has been produced and maintained through colonialism and the current economic dimensions of globalization (Deepak, 2011), which contribute to and sustain interlocking forms of global and local oppression. Tools for resistance to these forms of oppression can be found in the social and technological dimensions of globalization that facilitate collective agency and the creation of partnerships with allies to mobilize locally and globally to fight against these inequalities (Deepak, 2014).

The perspective is grounded in postcolonial feminist theory, which rejects colonial and development discourses that characterize women from the global South as passive victims of timeless, oppressive cultural and religious traditions in need of being rescued by white men, and sometimes women, on a civilizing mission (Chatterjee, 1993; Mohanty, 1991; Spivak, 1995; Syed & Ali, 2011, as cited in Deepak, 2011).This rejection of oppressive discourse includes nationalist discourse that positions women in the global South as willing participants in oppressive patriarchal practices (Spivak, 1995), often defended as cultural in origin (Deepak, 2011, 2014). Nationalist discourse creates an ideal woman who is demure, spiritual, and devoted to nation and family in opposition to the Western woman, constructed as selfish, promiscuous, brazen, and materialistic (Chatterjee, 1993, as cited in Deepak, 2011, 2014).

Postcolonial feminist theory highlights multiple sites of oppression through colonialism, nationalism, fundamentalism, racism, patriarchies, and global economic structures, while affirming the agency of women in the global South. This agency is recognized as partial and limited, just as in the case of women in the global North (Deepak, 2011, 2014).

In applying the perspective to the issue of immigrant and refugee mental health, three questions are used for analysis: (1) How does globalization and global inequality play a role in the interlocking forms of oppression in this issue? (2) How do women (and men) collectively resist these forms of oppression in ways that promote mental health? (3) How are social workers and mental health providers implicated in these systems of oppression, and how can we act as allies in promoting the mental health of refugees and immigrants?

RISK FACTORS FOR POOR MENTAL HEALTH OUTCOMES

A primary reason immigrants and refugees migrate is to create a better life and to provide opportunities for their families (IOM, n.d.), who remain in their country of origin in the home and for those in the host countries. Achieving this goal requires the physical, emotional, and economic security that enables immigrants and refugees to protect and provide for their families. The inability to protect family members from psychological and physical harm as well as the difficulty in adequately providing for family members results in risk factors for poor mental health outcomes.

Immigrants and refugees living in the United States and Canada have identified these risk factors for poor mental health outcomes: (a) experiences of racism and discrimination (George, Thomson, Chaze, & Guruge, 2015; Immigrant Services Association of Nova Scotia, 2014; Leong, Park, & Kalibatseva, 2013; Salas, Ayon, & Gurrola, 2013); (b) the stresses associated with the ability to find and maintain employment, transportation, and basic necessities to provide for their families (Deeb-Sossa et al., 2009; George et al., 2015); and (c) separation from family members (Deeb-Sossa et al., 2009; Koball et al., 2015). These risk factors are shaped by the context of globalization and global inequality manifested in patriarchal global economic oppression and racialized U.S. immigration policies of detention and deportation.

GLOBALIZATION AND GLOBAL INEQUALITY

Globalization is a core component of the social and economic landscape of migrants' experiences. It is an "intensified global interconnectedness . . . via the mobility and flows of culture, capital, information, resistance, technologies, production [and] people" (Gunewardena & Kingsolver, 2007, pp. 7–8). The economic dimensions of globalization are manifested in economic policies that include cuts to social services and the privatization of public services, such as health, education, and social welfare leading to increases in inequality, economic insecurity, vulnerability, and poverty, with vulnerable and marginalized populations in the global South more harshly impacted (Fudge, 2011; Petrozziello, 2013).

THE FEMINIZATION OF MIGRATION AND GLOBAL CARE CHAINS. As a consequence of the economic dimensions of globalization and the dislocation of men as primary providers, an increasing number of poor women from the global South are migrating independently as primary providers for themselves and their transnational families rather than as family "dependents" (Fudge, 2011; Petrozziello, 2013). This dynamic is referred to as the feminization of migration.

The United States is home to the largest number of international migrants (47 million), which is about a fifth of the world's total (UN Women, 2015). In 2015, the percentage of female migrants was highest in Europe (52.4%) and Northern America (51.2%), while it is much lower in Asia (42%) and Africa (46.1%) (UN Women, 2015). The higher percentage of female migrants in the global North has been attributed to the demand for female migrant labor because of a care deficit caused by a combination of factors, for example, increasing life expectancy, an increase in women's labor force participation, changes in family structure, declining fertility rates, shortages of public care because of cuts in social protections, and the privatization of social care (Fudge, 2011). Because most governments in the global North have not addressed this care crisis, households continue to assume this responsibility. An affordable option for middle-class and upper-class households has been to hire a female migrant worker to provide care services (Petrozziello, 2013).

These migrants transfer their own caregiving responsibilities in their home countries to someone else in the family or outsource it to internal migrants in the home country (GFMD, 2015). In the global North, jobs as nannies, domestic workers, and home health care aides are the worst possible in terms of pay, working conditions, legal protections, and social recognition (UN-INSTRAW, 2007). The underpaid and unprotected care work that is provided by immigrant women helps to keep U.S. families stable and productive, while at the same time, U.S. immigration policies of detention and deportation and the threats of these policies separate families, threaten their economic and psychological stability, and create a climate of fear.

U.S. IMMIGRATION POLICIES OF DETENTION AND DEPORTATION

U.S. immigration laws are created for the purpose of enforcement rather than the rights of children and their families (Women's Refugee Commission, 2015). Two of the policies that are particularly stressful to immigrants and refugees and their families are family detention and deportation.

DETENTION. Immigration detention is the policy of placing legal and undocumented immigrants in confinement until a decision is made about their status, either asylum or deportation. The United States has the largest immigration detention system in the world, detaining nearly 500,000 individuals each year, including families, and is almost completely privatized (Global Detention Project, as cited in Schueths, 2016). In 2009, Congress implemented a yearly detention bed quota that requires Immigration and Customs Enforcement (ICE) to maintain 34,000 beds at any time. No other law enforcement agency operates on a quota system (Schueths, 2016).

These policies and the threat of their enforcement affect the mental health of families, communities, and children in a variety of ways. Undocumented immigrants report generalized anxiety and stress and limited participation in community life, interaction with service providers and police for fear of being deported. In addition, they report depression, withdrawal, inability to focus, and acting out among children who experience detention and deportation of family and community members (HIP, 2013).

WOMEN AND CHILDREN IN DETENTION. The practice of family detention in the United States was minimal until the summer of 2014, when there was a rapid increase of Central American asylum-seeking families fleeing extreme violence in their home countries. In response to this situation, the 95 beds for family detention were increased to 3,700, new detention centers were built, and the numbers of women and children in detention dramatically increased, despite the fact that international law rejects immigration detention for children and discourages it for families (American Civil Liberties Union [ACLU], 2015; Human Rights First, 2015).

Family detention has a damaging impact on the mental health of asylum seekers and is particularly traumatizing for mothers and children, even for very short periods of time (Human Rights First, 2015). Women in detention report suicidal thoughts, depression in themselves and their children, weight loss in young children, sexual assault by guards, and inadequate access to healthcare, child care, and medical and mental health care (Lutheran Immigration Refugee Service & Women's Refugee Commission, 2014).

DEPORTATION. In 2013, there were 438,421 deportations in the United States; in approximately 83% of those cases, individuals did not have a hearing, did not meet with an immigration judge, and were deported through administrative processes by the presiding immigration officer (ACLU, 2015). These deportations included 72,000 parents who said they had U.S.-born children (Foley, 2014). Of those deported without a hearing, some had U.S.-citizen children and never had the opportunity to call an attorney or arrange for their children's care. Others were fleeing persecution or violence and were returned to the same danger. Some were in the United States lawfully and should not have been deported (ACLU, 2015).

For mixed-status families, in which one or both parents are undocumented, the situation is complex because of the different rights each family member has under U.S. law. The estimated number of U.S.-citizen children who have families with mixed immigration status is 4.5 million (HIP, 2013). Between 2010 and 2012, almost 205,000 parents of U.S.-citizen children were deported (Wessler, 2012). Undocumented parents facing deportation may confront the decision of whether to leave their U.S.-citizen child in the United States with a documented relative for a chance at a better life or to return to the home country together; some of these parents do not have the privilege of making this decision, and their children are placed in foster care.

Through the Adoption and Safe Families Acts (AFSA) of 1997, strict timelines were created to ensure that courts file for the termination of parental rights in cases when a child has been in care for 15 of the previous 22 months; states can begin these proceedings before 22 months if parents are not complying with reunification plans (Wessler, 2011). For deported parents and those in detention or going through immigration proceedings, the timelines created by AFSA are insufficient for parents to comply with child welfare requirements that would lead to reunification (Women's Refugee Commission, 2015).

In addition, social services in Mexico cannot be useful to deported mothers unless the mothers have reported the birth of their child in the United States to Mexican authorities prior to their deportation. These Mexican agencies are working diligently with U.S. social services to make this information available to Mexican mothers who risk deportation. Without such a report and the resultant protection, the mother deported to Mexico cannot engage the Mexican authorities to help her regain the custody of her child (IMUMI, 2015, personal communication).

In sum, a host of risk factors for poor mental health outcomes stem from anti-immigration racism reflected in; (a) patriarchal global economic oppression manifested in a contradictory demand for migrant women from the global South to engage in care work without proper compensation or legal rights, and (b) U.S. immigration policies of detention and deportation that harm and separate families from the global South. In response, immigrants and refugees engage in courageous acts of collective resistance and activism; it is these acts of collective empowerment that promote mental health (MacDonnell, Dastjerdi, Bokore, Tharao, & Khanlou, 2012; Wong, Wong, & Fung, 2010).

MENTAL HEALTH PROMOTION THROUGH COLLECTIVE RESISTANCE AND EMPOWERMENT

Through coordinated collective resistance, immigrants and refugees create and participate in spaces in which they build their social support and social capital, build trust with organizational allies, contribute to their communities, and develop and enhance leadership skills. Research indicates that these forms of collective empowerment and capacity building are key strategies for mental health promotion for refugee and immigrant women (Wong, Wong, & Fung, 2010).

RESISTANCE TO ECONOMIC INSECURITY

IMMIGRANT-RUN WORKER-OWNED COOPERATIVES. Worker cooperatives are for-profit businesses that are owned and managed democratically by employees. For marginalized immigrant and refugee women and men, who are usually poorly paid and exploited in service, construction, landscaping, and domestic work, participating in worker cooperatives is a strong model of economic empowerment (Ji & Robinson, 2012) and consequently, also a strong model of collective empowerment.

Immigrant and refugee women have successfully formed worker cooperatives with the support of external or community nonprofit organizations, such as the Beyond Care Childcare Cooperative (BCCC) and the Center for Family Life in Sunset Park (CFFL), Brooklyn, a neighborhood-based family and social services organization.

BCCC was set up in 2008 by 16 worker-owners but now has 30 members, all immigrant women mothers, most of whom have had experience working as babysitters, after-school program employees, or nannies. Members are guided by their commitment to fairness in wages and treatment and are able to set their own schedules and have more time to spend with their families. The model includes technical assistance and training on cooperative values, effective group work, skills and knowledge needed for the particular business, and business development (Voinea, 2014).

RESISTING DEPORTATION AND DETENTION

Immigrants and refugees resist deportation and detention through participation in campaigns that advocate for changes in U.S. immigration and labor policy and the protection of immigrant and refugee families (Cervantes, Hafiz, Kline, Kuhner, & Morrow, 2015). One of these campaigns is coordinated through We Belong Together, a binational organization that was formed as a partnership between the National Domestic Workers Alliance and the National Asian Pacific American Women's Forum, with the participation of women's organizations, immigrant rights groups, and children and families across the United States. We Belong Together uses a mix of policy advocacy, community organizing, and civil disobedience to frame the issue of immigration reform as a human rights issue that is, at its core, about keeping families together.

The immigration reforms the organization demands are (a) a broad and clear roadmap to citizenship that recognizes the contributions of women's work and women workers, (b) to keep all families together, (c) to recognize women's work in future employment categories and protect women workers on the job, (d) to ensure protections for survivors of violence and trafficking, (e) to protect families and ensure due process, (f) to promote immigrant integration that includes and empowers women (We Belong Together, n.d.).

Immigrants and refugees participate through their membership, by sharing their experiences which then lead to organizational demands, and by organizing and participating in collective political action through marches. For example, in the *100 Women 100 Miles Pilgrimage*, one hundred women, ages 4 through 73, marched from a detention center in York County, Pennsylvania, to Washington, D.C., in seven days to welcome Pope Francis during his first visit to the United States "carrying stories from a site of human suffering to the Pope with a message of human dignity" (We Belong Together, n.d.).

BECOMING STRONGER ALLIES

We become part of the systems of oppression that threaten the mental health of immigrant and refugee families when we ignore the larger historical, political, and economic contexts that are creating serious risk factors for poor mental health outcomes. For U.S. citizens, it is a privilege to ignore the daily threats to physical, emotional, and economic security faced by immigrant and refugee families and communities (American Friends Service Committee [AFSC], n.d.). By recognizing the privileges associated with citizenship, we can become stronger allies in the mental health promotion of refugees and immigrants.

As U.S. citizens and documented U.S. residents, we can leverage our privilege to become stronger allies by partnering with community-based organizations and collective movements that challenge harmful policies, practices, and discourse that threaten the mental health of immigrant and refugee families. These policies include immigration, labor, and economic policy. Finally, we can integrate the commitment to becoming stronger allies into our practice through our roles as mental health providers, social workers, community organizers, and administrators.

IMPLICATIONS FOR MENTAL HEALTH PROVIDERS

A postcolonial feminist social work perspective in understanding immigrant and refugee mental health highlights the experiences of women without erasing those of men and enables a dual focus on multiple sites of oppression and the affirmation of individual and collective agency. This perspective has been used to rethink the risk factors for poor mental health as embedded in oppressive structural, historical, and political factors rather than solely in individual experiences. In addition, the focus of the perspective on collective resistance to oppression helps to refocus mental health treatment and interventions to include mental health promotion in the form of collective empowerment. In the examples provided, worker cooperatives and participation in immigrant-rights advocacy helped to increase economic, emotional, and physical security. Both worker cooperatives and immigrant-rights advocacy incorporate social integration and leadership opportunities.

Whether one is working as a mental health provider with individual clients, families, and groups or as a social worker community organizer or program administrator, the application of a postcolonial feminist social work perspective enables an expanded understanding for mental health assessment and treatment. The structural nature of the threats to immigrant and refugee mental health and the ways in which communities and individuals resist these threats are crucially important components of assessment and treatment.

Organizations that recognize and address these structural threats to mental health are more effective in serving the mental health needs of children and families. For example, organizations found to be most successful in serving children after a parental detention or deportation were those that built trust with families "by providing vital support services, building close relationships with immigrant communities, engaging in immigrant-rights advocacy, and providing immigration legal assistance" (Koball et al., 2015, p. 34). From the perspective of a program administrator in mental health services, a recognition of the importance of accessing these services and engaging in immigrant-rights advocacy is critically important in building relationships of trust that can deepen individual clinical services. Program administrators and social work community organizers can address this by building partnerships with community-based organizations that provide these essential services.

The meaningful participation of immigrants and refugees in challenging immigration and labor policies is in itself a path toward healing. Advocates for survivors of human labor trafficking recommend that social service providers recognize "the value of labor organizing and leadership development in the healing process" (Williams, 2015, p. 7). Mental health providers that are mindful of the benefits of labor organizing and leadership development in the healing process can identify opportunities in which clients can participate in these activities if they so choose.

By recognizing the connection between collective empowerment and mental health, we can be attuned to seeking out and recognizing individual and collective resistance when it occurs and mindful of connecting individual clients to opportunities for community involvement and collective connection. This approach is supported by a study on the mental health and well-being of immigrant and refugee women that concluded there was a need to "(1) create spaces and supports for women to express their agency individually and collectively to foster change at individual, family, community and structural/social levels and (2) address strategies that affirm their positive contributions to communities and systems" (MacDonnell, Dastjerdi, Bokore, Tharao, & Khanlou, 2012, p. 9). Providers also can provide psychoeducation and educational groups to help immigrants and refugees begin to feel more empowered with information and with concepts that continuously arise in conversations with community organizations and other community partners. Training immigrants and refugee women and men to facilitate these groups within the community would be a way of providing leadership opportunities in which they can make a positive contribution to their communities.

Finally, by increasing our knowledge and awareness of community-based organizations and innovative programs that promote immigrant and refugee mental health through civic engagement and worker cooperatives, we can link individuals and families to these opportunities and work to create opportunities for leadership development and social and economic growth and development within our own programs. Social work community organizers can play a vital role in this process, by researching successful models and reaching out to immigrant and refugee community stakeholders to participate in developing these programs. By sharing our knowledge and experiences with our personal and professional networks and by learning from immigrant and refugee community leaders, activists, and organizers, we can continue to become better allies through these relationships.

REFLECTIVE QUESTIONS

1. As you reflect on this article, what issues for women, men, and children become critical concerns for the mental health field in general and for your social work practice specifically?

2. What would you suggest for the most effective method of accomplishing the registration of births in the United States, with Mexican authorities, to protect the bond between children and their families in case of deportation? How might social workers and other helping professionals support those in this situation? Consider the use of technology, for example, Skype, Facebook, the Internet, and so forth.

3. What would you describe as the advantages and limitations for the collective empowerment of women as a method for helping families in host and home countries?

4. How would labor organizing and leadership development contribute to the healing process for formerly trafficked women and men?

SUMMATIVE POINTS

- Postcolonial feminist social work perspectives can be used to frame social justice and advocacy efforts in supporting immigrant and refugee mental health.

- Detention and deportation are common practices integrated into immigration laws that are particularly stressful for the immigrant and refugee populations and which can exacerbate adverse mental health symptoms.

- Providers and the general society can become stronger allies against immigration practices that are harmful to the larger society.

- The author suggests that a postcolonial feminist social work perspective in understanding immigrant and refugee mental health highlights the experiences of women without erasing those of men and enables a dual focus on multiple sites of oppression and the affirmation of individual and collective agency.

REFERENCES

American Civil Liberties Union. (2015). *Immigrant family detention in the US*. Retrieved from https://www.aclu.org/files/field_document/ACLU%20-%20Family%20Detention.pdf

American Friends Service Committee. (n.d.). *Citizen privilege and ally basics*. Retrieved from http://afsc.org/document/citizen-privilege-and-ally-basics

Cervantes, W., Hafiz, S., Kline, V., Kuhner, G., & Morrow, L. (2015). *The heart of the matter: Women, children and the way forward on immigration policy*. We Belong Together: Women for Common Sense Immigration Policies. Retrieved from http://www.webelongtogether.org/new-report-the-heart-of-the-matter-women-children-and-the-way-forward-on-immigration-policy

Chatterjee, P. (1993). *The nation and its fragments*. Princeton, NJ: Princeton University.

Deeb-Sossa, N., Sribney, W. M., Elliott, K., Girodana, C., Sala, M., & Aguilar-Gaxiola, S. (2009). *Building partnerships: Conversations with Latino/a migrant workers about mental health needs and community strengths*. Sacramento, CA: UC Davis Center for Reducing Health Disparities.

Deepak, A. C. (2011). Sustainability and population growth in the context of globalization: A postcolonial feminist social work perspective. *Journal of Research on Women and Gender, 3*, 1–22.

Deepak, A. C. (2014). A postcolonial feminist social work perspective on global food insecurity. *Affilia: Journal of Women and Social Work, 29(2)*, 153–164.

Foley, E. (2014, June). Deportation separated thousands of U.S.-born children from their parents in 2013. *Huffington Post*. Retrieved from http://www.huffingtonpost.com/2014/06/25/parents-deportation_n_5531552.html

Fudge, J. (2011). *Gender and migration: Workers at the interface of migration and development*. A special panel event by the United Nations Entity for Gender Equality and Women's Empowerment (UN Women) and the International Labor Organization (ILO) at the fourth United Nations Conference on Least Developed Countries (LDC-IV). Decent Work for Migrant Care Workers. Retrieved from http://www.ilo.org/wcmsp5/groups/public/@dgreports/@dcomm/documents/meetingdocument/wcms_155339.pdf

George, U., Thomson, M. S., Chaze, F., & Guruge, S. (2015). Immigrant mental health, a public health issue: Looking back and moving forward. *International Journal of Environmental Research and Public Health, 12*, 13624–13648.

GFMD. (2015). *Global forum on migration and development*. Retrieved from gfmd.org/int

Gunewardena, N., & Kingsolver, A. (2007). Introduction. In N. Gunewardena & A. Kingsolver. (Eds.), *The gender of globalization: Women navigating cultural and economic marginalities* (pp. 3–21). Santa Fe, NM: School for Advanced Research Press.

Human Impact Factor. (2013). *Family unity, family health: How family-focused immigration reform will mean better health for children and families*. Retrieved from http://www.familyunityfamilyhealth.org/

Human Rights First. (2015). *U.S. detention of families seeking asylum: A one-year update*. New York: Author.

Immigrant Services Association of Nova Scotia. (2014). *Newcomer community wellness project: Immigrants' perspectives of their mental health and wellness*. Halifax, Nova Scotia, Canada: Immigrant Services Association of Nova Scotia.

IMUMI. (n.d.). Imumi website. Retrieved from http://www.imumi.org.

IOM. (n.d.). *International organization of migration trends*. Retrieved from http://www.iom.int

Ji, M., & Robinson, T. (2012). *Immigrant worker cooperatives: A user's manual*. Retrieved from http://american.coop/sites/default/files/Workers_Coop_Manual_FINAL_May_31_copy.pdf

Koball, H., Capps, R., Perreira, K., Campetella, A., Hooker, S., Pedroza, J. M., Monson, W., . . . Huerta, S. (2015). *Health and social service needs of US-citizen children with detained or deported immigrant parents*. Washington, DC: Urban Institute & Migration Policy Institute.

Leong, F., Park, Y. S., & Kalibatseva, Z. (2013). Disentangling immigrant status in mental health: Psychological protective and risk factors among Latinos and Asian American immigrants. *American Journal of Orthopsychiatry, 2*(3), 361–371.

Lutheran Immigration Refugee Service & Women's Refugee Commission. (2014). *Locking up family values, again: A report on the renewed practice of family immigration detention*. Retrieved from https://womensrefugeecommission.org/resources/document/1085-locking-up-family-values-again?catid=237

MacDonnell, J. A., Dastjerdi, M., Bokore, N., & Khanlou, N. (2012). Becoming resilient: Promoting the mental health and wellbeing of immigrant women in a Canadian context. *Nursing Research and Practice, Special Issue on Migration and Health*. Retrieved from http://www.hindawi.com/journals/nrp/2012/576586/

MacDonnell, J. A., Dastjerdi, M., Bokore, N., Tharao, W., & Khanlou, N. (2012). *Exploring how immigrant women conceptualize activism: Implications for mental health promotion. Final Report*. Retrieved from https://www.researchgate.net/publication/265291981_Exploring_How_Immigrant_Women_Conceptualize_Activism_Implications_for_Mental_Health_Promotion_Final_Report

Mohanty, C. (1991). Under western eyes: Feminist scholarship and colonial discourses. In C. Mohanty, A. Russo, & T. Lourdes (Eds.), *Third world women and the politics of feminism* (pp. 51–79). Indianapolis, IN: Indiana University Press.

Petrozziello, A. J. (2013). *Gender on the move: Working on the migration-development nexus from a gender perspective*. Retrieved from http://www.unwomen.org/en/digital-library/publications/2013/12/gender-on-the-move

Salas, L. M., Ayon, C., & Gurrola, M. (2013). Estamos traumados: The impact of anti-immigrant sentiment and policies on the mental health of Mexican immigrant families. *Journal of Community Psychology, 41*(8), 1005–1020.

Schueths, A. (2016, April 25). The new Juan Crow: Who benefits from immigration detention? *Sociology in Focus*. Retrieved from http://sociologyinfocus.com/2016/04/the-new-juan-crow-who-benefits-from-immigration-detention/

Spivak, G. (1995). Can the Subaltern speak? In B. Ashcroft, G. Griffins, & H. Tiffin (Eds.), *The postcolonial studies reader* (pp. 24–28). London: Routledge.

Syed, J., & Ali, F. (2011). The white women's burden: From colonial civilization to third world development. *Third World Quarterly, 32*, 349–365.

We Belong Together. (n.d.). We Belong Together About. http://www.webelongtogether.org/about

UN-INSTRAW. (2007). *Feminization of migration: Gender, remittances and development.* Retrieved from http://www.renate-europe.net/wp-content/uploads/2014/01/Feminization_of_Migration-INSTRAW2007.pdf

UN Women. (2015). *Progress of the World's Women 2015-2016: Transforming economies, realizing rights.* Retrieved from http://progress.unwomen.org/en/2015/

Voinea, D. V. (2014). A demographic portrait of Romanian immigrants in California. *Social Sciences and Education Research Review, 1*(1), 63–70.

Wessler, S. F. (2011). *Shattered families: The perilous intersection of immigration enforcement and the child welfare system.* Applied Research Center. Retrieved from https://www.raceforward.org/research/reports/shattered-families

Wessler, S. F. (2012). *Primary data: Deportations of parents of US citizen kids. Colorlines.* Retrieved from http://www.colorlines.com/articles/primary-data-deportations-parents-us-citizen-kids

Williams, T. (2015). *Beyond survival: Organizing to end human trafficking of domestic workers.* New York: National Domestic Workers Alliance.

Women's Refugee Commission. (2015). Family separation as a result of immigration policies in the United States. In *Childhood and migration in Central and North America: Causes, policies, practices and challenges.* San Francisco: Center for Gender & Refugee Studies at the University of California Hastings College of Law.

Wong, Y. R., Wong, J. P., & Fung, K. P. (2010). Promoting mental health through empowerment and community capacity building among East and Southeast Asian immigrant and refugee women. *Canadian Issues: Immigrant Mental Health, Summer Issue*, 108–113.

INTERVENTION MODALITIES USING AN INTEGRATIVE APPROACH

> "I handed my passport to the immigration officer, and he looked at it and looked at me and said, 'What are you?'"
>
> ~ **Grace Hopper**

Learning Objectives

Discuss six client systems and the respective service models available in the field that use an integrative approach to working with transnational populations.

INTRODUCTION

Unit III: Intervention Modalities Using an Integrative Approach consists of six chapters that explore the various client systems that can be engaged in the field: individuals (Chapter 7: "Practice With Individuals," Hilado), couples and families (Chapter 8: "Practice With Families," Lundy), groups (Chapter 9: "Support and Psychoeducational Groups for Immigrant Women," Lundy, Rodgers, Sánchez, Egan & Simon), communities (Chapter 10: "Community Practice," Goodman, Letiecq, Vesely, Marquez, & Leyva), organizations (Chapter 11: "Organizational Practice," Hilado), and local/volunteer workforces (Chapter 12: "Preparing a Local and Volunteer Workforce," Sokhem et al.). We firmly believe that responsive and culturally sensitive transnational practice needs to incorporate an integrative modality as well as an integrative theoretical framework, grounded in critical thinking and strengthened by the recognition of dynamic ecological systems that directly affect the perceptions and experiences of new immigrants and refugees. As such, each of the chapters discusses a model of practice that embodies critical integrative concepts applied to different interventions by client system type or modality and effective strategies for meeting those needs using an integrative approach.

One common thread is the role of culture when working with immigrant and refugee populations, irrespective of modality. Culture—inclusive of values, beliefs, traditions— shapes how all human beings understand themselves, the relationships around them, and their world. Each chapter gives an understanding of approaches to different client systems levels but infuses the relevance of the culture and cultural understanding and honors cultural beliefs that support practice with immigrants and refugees. The specific social environments to which immigrants enter and the policies that govern immigrants and refugees are equally relevant to the conversation, and you will see these discussions unfold in each chapter. As these discussions unfold, Unit III builds on the conceptual and theoretical discussions of the previous section and sets the foundation for examining the ways in which integrative models are applied to specific needs and subgroups within the immigrant and refugee population.

Chapter 7

PRACTICE WITH INDIVIDUALS

AIMEE HILADO

KEY TERMS

individual therapy, trauma, mental health, cultural sensitive practice, Western versus non-Western approaches, integrative practice

---

CHAPTER HIGHLIGHTS

- Discussion of the various historical approaches to clinical practice with individuals and the applicability of Western models of treatment with non-Western populations

- Examination of the unique needs among trauma-exposed immigrants and refugees seeking individual clinical services

- Exploration of factors that support culturally sensitive direct practice

INTRODUCTION

Delivering therapeutic services to individuals is one treatment modality that has been used to address a diverse range of needs, including the increase of coping and problem-solving skills, addressing grief and loss, and managing symptoms of a severe mental illness. The words **direct practice** or **individual practice** encompass a range of services that may include case management and referral support to more specific interventions involving diagnosis, treatment, and evaluation. For the purpose of this chapter, individuals are the primary client system and the central topic is migrant mental health. Specifically, I discuss direct practice in the form of clinical interventions used to address adverse mental health symptoms experienced among trauma-exposed immigrants and refugees. As noted by Dow (2011), "migration is a stressful event regardless of whether a person immigrates to a new country voluntarily or involuntarily" (p. 210), thus attention to an immigrant or refugee's migration experiences is interwoven through the discussions of best practices with individuals currently used in the field.

To begin, the chapter provides a synopsis on the evolution of individual therapy practice, starting with the work of Sigmund Freud to more recent approaches involving cognitive-behavioral and mindfulness frameworks. Historically, much of the theories guiding individual practice across diverse disciplines (including psychiatry, psychology, social work, and counseling) were informed by models based on Western ideologies and developed in the context of middle- to upper-class societies in developed, industrialized countries. The chapter seeks to highlight important practice themes relevant to trauma-experienced clients, while reconciling the potential disconnect between Western-based therapy models and non-Western populations, especially as it applies to the term *mental health* and cultural perspectives around that term. The therapy models call on professionals to maintain a phenomenological stance that understands the client's circumstances and sense of reality as the core foundation of the therapeutic encounter. Moreover, a discussion of key considerations for professionals and practice settings is provided to help enhance competence in providing culturally sensitive clinical services to immigrant and refugee clients.

THE EVOLUTION OF PRACTICE WITH INDIVIDUALS

Therapy[1] has an extensive history of being an effective vehicle for addressing personal issues that disrupt and impede one's ability to live a full and active life. The fields of psychology, psychiatry, social work, and counseling have long studied and developed various approaches to conceptualizing psychopathology—its causes, its developmental course, its treatment—and contributed theoretical and practice frameworks to guide professionals[2] based on the discipline's respective orientation. To ground the discussion in direct practice (hereafter *therapy*), it is important to examine the contributions of several prominent theorists and movements that serve as the foundation for our current frameworks guiding therapy services across the globe.

ORIGINS OF THE THERAPEUTIC INTERVENTION. The beginnings of what is understood as a *therapeutic intervention* today began before the turn of the 20th century. Psychoanalysis, the "child of Sigmund Freud's genius," provided the foundation for our understanding of the psyche that was groundbreaking and continues to remain relevant (Sadock & Sadock, 2007, p. 190). As stated by Sadock and Sadock (2007), "the science of psychoanalysis is the bedrock of **psychodynamic** understanding and forms the fundamental theoretical frame of reference for a variety of forms of therapeutic intervention . . ." (p. 190). Freud's work laid bare the opportunity to understand human behavior and motivation in terms of internal and biological drives, unconscious mental activity, and the role of childhood experiences in shaping the adult personality. He also argued that "symptoms, thoughts, feelings and behavior could all be viewed as the final common pathway of meaningful psychological processes, many of which were unconscious" (p. 190).

---

[1]The terms *clinical practice*, *direct practice*, or *practice with individuals* have also been used to reference therapy and will be used interchangeably in this chapter.
[2]Alternate titles for professionals addressing psychological disruptions or adverse mental health symptoms include *psychoanalysists, psychotherapists, therapists, clinicians, practitioners, mental health professionals, clinical social workers,* or *marriage family therapists.*

The therapeutic relationship between client and analyst (in psychoanalysis) created an opportunity to explore unconscious thoughts that were the driving force behind the symptoms, thoughts, feelings, and behaviors exhibited in one's wakened state. Transference, dream interpretation, and free association were hallmarks of the Freudian approach that served as vehicles for exploring psychological disturbances in treatment, typically involving multiple sessions per week with the analyst (Schriver, 2010). From his work, other schools were developed, with each theorist expanding and/or revising Freud's theory or completing rejecting his frameworks, resulting in the creation of new schools of thinking about psychoanalysis and psychology. As the fields of psychology and psychiatry continued to evolve with scientific advancements, rigorous field studies, and dialogues across disciplines, *psychosocial* approaches to understanding affect and behavior began to emerge from other disciplines, including anthropology, sociology, and social work.

Beginning as early as the 1950s with the work of Erik Erikson, disciplines were moving away from the belief that affect and behavior were solely rooted in an intrapsychic process (i.e., a process in the mind) to a more inclusive view of the forces that shape human beings. Termed the *psychosocial sciences*, varying disciplines contributed explanations to human behavior, affect, and even motivation. Psychosocial approaches continued to examine biological predispositions, development in the early years, and psychological processes similar to psychoanalysis but also expanded the scope of theory to include other factors, such as developmental stages past adolescence, accounting changes through older adulthood. New psychosocial theories also concentrated on the totality of experiences throughout the lifespan—observed, learned or conditioned—(not solely the experiences in early childhood) that equally shape the person. Jean Piaget (1896–1980) contributed a great deal around cognitive development and the stages of intellectual development, broadening the focus on underlying or internal motivation and early experiences as the determinant of the adult personality. Instead, Piaget's concepts focused on "thoughts, including automatic assumptions, beliefs, plans and intentions" (Sadock & Sadock, 2007) that were developed over time. These thought patterns could be productive or counter-productive, and it was the counter-productive thought patterns that adversely impacted functioning when sustained over time. Therapy, in turn, focused on thought patterns (adaptive and maladaptive) and the client's current sense of reality rather than an over-reliance on unpacking early experiences that lead to the issues at present.

Piaget's work led to more developmentally based psychotherapy, coined by Stanley Greenspan (1941–2010), that provided new understandings of human development. The capacity to think, feel, and exist corresponds directly with the developmental abilities linked to one's life stage; Western-oriented in its social expectations for each life stage yet based on biological science and the universal physical and cognitive milestones achieved throughout the lifespan irrespective of culture. As such, therapy from this vantage integrates extensive knowledge around human development and using age-appropriate strategies that match the capacity of the client at any given time in treatment or moves clients to a level of functioning expected for her life stage.

Attachment theories linked to John Bowlby (1907–1990) and Mary Ainsworth (1913–1999) emphasized the importance of the attachment relationship between mother and child and the idea that deficits in this bond could lead to psychological disruptions later in development. Based on this school of theory, psychotherapy requires establishing or repairing attachment relationships that could then facilitate growth in other areas of development. Similar to other theorists, relationships developed in the early years were valued. At the same time, attachment theorists also understood that attachment relationships—even with one's therapist and not solely a mother figure—were opportunities for healing and growth.

Finally, the learning theories deeply influenced our present day therapy approaches, as it has informed us of the ways in which people learn, which can in turn impact human behavior and by extension, psychological well-being (Sadock & Sadock, 2007). The work of Ivan Pavlov (1849–1936) involving classical conditioning (passive/retrained observation and reinforcement of behavior), J. B. Watsons' (1878–1958) work on generalizing and discrimination of different stimuli, and B. F. Skinner's (1904–1990) work around operant conditioning (conditioning behavior) all suggest that human behavior, and the feelings associated with them, are malleable. More precisely, human behavior is a product of biological underpinnings interacting with a changing social environment (relationships, sociopolitical structures, and physical space) that shape how and why people feel, act, and react as they do. In treatment, the focus of therapy would revolve around addressing troublesome behaviors and modeling/conditioning more productive behaviors that would support the client's well-being.

Collectively, these prominent individuals and their respective theoretical schools have shaped how mental health professionals conceptualize human behavior, psychopathology, and human motivation today. They provided a framework for understanding the unique ways in which people come to be, based on the social context, values, and beliefs of their respective times. And as a result, therapeutic approaches became varied to reflect how needs and problems were understood. The strategies employed to address problems and needs also took different forms. Some approaches focused on the relationship between professional and client, and change could be an outgrowth only if a strong trusting relationship was established first (attachment). Other approaches focused on thought patterns in the present (cognitive theories). Still others focused on free association and letting the client come to an understanding of self through self-exploration, with the professional serving only as a witness (psychoanalysis).

Treatment approaches aside, uniformly the frameworks noted exemplify theories based on Western ideals and belief systems reflecting understandings within middle- and upper-class societies. Despite the intrinsic value in having a long history of theory and research to guide mental health professionals, application of such frameworks with non-Western, ethnically diverse populations requires caution. The richness of the frameworks and the scientific basis for understanding behavior is invaluable, yet such perspectives cannot apply to all societies without a degree of adaptation. The value and meaning espoused in Western theories and associated with developmental periods, early relationships, and psychopathology are at times in conflict with the belief systems of non-Western cultures. And such conflicts can lead to disconnect and early termination in treatment because of the mismatch between practitioner perspectives and client needs. In order to engage immigrant and refugee populations from non-Western communities in therapy, attention to the relevance of our historical approaches to practice requires thoughtful consideration; something that will be discussed further in this chapter.

CENTRAL THEMES WHEN CONDUCTING THERAPY WITH TRAUMA-EXPOSED IMMIGRANTS AND REFUGEES

Immigrants and refugees enter new countries with the hopes of building (for some, rebuilding) their lives with opportunities that may not have been available in their country of origin. There are a number of factors that influence the degree to which an immigrant or refugee can fully integrate and adapt to life in a new country—language skills, social capital, social support—however, the focus of this chapter is on mental health as a critical component of each migration story. According to Pumariega, Rothe, and Pumariega (2005), "mental health factors, most of which go unrecognized and untreated, can adversely affect the immigrant's successful adaptation and functioning after immigration" (p. 590). Therefore, the goal of therapy is to serve as one support in stabilizing mental health problems that are impediments to the cultural adjustment of new immigrants in a new country.

PRIORITY OF RESETTLEMENT NEEDS. There are necessary nonclinical steps that need to be addressed prior to engaging immigrant or refugee clients in therapy, particularly those who have been exposed to violence-related trauma, loss, and those who are newly arrived in a country. For the purpose of this chapter, a newly arrived person would be someone who has been in the country only 6 to 8 months. Practitioners working with new arrivals should anticipate working on the primacy of resettlement needs—for example, accessing stable housing, employment, navigating groceries, medical facilities, and so forth—before engaging the client in clinical services for adverse mental health symptoms or psychological disturbances. This is especially important for those who lack supportive networks, be they social service agencies or family/community networks. Those resettlement needs will trump any desire to be reflective of trauma-related systems, thus meeting basic needs will be the precursor to therapy.

The following questions provide a culturally sensitive approach to engaging the client in a discussion about his or her resettlement experiences, while allowing the professionals to access critical information that may support his or her adjustment to a new country:

- How are you adjusting to your new city?
- What has surprised you most about your new community?
- Is there anything about your current city that reminds you of your home country? What is it?
- What information or skills do you need at this time to help you navigate your new community?
- What worries you the most as you start a new chapter of your life in a new country?

Once basic needs are met, there may be an increased likelihood of mental health service utilization (Chen, Kazanjian, & Wong, 2009; Derr, 2016; Wong et al., 2006). At that time, the following themes may arise in therapy: pre-migration and post-migration stressors and experiences of profound loss and trauma.

PRE-MIGRATION AND POST-MIGRATION STRESSORS. The pre- and post-migration experiences are worth exploring in the pursuit of addressing mental health problems, as there is a direct connection between experiences and effects (Murphy, 1955; Neuner, Schauer, Klaschik, Karunakara, & Elbert, 2004). According to the seminal work of Westermeyer (as cited in Fazel, 2005) refugees who remained longest in camps had higher rates of psychopathology and that refugees resettled in Western countries were approximately ten times more likely to develop post-traumatic stress symptoms than the general population (as cited in Fazel, 2005). The experiences upon arrival in the resettlement country—such as level of stress in adjustment, changes in one's socioeconomic status, and the experiences with the receiving community—matter as well. The rates of developing schizophrenia and other psychosis were high for those immigrants who experienced a significant level of psychological stress and both physical and psychological dysfunction during the first two years of resettlement (Kisely, Terashima, & Langille, 2008). This indicates that stress in the initial resettlement period could have far-reaching health effects; therefore immediate services and resources to combat post-migration stress is valuable. Related to socioeconomic status and education, it has been shown that immigrants experience higher levels of distress and adverse mental health symptoms when they learn their credentials from their home country are not recognized or experience a decrease in socioeconomic status because of an inability to find positions that matched those positions previously held (Dow, 2011). And even accommodation conditions were sufficient post-migration factors that were related to poor mental health outcomes; poor derelict housing in areas understood as unsafe increased mental health problems (Porter & Haslam, 2005).

Moreover, an unwelcoming host community can lead to higher levels of stress that may serve as a precursor to more substantial health and mental health problems in the future. Neighborhoods perceived as unsafe or violent could undermine a sense of social cohesion (Beiser, Hou, Hyman, & Tousignant, 2002), which can exacerbate acculturative stress already experienced. Immigrants who experience race-based traumatic stress, such as discrimination, have higher levels of isolation and risk behaviors, such as alcohol and drug use and involvement in fights (Flores, Tschann, Dimas, Pasch, & de Groat, 2010; Pumariega et al., 2005). Targeting based on negative portrayals in the media (Pickering, 2001) and national security concerns tied to terrorism (Hugo, 2002) have led to higher rates in adjustment stress that correlates with higher levels of depression, anxiety, and other mental health problems (Finch, Kolody, & Vega, 2000; Yeh, 2003). In the process of learning how to support the mental health needs of immigrants and refugees, the evidence in the literature is clear in elucidating the realities of pre- and post-migration experiences, while informing of the critical nature of including such experiences in the therapeutic encounter. These are the variables that influence an immigrant or refugee's level of functioning and sense of reality and can be the source of adverse mental health symptoms that impede adjustment and integration.

The following questions allow the professional to understand the experiences within the client's home country, experiences in transit, and experiences on arrival that may impact adjustment in a new country:

- What was it like in your home country?
- What factors led you to leave your home country?
- Where did you go after leaving your country? What was it like in that host country?
- [For those resettled in a new country] What was it like coming to this [destination] country?
- Did you have any expectations or assumptions of what it would be like in this country? What matched your expectation and what was surprising?
- What was the most rewarding and the most challenging part of your migration experiences?

EXPERIENCES OF PROFOUND LOSS AND TRAUMA. The migration experience of immigrants and refugees is weighted with distinct occurrences of loss (sometimes temporary but oftentimes permanent)—loss of country, culture, support systems, loved ones. Despite the opportunities that await upon arrival, many immigrant clients seeking therapy will need to mourn many losses as part of the healing and adjustment process. As noted by Dow (2011), the loss is often profound and can cause a considerable amount of stress that may progress to more severe mental health problems when not adequately addressed. The separation from loved ones is also viewed as loss that can be temporary or permanent but equally unwelcomed (Khawaja, White, Schweitzer, & Greenslade, 2008).

Trauma, a deeply distressing or disturbing experience, is often interrelated with this concept of profound loss. Trauma is a loss of one's sense of personhood and the social bonds that should tie all human beings together (Gorman, 2001). Trauma also evokes a loss in the belief in the dignity and worth of all human beings (www.nasw.org, n.d.). And as eloquently stated by Judith Herman (1992), trauma robs the victim of a sense of power and control over her[3] own life; therefore, the guiding principle of recovery is to restore power and control to the survivor. In Herman's work (1992), she described the ways in which trauma has a deleterious effect on one's ability to trust others because

---

[3]The pronoun "her" will be used, based on J. Herman's work, but should be understood as applying to both male and female clients. According to the UNHCR general reports (UNHCR.org, 2012), a high percentage of refugees and internally displaced persons are women and children; however, a proportion of this group include men; all of whom may be in need of culturally mental health services.

of the loss of power and control at the hands of another. For immigrants and refugees, particularly those forced from their homes because of a threat to their safety and livelihood, the power and influence of trauma is clear. It defines how they understand themselves and others. It defines engagement and hope for the future. And it defines, to a certain degree, their understanding of any psychological disturbances they are experiencing.

The goals of trauma-focused therapy should be on establishing *safety*, *reconstruction* of one's life story so that it is not consumed by the traumatic memories, and *reconnection* to the parts of oneself that are most valuable and choosing to take back meaning in one's life (Herman, 1992). Therapy must be collaborative to achieve these goals, and in doing so, the episodes of loss that may be related to the client's trauma history can be recognized and mourned as part of the healing process. The experience of trauma should not be pathologized so that there is the underlying assumption that if a person has a trauma history, immediately she is in need of therapy. Great resilience in the human spirit can be found in even the direst of human conditions and circumstances. Nonetheless, the attention to the unfortunate consequences of trauma and loss are pertinent in the provision of therapy with immigrant and refugee populations.

The following questions will allow the professional to explore experiences of trauma and loss while identifying culturally appropriate responses and methods of healing/recovering from trauma and loss:

- Did you witness or directly experience any deeply distressing events in your home country or during your travels to get to this country? Can you share some of those experiences with me?

- What are the memories that are most difficult for you to think about?

- Was there anyone important (family, friends) whom you left behind or anyone you lost given what was happening in your country?

- In your culture, what do people do after experiencing such losses and surviving such terrible events (if applicable)?

- What supports do you need now to help you heal from those experiences?

NOTE: It is important to educate clients on the nature of trauma and profound grief/loss. While there are ways of reducing the sadness and related adverse symptoms, the memories will never be entirely erased; a point to be clearly communicated in therapy.

PRACTICE CONSIDERATIONS WITH TRAUMA-EXPOSED IMMIGRANTS AND REFUGEES

The theoretical framework chosen to guide a professional's clinical practice with an immigrant or refugee client will be effective, based on the cultural-appropriateness of the framework/model but also other additional influences to be discussed in the following sections. There are a number of factors that may present challenges to addressing migrant mental health, including language, cultural differences, family, and community structures that impact adjustment and integration into a new country (Kirmayer et al., 2011). This reality places responsibility on the shoulders of the provider, as so much happens even before therapy begins.

First and foremost, the provision of mental health services to culturally diverse populations requires a great deal of critical thinking and self-awareness of one's own cultural *incompetence*, fully recognizing that no professional can fully understand the history and complex cultural traditions that shape the actions and reactions of any individual, family, or community. The complexity of understanding a client's circumstances to enhance functioning is only compounded with a greater need for sensitivity and cultural understanding when working with an immigrant client who has lived in protracted circumstances of displacement and uncertainty and prolonged exposure to violence and loss. From this position of self-awareness, individual therapy then requires particular attention to areas we discuss in the following sections.

ADAPTING WESTERN THEORETICAL FRAMEWORKS FOR USE WITH NON-WESTERN POPULATIONS. The disciplines preparing the future mental health professionals of tomorrow continue to rely on a foundation on Western theoretical models that outline a range of psychopathological as defined by the **International Statistical Classification of Diseases and Related Health Problems (ICD)**, a medical classification list by the World Health Organization (WHO), and the corresponding **Diagnostic and Statistical Manual of Mental Disorders (DSM)** now in its fifth Edition (DSM-5). Through the years, both the ICD and DSM have increased inclusion of "culturally-bound" symptoms that document symptoms as they are understood through cultural terms relevant to specific ethnic groups across the globe. There has also been an increase in training programs focusing on the integration of multicultural concepts (Kuo & Arcuri, 2014) to facilitate greater dialogue around issues of culture and diversity in the clinical engagement, assessment, treatment, and the evaluation process with non-Western clients.

Culturally sensitive practice with non-Western, multicultural populations require a set of skills wherein mental health professionals critically appraise the relevance of treatment approaches and its applicability based on the client's cultural background and experience. It also requires forging a thoughtful treatment plan that integrates client expectations and culture, the client's circumstances, and a collusion of relevant Western frameworks that are culturally sensitive and flexible to the unique needs and belief systems of the client being served. It would be remiss to say Western theories didn't hold value when applied with non-Western populations, as that is simply untrue. Current frameworks for understanding psychopathology (Freud, Adler, Kohut, Jung), developmental processes (Erikson, Piaget, Greenspan), attachment relationships (Bowlby, Ainsworth), and behavior (Pavlov, Skinner) all provide insights into the biological and psychological processes in interaction with social experiences— irrespective of culture—that shape how all human beings function.

The attention must therefore be placed on the specifics of the treatment modality, recognizing that no one theory can explain all human suffering, functioning, and ways of being. As suggested in this book, an integrative approach to practice can enhance the relevance and effectiveness of clinical work. Such a method allows the professional to synthesize the qualities of different theories that, together, would orchestrate a clinical practice approach that is responsive to the client needs, remains based on scientific discourse, and is adaptive to our ever-changing social and practice context. To illustrate, the following approaches can apply in therapy:

- *Explore and compare cultural definitions for adverse symptoms with the DSM-5 or ICD-10 culture-bound syndrome descriptions, standard DSM-5/ICD-10 descriptions, and other interpretations of the symptoms:* The exploration of varied understandings for the same symptoms/disease allows for the therapist and client to find common ground and a common language for understanding needs and potential treatments that can integrate culturally appropriate healing techniques and knowledge of Western medical approaches to address the same symptoms.

- *Applying Erik Erikson's Eight Stages of Man/psychosocial development across the lifespan:* The therapist can apply Erikson's stage theory to the client's current age and discuss the expectation of that given stage according to the theory. The therapist can then explore what the client believes should be attained at her current developmental stage and any deficits that exist in meeting her expectations and explore what steps are necessary for her to feel like the goals of her life stage are met. In collaboration, the therapist and client can discuss individual steps she can take as well as acquire supports in her family, community, or the organization to achieve her goals.

- *Applying attachment theory and the importance of secure attachments:* Attachment theorists believe that early relationships with caregivers is critical in shaping relational patterns and personality development. The therapist can explore early maternal-child relationships, but if this does not seem to align with the client's culture, the therapist can explore other attachment relationships that helped shaped the client's sense of self and her support network—resources that could help her cope in difficult situations. In the absence of any meaningful relationships, the therapist can help the client define what she needs in a secure attachment relationship and find ways of building those relationships with others in the present.

- *Applying cognitive-behavioral theory (CBT) approaches:* Together, the therapist and client can identify problematic thought patterns or behaviors that impede the client from living without discomfort—discomfort with self or with others. Classic CBT approaches have typically included techniques such as homework (tracking behaviors or thought patterns), ongoing questioning the evidence, and self-regulation through breathing exercises. Some clients may have never been exposed to these types of activities and may not be able to comply with the suggested work outside of the therapy sessions. To address this, the therapist can first provide education around how thought patterns and behaviors can be changed using this approach. To make the activities more culturally sensitive, the therapist can encourage partnership and accountability by including a family member or friend (with the client's permission) to aid in executing the tasks. Making the activities more communal can help with compliance and execution, especially if communal activities align better with the client's culture and approach to solving problems.

Each example demonstrates how therapy can be rooted in Western models of clinical practice but also integrate the client's culture and perspective on receiving help. This approach remains client and culture focused but retains a theoretical framework for conceptualizing the client's need. In many cases, the therapist will need to integrate different theoretical models to address the full scope of presenting problems, yet the same thoughtful consideration of theory and adaptation to be more culturally sensitive will still apply. Naturally, integrative approaches must be documented and studied to examine efficacy, and this is likely happening already given the dialogue around multiculturalism and integration of cultural diversity topics across disciplines. Nevertheless, integrative work is intended to be intentional rather than eclectic, and supportive of the need for innovations in practice that are a direct response to the swelling migration patterns across the globe. As noted by Elsass (1997), treating clients in isolation is the "most frequent cross-cultural psychotherapeutic error" (p. 118, as cited in Gorman, 2001) and one that can be avoided when an integrative, culturally centered approach is applied. The dialogue here offers suggestions that can meet this practice need in the population.

ALTERNATE DEFINITIONS OF MENTAL HEALTH AND TRAUMA. Mental health and mental health service definitions in other countries conflict with what we understand in industrialized Western countries. Kirmayer et al. (2011) states that "in many developing countries, mental health services are associated only with custodial or hospital treatment of the most severely ill and psychotic patients" (p. 962). The stigma around the term "mental health" remains in most countries, and most prospective clients will be reluctant to attribute any symptoms to a mental disorder given the cultural repercussions that affect not only the individual but siblings and other family members as well (Chen, Kazanjian, & Wong, 2009; Fenta, Hyman, & Noh, 2007; Whitley, Kirmayer, & Groleau, 2006; Wong et al., 2006). Additionally, all cultures describe mental health symptomatology with its own history and reasoning for why symptoms present as they do. Whereas Western cultures may view symptoms of psychosis as problematic, other cultures have explanations that are more affirmative, even believing symptoms to have "gift-like" qualities (Gaw, 1993).

What is understood as "normal" varies dramatically between cultures, and the absence of symptoms does not suggest there is no need (Sadock & Sadock, 2007); thus investigative work around the cultural definitions of typical/atypical behavior and mental health needs must be consistent and the findings discussed with the client. There must also be information-sharing around the cultural beliefs tied to the use of psychotropic medications to treat psychological disturbances. In some cases, it is one's sociocultural beliefs that impact individual attitudes about taking medication (Ng & Klimidis, 2008). And as cross-cultural practice increases across the globe, the integration of culturally bound practices and symptoms has made inroads into our ongoing discussions (see discussion on ICD and DSM classifications) around supporting mental health and policies that govern mental health practice.

PRACTICE STRATEGIES

Explore cultural definitions of mental health using the following probes:

- Is there an equivalent term or way of understanding mental health in your culture?

- What does the term "mental health" mean to you and your community?

- How does your culture explain the symptoms you are describing and what is the recommended treatment?

- What Western treatments (describe explicitly) would you be willing to consider to treat your symptoms?

Note: Cultural definitions and education around mental health terminology can create more understanding around the purpose of therapy while strengthening the therapeutic relationship.

PROVIDING EDUCATION ON MENTAL HEALTH AND RELATED SERVICES. Professionals providing therapeutic services to immigrants and refugees must add an additional step to their therapeutic encounter by educating clients on the meaning (and myths) around what is mental health and the nature of clinical interventions to address mental health problems. Professionals can explain how the brain responds to trauma and the adverse symptoms that come with a neurological response (i.e., hypervigilance, flashbacks, insomnia). Additionally, professionals can help normalize fears around adverse mental health symptoms, reiterating that the symptoms are a by-product of terrible traumatic experiences and not the fault of the client. There is a great deal of misinformation and culturally informed perspectives around the term mental health. As such, professionals cannot assume any client has had exposure to mental health or health terminology, and for those who have heard the term mental health, it is likely the concept has been culturally defined (Helsel & Mochel, 2002; Pumariega et al., 2005). Beyond symptom reduction, a goal of therapy should include increasing the client's understanding of mental health and for the client to prioritize mental health as a means of supporting overall well-being.

When it comes to therapy, professionals must also approach the topic with sensitivity and avoid assumptions that the client understands the protocol of clinical treatment. Each theoretical framework lends toward different treatment approaches and techniques, so either a client may have been exposed to different treatment strategies based on the preference of their provider or have zero exposure, if this is the first time she may have sought treatment. A discussion of confidentiality is also critical in building a trusting therapeutic alliance. For many immigrant and refugee clients, speaking to someone outside of the family about such intimate life details is culturally inappropriate. Assurances and confidentiality documents (translated into the language of the client) stating that no information will be shared with anyone—including spouses and other family members—without explicit permission from the client need to be clear. This is certainly the case when in-person interpretation is used and the interpreter is from the same community, as is often the case. A thorough explanation of symptoms, methods, and confidentiality clauses should be explained ongoing throughout the treatment process; mediums, such as workshops or handouts, could be useful to this end. Ideally, these steps will encourage clients to be empowered in the treatment process and able to articulate what is and isn't working. At the same time, the hope is that clients will also be able to appreciate the purpose of the treatment methods and remain engaged in the services so that the intended outcomes of the selected interventions can be realized.

PRACTICE STRATEGIES

- Deliver information in the language of the client in therapy sessions and group workshops to ensure clients understand the concepts used to support mental health.

- Confirm comprehension by asking clients to summarize their understanding of the information and clarifying as needed.

- Provide additional materials in written form in the language of the client so that information can be reviewed as needed.

ATTENDING TO META-LEVEL TREATMENT THERAPY FACTORS. Gorman (2001) elucidated the essential nature of attending to "meta-level" considerations in therapy in addition to client context. This includes "nonverbal signals, communication styles, significance of self-disclosures and expression of feelings, power and role differentials, gender and age factors, the physical setting, and the attributional ways of perceiving problems and the giving or receiving of help" (p. 445). Many of these meta-level considerations relate to cultural ideologies and practices as well as communication patterns that are culturally defined. Other factors, such as space and perceptions of problems, are based on the past experiences of clients, broadly speaking. The physical space of therapy may trigger both positive and harmful memories for the clients; therefore it is important to maintain a space that is as neutral as possible. This includes removing of any personal items or photographs that could elicit difficult memories of relationships, family members, or loss; keeping the color of the walls neutral; and making the space as comfortable and open as possible with the spacing of furniture and the type of furniture in the space. Past experiences that resulted in betrayal or victimization (the extreme example is survivors of torture) will directly shape the degree to which help is understood and accepted (Gorman, 2001); thus thoughtful consideration of the language and the efforts to build a trusting relationship through consistent appointments or self-disclosure need to be considered in the treatment process.

Additionally, Gorman (2001) discussed the essential task of exploring strengths and supports in addition to risk, fear of uncertainty, and vulnerabilities in the client's own terms, which may also be culturally influenced. Therapy is intended to validate a client's experiences as genuine and authentic, irrespective of culture or circumstances. Allowing clients to define needs on their terms lends toward a more honest account of the problem and a clearer path for deciding on the most appropriate treatment options in therapy. The therapeutic encounter is intended to be collaborative, and having this level of honest dialogue at the outset will only be more supportive of productive outcomes for client and clinician in the process. The meta-level considerations of therapy discussed here are not exhaustive and should instead highlight the need to look at the forces that influence treatment outcomes that are not overt. These factors are subtle yet substantial in influencing receptiveness to treatment and the outcomes itself.

PRACTICE STRATEGIES

- During the initial intake or first therapy session, confirm that the client feels comfortable in the space and pay attention to any nonverbal cues that require additional probing.

- Explore the client's experience in sharing personal details with someone outside of the community and affirm respect for cultural differences.

- Provide a thorough explanation of the grounds for confidentiality and the nature of the therapeutic relationship to address any concerns around power dynamics in the therapy space.

- When personal questions are asked, the professional should use discretion in self-disclosure. Instead, explore why personal details about the professional are important to the client.

- At the end of the session, ask the client how she felt the session went and what can be done to make her feel more comfortable.

THE ROLE OF FAMILY AND COMMUNITY. Direct practice with individuals must integrate elements of the client's social context to be effective. Specifically, attention must be given to the contextual and practical issues (e.g., interpersonal relationships, feelings of discrimination, social support systems, stable housing) that influence the level of adverse psychological symptoms, intercultural understanding, and even the relationship between client and professional (Kleinman & Benson, 2006). Equal attention should be given to the sociocultural context (combining social and cultural factors) surrounding the individual, including relationships with her spouse, family members, ethnic community, and spiritual leaders wherein "the presence of welcoming links within ethnic communities or religious congregations can buffer the effects of migration losses, isolations and discrimination" (Kirmayer et al., 2011). These are all prominent themes in practice with individuals.

Unfortunately, the migration experience itself can place undo pressure on family structures or separate families completely, and as a result, there may be an adjustment of roles and responsibilities within the family. Children may take the role of interpreter for the family, as they often acquire the language quicker than other family members (Pumariega et al., 2005). Migration may also lead to the restructuring of caregiving roles with children and grandchildren caring more for seniors (Lai & Surood, 2008) or the women becoming the breadwinner of the household (Darvishpour, 2002). These alternative family structures can be particularly disruptive in patriarchal societies. In some cases, the burden of being the global breadwinner and sending monies to family abroad becomes so great that families in the destination country will cut ties out of guilt in not being able to help.

Many non-Western cultures value interdependence among family and community units, thus the experiences within the family structures can (and oftentimes do) influence the larger social communities immigrants and refugees find themselves within. For example, children often learn the language and adapt to new cultures more readily than their parents, and this can manifest in a number of ways that impact the family. Children may feel a need for greater independence and may stop listening to their parents, fulfilling roles they may have maintained abroad (cleaning, caring for siblings, etc.) or contributing to the household income. Parents may feel unable to maintain the same family boundaries, as they can no longer discipline their children in the way they would in their country of origin or by virtue of the fact that they may need to rely on their children navigating other resources on their behalf. These patterns, if replicated in families across an ethnic community, can have negative implications for the family and community together. Often, such changes can signal feelings of homesickness and loss of culture for entire ethnic communities, further complicating and burdening the adjustment process.

All this is to say that there is relevance in considering family and community roles within the context of practice with individuals. Integrating family and community belief systems is culturally appropriate and cogent as both structures align with the cultural underpinnings of health and social support of the individual's culture of origin. Allowances for these discussions in therapy and inclusion of relevant family or community members in the therapeutic process could be beneficial to both individual and family/community system.

PRACTICE STRATEGIES

- Begin by exploring how problems or needs are typically addressed in the client's culture.

- Explore how the client feels about seeking services outside her family or community (if this is contrary to cultural norms).

- To understand context greater, the professional should ask how the family is adjusting to life in a new country (if applicable) and if there have been any major changes in roles or family dynamics since arrival.

- Ask the client if she would be more comfortable with family or community members present for the sessions and explore the benefits and challenges of their inclusion.

- Integrate the client's suggestions into therapy in a culturally meaningful way.

THE ROLE OF THE INTERPRETER/CULTURAL BROKER. The interpreter (telephonic or in person) is an invaluable component of the therapeutic encounter with immigrants or refugees who does not speak the language of their resettlement country. The words as well as the affect shared between client and provider must be communicated accurately in order for the process to be impactful. In many cases, interpreters serve as cultural brokers who help clients and providers understand differences in the meaning of the words used in therapy, while offering suggestions on how to bridge the linguistic and cultural divide. Concretely, interpreters can inform the provider of nonverbal communication messages that are present in treatment and increase the provider's awareness of cultural factors that may support or impede the therapeutic process. As supported by Kirmayer et al. (2011), the effectiveness of treatment can be greatly enhanced when trained interpreters and cultural brokers can address "any linguistic or cultural differences that impede communication and mutual understanding" (p. 959). Additionally, the interpreter becomes a witness to the therapeutic alliance and the process of change, which could be meaningful to the client who has both a provider and person speaking her native tongue validating her experiences, even if the interpreter is simply conveying information. The support for the client is physically evident with the triad in the room.

The decision to use telephonic versus in-person interpreters depends on a number of factors, including the program's budget and the respective provider or program's framework for practice, but both modalities have benefits and challenges that should be considered. Telephonic interpretation involves contracts with outside companies who certify interpreters after extensive training and testing, thereby ensuring contracted interpreters meet the standards for medical interpretation in their given language. The use of telephonic interpreters allows for consistent therapy sessions with interpreters who understand health and mental health terminology. Telephonic interpreters, however, are expensive and are often unable to pick up on nonverbal cues, including facial expressions and body language, that can directly contradict statements being made; thus the clinician needs to be keenly aware of any subtle, culturally derived communications patterns that could redirect treatment.

In contrast, in-person interpreters are able to identify any incongruence between client statement and body/facial cues. The challenge with in-person interpreters, however, could be capacity, as many nonprofit service agencies use this interpretation format agency-wide, so interpreters may be spread across multiple programs and serve multiple roles within the organization. This creates issues with trust and confidentiality as well as consistency of treatment, as the same interpreter may serve a client in the mental health program as well as those receiving, say, employment or case management services. Additionally, the interpreter may be a member of the client's community, which presents added areas of confidentiality and boundaries that must be addressed. Notwithstanding the benefits and challenges of both interpretation formats, the same emphasis on the importance of this role and its influence on treatment outcomes must still be acknowledged. It has been studied that inadequate interpreters and linguistic and cultural barriers faced by new immigrants have been a major deterrent in accessing quality mental health services with long-term implications (Bauer, Rodrguez, Szkupinski Quiroga, & Flores-Ortiz, 2000; Ku & Waidmann, 2003). As such, providers should attempt to account for this variable, given its influence on treatment outcomes.

PRACTICE STRATEGIES

- The interpreter plays the primary role as a conduit of information, who does not alter what is being said and interprets using first person language and reflects the tone, volume, and inflection of the speaker.

- The interpreter must also play the role of the clarifier, ensuring that both parties understand the information shared in the conversation and asking for permission to interrupt the conversation to ensure clarity and pacing of the discussion.

- The interpreter plays the role of the cultural broker, providing the therapist with relevant cultural context and expressing cultural concerns that could impede mutual understanding.

- Therapists should meet with the assigned interpreter (in the case of in-person interpretation) prior to and after sessions to ensure the format and goals of therapy are consistent and there is clear understanding of what was exchanged in session.

- All parties should be encouraged to ask for explanations or clarification as needed.

THE IMPORTANCE OF CULTURE. Culture shapes the belief systems of our clients and frames their understanding of experiences as well as their sense of reality. The importance of culture cannot be understated in direct practice, as it influences every aspect of the therapeutic encounter. The level of engagement, the buy-in to remain consistent in treatment even when improvement is gradual, and the ability to trust another person who is outside of the client's cultural community all revolve around one's culture and the client's ability to adapt her belief systems to accommodate treatment methods that may not be aligned with her culture of origin. Spirituality is deeply connected to culture and in many cases religious or spiritual practices, such as prayer and meditation, are culturally relevant and appropriate responses to grief, fear, and stress (Colic-Peisker & Tilbury, 2003). Acknowledgment, inquiry, and validation of cultural traditions throughout the therapeutic process will substantiate the client's sense of self and honor her cultural heritage. At the same time, such reflective moments provide opportunities for the practitioner to develop cultural sensitivity simultaneously. The therapeutic alliance can only strengthen with such efforts that will promote a greater sense of self-efficacy for all parties involved, another positive by-product of the therapeutic intervention.

PRACTICE STRATEGIES

- Allow time in the therapy session to learn more about the client's culture by having the client describe common traditions and special events held dear to the client.

- Ask the client to bring artifacts, pictures, or symbols of her culture to session.

- Integrate an understanding and respect for the client's culture throughout the treatment planning and intervention process.

ACKNOWLEDGING RESILIENCE. The field of resilience has spanned over 40 years with major research developments and contributions throughout that time (see studies by Luthar, 2006). Resilience is the maintenance of positive adaptation and development in the face of significant adverse experiences (Luthar, Cicchetti, & Becker, 2000), focusing on individual competence and the balance between risk and protective factors that influence vulnerability and coping skills (Luthar, 2006). Resilience allows people to develop and move forward in the face of disappointment and struggle, and it is a quality that is valuable and recognized across a broad range of human service disciplines (Howe, Smajdor, & Stöckl, 2012; Kaminsky, McCabe, Langlieb, & Everly, 2007; Prilleltensky, 2005). Resilience is what allows survivors of torture, survivors of life-threatening illness, and survivors of massive losses (family, country, culture) to remain alive despite insidious effects of their experiences.

For immigrants and refugees, resilience is an important component of their migration narrative. It takes resilience to leave one's country in search of new opportunities. It takes resilience and grit to survive some of the living conditions they endured for protracted periods. And it takes resilience to be willing to rebuild their lives in the midst of profound loss and trauma. The topic of resilience can be capitalized in therapy, focusing on client strengths and empowering her to take control of the changes she wants in their life. It takes a great deal of strength and dedication to explore immigration options, file applications, and settle in a new country, and this should be acknowledged in the therapeutic encounter. Acknowledging resilience allows the therapist to illuminate the client's inherent capabilities and build upon preexisting skills to move her forward.

PRACTICE STRATEGIES

Examine and validate resilience using the following activities:

- Document and share events and circumstances when the client demonstrated resilience (pre- and post-arrival).

- Allow the client to describe a time when she felt empowered and strong and overcame adversity. Then validate that this is resilience.

- Work with the client to readjust the words used to describe her circumstances to reflect more strength-based language that exemplifies resilience in her own terms.

- Consistently validate and affirm the survivor narrative and belief in the client's ability to reach her goals.

CULTURALLY SENSITIVE DIRECT PRACTICE WITH IMMIGRANTS AND REFUGEES

In sum, this chapter details the nature of individual practice with trauma-exposed immigrants and refugees with mental health needs and the important considerations necessary for meaningful and impactful practice. Mental health professionals have access to a long history of theory and research to inform current day practices but must integrate cultural sensitivity, critical thinking, expansion of the therapeutic relationship to include family and community, and a spirit of collaboration. Learn the client's culture as the client learns of the workings of her resettlement country. Moreover, there are common elements that can support any therapeutic intervention irrespective of culture. Similar to discussions in attachment theory, it is with warm, empathic, and consistent relationships that we see people thrive. Building trust within a therapeutic encounter with immigrants and refugees may take the form of consistent appointments or securing a critical medical appointment on her behalf, but the outcomes are the same; the client builds a belief that the professional is here to help and wants to support the client in whatever manner will help improve her life and ability to function. Trauma-experienced immigrants and refugees oftentimes have experienced the worst side of humanity, which has engrained a deep mistrust in their government, their community, and their neighbors. As noted in Article 1 of the United Nations Declaration for Human Rights, "All human beings are born free and equal in dignity and rights" (www.un.org, n.d.), and therapy can help restore the belief that this is indeed true. Through culturally sensitive, responsive, and compassionate direct practice with individuals, professionals can help rebuild lives and strengthen life skills for a brighter future.

REFLECTIVE QUESTIONS

1. Micro practice: Based on the chapter, what can professionals do to ensure they provide culturally sensitive and responsive therapy services to immigrant clients? Using the concepts in this chapter, what do you feel is the most important quality of a therapist working with a trauma-exposed population?

2. Macro practice: How can the implications for mental health practitioners inform practice with other client systems—that is, communities and organizations? What policies can/should be developed to address these areas of best practices when providing mental health services to immigrant and refugee clients?

CRITICAL THINKING EXERCISES (BASED ON BOX 7.1 CASE ILLUSTRATIONS)

1. The three clients described in this chapter responded to their symptoms and treatment in varied ways. What do you believe are the critical contextual factors that influenced their reactions and the type of services needed?

BOX 7.1 Case Illustrations: Varying Practice Reactions Based on Client Profile

Client 1: Ahmed	Client 2: Riziki	Client 3: Idalmis
40-year-old male, refugee from Iraq	27-year-old female, refugee from the Democratic Republic of Congo	62-year-old female, asylum seeker from Columbia

Diagnosis: post-traumatic stress disorder (relevant symptoms: hypervigilance, nightmares, depressed mood, flashbacks)

Treatment modality: bi-weekly 50-minutes sessions using narrative exposure therapy (NET) with trauma-focused cognitive behavioral techniques (TF-CBT) to reduce problematic systems. Medical case management services were provided to support compounding health issues and any relevant adjustment needs, for example, food stamps, bus cards, housing issues.

Treatment reactions/issues

Ahmed had been exposed to psychological screenings in Iraq and the medical field prior to arrival in the United States. He was an interpreter for U.S. allied forces and was able to attend therapy sessions without the aid of an interpreter. As such, he understood much of the terminology around mental health, the role of medication in treating his insomnia and depression symptoms, and the purpose of treatment. In therapy, Ahmed was able to discuss the loss of loved ones to violence and the challenges of adjusting to life in a new country. Using a combination of the psychotropic medication and the modalities mentioned, we were able to implement coping strategies (e.g., deep breathing, reframing, reflective practice) using TF-CBT approaches. Ahmed was also able to alter his narrative (NET) from one who was powerless to a survivor who has opportunities to move forward with his life and not be defined by his losses in Iraq. The use of testimony (trauma theory) was also useful, as he felt empowered sharing his story of loss and survival with non-refugees in the community.

Treatment reactions/issues

Riziki lost both her parents to militants who stormed her village in the DRC but was able to reach a refugee camp in Kenya with her younger sister and aunt. Life in the refugee camp was difficult, as there was very little food, clean water, and opportunity to work. Without the protection of her parents or male family members, she was assaulted in the camp when she was left alone in her tent. When she was approved for resettlement with her sister, Riziki was excited and she arrived optimistic and hopeful for her future. During her standard mental health screening, Riziki openly discussed the loss of her parents and being raped. She noted flashbacks and occasional nightmares but clearly stated that those events did not define her. She was willing to participate in therapy but refused any medication to address her sleep problems. TF-CBT techniques were used to help her cope with flashbacks, while she continued to rely on prayer and her community when she was sad. We also created a space for her to grieve her loss/pain and find her voice as an empowered woman with a bright future as her new narrative.

Treatment reactions/issues

Idalmis arrived with a great deal of anxiety about her adjustment to life in a new country later in life. She was battling with her memories of the past, which included family members and neighbors being kidnapped and the increasing violence in her community that led her to flee. At the same time, she missed her old community and culture, and she felt isolated without a community of Columbians near her and only her spouse. Idalmis also had health problems; she had been diagnosis with congenital heart failure as well as painful arthritis in her hands, elbows, and knees. When we began treatment, our focus was on stabilizing her health while simultaneously addressing issues from her past and present that exacerbated her adverse mental health symptoms. Idalmis did not enjoy the mindfulness strategies but was able to integrate reframing exercises for when she felt she would survive in a new city. We also changed her narrative of being isolated and "too old" to one that focused on how to live in a new city by using both narrative work and inputting concrete supports; we connected her with other Columbian families to develop a support network outside of the agency and senior programs that could help with her coordinating health and social needs that would aid her adjustment.

SUMMATIVE POINTS

- Therapy, direct practice, and practice with individuals all encompass similar efforts to improve mental health functioning for individual clients.

- Delivering culturally appropriate therapeutic services requires important considerations, including awareness of the disconnect between Western models of treatment and non-Western beliefs around mental health, the role of culture, and the role of interpreters.

- Practitioners engaged in therapy services with immigrants and refugees should be aware of the relevance of pre-migration, migration, and post-migration experiences as well as the impact of trauma and loss in the lives of immigrant clients.

- Practice should also include purposeful recognition of the resilience and strength that is developed through the migration experience and how those qualities can aid when other challenges are faced in the destination country.

- Effective practice with immigrants and refugees requires professionals to practice from a place of cultural incompetence and humility in what is not known about our client's cultural history and traditions. The therapeutic process with immigrants creates opportunities for learning and growth in both the client and the professional/provider.

GLOSSARY

direct/individual practice. A modality in which interventions focus on the individual. Related terms include clinical practice, therapy, psychotherapy.

International Statistical Classification of Diseases and Related Health Problems (ICD). A medical classification list by the World Health Organization (WHO).

Diagnostic and Statistical Manual of Mental Disorders (DSM). A derivative of the ICD classification system commonly used in the United States and now in its fifth Edition (DSM-5).

psychodynamic. An approach to psychology that emphasizes systematic study of the psychological forces that underlie human behavior, feelings, and emotions and how they might relate to early experience.

REFERENCES

Bauer, H. M., Rodrguez, M. A., Szkupinski Quiroga, S., & Flores-Ortiz, Y. G. (2000). Barriers to health care for abused Latina and Asian immigrant women. *Journal of Health Care for the Poor & Underserved, 11*(1), 33–44.

Beiser, M., Hou, F., Hyman, I., & Tousignant, M. (2002). Poverty, family process, and the mental health of immigrant children in Canada. *American Journal of Public Health, 92*(2), 220–227.

Chen, A. W., Kazanjian, A., & Wong, H. (2009). Why do Chinese Canadians not consult mental health services: Health status, language, or culture? *Transcultural Psychiatry, 46*, 623–641.

Colic-Peisker, V., & Tilbury, F. (2003). Active and passive resettlement: The influence of social support services and refugees own resources on resettlement style. *International Migration, 41*, 61–89.

Darvishpour, M. (2002). Immigrant women challenge the role of men: How the changing power relationships with Iranian families in Sweden intensifies family conflicts after immigration. *Journal of Comparative Family Studies, 33*(2), 271–296.

Derr, A. S. (2016). Mental health service use among immigrants in the United States: A systematic review. *Psychiatric Services, 67*(3), 265–274. doi: 10.1176/appi.ps.201500004

Dow, H. D. (2011). An overview of stressors faced by immigrants and refugees: A guide for mental heath practitioners. *Home Health Care Management & Practice, 23*(3), 210–217. doi: 10.1177/1084822310390878

Fazel, M. (2005). Prevalence of serious mental disorder in 7000 refugees resettled in western countries: A systematic review. *Lancet, 365*, 1309-1314.

Fenta, H., Hyman, I., & Noh, S. (2007). Health service utilization by Ethiopian immigrants and refugees in Toronto. *Journal of Immigrant Minority Health, 9*, 349–357.

Finch, B., Kolody, B., & Vega, W. (2000). Perceived discrimination and depression among Mexican-origin adults in Calif. *Journal of Health and Social Behavior, 41*(3), 295–313.

Flores, E., Tschann, J. M., Dimas, J. M., Pasch, L. A., & de Groat, C. L. (2010). Perceived racial/ethnic discrimination, posttraumatic stress symptoms, and health risk behaviors among Mexican American adolescents. *Journal of Counseling Psychology, 57*(3), 264–273.

Gaw, A. (1993). *Culture, ethnicity and mental illness.* Washington, DC: American Psychiatric Press.

Gorman, W. (2001). Refugee survivors of torture: Trauma and treatment. *Professional Psychology: Research and Practice, 32*(5), 443–451. doi: 10.1037//0735.7028.32.5.443

Helsel, D., & Mochel, M. (2002). Afterbirths in the afterlife: Cultural meaning of placental disposal in a Hmong American community. *Journal of Transcultural Nursing, 13*(4), 282–286.

Herman, J. L. (1992). *Trauma and recovery: The aftermath of violence.* New York: Basic Books.

Howe, A., Smajdor, A., & Stöckl, A. (2012). Towards an understanding of resilience and its relevance to medical training. *Medical Education, 46*(4), 349–356.

Hugo, G. (2002). Australian immigration policy: The significance of the events of September 11. *International Migration Review, 36*(1), 37–40.

Kaminsky, M., McCabe, O. L., Langlieb, A. M., & Everly, G. S., Jr. (2007). An evidence-informed model of human resistance, resilience, and recovery: The Johns Hopkins' outcome-driven paradigm for disaster mental health services. *Brief Treatment and Crisis Intervention, 7*(1), 1.

Khawaja, N. G., White, K. M., Schweitzer, R., & Greenslade, J. (2008). Difficulties and coping strategies of Sudanese refugees: A qualitative approach. *Transcultural Psychiatry, 45*(3), 489–512. doi: 10.117/13634615080894678

Kirmayer, L. J., Narasiah, L., Munos, M., Rashid, M., Ryder, A. G., Guzer, J., . . . Pottie, K. (2011). Common mental health problems in immigrants and refugees: General approach in primary care. *Canadian Medical Association Journal, 183*(12), E959–E967. doi: 10.1503/cmaj.090292

Kisely, S., Terashima, M., & Langille, D. (2008). A population-based analysis of the health experience of African Nova Scotians. *Canadian Medical Association Journal, 179*, 653–658.

Kleinman, A., & Benson, P. (2006). Anthropology in the clinic: The problem of cultural competency and how to fix it. *PLOS Medicine, 3*, E294.

Ku, L., & Waidmann, T. (2003). *How race/ethnicity, immigration status, and language affect health insurance coverage, access to care and quality of care among the low-income population.* Washington, DC: Kaiser Commission on Medicaid and the Uninsured.

Kuo, B. C. H., & Arcuri, A. (2014). Multicultural therapy practicum involving refugees: Description and illustration of a training model. *The Counseling Psychologist, 42*(7), 1021–1052. doi: 10.1177/0011000013491610

Lai, D., & Surood, S. (2008). Predictors of depression in aging South Asian Canadians. *Journal of Cross Cultural Gerontology, 23*, 57–75.

Luthar, S. S. (2006). Resilience in development: A synthesis of research across five decades. In D. Cicchetti & D. J. Cohen (Eds.), *Developmental psychopathology, Volume 3: Risk, disorder, and adaptation* (2nd ed., pp. 739–795). Hoboken, NJ: John Wiley & Sons.

Luthar, S. S., Cicchetti, D., & Becker, B. (2000). The construct of resilience: A critical evaluation and guidelines for future work. *Child Development, 71*(3), 543–562. doi: 10.1111/1467-8624.00164

Murphy, H. B. M. (1955). *Flight and resettlement.* Paris, France: UNESCO.

NASW.org. (n.d.). NASW website. Retrieved from https://www.nasw.org/

Neuner, F., Schauer, M., Klaschik, C., Karunakara, U., & Elbert, T. A. (2004). A comparison of narrative exposure therapy, supportive counseling, and psychoeducation for treating posttraumatic stress disorder in African refugee settlement. *Journal of Consulting and Clinical Psychology, 72*, 579–587.

Ng, C. H., & Klimidis, S. (2008). Cultural factors and the use of psychotropic medication. In C. H. Ng, K. Lin, B. S. Sing, & E. Y. K. Chiu (Eds.), *Ethno-psychopharmacology: Advances in current practices* (pp. 123–134). Cambridge, UK: Cambridge University Press.

Pickering, M. (2001). *Stereotyping: The politics of representation.* New York: Palgrave.

Porter, M., & Haslam, N. (2005). Predisplacement and postdisplacement factors associated with mental health of refugees and internally displaced persons: A meta analysis. *Journal of the American Medical Association, 294*, 602–612.

Prilleltensky, I. (2005). Promoting well-being: Time for a paradigm shift in health and human services [Supplemental material]. *Scandinavian Journal of Public Health, 33*(66), 53–60.

Pumariega, A. J., Rothe, E., & Pumariega, J. B. (2005). Mental health of immigrants and refugees. *Community Mental Health Journal, 41*(5), 581–597. doi: 10.1007/s10597-005-6363-1

Sadock, B. J., & Sadock, V. A. (2007). *Kaplan & Sadock's synopsis of psychiatry: Behavioral science/clinical psychiatry* (10th ed.). Alphen aan den Rijn, Netherlands: Wolters Kluwer.

Schriver, J. M. (2010). *Human behavior and the social environment: Shifting paradigms in essential knowledge for social work practice* (5th ed.). Boston: Allyn and Bacon.

UNHCR. (2012). Displacement: The new 21st century challenge. *UNHCR: Global Trends 2012.* http://fas.org/irp/agency/dhs/fema/displace.pdf

Whitley, R., Kirmayer, L. J., & Groleau, D. (2006). Understanding immigrants' reluctance to use mental health services: A qualitative study from Montreal. *Canadian Journal of Psychiatry, 51,* 205–209.

Wong, E. C., Marshall, G. N., Schell, T. L., Elliott, M. N., Hambarsoomians, K., Chun, C. A., & Berthold, S. M. (2006). Barriers to mental health care utilization for U.S. Cambodian refugees. *Journal of Consultation Clinical Psychology, 74,* 1116–1120.

Yeh, C. J. (2003). Age, acculturation, cultural adjustment, and mental health symptoms of Chinese, Korean, and Japanese immigrant youths. *Cultural Diversity and Ethnic Minority Psychology, 9*(1), 34.

Chapter 8

PRACTICE WITH FAMILIES

MARTA LUNDY

Just actions respect the dignity and worth of each and every individual.

Justice is impersonal and nonjudgmental.

Social justice must be measured in terms of whether individuals are benefited or violated.

Individuals are often violated for the "sake of the common good."

Leroy H. Pelton, *Journal of Social Work Education*

ABSTRACT

The stages of migration indicate the mixed reality of many immigrants and refugees and provide a framework for better understanding the complex experience of migration for each family member and for the family system as a whole. Because of the ever-increasing global risks that are driving migration and the challenging trajectory of resettlement after arriving in a destination country, it is imperative to build solidarity with clients and within family systems. The family system provides a set of expectations as well as continuous resources for family members. Family systems are the organizing and stabilizing units for many peoples of the world; therefore, service providers may be more instrumental by building and supporting the family system. This chapter intends to further that goal by (a) documenting research that supports the importance of the family for immigrants and refugees, (b) describing the stages of migration and its impact on the family system, (c) identifying the potential harm that might ensue when these connections are impaired and/or fractured, and (d) discussing methods that might be used to maintain connection between intact and transnational families, including family systems theory.

KEY TERMS

family systems, resilience, stages of migration, immigrants, refugees, intergenerational transmission process, systemic theory, circular causality

CHAPTER HIGHLIGHTS

- Resilience and strengths are factors within individuals and families that can buffer the impact of migration and mitigate the challenges of migration.
- Greater understanding of the common stages of migration for immigrants and refugees prepares providers for the potential needs of the clients.
- Family systems establish individual and familial expectations as well as provide a ready resource for family members.
- Family systems provide extensive support and connection for immigrants and refugees, often relieving some of the stress of the stages of migration.
- Family systems may extend the trauma of migration throughout future generations unless there is comprehensive assessment and prevention provided to vulnerable family members who have had such experiences.

According to Zong and Batalova (2016), migration to the United States has exponentially increased over the last 25 years. For example, in 1970, there were 9.6 million immigrants; in 2000, there were 31.1 million; by 2010, the numbers of immigrants in the United States had increased to 40 million foreign born, and in 2014, there were 42.4 million foreign born immigrants living in the United States. These numbers have changed the diversity of the country and contributed to the economy. Mexican immigrants account for 28% of the 42.4 million foreign born population, making them by far the largest immigrant group in the country (Zong & Batalova, 2016).

When families experience economic insecurity and sociocultural hardship and violence, they seek resolution. As identified above, in much of the world that has been the situation for the last several decades, and the result has been worldwide relocation, people striving to have a safe home, make a liveable wage, and create a future for themselves and future generations. Often individuals and/or segments of families leave a specific part of the world in search of a better life, but many family members remain. This is not only emotionally difficult but creates a hole in the fabric of family life.

When families face massive changes because of relocation, and when the movement is demanded because of life-endangering situations and events, different family members may evaluate the situation differently. "The power of family [counseling] derives from bringing parents and children together to transform their interactions. Instead of isolating individuals from the emotional origin of their conflict, problems are addressed at their source" (Nichols, 2011, p. 8). With this in mind, this chapter will address not only the resilience of the family system but also the myriad problems and difficulties that may arise because of migration, including relocating halfway around the world.

LITERATURE REVIEW

A description of a family system can be as diverse or as similar as one can imagine—of polar opposites or mirror images across generations—and maintain the definition of family. Immigrant families are no different from others, although with some unfortunate commonalities—for example, displacement because of economic insecurity, war, and/or tribal conflict; relocation because of life threatening oppression; the likelihood that families become transnational; and the decision of where to relocate. Throughout U.S. history, immigrants have arrived in poverty needing employment, possibly fleeing violence and discrimination but surely looking for a new beginning, opportunities, and resources that did not seem currently available in their country of origin. The 21st century shares this picture—immigrants and refugees seeking economic and social security and looking for opportunities for their family to grow in a safe environment, seeking a better life. An examination of migration patterns and stages of migration will provide insight into the struggles of the family unit, proving its resilience and willingness to work to accomplish relocation change, all the while trying to maintain relationships in some of the most difficult of circumstances and often across thousands of miles.

For this chapter, there are three overarching goals. First, an examination of the family requires a theoretical framework; the most common for understanding how families manage is family systems theory, although the complexity of transnational family systems and migration requires an adapted integrative approach, which will be discussed. Second, the stages of migration provide an overview of the lived reality of many immigrant and refugee individuals and families as well as a lens for achieving a better understanding of the complex experience of migration for each family member and for the family system as a whole. This experience often leaves emotional scars in the form of trauma and emotional vulnerability, requiring specific attention to the family system. Third, although the relocation of people crosses almost every international border, from Bosnia to Nigeria, Latin America to China, Asia to the Middle East, the largest numbers to migrate into the United States are Mexicans, therefore, this population will be included as examples of the various experiences of migrants, providing a template for collaborative integrative transnational practice.

Years ago, the first generation to migrate to the United States from Mexico simply walked across the border, which in some cities in the southern part of the United States literally meant crossing the street. No difficulties, no inspection, no need for visas or additional documents, and no refusal. But for successive generations, not only are more people migrating but the journey north from Mexico and Central America to the United States and globally, from one country of war and violence to another country for security, the difficulties of migrating have increased exponentially with the potential for high risk and severely dangerous pathways. Migration and the forces driving it are producing a set of intractable challenges that cross international borders. These challenges are experienced immediately at the level of the family and include the following: persistent or periodic ruptures in families and social support because of mobility and migration, poverty and economic insecurity, vulnerability related to legal status, exposure to violence and exploitation, and social and linguistic isolation (Falicov, 2014). It is with this backdrop of experiences that immigrants arrive in the United States.

Literature on the lived experiences of immigrants indicates that they come to the United States as a host country to live and find work, but the experience is laden with multiple barriers against providing a full family life. Barriers include language, lack of job skills, unfamiliarity with urban living, and commonly, discrimination and exploitation in the workplace (Parra-Cardona, Bulock, Imig, Villarruel, & Gold, 2006). Additional areas of discrimination and dissatisfaction are faced when interacting with health care settings, social services agencies, and schools. Many Mexican immigrants report no health insurance and discrimination because of language at work and school. Bacallao and Smokowski describe the hardships experienced by Mexican family systems after immigration, "families mourned the loss of family connections and familial support" (2007, p. 12). In addition, because of poor wages, they also have had to "adjust to juggling multiple jobs and stressful work conditions, which left little time for family relationships (2007, p 12)," the life-sustaining connections that they need and love.

The effect of these experiences reverberates throughout the family system, influencing societal, interpersonal, and intrafamilial relationships and expectations. Providers must prepare for the potential difficulties they may encounter when working with immigrant and refugee individuals and families—that is, a fractured family system, stress and possible trauma from the experiences of migration, and stressful anticipation of what is before the immigrants and refugees as they try to resettle in a new country. But in addition, other problems may loom over the family members who have had generations of immigrants cross before them. Providers also must prepare to assess for the presence of the intergenerational transmission of trauma based on the experiences of preceding generations of immigrant family members (Danieli, 1998; Lev-Wiesel, 2007; Weiss & Weiss, 2000). This chapter will include suggestions for providers to use that might facilitate repair to family systems.

RELEVANCE OF THE FAMILY FOR IMMIGRANTS AND REFUGEES

We are continuing to learn how transnational families maintain their connections with migrated family members. Technology helps to maintain the extended family through "remittances, mail packages, phone cards, e-mails, and occasional visits" (Falicov, 2007, p. 158), not to mention Skype, Facebook, and other social media. Transnational family systems are certainly the norm between the global North and South, and increasingly around the world (Falicov, 2007, p. 158). Family members around the globe are able to stay connected, maintaining relationships, but the questions remain: *How do these relationships evolve and endure, and what are the strengths and pressures of these situations?*

Immediate and extended family systems can provide emotional, physical, and financial support, even if limited. The stabilization of a well-functioning, supportive family system is relevant throughout all collectivistic cultures and societies. Gaining a better understanding and having methods for facilitating intrafamilial discussions will enable providers to be more purposeful in their work (Figley, 1988; Minuchin, n.d.). Facilitating family systems to understand and manage the experiences of migration becomes a powerful endeavor in communication and connection for the entire family system. We know the relevance of the family system and have a realization regarding the role of social media; however, we continue to see many family members with usual problems—for example, isolation, loneliness, limited social network—which creates a fractured experience among family members. These family members may or may not stay connected, depending upon resources and the difficulty of staying connected—for example, the cost of a phone, time difference between countries, other work responsibilities, time to make a call, and the demands of living in the United States (McGuire & Martin, 2007).

STAGES OF MIGRATION

Immigration is often explained as the result of the push and pull of economies, with one country's economy *pushing* individuals and families out of the country because of poor wages, lack of economic security, and lack of safety, whereas another is *pulling* individuals and families toward them with the availability of jobs and the need for workers. Immigrants are forced to relocate in order to feed their families, provide medical care for aging parents, and establish security for the lives of family members.

A realization of the prevalence of migration and the demands of host countries on the migrant are critical to understanding the demands on the family system and the probable services needed to support individuals and families.

> Migration is a complex process, involving a heterogeneity of causes, experiences, cultural adjustment and stages, that influence the mental health of migrants. The stresses of the migration process itself combined with a lack of social support, a discrepancy between achievement and expectations, economic hardships, racial discrimination and harassment, and a lack of access to proper housing, medical care, and religious practice can lead to poor self-esteem, an inability to adjust, and poor physical and mental health. (Bhugra & Becker, 2005, pp. 18–24)

In addition, the history of the process of migration for the individual and family systems "usually paves the way to understanding relational stresses that may have ensued" (Falicov, 2014, p. 102). Figure 8.1 maps out the stages of migration that reflect the experiences of all immigrants, both documented and undocumented.

Pre-Migration or Family Decision Making

For many families, "the decision to migrate takes many defeating scenarios in their countries of origin before deciding that migration is the only and best path at the time" (Falicov, 2014, pp. 53–65). As described above, there are social, economic, political, and safety factors that all play a critical part in the decision-making process for families.

Figure 8.1 Diagram of Stages of Migration

(Drachman, 1997; Pine & Drachman, 2005)

Pre-migration Families discuss, plan, decide who goes or immediately flees danger
Transit Often long, dangerous, exploitive journey and/or refugee resettlement camp
Detention and/or Incarceration and/or Deportation Disappointments & delays of the journey
Repeat the Journey Often returned to home country w/o funds &/or badly hurt
Arrive at Destination Country Learn English, locate employment & housing
Resettlement Learn new culture, language, make connections, mourn losses

It also is important to remember that not all families and cultures are static; rather, families are complex, varied, and ever-changing systems (Falicov, 2014).

Generally, there are three primary stages for migration: pre-migration, migration, and post-migration (Drachman, 1992). However, these can be further defined into five, which include specific but common events: pre-migration, transit, detention and/or incarceration and/or deportation, transnational migration to find an accepting country, and resettlement or life in a host country. These provide specific situations that many family systems have to navigate that offer difficult but also hopeful decision points that can be explored. For example, the pre-migration deliberation and decision-making process can include all or only a few family members. The needs of individuals and families drive the discussions and decisions, and often families make collective decisions about who migrates, where they will go, and how the process will be managed. For other families, the decision-making may be more parent driven, and some children/ youth may not feel included and/or part of this process. Although understandable, especially for young children, nonetheless, this potentially alienating process can have reverberations later on within the life of the family system. Further, repeated attempts to locate and remain in a host country create potentially conflictual intergenerational confusion.

Transit

The actual transit is different across families and countries, with the relevant global contexts and considerations required to gain a full understanding. Using Mexican and Central American immigrants as an example, the process of leaving Mexico for the United States is extremely dangerous with bandits and local gangs along the way, corrupt police, and the drug cartels, to mention a few of the dangers. Often local merchants charge higher prices for necessary traveling commodities—for example, water, food, and clothing. Mexicans describe witnessing abuse and being helpless to intervene as well as experiencing brutalization and exploitation by others, often with too little food and water, no one to trust, and a long, hot, desolate desert to overcome (Kino Border Initiative, personal communication, Nogales, Mexico). Often, if identified and/ or found to be crossing without the proper documents required by the United States, immigrants are detained by the U.S. Border Patrol and put in detention or incarceration for varying amounts of time, depending on the categories within the system.

In other countries, we have witnessed similar processes whereby refugees and immigrants who are fleeing for better living conditions, greater safety and security, and a place to raise their families, are given only the most difficult paths to travel, are denied entry to some destination countries even as they arrive at the border, and/or are put in detention or placed in UNHCR Refugee Resettlement camps, where the conditions are often insufficient and unsafe. Most recently, the world has witnessed a mass exodus of refugees traveling across the EU, from 10 of the most dangerous countries: Syria, Afghanistan, Iraq, Kosovo, Albania, Pakistan, Eritrea, Nigeria, Iran, and the Ukraine, in the most unsafe conditions, with no resources, often walking for days, across country after country, seeking safety and refuge (BBC, 2016). Often, they are turned away or pushed out by high and lethal barbed wire fences recently constructed to keep them out. The most generous of countries feel the strain of the masses of men, women, and children who require shelter, food, water, education, and work, to name the most prominent needs.

Resettlement

For many family members across the globe, resettlement has concrete implications: obtain secure housing, find employment, and learn the language. Each of these is an enormous demand. For most, there is no time to process their recent migration experiences. They must move steadily forward in their progress to remain in the country of destination. But for many, the United States was not their preferred destination country, and they have no one here to turn to . . . no relatives who have come before, no referrals for getting a job, and too little support for how to manage. But they have to make this work, and there is no time to mourn what might have been and who has been left behind. Immigrants and refugees must accommodate whatever happens, or they will perish.

TRANSNATIONAL FAMILIES

For Mexicans, there can be an effort to establish a transnational lifestyle. Some members of the family make the journey several times and return home over the course of months and/or years, sending regular remittances and bringing proceeds home for the family to use and enjoy. But when the funds are depleted, the family member, usually the male head of household, will return again to the United States to earn more wages for the family, once again separating the family. These are harrowing circumstances for everyone because of the extreme dangers faced by the migrant. More recently, because of U.S. high tech surveillance and patrol of the border and the presence of the Mexican drug cartels, these types of transnational crossings are strikingly more dangerous and less likely to occur (U.S. Border Patrol presentation, personal communication, 2015, 2016).

More frequently, we now see that there are generations and parts of family systems in both countries—for example, grandparents, parents, and extended family in the country of origin or in a resettlement camp and children and successive generations in the host country. These family systems have been separated and in many cases, fractured or broken by the circumstances, and many need to find methods for reconnecting with their extended family systems. The potential to reunite and/or restore some of the traditions and relationships among family systems is a potentially empowering and life-giving process.

THEORETICAL FRAMEWORK: INTEGRATIVE FAMILY SYSTEMS MODELS

The family system provides a set of expectations as well as continuous resources for family members, especially in collective cultures in which the family is the organizing and stabilizing unit. An integrative family systems model is extremely relevant for working with immigrant and refugee client systems. This theoretical framework has been primarily conceptualized from an individualistic Western perspective; therefore, these theories require adaptation in order to be fully applicable to the needs of specific immigrant and refugee families.

In order to be fully prepared to work with intergenerational, transnational, and fractured family systems, engage individuals, facilitate enactments among family members—that is, interactive discussion and conversation—and identify family interaction patterns and problems, providers will need to accommodate these complex family systems. Most specifically, a combination of commonly used theories will be most flexible for meeting the specific issues and needs of the client family system. Currently, there are hundreds of different theories and integrative theoretical models; we are recommending seven specific theories that relate well to the context of transnational family systems. Each provider will have to identify what is needed for the specific family system with their unique needs, consider which aspects require theoretical adaptation to the precise circumstances of the family system, and to evaluate their own level of skill to determine which theories to incorporate. For example, practitioners need to cautiously evaluate the family system with the reality that all systems in immigrant and refugee families are severely overburdened and stressed with acculturation expectations and language barriers and understandably in overload which may create the appearance of dysfunction (Rasheed, Rasheed, & Marley, 2011). This is damaging to the relationship and assumes there is dysfunction before gaining an understanding of the culture and the cultural mandates for health and well-being and the familial structure of the client system. At that point, the provider can determine the models most relevant to the circumstance—for example, ecological systems theory, empowerment model, multigenerational and structural family systems models, solution focused family system therapy, and narrative theory, each of which is oriented to facilitate productive practitioner engagement and effective family member interaction and communication. These models each provide specific interventions that are designed to move families toward better communication and understanding and thereby closer connections. Other relevant models and/or theories may be included as needed by the client system but will not be discussed here, although they are found in other chapters of this text.

BRIEF DESCRIPTION OF CONCEPTS AND THEORIES

Core theories for working with immigrant and refugee clients, regardless of the practice orientation, are intensive case management, ecological system theory, and social justice. These theories establish the foundation on which all other work depends, adapting every theory to these core components. The definitions of these concepts and theories are derived from the *Encyclopedia of Social Work* (Hall, 2016).

Intensive Case Management

Concrete needs and services and referrals to resources are often the introductions for ongoing provider/client relationships, which include attention to immediate needs for food, water, but also medical examination, medications, surgery, and/or psychiatric examinations, and so forth. Immigrants and refugees often come with serious injuries that have never received medical attention and mental health conditions that with proper care can greatly ease the psychological burdens on the individual and family systems. "Systematic enquiry into the migration trajectory and subsequent follow-up on culturally appropriate indicators of social, vocational, and family functioning will allow clinicians to recognize problems in adaptation and undertake mental health promotion, prevention or treatment interventions in a timely fashion" (Kirmayer et al., 2011, p. E962). These are necessary resources, which when attended to with priority, give a strong message that the provider is aware, responsive, resourceful, and ready to help. This not only lays the foundation for a working relationship but provides grounding for the person to move into resettlement of their new life.

Social Justice

Social justice is a core concept of social work values and ethics, and guides social work practice and policy. In the *Encyclopedia of Social Work*, Barker (2016) defines it as "an ideal condition in which all members of a society have the same rights, protections, opportunities, obligations, and social benefits. Implicit in this concept is the notion that historical inequities should be acknowledged and remedied through specific measures" (p. 405; see also Franklin, 2016, p. 1).

Ecological Systems Theory

Ecological concepts maintain a focus on the reciprocal relationship between the client system and the environment, and the reciprocity and influence that each has on the other. This theory has provided an alternative to the medical and disease model that has been pervasive in social work, reframing client situations with full consideration for the environment in which they are located (Gitterman & Germain, 2016, p. 1).

Empowerment Model

Empowerment is used in both generalist and advanced practice to counter conditions of powerlessness. Providers collaborate with clients to form an empowering relationship, emphasizing opportunities for clients to experience power and collaboration and teaching tools and skills to build empowerment (Parsons & East, 2013, pp. 1–3).

In addition to the core concepts, family systems theories guide both the clinical and research work of the practitioner. Following are the two core theories that comprise an integrative transnational model for working with immigrant and refugee families.

Multigenerational Family Therapy

"Central to . . . this theory is . . . belief in the influence of one's family of origin on present-day functioning, for example, how we form attachments, deal with anxiety, manage intimacy, deal with and resolve conflict . . . " (Rasheed et al., 2011, p. 171). All of these interactions are learned within the family of origin system, and we continue using them throughout successive relationships, whether they are constructive or destructive. Fortunately, a careful examination of the behavior patterns of our families of origin in relation to our own current patterns of relating can begin the process toward productive change.

The relevant Bowenian concept for this chapter is the intergenerational transmission process. While research has not been complete, practice discussions continue to address the potential for the intergenerational transmission of trauma. It is apparent that practitioners have consistently identified some clients for whom this is a significant problem. Because we cannot make the connections across generations unless we ask difficult and seemingly intrusive questions, we do have to ask, even if it feels uncomfortable.

Structural Family Therapy

Structural family therapy has a strong social justice component, advocating for immediately useful applications for family difficulties. It is essentially a practical, problem-focused, and interactive therapy to bring family members in connection with one another. The focus is on the structure and balance among family members, and the three primary subsystems that exist within a family system—that is, spousal, parental, and siblings. Within those subsystems, the provider examines boundaries and roles among the individuals and across the subsystems. The only way to be truly helpful is to learn from our clients about their experiences. With that knowledge, we can facilitate our client's goals for change and growth and also provide relief from despair and isolation within the family system (Rasheed, Rasheed, & Marley, 2011).

Two more recent theories follow, each with a specific focus and perspective engaging client family systems.

Narrative Theory

Narrative theory is a postmodern, person-centered practice approach that promotes change through the exploration of narrative, "a story of self . . . [and] the meanings attributed to life events . . . " (Hall, *Encyclopedia of Social Work*, p. 1). The discourse of family, region, culture, and so forth, determines the meaning and generally is meant to continue the current dominant social and political structure, not the needs of the person. The practitioner artfully asks clarifying and reformulated questions, providing the client system with the opportunity to rethink and reformulate her understanding and interpretation of life events.

Solution Focused Family Therapy

Solution focused family therapy is oriented toward the family system, not only as the expert about the difficulties experienced by family members but also the instrument of change—that is, it is the family who knows when and what behaviors "change the problem" (Rasheed, Rasheed, & Marley, 2011, p. 265). Solution focused theory explores and encourages the family to identify what they are doing when the problem does not occur. For the family system that is disinclined to examine the problem and has no history of self-reflection, this can be an affirming experience. The practitioner is the listener who asks the family to continue what they are doing when the problem does not occur. Although this is in contrast to many other theories, research with U.S. families suggests that this intervention remains effective long after termination (Rasheed et al., 2011).

These theories provide a foundation for collaborating with individuals and families on gaining more clarity about the family system. Not all theories will be relevant for all families, but certainly some will open a pathway for resourceful methods for connecting with the family and healing them to reconnect with family members around the world.

COMMON PROBLEMS AND POTENTIAL HARM WITH IMPAIRED FAMILY CONNECTIONS

Although there are many immigrants, refugees, and asylees who do not experience physical and/or mental health problems, the difficulties of the migration experience are known to create many common problems. For example, refugees who have lived in displacement or resettlement camps and/or have been caught in warfare generally require immediate medical care, sometimes surgery for wounds that have never been addressed, malnutrition, and so forth. Migrants and refugees also experience depression, loneliness, isolation, language barriers, loss of everything familiar, with accompanying suicidal ideation or attempts, substance and/or alcohol abuse, parent/child conflict, domestic and interpersonal violence, and a long list of trauma and traumatic stress related events (Cohen, 2010; Fortuna, Porche, & Alegria, 2008; Kirmayer et al., 2011). The common difficulties of poverty, racism, and discrimination in the host country and/or colorism from family and extended family exacerbate the problems of being in a new, unknown, and demanding culture.

For Mexican, Central and South American immigrants, the hardships also are well known and too common. Without legal papers, immigrants and refugees may arrive in the destination country having experienced layers of vulnerability because of the presence of coyotes, exploitive stores where bottled water costs an exorbitant price, and desert crossing with hot and cold weather extremes, all the while expending efforts to evade the U.S. Border Patrol. The common occurrences of robbery, armed assault, threats, exploitation and brutality, being chased by militia and watched by aerial drones contribute to a heightened state of distress. For refugees from African, Middle Eastern, and European countries, the violence often is even more direct. Armed men come into your home and assault family members, killing and maiming them in front of children and grandparents. Children are recruited at young ages for the armed forces. Family members are taken to fight in a war they don't understand, and making a living for the family is either difficult or impossible.

The emotional impact of migration is significant and often unexpected by the family system. Although the plans may have seemed clear at the time of separation, the reality of migration is complex. People change. It can be difficult to stay connected and close as work requires long hours often with longer commutes, time passes with too few resources to remain steadily in contact, and often, there is too little good news to share. The impact or the immediate imperative of the decision to leave one's family and country, the journey, and the resulting conditions include hardships unimaginable to the individual or family before the trip is experienced. For Mexican and Central and South American immigrants specifically "poverty prior to migration together with entry to the US without authorization was strongly associated with [the] likelihood of exposures to trauma in both adolescent children and their parents" (Perreira & Ornelas, 2013, p. 997).

The described experiences may lead to extensive trauma, traumatic stress, and the suppression of memories of events too horrible to contemplate for the individuals who were witnesses. It is often easier to "forget," and certainly the need to settle into the host country and manage the responsibilities of resettlement make it more likely that the experiences of migration can be pushed off, allocated to another time and place.

Strengths and Resilience

Focusing only on problems can perpetuate oppression as the strengths of certain cultures are not acknowledged (Waller & Yellow Bird as cited in Lietz, 2006). A perspective that is skewed toward only seeing problems misses ways in which people can benefit or grow stronger when they face challenges in their lives (McMillen as cited in Lietz, 2006, p. 575). An examination of resilience begins with a definition: "Resilience is characterized by successful outcomes despite serious threats to adaptation and development. Resilience is neither an individual trait nor a static process; rather it is a dynamic process that requires both the exposure to risk and the manifestation of positive adjustment despite experiences of adversity and trauma" (Masten, Best, & Garmezy; Masten et al; and Luthar & Cicchetti as cited in Cardoso & Thompson, 2010, p. 257).

Refugees and immigrants bring numerous strengths and resilience, much of which is derived from the family system and the continuous support of family of origin as well as extended family systems. As previously noted, immigrants and refugees are often from collective societies in which the central organizing unit is the family system. According to Perreira and Ornelas (Ornelas & Perreira, 2011; Perreira & Ornelas, 2013), there is a nearly ubiquitous finding among researchers on mental health among immigrants: "factors contributing to resilience include social support among parents as well as acculturation, time in U.S., and familism among children (Cook et al., 2009; Kuperminc et al., 2009; Ornelas & Perreira, 2011, 2013). Additional strengths include an ability to cope with adversity. Often refugees and immigrants have been able to maintain some sense of hope and belief that things will work out if they just forbear it. Generally, there are strong family values and a strong faith, a focus on goals and objectives for their lives, and a sense of responsibility for future generations. The strengths come from a sense of community and social networks that are critical to their success and also provide emotional sustenance. The collective natures of the societies that many refugees and immigrants come from provides a sense that working together, things can get better. The isolation so often experienced by immigrants and refugees in host countries can be mitigated by their sense of social networks. Assistance in helping refugees and immigrants to locate and maintain, and/or develop these social networks with family systems cannot be stressed enough.

Walsh (1998) described resilience as "the capacity to rebound from adversity strengthened and more resourceful" (Rasheed, Rasheed, & Marley, 2011, p. 440). Parra Cardona, Bulock, Imig, Villarruel, and Gold (2006) found that Mexican immigrants deal with challenges and hardships by staying together as a family and *trabajando duro* (working hard) to improve their living situations and to provide their children with a better life and more educational opportunities. Although the challenges of migration are obvious and the list of indignities, discrimination, and exploitation is long and often brutal, there is overwhelming evidence that immigrants and refugees are amazingly resourceful, hardworking, and hopeful. Resilience comes from a deep well that is maintained by faith, a caring and supportive family system, hard work, and determination to succeed in spite of the seemingly Sisyphian crater in front of them (see De Haan, Hawley, & Deal, 2002; Saleebey, 1992, 1996, 2002; Walsh, 1998, 2002). Walsh identified a family resilience framework from her experience working with many families, "The family resilience framework is a strengths-based approach rooted in the belief that individuals and families can adapt and manage basic or complex life situations when existing strengths, skills, abilities, and resources are identified, nurtured, and built upon" (2003, p. 11), which was supported by the work of Saleebey (1992, 1996, 2002), who believed that the strengths perspective facilitated the abilities of client systems.

Families seek providers because of problems from the environment as well as internal family difficulties. Although it is logical to begin with environmental problems first for immigrant and refugee family systems, assessing whether their concrete needs for food, housing, employment, and so forth, are being fulfilled, it also is imperative for providers to examine whether there are psychological and/or emotional and interpersonal problems that may be preventing the family from resolving other basic issues. Providers must always assess the various levels of potential need and problem area to ensure an ability to be useful. The following discussion seeks to identify interpersonal and intrafamilial problems that may create difficulties that are discussed in the literature and to provide a method for becoming more informed.

First, specific problem areas will be identified, followed by a presentation of one example of an integrated family systems model, and then an overview for how to proceed when facilitating family engagement, discussion, and resolution of problems.

INTEGRATED FAMILY SYSTEMS MODEL

An integrative model provides different perspectives and concepts for engagement and assessment as well as various interventions to facilitate family information sharing and subsequent change and methods of consolidation. For example, a careful assessment of family patterns, rules, resilience as well as expectations and limitations of family members enables the provider to gain a fuller picture of the family system. Applying a combined intergenerational, structural, and narrative family approach collects information through the utilization of a genogram and family narrative; assesses members' interaction patterns, communication styles, hierarchy, intergenerational transmission, and structure; and intervenes by identification of patterns, listening to the family narrative and observing enactments, reframing problems, providing information, and facilitating the family members to become more self-aware, thus becoming more differentiated and individually secure, which leads to greater connection. See Table 8.1 for more information.

Collective family systems often rely on the extended family system for moral, philosophical, and economic support. Those are more or less the family rules: Earlier generations guide and direct subsequent generations and identify family expectations— elders guide youth. And while these rules provide support for all members of the family, they also can result in heavy responsibilities and damaging results. Early in the history of family therapy, Bowen (1978) spoke of the intergenerational transmission of family experiences and messages—that is, the passage of problems from one generation to another. Efforts to understand the experiences of the immigrant, refugee, and/or asylee and to facilitate a productive life with a future requires various perspectives.

INTERGENERATIONAL TRANSMISSION OF TRAUMA

Although it remains a controversial topic with need for further examination and clarification, researchers and clinicians continue to try to understand the presence and complexity of transgenerational familial influences and the degree and manner

Table 8.1 Core Theories and Concepts in Family Systems Practice

Intensive Case Management

Concrete needs and services and referrals to resources
Attention to immediate needs for food and water
Medical examination and medications
Surgery
Psychiatric examinations for mental illness

Social Justice

Assess for social and economic rights, protections, opportunities, and social benefits

Ecological Systems Theory

Reciprocal relationship between the client system and the environment
Alternative to the medical and disease model

Empowerment Model

Counter conditions of powerlessness
Collaborate with clients to form an empowering relationship
Emphasize opportunities to experience power and collaboration

Intergenerational Family Therapy

Influence of one's family of origin on present-day functioning
Identifies relationship patterns, themes, and issues from our families of origin as part of our current relationships with others, continuing throughout generations, known as the intergenerational transmission process

Structural Family Therapy

Strong social justice advocate
Practical, problem-focused, and interactive therapy to bring family members in connection with one another
Focus on structure and balance among family members
Examines hierarchy
Focus on three primary subsystems within a family system—that is, spousal, parental, and siblings
Examine boundaries and roles

Solution Focused Family Therapy

Focus on family system as expert on difficulties but also the instrument of change
Explores and encourages family identification of when the problem does not occur
Disinclined to examine the problem
Practitioner listens, asks family to continue doing whatever when problem does not occur

Narrative Therapy

Postmodern, person-centered practice
Promotes change through the exploration of narrative . . . a story of self . . . the meanings attributed to life events

of influence of the intergenerational transmission of distress and/or trauma. One recurring theoretical concept that has been used to understand and respond to the individual and family experience has been Bowen's (1978) intergenerational transmission of trauma, with the understanding that the unprocessed experiences of a parent and/or grandparent may be projected onto successive generations through individual behaviors and interactions among the family system.

"Traumatic events often have severe negative consequences for those who were directly exposed to them as well as to others, particularly family members, who were not directly exposed to that event" (Figley, 1995, p. 10). Although the research has been sporadic and often inconclusive on many of these issues, there has been a continuing awareness of the manifestations of unresolved trauma in the children and grandchildren of families who have experienced alarming traumatic events. Since the Jewish holocaust that began in Germany and spread worldwide in the 1930s and 1940s, many have examined the phenomenon in an effort to understand individual and family functioning. Danieli (1998), Weiss and Weiss (2000), Lev-Wiesel (2007), and others have examined the impact of secondary trauma and the intergenerational transmission of trauma across generations. Often subsequent generations seem to have absorbed the pain of their elders and live out a life that is marked by suffering (Bowen, n.d.; Danieli, 1998; Lev-Wiesel, 2007).

Other researchers have been presented with similar possible explanations for recurring behaviors in subsequent generations, and many have generated outcome studies. Stith, Rosen, Middleton, Busch, Lundeberg, and Carlton have been concerned with the intergenerational transmission of spouse abuse. They conducted a meta-analysis and found "a weak-to-moderate relationship between growing up in an abusive family and becoming involved in a violent marital relationship (2000, p. 640). They did find gender effects, for example, "there is a stronger relationship between growing up in a violent home and becoming a perpetrator of spouse abuse for men than for women and for becoming a victim of spouse abuse for women than for men" (Stith et al., 2000, p. 648). Stith et al. (2000) came to the conclusion that the intergenerational transmission hypothesis requires more complex studies to better understand and reach a definitive conclusion.

Dekel and Goldblatt (2008), in their examination of PTSD in war veteran fathers and the impact on their sons, conducted a review of the literature, including research and clinical theory, and provided a template for examining what we know and how to proceed with future investigation into the phenomenon of intergenerational transmission. The variables are extensive, for example, gender, age, birth order, timing of father's injury, type of transmission—for example, distress, family functioning, self-esteem, and direct or indirect transmission. As the reviewers note, not all studies examine all variables and the perspective may be different, requiring further research.

There are examples of other problems among subsequent generations of families who have experienced mass discrimination and abuse—for example, the children of Japanese parents interned in camps in the United States during WWII (Nagata & Cheng, 2003), indications of traumatic behaviors in subsequent generations of the children of slaves (Mullan-Gonzalez, 2012), and more recently, studies have examined the potential for intergenerational transmission of trauma in first-generation children from the migration experiences of their immigrant parents (Lin & Suyemoto, 2016;

Phipps & Degges-White, 2014; Sirikantraporn, 2016). It remains a possible area of inquiry in order to facilitate healing among families but requires further research across clearly defined variables in order for any conclusive outcome.

Putting intergenerational transmission of trauma and the questions it raises aside, family systems providers are responsible to all generations. We must facilitate the entire immigrant and refugee family learning about the experiences as well as emotional responses to migration events and their impact on the family system. Raising questions about the grandparent and parent experiences and exploring that impact within current generations seems a worthwhile part of every assessment. If it isn't a difficulty reverberating within the family system, the provider will soon know, but the questions will have been asked should memories surface in the future. Also, it seems to be a powerful experience when adult children learn about the difficulties of their parents who struggled to migrate to a safe host country and endured hardships while establishing a secure and hopeful family environment for their children (student papers, personal communication, 2010–2015). The knowledge of the efforts and strengths of the family system to provide opportunities for immigrant, refugee, and asylee children places additional responsibilities on young family members to work hard, extend themselves for others, and exemplify a life that supports the sacrifices of their elders. The intensity of the relationships may change in powerful and constructive ways. If children and/or adult children never learn about the trajectory of their parents' lives, never know about the sacrifices, don't understand the idiosyncracies of their parents' behaviors often caused by the migration journey and/or the process of resettlement, there may be tension, confusion, and/or resentment among family members that providers may be able to identify and alleviate by providing a space for these narratives.

PROVIDER RESPONSE AND THE APPLICATION OF PRACTICE PRINCIPALS

It is important to note that although not every immigrant, refugee, or asylee will have experienced tragedy and trauma, it is incumbent upon providers to assess and discover what the issues may be for each individual and family. Before that process can begin, Bowen and others (1978) compel us to first know our own family history, including our own intergenerational family messages that often dictate how and what we feel, if and how we process emotions, our communication style, values, religion, and much more. This suggestion repeats imperatives given by family systems therapists, practitioners, and researchers over the decades (Bowen, 1978; Falicov, 2015; Figley, 1995). Bowen wrote explicitly about the family of origin of the practitioner and warned that practitioners are likely to be unknowingly influenced by their own family of origin messages if they are not known and understood (Bowen, 1978). This same process provides useful information for the client, often helping the client system to "see" how their own family of origin messages have influenced their lives without realization. Nichols (2008–2016) identified several core terms that are directly relevant for understanding the interpersonal behaviors among families and assisting them in identifying and healing from family and/or individual problems (Nichols, 2013, pp. 111–130; see Table 8.2, Definitions of Family Systems Concepts).

Table 8.2 Definitions of Family Systems Concepts and Related Others

Boundaries	Ability and willingness to separate the family system from influences that are unhealthy and to separate from other members of the family system if they become unhealthy.
Circular causality	Not linear. Influences and interactions flow from each part to all other parts within a family system, not from only one direction.
	Verbal and non-verbal expressions of thoughts and feelings.
Culture	Common patterns of behavior and experience derived from the settings in which people live; members of the same culture do not necessarily share same values and assumptions.
Differentiation	The ability and stability to maintain one's ideas, feelings, and meanings of events even when all others within the family system may disagree.
Emotional cut-off	Limiting and/or completely discontinuing all contact with a member of the family of origin or extended family because of interpersonal emotional difficulties.
Enactment	Facilitating the interpersonal and/or familial discussion of events and/or topics in order to observe patterns of communication and interaction.
Family structure	Power systems, for example, power over or power to, and hierarchy that characterizes the family system.
Hierarchy	The balance of power within any system but specifically within families, the utilization of power within the parental subsystem.
Interaction patterns	Patterns of interpersonal behaviors, communication, responsiveness or lack thereof.
	All provide evidence of repeated types of various methods of communication among family members.
	Often, there is no one cause or reason for a problem but rather a series of actions and reactions among family members that create and sustain difficulties. Not a linear model but rather interactive in multiple interpersonal directions. Not conceived exclusively from prior events.

(Continued)

(Continued)

Intergenerational transmission	Messages and patterns from earlier generations transmit expectations for education, profession, family values, behaviors and/or emotional responses to successive generations, including any traumatic events and the inability of the previous generation to deal with the traumatic stress, hurtful nature of the event, and/or perceived threat to the family system.
Reframe	Describe a situation or relationship pattern within the family system in positive and easily understood terms.
Spirituality	A belief system that provides direction and strength to the family.

HELPING FAMILIES NAVIGATE PROBLEMS

There is a long and solid tradition within clinical practice to ask if there may be problems in areas of common difficulties in order to provide a venue for the client to express their concerns, if they have any, and to know that there is interest and openness—that they can discuss these issues if they should arise in the future.

Family systems theory is extremely relevant for collectivist cultures where the family unit is the primary social system, including multiple generations as well as extended family and others as integral parts of the family system. In family systems, people are "embedded in a network of relationships . . . and are part of something larger than themselves" (Nichols, 2008, p. 7). Often families live near one another, making close relationships and activities especially possible. When these relationships are severed, for whatever reasons and purposes, it is important for them to be identified, discussed, and understood. It is at that juncture that individuals and families have options. See Table 8.3 for an elaboration on the four phases of working through family trauma.

When families experience economic hardship and violence because of conditions within a country, they seek a resolution. In much of the world, this has been the

---

Table 8.3 Four Phases for Working With Family Trauma

1. **Engage everyone in the family. Build a commitment to therapeutic objectives: family works together.**
2. **Reframe the problem.**
3. **Construct/develop an integrative model of healing.**
4. **Prepare and close.**

situation for several decades, and the result is large numbers of immigrants and refugees worldwide striving to relocate to safety, without the economic ability to remain connected to others. This is not only emotionally difficult but also leaves a hole in the fabric of the family life. When families face massive changes because of relocation and when the movement is required because of life-endangering situations and events, whether it be economic survival or relief from conflict, different family members may evaluate the situation differently. Some may feel abandoned; some may be angry; others may be forlorn. "The power of family [counseling] derives from bringing parents and children together to transform their interactions. Instead of isolating individuals from the emotional origin of their conflict problems are addressed at their core" (Nichols, 2016, p. 8). It is from this perspective that mental health providers can address both the resilience of the family system but also the myriad problems and difficulties that might arise because of the stages of migration, including relocating from halfway around the world.

One of the primary methods for establishing an environment in which difficult questions can be asked is to engage with the client and develop a relationship. That requires knowledge of the culture of the client and a thorough assessment of one's own biases and behaviors. Some common behaviors—for example, shaking hands, calling clients by their first names—will not be well received by many cultures that are more formal and/or by clients who have had poor experiences in forming relationships. Meet the client system where the clients are and be open to their cues, with a plan to describe your lack of knowledge about their culture at the beginning of the first meeting.

Maintain a flexible attitude with a preference for client self-determination. One of the most flexible methods for relating with clients is to engage with *unbounded or inclusive solidarity*, a term described by Amnesty International (Breton, 2011) that is immediately and directly applicable. Facilitate family members to discuss the experiences that are most difficult for them during the migration, for example, the dangers, hardships, and the most worrisome issues that stay with them. Help each to talk about the loneliness and the losses as well as the wonderful but brief friendships that were ignited along the way, as it was relevant for them.

CASE EXAMPLE

Working With Family Systems

Although the difficulties family members have endured may be extensive, the need to be accepted and forgiven for whatever behaviors or actions the person may feel were less than honorable and be reunited with family remains a powerful and too often overlooked resource for individual health. The following four phases in family systems practice have been identified and adapted as methods to help family members and the family system as a whole to maintain its integrity and bonds and/or to develop new connections (Figley, 1988):

1. Engage everyone in the family. Build a commitment to therapeutic objectives: Family works together.

2. Reframe the problem(s).

3. Construct/develop an integrative model of healing.

4. Prepare and close.

Engage Everyone in the Family

The various steps provide a flexible template for how to proceed, always alert for whether the individual and/or family system may require additional services and/or interventions. As is well documented, the first task of any therapeutic encounter is to engage the family. Develop a comfort level by greeting and engaging everyone in the family, individually. Introduce yourself and ask about that person's experience. No one gets to speak for that person. Include children of all ages who otherwise are not part of this process and hence often do not feel like an integral part of the family system. Move to easy direct eye contact position, especially if the child is quite small. Each person, in his/her own time, provides a perspective and experience in how the family is relating. Promote understanding, encourage constructive disagreement, and support acceptance and family support. Begin by not allowing interruptions or insults or disrespect of any kind. Note contradictions; always make sure that the person who is interrupted is able to complete his/her statement. In addition, help the family to compile a list of wanted and unwanted consequences of the circumstances and/or trauma, for example, the family stays together or separates. Encourage disclosure, reflection, and family working together for the family.

Reframe the Problem

After the family system functioning becomes more clear, promote new rules to build communication and establish a safe space for self-disclosure. Shift attention from "victim" to "survivor" to "family system." Recognize and redirect and/or do not allow victim blaming. Use education, psychoeducation, and so forth, to help family members communicate "move toward forgiveness. . . . " Families need to become aware of the stress of migration and the recurring feelings of helplessness of the migrant to find work that pays well and consistently. Identify how family members feel and how this translates into behavior. Identify family members who feel inadequate to help or feel like failures because they didn't see the problem. Help the survivor(s) realize the individual family members may not be avoiding, dislike, or blame them but rather feel inadequate to the task and unable to help. Reframe tragedy as challenge for the family to work on together.

Assess the ability of the individual and family system to sit with the trauma and based on the assessment, facilitate recall of all facets of the trauma. Clarify insights. Correct distortions and blaming. Support new, more generous perspectives. Identify ideas with the most endorsement. Acknowledge supportive explanations. It is critical to allow the family to struggle with the various views of the trauma and its wake and the collective meanings for family members.

Review the specific objectives of the work and encourage family members to recognize their accomplishments. Guide family members to articulate the meaning of the trauma. Reach out to extended family; use social media, an often-critical component toward family connection. Encourage family and extended family to stay informed about each other by using social media. If possible, set up an appointed computer in your agency that is available for client sessions and client use to maintain family communication and connection.

Ask each family member to answer four survivor questions:

1. What happened?

2. Why did it happen?

3. Why did I, myself, act as I did throughout this ordeal?

4. If something equally as challenging happens in the future, how do I want to cope in the future? How will I cope better?

Help families rethink the definitions of victim, villain, and hero.

Construct an Integrative Model for Healing

As the family becomes stronger, the individual and family unit need to discuss a theory of healing. What behaviors, discussions, and/or methods do individual family members think would facilitate the assimilation of this intergenerational phenomenon that has impacted the family? Families are remarkably creative in discovering methods to heal and to incorporate events into the fabric of the families' life. For example, some families might attend a grave site together or visit a memorial to the holocaust and/or travel to the site of migration or entry and collectively share the remembering and healing. Others might have a family dinner where toasts and laughter engage the family system with the events of the family life, thereby promising renewal but not forgetting. The methods are endless and dependent only on the needs and wishes of the family system.

Prepare and Close

The understanding of different responses and meaning systems and the repair of differences is the beginning of new familial relationships. Stress this beginning and engage the family members in a discussion of how each would like their new relationships to unfold, what they will do together, and how they will manage future differences. Preparation in maintaining open, engaged relationships is critical to the final phase of the work, along with providing closure to the current process. Facilitate family members in a discussion about what this process meant to them.

CONCLUSIONS AND IMPLICATIONS

Although questions remain about the reality of and benefit to exploring intergenerational transmission of distress and/or trauma, there is little doubt that facilitating open and engaged family relationships is useful and can be supportive for family members. Providers must be prepared for the difficult work of facilitating conversation among family members about issues that they may not have ever considered or discussed before. The potential outcome is to build strong family support in the face of overwhelming experiences and heavy responsibilities. Concurrently, providers need to identify and support individual and familial resilience so these resources need only be remembered and drawn from when confronted with adversity.

There is a need for much more complex research methods in order to clarify the presence of phenomenon, for example, intergenerational transmission of trauma, and the utility of specific intervention methods. Clearly there is interest in knowing more and in acquiring the skills to help families regain balance and control and provide needed support.

REFLECTIVE QUESTIONS

1. Micro practice: How would you prepare yourself as a practitioner to ask questions that will be sensitive and difficult for the family to address?

2. Micro practice: In what ways will you prepare yourself to manage your own family of origin messages when working with immigrant and refugee families that might have similar or overlapping family histories?

3. Macro practice: What methods of advocacy for clients and practitioners would you employ within your agency?

SUMMATIVE POINTS

- Collective societies rely heavily on the organizing and supportive unit of the family.

- Family systems theories facilitate family members to have more constructive communication, more enhancing interpersonal interaction patterns, and provide a more supportive family environment.

- The potential for having had a traumatic experience is great in immigrant and refugee family systems, making it a relevant question to be asked.

REFERENCES

Bacallao, M. L., & Smokowski, P. R. (2007). The costs of getting ahead: Mexican family system changes after immigration. *Family Relations, 56*(1), 52–66.

Barker, R. (2016). Social justice. In C. Franklin (Ed.). *Encyclopedia of social work* (p. 1). New York: National Association of Social Workers Press and Oxford University Press.

Bhugra, D., & Becker, M. A. (2005). Migration, cultural bereavement and cultural identity. *World Psychiatry, 4*(1), 18–24.

Bowen, M. (n.d.). Multigenerational family therapy: Multigenerational transmission process. www.thebowencenter.org

Bowen, M. (1978). *Family therapy in clinical practice*. New York: Jason Aronson.

Breton, M. (2011). Citizenship consciousness, nonbounded solidarity, and social justice. *Social Work with Groups, 31*, 35–50.

British Broadcasting Company. (2016, March 4). *Migrant crisis: Migration to Europe explained in seven charts*. www.bbc.com/news/world-Europe-34131911

Brown, L. (2008). *Cultural competence in trauma therapy: Beyond the flashback*. Washington, DC: American Psychological Association.

Cardoso, J. B., & Thompson, S. J. (2010). Common themes of resilience among Latino immigrant families: A systematic review of the literature. *Families in Society, 91*(3), 257–265.

Cohen, E. (2010). A social worker's tool kit for working with immigrant families: Healing the damage, trauma and immigrant families in the child welfare system. www.americanhumane.org

Cook, B., Alegria, M., Lin J. Y., & Guo, J. (2009). Pathways and Correlates Connecting Latinos' Mental Health with Exposure to the United States. *American Journal of Public Health, 99*, 2247–2254.

Danieli, Y. (1998). *Intergenerational handbook of multigenerational legacies of trauma*. New York: Plenum.

De Haan, L., Hawley, D., & Deal, J. (2002). Operationalizing family resilience: A methodological strategy. *The American Journal of Family Therapy, 30*, 275–291.

Dekel, R., & Goldblatt, H. (2008). Is there intergenerational transmission of trauma? The case of combat veterans' children. *American Journal of Orthopsychiatry, 78*(3), 281–290. doi: 10.1037/a0013955.

Drachman, D. (1992). A stage-of-migration framework for service to immigrant populations. *Social Work, 37*(1), 68–72.

Falicov, C. J. (2007). Working with transnational immigrants: Expanding meanings of family, community, and culture. *Family Process, 46*(2), 157–171.

Falicov, C. J. (2015). *Latino families in therapy* (2nd ed.). New York: Guilford.

Figley, C. R. (1988). A five-phase treatment of post-traumatic stress disorder in families. *Journal of Traumatic Stress, 1*(1), 127–141.

Figley, C. R. (1995). *Compassion fatigue*. New York: Routledge.

Fortuna, L. V., Porche, M. V., & Alegria, M. (2008). Political violence, psychosocial trauma, and the context of mental health services among immigrant Latinos in the U.S. *Ethnic Health, 13*(5), 435–463.

Franklin, C. (Ed.). (2016). *Encyclopedia of social work*. New York: Oxford University Press and National Association of Social Workers.

Gitterman, A., & Germain, C. B. (2016). Ecological framework. In C. Franklin (Ed.), *Encyclopedia of social work*. New York: Oxford University Press and National Association of Social Workers.

Hall, J. C. (2016). Narrative therapy. In C. Franklin (Ed.), *Encyclopedia of social work*. New York, NY: Oxford University Press and National Association of Social Workers.

Kirmayer, L. J., Narasiah, L., Munoz, M., Rashid, M., Ryder, A. G., Guzder, J., Hassan, G., Rousseau, C., & Pottie, K. (2011). Common mental health problems in immigrants and refugees: General approach in primary care. *Canadian Medical Association Journal, 183*(12), E959–E967. doi: 10.1503/cmaj.090292

Kuperminc, G. P., Jurkovic, G. J., & Casey, S. (2009). Relation of filial responsibility to the personal and social adjustment of Latino adolescents from immigrant families. *Journal of Family Psychology, 23*(1), 14–22.

Lev-Wiesel, R. (2007). Intergenerational transmission of trauma across three generations: A preliminary study. *Qualitative Social Work, 6*(1), 75–94.

Lietz, C. A. (2006). Uncovering stories of family resilience: A mixed methods study of resilient families, part 1. *Families in Society, 87*(4), 575–581.

Lin, N. J., & Suyemoto, K. L. (2016). So you, my children, can have a better life: A Cambodian American perspective on the phenomenology of intergenerational communication about trauma. *Journal of Aggression, Maltreatment & Trauma, 25*(4), 400–420.

McGuire, S., & Martin, K. (2007). Fractured migrant families: Paradoxes of hope and devastation. *Family Community Health,* (3), 178–188. doi: 10.1097/01.FCH.0000277761.31913.f3

Minuchin, S. (n.d.). *Structural family therapy.* www.minuchincenter.org

Mullan-Gonzalez, J. (2012). Slavery and the intergenerational transmission of trauma in inner city African American male youth: A model program—from the cotton fields to the concrete jungle. *Dissertation Abstracts International* DAI-B 74/02(E).

Nagata, D. K., & Cheng, W. J. Y. (2003). Intergenerational communication of race-related trauma by Japanese American former internees. *American Journal of Orthopsychiatry, 73*(3), 266–278. http://www.nimh.nih.gov/health/topics/post-traumatic-stress-disorder-ptsd/index.shtml

Nichols, M. P. (2008). *Family therapy: Concepts and methods* (8th ed.). Boston, MA: Pearson Publishers.

Nichols, M. P. (2011). *Family therapy: Concepts and methods* (10th ed.). Boston, MA: Pearson Publishers.

Nichols, M. P. (2016). *Family Therapy: Concepts and methods* (11th ed.). Boston, MA: Pearson Publishers.

Ornelas, I. J., & Perreira, K. M. (2011). The role of migration in the development of depressive symptoms among Latino immigrant parents in the USA. *Social Science & Medicine, 73*(8), 1169–1177.

Parra Cardona, J. R., Bulock, L. A., Imig, D. R., Villarruel, F. A., & Gold, S. J. (2006). "Trabajando duro todos los dias": Learning from the life experiences of Mexican-Origin migrant families. *Family Relations, 55,* 361–375.

Parsons, R. J., & East, J. (2013). Empowerment practice. In C. Franklin (Ed.), *Encyclopedia of social work* (pp. 1–9). New York: Oxford University Press and National Association of Social Workers.

Pelton, L. H. (2001). Social justice and social work. *Journal of Social Work Education, 37*(3), 433–439.

Perreira, K. M., & Ornelas, I. (2013). Painful passages: Traumatic experiences and post-traumatic stress among U.S. immigrant Latino adolescents and their primary caregivers. *International Migration Review, 47*(4), 976–1005.

Phipps, R. M., & Degges-White, S. (2014). Application: Theory to culturally competent practice. *Journal of Multicultural Counseling and Development, 42,* 174–187.

Pine, B. A., & Drachman, D. (2005). Effective child welfare practice with immigrant and refugee children and their families. *Child Welfare*, *84*(5), 537–62.

Rasheed, J. M., Rasheed, M. N., & Marley, J. A. (2011). *Family therapy: Models and techniques*. Thousand Oaks, CA: Sage.

Saleebey, D. (1992). The strengths perspective in social work practice. New York: Longman.

Saleebey, D. (1996). The strengths perspective in social work practice: Extensions and cautions. *Social Work*, *41*, 296–305.

Saleebey, D. (Ed.). (2002). *The strengths perspective in social work practice* (3rd ed.). Boston, MA: Allyn & Bacon.

Shields, S. A. (2008). Gender: An intersectionality perspective. *Sex Roles*, *59*, 301–311.

Sirikantraporn, K. (2016). Introduction: Multicultural perspectives of intergenerational transmission of trauma. *Journal of Aggression, Maltreatment & Trauma*, *25*(4), 347.

Stith, S. M., Rosen, K. H., Middleton, K. A., Busch, A. L., Lundeberg, K., & Carlton, R. P. (2000). The intergenerational transmission of spouse abuse: A meta-analysis. *Journal of Marriage and Family*, *62*(3), 640–654.

Walsh, F. (1998). *Strengthening family resilience*. New York: Guilford Press.

Walsh, F. (2002). A family resilience framework: Innovative practice applications. *Family Relations*, *51*, 130–137.

Walsh, F. (2003). Family resilience: A framework for clinical practice. *Family process*, *42*(1), 1–18.

Weiss, M., & Weiss, S. (2000). Second generation to Holocaust survivors: Enhanced differentiation of trauma transmission. *American Journal of Psychotherapy*, *54*(3), 372–386.

Zing, J., & Batalova, J. (2016, April 14). Frequently requested statistics on immigrants and immigration in the United States. *Migration Policy Institute*. www.migrationpolicy.org/article/frequently-requested-statistics-immigrants-and-immigration-united-states

Chapter 9

SUPPORT AND PSYCHOEDUCATIONAL GROUPS FOR IMMIGRANT WOMEN

A Working Model

MARTA LUNDY, PATRICK RODGERS, CELESTE SÁNCHEZ, ANDREW EGAN, AND SHIRLEY SIMON

This chapter is dedicated to the women who lived through
difficult and disruptive migration experiences and
have shared their stories so that we might learn.

ABSTRACT

The purpose of this chapter is to provide an overview of Mexican women's experiences of migration, both historically and currently, and to describe a specific group work model focusing on Latinas who have migrated to the United States. The aim of the groups is to enhance women immigrants' knowledge about core concepts of individual and family communication, self-esteem and assertiveness, domestic violence, conflict and resolution, and the faces of migration and also to enable them to process the impact of their own migration experience. In addition, the goal of the group is to enable each woman to develop a personal social support system within her own community. Specific examples of these support groups are shared.

> **KEY TERMS**
>
> immigrant, solidarity, accompaniment, support group, self-help group, women's group, Latinas

All questions should be referred to Marta Lundy, PhD, LCSW, Professor, School of Social Work, Loyola University Chicago, Maguire Hall, 1 East Pearson, Chicago, IL. 60611, mlundy@luc.edu

- Describe the impact of migration on Latina women.
- Describe the history of an effective group modality for immigrant women.
- Identify and describe the process of an effective group modality for immigrant Latinas.
- Identify and describe the topics for weekly group presentations.

"Attempting to liberate the oppressed without their reflective participation in the act of liberation is to treat them as objects that must be saved from a burning building" (Freire, 1968/1997).

In the United States, there are 41.3 million immigrants or the equivalent of 13% of the overall population (Zong & Batalova, 2015). More than 20 million immigrant women and girls live in the United States, with Mexico as the single largest country of origin for female immigrants, approximately 26% (American Immigration Council, 2014). In addition, 5.6 million unauthorized Mexican immigrants were living in the United States in 2014 (Krogstad & Passel, 2015). Although the influx of immigrants from Mexico has decreased in recent years, nonetheless, migration from Mexico continues. The decision to migrate is personal and motivated by various individual, familial, and societal reasons. For many migrants, their economic and political insecurity, and/or general exposure to violence is so severe that leaving their country of origin is one of the few options for their individual and family well-being (Pew Hispanic Research, 2015). Migration journeys can be as simple as getting on a plane or riding a bus, but more often they are arduous, dangerous, and sometimes traumatic. Once resettled, integrating into a new society presents many cultural, emotional, linguistic, social, legal, and financial challenges and demands the immediate attention of immigrants and their families. The barriers and realities they face throughout their migration journey are not subdued once they arrive in the United States. The migration process and the various difficulties, traumas, and adjustments that occur often are the last issues to be addressed when women and/or families are locating housing, finding employment, and managing English fluency, among other everyday activities. Generally, if at all, the migration experience is allocated attention long after all of the daily living issues have been attended to, sometimes it is years before the migration experience is fully discussed, sometimes it is never given attention again. Current research suggests that these experiences may become intergenerational trauma, with the unspoken traumatic experiences in the migration journey of the parent becoming a hazard felt by the youth in the family (Gonzalez, Lord, Rex-Kill, & Francois, 2012; Perreira & Ornelas, 2013). Clearly, having the opportunity to process, work through, and be comforted as you recall that experience is a useful endeavor.

Social workers and other mental health providers can be important agents of change for immigrant populations. Group work is an ideal modality for social workers to help cultivate a safe space, allowing immigrants to reflect and share their migration narratives while learning new skills to understand and manage thoughts and feelings, while discussing the difficulties they encounter integrating into their new communities and host countries. Facilitated support groups for women immigrants enable the development of social support, psychoeducational learning, and mutual solidarity through members' shared experiences. In order to demonstrate the use of groups with immigrants, we will discuss the application of *El Manual de Salud Emocional* (*The Emotional Health Manual*), a guide originally developed to address the emotional well-being of Mexican women affected by migration. The text is highly adaptable and has been used transnationally in guiding support groups at varying stages of migration and resettlement adjustment. For this chapter, we will first discuss the history of the manual and its use in the United States, the relevance of group work for this population, including a brief explanation of the types and developmental stages of groups, and finally, the specific adaptation and revision of the manual for use in a host country, most specifically in the United States.

HISTORY AND FOCUS OF *EL MANUAL DE SALUD EMOCIONAL (MANUAL OF EMOTIONAL HEALTH)*

El Manual de Salud Emocional was published by Jesuit Migrant Services in Mexico City, in 2011. It was created as an intervention to inform and empower Mexican women who remained in their communities of origin while their husbands and loved ones migrated, typically to the United States. The manual is focused on creating mutual aid and solidarity among group members as well as reflecting the central tenets of Jesuit principles, accompaniment, and hospitality. The groups that have been provided in Mexico and the United States have as their primary focus a sense of welcome and service to the needs of women. Accompaniment is a healing partnership that emerges through the mutual recognition of the inherent human dignity between a helping person and those who suffer; it arises when space is given to talk, share, and simply be (O'Neill & Sophn, 1998). "In accompaniment work, we move beyond a mere delivery of services through offering companionship, active listening and solidarity, focusing on individual's personal needs and concerns" (Hampson, Crea, Calvo, & Alvarez, 2014, p. 7).

As the mechanism for achieving the group goals, the original manual addresses 17 themes around psycho-emotional and intrafamilial health, leading to individual and group affirmation and empowerment. Jaqueline Garcia Salamanca, a Mexican psychologist, implemented this emotional health program by collaboratively authoring the manual with and for women in rural communities affected by migration in Mexico.

The themes of the manual have been successfully implemented in rural areas of Mexico, in the states of Puebla and Veracruz. Community organizers and advocates like Jaqueline Garcia from Jesuit Migrant Services, Mexico City, brought the manual to rural communities and elicited the support of local governments, churches, and community networks. Most importantly, they invited and welcomed local women to join the group. The group progressed, and bonds of trust were formed as each member shared her experiences with the others. The women bravely stood together in solidarity as they were witness to each other's journey of healing from the effects of migration and feeling "left behind." The groups were formed for women who, because of the migration of their partners, husbands, and sons, were often overwhelmed when left with the tasks of a sudden role reversal of traditional gender norms—for example, single parenting, household responsibilities, and family and community expectations. They were able to find a community as the result of the group, and this experience empowered the women to gain resources from one another, name their emotional and interpersonal experiences, and find their own voice.

For many, the group allowed them to embrace/experience a sense of leadership. After the successful completion of the seventeen themed sessions, key members wished to continue their participation in the group. The manual provides a model for replication of the support group experience. Although it will not be discussed in this chapter, there is an additional group component identified as *Train the Trainers*, a 15-week group that teaches women with nascent leadership skills how to effectively respond to and facilitate future community groups. Women who were positively affected by their group experience can become trained and start new groups for other women in the same or in a neighboring community and thus offer the benefit of the groups to other remote areas affected by migration. This model was effective in Mexico in part because the activities in the manual resonated with the population—that is, each week followed a specific theme and with it were interactive games and well known playground songs that were familiar to all of the women. These activities helped nurture the group experience as well as provide fun. The manual was introduced to social workers in the United States. We saw this manual as a relevant, effective tool, because the process of migration is extensive. Just as migration has an emotional toll on those in communities of origin, those involved in migration journeys and trying to resettle endure stress of their own. The groups and the activities presented in the manual were seen as a way to help women along the continuum of migration to address the effects of migration, reduce isolation, and provide a nurturing community to help women work through many of the experiences in migration. The goal of the manual is to facilitate groups that provide a shared space where women can empower themselves and other members, especially because many of them have endured isolation and the inability to express their emotions. Participating in a group offers the women the ability to develop a sense of community.

REVISIONS OF MANUAL FOR IMMIGRANT WOMEN IN THE UNITED STATES

This manual, developed in Mexico, by and for Mexicans, has now been revised and adapted for use with immigrant Latina women who have migrated to a host country, specifically Chicago, Illinois, United States. Support groups based on this manual have been implemented for women who have migrated by themselves or with children and families, are new or older arrivals, and have varying immigration histories and statuses. The groups in the United States have been support groups with facilitators, but the ultimate goal is for these groups to develop into self-help groups with peer leadership, as they have in Mexico. The manual's content is applicable for other immigrant groups with limited adaptation required. This adaptation and implementation for a different population and/or country and in a different stage of migration was possible after the methodology was analyzed, revised, and constructed to fit within the given context and needs of the potential members of a group.

Social work principles of client self-determination, person-in-context, and advocacy contribute to the core philosophy of the text. Critical to this approach is the acknowledgment of the strengths and resilience of the women who are part of the group, who have made new lives for themselves and their families, and who continue to navigate a host country that often is characterized by discrimination and oppression. In addition, the manual is grounded in the Jesuit concepts of accompaniment—that is, a healing partnership that emerges through the mutual recognition of the inherent human dignity between a helping person and those who suffer; it arises when space is given to talk, share, and simply be (O'Neill & Sophn, 1998). "In accompaniment work, we move beyond a mere delivery of services through offering companionship, active listening and solidarity, focusing on individual's personal needs and concerns" (Hampson, Crea, Calvo, & Alvarez, 2014, p. 7). These groups also were founded on and included principles of solidarity—that is, working toward the same goals, collaboration with mutual trust and respect without an imbalance of power in the relationship, and empowerment and the identification of personal agency—that is, each person has strengths, although there are times when we need to be reminded.

The manual and its methodology is based on Freire's (1968/1997) popular education as well as Gestalt and family theories, psychoeducational principles, and support group methodology. This allows the development and implementation of themes and sessions that are linked with familiar emotions, communication styles, mourning, and emotional health issues. This methodology is interwoven with time for activities, collective reflection, and "self-realization," moments that enable the women to process personal issues and allow the expression of feelings and experiences.

The manual was adapted and revised over a two-year period. During that time, we provided groups and learned from the women in the groups in order to be effective with women who have migrated to a host country. This process provided the collaborators with insight into instructions, activities, and concepts that needed to be adapted or revised for clarification and effectiveness. The themes remained primarily the same psycho-emotional, educational, and intra-familial mental health issues as in the original version; however, one chapter was deleted, and four additional chapters focusing on themes relevant to immigrant women living in a destination country were added. The four additional chapters addressed the following topics: assertiveness, detention and deportation, and the face of migration—three particularly relevant themes for immigrant women, and a final consolidation chapter at the end of the manual. In addition, all of the vignettes, activities, and examples were revised and/or adapted for this immigrant population. Since the original manual was completed in 2011, many of the chapters were updated with additional current material. Citations and references also were updated. Although this revision is specific to the United

States, it is intended for easy adaptation for different immigrant populations and for use by other host countries. The original manual went through extensive revisions before being published, in order to identify which activities most resonated with immigrant women in a host country. This process provided the collaborators with insight into instructions, activities, and concepts that needed to be reworked for clarification and effectiveness.

The manual was introduced to social workers in the United States through the Migration Sub-Specialization Program at Loyola University Chicago, School of Social Work, in collaboration with Catholic Charities of Chicago, Offices of Latino Affairs. We believe that this manual can be as effective a tool for immigrant Latinas in a destination country as it has been for Mexican women. The group work model and the manual offer an opportunity for affirmation and support for immigrant Latinas in the United States.

STAGES OF MIGRATION AND RESULTANT DIFFICULTIES

STAGES OF MIGRATION. Because the purpose of these groups is to facilitate a space for women to process and better understand their experiences as affected by the life-changing process of migration, a thorough understanding of the stages of migration is relevant and necessary. Drachman (1992) and Pine and Drachman (2005) identify the multiple stages typical of the migration experience for many families: pre-migration, transit, resettlement, and/or return to country of origin.

In the pre-migration stage, many life-changing decisions are made. Individuals and families come to the conclusion that it is necessary to migrate based on economic imperatives or unstable, dangerous environments (Drachman, 1995; Pine & Drachman, 2005) and also because of the education and health needs of different family members. There is a significant feeling of loss for those who migrate, especially if one person alone will represent the family on this journey. While this may be an accepted family expectation, it is likely to be a frightening and lonely reality. Migrants feel the emotional separation from family and friends, and they are likely to be forlorn about leaving everything that is familiar to them: their family, friends, language, culture, and the familiar streets they walked.

The transit stage encompasses the duration of the journey including the dangers and hardships experienced on the way to a new destination. Lack of safety, security, comfort, insufficient food and water, and economic hardship as well as assault, robbery, mugging, exploitation, and witnessing ferocious brutality are always a potential in this journey, which often results in many failed attempts to arrive in a host country and experiences of trauma.

According to Pine and Drachman (2005), the resettlement stage is complicated. The immigrant is faced with the loss of language and culture; they have to establish new networks in order to find housing and employment, and the demands to accomplish these tasks often are driven by immediate need. The immigrants frequently endure a cold reception, discrimination, and racism from the native residents (Yakushko & Chronister, 2005). If families migrate together, family members adapt or acculturate at their own pace, which may cause tension within the family (Birman & Poff, 2011). For some unauthorized migrants, a return to their country of origin would prohibit a return to the United States or minimally, a rigorous, dangerous return trip to the United States. Oftentimes, immigrants make the decision to return home or are deported. This suggests a complicated discussion at this stage of migration, providing opportunities to fully process the implications of their decisions. Individual, couple, family, and group interventions may be options for navigating the healing process. Mental health professionals must be trained in assessing and providing relevant interventions in order for the individual and family systems to move on, weaving these experiences into the fabric of their lives.

WOMEN'S HISTORICAL AND CURRENT EXPERIENCES OF MIGRATION

Until the early 2000s, migration was typically discussed using the experiences of men and boys (Boyd & Grieco, 2003). Those who migrated were men who were seeking employment opportunities in the North, in order to work and send remittances back home to their families. Often, couples migrated in order to establish work and home and would then send for their children, who remained in their native country with relatives or others. Children were not brought along because of the dangers of the journey and the significant amount of time in the destination country that would be spent on establishing stability. This process greatly impacted the entire family. In general, women's experiences were identified. Women were assumed to maintain traditional gender roles even in the destination country, within the context of expressing concerns for their children, while their own responses and roles historically were not addressed.

To date, there has been a significant amount of scholarship demonstrating the negative impact that migration has on women (O'Mahony & Donnelly, 2007), and how this stress makes them susceptible to a number of physical, social, and emotional vulnerabilities. Yoshihama and Chronister (2005) assert that the immigration experience and accompanying acculturation stress can profoundly impact the social, emotional, and physical health of immigrant women, which untreated can adversely affect them, their families, and communities. In addition, Delara (2016) asserts a similar view,

> The pattern of immigrants' mental well-being seems to differ from a healthy immigrant effect . . . there is a decline in both mental health and physical health of immigrants over time. This decline has been attributed to many factors including socioeconomic status, financial and employment constrains, resettlement and acculturation challenges, multiple responsibilities, discriminatory treatment, and difficulty obtaining services in a timely manner due to language differences. (pp. 1–2)

In response to this, it is essential for mental health practitioners to find meaningful ways to provide support services for this population and in particular to identify the best modality for providing services for affected migrant women. Group work, with its focus on mutual aid, universalization, cohesion, and instillation of hope (Yalom & Leszcz, 2005) is one such modality. Effective groups facilitate connection and invite participation and self-disclosure in a safe, nonjudgmental setting. Gathering together individuals with similar experiences and providing a structure and environment conducive to reflection, candid sharing of feelings, and open, honest discussion is especially relevant for immigrant women, who experience isolation, difference, and a lack of community.

RELEVANCE OF GROUP WORK WITH IMMIGRANT WOMEN

According to Toseland and Rivas (2012), one definition of group work is "Goal-directed activity with small treatment and task groups, aimed at meeting socioemotional needs and accomplishing tasks. This activity is directed toward individual members of a group and to the group as a whole within a system of service delivery" (p. 11). There are a variety of types of groups, including self-help, support, psychoeducational, and remedial-therapy groups, addressing issues such as depression, anxiety, substance use, domestic violence, or parenting. Another outcome of effective groups is to "develop leadership skills for members, to take increasing responsibility for the group's development. Further, groups can learn to change the social environment, including helping members to gain greater control over the organizations and communities that affect their lives" (Toseland & Rivas, 2012, p. 11). Each type of group can be used for specific purposes based on the needs of the group participants and the skills and experience of the group leader and/or facilitator.

For the purposes of working with immigrant women, we chose an adapted support group model. This type of group provides an organizational structure and a facilitator to guide and focus the group. It is characterized by the facilitator's willingness to step back as each woman becomes more engaged, comfortable, and skilled in stating her own concerns and experiences and discussing them with other group members. In fact, the facilitator in these groups encourages the women to "own their own group" by encouraging them to take increasingly greater responsibility for the group functioning. As the group members become more comfortable and empowered, the facilitator assumes a less central position and allows the members to take a larger role in directing and engaging in the group activities. This type of group aims to enhance cohesion and mutual aid among its members. Participants are encouraged to take what they have learned from the support group and initiate, develop, and lead self-help groups in their home communities. Planned for use in the United States in the fall of 2016, there will be a *Train the Trainers* group available for all women who have completed the groups and who want to become a facilitator for a group.

Group work is an effective intervention strategy that can help accomplish the therapeutic goals of reducing immigration stress. Gonzalez, Lord, Rex-Kill, and

Francois (2016) suggest that group work reduces social isolation faced by many immigrants, while strengthening solidarity among its members. Research suggests that women acculturate better when they have social support networks that provide a space to share their stories, be heard, and establish a sense of belonging, mutual care, and understanding (Rayle, Sand, Brucato, & Ortega, 2006). Group work provides the structure and space for social networks to emerge. For many Latinas, attending a group is comfortable and familiar, similar to the gatherings of the extended family. It is best understood using the concept of *familismo*, the reliance and trust in the family system. Across Latino cultures, the family is of prime importance and the group can become an extension of the family (Forehand & Kotchisk, 1996; Santiago-Rivera et al., as cited in Rayle et al., 2006, p. 8). In addition, group members can become a social support network, a place of solidarity and can "provide an opportunity for members to reflect on their shared migration experiences to the United States" (Gonzalez, Lord, Rex-Kill, & Francois, 2012, p. 18). There may be no better outlet for immigrants to reflect upon and discuss these experiences.

When leading a group for immigrant women, practitioners should carefully consider and examine the theoretical framework in order to achieve the purposes of the group. The theoretical framework guides the group in examining issues of migration and its impact on the women migrants. For example, Yakushko and Chronister (2005) suggest using Bronfenbrenner's ecological framework to understand the many different levels on which the process of migration affects the individual. This framework helps to identify the strengths of the individual and to understand other systems that intersect with their acculturation process including families, neighbors and neighborhoods, communities, governments, and relevant laws. Schiller (1997) suggests using a feminist framework, asserting that group development is typically different for women than men. Her relational model stresses that women, through sharing common experiences and building trust and cohesion, come together and empathize with each other before they risk engaging in conflict. This is said to be unlike male groups, which may experience conflict first, before mutual aid is established. Knowledge of Schiller's model of group development is important when working with immigrant Latinas, because it emphasizes the unique relational needs of women and the importance of trust and connection prior to risking confrontation or conflict. Group facilitators, who appreciate this model, will spend time early in the group's development encouraging participation, cohesion, and emotional safety.

When planning the structure of the group, the frequency and length of sessions, dates, times, and typical agendas all need to be addressed. Each of the groups for immigrant women meets once a week for one and a half hours. This allows adequate time for check-in, presentation of a theme, group activity, summary, and closure. Usually, there is one theme presented each week. The participants in the group, both facilitators and members, determine exactly when the groups will meet, identifying the time that best fits everyone's schedule. Because refreshments can enhance socialization and help create a welcoming atmosphere, food and beverages are usually available at group meetings. The type and funding of refreshments are discussed and determined by the members of each group, thereby encouraging group decision-making and demonstrating the group's ability to act as a cohesive unit.

TOPICS AND ACTIVITIES FOR THE IMMIGRANT WOMEN'S GROUPS

The manual is divided into 19 themes, with a final 20th week for consolidation of all of the material (See Table 9.1 Content of Manual). Each group covers nine or 10 themes over an eight-week period of weekly sessions with a final, ninth week for assessment and celebration. A nine-week model was selected because of student availability to facilitate the groups and participant availability to attend. The Latina women/mothers have family obligations—for example, family gatherings, holiday festivities, summer responsibilities—as well as employment and other activities that circumscribe their availability. In addition, the groups are all conducted in predominantly Latino populated areas of the city. The groups are intended to be conveniently located and easily accessible for the participants. See Table 9.1 for details in the *Manual of Emotional Health* that are useful in working with immigrant women groups.

At the beginning and end of each group session, the facilitators ask each woman to identify her feelings. We have two purposes for this request. We want the women to examine a list of feelings and enlarge their knowledge and identification of their own feelings throughout the group process (see Table 9.3 Feelings List), and we want to capture whether there is a change in how the women feel and the words they choose

Table 9.1 Table of Contents of *Manual of Emotional Health*
MANUAL DE SALUD EMOCIONAL (Spanish / English) Manual of Emotional Health
Tema 1 Qué es un GRUPO DE AUTOAYUDA (GDA) y cómo funciona Theme 1 What is a SELF-HELP GROUP (GDA) and how does it work?
Tema 2 Costos emocionales de la migración Theme 2 Emotional costs of migration
Tema 3 El duelo en la migración (primera parte) Theme 3 The grief in migration (Part 1)
Tema 4 El duelo en la migración (segunda parte) Theme 4 The grief in migration (Part 2)
Tema 5 Manejo de emociones (primera parte) Theme 5 Management of emotions (Part 1)
Tema 6 Manejo de emociones (segunda parte) Theme 6 Management of emotions (Part 2)
Tema 7 Autoestima (primera parte) Theme 7 Self-esteem (Part 1)

(Continued)

(Continued)

Tema 8 Autoestima (segunda parte) Theme 8 Self-esteem (Part 2)
Tema 9 Asertividad Theme 9 Assertiveness
Tema 10 Comunicacion familiar communication Theme 10 Family
Tema 11 Resolución de conflictos dentro de la familia migrante (primera parte) Theme 11 Resolutions for conflicts within the migrant family (Part 1)
Tema 12 Resolución de conflictos dentro de la familia migrante (segunda parte) Theme 12 Resolutions for conflicts within the migrant family (Part 2)
Tema 13 Maltrato infantile/child abuse Theme 13 Gender violence
Tema 14 Rostros de la violencia Theme 14 Faces of violence
Tema 15 El círculo de la violencia y centros de asistencia Theme 15 Cycle of violence and resources
Tema 16 Sexualidad y derechos sexuales Theme 16 Sexuality and sexual rights
Tema 17 Deportación y detención Theme 17 Deportation and detention
Tema 18 Rostros de migracion Theme 18 Face of migration
Tema 19 Consolidación y Rescisión Theme 19 Consolidation & termination

to describe their affective experience over time. We also ask the group facilitators to respond to a series of questions in a confidential questionnaire at the end of each group session, in order to reflect on the purpose and functioning of the group. This provides a basis for discussion after each facilitated group during a debriefing session with facilitators once a week with the faculty supervisor. Students facilitate one and sometimes two groups. (See Table 9.4 for Facilitator Reflection.)

The final meeting for the participants is a volunteer focus group, in which the women discuss what the group meant to them and share feedback, suggestions, and comments on what was most and least important to them and what they might like included or omitted from the content of the groups. Following the focus group, there is a celebration that includes a certificate of attendance for each member of the group.

Table 9.2 Developmental Stages of Group Work

Stages	Purpose & Plan
Stage 1	Planning: Define group purpose, determine location, membership size, and procedures. Assess current research, establish evaluation, & monitor systems.
Stage 2	Beginning: Introduce group, establish member inclusion, define purpose, set goals.
Stage 3	Assessment: Monitor both individual and group process. Collect data, if relevant. Provide time for reflection and writing activities.
Stage 4	Middle: Continue preparation, empower group members, monitor group progress and achievement.
Stage 5	Ending: Prepare for planned and unplanned termination and early termination, discuss feelings at end, learn from members, and make relevant referrals.
Stage 6	Evaluation: Data review, review each group phase, write case study. Analyze if purpose was achieved through measurements.

Group Facilitators

All of the groups but two have been conducted in Spanish by Mexican psychology exchange students who come every semester from Iberoamericano University in Mexico City to complete the required community service work at Catholic Charities of Chicago, Immigration Services, in collaboration with Loyola University School of Social Work, Chicago. Two additional groups were conducted in Spanish by a social work student, and these groups became the first to complete all 20 weeks of the manual and have women who are eager to become group facilitators. Dr. Graciela Polanco, from the Department of Psychology at Iberoamericana University, has a long history of collaboration with Loyola University Chicago, School of Social Work and Catholic Charities of the Archdiocese of Chicago. She informs students about the opportunity for this learning experience and decides which students are prepared and have enough experience to complete this work. Dr. Maria Vidal de Haymes, creator of the Migration Studies subspecialization, Loyola School of Social Work, provides an orientation for students throughout the semester, including various speakers on the topics of migration, history of Mexicans in migration, and an overview of the sociodemographic, economic, cultural, political, and social issues that propel Mexicans and others to migrate from their native country to a host country. Training and supervision of the group facilitators and the research on immigrant women's groups has been conducted by Dr. Marta Lundy, cocreator of the Migration Studies subspecialization, Loyola

Table 9.3 Feelings List

FEELINGS (n = 67)

Aggressive	Naughty	Confident
Agony	Indifferent	Happy
Anxious	Overwhelmed	Cheerful
Arrogant	Pessimistic	Optimistic
Bored	Depressed	Thankful
Cautious	Other	Prudent
Cold	Alone	Terrified
Concentrated	Humble	Exhausted
Confident	Surprised	Interested
Curious	Satisfied	Cheerful
Appeased	Meditative	Hysterical
Confused	Calm	Revengeful
Determined	Fearful	Innocent
Disappointed	In love	Embarrassed
Upset	Stubborn	Injured/hurt
Undecided	Sad	Horrified
Envious	Optimistic	Guilty
Bitter	Prudent	Negative
Ashamed	Frustrated	Ecstatic
Enraged	Intrigued	Tired
Hurt	Distraught	Sore
Incredulous	Thankful	
Desperate	Paranoid	

School of Social Work. These students have experience conducting some groups; knowledge about issues of psychology, trauma, isolation, and family separation; and provide a familiar, welcoming presence for the Mexican immigrant women. It appears to be a meaningful experience for the women.

Table 9.4 List of Substantive Area, Psychoeducational Component, Activities, and Reflection

Each week has a beginning and ending discussion of the previous week, and facilitators ask the women to reflect on what they learned and how they are feeling at that time. Those are critical components, although for brevity they are not included on the table.

Theme	Topic	Activities	
1 Self-help	Welcome, getting to know one another	Balloon activity: Each member inflates a balloon, members attempt to keep their own and all other balloons afloat. (n = 1)	DISCUSSION AND REFLECTION
	Principles & process of self-help group		
2 Emotional health	Importance of self-care and emotional health	Self-care: Members brainstorm self-care definitions and learn about different types of self-care. (n = 3)	
3 & 4 Grief of migration	Stages of acculturation	The scream: Members are invited to scream as loud as possible. How do we experience grief and identify acculturation stress? (Theme 3, n = 2) (Theme 4, n = 1)	
	Emotional effects of migration		
5 & 6 Manage emotions	Identifying and managing emotions	Diagram of emotions: Determine emotions of certain characters. Managing emotions: Use clay to let go of negative emotions. (Theme 5, n = 2) (Theme 6, n = 2)	
	Conflict resolution skills		
7 & 8 Self-esteem	Strengthen self-esteem	Luggage for my journey: List positive aspects of personal life that you would take on a "journey" inside a picture of luggage. Reflect on characteristics of empowerment and past experiences. (Theme 7, n = 3) (Theme 8, n = 1)	
	Right to have control over your future and to transform your life		
9 Communication	Types of communication	The drop that shed the cup: Facilitator pours water into cups until member says stop. Cup overflows if member doesn't speak up. (n = 2)	
	Assertive communication strategies		

(Continued)

	DISCUSSION AND REFLECTION	DISCUSSION AND REFLECTION
10 Family relations	Communication patterns in families Promote healthy family relationships	Sale of ridiculous things: Each member must attempt to "sell" their ridiculous product to the rest of the group. ($n = 3$)
11 & 12 Conflict resolution	Family conflicts caused by migration Conflict resolution in families	Conflicts in migration: Members draw picture of personal conflict. The rope of conflict: Members link arms back to back and attempt to pick up small piles of candy without separating. (Theme 11, $n = 2$) (Theme 12, $n = 1$)
13 Gender violence	Types of gender violence Attitudes that promote/prevent violence	Double turn: Members are given two pictures of a clock, on one they mark their schedule and on the other that of their partner. ($n = 3$)
14 Face of violence	Types of violence Effects of the cycle of violence	The war: Members make balls of paper and throw them at each other while facilitators observe their behavior. ($n = 3$)
15 Cycle of violence	Interpersonal interactions of power and control in relationships	Cycle of violence: Members form a circle around one member in the middle and do not allow the person in the middle to exit. ($n = 6$)
16 Sexual rights	Sexual and reproductive rights Promote healthy sexual relationships	Sexuality myths: Divide members into two groups and facilitators will read statements. Teams will identify as true or false. ($n = 3$)
17 Detention deportation	Rights regarding detention and deportation	Family care plan: Members divide into groups and develop plans to keep their families safe during detention and deportation. ($n = 2$)
18 Faces of migration	Realities of migration in the United States	The face of migration: Discuss the stages of migration and relevant statistics about migrants in the United States. ($n = 1$)
19 Conclusion	Overview of the themes covered Consolidation and termination	Which ending do you choose? Members divide into small groups and act out different endings to the same story. ($n = 1$)

Group Process

The support groups are closed groups—that is, there are consistent, ongoing members and no new participants are added after the second week. We include the second week because it is not unusual for a woman to want to bring her friend, neighbor, or cousin to the group after attending the first meeting. Contracting for attendance and participation is addressed during the first two sessions. This includes a discussion of group purpose, goals, time, length and structure of sessions, expectations of members and facilitators, and issues of confidentiality. All members are asked to pledge to maintain the confidentiality of all other group members, including not talking about members among themselves when others might overhear. Initially, easily mastered activities and discussions are facilitated in order to foster participation and provide a sense of accomplishment and success.

Each group meeting begins with a check-in reflection about the previous group. Women are asked to comment on what they remember, and questions are elicited from the members about their feelings and what they learned. The new topic is introduced, incorporating general and more specific information, activities, and group discussion. Each group ends with a consistent closing reflection about how each woman feels and what she thinks she has learned.

Because the first two meetings may include new members, the definition of a support group with a facilitator is included as well as the importance of affirmation and support for all members is discussed in both the first and second sessions. This reinforces the sense of community and affirmational, empowering support provided by the group members for one another. The first half of the manual covers basic skills, for example, self-esteem, assertiveness, empowerment, family communication as well as the grief and emotional costs of migration and the management of emotions. These topics flow together easily, and provide a common experience for all of the women to share. The second half of the group moves into issues that may be more emotionally evocative and therefore more engaged and invested in the clinical process. By this time, it is anticipated that the women will have developed a cohesive core and a relative level of trust, which allows for a more open and honest discussion of these issues. Topics such as family conflict and conflict resolution, domestic violence, child abuse, sexuality, detention and deportation, and the faces of migration are all included in the final group sessions.

Activities for the Various Themes

As indicated above, each week has a different theme (see Table 9.4 of Topics, Activities, and Reflection). For particularly complex topics, more than one week may be dedicated to cover the relevant issues—for example, domestic violence, the pain of migration, and self-esteem. For each theme, the manual contains several different mini-lectures and accompanying activities. These activities may incorporate verbal and nonverbal interactions, including drawing, writing a reflection, discussing a vignette, or acting out a scenario. All of the activities encourage and facilitate participation by every member of the group, and all are directly relevant to the specific theme. For example, one activity requires each woman to keep her own and everyone else's inflated balloon in the air, demonstrating cooperation and cohesion and highlighting how difficult it is to pay attention to everyone's balloon, symbolically, others' issues and needs, as well as one's own! It is consistently perceived as great fun, while also providing a very instructive example of interdependent caring, which is then discussed in the group. Another activity that seems to have been very meaningful to the group participants has been drawing their remembered personal migration journey. Women keep these drawings to share with their families and describe this activity as very useful and immediately meaningful. Figure 9.2 is a sample of the materials distributed to participants.

Evaluation

To determine the utility of this group work model for immigrant women, we have conducted focus groups during the last session of each nine-week group. We asked the participants to comment on their experiences in the group as well as whether there had been an impact on their lives. The focus groups have been conducted by trained masters in social work students. The focus group follows a specific protocol (see Figure 9.1), and no one has ever seemed upset or disturbed by this protocol. All of the focus group discussions have been audio-recorded, transcribed, and translated by native Spanish speakers. The following are de-identified comments by the women in the focus groups.

Figure 9.1 Developmental Stages of Group Work

Interview Script: Women's Group

Thank you for agreeing to participate in the focus group. As you know from having read the consent form, your participation is voluntary, you can end at any time, and you do not have to answer any questions if you don't want to. I would like to request that you not discuss any responses outside of the focus group, not your own or those of others. Thank you for agreeing to this very important request.

How would you describe your experience in the group?
- Stronger ties among the women?
- Strengthened solidarity among women?
- Better understanding of one another?
- Greater awareness of your own feelings?
- Better able to know and to describe your own feelings?
- More acceptance of your own feelings?

How would you describe the influence of the group experience on your family?
- Did your family notice anything different about you?
- Greater awareness of emotions?
- More tolerance for deep self-reflection?
- Greater personal forgiveness?
- More harmonious relationships with family members?
- More personal conversations with family members?

How would you describe your ability to identify and take care of your own needs?

- Greater awareness of what you want?
- More self-assertiveness?
- Feeling less insecure about your own feelings?

How would you describe what, if anything, you learned about yourself?

- Have you recognized old patterns, worries?
- Have you become more aware of your own emotional needs?
- Have you become more open to your intimate emotional struggles?
- Have you become more accepting of your personal emotional states?

How would you describe your awareness of yourself as a person with rights?

- Awareness of your power to make demands?
- Awareness of the right to access health information?
- Awareness of your right for more information?
- Awareness of your right to express concerns, emotions, desires, needs?

How would you describe any changes about your expectations for women?

- Gender changes in the family?
- Gender changes in the work place?
- Gender changes in your personal views?

How would you describe your interest in leading a similar group for women?

Figure 9.2 Sample Flier Distributed to all Potential Participants of the Women's Group

Estás invitada...

~Mujeres Floreciendo~

Bienestar físico y emocional

The **CATHOLIC CHARITIES** OF THE ARCHDIOCESE OF CHICAGO

Mujeres compartiendo en un lugar para relajarse y dialogar

¿Cuándo?

¿Dónde?¿Duración?

　　　Contaremos con cuidado para sus niños durante la hora y media que dura la reunión

Para registrarse acuda a las oficinas de Caridades Católicas en la oficin

Para más información llame al:

Una colaboración entre Caridades Católicas de la Arquidiócesis de Chicago, Servicio Jesuita Migrante y Universidad Loyola Chicago.

Emotions: "Sometimes one thinks they are wrong or crazy. I learned how to recognize that everyone has emotions; it's just that sometimes we don't know how to identify or express them."

Confidentiality: "For me, I liked many things about the program, beginning with confidentiality. That everything stayed within the group. That, more than anything, was very important to me. You rearticulate at the beginning of every session that what is said here, stays here, that we can't go around divulging information outside of the group. More than anything, this group made me trust that I could say very personal things."

Handling conflict: "That was a very big change, and for the better. Because you have learned how to control your emotions. [I] was quick to anger . . . light up like a cigarette, and this group has been very helpful. Sometimes we don't know how to express ourselves and these classes help you do that."

Understand your rights: "I think we know what our rights are, but we don't believe that we have a right to demand them and to ask for them. Now . . . we recognize what we want and how to say what we want."

Self-esteem: "For me, I liked that theme of, how was it? One should value themselves. That you should value yourself and you should have things very clear and you should think things over. That, self-esteem, that's the word, self-esteem should be higher. That is going to help our families. And for our children, we should help them have better self esteem. That is what I liked about the program."

"Well, before it was all about our children. First, our children, and then our children, and then our husband, and then our children. We never thought about ourselves. What we wanted. Now, now we know how to recognize the necessities that we have. We recognize what we want and how to say what we want."

Communication: "For me, I also liked many things. Personally, I also really liked the class when we identified our pains and our experiences of knowing how to listen, how to understand. When we learned how to express that we wanted to be listened to, that other people try to understand us, and that our spouses support us like we support them. We learned to share more with our children. I believe the last one is very important, that we learn here how to say and to practice all of this with our children. For me, the balance with my children has worked."

Learning to listen: "One has to learn how to treat them [our children]. How to teach them to respect themselves so that in the future they feel secure about themselves."

"Learning to listen to our children. That is very important. Sometimes as parents, we think no one else knows the right thing to do. Our children also have needs; they also need to express how they feel. One has to learn how to treat [children], how to teach them to respect themselves so that in the future, they feel secure about themselves."

Immigration: "When we arrived here from our country, we all passed through a process of adaptation, a process of pain, and sometimes we never realized it. That is what we learned here. And that affected me very much, because you can live through all of that but never realize it. Here the facilitators helped us identify all of these things and many more. They let all of us speak."

DISCUSSION AND IMPLICATIONS FOR FUTURE GROUPS

We have been gratified to learn that the women participants have reported that the themes and discussions are relevant and useful. The preliminary results suggest that the topics resonate with the women's experiences, that the group model feels supportive and productive, and that the effects positively influence their family lives. The secondary purpose of the group, while providing a rich, validating experience for the women who attend, is the hope to identify women who want to complete the *Train the Trainers*, learn to facilitate groups, and then facilitate additional groups in their communities. We have had some success with a few women who are interested in pursuing this opportunity, and we hope to engage more women in this process.

The utility of the groups suggests a wider variety of applications—for example, for youth and possibly for men—and also suggests ways in which we can evaluate the purposes of the groups and develop more methods for the women to identify and evaluate their own needs. Below are some implications of the group model that might be used for future groups and/or research and some projects that we are planning. We continue to process and analyze the group experience for immigrant Latina women, and we plan to continue the groups as long as the women express an interest. Also included is a sample of one adaptation of the manual for a youth group.

Comparative Study Across Groups

The preliminary results are encouraging for the potential utility of these groups and suggest further study and analyses on the use of groups for specific immigrant populations and/or problems. Considering the nature of collective societies of large numbers of populations—for example, immigrants from the Middle East as well as various African, Asian, European, and Eastern Asian countries—and others who share a more collective organizational family structure, it is possible that groups may be useful and also may provide an empowering and affirming experience for many immigrant groups, including youth and men as well as women. In our work we have found that gathering within a group structure is particularly syntonic with traditional cultural activities involving group membership and that this is similar across many immigrant groups. It is our plan to offer these groups to different immigrant women and men and to evaluate if and how these groups are useful for other immigrant populations in the United States. In addition, groups similar to the ones described in this chapter are being conducted in Guadalajara, Mexico. We are evaluating the similarities and differences among the groups, the evolution of the knowledge and experiences of the women, and the methods that are used to conduct the groups. Our goal is to facilitate groups that provide an opportunity to process the experience of migration while developing emotional, situational, and concrete knowledge and support for women who have migration as one of their significant personal and/or familial experiences. We are in discussions with group participants/facilitators in Mexico to develop opportunities for the women in the groups in Mexico and the United States to meet one another and gain a better understanding of their different and similar life experiences with migration.

We think this would be a very powerful and affirming experience.

Inclusion of Additional Topics/Themes

Future plans include the assessment of whether women want more and/or different content in the groups. For example, a couple of women have asked about educational content on sexuality and reproduction in order to be more informed and to know how to approach these topics with their adolescent children. Other topics that we want to include are raising bicultural children, working through problems with blended families, and maintaining connections with transnational families.

Inclusion of Questionnaires and Future Projects

Although we were initially reluctant to ask for personal information, we have since learned that women feel relatively free to provide basic demographic information. We will be able to collect more information. We are encouraged to move toward the use of more instrumentation that might benefit the women. For example, we are planning to use instruments that may provide additional information for women about their current emotional state. For example, *The Danger Assessment for Latinas* (Messing, Amanor-Boadu, Cavanaugh, Glass, & Campbell, 2013) may help to better prepare women for their life circumstances and for facilitators to make referrals. We want to include the

Domestic Violence Safety Plan (NCADV) and questionnaires about depression and self-esteem so women may be able to better identify and evaluate their own progress and request additional support if they realize they need it. We also are planning for the utilization of the group manual by other immigrant groups—for example, Congolese immigrant women. We are excited to increase the potential utility of this manual and to provide additional information for the participants. We are eager to evaluate the utility of these informational additions in the coming year.

AN EXPERIMENT IN ADAPTING THE MANUAL: GROUPS FOR YOUTH AND THE INTERGENERATIONAL TRANSMISSION OF TRAUMA

Considering Bowen's theory, that we are each the product of events that happened in previous generations and that those events impact our current lives, for first generation immigrants this becomes especially important and critical to address. The idea was to use the topics in the manual to help teenagers learn to know themselves better, with the ultimate goal of helping to create a positive self-image and self-identity.

The following example is a brief description of how the manual can be adapted to suit a specific population. We offer this as an example of the adaptability and utility of this manual and the potential for group work. A social work student working in a field placement in Chicago successfully adapted the manual with a male, adolescent immigrant population. Immigrant and first generation youth are greatly affected by the culture of the host country, which creates a dual identity. The youths' individual experience and their collective acculturation traumas were discussed, and cohesion and mutual aide emerged as the result of the manual's group process. Finding one's identity and a place to fit in often become recurring themes in practice with youth. This group began after a student who formally was involved with gang activity and an honor roll student were talking about their experiences coming from Mexico to the United States as undocumented youth. The mutual need and the cohesion between the two individuals was easily apparent. The unfortunate traumas that they had personally faced and those of their parents could then be addressed within the group.

Since the manual had already been adapted for U.S. immigrants, it could be used for group work with youth or teens, all of whom were either immigrants themselves or first generation. The group consisted of six boys, all self-identifying as either Latino or Hispanic, age range from 14 to 17. The theme of managing emotions was chosen for the beginning orientation for the group. The facilitator made appropriate language, time considerations, and activity changes. One example was to change words like husband and wife to mother or father and boyfriend or girlfriend to partner during the activities and to manage the time to fit the school schedule. The vocabulary changes provide a modicum of anonymity for the teens and normalize behaviors. Other beneficial observations are (a) provide food and drink, (b) provide written and verbal description of activities and case studies to accommodate different learning styles and levels, (c) adapt discussion questions to current events relevant to youth, (d) never assume that participants understand the meaning of all the words, and (e) clearly define potentially unfamiliar concepts and thoughts. In addition, critical to the process is for the facilitator to be especially aware of his or her own beliefs, biases, and expectations and to be open to questions and discussion.

In the future, the groups would be separated into two, one for immigrants and another for first generation youth. There are obvious differences that each population faces, starting with the legal restrictions and remedies that are applicable to them. Separating the groups might provide more cohesion that could lead to the teenagers understanding solidarity and alleviate some of the loneliness that they expressed.

The potential utility of these groups and the adaptability of the manual for specific group needs make this method of providing supportive and welcoming services particularly well suited to the various groups, problems, and needs of the vast and diverse immigrants who have joined us in the United States.

REFLECTIVE QUESTIONS

1. Describe the ways that group work is an effective modality for change and healing and when might it be more effective than individual intervention?

2. As a practitioner, how would you get to know the needs of your group in order to implement effective activities for a manualized curricula?

3. Describe how group workers engage individual members in order to contribute to the overall building of mutual aid and solidarity within a group.

4. What are some methods with which supportive group work can encourage members to face their own issues/traumas regarding their migration narratives?

CASE STUDY

Claudia does not have enough money to support her family. She realizes in order to provide for her family she must migrate to the United States. Claudia, 30 years old, is the mother of four young children. She will have to entrust her children with her aging parents. Her husband, Toño, migrated to North Carolina three and a half years ago. He works on a farm earning less than $600 a month and is only able to send back $200 a month, which provides relief for Claudia and her family, but it is not enough.

Claudia is afraid of reuniting with Toño. When he drinks, he hits her. The violence has escalated over time. Claudia depended on their separation for safety and security, but now she feels she must go with him to try to earn money for the family, even if it means she might have to encounter the abuse once more.

Claudia has to cross into the United States without documents. Since Toño migrated north to the United States, the U.S. Border Patrol has intensified, leaving only the most dangerous routes for travel—through the Sonora desert, or the mountainous areas, which are even more remote. Many people get detained in a U.S. prison, even crossing over the first time. Her father knows a coyote, someone who can get Claudia over to the other side. The cost is $9,000, more than it has ever been before. The cost keeps escalating, making the family debt even larger. The fees are more for women, because there is an extra fee added for "rape insurance," although there is no guarantee that the woman won't be raped. Women are extremely vulnerable while in transit.

In addition, crossing the desert is dangerous. There are extreme weather shifts; it is sweltering during the day, often over 100 degrees, and drops to nearly freezing at night. It is impossible to carry enough water for the duration of the trip, making dehydration a very large problem. Claudia also is worried about developing blisters or getting lost. These are factors that could prevent a successful crossing; in fact, they can be lethal.

Claudia has to weigh all of the factors, including leaving her young children behind. Is it worth it? Does she really have a choice?

The content of this vignette is a reality that many women in Mexico face.

Macro Issues

- Is there a way for her to stay? How will she be able to do it all, care for children, aging parents, make more money to pay the bills? Is there a government structure in Mexico that helps single mothers to manage, to feed their children? Are there programs to help her to increase her education and ability to earn a living wage?

Micro Issues

- What thoughts and feelings would you expect to be going through Claudia's mind?

- How would you advise a social work practitioner to respond to Claudia? There is a need for self-reflection, assessment of resilience and strengths, and affirmation, that Claudia is doing all that she can.

- Describe your own feelings after reading this? What would you do if you were talking with Claudia?

SUMMATIVE POINTS

- Support groups provide affirmation and acknowledgment, thereby building sources of human agency and resilience within communities.

- Support groups develop a social network, providing solidarity and mutual support that strengthens individuals, families, and communities.

REFERENCES

American Immigration Council. (2014). *Immigrant women in the United States: A portrait of demographic diversity*. http://www.immigrationpolicy.org/just- facts/immigrant-women-united-states-portrait-demographic-diversity

Birman, D., & Poff, M. (2011). *Intergenerational differences in acculturation* (pp. 1–7). Retrieved from http://www.child-encyclopedia.com/

Boyd, M., & Grieco, E. (2003, March 1). *Women and migration: Incorporating gender into international migration theory.* Migration Policy Institute www.mpi.org

Delara, M. (2016). Social determinants of immigrant women's mental health. *Advances in Public Health*, an online journal. Article ID 9730162. http://dx.doi.org/10.1155/2016/9730162

Drachman, D. (1992). A stage-of-migration framework for service to immigrant populations. *Social Work*, *37*(1), 68–72.

Freire, P. (1997). *Pedagogy of the oppressed.* New York: Continum. (Original work published 1968)

Gonzalez, A., Lord, G., Rex-Kill, B., & Francois, J. J. (2012). Parents beyond borders: A social group work curriculum for supporting immigrant parents and building solidarity. *Social Work with Groups*, *35*, 18–34.

Hampson, J., Crea, T. M., Calvo, R. & Alvarez, F. (2014). The value of accompaniment: Faith and responses to displacement. *Forced Migration Review*, *48*, 7–8.

Krogstad, J. M., & Passell, J. S. (2015, November). *5 facts about illegal immigration in the U.S Pew Research Center.* http://www.pewresearch.org/fact-tank/2015/11/19/5-facts-about-illegal-immigration-in-the-u-s/

Messing, J. T., Amanor-Boadu, Y., Cavanaugh, C. E., Glass, N. E., & Campbell, J. C. (2013). Culturally competent intimate partner violence risk assessment: Adapting the danger assessment for immigrant women. *Social Work Research*, *37*(3), 263–275.

O'Mahony, J. M., & Donnelly, T. T. (2007). The influence of culture on immigrant women's mental health care experiences from the perspectives of health care providers. *Issues in Mental Health & Nursing*, *28*(5), 453–471.

O'Neill, W. R., S. J., & Sophn, W. C. (1998). Rights of passage: The ethics of immigration and refugee policy. *Theological Studies*, *59*, 84–106.

Perreira, K. M., & Ornelas, I. (2013). Painful passages: Traumatic experiences and post-traumatic stress among U.S. immigrant Latino adolescents and their primary caregivers. *International Migration Review*, *47*(4), 976–1005.

Pine, B. A., & Drachman, D. (2005). Effective child welfare practice with immigrant and refugee children and their families. *Child Welfare*, *84*(5), 537–562.

Rayle, A. D., Sand, J. K., Brucato, T., & Ortega, J. (2006). The "comadre" group approach: A wellness-based group model for monolingual Mexican women. *The Journal for Specialists in Group Work*, *31*(1), 5–24.

Schiller, L. Y. (1997). Rethinking stages of development in women's groups: Implications for practice. *Social Work with Groups*, *20*(3), 3–19.

Stepler, R., & Brown, A. (2016, April, 19). Statistical portrait of Hispanics in the United States. *Pew Research Center.* Retrieved from http://www.pewhispanic.org/2016/04/19/statistical-portrait-of-hispanics-in-the-united-states-key-charts/

Toseland, R. W., & Rivas, R. F. (2012). *An introduction to group work practice*. New York, NY: Pearson.

U.S. Census Bureau. (2011). *American community survey*. www.census.gov/acs/www/

Yakushko, O., & Chronister, K. M. (2005). Immigrant women and counseling: The invisible others. *Journal of Counseling & Development, 83*(3), 292–298.

Yalom, I. D., & Leszcz, M. (2005). *The theory and practice of group psychotherapy* (5th ed.). New York, NY: Basic Books.

Yoshihama, O., & Chronister, K. M. (2005). Immigrant women and counseling: The invisible others. *Journal of Counseling & Development, 83*, 292–298.

Zong, J., & Batalova, J. (2015). *Frequently requested statistics on immigrants and immigration in the United States*. Migration Policy Institute. http://www.migrationpolicy.org

Chapter 10

COMMUNITY PRACTICE

RACHAEL D. GOODMAN, BETHANY LETIECQ, COLLEEN VESELY,
MARLENE MARQUEZ, AND KRISHNA J. LEYVA

KEY TERMS

communities of resistance, critical consciousness, transnational, immigrants,
community practice, working in partnership with transnational population,
marginalized populations, critical and liberatory psychological perspectives

---

CHAPTER HIGHLIGHTS

- Transnational populations are part of at least two geographic communities—their home community where they lived pre-migration and their new community where they live post-migration. Both communities may influence the lives of immigrants and refugees, even if they are only physically present in their new community.

- For refugees and immigrants, the experience of community in their new home contains resources and sources of stress—both of which are critical for community practitioners to understand within a particular context.

- Community practices, as compared to individually focused services, are compelling, powerful, and meaningful avenues for intervention, particularly with transnational and other marginalized populations.

- Viewing community as a unit of intervention draws on the ways in which people are already organized and have a sense of identity.

- Community practitioners should strive for awareness of the systemic and sociopolitical issues that impact our clients, including power differentials, structures of oppression, and historical and contemporary experiences of marginalization.

- Community practices should build on existing strengths of individuals, families, and communities.

THE MEANING OF COMMUNITY

The communities to which we belong have profound implications for our sense of identity, our resources and strengths, and our challenges. Community, however, is not static: The communities with which we identify are varied and changing. This is particularly true for transnational populations, for whom community shifts in part because physical location shifts during migration. For the purpose of this chapter, we draw on Wallerstein, Duran, Minkler, and Foley's (2005) definition of community as "people who have a shared identity, whether that identity is based on geography, political affiliation, culture, race or ethnicity, faith or religion, sovereign tribal nationhood, institutional connections such as schools or workplaces, or other shared identification with a group" (p. 33). We note that sometimes this shared identity is ascribed *to* individuals and groups instead of self-selected. For instance, this is the case with individuals from different countries who arrive in a resettlement country and are now collectively identified as "refugees," despite often having little else in common.

In thinking about transnational populations, we can see that they are part of at least two geographic communities—their home community where they lived pre-migration and their new community where they live post-migration. Both communities may influence the lives of immigrants and refugees, even if they are only physically present in their new community. Oftentimes, remaining connected to family members in one's country of origin (COO) offers a source of emotional support and connection. These connections may inspire a sense of purpose, where family members resolve to make a better life for their families, while keeping members safe and out of harm's way. However, particularly for immigrants and refugees whose families remain in danger in their COOs, this can be a source of significant worry, concern, and stress. Being psychologically connected to communities in differing geographic spaces may foment feelings of ambivalence, ambiguity, and loss (Falicov, 2002).

Relocating to a new geographic community may engender other shifts in identity and community. For instance, one is now identified as an immigrant or refugee—a new identity that may connect that individual to a community of refugees or immigrants. While this can give rise to the possibility of solidarity and support as a member of this group, this identity may also put someone at risk for discrimination and other challenges, given the way this community or group is perceived and often stereotyped. Other identity shifts could relate to one's situatedness in a new culture and context, where there may be changes to economic opportunity and human rights.

For refugees and immigrants, the experience of community in their new home contains resources and sources of stress—both of which are critical for community practitioners to understand within a particular context. Communities might have resources that can help support transnational populations, such as food banks, early childhood education and care centers, adult language classes, and resettlement services. However, such services must be known to the community, available when community members need them, and accessible in terms of cost and transportation. Other contextual community factors that can support transnational populations are the presence of peers who speak the same language or family members who arrived before, paving the way for future members.

Community factors may also be sources of stress and challenge, particularly when receiving communities are geographically isolated, engage in discriminatory practices and fuel attitudes of nativism and hostility toward immigrants, and have limited social services, resources, and infrastructure. Some of the fastest growing settlements are in rural counties, far from traditional immigrant hubs. These new settlements often are ill-equipped to meet the needs of immigrant and refugee families, lacking infrastructure and personnel with knowledge of immigration policies and laws, language proficiencies, and access to adequate resources (Grzywacz et al., 2010; Letiecq, Grzywacz, Gray, & Eudave, 2014).

WHY COMMUNITY PRACTICE?

We find community practices, as compared to individually focused services, to be compelling, powerful, and meaningful avenues for intervention, particularly with transnational and other marginalized populations. Frequently, community-based services run counter to the ways in which social services are set up—particularly in the United States, where individuality is emphasized and personal responsibility and self-sufficiency are seen as ideal characteristics. Many from the refugee and immigrant communities may not trust and/or seek individual services (e.g., individual counseling; Chung, Bemak, Ortiz, & Sandoval-Perez, 2008), and may prefer joining in community-based services that offer more communal and accessible points of intervention. Indeed, Dass-Brailsford (2007) recommends outreach in which service providers visit community centers and homes to foster trust and familiarity among refugees. Letiecq and Schmalzbauer (2012), in their community-based efforts, found that social gatherings, dances, and parties both served to mitigate immigrants' feelings of social isolation, while also providing safe, alternative contexts in which to connect community members to services and resources.

Traditionally delivered, individually focused interventions may not be congruent with the collectivist cultures from which many transnational populations hail (Falicov, 2002; Hall, 2001). Over the past two decades, community-focused interventions that are developed in concert with community members have been found to offer more culturally appropriate and responsive practices. For example, some interventions have drawn upon the ideals of interconnectedness and care for one another, which not only better aligned with cultural values of the communities being served but also facilitated natural support systems (e.g., Watkins & Shulman, 2008). Research shows that social support is critical for resilience and healing (e.g., Betancourt et al., 2015; Peddle, 2007), enhancing the benefits of this type of intervention as compared to individually focused interventions.

Importantly, community practice often takes an ecological or systemic view and examines critically the roles systems and social structures play in hindering or facilitating individual and family functioning. Such a focus encourages practitioners to work toward changing existing structures, policies, and practices on a systemic or structural level, while also supporting individual well-being. Action for structural change can be more powerful than simply adding intervention programs because "the more enduring contexts of family, school, workplace, and established community settings exert powerful and long-lasting impacts on individual health and well-being" (Harvey, 2007, p. 18).

Finally, viewing community as a unit of intervention draws on the ways in which people are already organized and have a sense of identity (Israel, Schulz, Parker, & Becker, 1998). As noted above, group identity and community is complicated for transnational populations, given their displacement or relocation and changes in identity. Further, they may have been persecuted or discriminated against because of their group identity (Kira & Tummala-Narra, 2015). For instance, refugees often experience torture or sexual assault as means of destroying community cohesion (Dass-Brailsford, 2007). Thus, community work can be a powerful counter to these violence exposures and traumas and engender healing, resilience, and growth. Facilitating a collective identity as a part of community work can build solidarity among marginalized groups to engage in collective action. This collective action could help communities heal from the wounds of trauma through interpersonal connection and care. Further, communities might undertake collective action that addresses the injustices facing their communities—thus extending the impact of their collective identity beyond healing to liberation and justice ends.

THEORETICAL FOUNDATIONS

Our work is grounded in *critical* and *liberatory psychological perspectives* (Martín-Baró, 1994; Prilleltensky, 1998) that require our practice acknowledge and address the ways in which systems operate to harm and oppress those we wish to serve. From this framework, we aim to deconstruct and understand the impact of historical and ongoing oppression, so that the cause of distress is linked to systemic forces instead of viewed as individual failings. Further, we seek to co-construct knowledge and interventions that reflect the values and strengths of the communities we serve. Our intention is not to impose interventions based on our worldviews but to co-create pathways for healing that bolster individual, family, and community resilience. For instance, Watkins and Shulman (2008) described how *communities of resistance*, a liberation-based practice, can bring marginalized individuals together to question and reject the "processes in the dominant culture that have attributed negative meanings to one's very existence" and help members "recover from toxic internalizations and feelings of inferiority, emptiness, and meaninglessness" (p. 217).

An *ecological systems perspective* is also a useful guide for understanding community and the ways in which we engage with transnational populations in community practice. Bronfenbrenner (1977), a major theorist of the ecological system perspective, offered a framework that has been used in a multitude of human and social service professions, such as counseling and social work, and that explicitly takes into consideration the contextual factors that influence individuals, families, and communities. While this is in many ways intuitive and resonates with our own experiences as individuals who are influenced by where we are located and the systems in which we interact, there is also a history in many social science and human service fields that discounts ecological factors and over-emphasizes the role of the individual. This deficit-based lens is problematic, because it locates problems within the individual—or sometimes within families or culture—rather than considering the complex genesis and ecologies of social problems. This is particularly problematic when working with immigrants and refugees, who are subject to immigration laws and policies that determine their eligibility and level of engagement in many social, health care, and educational services. Because of the ways in which their lives are structured and regulated by larger, macro-level forces, individual agency to address and improve their circumstances is particularly constrained and controlled. Thus, in our work, we examine the ways such communities resist and develop resilience in the face of systemic barriers and injustices as well as how we can transform systems to be supportive, equitable, and just.

We use these theories to guide and frame our community practices with refugees and immigrants in ways that increase effectiveness, ensure ecological and cultural validity, and address structural barriers and supports. As noted, trauma-exposed transnational populations have complex needs and face myriad challenges, while also possessing enduring strengths that foster resilience. In this chapter, we delineate community "best practices" and offer examples of how practitioners can strategically partner with communities using a community-based participatory approach to facilitate supportive environments that foster well-being. As Harvey (2007) noted, we know that most individuals who've been exposed to traumatic events recover, but "[n]eeded now is knowledge about how to create and sustain [supportive] environments" (p. 15). We conclude with implications for working in community-based settings.

COMMUNITY "BEST PRACTICES": WORKING IN PARTNERSHIP WITH TRANSNATIONAL POPULATIONS

Collaborative and Community Driven

Engaging the community we wish to serve in a collaborative partnership should not be a radical concept, but it often is. Many service providers are trained and service systems are set up so that practitioners deliver a solution to an individual, family, or community based on practitioners' understanding of a particular problem. This method of practice is rife with the possibility of errors and missed opportunities to advance community health, often because of a misalignment between practitioner "knowings" and community "realities." Practitioners may err in the way they understand and define the problem or problems or in the solutions or interventions they select, without critical inputs from the community. Such didactic and paternalistic approaches—often with the best of intentions—can unintentionally employ deficit-based models, miss the complex and nuanced circumstances of immigrant and refugee communities, or simply fail to meet community members where they are. Collaborative partnerships, instead, seek to engage community members in the process of identifying problems or needs as well as developing and implementing solutions. Critically, such partnerships locate control for the project jointly between the community and "intervening" entities (e.g., university researchers, clinical practitioners, school counselors). Critical practitioners argue that centering and empowering those historically silenced and marginalized to lead is necessary to developing inclusive and democratic partnerships (Martín-Baró, 1994; Prilleltensky, 1998; Watkins & Shulman, 2008).

Critically Conscious

Community practitioners should strive for awareness of the systemic and sociopolitical issues that impact our clients, including power differentials, structures of oppression, and historical and contemporary experiences of marginalization. Known as "critical consciousness" (Freire, 2001), this awareness is particularly important when working with immigrants and refugees, given the structural conditions and forms of oppression faced by transnational populations. We can facilitate critical consciousness within ourselves and others, through self-reflection and reflexive dialogue on unconscious, implicit biases and power differentials between and within service providers and community members. Using this perspective, we can locate the problems experienced by a community within the broader systems and power structures and bring to the fore the ways in which we are all complicit in perpetuating systemic inequality and injustice. This consciousness gives rise to the need for advocacy action (discussed further below) as a part of community practice or what Freire called the "praxis component" of critical consciousness.

Culturally Aligned and Culture Centered

The importance of understanding our clients' cultures is now well accepted across human service professions. There remain myriad challenges to actually aligning our interventions with those cultural beliefs and practices of our clients, including Eurocentric training models, cultural and racial bias, and the growing focus on empirically supported interventions that tend to be Eurocentric in nature. Building on the notion of *culturally sensitive therapies* (CST; Hall, 2001), *culturally supported interventions* (CSI; Wallerstein et al., 2005) focus on ensuring that our practices are valid and meaningful according to the culture of our clients. Further, *culture-centered practices* position the traditions and healing practices of our clients at the center of our work, such that we support and facilitate the ways in which our clients view well-being and the means for moving toward well-being. For example, Joseph Gone (2013) writes about culture-as-treatment for indigenous communities who have had their culture assaulted and criminalized; he notes that the act of engaging in cultural practices can itself be a form of healing. A similar framework might be applied within transnational populations who've experienced group identity-based trauma and may face cultural or religious discrimination.

Contextually Responsive

As noted, the experiences of transnational populations are influenced by the ecologies in which they reside and must be not only culturally appropriate but *contextually* responsive. Scaled-up, *one-size-fits-all* approaches rarely address the specific needs of a community or build on their unique strengths. For instance, high cost of living in an urban resettlement community might engender the need for housing support and advocacy services but not in a rural community with lower housing costs. Further, local policies and practices can facilitate the well-being of transnational communities, such as the availability of driver's licenses to undocumented immigrants in some U.S. cities, or can hinder community well-being, such as anti-immigrant legislation in various U.S. cities and states (e.g., S.B. 1070 in Arizona).

Strengths Focused

Community practices should build on existing strengths of individuals, families, and communities. This is an important counter to the deficit focus that is common when working with marginalized communities. A deficit or problem-based focus is also common when working with trauma-exposed communities, as is often the case with transnational populations. While not ignoring problems transnational communities face, practitioners should note ways in which communities have successfully resisted and persisted in difficult circumstances. For instance, refugees and immigrants may possess and enact special qualities and skills, such as multilingualism and multiculturalism, perseverance, courage, creativity, determination, and flexibility as they journey from their home and build a life in a new country. Practitioners should note what individual, familial, cultural, and community-based practices, values, and beliefs help to sustain this community despite, for example, facing multiple stressors of discrimination, few job prospects, and family separation. Understanding and drawing upon a community's "meaning making" is essential to position our work in a strengths-based paradigm that is community driven and responsive.

Holistic and Ecological

As noted in our use of ecological systems theory, best community practice involves intervention at multiple levels, including concerns such as individual mental health, family financial security, local policies, and institutional practices (Harvey, 2007). It is critical that we are holistic in our perspective, noting the concerns, needs, and strengths of the whole person/family/community. Often, practitioners can become focused on their area of interest at the expense of other important, intersecting areas of concern. For instance, as a mental health counselor specializing in trauma, I might want to focus on healing for intimate partner violence; however, my client may be more concerned about a recent eviction notice and finding a job to support her three children. Thus, I must be flexible and responsive to the holistic experience of my client. I must address both traumatic events and ongoing stressors, understanding that these experiences and sequelae intersect and interact with one another (Miller & Rasmussen, 2010).

Trauma Informed

Best practices also ensure that an understanding of trauma exposures, symptoms, and models for recovery are embedded in the lens we use in our practice. Trauma-informed social service and mental health service delivery models are critical, because trauma is often misunderstood. For instance, children exhibiting "behavior problems" in schools may be labeled as oppositional or thought to have a learning or attention problem when, in fact, they are exhibiting symptoms of trauma (Goodman & West-Olatunji, 2010). If a school social worker misdiagnoses or mislabels a student's problems, this can prevent that student from receiving appropriate services and may also further marginalize or stigmatize the student. Trauma-exposed individuals may seek treatment for concerns seemingly unrelated to trauma. Thus, a trauma-informed lens ensures we assess for trauma symptoms among everyone with whom we work. Transnational populations are at high risk for trauma exposure and may face additional barriers to seeking treatment, such as fear of stigma, discrimination by service providers, or lack of access to services that are culturally and linguistically appropriate (Kenny & Lockwood-Kenny, 2011; Yako & Biswas, 2014). Our trauma-informed approach must also be culturally appropriate since we know that there are multiple ways in which trauma manifests across cultures—manifestations that remain understudied and perhaps misunderstood (Marsella, 2010). Not addressing trauma may result in failed interventions.

Advocacy Focused

As community practitioners, we must include advocacy action to address and transform the systems and structures in which we practice that may unintentionally and negatively impact our clients. This is a critical and often overlooked component of practice, but we must interrogate how we are complicit in perpetuating injustices and deficit-based practices that unintentionally harm rather than support and promote community well-being. While persistence and resistance on the individual and familial level is necessary in concert with our community practice, we must acknowledge the professional imperative for advocacy, systems change, and the development and implementation of just policies and practices residing in the macro-level spaces of our work. As Menjívar and Abrego (2012) demonstrated, immigrant communities experience legal violence in the forms of anti-immigrant policies and practices. Further, transnational populations may experience institutional betrayal trauma in which existing trauma is exacerbated by the failures of the systems that are supposed to support them (Goodman, Vesely, Letiecq, & Cleaveland, in press; Smith & Freyd, 2013). Without attention to these policy and systems issues, we will not create supportive and sustained pathways to well-being for the most marginalized.

APPLICATION OF COMMUNITY-BASED PRACTICES

In this next section, we present an approach referred to as community-based participatory research (CBPR) that draws upon the community best practices specified above. While there is a great deal written on CBPR principles and approaches (see, for example, Israel, Eng, Schulz, & Parker, 2005; Minkler & Wallerstein, 2008), for the purposes of this chapter, we focus on our community-based efforts to actualize best practices by establishing community advisory boards and strategic community partnerships to inform a shared research and action agenda (Faridi et al., 2007; Israel et al., 2005; Letiecq & Schmalzbauer, 2012; Minkler & Wallerstein, 2008). Below we describe examples from our work as a means of engaging in community practice with immigrants and refugees. As with any democratic, participatory, community-based engagement, we acknowledge that we have not perfected our practice, but we aspire to actualize best practice principles in our work (Ospina et al., 2004). As such, we discuss emergent challenges and reflect on implications of this work for future practice.

Community-Based Case Examples

We draw upon our work with two communities in the D.C.-metro region where we are situated: refugee/asylee women (mainly from Asia and Africa) and Latina immigrants (mainly undocumented women from Central America). Importantly, community best practices often call for community-driven efforts, where the community identifies a need that they wish to work on and then seeks collaboration with university researchers and/or practitioners in the field. However, in both cases, we reached out to community agencies already working with immigrant and refugee communities and offered our services and to partner with community members and work on issues important to them. In both cases, our community agency partners connected us to groups of women identified as natural leaders or natural helpers in the community. We held initial meetings where we shared our goals of building trusted relationships and equitable partnerships to address community-determined challenges by (a) conducting culturally responsive and attuned research; and (b) developing and implementing evidence-based interventions in partnership with the communities we wished to serve. Our long-term goals are to build sustainable, culturally, and contextually responsive practices that empower vulnerable communities and promote health equity and justice.

After lengthy discussion, both communities of women expressed interest in forming community advisory boards (CABs) to guide our work. Thus, in 2014, two boards were formed: Hand-to-Hand CAB, made up of six refugee/asylee women from Asia and Africa, and Amigas de la Comunidad CAB, made up of ten Latinas mainly from Central America. Other CAB members included our community agency partners, trusted community organizers, and university research team members (faculty, graduate/undergraduate students).

CAB DEVELOPMENT. After the CABs were established, members agreed to meet weekly to build rapport and trust within the group and to build group identity, solidarity, and purpose. Rapport and trust building were important so CAB members would feel comfortable sharing personal information about their families and communities. As a part of this process, we worked collectively to establish that all members had knowledge and expertise to share and that we wished to center our efforts on the most marginalized in the group to empower them to determine which problems in the community should be our focus. We discussed ways to share power and resources and acknowledged that we (as university researchers with grant funding) held the project purse strings. With both groups, the collective agreed that participation in the CAB would be facilitated by a stipend ($20–40/meeting) and the provision of meals and child care (if needed).

An important component of the development of both CABs was establishing a group identity so that our purpose was clear both within the group and within the broader communities we wished to serve. Over the course of several meetings, each CAB created a name and mission statement. We produced business cards and letters to be shared with community members explaining the mission of each CAB. Members of Amigas de la Comunidad also worked with a graphic design student to develop a logo for CAB T-shirts, tote bags, and a banner to be displayed at community gatherings. These efforts also served to establish professional dispositions; however, after separate struggles within each CAB (e.g., interpersonal conflict, accusations of gossiping about members outside the group, accusations about a theft of a jacket following a CAB meeting), we also worked collectively to establish a set of *ground rules* (e.g., treating each other with respect, no gossiping), which were written up as CAB contracts and signed by all members. We discussed the importance of adhering to the rules so as not to undermine our ability to build trust, solidarity, and work in the community.

ADDRESSING ONGOING CHALLENGES. Language is a challenge facing both CABs. In Amigas de la Comunidad CAB, the researchers (who have limited Spanish proficiency) used translators so that the meetings could be conducted in Spanish (since most CAB members had limited English proficiency). When the fourth author (MM) joined the team, she led many meetings in Spanish and translated for the other researchers, since she is a native Spanish speaker and proficient in English. In Hand-to-Hand CAB, the language challenges were different in that there were multiple first languages spoken by CAB members (e.g., Dari, Urdu, and French), so the process of communication required multiple translations by CAB members and sometimes student research assistants. In both CABs, communication was challenging for the person who was trying to translate, because multiple conversations were happening and there were few pauses to translate. Often, progress was slow, since we needed to translate as well as repeat what was said.

Determining the direction and agenda for the CABs was also a challenge, in part because of the language difficulties but also because of diversity of perspectives, experiences, and personalities within each CAB. In Amigas de la Comunidad CAB, all the CAB members lived in the same community, so there was some shared understanding about the problems facing their community, but there were also differences (e.g., immigration status, country of origin, literacy, and family separation). In Hand-to-Hand CAB, there was even greater diversity among the women, including language, place of residence in the D.C.-metro region, region of origin, and immigration status. We realized during our process that both CABs were examples of a fairly new type of CBPR work in which we were working with communities that were not necessarily communities until they arrived in the United States. Developing shared goals involved different techniques, such as unstructured time during meetings for women to voice their personal concerns and share what was happening in their communities. At times, we would reorient the discussion and ask the group members to focus on specific tasks, such as identifying action steps. We also found participation in the group was not equal, with some members dominating group meetings. In the Hand-to-Hand CAB, some members who had more limited English skills and fewer years of formal education completed appeared to struggle to have their voices heard in the group. While our (research team) initial aim was for both groups to be led by our community partners, we found that negotiating space for everyone to talk and to hear everyone's perspective required more facilitation on the part of the research team. We continue to develop leadership skills within the group (including our own).

Within the Amigas de la Comunidad CAB, trust was a significant concern because of the lack of legal immigration status among most of the members. Confidentially and persistence were key components to gaining trust, since many in the immigrant community are afraid that if they speak about the problems they are experiencing that there will be negative consequences for them and their families. Many are afraid of being deported from the United States and feel it is safer to stay *in the shadows* instead of being involved in their community. We gained each other's trust by being there regularly (either weekly or eventually monthly) and by listening to each other. Through this process, some exhibited trust by sharing their personal stories in CAB meetings, but many remained less willing to open up in public spaces.

Early on, it became clear that agenda-setting would often take a back seat to listening to immediate and pressing concerns of each member and working as a collective to problem solve and facilitate acquisition of resources if possible. For example, one CAB member came to a meeting reporting that her food stamps had been cut off. We discussed in the group who she should call and discussed how we could support her to meet her food needs for her family during the lapse (e.g., identifying local food banks). When CAB members or other community members reported similar time-sensitive challenges, such as eviction notices, we looked for ways to support those individuals through support or advocacy action (e.g., providing a translator for seeking help at social services, calling the resettlement agency to seek an extension of support services). Other members often shared dire circumstances of their friends and family members and sought ways we could respond as a group. On one occasion, a CAB member shared that her friend's son drowned while trying to cross the Rio Grande river and that she needed to raise money to return his body to Guatemala. As a group, we supported her friend emotionally and helped her raise the money that she needed. With each opportunity to meet CAB members (and by extension, their family and friends) where they are, we (research team members) learn about the lived experiences of our community partners, the nuances of cultures often lumped together as if the same (e.g., Guatemalan versus El Salvadorian), and become more critically conscious of our assumptions, biases, and feelings of inadequacy and helplessness to address the challenges faced by our community partners. We also are gaining more focus and seeing where we collectively have capacity to intervene in meaningful ways.

Research and Action Steps

In conjunction with CAB development, we have been working collectively to conduct research and gather data to inform on-going action steps and future intervention efforts. As is typical with CBPR approaches (Israel et al., 2005), we have used multiple methods. For example, as we worked to build relationships and trust as a CAB, language barriers, agenda setting, and the cacophony that comes with holding meetings and providing child care in the same spaces precluded deeper connections from forming between community partners and research team members. When the research team shared our desire to know our partners better, they invited us into their homes for one-on-one in-depth interviews. At CAB meetings, we collectively discussed the kinds of questions that would be important to cover during these interviews, confidentiality, and how we could benefit collectively from these data gathering processes. Then we, as a research team, developed consent forms, formalized an interview protocol, gained institutional review board approval, hired translators, and conducted in-depth interviews lasting between one and two hours (with some interviews taking place over several visits). The research team also took copious field notes during CAB meetings, conducted environmental scans with our community partners, and conducted interviews and focus groups with community agency workers to gain their perspectives about the challenges and opportunities facing the immigrant and refugee communities in the region as well as agency capacities to garner resources and intervene.

While conducting our research and sharing emergent findings with CAB members, action steps were identified that we could carry out collectively in the short term and long term. In the short term, Hand-to-Hand CAB organized resource drives to get much needed items like clothing and diapers to newly resettled families. Realizing the limitations of our organization to address these needs, we began developing a resource guide that is given out with donations to help connect families to organizations that offer donations and those that offer reputation and low-cost services such as language classes or driver's education. In partnership with a resettlement agency, we held a problem-solving workshop in which women from the community were invited to the agency to learn problem-solving skills. CAB members were responsible for recruitment, which led to a much greater than expected turnout. The large turnout actually engendered a number of challenges, since there was great diversity among languages spoken, needs, and time in the United States. This was an important learning opportunity for our group, and we processed the problems and decided ways in which we could proceed differently and more effectively in the future, such as holding different workshops for different languages and different needs and providing more concrete resources (e.g., a phone number of who to call if your food stamps are cut off).

For the Amigas de la Comunidad CAB, a major component of the actions undertaken were related to the quantitative survey. CAB members spent months spreading the word in the community about our organization in order to build trust, since there is particular fear and mistrust among the undocumented immigrant community about deportation and about being scammed. As we recruited and then met with community members, we were able to share with them information from the resource guide we produced in conjunction with a community agency. For those who had young children, we were able to provide them with information about education and child care services. Several CAB members attended community meetings held by a local human rights commission and the superintendent of their local school system to share their stories and engage in advocacy. We also shared the preliminary results of our quantitative findings at a community meeting, which resulted in further discussion about concerns and action steps desired by community members.

Research and Action Outcomes

The trauma and stressors women faced intersected and were cumulative in nature, as they overlapped multiple domains (e.g., housing, employment, health care, child care, education) of women's lives across contexts (e.g., country of origin, U.S. community) and time (i.e., pre-migration, during migration, post-migration). The women and families in these communities had complex histories of trauma linked to their experiences in their COOs as well as their migration to the United States. Across undocumented immigrants, refugees, and asylees, the majority of women noted the role of fear in leaving their COOs. Refugee and asylee women left their COOs because of persecution, leaving themselves or their families' lives in danger; while many of the undocumented immigrant women fled impoverished societies of drugs, gangs, and violence in their COOs and came to the United States to protect themselves and their children from these dangerous situations. In addition, undocumented and refugee/asylee women alike faced harrowing journeys from their COOs, in which rape, extortion, robbery, and physical assault were not uncommon.

Upon arriving in the United States, women across both communities faced ongoing stressors, primarily related to inadequate housing, economic stability, and employment as well as child and health care, exacerbating their previous traumatic experiences and further compromising their individual and family well-being (Goodman et al., in press; Vesely, Goodman, Ewaida, & Kearney, 2014) and ability to build resilience. Moreover, we observed both developmental and contextual mediators of resilient responses (Harvey, 2007) among the women. In particular, women's experiences of stress and building resilience were connected to their personal and familial resources, including aspects of human, social, and navigational capital. For example, some women arrived in the United States with higher education, English proficiency, and/or connections to other family and community members who, in addition to providing emotional support, could link them to necessary resources. However, other women entered the United States with little to no formal schooling or experiences navigating institutions, limited or no literacy skills in their language of origin as well as in English, limited or no formal employment experience, as well as limited connections vis-à-vis family and friends to opportunity structures.

Women's experiences were also shaped by their social and geographic situatedness and their resulting interactions with institutions, policies, and laws. These "structural ecologies" or the institutions and services available to these women and their families and how they support family functioning and resilience building are often less understood. Specifically, documentation was an important component of situatedness for the women in this study. For undocumented immigrant women, not having papers often meant limited access to public benefits and supports coupled with living in fear of deportation. For others, despite holding refugee or asylee status, which afforded access to important financial and material supports, with shifting funding and heightened anti-immigrant sentiment, interactions with public service agencies often left these women feeling a sense of institutional betrayal trauma (Smith & Freyd, 2013). This experience of feeling betrayed because of a "wrongdoing by an institution upon which an individual relies" (Goodman et al., in press) further complicated the existing stress and trauma these women already faced from their migration experiences.

In the face of this accumulation of stress and trauma as women began adapting to life in the United States, they coped and built resilience. They employed a number of coping strategies. First, women across both communities often worked to *reframe their perceptions*. While refugee women described feeling let down or a sense of betrayal by the U.S. government vis-à-vis U.S. institutions, in terms of expectations, they were often able to reframe their experiences in the U.S. as being "better than back home," as for many the governments in their COOs provided no support for individuals and families. For undocumented women who lamented over living in fear of deportation, they reframed this perception, noting that this fear in the United States was more manageable than the fear they lived in back home as they navigated violence related to drugs and gangs. Second, women engaged in *(re)building social and navigational capital* by building and rebuilding relationships among family and friends in the United States and back home as well as making new connections with others from like linguistic and cultural backgrounds in the United States. These links in the United States had the potential to provide women connections to resources they may not have accessed on their own as well as insight into how to navigate the U.S. systems; however, these relationships were sometimes challenged because of issues of trust, as women feared gossip and betrayal by other women in the community. Moreover, relationships with family members, particularly those back home, often provided important support, but they could also be sources of additional stress and worry due to separation.

Third and finally, for the women in both communities who were a part of the CABs, they described and we observed how the CAB process itself over the initial 12 to 18 months of work together on behalf of the community shaped CAB members' coping and resilience. For example, we witnessed over the first 18 months of our work how women were able to build lives in the United States, even in the face of stress and trauma. Bolour exemplifies this growth and resilience that highlights the positive unintended consequence of the CAB itself—which is, through meeting regularly to do work on behalf of the community, CAB members were able to build resilience. When we first met Bolour, she had very limited English, she presented symptoms of depression and was experiencing suicide ideation, she had little to no understanding of U.S. systems, no employment, and was concerned about being evicted from her home. In addition her adolescent son was refusing to go to school after being treated negatively by the physical education teacher at his school. In the face of all she had going on, Bolour was still able to develop a social capital via a small network of friends from like linguistic and cultural backgrounds, including another CAB member, who provided her translation support as well as emotional support during the CAB and her earliest months in the United States. Over time, we witnessed Bolour find employment and garner the services she needed as well as improve her English skills. Through initial and follow-up interviews as well as informal conversations with CAB members, they noted that working in service of their community and meeting regularly to accomplish this work was not only an intervention for their community but for themselves as well. They attributed some of their adaptive success to the CAB process.

IMPLICATIONS FOR PROFESSIONALS
WORKING IN COMMUNITY-BASED SETTINGS

Using the lessons learned from our work and that of others, there are a number of implications for professionals working in community-based settings. We group these implications in terms of identity factors, community-based processes, and practitioner factors.

Identity Factors

It is critical that practitioners attend to the *intersectionality of identity*, meaning that an individual's concerns will not be based solely on one aspect of her identity (e.g., female gender) but will intersect with the other aspects of her identity (e.g., female, country of origin, religion, socioeconomic status, and more). Thus we can't equate all women's experiences as the same, although there might be points of similarity based on sexism and patriarchy experienced by women, but these will operate differently for an Asian, Muslim woman than for a Salvadoran, Catholic woman. Additionally, there are important *within-group differences* to which practitioners must attend. It is critical that practitioners don't make assumptions about similarities or generalize what we know about some individuals to an entire group. For instance, some refugee children will have spent most of their lives in a refugee camp, while others will not have ever been to a refugee camp. Thus, we much be attuned to the ways in which the experiences of transnational communities are both similar and unique, educating ourselves and customizing our practices to the specific needs and experiences of individuals, families, and communities.

Community-Based Processes

In this work, we find that *setting expectations* for the work that we will do together as a community-based group of practitioners and community members is critical. We also find that we must reiterate our abilities and limitations, as practitioners, throughout the process to ensure that we are clear about our intentions and to address concerns that may arise. Similar to informed consent processes in clinical work, this process does not only occur at the beginning of a working relationship but must be an ongoing discussion. That expectations are clear to members of the community must not be taken for granted since there can be many barriers, including that our way of working may be counter to community members' experiences with other service providers or that there may be difficulty in understanding one another when working across cultures and first languages.

Attending to the people and processes of this work is also crucial. For instance, identifying *community stakeholders* early on in the work aids in the process of understanding the community, identifying additional partners, and building a community organization to facilitate the work and ensure that it's community driven. We also find that attending to *interpersonal dynamics* is a necessary part of community-based work. As with any group of people, it is likely that conflicts will arise or that some members will intentionally or unintentionally marginalize other members. Setting ground rules may help address these concerns. It is also helpful to address how members will share ideas and to look for ways to bring in the voices of marginalized members, which might be accomplished by having smaller group discussions and then bringing that back to the larger group.

Practitioner Factors

Finally, practitioners involved in community work should anticipate *sustained engagement*. It is critical to the development of collaborative, trusting partnerships that practitioners are willing to invest time on a regular basis to meeting with community members. Often this is best done within the community's own spaces, as this can show respect for the community and also increase connection and understanding between community members and practitioners. Given that trusting relationships take time to develop—particularly when there may be barriers related to appropriate mistrust of service providers or cultural differences—*patience* on the part of the service providers is of great importance. Patience involves allowing time and space processes and understandings to unfold and is related to another important practitioner characteristic: *flexibility*. As noted, liberatory, ecosystemic community-based practice should be community driven, meaning that service providers need to remain extremely flexible throughout the process; we must be willing to shift and change in response to changing community needs and concerns as well as our own developing understandings and awareness. We must also approach this process with a great deal of *humility*—remembering that while we as practitioners bring in a set of skills and understandings, there is also much that we don't know and may never fully understand as, oftentimes, individuals who are not members of the communities we serve. Finally, as we engage in this challenging and rewarding work, we must attend to our own needs for *balance* and self-care and we must set appropriate *boundaries*. As we know, human and social service providers are at risk for burnout and secondary traumatic stress, particularly when working with traumatized or marginalized communities. Given the less structured and often more intimate nature of community-based work, as compared to more traditional social services, practitioners must be particularly careful to attend to their own needs for support and downtime. Further, while our roles are flexible and changing, we must also be clear and thoughtful about our roles, ways of engaging, and personal sharing so that—in our desire to develop connection and help—we don't create dependencies or inappropriate relationships that could lead to disappointment or even harm if we are not able to fulfill expectations.

In sum, we find community-based work to be particularly well suited for working with transnational populations because of their unique concerns and experiences as well as the opportunity to enact justice-based, culture-centered, and localized initiatives for healing and well-being. Such efforts can lead to sustainable programs that improve not only the lives of individuals and families but entire communities.

SUMMATIVE POINTS (FINAL TAKE-AWAY MESSAGES)

- Best practices ensure that an understanding of trauma exposures, symptoms, and models for recovery are embedded in the lens we use in our practice with transnational and immigrant families.

- Community-based work is well suited for working with transnational populations, because of their unique concerns and experiences as

well as the opportunity to enact justice-based, culture-centered, and localized initiatives for healing and well-being.

- As we engage in this challenging and rewarding work, we must attend to our own needs for balance and self-care, examine our biases and assumptions, and set appropriate boundaries.

CASE EXERCISES

Application Exercise 1: Community Resilience Genogram

This exercise builds on previous iterations of genograms, such as the Transgenerational Trauma and Resilience Genogram (Goodman, 2013), the Critical Genogram (Kosutic et al., 2009), the Community Genogram (Ivey & Ivey, 1999), the Multicultural Genogram (Thomas, 1998), and the GLBT (gay, lesbian, bisexual, transgender) genogram (Chen-Hayes, 2003). These genograms build on work in family systems therapy that used genograms as a tool to assess family patterns across generations (McGoldrick & Gerson, 1985; McGoldrick, Gerson, & Petry, 2008). The more recent iterations of the genogram have emphasized a broader view of family (e.g., chosen versus biological); an individual's situatedness within a community instead of just within a family; intersectional aspects of identity (e.g., gender, sexual orientation, culture, race, ethnicity); sociopolitical experiences (e.g., racism, discrimination, economic disparities); forms of resilience (e.g., inclusion of strengths versus deficit focus); and free-form visual representations instead of prescriptive structures that might limit accurate and comprehensive representations.

The exercise can be used individually or within a group or larger community. The following are steps that can be followed or adapted to develop a community resilience genogram (CRG). We recommend placing visual representations in spaces that can be viewed by community members and using media (e.g., photos, painted murals) that are selected by the community.

1. **How we'll work**: Together with the community, explain the idea of the CRG as a way of developing a sense of collective identity, honoring both similarities and differences, identifying strengths and ways the community overcomes challenges, and explicating the nature of the challenges faced. Note any additional ways in which the CRG might function in this community, making sure this exercise aligns with the expressed interests of the community with whom you're working and collaboratively adapting the CRG. Determine how the CRG will be created and how it will be represented visually (e.g., community members draw pictures, bring in objects or photos, write together on a large paper). Determine if and how the CRG might be displayed, shared, or otherwise used by the community.

2. **Who we are**: Begin the activity by asking for members of the community to brainstorm what defines them as a community. What are the characteristics? Is it geographic location? Is it internally or externally defined (e.g., immigration status)? What are commonalities (e.g., as

people making a life in a new country)? What are some areas of difference (e.g., country of origin, economic resources, languages)? Visually represent these ideas, usually as the center of the CRG.

3. **Who is involved**: Identify important people, agencies, or organizations that are part of or influence this community. It may be helpful to use Bronfenbrenner's ecological model, moving from the immediate community out through the broader systems (e.g., exosystem, macrosystem) and visually representing these components within concentric circles that represent each system level.

4. **Our challenges**: Identify the areas of challenge faced by the community and its members. How do the components from Step 3 exert stress or create difficulties for the community? This would visually represent with lines that are labeled with the dynamic (e.g., line from social service agency to community labeled "non-multilingual staff limits access"). Think broadly about challenges that the community carries with them as well. This might include past traumatic events of individual members (e.g., fleeing gang violence, religious persecution and death threats, history of sexual assault during border crossing). It might also include daily stressors (e.g., difficult paying rent, difficulty accessing English language classes).

5. **Our strengths**: Importantly, the focus should not shift to a strengths and resilience focus. While the struggles faced by communities might be the impetus for coming together to seek services or make community change and the difficult trauma and stress experiences cannot be ignored, the focus must not focus solely on problems but also on honoring the ways in which individuals, families, and communities have survived, coped, persisted, and sometimes thrived despite these challenges. There may be opportunities to link agencies to the communities through lines showing the support they have provided (e.g., line from resettlement agency to community showing provision of language learning services). These same organizations may be sources of both stress and support, so it is helpful to note more than one type of relationship can and probably does exist (e.g., helpful service for finding a job but time limited or difficult to access because of location).

6. **What this means**: The next step involves processing with the community members what the CRG means. Questions can focus on new insights that might be gained, with particular attention to the needs of the community and purpose of the activity. The CRG can be an intervention to building a sense of solidarity for shared experiences, developing greater empathy and understanding, and acknowledging and fostering strengths and forms of resilience. It may be used to identify areas of focus for community action.

7. **What's next**: After processing, next steps should be identified. If the purpose was awareness raising and community building, then a next step might be to place the CRG in a location where it could be viewed by others and have some follow-up discussion. If the purpose was to identify areas to take action, the next steps might be to (a) identify area(s) of focus, (b) identify members to lead and assist with efforts, (c) identify additional partners that could support efforts, and (d) move forward with action planning and tasks as appropriate. Perhaps what is identified is that the community needs a better sense of what resources are available, so resource mapping could be used (see Exercise 2). Or perhaps the community identifies that there is a need for more data on the housing and mental health experiences of community in order to engage in advocacy action, so they might seek to engage in data collection and advocacy work and seek partners to assist, such as universities.

Application Exercise 2: Community Resource Mapping

This exercise focuses on building our understanding of the resources available to a particular transnational community and the limitations or gaps in these resources. This activity might focus on a particular need (e.g., mental health services) or might be broad and include any assets or supports. A community resource can be a person or group of people, an organization (e.g., business, nonprofit, university), or a physical place or structure (Berkowitz & Wadud, 2013). To engage in community resource mapping, the following steps can be adapted for your particular community organization:

1. **Identify the parameters**. What is the community of interest? Is this based on a population, geographic location, or some other criterion? What is the topic for the resource mapping? Is it broad (to include all possible assets) or specific and narrow (e.g., economic supports)? For instance, we might be interested in what support services are available to address the needs of undocumented immigrant families who are impacted by recent reunification and who live in a particular county.

2. **Identify resources for the tasks of resources mapping**. Who will be involved? Who will lead the effort and who will support the effort? What documents can be drawn upon that provide guidance for your particular focus (e.g., online resources, guidebooks)? What information already exists that can be used, perhaps from similar activities conducted in the past?

3. **Develop a framework**. What information will be gathered or what questions will be asked? How will this information be gathered (e.g., sending e-mails, in person)? How will this information be collected, stored, and processed? How will it be shared with others? Can it be visually displayed, via a tool like an actual map? It is ideal to pilot the collection, storage, and processes prior to engaging in a major effort so that you can ensure that the work you're doing will be of high quality and will be in a form that is useful for your purposes.

4. **Collect, store, process**. Ideally, with the support of a team, engage in the process of collecting, storing, and processing the information. Engage in an iterative process of analysis so that you are conducting initial reviews of the information as it's submitted. This ensures you catch any errors and can allow you to tweak anything that is problematic.

5. **Analyze**. Based on your purpose(s), conduct an analysis of the resources you've collected. A visual representation may help identify geographic holes in services (e.g., no food pantry on the west side of the district). Matching the resources up to the needs within the community may help to identify and address emerging needs in the community and fill those needs.

The results of the exercise can assist community service providers by enhancing their understanding of what resources are already available to their clients. Further, it might help identify areas for partnership where an agency with expertise in a particular area is able to offer a workshop or other service to the clients of another agency. Gaps in services can also be identified. Members of the resource mapping exercise and others in the community may be able to then use this information to advocate for needed resources for their clients and communities. Overall, this mapping exercise can assist in linking clients with resources, agencies, and service providers with one another and decision makers with important information that can improve community services and community well-being.

REFERENCES

Berkowitz, B., & Wadud, E. (2013). Section 8: Identifying community assets and resources in Chapter 3: Assessing community needs and resources. *The Community Toolbox*. Retrieved from http://ctb.ku.edu/en/tablecontents/sub_section_main_1043.aspx

Betancourt, T. S., Abdi, S., Ito, B. S., Lilienthal, G. M., Agalab, N., & Ellis, H. (2015). We left one war and came to another: Resource loss, acculturative stress, and caregiver–child relationships in Somali refugee families. *Cultural Diversity and Ethnic Minority Psychology, 21*, 114–125. doi: 10.1037/a0037538

Bronfenbrenner, U. (1977). Toward an experimental ecology of human development. *American Psychologist, 32*, 513–531. doi: 10.1037/0003-066X.32.7.513

Chen-Hayes, S. F. (2003). The sexual orientation and gender identity/gender expression genogram. In J. S. Whitman & C. J. Boyd (Eds.), *The therapist's notebook for lesbian, gay, and bisexual clients* (pp. 166–173). Binghamton, NY: The Hawthorne Press.

Chung, R. C.-Y., Bemak, F., Ortiz, D. P., & Sandoval-Perez, P. A. (2008). Promoting the mental health of immigrants: A multicultural/social justice perspective. *Journal of Counseling & Development, 86*, 310–317.

Dass-Brailsford, P. (2007). *A practical approach to trauma: Empowering interventions.* Los Angeles, CA: Sage.

Falicov, C. J. (2002). Ambiguous loss: Risk and resilience in Latino immigrant families. In M. Suarez-Orozco & M. Paez (Eds.), *Latinos: Remaking America* (pp. 274–288). Berkeley: University of California Press.

Faridi, Z., Grunbaum, J. A., Gray, B. S., Franks, A., & Simoes, E. (2007). Community-based participatory research: Necessary next steps. *Preventing Chronic Disease: Public Health Research, Practice, and Policy, 4*(3), 1–5 [series online]. Retrieved January 11, 2009, from http://www.cdc.gov/pcd/issues/2007/jul/06_0182.htm

Freire, P. (2001). *Pedagogy of the oppressed.* New York, NY: Continuum.

Gone, J. P. (2013). Redressing first nations historical trauma: Theorizing mechanisms for indigenous culture as mental health treatment. *Transcultural Psychiatry, 50*, 683–706. doi: 10.1177/1363461513487669

Goodman, R. D. (2013). The transgenerational trauma and resilience genogram. *Counselling Psychology Quarterly, 26*, 386–405. doi: 10.1080/09515070.2013.820172

Goodman, R. D., Vesely, C., Letiecq, B., & Cleaveland, C. (in press). Trauma and resilience among refugee and undocumented immigrant women. *Journal of Counseling & Development.*

Goodman, R. D., & West-Olatunji, C. A. (2010). Educational hegemony, traumatic stress, and African American and Latino American students. *Journal of Multicultural Counseling & Development, 38*, 176–186. doi: 10.1002/j.2161-1912.2010.tb00125.x

Grzywacz, J. G., Quandt, S. A., Chen, H., Isom, S., Kiang, L., Vallejos, Q., & Arcury, T. A. (2010). Depressive symptoms among Latino farmworkers across the agricultural season: Structural and situational influences. *Cultural Diversity and Ethnic Minority Psychology, 16*, 335–343.

Hall, G. C. N. (2001). Psychotherapy research with ethnic minorities: Empirical, ethical, and conceptual issues. *Journal of Consulting and Clinical Psychology, 69*, 502–510. doi: 10.1037//0022-006X.69.3.502

Harvey, M. R. (2007). Towards an ecological understanding of resilience in trauma survivors: Implications for theory, research, and practice. *Journal of Aggression, Maltreatment & Trauma, 14*, 9–32. doi: 10.1300/J146v14n01_02

Israel, B., Eng, E., Schulz, A., & Parker, E. (2005). Introduction. In B. A. Israel, E. Eng, A. J. Shulz, & E. A. Parker (Eds.), *Methods in community-based participatory research for health* (pp. 4–37). San Francisco, CA: Jossey-Bass.

Israel, B. A., Schulz, A. J., Parker, E. A., & Becker, A. B. (1998). Review of community-based research: Assessing partnership approaches to improve public health. *Annual Review of Public Health, 19*, 173–202.

Ivey, A. E., & Ivey, M. B. (1999, February). Integrating cultural and contextual issues into the interview: The community genogram. *Counseling Today*, pp. 38, 40.

Kenny, P., & Lockwood-Kenny, K. (2011). A mixed blessing: Karen resettlement to the United States. *Journal of Refugee Studies, 24*, 217–238. doi: 10.1093/jrs/fer009

Kira, I., & Tummala-Narra, P. (2015). Psychotherapy with refugees: Emerging paradigm. *Journal of Loss and Trauma, 20*, 449–467. doi: 10.1080/15325024.2014.949145

Kosutic, I., Garcia, M., Graves, T., Barnett, F., Hall, J., Haley, E., . . . Kaiser, B. (2009). The Critical Genogram: A tool for promoting critical consciousness. *Journal of Feminist Family Therapy, 21*, 151–176.

Letiecq, B., & Schmalzbauer, L. (2012). Community-based participatory research with Mexican migrants in a new rural destination: A good fit? *Action Research Journal, 10*(3), 244–259. doi: 10.1177/147675031244357

Letiecq, B. L., Grzywacz, J. G., Gray, K. M., & Eudave, Y. M. (2014). Depression among Mexican men on the migration frontier: The role of family separation and other structural and situational stressors. *Journal of Immigrant and Minority Health, 16*, 193–200. doi: 10.1007/s10903-013-9918-1

Marsella, A. J. (2010). Ethnocultural aspects of PTSD: An overview of concepts, issues, and treatments. *Traumatology, 16*, 17–26. doi: 10.1177/1534765610388062

Martín-Baró, I. (1994). *Writings for a liberation psychology*. Cambridge, MA: Harvard University Press.

McGoldrick, M., & Gerson, R. (1985). *Genograms in family assessment*. New York: W. W. Norton.

McGoldrick, M., Gerson, R., & Petry, S. (2008). *Genograms in family assessment* (3rd ed.). New York: W. W. Norton.

Menjívar, C., & Abrego, L. J. (2012). Legal violence: Immigration law and the lives of Central American immigrants. *American Journal of Sociology, 117*, 1380–1421. doi: 10.1086/663575

Miller, K. E., & Rasmussen, A. (2010). War exposure, daily stressors, and mental health in conflict and post-conflict settings: Bridging the divide between trauma-focused and psychosocial frameworks. S*ocial Science & Medicine, 70*, 7–16. doi: 10.1016/j.socscimed.2009.09.029

Minkler, M., & Wallerstein, N. (2008). *Community-based participatory research for health: From process to outcome* (2nd ed.). San Francisco, CA: Jossey-Bass.

Ospina, S., Dodge, J., Godsoe, B., Minieri, J., Reza, S., & Schall, E. (2004). From consent to mutual inquiry: Balancing democracy and authority in action research. *Action Research Journal, 2*(1), 47–69.

Peddle, N. (2007). Assessing trauma impact, recovery, and resiliency in refugees of war. *Journal of Aggression, Maltreatment & Trauma, 14*, 185–204. doi: 10.1300/J146v14n01_10

Prilleltensky, I. (1998). Critical psychology foundations for the promotion of mental health. *Annual Review of Critical Psychology, 1*, 100–118.

Smith, C. P., & Freyd, J. J. (2013). Dangerous safe havens: Institutional betrayal exacerbates sexual trauma. *Journal of Traumatic Stress, 26*, 119–124. doi: 10.1002/jts.21778

Thomas, A. J. (1998). Understanding culture and worldview in family systems. *The Family Journal, 6*, 24–32.

Vesely, C. K., Goodman, R. D., Ewaida, M., & Kearney, K. (2014). A better life? Immigrant mothers' experiences building economic security. *Journal of Family and Economic Issues, 36*, 514–530. doi: 10.1007/s10834-014-9422-3

Wallerstein, N., Duran, B., Minkler, M., & Foley, K. (2005). Developing and maintaining partnerships with communities (pp. 31–51). In B. A. Israel, E. Eng, A. J. Shulz, & E. A. Parker (Eds.), *Methods in community-based participatory research for health*. San Francisco, CA: Jossey-Bass.

Watkins, M., & Shulman, H. (2008). *Toward psychologies of liberation*. New York, NY: Palgrave Macmillan.

Yako, R. M., & Biswas, B. (2014). "We came to this country for the future of our children. We have no future": Acculturative stress among Iraqi refugees in the United States. *International Journal of Intercultural Relations, 38*, 133–141. doi: 10.1016/j.ijintrel.2013.08.003

Chapter 11

ORGANIZATIONAL PRACTICE

AIMEE HILADO

KEY TERMS

organizations, cultural mergence model, trauma, mental health, adjustment, well-being

---

CHAPTER HIGHLIGHTS

- Description of organizational structures serving immigrants and refugees.
- Integrating mental health practice within organization settings.
- Introduction to the *cultural mergence model*: A practice framework for delivering mental health services to trauma-experienced populations.
- Discussion of implications for direct service settings.

INTRODUCTION

This chapter examines the role of organizations as an intervention modality for immigrants and refugees. Organizations provide invaluable supports to aid adjustment in a new country by addressing the multi-level areas of need—physical, psychological, social, family, education, and vocational—often present among new immigrant and refugee arrivals. The chapter begins with basic definitions related to organizations that will serve as a foundation to discussing the relevance of immigrant and refugee-serving organizations. The chapter also focuses on the impact of trauma among a subgroup of immigrants in the United States—refugee populations—and the lessons that can be gained from the service framework used by refugee resettlement organizations[1] to aid

---

[1]In the United States, *refugee resettlement organizations* are specific organizations that have formal agreements with one of nine U.S. private agencies and one state agency. These national agencies have cooperative agreements with the U.S. Department of State to provide reception and placement services for refugees arriving in the country through the U.S. Refugee Resettlement Program. Other organizations serving immigrants who do not have refugee status fall under different service guidelines than those mandated by the U.S. Department of State.

in refugee adjustment to a new society. Building on these topics, the focal point of the chapter is the role of mental health programs that can serve as another resource for supporting adaptation and integration of trauma-exposed people in a new country. And in context of mental health programming, the cultural mergence model is introduced as a practice model for delivering mental health services within a refugee resettlement setting; a model that stabilizes all areas of health and well-being within an organization context. Although refugee-serving organizations (and human services organizations generally) will range in the services they provide, very few embed mental health programs as a core service component within the organization structure. This chapter highlights an exception to this, wherein a mental health program is built *into* a refugee resettlement organization and there are internal procedures that allow refugee clients to readily engage with mental health providers onsite. To this end, the model and major benefits of this structure will be discussed in detail for those seeking organizational practice methods to address the health and mental health needs of trauma-experienced populations.

Current Context of Global Migration

Global migration numbers are increasing worldwide as millions face the threat of war, famine, and economic downturn. Many more leave in pursuit of freedom and opportunities that are nonexistent in their home countries. Some face hardships of oppressive governments that stifle growth, development, and promote gross violations of human rights. And the most vulnerable of immigrants are arriving with profound trauma histories riddled with stories of persecution for religious, ethnic, or political affiliation. Some are victims of gender-based violence, while others are simply in countries that cannot provide for the basic needs of its citizens. Moreover, natural disasters and global warming further threaten those living in impoverished regions throughout the world. The types of organizations, and the services they provide to new immigrants and refugees, must therefore account for these diverse flight reasons and the trauma histories that accompany new arrivals.

The nature of forced and survival migration—a common characteristic of today's migrant experience globally—lends itself to a discussion of the physical and psychological sequelae of trauma from remaining in protracted uncertain situations. Trauma is an assault on the mind that can change the architecture of the brain so that typical ways of thinking and feeling can be altered permanently. Psychological distress can take the form of depression, anxiety, chronic illness, and post-traumatic stress disorder (Dow, 2011). The severity and duration of exposure to traumatic experiences, combined with the biological composition and resilience of a person, will ultimately determine the negative effects of trauma (Herman, 1992), but the adverse impact of trauma is unquestionable. Broadly, trauma has an ability to attack one's sense of personhood, our belief in the social bonds between human beings, and the values that govern what we believe should exist for all peoples, leaving one feeling dehumanized, disempowered, deprived, and vulnerable (Gorman, 2001). The result is multiple areas of impact—physical, psychological, social—on a person's ability to function.

There is a robust relationship between trauma and adverse psychological symptoms, with implications for long-term mental health problems when symptoms are left untreated (Alexander, Eyerman, Giesen, Smelser, & Sztompka, 2004; Barnes, Harrison,

& Heneghan, 2004; Daniels, 2002; Fong, 2004). For refugees, they often arrive in their destination country with health needs that exacerbate an already fragile mental state (Alexander et al., 2004; Daniels, 2002; Fong, 2004). Many have health issues because of living in unsanitary, under-resourced refugee camps for extended periods of time without access to proper healthcare (Tiong et al., 2006), nutritious food, and clean water (Burnett & Peel, 2001). To add further complications, new immigrant and refugee arrivals are struggling to acculturate to a new society quickly (Alexander et al., 2004), learn the language, find employment, and become self-sufficient (Daniels, 2002; Lie, Sveaass, & Eilertsen, 2004; Somasundaram & Jamunanantha, 2002).

The combination of complex health and mental health needs, coupled with migration stressors, makes adjustment and integration increasingly challenging for new arrivals. Recent studies show that refugees experience higher rates of certain illnesses (e.g., PTSD, depression, psychosis, tuberculosis, and hypertension) than other populations in the United States (Barnes et al., 2004; Szajna & Ward, 2014) and that such needs are not adequately addressed with current health and mental health interventions (Murray, Davidson, & Schweitzer, 2010). Barriers such as low levels of education, low English-language skills, and low vocational skills are additional formidable stressors that can again make adjustment even more difficult (Huijts, Kleijn, van Emmerik, Noordhof, & Smith, 2012). Moreover, there are limited financial supports offered to new immigrants and the expectations for self-sufficiency (i.e., independent from substantial public aid/ services and basic needs of clothing, food, and shelter are met) are often unrealistic. For some, the resettlement process in a new country (and the pressures to adjust quickly and become self-sufficient) can be experienced as trauma and sadly, some consider resettlement in a new country even more traumatic than their experiences abroad.

Organizational Practice: Supporting Forcibly Displaced Persons Worldwide

Organizations serve as a lifeline to trauma-exposed new immigrants and refugees who need to access information and resources, especially during that first year upon arrival to their destination country. To understand the full value and influence of organizations that serve these groups, it is critical to first define the term *organization* and the context behind practice within organization settings (organizational practice). Organizations form the contexts in which much of our daily lives are carried out as we constantly interface with formal and informal organizational settings. As social units (or human groupings), **organizations** are deliberately constructed and reconstructed to seek specific goals, oftentimes involving more than two people and with a goal and mission that can be met by the members of the group (Schriver, 2010). In many ways, our well-being and basic survival is linked to organizational structures. Our basic subsistence is met by the availability of groceries, clothing stores, banks, and housing accommodations. We meet our health and well-being needs by interfacing with hospitals, clinics, and pharmacies. We are socialized through schools and community organization settings. Our spiritual needs are met with religious and spiritual organizations. And our ability to sustain ourselves financially is met with the different employment opportunities housed within an organization structure. Thus, this discussion of organizational practice is included, because we know all people (including immigrants and refugees) depend on organizations to function in their daily lives. As such, the organization structure, its goals, and its approach to service delivery matter. Mismatch between the organization goals, client needs, and the cultural appropriateness of service delivery can result in lower service utilization. Even worse, a mismatch may foster higher levels of isolation or desperation for resources among those most in need of culturally sensitive services.

Organizations are thus positioned with a unique opportunity to address the adverse trauma symptoms and adjustment needs of new immigrants when it can provide comprehensive, multi-level (i.e., focuses on individual, family, community), and culturally tailored services to its client population. Organizations can focus on relevant pre-migration, transit experiences, and post-migration needs (Kirmayer et al., 2011) by training staff to engage clients with cultural sensitivity and awareness of trauma stressors. Organizations can also inform clients about the realities of living in a new country, including issues around racism, discrimination, and employment opportunities (Dow, 2011; Porter & Haslam, 2005; Pumariega, Rothe, & Pumariega, 2005) that further impact adjustment. Negative attitudes generated by the media (Pickering, 2001), post-9/11 concerns over national security (Van Selm, 2003), and terrorism (Hugo, 2002) are additional sociocultural and sociopolitical stressors on an already vulnerable under-included population adjusting to life in a new country. That being said, organizations can educate on immigrant rights and ways of remaining vigilant and safe despite the heated rhetoric around immigration in communities worldwide. Altogether, organizations can address these diverse issues in an organized, trauma-informed, and culturally aligned manner with an informed staff, mechanisms to disseminate information to clients in their native language, and by fostering an environment of safety and acceptance. Finally, organizations—as a collective institution with a unified voice—can validate the experiences of those who have been oppressed through wider advocacy efforts to ensure new immigrants have opportunities to live lives of dignity that go beyond any one individual story.

Immigrant-serving social service organizations are often designed to implement services that promote acculturation in the new country through the provision of a wide array of language, education, immigration, and vocational training programs. There are **refugee resettlement organizations** that contract specifically with the U.S. Department of State to resettle refugees registered with the United Nations High Commissioner for Refugees (UNHCR). Such agencies tend to have comprehensive services, including case management, English-language training programs, employment programs, and housing assistance as part of a government mandate. **Mutual aid associations** are also immigrant-serving organizations who partner with refugee resettlement agencies or operate independently to serve immigrants in the larger communities. Many are ethnic/culture-specific and provide targeted services, such as English and job placement as well as workshops on navigating the school systems, health care systems, and the financial banking systems. Beyond these immigrant-specific organizations, there are other multi-service agencies available offering a range of resources including health clinics and cultural programming to more targeted needs, such as substance abuse, domestic violence, or immigration services.

Ultimately, when an organization has a clear understanding of its service population and it organizes staff in a way to address that population's needs, service delivery will be thoughtful and comprehensive. Many immigrant-serving organizations are structured with a bureaucratic hierarchy that aligns management and programs to be goal-specific but collaborative. Additionally, many organizations are shifting toward research-informed, evidence-based practice designs to ensure program practices are documented and evaluated. These structures allow for service delivery to match the needs of the service population but incorporate accountability mechanisms to measure impact and effectiveness. Of course, there are challenges to meet the changing service delivery needs as the demographics of arriving populations continue to bring new cultural and linguistic demands that could influence access and utilization (Sue, Zane, Nagayama Hall, & Berger, 2009). These barriers, however, should not deter organizations, as the needs could be addressed when organization structures can adapt and learn about new cultures and hire and train staff to match the qualities/cultures of arriving groups.

Embedding Mental Health Programs Within Immigrant-Serving Organizations

There are untoward consequences when immigrant-serving organizations fail to recognize the importance of mental health in their program design and service delivery structure. Mental health problems can thwart gains in any one of the many supportive programs (e.g., language training programs, vocational training programs, etc.), when those gains cannot be sustained as a result of the adverse mental health symptoms. According to Murray, Davidson, and Schweitzer (2010), there is an ongoing need to develop "culturally appropriate mental health services for socially under-included and marginalized populations," and the authors go on to note a specific need for refugee groups given a general shared experience of physical and emotional trauma and forced relocation (p. 576). The review of alternative program structures and practice frameworks with a trauma focus is thus warranted.

Accordingly, I want to build on the concepts presented and examine the trauma commonly associated with the refugee experience and the role of organizations in supporting refugee adjustment and healing. I will specifically examine the benefits of mental health programs *embedded within* refugee resettlement organizations; an organization structure that puts mental health providers directly in contact with newly arrived refugees alongside staff overseeing other refugee programs (general case management, employment, housing, language training) from the moment refugees arrive in their new home country. Finally, I want to focus on details of a practice framework for delivering culturally sensitive mental health services within the context of a refugee resettlement organization. Although not all immigrant-serving organizations have an embedded mental health program, it is worth discussing the relevance of equipping immigrant-serving organizations with mental health knowledge to support the overall well-being and integration of trauma-exposed clients in a new community. Many of the concepts and approaches can certainly be adapted to any service setting so there is a general utility in its review.

This shift is not to understate the trauma experiences and mental health needs of immigrants generally; asylum seekers, documented, and undocumented immigrants are in many ways equally trauma exposed in their respective migration journey. And while not every immigrant is a refugee,[2] every refugee is an immigrant and one who typically arrives to a resettlement country after experiencing trauma to a disproportionately higher degree than the general immigrant population (Szajna & Ward, 2014). This is, in part, the rationale for focusing on refugees as a subgroup of the larger immigrant population and examining the value of mental health service delivery to refugees within the context of a U.S. authorized refugee resettlement organization; we can expect adverse trauma symptoms to impact the adjustment process given the general experience of those designated with refugee status. Again, the detailed information on mental health service delivery models implemented with refugees can be applied to other immigrant groups (documented and undocumented) and asylum seekers as well. It is understood that the cumulative impact of trauma on the health and mental health for all immigrants can compromise the readiness with which immigrants begin that journey of rebuilding their lives and can undermine progress in developing skills to integrate into a new country and their ability to cope with challenges that arise in that process. Organizations can play a critical role in that journey; a role that needs to be better understood.

THE CULTURAL MERGENCE MODEL

Historical Context

The **cultural mergence model** was designed and implemented in 2011 to guide the delivery of mental health services as part of the core services offered at a Chicago-based refugee resettlement organization. Using trauma-informed and culturally respectful techniques, the cultural mergence model (hereafter model) was embedded into the mental health program, aptly named *The Wellness Program*, established in direct response to the lack of community mental health providers who had both the linguistic capacity and the cultural knowledge to work with arriving refugee populations at the time as well as the decreasing funds for community mental health programs for immigrant and refugee populations.

Intersections Between the Model and Organizational Practice

The model offers a way of addressing acute mental health conditions among refugee arrivals against the background of organizational practice and the importance of having both conceptual and applied integrative frameworks for practice. The program's delivery

---

[2]A *refugee* being a person who owing to a well-founded fear of persecution leaves her country of origin, crosses an international border, and seeks the protection of the United Nations and the privileges allowed in her temporary host country (UNHCR.org, n.d.). Those having the refugee experiences— those forced to migrate for safety and survival—have particular physical and psychological risk factors related to trauma that may aggravate the adjustment process and increase the likelihood of exhibiting adverse symptoms.

approach was designed as intensive but with sensitive prevention and intervention strategies, typically delivered with in the first six to eight months of a refugee's arrival in Chicago. To date, there are very few refugee resettlement organizations across the country with an embedded mental health program wherein mental health professionals are working alongside case managers, medical caseworkers, English-language teachers, and employment counselors (i.e., general adjustment programs[3]) within one organization. The model, by virtue of its ability to stabilize health and mental health needs, also seeks to increase gains in an organization's other programs (e.g., English language training programs, employment training programs, youth and senior programs), also intended to assist with integration into a new country. It requires general staff, not exclusively the mental health providers, to have a working knowledge of trauma-related mental health symptoms. For example, refugees in language training programs may have difficulty concentrating or integrating knowledge because of mental health problems and other stressors, so language teachers can make referrals to the mental health program as needs arise. Employment program staff, responsible for helping refugees find jobs, may pay attention to triggers on the job site, such as harsh sounds, extreme temperatures, or manual labor tasks that can remind refugee clients of trauma experiences in their past. Case managers may identify during the initial intake interviews that trauma-symptoms are so severe that a refugee will not be able to work. In such cases, caseworkers can step in and file the appropriate disability applications while referring to mental health services. And the mental health providers in the organization can consult, observe, and enroll in direct services (individual, couple, group, family therapy) when mental health problems need to be addressed with minimal delay.

Thus, the Wellness Program and its model was designed to capitalize on the strengths of the different adjustment programs already in operation within the larger organization. From an ecological perspective and knowing the stigma of mental health remains, the program and its model relies on *all* organization programs sharing a unified language when it comes to talking about mental health symptoms; that these symptoms were a product of terrible experiences and that clients can access a program onsite with mental health professionals who can help. Consequently, collaborative approaches across programs and full recognition of the adverse effects of trauma gives greater insight to developing comprehensive plans that will stabilize health and help refugees become self-sufficient. And in the process, each respective adjustment program collectively achieves the overarching organization's goals of providing culturally appropriate and responsive services to refugees that enable them to build lives of safety, dignity, and self-reliance.

Literature Informing the Cultural Mergence Model

I designed the model as a practice framework for delivering mental health services within or in close collaboration with resettlement or immigrant-serving organization settings, accounting for the need for more practice models that are contextually

---

[3]*Adjustment programs* refer to an array of services that help new immigrants integrate into a new society, including case management services to aid with navigating public benefit and social service systems, English-language training programs, employment services for securing a job, and housing programs to help new immigrants secure affordable housing.

responsive and strength based. The model provides a conceptualization of the physical, psychological, social, and economic needs among trauma-experienced immigrants and refugees (hereafter refugees) and away from the central focus on singular traumatic experiences, as has been the case. Trauma has typically been at the center of interventions, as the focus has historically been on psychological disturbances associated with a person or community's trauma history. While there is validity in recognizing the adverse impact and symptoms associated with trauma, for years there has been a question on the appropriateness of the "trauma model" along with other Western frameworks for assessing mental health with non-Western populations (Bracken, 2002). Gozdiak (2004) has criticized the medicalization of trauma: "Biomedicine may actually diminish the capacity of human beings to deal with anxiety and suffering, deny their resilience, render them incapacitated by their trauma, and indefinitely dependent on external actors for their psychosocial survival" (p. 206). The model seeks to shift away from the deficit-based understanding of trauma. Instead, there is a growing attention toward recognizing the refugees' experiences and challenges in the resettlement context as a means of fostering strength and resilience for both individual and community (Papadopoulos, 2007). This requires recognition of the sociocultural context—that is, changes in cultural systems, changes in socioeconomic systems, and the creation of new social support systems that impact overall well-being.

The model still elucidates the relevance of mental health needs and services when working with refugee groups but accounts for more stressors while answering the call to move away from allowing trauma to be the primary defining quality of psychological disturbances. Furthermore, the model grounds itself on critical thinking, adaptability, and consideration of the dynamic ecological systems at play (individual, family, community, global systems) that affect the quality of adjustment (Rasco & Miller, 2004) in the context of the clients served by the model. Conclusively, the model provides a pragmatic way of organizing multi-level, culturally sensitive, therapeutic interventions within an organizational context. There is no singular theoretical foundation for the model. Instead, the model employs an integrative approach to theory application that guides engagement and therapy while accounting for the pre- and post-migration stressors that directly influence health and adjustment outcomes.

The model name itself—cultural mergence—is derived from the inextricable understanding of the need for cross-cultural proficiency within a multicultural paradigm when delivering mental health service to refugees or any new immigrant. Migration itself results in three specific transitions: A change in personal ties and the creation of new networks, movement from one socioeconomic system to another (sometimes a lowering of status), and a shift from one cultural system to another (Bhugra, 2004). In the process of delivering culturally appropriate mental health services within an organizational practice framework, there is value in examining the merging of cultures between refugee client and professional as an intrinsic part of the process. The mental health professional must learn, grow, and adapt in the same manner required of the refugee participant, thereby producing gains for both parties. There is a "mergence" of culture, environmental contexts, theory, and clinical techniques through the therapeutic relationship built between mental health professional and participant/client. Notwithstanding the complexity of each individual's experience, the model adapts to the varying degree of need and the client's circumstances, making this model both culturally sensitive but flexible for diverse ethnic groups and circumstances. It gives full recognition of the importance of pre-migration, migration, and post-migration resettlement factors and stressors for understanding the physical and psychological manifestations of trauma and its related impact on adjustment. And the model understands the unique cultural definitions of mental health that exist and the need to create a shared definition for mental health between professional and participant in order for services to be used.

Furthermore, the model had to be cognizant of the particular circumstances of refugee resettlement that would directly influence mental health service utilization. According to Murray et al. (2010), the effectiveness of mental health interventions following resettlement is likely to be dependent on "the extent to which those interventions relate directly to the educational, socio-economic, and socio-political stresses that refugees encounter as well as their ability to alleviate the lingering symptoms of traumatic stress" (p. 8). The services must fit the refugee client's definition of what mental health symptoms are problematic and needing attention. To be relevant, mental health services also have to recognize the inter-relatedness of social, economic, political, and even legal dimensions associated with resettlement (Al-Shiyab, 2009). Refugees are not simply seeking to heal past psychological and physical wounds (although that is critical), but they are also reconciling loss in the present with hope for the future. So building on Judith Herman's (1992) work, the model seeks to provide safety, a space for reconstructing one's trauma narrative, and reconnecting with the present and future hopes to give space to process the past and consider dreams in the future in a manner that is culturally admissible to the client. In this process, the model seeks to validate and empower participants through recognition of their resilience and to substantiate their experiences with compassion and respect in a meaningful way. As stated by Murray et al. (2010), "effective interventions can utilize culturally appropriate ways of engaging with refugees that do not pathologize but rather honor cultural systems and values to foster recovery and resilience processes" (p. 3). These perspectives are integrated in the model's design and intent to provide responsive, culturally aligned mental health resources that could be widely accepted within the refugee community.

Major Model Components

To begin, the cultural mergence model provides a framework for delivering mental health services within a refugee-resettlement organization context. At the same time, it illuminates the nature of the therapeutic relationship between refugee/immigrant participant (hereafter client) and the practitioner (hereafter mental health professional); a relationship that is invaluable in addressing the mental health problems of refugee clients. These next sections outline the details of the various model components and its relation to the goals of the model. When appropriate, other staff members (other than the mental health professional) within the respective organization can be enlisted to support stabilization efforts that will complement clinical interventions addressing the mental health needs of the client.

Figure 11.1 illustrates the entire model, mapping the interactive relationship from initial engagement to resolving client needs, and the outcomes for client and professional as

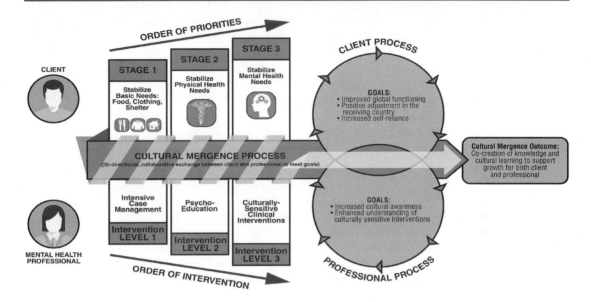

Figure 11.1 The Cultural Mergence Model: A Practice Model for Serving Trauma-Exposed New Immigrants

an outgrowth of addressing the client's needs. To be clear at the outset, not all trauma-experienced immigrants or refugees would require mental health services or find use in the model that integrates mental health as an underscore to the service framework. For those immigrants that *do* come with a trauma history and adverse mental health symptoms that impede her[4] ability to navigate the demands of daily life, the model's stepped approach is sensitive and supportive. And as you will see with each description, the model embodies this goal of honoring culture and empowerment through its multi-level, integrated intervention approach to providing mental health services to trauma-exposed refugees.

UNIVERSAL SCREENING. Universal screening for mental health needs (not shown in the figure) allows an organization and its affiliated mental health program (if applicable) an opportunity to quickly identify mental health needs among new arrivals before the needs/problems immobilize the client to a level that deters any successful adjustment outcomes. Importantly, it is the screening process that initiates the program enrollments that would lead to the application of the model. In the Wellness Program, every refugee adult (18+ years) is screened for mental health needs. And while screening is not intended to be diagnostic, it affords a comprehensive look at general areas of functioning that need attention to stabilize overall health.

There are a number of validated mental health screening instruments available for use with immigrant and refugee populations. The Refugee Health Screener-15 (RHS-15)

---

[4]The pronoun "her" will be used to reference all immigrant and refugee clients with full recognition that women or those who identify as a woman are not the only persons who immigrate to new countries and seek mental health services.

and the Harvard Trauma Questionnaire (HTQ) have been commonly used to identify symptoms of post-traumatic stress disorder (PTSD) and other related symptoms. The New Mexico Refugee Symptom Checklist-121 (NMRSCL-121) was developed to identify physical and emotional symptoms and the Hopkins Symptom Checklist-25 (HSCL-25) has been adapted for immigrant populations to look for anxiety and depressions but not PTSD. Additionally, there are a multitude of other instruments used in the mental health field to address other mental disorders, not necessarily normed to multicultural populations or specific to immigrants and refugees. The Posttraumatic Symptom Scale-Self Report (PSS-SR) is one example of a tool that identifies PTSD but in general Western populations, specifically, populations in the United States.

The Wellness Program uses a comprehensive universal mental health screening instrument that combines several validated tools currently used in health and mental health settings and adapted for internal use with refugee populations. It is administered within 30 to 45 days of a refugee's arrival date in Chicago, and the findings will determine enrollment in mental health services or referrals to other supportive programs in the agency. The Wellness Program screener is able to identify symptoms of depression, anxiety, psychosis, PTSD, intimate partner/domestic violence, and substance abuse. The instrument also has specific questions on women's reproductive health, needs among pregnant or new mothers, and scales for emotional and health states. Together, the screening instrument requires 35 to 45 minutes to administer and yields a great deal of information about a person's current level of functioning.

The delayed administration of the instrument is intentional, as refugees often experience a "honeymoon" period (see Lysgaard U-curve of adjustment) within the first weeks of arrival in a new country. During this time, adverse symptoms are often masked by the excitement, nervousness, and the adrenaline surge that comes with being in a new place. Additionally, newly arrived refugees are inundated with a number of required intake interviews, public benefit and identification appointments, and health appointments. Screening completed too early may result in false negative or false positive scores in which the refugees either feel no symptoms, although symptoms are actually present, or they describe symptoms of a severe mental illness, when those symptoms are in reality a product of the extreme stress tied to general adjustment. Accordingly, the timing of the screener matters, but even if a refugee client screens without a need during the 30- to 45-day window, this will not bar a client from receiving mental health services in the future. Refugee clients who present with adverse symptoms or needs later in the adjustment period can be rescreened, enrolled, and the model of service will apply.

The strength of universal screening is that it is a part of an organization-wide effort to normalize mental health terminology for new refugee arrivals. Even before the screening is administered, newly arrived refugees are already being exposed to the mental health language to help reduce stigma. As context, refugees in the United States are required to complete a series of cultural orientation sessions to socialize newcomers to the country as mandated by the U.S. Department of State, which oversees the U.S. refugee resettlement program. Newly arrived refugees attend cultural orientation within the first week of their arrival and at that time, all arrivals will be introduced to the Wellness Program and mental health terminology and symptoms. They will also be informed that all arrivals will be screened by a clinical social worker in the program who will be asking them questions about how they are feeling and adjusting to life in Chicago.

To ensure no one refugee feels targeted for her mental health symptoms (again, related to stigma and misperceptions around the concept of mental health), the mental health screening process is built into the resettlement agency's core adjustment services. This means the screener is just one step in a comprehensive protocol of intakes and follow-ups during the first 90-days post-arrival to ensure the resources and services necessary for successful integration are inputted during this critical time. At 90-days, refugees meet with an agency mental health professional again to ensure any mental health needs, not currently addressed, are given attention. Likewise in the spirit of normalizing mental health needs, all staff within the larger organization are trained to recognize mental health needs, use a common language to describe mental health symptoms, and refer to the Wellness Program accordingly. Again, there are clear benefits of an embedded mental health program within a larger refugee resettlement organization.

Mental health is a core component of how the respective organization understands the functioning of newly arrived refugees and the quality of their adjustment to life in a new country. It is an organizational practice approach that has clear protocols to promote mental health stabilization—mental health content at orientation, universal screening at 30- to 45-days post arrival, follow-up procedures at 90-days post arrival—and all work together to normalize mental health language into how refugees understand health and what is necessary to thrive in general. Clients who understand their symptoms better may feel greater agency to participate and find answers to their needs and maintain good health.

MODEL ACTIVITIES. After the screening process is completed and clients are identified, in brief, the following flow of activities applies. The client presents with three stages of need that are listed based on order of priority upon arrival in her resettlement country; the levels range from most critical at arrival (Stage 1: Stabilize basic needs) to less critical at arrival (Stage 3: Stabilize mental health needs) based on perceptions of the client, which may include a client's lack of understanding around the term mental health. Matching the client's priorities, the mental health professional will engage in three levels of interventions to meet each client priority stage from providing intensive case management (Level 1) to providing clinical interventions—that is, mental health services (Level 3). In the process, the client attends to her basic adjustment needs, and builds social supports and a general sense of stability to address other vulnerable areas that may impede adjustment and overall well-being. Through the collaborative exchange (bi-directional) between client and professional, both parties experience gains. The client gains improved global functioning across the dimensions of health, mental health, and sociocultural adjustment and increased self-reliance. The mental health professional, in turn, should develop an increased level of cultural awareness with a greater understanding of the impact and efficacy of the culturally sensitive interventions employed through the model. Finally, outcome of the model process is the **cultural mergence outcome**—that is, the co-creation of knowledge and cultural learning to support the growth in both the client and the mental health professional.

MULTILEVEL ELEMENTS OF THE CULTURAL MERGENCE MODEL

I. Client Priorities (Stage 1 to Stage 3)

The course of adjustment to life in a new country is not linear. New immigrants experience the roller coaster of emotions and experiences (Lysgaard, 1955) that make each day both exciting and challenging. One true fact is that mental health is often an afterthought. For so many, the history of trauma and its related symptoms are experienced with a sense of normalcy and in some cases, the collective trauma within communities only further normalizes those trauma experiences. This reality places a potential challenge to addressing mental health needs among new refugee arrivals that may undermine successful adjustment, as the focus is on the primacy of resettlement and survival needs that relegate mental health needs and seeking treatment to an afterthought. Unfortunately, refugees may not fully grasp that adverse mental health symptoms may directly interfere with efforts to stabilize basic needs if those symptoms get in the way of executing tasks or accessing resources. Given this reality, the model underscores the client priorities and its respective order of importance as determined by the client. The priorities are addressed in epigenetic stages that begin with the most basic needs of clients to the more complex areas that impact functioning, specifically, mental health if applicable.

STAGE 1: BASIC NEEDS: FOOD, CLOTHING, SHELTER. For refugees, there is a focus on the primacy of resettlement needs and information gathering as essential components of stabilizing mental health and well-being. Following Maslow's Hierarchy of Needs (1943), new immigrants follow the same priority structure. Addressing the physiological needs of accessing food, clothing, and shelter (and employment to maintain access to each) are a critical priority in resettlement agencies during the first 90-days post arrival. Integrated into meeting these basic needs is a focus on English proficiency as language abilities are equally critical to new immigrants; language skills support the building of new support systems that are vital to adjustment, including accessing public resources (social security, public benefits programs, etc.) and navigating different service providers (doctors, job recruiters, etc.) and other social systems (education programs, banks, etc.). Basic needs vary, as do the degree of skills and resources new immigrants have upon arrival. For those with higher levels of education, they experience worst post-migration outcomes as a result of not finding comparable work opportunities (Porter & Haslam, 2005). This distinction aside, all new refugees are learning about a new environment and adapting to new cultures and systems, a process that can create anxiety and feelings of insecurity irrespective of one's social capital upon arrival.

STAGE 2: STABILIZE PHYSICAL HEALTH NEEDS. Generally, refugees enter unfavorable living conditions when displaced in host countries and awaiting resettlement options.

Whether relocated to refugee camps in Kenya or Thailand or relocated to urban cities in Egypt, Jordan, or Malaysia, there is a general lack of access to quality medical care and medication. Some research has documented the difficulty in accessing specialists (Huang, Yu, & Ledsky, 2006), language barriers (Jacobs, Shepard, Suaya, & Stone, 2004), or the extraordinary costs of accessing care and medication (Goldman, Joyce, & Zheng, 2007; Schaafsma, Raynorr, & Jong-van den Berg, 2003) that deter refugees from seeking or accessing health services. As many refugees entering the United States currently arrive from active conflict zones, the Wellness Program is seeing an increase in clients who are physically compromised with shrapnel in their bodies from explosions. Others arrive with symptoms of malnutrition and gastrointestinal problems. There are women who arrive pregnant in their second trimester without having any prenatal care prior to arrival—a state in which hospitals automatically categorize the pregnancy as "high risk," limiting delivery to only designated hospitals equipped to meet this criteria. Finally, we are seeing refugee arrivals that only learn upon arrival that they are HIV positive and have had no treatment.

The physical health problems of refugees worldwide are escalating as conflicts rage, resources dwindle, and people are displaced to substandard living conditions. It is a recipe for poor health outcomes overall, as there is a direct correlation between physical health problems and the prevalence of adverse mental health symptoms (Hilado & Kim, n.d.). And while identification of health and mental health problems is imperative to stabilizing health and general functioning, it is not always easy to identify. Mental health problems can manifest as physical ailments, whether somatic or repressed, making treatment challenging and misdirected (Aragona et al., 2005; Ritsner, Ponozovsky, Kurs, & Modai, 2000; Ryder et al., 2008). Likewise, poor physical health can adversely impact mood and the ability to maintain self-sufficiency, which is critical for new arrivals. Accordingly, the task of stabilizing physical health needs paves the way for addressing interrelated mental health symptoms that further influence the adjustment process.

STAGE 3: STABILIZE MENTAL HEALTH NEEDS. Once basic physiological and survival needs are met and physical health problems are addressed and stabilized, there is an increased likelihood and openness to addressing previous trauma that may be the source of mental health problems. To begin, it is critical we define mental health. According to the World Health Organization (WHO, 2016), mental health is defined as "a state of well-being in which every individual realizes his or her own potential, can cope with the normal stresses of life, can work productively and fruitfully, and is able to make a contribution to her or his community." The positive dimension of mental health is stressed in WHO's definition of health as contained in its constitution: "Health is a state of complete physical, mental and social well-being and not merely the absence of disease or infirmity" (WHO, 2016). Addressing mental health needs, when applicable, builds on a foundation of health that the model seeks to afford its participants. Through linguistically and culturally sensitive therapy approaches, client experiences are affirmed while the professional seeks to reduce symptoms, in collaboration with the client, that impair and negatively impact the client's life. Simultaneously, this stage seeks to illuminate the client's sense of self-agency and resilience, empowering them to maintain their health and well-being upon termination of services and beyond the services offered within the resettlement organization.

II. Professional Process (Intervention Level 1 to Level 3)

The cultural mergence model reflects the client and professional interactive exchange that produces outcomes for both parties. Specific to the mental health professional, however, there are three graduated intervention levels that complement the various needs (i.e., stages) presented by the client.

LEVEL 1: INTENSIVE CASE MANAGEMENT. To meet the Stage 1 (basic needs) of the client, there may be partnership between the mental health professional and case management staff in the larger resettlement organization. Intensive case management can include an array of activities to meet the basic life needs described, including securing public benefits (e.g., identification cards, Employment Authorization certificates, food stamps, Temporary Assistance for Needy Families (TANF), Social Security benefits), coordinating housing and education around how to pay rent, coordinating with employment programs to help clients secure a job, and referrals to English language training. The intensive case management component may also include seeking medical referrals for specialized health conditions, addressing vision or dental needs, or any legal or immigration services that may apply to the client. Activities in this level may continue throughout the process toward delivering clinical services (Level 3); however, energy and attention at the front-end of the service model ensures major survival needs are met before proceeding to the next level of intervention.

LEVEL 2: PSYCHO-EDUCATION. Cultivating self-agency and resilience can occur when we equip clients with information about their health and the health resources around them. Multilevel interventions that focus on prevention to intensive interventions are valuable in resettlement contexts, as it can lessen or delay adverse health and mental health symptoms as well as improve access to resources (Weine, 2011). In the model, preventive supports come in the form of client-specific psychoeducation workshops. Generally, participants in interventions seek tangible supports, such as learning a new skill or attaining knowledge, suggesting value when participants could learn more about Western ideologies related to mental well-being (van der Velde, Williamson, & Ogilvie, 2009). The model meets what Weine (2011) believes are useful structures for preventive mental health interventions for refugees, as the workshops are accessible for clients to attend (i.e., in the same location as other resettlement services), culturally tailored, and adaptable to client education and language abilities. In the Wellness Program, topics most useful to refugee arrivals include understanding trauma symptoms, nutrition topics to help manage diabetes and hypertension, information on taking medication correctly and refilling prescriptions, and stress management.

There is documented success of other preventative health programs when clients are given information about how to help sustain their own health. To illustrate, one intervention provided health information related to mammography, pap smears, and mental health services to address trauma through workshops targeting Congolese and Somali refugee women in the United States. Findings of that intervention showed an increase in knowledge and desire to pursue services (Piwowarczyk et al., 2013). Ultimately, the model seeks to further stabilize client needs and physical health (Stages 1 and 2) by providing both the concrete services and resources to meet basic health and adjustment needs but also providing information about how to maintain their health and well-being and how to access other services when needed.

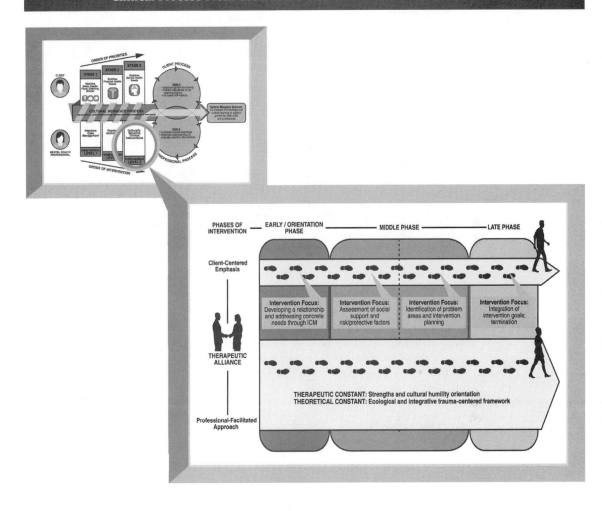

LEVEL 3: CULTURALLY SENSITIVE CLINICAL INTERVENTION. The multilevel supports of Intervention Level 1 and Level 2 are the foundation for facilitating clinical interventions to address adverse mental health symptoms among refugees or any trauma-exposed immigrant in Level 3. Intervention Level 3 involves the mental health service component of the model and is employed by trained and licensed mental health professionals (i.e., psychiatrists, licensed clinical social workers, psychologists, counselors, marriage family therapists). This is the premise of the model as a practice framework for delivering mental health services. Figure 11.2 illustrates the detailed activities in Level 3 that are part of the larger model. Not all refugees will require extensive mental health interventions, as it is possible for adverse psychological symptoms (e.g., mild generalized anxiety, excessive stress or nervousness upon arrival,

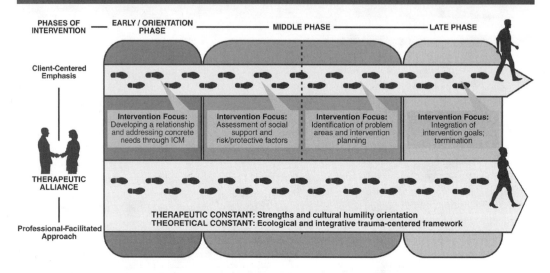

Figure 11.3 Intervention Level 3: Culturally Sensitive Clinical Interventions

mild adjustment disorder) to be addressed with Intervention Levels 1 and 2. At the same time, this illustrates the model's multipoint opportunities to stabilize health and mental health. For those who need more intensive mental health services, Level 3 is available and will build on the gains met through the previous intervention activities. It is important to note that the model is employed for all those needing mental health services, but the level of need will always vary; therefore, the model can adapt to what the client needs at any given time.

THE CLINICAL PROCESS OF ADDRESSING MENTAL HEALTH NEEDS (LEVEL 3)

Delving further, Level 3 (culturally sensitive clinical interventions) is an interactive relational process between the client and the mental health professional who form a therapeutic alliance (i.e., restorative clinical relationship) to address a range of mental health needs from generalized, mild problems to severe psychological diseases (see Figure 11.3). Gonsalves (1992) acknowledged that mental health interventions and the roles of practitioners delivering them must change with the client's changing therapeutic needs and be evaluated at the different stages of development, and the same applies to the model. The work within the therapeutic alliance is facilitated by the professional (professional-facilitated approach) and centered on the client's[5] needs, level of comfort in the session, and individual goals that may change over time (client-centered emphasis). Together, the two will navigate the three phases of intervention—

[5]The "client" can include varying types of client systems—including couples, families, and community. The model is flexible for allowing different intervention styles based on the client system. For this basic introduction, the client will be used in the singular involving one participant.

each with its distinct goals that should be evaluated from initial engagement to termination.[6]

The phases of clinical intervention in the model follow standard practice formats—the early/orientation phase, the middle phase, and the late/termination phase—and at each phase, there are specific goals that should be addressed. During the early/orientation phase, the client and practitioner focus on developing a relationship and addressing concrete needs through intensive case management (Intervention Level 1). The coordination of services to meet resettlement needs can also be a trust-building mechanism that strengthens the therapeutic alliance.

During the middle phase of treatment, there are two foci: (a) assessment of social support and risk and protective factors that may mitigate or aggravate mental health problems, and (b) identification of problem areas and intervention planning. Critical to this phase is honoring cultural practices and traditions that may involve recognizing community or spiritual leaders—including relevant family members—building in community supports, and identifying ways of building new social support networks that can buffer the impact of risk factors and decrease isolation in the resettlement country. At this stage, it is also critical to avoid pathologizing trauma or corresponding symptoms. Clients have a right to self-determination (i.e., in this case, client authority in treatment planning), and the professional needs to work within what is respectful of the client's experience, understanding of need, and what the professional understands as intervention options. Ultimately, the relationship must revolve around a collaborative effort to enhance client functioning and well-being, with client desires placed at the center of the decision-making process.

The final phase of intervention—late or termination phase—revolves around the integration of intervention goals to reduce problematic symptoms and enhance coping and problem-solving skills. This phase also prioritizes a change in any deficit-based personal narratives, moving clients away from self-identification as a victim and to a survivor narrative instead. Clients are encouraged to recognize the past experiences that shape the present but to avoid allowing the past to define their futures. This emphasis employs strength-based approaches (Epstein et al., 2003) to conceptualizing one's life and in doing so, empowering clients to see the opportunities for health and growth beyond the therapy sessions.

To achieve the goals outlined throughout the intervention, the professional-facilitated intervention approach of the model encompasses two building blocks: the therapeutic constant and the theoretical constant. Both guide the nature of engagement with the client and inform the language, clinical techniques, and conceptualization of the client's problem; each taking a positive, holistic approach to understanding client needs and finding solutions. Furthermore, the professional enters the encounter from a place of

---

[6]In the Wellness Program, progress measures are periodically administered to track changes in the client's level of functioning areas (including mood, sleep, and social functioning) based on client self-reports. A pre-test is administered at the first session, followed by midterm reports every six to eight sessions. A post-test is completed at termination and together, the information from the various data points are analyzed to examine model efficacy.

cultural humility and curiosity as he or she accepts the lack of complete knowledge of any one client's experiences or cultural history.

BUILDING BLOCK A: THERAPEUTIC CONSTANT. Professionals applying the model must be guided by a strengths-based (Epstein et al., 2003) and cultural humility orientation (Tervalon & Murray-Garcia, 1998) in each therapeutic encounter, and there is no one prescriptive way of doing this. Instead, the model encourages professionals to find ways of highlighting client's innate capabilities to understand her problems and move toward reframing the program problems and/or circumstances in a positive/ optimistic manner (strengths framework). The cultural humility orientation requires professionals to come from a place of curiosity and career-long learning about different cultures and different cultural experiences rather than a place of cultural competence when engaging clients of unique, diverse backgrounds. Such perspectives on the client and the client's needs allow the professional to see the person beyond the problem. As stated by Papadopoulos (2007), it is important we collectively move away from medical models of psychological distress that emphasize stress-related trauma and move toward psychosocial models that focus on positive personal change. In doing so, practitioners are able to help clients regain a sense of control over their lives within a culturally appropriate framework. We also want to again recognize the role of community leaders and build capacity beyond the program (Papadopoulos, 2007), thereby giving a sense of agency in the client's larger social community and diminishing any sense of dependence on the therapeutic alliance alone. The practice with refugees requires professionals to rethink the common psychotherapy models available as professionals move to accommodate culture, linguistic background, meanings of emotions, and the cultural context of the host country in conjunction with the client's culture of origin (Miller, 1999).

BUILDING BLOCK B: THEORETICAL CONSTANT. The model employs an ecological and integrative trauma-centered framework as the theoretical basis to guide interventions, which recognizes the potential disconnect between Western-oriented theoretical frameworks when used with non-Western populations. The ecological approach suggests attention be paid to the related systems that revolve around an individual that may impact functioning—including family, group, community, and the larger social systems—including relevant political, legal, social, and financial systems that impact the daily lives of participants. Moreover, the use of a trauma-centered framework gives attention to any relevant trauma history—pre-migration, migration, post-migration—that may influence behavior (i.e., actions and reactions to stimuli) and ways of perceiving one's environment. These two elements provide the theoretical foundation that should frame all engagement activities and account for both the active and passive style of coping among refugees (Colic-Peisker & Tilbury, 2003). Active and purposive coping strategies include active involvement in political activities and confronting the source of conflict directly. Passive and the more ineffective strategies involve avoidance, failure to confront the trauma, or stating it is out of one's control (Colic-Peisker & Tilbury, 2003). Consequently, each coping style can be addressed with a combination of therapeutic engagement strategies informed by other theories of practice.

The specific theoretical approaches/techniques can vary based on the client needs, so long as the approaches encompass the therapeutic constant variables (strengths based and cultural humility) and the theoretical constants (ecological and trauma centered) described. An integrative approach to clinical practices recognizes the value in different theoretical approaches within the treatment room. The literature suggests there are a variety of evaluated treatment methods that have shown successful outcomes among immigrant and refugee populations including cognitive behavioral treatments (D'Ardenne, Ruaro, Cestari, Fakhoury, & Priebe, 2007; Ehntholt, Smith, & Yule, 2005; Fox, Rossetti, Burns, & Popovich, 2005), expressive therapies (Baker & Jones, 2006; Rousseau, Benoit, Lacrois, & Gauthier, 2008), and family and community interventions (Goodkind, 2005), but these are typically limited to specific groups by age and ethnic group. Interpersonal therapy in group formats (Bolton et al., 2007) and narrative exposure therapy (Neuner, Schauer, Klaschik, Karunakara, & Elbert, 2004) have also been equally successful when applied with refugee populations.

The Wellness Program therapists have documented and are studying the use of several therapeutic techniques—exploration of trauma story (narrative theory), exploration of positive relationships/support networks (object relations theory), scaling fear and targeting pervasive negative thought patterns (trauma-focused cognitive-behavioral theory), application of relaxation exercises (mindfulness)—that support symptom reduction and enhance coping strategies while paying attention to environmental factors and trauma narratives. The model allows for the use of several frameworks at any given session or changing approaches throughout the duration of the therapeutic relationship while integrating religion/spirituality, social support, reframing, and future orientation, which have been proven supportive in refugee adjustment (Khawaja, White, Schweitzer, & Greenslade, 2008). This idea of integrative approaches simply recognizes the gap in any one theory; no one theory can explain or support the complex needs oftentimes presented among newly arrived refugees (or broadly, immigrants). Future research will allow for studies on effective techniques and integrative approaches, but also the key consideration is evaluating cultural appropriateness of Western models with non-Western trauma-exposed populations.

III. The Cultural Mergence Process: An Interactive, Transformative, Relational Process

The client priorities organized by Stages 1 through 3 and the mental health professional's intervention Levels 1 through 3 interact together through what I term the *cultural mergence process*: the bi-directional, collaborative exchange of information, strategies to support adjustment and health, and feedback between the client and professional to meet respective goals for both parties. The process happens in the context of a trusting therapeutic relationship, resulting in a transformative undertaking that can leave both the client and professional improved with a greater understanding of culture, mental health, and the skills necessary to live active lives. Client may experience gains in the areas of self-sufficiency, self-agency, and self-actualization, while the mental health professional develops greater cultural sensitivity and self-awareness in support of the client and others with similar experiences.

Consequently, the model embodies major tenets of what is understood as culturally sensitive practice with new immigrants and refugees. First, the bi-directional exchange process between client and professional is client centered and places the client's cultural perspective at the center of the engagement. Furthermore, the model is supportive of client outcomes beyond the therapeutic alliance. The therapeutic relationship enables the client to develop skills for establishing social support networks outside of the program/services, and this is understood as valuable to coping across diverse ethnic communities (Khawaja et al., 2008), as non-Western clients often thrive in community settings that are more aligned with home culture practices. The model values this, knowing that social support has been well understood as a critical protective factor that buffers the impact of violence and persecution that can be felt at an individual and community level (McMichael & Maderson, 2004).

Secondly, the model meets clients where they are, a hallmark of the social work profession, meaning that mental health professionals begin the engagement process prioritizing the client's sense of self and reality. Many newly arrived immigrants and refugees are managing loss of those left behind but also playing the role of the "global breadwinner"—that is, the person living abroad, believed to have access to more resources, who sends money and goods back to family in her home country (Simich, Hamilton, & Khamisa Baya, 2006, p. 622). The focus again requires initial attention to the primacy of resettlement needs, including housing, shelter, feelings of loss of loved ones and separation of family (Khawaja et al., 2008), and the impact on life activities—for example, education and employment (Khawaja et al., 2008), as these are the initial primary foci of the client. Mental health interventions can build from there. Notwithstanding the natural stressors that come with migration, the majority of refugees can successfully adapt to stressors and trauma (Khawaja et al., 2008). For this reason, the model exemplifies a practice framework that carries an intrinsic belief in the resilience and capabilities of trauma-exposed clients. The model also examines problems in adaptation from all angles of adjustment and intervenes with strategies to promote mental health, by using the capabilities of the client and time-focused treatments to enhance functioning in a culturally acceptable manner.

OUTCOMES AND IMPLICATIONS

Five years of operations in the Wellness Program, ongoing data analysis, and findings reflected in the literature only elucidated the need for more integrated and embedded mental health efforts for trauma-experienced immigrants. The work also calls for more research around impactful integrative models and effective interventions with this population. This gap aside and all discussions considered, the model offers a practice framework for professionals that is respectful of cultural difference, mindful of the power and influence of sociocultural experiences (past and present), and acknowledges the potentially damaging impact of trauma on one's ability to live a full and productive life. The model framework for mental health interventions emphasizes the resilience of participants and the strength of the human spirit to overcome the worst adversity and circumstances. There is a focus on ecological contexts, recognizing that multiple systems (individual, family, community, organization) play a role in health stabilization and service utilization. And empowerment leads to great engagement (van der Velde, Williamson, & Ogilvie, 2009) and active help-seeking behaviors to support overall well-being. The framework has shown promising gains among the clients served by the Wellness Program in its tenure that will be shared as the program continues to test efficacy.

Naturally, there are systemic barriers that need to be addressed when delivering mental health services to this under-included group in the general population. As service providers, there is a need to combat barriers to mental health service utilization, including a general distrust of authority and/or systems, stigma of mental health services, linguistic and cultural barriers, and prioritization of resettlement stressors (Ellis, Miller, Baldwin, & Abdi, 2011; Hilado & Allweiss, see Chapter 3 of this book). Despite these barriers, this pragmatic approach to addressing mental health needs within a resettlement organization context has benefits to clients, mental health professionals, as well as the larger organization. According to Lie, Sveaass, and Eilertsen (2004), interventions are "the reconstruction of meaningful lives and the general process of rehabilitation taking place in environments alien to the refugee, making . . . the creat[ion] of structures even more important" (p. 346). The organizations and mental health programs within them are the environments/structures wherein change can and does happen. And by virtue of the interface between mental health programs and the larger organizational structure, a more "trauma-informed system" can be gained. This may include basic staff training and awareness about trauma as well as knowledge of best practices in trauma-informed care in the field (Lang, Vanderploeg, & Campbell, 2015).

Not all organizations can embed a mental health program; however, there are elements of the cultural mergence model—the approach to prioritizing client needs in order to make discussions around mental health programs accessible; the graduated, tiered intervention supports that provide concrete resources, information, and clinical interventions; the therapeutic engagement model with benefits for both client and professional—that can be replicated in other immigrant-serving organizations or mental health programs working closely with immigrant-serving organizations. In the interest of providing culturally relevant and supportive mental health services to the most vulnerable new immigrant populations, the model offers common sense options in service delivery that are relevant to the needs of *all* immigrant arrivals. Therefore and given the importance of organizational practice and mental health services, consideration of integrative, culturally responsive models are worth examining.

REFLECTIVE QUESTIONS

1. Micro practice: What role can the organization play in encouraging mental health service utilization for individuals who have mental health problems?

2. Macro practice: Given the role of organizations in supporting immigrant and refugee adjustment in a host country, how can the content in this chapter inform policy decisions impacting new immigrants and refugees in your country?

3. Macro practice: What components of the cultural mergence model are culturally appropriate for diverse groups? How can the model be adapted to other service organizations or community settings?

APPLICATION WITH TRAUMA-EXPOSED NEW IMMIGRANTS

CASE STUDY: "MAZOKA"

Mazoka is a 32-year-old refugee from Somalia who lived in a Kenyan refugee camp for six years prior to resettlement in the United States with no family. Upon arrival, she shared information about being sexually assaulted in the refugee camp and losing many loved ones from the time she fled Somalia to the refugee camps and the friends she lost to disease, malnutrition, and violence even after arriving in Kenya. Mazoka discussed symptoms of depression, reoccurring nightmares, feeling anxious in crowded areas, and being hyper-vigilant when home alone. The mental health professional evaluating her provided education around post-traumatic stress disorder, a diagnosis that could explain many of her symptoms. When it was suggested that Mazoka begin a combination of therapy and seeing the psychiatrist, she immediately declined services saying that she needed to find a job first and find a roommate to help pay the rent in her studio apartment. Mazoka also stated that she just needs some Somali friends and she will feel better, as she was not sure she could share so much private information with someone who was not from the community.

CRITICAL THINKING EXERCISES: THE CASE OF MAZOKA

1. Based on the case provided, how can the cultural mergence model be applied to support Mazoka? What elements do you think were the most appropriate and culturally sensitive to her circumstances?

2. How can the model support her sense of agency outside of her resettlement organization and the mental health program?

3. What other areas of support could be given to Mazoka to aid in her adjustment and healing?

SUMMATIVE POINTS

- Immigrant and refugee-serving organizations, particularly those that have an embedded mental health program, have a framework for addressing adjustment/resettlement needs alongside mental health needs simultaneously.

- The cultural mergence model is a practice framework for supporting mental health while attending to the primacy of resettlement priorities through case management, education, and culturally sensitive clinical interventions.

- Integrative theoretical approaches must be used to deliver appropriate mental health services to immigrant populations, as Western therapeutic models are not always able to address the cultural diversity and belief systems of the arriving populations.

- All trauma-informed interventions should integrate a strength-based approach to understanding an immigrant's pre-migration, migration, and post-migration experiences, while practicing cultural humility by acknowledging the cultural learning that needs to happen when working with new immigrant groups.

GLOSSARY

organizations. Social units or human groups that are deliberately constructed and reconstructed to meet specific goals and include a goal and mission to be met by members.

immigrant-serving social service organizations. Organizations that provide services targeted to support the needs of immigrants, typically involving services that match the language and cultural beliefs of a specific group.

refugee resettlement organizations. Organizations contracted through affiliates of the U.S. Department of State (specific to the United States) that provide a range of adjustment services to refugee populations.

mutual aid associations. Community-based, ethnic-specific organizations that collaborate with refugee resettlement agencies or operate independently as a not-for-profit social care organization for immigrants and refugees.

cultural mergence model. A trauma-informed multilevel service delivery framework that organizes activities to address mental health needs among trauma-exposed immigrants and refugees.

cultural mergence outcome. The co-creation of knowledge and cultural learning to support the growth of both client and professional.

REFERENCES

Al-Shiyab, A. (2009). *The legal, economic, and social conditions of Iraqi residents in the Hashemite Kingdom of Jordan*. Yarmouk University, Jordan.

Alexander, J. C., Eyerman, R., Giesen, B., Smelser, N. J., & Sztompka, P. (2004). *Cultural trauma and collective identity*. Oakland: University of California Press.

Aragona, M., Tarsitani, L., Colosimo, F., Martinelli, B., Raad, H., Maisano, B., & Geraci, S. (2005). Somatization in primary care: A comparative survey of immigrants from various ethnic groups in Rome, Italy. *The International Journal of Psychiatry in Medicine, 35*(3), 241–248. doi: 10.2190/2G8N-MNNE-PGGP-PJJQ

Baker, F., & Jones, C. (2006). The effect of music therapy services on classroom behaviors of newly arrived refugee students in Australia—A pilot study. *Emotional and Behavioural Difficulties, 11*, 249–260.

Barnes, D. M., Harrison, C., & Heneghan, R. (2004). Health risk and promotion behaviors in refugee populations. *Journal of Health Care for the Poor and Underserved, 15*(3), 347–356. doi: 10.1353/hpu.2004.0034

Barret, P. M., Moore, A. F., & Sonderegger, R. (2000). The FRIENDS program for young former-Yugoslavian refugees in Australia: A pilot study. *Behaviour Change, 17*, 124–133.

Bhugra, D. (2004). Migration, distress and cultural identity. *British Medical Bulletin, 69*(1), 129–141. doi: 10.1093/bmb/ldh007

Bolton, P., Bass, J., Betancourt, T., Speelman, L., Onyango, G., Clourgherty, K. F., . . . Verdeli, H. (2007). Interventions for depression symptoms among adolescent survivors of war and displacement in Northern Uganda. *Journal of the American Medical Association, 298,* 519–527.

Bracken, P. G. (2002). *Trauma: Culture, meaning and philosophy.* London: Whurr Publishers.

Burnett, A., & Peel, M. (2001). Health needs of asylum seekers and refugees. *British Medical Journal, 322*(7285), 544–547.

Colic-Peisker, V., & Tilbury, F. (2003). Active and passive resettlement: The influence of social support services and refugees own resources on resettlement style. *International Migration, 41,* 61–89.

d'Ardenne, P., Ruaro, L., Cestari, L., Fakhoury, W., & Priebe, S. (2007). Does interpreter-mediated CBT with traumatized refugee people work: A comparison of patient outcomes in East London. *Behavioural and Cognitive Psychotherapy, 35,* 293–301.

Daniels, R. (2002). *Coming to America: A history of immigration and ethnicity in American life* (2nd ed.). New York, NY: Harper Perennial.

Deming, W. E. (9182). *Out of crisis.* Cambridge, MA: Massachusetts Institute of Technology, Center for Advanced Engineering Study.

Dow, H. D. (2011). An overview of stressors faced by immigrants and refugees: A guide for mental heath practitioners. *Home Health Care Management & Practice, 23*(3), 210–217. doi: 10.1177/1084822310390878

Ehntholt, K. A., Smith, P. A., & Yule, W. (2005). School-based cognitive-behavioural therapy group intervention for refugee children who have experienced war-related trauma. *Clinical Child Psychology and Psychiatry, 10,* 235–250.

Ellis, B. H., Miller, A. B., Baldwin, H., & Abdi, S. (2011). New directions in refugee youth mental health services: Overcoming barriers to engagement. *Journal of Child and Adolescent Trauma, 4,* 69–85. doi: 10.10801/19361521.2011.545047

Epstein, M. H., Harniss, M. K., Robbins, V., Wheeler, L., Cyrulik, S., Kriz, M., & Nelson, J. R. (2003). Strength-based approaches to assessment in schools. In M. D. Weist, S. W. Evans, & N. A. Lever (Eds.), *Handbook of school mental health: Advancing practice and research* (pp. 285–299). Springer Publications.

Fong, R. (2004). Overview of immigrant and refugee children and families. In R. Fong (Ed.), *Culturally competent practice with immigrant and refugee children and families* (pp. 1–18). New York: The Guildford Press.

Fox, P. G., Rossetti, J., Burns, K. R., & Popovich, J. (2005). Southeast Asian refugee children: A school-based mental health intervention. *The International Journal of Psychiatric Nursing Research, 11,* 1227–1237.

Goldman, D. P., Joyce, G. F., & Zheng, Y. (2007). Prescription drug cost sharing: Associations with medication and medical utilization and spending and health. *Journal of the American Medical Association, 298*(1), 61–69. doi: 10.1001/jama.298.1.61.

Gonsalves, C. J. (1992). Psychological stages of the refugee process. A model for therapeutic interventions. *Professional Psychology: Research and Practice, 23,* 382–389.

Goodkind, J. R. (2005). Effectiveness of a community-based advocacy and learning program for Hmong refugees. *American Journal of Community Psychology, 36*(3–4), 387–408.

Gorman, W. (2001). Refugee survivors of torture: Trauma and treatment. *Professional Psychology: Research and Practice, 32*(5), 443–451. doi: 10.1037//0735.7028.32.5.443

Gozdiak, E. M. (2004). Training refugee mental health providers: Ethnography as a bridge to multicultural practice. Human Organization, 63, 203–210.

Herman, J. L. (1992). *Trauma and recovery: The aftermath of violence*. New York: Basic Books.

Hilado, A., & Kim, C. (n.d.). *Examining the effects of pre- and post-arrival experiences on mental health functioning among refugees*. Unpublished manuscript.

Howard, L. M., Trevillion, K., & Agnew-Davies, R. (2010). Domestic violence and mental health. *International Review of Psychiatry, 22*(5). Retrieved from http://ehis.ebscohost.com.proxy.uchicago .edu/eds/pdfviewer/pdfviewer?sid=63f8ace5-b925-4daf-9874-e23d47e06624%40sessionmgr198 &vid=3&hid=109

Huang, Z. J., Yu, S. M., & Ledsky, R. (2006). Health status and health service access and use among children in U.S. immigrant families. *American Journal of Public Health, 96*(4), 634–640. doi: 10.2105/AJPH.2004.049791

Hugo, G. (2002). Australian immigration policy: The significance of the events of September 11. *International Migration Review, 36*(1), 37–40.

Huijts, I., Kleijn, W. C., van Emmerik, A. A. P., Nordhof, A., & Smith, A. J. M. (2012). Dealing with man-made trauma: The relationship between coping style, posttraumatic stress, and quality of life in resettled, traumatized refugees in the Netherlands. *Journal of Traumatic Stress, 25*, 71–78.

Jacobs, E. A., Shepard, D. S., Suaya, J. A., & Stone, E. (2004). Overcoming language barriers in health care: Costs and benefits of interpreter services. *American Journal of Public Health, 94*(5), 866–869. doi: 10.2105/AJPH.94.5.866

Katz, D., & Kahn, R. L. (1966). *The social psychology of organizations*. New York: Wiley.

Khawaja, N. G., White, K. M., Schweitzer, R., & Greenslade, J. (2008). Difficulties and coping strategies of Sudanese refugees: A qualitative approach. *Transcultural Psychiatry, 45*(3), 489–512. doi: 10.117/13634615080894678

Kirmayer, L. J., Narasiah, L., Munos, M., Rashid, M., Ryder, A. G., Guzer, J., Hassan, G., . . . Pottie, K. (2011). Common mental health problems in immigrants and refugees: General approach in primary care. *Canadian Medial Association Journal, 183*(12), E959–E967. doi: 10.1503/ cmaj.090292

Lacroix, M., & Sabbah, C. (2011). Posttraumatic psychological distress and resettlement: The need for a different practice in assisting refugee families. *Journal of Family Social Work, 14*, 43–53. doi: 10.1080/10522158.2011.523789

Lang, J. M., Vanderploeg, J. J., & Campbell, C. (2015). Advancing trauma informed systems for children. Framing: Child Health and Development Institute of Connecticut.

Lie, B, Sveaass, N., & Eilertsen, D. E. (2004). Family, activity, and stress reactions in exile. *Community, Work, & Family, 7*(3), 327–350. doi: 10.1080/1366880042000295745

Lysgaard, S. (1955). Adjustment in a foreign society: Norwegian Fulbright grantees visiting the United States. *International Social Science Bulletin, 7*, 45–51.

Maslow, A. H. (1943). A theory of human motivation. *Psychological Review, 50*(4), 370–396.

McMichael, C., & Manderson, L. (2004). Somali women and well-being: Social networks and social capital among immigrant women in Australia. *Human Organization, 63*, 88–99.

Miller, K. E. (1999). Rethinking a familiar model: Psychotherapy and the mental health of refugees. *Journal of Contemporary Psychotherapy, 29*, 283–304.

Murray, K. E., Davidson, G. R., & Schweitzer, R. D. (2010). Review of refugee mental health interventions following resettlement: Best practices and recommendations. *American Journal of Orthopsychiatry, 80*(4), 576–585. doi: 10.1111/j.1939-0025.2010.01062.x

Neuner, F., Schauer, M., Klaschik, C., Karunakara, U., & Elbert, T. A. (2004). A comparison of narrative exposure therapy, supportive counseling, and psychoeducation for treating posttraumatic stress disorder in African refugee settlement. *Journal of Consulting and Clinical Psychology, 72*, 579–587.

Papadopoulos, R. K. (2007). Refugees, trauma and adversity-activated development. *European Journal of Psychotherapy and Counseling, 9*, 301–312.

Pickering, S. (2001). Common sense and original deviancy. News discourses and asylum seekers in Australia. *Journal of Refugee Studies, 14*(2), 169–186.

Piwowarczyk, L., Bishop, H., Saia, K., Crosby, S., Mudymba, F. T., Hashi, N. I., & Rag, A. (2013). Pilot evaluation of a health promotion program for African immigrant and refugee women: The UJAMBO Program. *Journal of Immigrant Minority Health, 15*, 219–223. doi: 10.1007/s10903-012-9611-9

Porter, M., & Haslam, N. (2005). Predisplacement and postdisplacement factors associated with mental health of refugees and internally displaced persons: A meta analysis. *Journal of the American Medical Association, 294*, 602–612.

Pumariega, A. J., Rothe, E., & Pumariega, J. B. (2005). Mental health of immigrants and refugees. *Community Mental Health Journal, 41*(5), 581–597. doi: 10.1007/s10597-005-6363-1

Rasco, L. M., & Miller, K. E. (2004). Innovations, challenges, and critical issues in the development of ecological mental health interventions with refugees. In K. E. Miller & L. M. Rasco (Eds.), *The mental health of refugees: Ecological approaches to healing and adaptation* (pp. 375–416). Mahwah, NJ: Lawrence Erlbaum.

Ritsner, M., Ponozovsky, A., Kurs, R., & Modai, I. (2000). Somatization in an immigrant population in Israel: A community survey of prevalence, risk factors, and help-seeking behavior. *The American Journal of Psychiatry, 157*(3), 385–392.

Rousseau, C., Benoit, M., Lacoix, L., & Gauthier, M. F. (2008). Evaluation of a sandplay program for preschools in multiethnic neighborhood. *The Journal of Child Psychology and Psychiatry, 50*(6), 743–750. Retrieved from http://www3.interscience.wiley.com/journal/121575257/abstract.

Runner, M., Yoshihama, M., & Novick, S. (2009). Intimate partner violence in immigrant and refugee communities: Challenges, promising practices, and recommendations. *Family Violence Prevention Fund*. Retrieved from http://www.futureswithoutviolence.org/userfiles/file/ImmigrantWomen/IPV_Report_March_2009.pdf

Ryder, A. G., Yang, J., Zhu, X., Yao, S., Yi, J., Heine, S. J., & Bagby, R. M. (2008). The cultural shaping of depression: Somatic symptoms in China, psychological symptoms in North America? *Journal of Abnormal Psychology, 117*(2), 300–313. doi: 10.1037/0021-843X.117.2.300

Schaafsma, E. S., Raynorr, D. K., & Jong-van den Berg, L. T. W. (2003). Accessing medication information by ethnic minorities: Barriers and possible solutions. *Pharmacy World and Science, 25*(5), 185–190.

Schriver, J. M. (2010). *Human behavior and the social environment: Shifting paradigms in essential knowledge for social work practice* (5th ed.). Boston: Allyn and Bacon.

Simich, L., Hamilton, H., & Khamisa Baya, B. (2006). Mental distress, economic hardship and expectations of life in Canada among Sudanese newcomers. *Transcultural Psychiatry, 43*(3), 418–444. doi: 10.1177/1363461506066985

Somasundaram, D., & Jamunanantha, C. S. (2002). Psychosocial consequences of war: Northern Sri Lankan experience. In J. de Jong (Ed.), *Trauma, war, and violence: Public mental health in socio-cultural context* (pp. 205–257). New York, NY: Kluwer Academic/Plenum Publishers.

Sue, S., Zane, N., Nagayama Hall, G. C., & Berger, L. K. (2009). The case for cultural competency in psychotherapeutic interventions. *Annual Review of Psychology, 60*, 525–548. doi: 10.1-10.24;10.1146/annurev.psych.60.110707.163651

Szajna, A., & Ward, J. (2014). Access to health care by refugees: A dimensional analysis. *Nursing Forum, 50*(2), 83–90.

Tervalon, M., & Murray-Garcia, J. (1998). Cultural humility versus cultural competence: A critical distinction in defining physician training outcomes in multicultural education. *Journal of Health Care for the Poor and Underserved, 9*(2), 117–125. doi: 10.1353/hpu.2010.0233

Tiong, A., Patel, M. S., Gardiner, J., Ryan, R., Linton, K. S., Walker, K. A., Scopel, J., & Biggs, B. (2006). Health issues in newly arrived African refugees attending general practice clinics in Melbourne. Medical Journal of Australia, 185(11–12), 602–606.

UNHCR.org. (n.d.). *Who we help: Refugees*. Retrieved from http://www.unhcr.org/en-us/refugees.html

Van der Velde, J., Williamson, D. L., & Ogilvie, L. D. (2009). Participatory action research: Practical strategies for actively engaging and maintaining participation in immigrant and refugee communities. *Qualitative Health Research, 19*(9), 1293–1302. doi: 10.1177.1049732309344207

Van Selm, J. (2003). Foreign policy considerations in dealing with Afghanistan's refugees: When security and protection collide. *Force Migration Review, 13*, 16–18.

Weine, S. M. (2011). Developing preventive mental health interventions for refugee families in resettlement. *Family Process, 50*(3), 410–430.

World Health Organization. (2016). *Health topics: Mental health*. Retrieved from http://www.who.int/topics/mental_health/en/

Chapter 12

PREPARING A LOCAL AND VOLUNTEER WORKFORCE

KONG SOKHEM, PRAK CHANKROESNA, NONG SOCHEAT, YUNG CHANTHAO, IM SREYTHA, ALASTAIR HILTON, AND KRISTIN BULLER

KEY TERMS

learning needs assessment, culturally appropriate training, local workforce, professional development

---

CHAPTER HIGHLIGHTS

- How to conduct a learning and training needs assessment (LTNA)
- Ethics of capacity building
- Best practices used in Cambodia
- How to train social workers in a context different than your own

---

INTRODUCTION

The goal of this chapter is twofold. The first purpose is to provide a practical guide to building a local workforce of professionals and paraprofessionals to deliver trauma-informed social services to a trauma-exposed population. The discussions are based on the first-hand experiences of the authors while implementing programs in Cambodia and drawing from their collective experiences in developing and implementing training programs across different countries. The chapter complements the text, recognizing that trauma may impact the lives of individuals, families, and communities across the globe that are equally in need of access to culturally sensitive, research-informed services. Second, this chapter intends to disseminate capacity-building models that will strengthen a local workforce to address local needs. The same lessons in cultural competence, effective models for service delivery, and trauma-informed interventions must be shared with a global audience to support *any* person or community negatively impacted by trauma, regardless of immigration status and country. Thus, the lessons shared in this chapter attempt to connect relevant field experiences to the larger global community.

Setting the Context

The authors collectively have over 70 years of experience delivering social work services and training in a range of settings, namely Cambodia, the United Kingdom, and the United States, and also we have worked together at various times in social welfare organizations in Cambodia in the last few years. Our individual and collective experiences in that country include working with adults and children affected by various forms of violence and trauma, including domestic violence, sexual abuse, and exploitation and other complex mental health problems that are a legacy of many post-conflict settings, not least those unleashed as a result of the terrors and deprivations of the Khmer Rouge regime from 1975 through 1979.

Some might assume that a generation after the fall of the Khmer Rouge there would be a significant reduction in the legacy of what many Cambodians refer to as "Pol Pot Times," but research continues to indicate that 40% of the population 18 years of age or older experience mental health and psychological problems (DeJong, 2002), with at least 14% of that population suffering from PTSD (Sonis et al., 2009; TPO Cambodia, n.d.). The relative paucity of research leaves many questions unanswered as to the longer term "ripples" caused across the social spectrum by direct and indirect experiences of violence during those years and beyond. Research and experience indicates that large numbers of the population have little or no access to well-resourced services (e.g., those in rural areas, older people, and parents) while many services are aimed at children and young people. Contemporary social problems within Cambodia include trafficking of women and girls for labor and sexual services, trafficking of men to the fishing industry (U.S. Department of State, 2015) (where many experience considerable abuse of all forms), violence within families and communities, alcohol and drug misuse, and rape and sexual violence against women, men, girls, and boys (Harbitz, 2016; Hilton, 2008), while children display sexually abusive and harmful behaviors, which are receiving more attention in recent times (ADHOC Cambodia Human Rights and Development Association, 2013).

Cambodia has experienced considerable growth and development in many areas recently. And Cambodia has literally thousands of nongovernmental organizations (NGOs). Approximately 4,953 registered NGOs and associations with an estimated 1,350 organizations remain active (INCL, 2016), delivering a range of social welfare and educational services, but the planning, coordination, and delivery of services has often been haphazard and characterized by short-term goals often driven by individuals (often non-Cambodians) with big hearts and deep pockets, although often without sufficient training or experience within their own countries of origin. The result is a patchwork of services with pockets of good practice, which are often centered in and around the main urban areas, such as Phnom Penh. It was not until 2010 that the Royal University of Phnom Penh (RUPP) in partnership with the University of Washington in Seattle launched a social work degree course (Royal University of Phnom Penh, n.d.; School of Social Work University of Washington, n.d.).

For the last two decades the Cambodian NGO sector has experienced a flood of short-term expatriot experts. From the authors' collective experiences, these were often training and capacity development initiatives that seemed to be taken from outside of Cambodia, many with little or no attention paid to the cultural, social, and historical context of Cambodia and very little or no follow-up beyond the initial delivery. The result of such training initiatives understandably is mixed, with one legacy being a considerable community of paraprofessional "social" workers with mixed levels of understanding of key issues and priorities often driven by a range of disparate factors. Long-term development, planning, and sustainability, so often in the present day repeated and recognized as a foundation of the world of development, was often and in many respects still is conspicuous by its absence.

It is against this background that the authors, five Cambodian citizens and two professionals from the United States living in Cambodia, set out to contribute to this book. The five Cambodian authors and one of the expatriots currently work together in a local NGO First Step Cambodia (FSC) (First Step Cambodia, n.d.), based in Phnom Penh, which provides social work services to boys and young men affected by and at risk for sexual violence and abuse. The Cambodian team has also developed and delivers a range of training to other Cambodians working in the social welfare field. The remaining expatriot worked in Cambodia for several years with some of the other authors, in a similar project, responding to the needs of victims of trauma.

From the outset, it was clear that the only way to contribute effectively would be to utilize our individual and collective relationships of trust, incorporating the experiences of all concerned in a meaningful way, as we have done throughout the last decade or so. The Cambodian perspective, as receivers of training and "capacity building" but also as service and training providers in their own right, forms the foundation of this chapter. The expatriot authors continue to learn and by doing so, helped structure the content and narrative through focused workshops, reflection, and further discussions.

The process in many respects mirrors two time-honored principals of social work— that is, community based/person-centered practice and qualitative research methods as a form of social inquiry. For example, this process entails working closely alongside individuals and communities to understand the world from their experience. Both require many of the same values, skills, and attention to detail; both require the researcher/practitioner to demonstrate respectful, empowering, and genuinely inclusive relationships that are built on strengths and an understanding that the process of learning is a mutual one. Ours is an approach that confronts the notion of "expert," which is usually assigned to foreigners, while also attributing knowledge and wisdom to all indigenous peoples and then exploring the assumptions and power dynamics that surround that. Our approach draws on "solution focused" theories of change, with a focus on understanding and building on strengths and identifying practical methods for resolving the problems. As practitioners from another country, we understand the impetus to be helpful to people who are suffering. And while it is understandable that practitioners might bring with them and want to provide solutions that have been proven in their own countries to be highly effective, it also is critically important that the solutions employed from the country in which one is working may be more relevant and constructive and therefore ultimately more useful.

Ecological Framework for Analysis:
An Integrative Approach to Training

Our approach to developing culturally sensitive training programs for local professionals relies on Bronfenbrenner's ecological model for human development (1979) as a tool for analysis, considering causes of social problems, risk factors, and also the impact of trauma in building a competent workforce. When building a workforce, the focus is on capacity building within the context of the local community and including the sociopolitical structures within that community and country. For the purposes of this chapter, the authors define **capacity building** as any process or method employed to develop skills, knowledge, ability, practice, and aptitude within the field of development. This includes but is not limited to presentations, training, individual and group clinical supervision, mentoring, and so forth.

Setting the Scene and Planning and
Building the Foundations for Effective Capacity Building

While the authors recognize the multiple scenarios in which capacity building can take place and understand that it is not possible to anticipate all situations, they advise that for all types of training the practitioners prepare to build a firm foundation. This preparation will increase the effectiveness of any activity, lead to greater understanding, avoid frustration, and ultimately succeed in your shared objectives. There can be a tendency for even the most well intentioned of "providers" of training to assume many things, not least the existing level of understanding and familiarity with technical terms, concepts, ideas, reasoning and what is considered best practice—as if what we have learned in our college classes in Western and so-called developed countries is both universally understood and appropriate. This may run parallel with the subconscious belief that we as providers and imparters of knowledge and wisdom have little to learn. Accept that you are a participant in a genuinely shared process, also with a great deal to learn; failure to do so will essentially result in poor results and a process that is little more than another form of colonialism.

In the following section we hope to provide concrete ways to thoughtfully complete this preparation process.

Professional Preparation Prior to Departure

Embarking on a journey to a new country to collaborate in community interventions requires a heightened level of professional preparedness for new experiences and new learning environments in order to be successful. The following section provides categories and critical thinking prompts to consider for those interested in working with other local organizations abroad.

SELF-REFLECTION AND MOTIVATION. Effective capacity building leans on the motivation and investment of those seeking to invest time, energy, and resources to build a local workforce. The sustainability of such work requires investment during the initial implementation phase of a training program but also the follow-up, required to ensure lessons are learned, retained, promoted, disseminated, and revised as needed. For anyone seeking to embark on such an investment, self-reflection around personal motivation and commitment to do the work is required. Why do you want to do this work at this time? Whose needs are being fulfilled and how have those needs been established? Is the process open, inclusive, and transparent? Ask yourself if your approach assumes a more hierarchical system. Such reflective questions may elucidate the level of personal investment in the process.

Equally relevant is an understanding of the context and communities where training programs will be conducted. Training professionals must be open to developing knowledge about learning styles in different settings. Western styles of learning often promote individualistic approaches, self-expression, analysis, and critical thinking, so much so that we often assume that this is universal, but in many countries this is not the case. As the Cambodian authors of this chapter remarked, "Please don't assume a shared understanding, confidence and the ability to speak out and share; create different and varied opportunities for sharing. There is a need to acknowledge our perspectives and our culture; pay attention to the personal and psychological safety of all concerned." Awareness of the continuum of beliefs from Western to non-Western traditions requires exploration, critical consciousness, and self-awareness.

Alongside motivation comes this idea of commitment and follow-through. As authors, we have seen the problematic approach of short-term approaches to training, where trainers "drop in" without adequate preparation, deliver training, and then leave without planning appropriate follow-up. A negative consequence of this approach is that the time and resources of all concerned will not be best utilized and the long-term impact will be negligible. We recommend that professionals conducting such programs support local professionals; remember that one cannot just translate a model to another context and assume it will work the same. Plan time for preparation, for becoming better acquainted with the culture and the varied ways of learning, and to identify the knowledge level of participants. Plan time for the training as well as how follow-up will occur to integrate learning. Cultural adaptation, flexibility, and diligence in finding effective ways to disseminate information will be necessary. Moreover, hold on to a persistent motivation and commitment to adapt the program in ways that are useful to that community and that inform future trainings, even if the endeavor requires more time and effort than initially considered. And seek out other training programs that are modeling this approach, learn from each other and support each other, as you may find you are going against the bigger norm of the drop-in training methods.

RELEVANT EXPERIENCES TO SUPPORT WORK ABROAD. The preparation for implementing training abroad begins before one arrives and continues once you are in the country in which you will be working. We suggest spending dedicated time, several months if possible, getting to know and understand the culture where you will be working. We have found this involves asking lots of questions and doing even more listening and observing. In addition, a focus on self-reflection and self-awareness is critical, and prospective trainers really benefit from having gained experience in their own settings. Ideas, models, and concepts can be helpful, but without in-depth experience of working with challenging families, communities, and traumatized individuals and an ability to explain, discuss, and reflect alongside those receiving training and your support in a meaningful way, those ideas and models are likely to remain elusive, confusing, and unhelpful to the vast majority. It will be a necessary asset as a trainer to be able to speak and pull from your own firsthand experience of implementing what it is you are teaching about. A balance between theory and relevant experience and practice is vital. This type of preparation—ideally before embarking on meaningful and long-term "capacity building"—we have found often requires on average at least six months experiencing one's own learning about the country, its people, and the culture. As the Cambodian authors testified during the process of writing this chapter, "Listen and learn, spend months learning about us and the way we do things." One can do research on the hosting organization, its history, development, and previous experiences of capacity building. Questions to guide your research include, How has it been utilized before? How has the current terms of reference for the work been negotiated? Were the staff at all levels involved in this process, or is this process largely driven by others—for example, donors or your employers? How were the views of those staff with high levels of time spent with service users but relatively less power within the organization included in the planning? Each of these questions are opportunities for reflection that can guide powerful collaborations, an approach that can be applied to any setting where capacity-building activities are planned.

This level of self-awareness and preparation also encourages training professionals to become informed around the personal goals for participation that may influence or shape the investment in and delivery of the training workshop. We have found it to be valuable to pay attention to different life experiences and histories—for example, the Khmer (or the indigenous population with whom you are working) and also your own. As for your own individual self-awareness, both personally (your gender, your life experience, your values) and professionally (be that a social worker, trainer, and/or development specialist), explore how this may influence the unique context and environment in which you find yourself, as this can inform your perspective about your audience and the community you seek to benefit. Also suggested is to treat this not as an experiment but with thoughtful respect to how the planning and implementation are affecting colleagues and participants. You may find that your psychological preparation for the work at hand can cultivate a greater sense of respect for the communities one will enter and a deeper understanding of one's purpose in delivering capacity-building programs to a local workforce.

STRATEGIES FOR EFFECTIVE IMPLEMENTATION. Develop training handouts that are relevant to the topics and population you will be working with and collaborate with your local colleagues to catch where language and concepts do not translate. There are certain training components that can enhance or detract from the purpose of the locally based capacity-building program. While our tendency might be to do what you would normally do in training and translate your existing resources, handouts, PowerPoints, and so forth, we caution you because we have found that no matter how effective you think they are in your own setting, they will very likely not be appropriate or as effective as you think. Instead, plan on carrying out an in-depth training and/or learning needs assessment as part of the development process (see model developed by FSC provided below), and then develop your presentation materials. After a thorough needs assessment, you will be much better placed to then determine which of your typical training materials are appropriate and/or how they could be adapted for the population you are working with. Where possible, plan to work with existing local training and service providers. Do your research and find out more about how people learn, the culture, and belief systems surrounding the issues related to the work the organization is involved in, which will also be addressed in the section below relating to the "training and learning needs assessment." Finally, explore and be aware of power dynamics within the Cambodian and organizational contexts and the way that may influence anything you do: how you are perceived as a foreigner, as a male/female, according to your age, and so forth. An underlying theme of the Cambodian authors' contributions to this chapter relate to the issue of "safety," captured in the comment that you need to "make plenty of time to create a safe environment and relationships for learning, like the client–social worker relationship. Without it, little will change." This also requires foreigners to deeply and honestly reflect on their own power in these settings.

Assuming that you have now arrived at your destination and have spent sufficient time learning about the country, its culture, people, history, and the organization in which you are placed and the services they are involved in providing, the training professional can now begin to think of activity/workshop programming. As recipients of training over many years and more recently as trainers in their own right, the Cambodian authors recognize and highly value the importance of gaining a deep understanding of what the precise needs of those receiving training are. In doing so, there is a mirroring in the process between provider and service user in which an in-depth assessment of needs may be carried out prior to services being delivered. Experiences within the field of capacity building are mixed, however, and it is not uncommon for little or no time to be spent researching the specific needs of participants beforehand.

One of the problems we encountered in many settings was either that little or no research or specific assessment of need was made before training and support was provided. In other situations, participants had attended training that was already designed and formulated by providers before being made available and as a consequence, rarely met many of the specific needs of the participants based on their work in that context. On the rare occasions that participants took part in any kind of process resembling an assessment before training, this was reported as being quite limited and one dimensional—for example, they were asked "what training was required," training professionals looked at lists of pre-existing training available, or participants completed an individual written form where questions focused on what training people required. In feedback received from participants taking part in FSC training events, many explained that their needs were rarely (if ever) taken into consideration before, and they considered the learning needs assessment a vital component of their learning experience. Others cited that they felt a greater sense of ownership and commitment to training once this was incorporated into the process.

Facilitating a Learning and Training Needs Assessment (LTNA)

Based on these experiences, other local research and a commitment to change the dynamics of this process, FSC therefore developed a flexible model for **learning and**

training needs assessment (LTNA) that can easily be applied in any setting using the most basic resources. The team has utilized this approach in numerous settings with very positive results. The model focuses almost entirely on potential participants' thoughts, ideas, experiences, beliefs, attitudes, and existing behavior rather than discussing "training" per se and introducing models, concepts, language, and jargon that is unfamiliar and effectively a barrier to understanding.

The section below describes the process and resources required.

BEFORE THE LTNA. Always take time to explore previous experiences of capacity building with specific attention to what has been useful/not useful and lessons learned from working with foreign consultants or issues with language capacity. The foreign authors of this article once met with a group of experienced practitioners in the gender-based violence field who had experience working with multiple consultants, experts, and trainers over a number of years. Whilst some of their experiences had been useful, many commented that they often felt intimidated and disempowered by the process when it was not inclusive, when understanding of language and concepts were assumed and beyond them, or the pace of learning was determined by resource and time driven agendas rather than the needs of the group. By paying attention to these experiences, you demonstrate from the outset that this process is centered on participants and their experiences, ideas, and existing strengths and understanding rather than some imported agenda. This also demonstrates respect for them as individuals and as a group and opens the door to infinite possibilities.

CARRYING OUT THE LTNA. Ideally, allow at least one full day with the team or group you plan to work with. Training professionals should plan to utilize a range of didactic engagement methods—for example, discussion in pairs and small groups and sharing and discussion in the wider group, and so forth. Additionally and when discussing sensitive topics, such as sexual violence or reproductive health, there should be separate physical spaces and opportunities available for men and women. In many cases, it may be culturally, religiously, and/or situationally inappropriate for mixed-gender groups to discuss sexual matters. More helpful and accurate responses may emerge if separation of the sexes will promote a safer environment for sharing. Similarly, take into account the specific roles of those taking part within the organization. For example, the process is likely to benefit from groups of caregivers and managers working separately at some stages of the LTNA, as existing power dynamics may restrict openness to sharing.

EXPLORING BELIEFS AND ATTITUDES. Dependent on the topic area, it is useful to spend time in pairs or small groups with focused discussion on the specific topic. For example, if you are carrying out a LTNA related to sexual violence against children, ask the group to discuss and write down on rectangular pieces of paper the existing beliefs that they and/or people in their community already have about the topic. This may also relate to what friends and family may say or believe, traditional ideas and beliefs about the causes of sexual violence, the impact and what are considered appropriate responses within that setting or culture, or things they have heard or read or been told in previous training events.

Provide a couple of examples for participants to help them understand the task—for example, in relation to sexual violence against boys:

- Sexual abuse of boys is rare.

- The abuse of boys is not serious and they recover quickly and without much support.

- Once abused, a victim will become a perpetrator.

- Women cannot and should not work with male victims.

- Women do not sexually abuse.

- If a boy is abused, he must be weak and/or gay.

This process can be easily applied to any specific topic, both widely and more focused. Once completed, use the pieces of paper similar as bricks and build a "wall of beliefs" on a suitable space. Ask the group to look at what they have produced and ask questions about things that are not clear, clarifying meanings and pointing out similarities and differences. What you have essentially produced is the basic foundation of your learning curriculum, which when analyzed and categorized later will relate to key areas of learning to address. For example, related to the topic of understanding the causes of abuse, several other ideas emerge—for example, responsibility/consent issues, impacts and effects, discrimination, and needs related to helping and supporting. Be prepared that some issues may not easily fit into categories and you will have to create new ones.

FOCUSING ON LIFE AND WORK EXPERIENCES. Similarly, the next exercise should also be carried out in creative ways, utilizing small groups or pairs. If you are working with a mixed group of men and women, provide opportunities for single-sex groups and pairs, which will create space for the unique experiences of men and women to emerge, which is vital if your training and capacity building is to be effective. Importantly, if you are working with a team or organization that includes managers alongside (e.g., caregivers), provide separate groups based on role and status. Not only will this reveal important and different needs, but it will also address any specific power dynamics within groups and encourage safer sharing. Anecdotally, staff with lower status may often be fearful of openly speaking out within the larger group for a range of reasons, not least that if they express openly their perceived weaknesses, this may negatively affect the way managers and others may treat them.

An example of how this process has been conducted is described briefly below. Similarly, the example of working with males experiencing sexual abuse will be used. Do also encourage them to share their ideas related to working with boys in general as well as victims of abuse. Many of the ideas people have about boys before they experience abuse—for example, they don't listen much, they can be too active—greatly influences their ideas and responses.

- Explain that you recognize that working with and supporting boys and young men in general and especially those affected by sexual abuse can be very challenging but also rewarding.

- Do provide examples of each. For example, it can be a struggle to know how to help. We may be fearful if boys become aggressive and/or concerned for our safety.

- Ask the group to discuss and record their likes and dislikes about working with boys. Ask them to include things they find easy or difficult in their work and other challenges.

- Explain that this can be related to many aspects of their current role or work. For example, topics might be building relationships and clear communication or more complex tasks like completing assessments and providing services and support.

Allow plenty of time for recording and displaying and sharing of their ideas within the larger group. Include opportunities for discussion and clarifying statements to gain a deeper understanding of specific issues. As above, this will build on the foundation of beliefs and provide a more nuanced understanding of the real-life experiences of the group and reveal often hidden issues, which simply asking about training needs is unlikely to reveal. Once analyzed and categorized, natural themes and topics may emerge, some of which are likely to overlap with data from the previous exercise.

SEEKING SPECIFIC QUESTIONS RELATED TO THE TOPIC. The third stage of the LTNA seeks to inquire more deeply into the needs of the group by asking them to identify what focused and specific questions they have about the issue or topic. Simply ask the group to spend time discussing what questions they would like to have answered. Explain that there are no "off limits" and that this is their opportunity to help create the detailed learning curriculum they need. Provide a couple of examples, as above, to encourage this. Encourage use of open and more specific questions related to the 5WH concept:

- Why? (e.g., Why do boys get abused?)

- Who? (e.g., Who are the abusers of boys?)

- Where? (e.g., Where and in what circumstances are boys abused?)

- What? (e.g., What are the needs of boys?)

- When? (e.g., When will I know that a child has recovered?)

- How? (e.g., How can I help an abused child?)

Similarly, as above, you can share, clarify, and discuss the meaning of the data, and this will provide additional, more detailed information to help you design the training and support systems for the group.

LEARNING AND ADDITIONAL SUPPORT. The final part of the LTNA process focuses on additional learning and supports that are required. You may be flexible in your approach based on the specific context and requirements of the group. Ask the group to reflect on their work so far and reflect on any gaps that may exist and/or additional learning and support they think they will need to achieve their goals. For example, this may relate to

- Identifying and sharing information about learning styles within the group

- Specific learning and other training they may think they need

- Identifying group and individual supervision and support needs and mechanisms. They may not be at all familiar with the concept of clinical supervision, therefore, consider providing a couple of examples that are jargon free

- Identify self-care needs

Once this process is complete, you will undoubtedly have a deep reservoir of information, ideas, and needs, many of which will overlap. This will enable you to reflect, write up, and categorize the data. Ideally, you should write a report, compiling all of the data, which will enable you to identify gaps, similarities, and differences and identify specific learning needs that may be different within the group. For example, there may be different learning needs for different demographic groups, caregivers, senior management, males and females, and so forth. Once this process has been completed, you should ideally return to the organization or group, share your findings, and begin the process of planning your capacity building with the organization involved. Figure 12.1 illustrates the essential aspects of the LTNA.

DEVELOPING LEARNING INTERVENTIONS, SUPPORT, TRAINING, AND RESOURCES. Following the LTNA, themes, topics, and needs will have emerged, which will enable you to combine your learning and to create a response to the needs identified. You may already have some materials available, but you will need to consider if they are appropriate for the setting in which the training is due to take place. On many occasions, the foreign authors have experienced situations where international organizations and individuals consider it appropriate to simply translate existing resources, which may often still include case studies based on Western scenarios and experiences. We would advise against this, if you wish your training and skills development to appropriately meet the needs of the group. Use the LTNA data to closely guide the process of development, staying "close to the data" and remaining relevant to the prospective audience.

THE FOLLOWING SUGGESTIONS ARE MADE TO GUIDE THE PROCESS OF DEVELOPMENT PRIOR TO DELIVERING TRAINING AND ALIGN WITH DISCUSSIONS IN PREVIOUS SECTIONS:

Professional Preparation

✓ Spend time to know and learn the local language, especially the specific language and meanings of words related to the specific subject you are focusing on in your

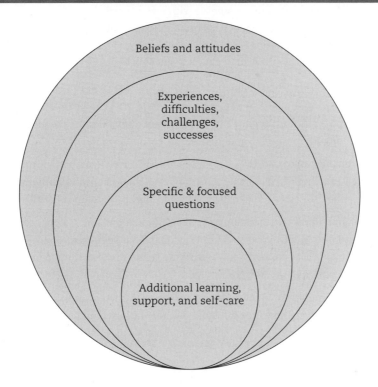

Figure 12.1 Components of Training and Learning Needs Assessments

Beliefs and attitudes

Experiences, difficulties, challenges, successes

Specific & focused questions

Additional learning, support, and self-care

work, whether that be mental health, social work, healing, or trauma, and so forth. One example of how the meaning of English words can change when translated is the word *puberty*, which when translated means "ready for marriage."

Collaboration With Local Organizations and Providers

✓ Include the organization and staff in the development of ideas and resources and thus avoid reinforcing the power dynamics present in the "expert–receiver of external wisdom" paradigm that is so common within the development sector.

✓ Build on the existing strengths of those due to receive training.

✓ Find out more about the relevant previous training and resources that have been developed and used with the team, read previous reports and evaluations that relate to capacity development within that setting, and make sure you incorporate those ideas in your planning and delivery.

✓ Always build into your training opportunities to explore existing ideas, beliefs, values, attitudes, and behavior on any given subject (e.g., healing from trauma) before introducing any new concepts and ideas. Without an understanding of what has gone before, our efforts at positive development are likely to have little meaning and be thwarted.

✓ Ensure that you spend time planning with interpreters and indigenous cofacilitators to ensure that the delivery of training is appropriate and that all resources (PowerPoint presentations, handouts, etc.) are also available in the native language.

Enhancing Training Sustainability and Relevance

✓ Where possible, do seek advice from local people and pilot the exercises and training, modifying approaches and exercises where appropriate.

✓ Plan sufficient time to deliver your training, especially where participants' first language is not English. As a general rule, for each hour of training with translation, double the time you need to deliver key concepts, discussion, and feedback.

✓ It is an important consideration to leave behind not only the memory of your training but sufficient resources to enable the indigenous staff to continue delivering and building on what you have provided. Try to ensure that you work in partnership with key staff to enable this to continue.

✓ Plan to thoroughly evaluate and identify lessons learned from your training and discuss with the team how they can build on those lessons in future.

Self-Reflective Practice

✓ Reflect on your own values and avoid imposing unfamiliar expectations on participants, for example, expecting them to immediately understand—participants are very likely to have ideas and solutions that are counter to your own beliefs. As a general rule, if suggestions are made consider the "do no harm" concept—for example, if ideas are unusual but are not harmful, discuss the merits of those but avoid imposing Western ideas simply because they exist.

✓ In many respects the process of developing a learning curriculum and suitable materials is likely to be a long process, so allow plenty of time.

DELIVERING EFFECTIVE TRAINING, SUPPORT, AND CAPACITY BUILDING. When working with the Cambodian team to prepare for this chapter, we asked them for feedback and ideas and what they considered to be helpful and effective as well as what was unhelpful and ineffective when developing capacity and delivering training. What emerged was a rich pool of ideas, suggestions, and guidelines, which are presented below. All are suggestions that we believe should be applied to any setting.

THE ROLE OF THE PROFESSIONAL. The training professional has a substantial responsibility in delivering information in a way that is accessible, relevant, and respectful of cultural difference and understanding. Professionals must work with participants to create a safe environment for trainees in order to address the personal and "internal" obstacles to learning. This may relate to many things—culture, life experiences, beliefs, personal perceptions—thus requiring physical space and specific times where sensitive or emotive topics are taught and discussed. Moreover, effective trainers question and challenge their own cultural assumptions about everything, including learning methods and style, empathy, the value and rights of children, children's rights, gender and rights issues, and so forth, and avoid assuming a universal understanding of that which is common to only the trainer. A component of this requires training professionals to compare personal experiences with that of the organization and participants and avoid making assumptions about what we think we know or should know from Western perspectives. Equally, training professionals should avoid the assumption that simply dropping in or "overlaying" new ideas, models, constructs, and paradigms is appropriate and easily understood. In our experience, people will often teach and provide and repeat the same things they do in their own countries (e.g., using case studies based on experiences in the United States or the United Kingdom) and assume participants will understand. Integration of local cases only enhances relevance and retention.

Finally and when possible, professionals should seek ongoing supervision and mentoring to reinforce learning. Such professional supports allow for opportunities to synthesize ideas, events, and concepts and facilitate critical thinking, as some practice contexts do not emphasize value in cultivating this skill or feel natural and comfortable processing in an open manner. Supervision and mentorship provide opportunities to help professionals discuss, explain, and compare similarities, differences, issues, options, ideas, choices, cultural attitudes, behaviors, and more. At the same time, the camaraderie allows professionals to model and help each other reflect on what they have learned, in turn applying that knowledge in personal and professional settings.

THE ROLE OF CULTURE. In delivering any sensitive content to persons of diverse ethnic backgrounds, the role of culture cannot be understated. Training professionals must always pay great attention to discovering and understanding the culture, history, values, beliefs, customs, and traditions in relation to whatever subject they are addressing—before, during, and after the process. This may apply, for example, to current understandings of relationships, gender issues, children, abuse, trauma, and the helping relationship. Explore current beliefs, thoughts, feelings, and attitudes about all relevant topics and incorporate that into the learning as part of the process; take time when introducing new ideas and compare these to traditional ideas, avoiding assumptions that the audience will understand new concepts easily and without comparison.

UNDERSTANDING YOUR AUDIENCE. Each participant will come with his or her own beliefs, values, and understanding of service delivery. The most effective trainer takes all of this into consideration in training delivery. One priority is to understand and never underestimate the issue of "saving face" and how this manifests itself within all relationships, including learning and sharing situations. Closely linked to safety above, failure to pay attention to this can seriously undermine the whole process. Additionally, the audience will present with diverse learning styles. Trainers must take time to discover and understand how the audience learns best and incorporate this knowledge into the professional's training approach. As the audience and topic changes, trainers must be flexible and creative in methods of teaching; understand the way individuals of differing abilities and groups learn best.

The logistics and delivery of training materials requires attention as well. When delivering any type of capacity-building activity, training professionals must pace the sessions and avoid including too much into each training and learning workshops. As all parties are learning new concepts with a new language, the pace needs to be appropriate. The staging of participants also needs attention. Participants should be separated into gender-based groups when carrying out learning needs assessments and teaching or discussing sensitive topics (e.g., talking about sexual matters). This understanding of how cultural ideas and attitudes about gender and roles will help mitigate any undo influence that could deter the learning process. Local case studies will again build relevance, as many of those used in training from outside are not familiar and make no sense at all. Terminology also should be inclusive, avoiding generalizations, particularly on the topic of gender-based violence, so that males are not solely viewed as perpetrators and women as victims. Without attention to this, participants may exclude the possibility of males being vulnerable and also abused and women being potential perpetrators. In the larger scheme, many of the predominant views within the field of international development often reflect and reinforce these unhelpful assumptions. They may be common, but they do not reflect the reality of collective experiences.

ENSURING USE OF ACCESSIBLE LANGUAGE. One of the most considerable challenges when delivering training and support is to ensure that ideas and concepts are accessible, connect with, and have meaning for those taking part. For many of us working in developing countries, our experience is that some practices within the international community often make assumptions about levels of understanding and use of terminology and language that often leave people isolated and marginalized from proceedings. For many who have worked in settings with survivors and traumatized populations, isolation and marginalization will also be a familiar experience, and we wish to avoid replicating this in any form.

It remains vital for us to recognize that with the great privilege of working overseas comes with a considerable responsibility to ensure that ideas, concepts, and language are shared in a manner that challenges and reduces this marginalization. Therefore, please avoid using complex jargon and technical terms or acronyms that are likely to not be fully or easily understood by interpreters or participants whose first language is not English. If you do use acronyms, please also briefly explain what they refer to and use standard English to subsequently explain your point where technical language and jargon are used. For example, use of the term *vicarious traumatization* is not easily interpreted.

USE OF IDIOMS. Our experiences also reveal that many native English speakers often, without realizing, slip into the use of familiar and culturally specific idioms that do not relate to the experiences of people from geographical, linguistic, and culturally diverse settings. For example, use of expressions such as *let's cut to the chase, let's wrap up now,* *it's not rocket science*, and *it's a piece of cake* are likely to have little meaning and will leave many confused, potentially feeling marginalized, within the event. As much as possible, please ensure that you avoid use of such terms or explain what they mean if you do use them. We also encourage you to learn the significance of the local idioms used and explore the meanings of those that are shared with you.

INTERPRETATION AND THE "PACE OF SPEECH." For those presenting at events where simultaneous interpretation is provided, please take into account that the Khmer and many other languages take longer to deliver than English, so please take your time when speaking, pausing briefly after making specific points, thus allowing the interpreter to catch up. If you are a naturally fast speaker, please try to adjust the pace of your speech to suit the environment. It is not uncommon for native speakers to unintentionally speak so fast that the delivery appears to be one long word in a sentence rather than separate words, each with their own meaning. In one training event provided by an international organization in Cambodia, participants who had a good understanding of English estimated that the interpreters accurately interpreted just 20% of what was spoken.

ASSISTING INTERPRETERS TO DELIVER HIGH QUALITY. Interpreters will need to be provided, in advance, with copies of PowerPoints and other resources to help them prepare. We would recommend that you meet with interpreters beforehand and provide brief notes related to your presentation to assist with this task.

TRANSLATION OF SUPPORTING MATERIALS. Please ensure that materials are translated from English to Khmer or the language of the participants and also "back translated" to English to check accuracy.

INCLUSION AND PARTICIPATION. Dependent on a range of factors and the type of presentation or training event (e.g., presentation), it may not be possible or appropriate to employ participatory methods. But where possible, you should plan to promote the voices and sharing of participants' experiences, opinions, and ideas at all events, as an important learning opportunity, to promote a collective experience and contribute to the process of nurturing positive alliances during and after the event. Trainers need to create different opportunities for sharing and asking, avoiding assumptions that during and after the training all participants will reach the same level.

THE IMPORTANCE OF EVALUATION AND FOLLOW-UP. Ensure that you build into the process of capacity building creative opportunities for evaluation, utilizing participatory methods similar to that which you employ during the LTNA. Share feedback and arrange follow-up days and opportunities for re-learning topics or concepts that require closer attention to detail. Where possible, this should include opportunities for observation of practice. Consider the implications of the evaluation and the implications for the organization and other stakeholders; gain feedback from managers and where possible, service users could and should be incorporated. Use the evaluation and follow-up to identify additional learning and support needs. If you introduce new theories, ideas, models, or ways of doing things, please do not just teach and go away! Build in follow-up (if not from you then from others). The vast majority of initial training is inadequate without follow-up, close supervision, and opportunities to discuss, relearn, and experience trial and error.

ENDINGS AND PLANNING FOR THE FUTURE. There is no doubt that when done properly, capacity development can be time consuming and resource heavy, but the authors believe that attention to detail and following the guidelines will ensure that your interventions are far more likely to be effective in the long term. Short-term drop-in trainings are rarely effective, and one might ask the question, if we know it is not effective, then why do we persist? Rather, a solutions-oriented focus emphasizes a shift from hierarchical therapeutic relationships to collaborative and cooperative relationships. Attention to solutions and collaboration can facilitate the learning, sharing, and growing experiences that can occur within "capacity building" fields.

In summary, carefully attend to these and other themes raised during this chapter, training, capacity development, supervision, and mentoring so that these do not become like another form of colonization, not of territory perhaps but of the mind. Endeavors to train a local workforce and bridge a gap in service delivery to local communities with trauma experiences require thoughtful reflection, collaborative relationships, attentiveness to cultural and historical contexts, and a prioritization of the participants' interests and needs. When a local workforce is developed with such attention, there is the possibility of considerable influence to social responses to need, larger practice and organizational policies, and ways of thinking about needs from a local perspective.

REFLECTIVE QUESTIONS

1. As you reflect on theory and practice, what assumptions, theoretical models, and treatment approaches do you practice from? Consider their origins and practical use—are they strength based? Are they appropriate for use in a different cultural context (If so how?), and/or could they be easily misused or misunderstood and result in inappropriate outcomes and discrimination? What are local beliefs, ideas, and attitudes in relation to the concept and ideas of "social work" and how may they influence what takes place? What assumptions do you have about the place you will be working and existing approaches that may need revising? What can you do to avoid the domination of Western ideas and concepts that may not be appropriate for that setting? What support and learning do you need, and where can you obtain that? Are you a good listener who is able to learn from others?

2. As you reflect on cultural differences, what do you need to learn about the culture you are going to be working with? How do you plan to do this? What assumptions do you make about the cultural context in which you will be working, and how will this affect your interactions and practice? What assumptions do you take with you? How will you ensure that your own ideas and assumptions do not dominate the discourse with indigenous colleagues and service users and result in inappropriate outcomes and practice? What are your own learning needs, and how will knowledge of the local culture enhance your own

learning and practice? How can you ensure an open dialogue that promotes sharing, reflection, learning, and mutual respect? Taking into consideration the issue of "gender issues" within that context, how can you ensure a balanced approach that takes into consideration the needs, vulnerabilities, and strengths of females and males—at all stages of life?

3. As you reflect on power dynamics, who holds the power in the relationships you will have with colleagues and service users? What are your thoughts and feelings about that? How do you plan to ensure to practice in a manner that is anti-discriminatory? How will you respond to situations of potential tension and conflict within the work setting?

4. As you reflect on your own learning needs, what support and learning needs do you have? How can you plan to ensure you receive that? What can you do to factor in and plan sufficient time for "self care" during this time—both individually and with your new colleagues?

SUMMATIVE POINTS

- Building a local workforce requires a level of introspection on the part of the training professional, a deep understanding of the community and cultural context, and an awareness of the diverse learning styles and needs of participants.

- Sustainability of capacity-building efforts requires close collaboration with local community stakeholders, including organizations, leaders in the community, and training professionals who are invested in maintaining and promoting culturally relevant workshops that help the larger community.

- The LTNA model provides a framework for considering the varied dimensions of executing culturally sensitive and accessible capacity-building workshops that can develop a local social services workforce.

GLOSSARY

capacity building. Any process or method employed to develop skills, knowledge, ability, practice, and capacity within the field of development.

learning and training needs assessment (LTNA). A model of training members of the community to provide services that can easily be applied in any setting and using the most basic resources.

REFERENCES

ADHOC Cambodia Human Rights and Development Association. (2013). *Issues of women's rights, child rights and migrant workers' rights in Cambodia*. http://www.adhoc-cambodia.org/?p=3440

Bronfenbrenner, U. (1979). *The ecology of human development.* Cambridge, MA: Harvard University Press.

De Jong, J. (Ed.). (2002). *Trauma, war and violence: Public mental health in socio-cultural context.* New York: Klumer. Academic Publishers.

First Step Cambodia. (n.d.). First Step Cambodia website. www.first-step-cambodia.org

Harbitz, M. (2016, January). *UN women Asia and the Pacific: Women in Cambodia continue to face violence. U.N. report says*. Retrieved from http://asiapacific.unwomen.org/en/news-and-events/stories/2016/01/women-in-cambodia-continue-to-face-violence

Hilton, A. (2008). *"I thought it could never happen to boys": Sexual abuse & exploitation of boys in Cambodia, an exploratory study*. Cambodia: Hagar and World Vision.

ICNL. (2016, June). *Civic freedom monitor: Cambodia*. NGO Law Monitor http://www.icnl.org/research/monitor/cambodia.html

Royal University of Phnom Penh. (n.d.). *Department of social work background*. http://www.rupp.edu.kh/fssh/social_work/?page=Background

School of Social Work University of Washington. (n.d.). *Cambodia partnership*. http://socialwork.uw.edu/programs/global-reach/cambodia-partnership

Sonis, J., Gibson, J. L., de Jong, J. T. V. M., Field, N. P., Hean, S., & Komproe, I. (2009). Probable post traumatic stress disorder and disability in Cambodia. Associations with perceived justice, desire for revenge and attitudes toward the Khmer Rouge trials. *Journal of the American Medical Association, 302*(5), 527–536.

TPO Cambodia. (n.d.). *The need for mental health care in Cambodia*. http://tpocambodia.org/the-need/

U.S. Department of State. (2015). *Cambodia 2015 trafficking in persons report*. http://www.state.gov/j/tip/rls/tiprpt/countries/2015/243409.htm

RESOURCES

Arbour, L. (2008). *Claiming the millennium development goals: A human rights approach*. New York and Geneva: United Nations. http://lib.ohchr.org/_layouts/15/WopiFrame.aspx?sourcedoc=/SPdocs/Claiming_MDGs_en.pdf&action=default&DefaultItemOpen=1

Gong-Guy, E., Cravens, R. B., & Patterson, T. E. (1991). Clinical issues in mental health service delivery to refugees. *American Psychologist, 46*(6), 642–648.

Janesick, V. (2011). *Stretching exercises for qualitative researchers*. Thousand Oaks, CA: Sage.

Mulroy, E. A. (2015). Community Needs Assessment. *Encyclopedia of social work*. http://socialwork.oxfordre.com/view/10.1093/acrefore/9780199975839.001.0001/acrefore-9780199975839-e-73

United Nations Publication. (2007). *Claiming the millennium development goals: A human rights approach*. New York: United Nations.

PRACTICE APPLICATIONS WITH VULNERABLE AND TRAUMA-EXPOSED IMMIGRANTS AND REFUGEES

"No administration could stop the tidal wave of immigration that swept over the land; no political party could restrain or control the enterprise of our people, and no reasonable man could desire to check the march of civilization."

~ Nelson A. Miles

Learning Objectives

Apply the integrative theoretical model to immigrant and refugee subgroups with a focus on trauma-exposed clients.

INTRODUCTION

UNIT IV: Practice Applications With Vulnerable and Trauma-Exposed Immigrants and Refugees. Building on theory and intervention modalities in the preceding sections, Unit IV provides concrete examples of the impact of using an integrative framework when working with immigrants and refugees, with attention to those who have experienced trauma. The chapters in Unit IV cover specific target groups, beginning with a discussion of trauma, its definitions, and the complex nature of its effects on transnational individuals and communities (Chapter 13: "Defining Trauma: Practice Application With Vulnerable and Trauma-Exposed Immigrant Populations and Survivors of Torture,"

Smith). The section also includes content on working with woman affected by violence (Chapter 14: "Practice Applications With Women," Fong et al.), practice with LGBTQ immigrants and refugees (Chapter 15: "Practice Applications With LGBTQ Immigrants and Refugees," Ramirez), and practice with immigrant and refugee youth (Chapter 16: "Practice Applications With Immigrant and Refugee Youth," Benson, Abdi, & Ford-Paz). For each chapter, the authors provide relevant definitions for their respective populations along with case scenarios and discussion that highlight the need for an integrative approach to intervention.

This section speaks to the necessity of providing clear conceptual models for working with vulnerable and trauma-exposed immigrants and refugees yet recognizes that vulnerability and trauma exist along a broad spectrum in which individuals, families, and communities can continue to thrive despite a complex trauma history. This section will highlight the relevance of genetics, coping strategies, resilience, and circumstance (normalized or acute), all of which influence one's ability to respond to traumatic experiences and move forward. The chapters also recognize the range of actions and reactions to environment that is salient for immigrants and refugees, behavior that may be culturally bound or a product of his or her pre-migration, migration, and post-migration experiences. This unit seeks to understand the impact of trauma on individual and group functioning. At the same time, all readers must recognize the diversity of reactions to new environments and the difficult and unique circumstances that present across the target populations identified. Special attention has been given to particularly marginalized groups (i.e., women, LGBTQ, youth), yet we do recognize all groups suffer when faced with survival or forced migration. Our intention is to highlight that some groups suffer disproportionately more because of global systems of oppression and injustice that impede equality across major segments of our society based on race, gender, class, religion, sexual orientation, and ability.

At the end of this section, readers should have a working knowledge of the varying needs in the target groups selected for this unit and the methods used to support practice using integrative theoretical approaches and cultural understanding that guide intervention.

Chapter 13

DEFINING TRAUMA

Practice Applications With Vulnerable and Trauma-Exposed Immigrant Populations and Survivors of Torture

HAWTHORNE E. SMITH

KEY TERMS

torture, forced émigrés, refugee trauma, complex marginalization, interdisciplinary care for trauma survivors

---

CHAPTER HIGHLIGHTS

- Description of the multi-faceted stressors confronting forced migrants
- Description of the detrimental effects of torture and human rights abuses
- Ways in which transnational migrants may be faced with marginalization in their daily lives
- Interdisciplinary, holistic, and resilience-based approaches to service provision for traumatized immigrants

---

When approached by the editors of this volume to contribute a chapter, I was eager to comply on behalf of our treatment team here at the Bellevue/NYU Program for Survivors of Torture (PSOT). It was immediately evident that we all shared a resilience and strength-based perspective regarding our clients. We understood that anyone can be a victim—just by being at the wrong place at the wrong time—but to be a survivor, one must find the inner force to confront challenges and to tenaciously cling to one's belief in possibilities, not just limitations. It was also clear that we recognized the ongoing nature of the trauma or trauma-related stress that transnational migrants face on a daily basis. These shared elements spoke to the potential of a fruitful collaboration.

As such, this chapter will endeavor to describe some of the ways in which multifaceted and reinforcing stressors are experienced and manifested in the lives of forced émigrés and survivors of torture. The chapter will also include a description of the role that holistic, interdisciplinary treatment can play in helping survivors to overcome the obstacles they face. This will be exemplified by describing the way we approach treatment provision at the Bellevue/NYU Program for Survivors of Torture and some of the lessons we have learned over these past 20 years.

REFUGEE TRAUMA AND THE CHALLENGES FACING FORCED ÉMIGRÉS AND TRANSNATIONAL MIGRANTS

When presenting information regarding clinical work with survivors of torture and refugee trauma to service providers, we have found it useful to initially engage them in a couple of brief experiential exercises. During one such exercise, the facilitator asks each member of the group to write down "between three and five of the most important things in the world" to them. These should be precious things that "make life worth living," in an emotional sense, and do not have to be "things" in the strictest sense of the word. The facilitator waits a few minutes for the responses.

The facilitator then collects the papers from the audience and without divulging names or identifying who wrote what, the facilitator reads through some of the responses from the papers he or she has collected. Often, audience members will write down the names of family members or loved ones. They may name a relationship, such as marriage or parenthood. Respondents may mention material things and possessions, such as an ancestral home. Other responses may describe aspirations (i.e., obtaining an advanced degree), passions (i.e., playing or enjoying music), achievements (i.e., professional success), or a general sense of well-being (i.e., good health, freedom, etc.). After reading through a number of these responses, the facilitator rips all of the papers to shreds. He or she then asks the audience to imagine for a moment that all of these precious things have been taken from them through violent means, and that they are currently powerless to reclaim any of them. This symbolizes the painful scenario that survivors of torture and refugee trauma who are now living in exile are facing (Smith & Keller, 2007).

Refugees who have survived traumatic events are assaulted with a continuous series of attacks on their psychological and emotional integrity (Bhui et al., 2003). Consequently, some theorists argue that the "post" in post-traumatic stress disorder can be misleading (Akukwe, Smith, & Wokocha, 2000; Briere, 2001; Elsass, 1997, 1998; Fondacaro & Mazzulla, 2015; Herman, 1992; Holtz, 1998). Survivors are not just reacting to an isolated traumatic experience from the past; they are reacting to a constant barrage of emotional and cultural challenges, including changes in how they perceive the world and themselves (Berliner, Mikkelson, Bovbjerg, & Wiking, 2004; Silove, Sinnerbrink, Field, Manicavasagar, & Steel, 1997). As such, theorists are currently debating other ways to conceptualize post-traumatic reactions. There have been calls in the literature to view PTSD more as a sign of a need for assistance rather than pathology per se (Quiroga & Jaranson, 2005). One such approach is the notion of *chronic traumatic stress*, which is described as "not a disorder, but rather the contextual experience of persistent traumatic events, both past and continued, that occur at any point across the lifespan, with sequelae that are perceived by the individual as impairing, regardless of symptom constellation or thresholds" (Fondacaro & Mazzulla, 2015).

The challenges facing refugees are distressing in nature and serve to exacerbate the psychological pain experienced by previously traumatized individuals (Genefke & Vesti, 1998; Quiroga & Jaranson, 2005). The stressors work to maintain the survivor's experience of trauma in the present tense. It has been argued that stimuli reminiscent of the trauma become generalized and can evoke psychological responses long after the initial trauma has passed (Gurris, 2001; Mollica et al., 2001; Randall & Lutz, 1991; Silove, Sinnerbrink, Field, Manicavasagar, & Steel, 1997; Straker, 1987). The stressors of being a refugee and living in exile are part and parcel of the human rights abuses from which our clients are endeavoring to recover. Exposure to war, torture, exile, and other traumatic events is tragically all too common, and recent global trends and statistics point to the fact that things are intensifying. The UNHCR (2015) states that 13.9 million people were newly displaced from their homes during the 2014 calendar year because of conflict and/or persecution. Among them were 11 million internally displaced people (Norwegian Refugee Council, 2015). This breaks down to an average of 42,500 people being forced to flee their homes every single day. When combined with the preexisting populations of refugees and internally displaced people, along with the 1.8 million people who applied for asylum worldwide in 2014 (including 121,000 in the United States), we see a staggering total of 59.5 million people across the globe who are currently living while forcibly displaced from their homes (UNHCR, 2015).

The psychological literature identifies three phases of traumatization that survivors of torture, war trauma, and exile endure. Initially, there is an increase in repression and persecution in the survivor's native country; then comes a period in which the survivor experiences or witnesses direct war trauma, torture, and/or other traumatic deprivations; and then the survivor is confronted with the difficult and long-term process of being uprooted and living in exile (van der Veer, 1998). This general scenario fits the experiences of the majority of clients we see at the Bellevue/NYU Program for Survivors of Torture. Among the "multi-traumatic situations" members of this population have survived (Elsass, 1997, p. 3) are severe violence and social upheaval in their home countries. These chaotic situations may have taken the form of ethnic or racial cleansing, religious intolerance, civil war, a rebel insurgency, tribal warfare, homophobic persecution, or some other form of social strife.

Many forced émigrés have been directly tortured, imprisoned, sexually assaulted, physically maimed, and may have lost family members in the conflict. In addition, there are many "indirect" forms of war-related trauma and human rights abuses that survivors endure. Witnessing random shootings, having family members or friends "disappeared," navigating harrowing circumstances and physical deprivation as one flees the besieged areas to find refuge, coping with mortal fear, guilt, and bereavement are also significant stressors that affect a survivor's ability to function on a daily basis (van der Veer, 1998; Volkan, 2004).

These survivors and refugees have generally lost most, if not all, of their worldly possessions. This includes not only material things but also applies to self-esteem, dreams, aspirations, feelings of emotional and physical security, and a sense of personal control (Fischman, 1998; Silove, Tarn, Bowles, & Reid, 1991). They have frequently lived as fugitives in their own country and escaped from their native lands under harrowing circumstances. Many refugees who have been forced to flee their war-torn homelands initially find refuge in neighboring countries that are often impoverished and chaotic themselves (de Jong, 2002).

All of these events precede the client's resettling in their final "host" country, with the forced adaptation this entails (Fondacaro & Mazzulla, 2015; Randall & Lutz, 1991; van der Veer, 1998). Survivors of torture and other transnational migrants who are living in exile as refugees are coping with multilevel stressors that serve to reinforce and complicate their ability to adapt emotionally (Kinzie, Leung, & Boehnlein, 1997). Some survivors have stated that, "Exile is the most painful form of torture" (Fischman & Ross, 1990, p. 139). Upon arrival in a new country, these forced immigrants are often subjected to harsh living conditions in refugee camps and/or detention centers. When they arrive in countries such as the United States, there may be further questions about their legal status. While refugees and individuals granted asylum have legal status, many asylum seekers are detained by immigration authorities and are kept in custody in detention facilities for several days, months, or years, while their cases are being adjudicated (Chester & Holtan, 1992; Fischman, 1998; Keller et al., 2003; Silove et al., 1991). Among forced émigrés seeking safety, these realities are frequently superimposed on the detrimental physical and psychological effects of the torture experience itself.

DETRIMENTAL EFFECTS OF TORTURE

The prevalence of torture in refugee communities has been estimated to be between 5% to 35% (Baker, 1992; Eisenman, Keller, & Kim, 2000; Montgomery & Foldspang, 1994). Eisenman et al. (2000) found a 6.6% prevalence of survivors of torture in a general outpatient medical clinic here at Bellevue Hospital. Other recent studies have reported higher prevalence rates, ranging from 8% to 11% (Crosby et al., 2006; Eisenman, Gelberg, Liu, & Shapiro, 2003). These percentages aside, the detrimental effects of torture are wide ranging and insidious. The goal of modern torture, beyond eliciting information or punishing particular individuals, is to undermine the psychic integrity of an entire community. The effects of torture and refugee trauma have been described in the literature as the "Four D's": disintegration of the psyche; dispossession through multiple, recurrent losses; dislocation from home and country; and disempowerment in terms of dealing with the internal and external world (Silove, Tarn, Bowles, & Reid, 1991).

One of the major misconceptions about survivors of torture and refugee trauma is that there is one clearly defined pattern of reactions to this broad array of stressors that makes it easy to identify survivors. In actuality, reactions often vary between individuals who have experienced similar types of trauma, including the multitraumatic situation of the consequences of wars (Elsass, 1997; Fabri, 2001; Jaranson, 1998). There is no "magic question" or "tell-tale sign" that will clearly differentiate between survivors and nonsurvivors with 100% specificity and sensitivity. There are, however, some general areas in which we may expect to see signs of distress. These signs can be physical, cognitive, emotional, behavioral, and spiritual. These effects overlap and can be self-reinforcing.

The physical symptoms of torture and refugee trauma are varied and may manifest themselves differently from client to client. There may be identifiable scars or disfigurements that document the trauma endured (i.e., cigarette burns, scars, missing teeth, and/or amputations). There may also be decrements in physical functioning because of the abuse suffered that leave no scars, such as impaired vision from violent blows to the head. Insomnia, nightmares, and other sleep difficulties are among the most frequently reported symptoms by torture survivors (Quiroga & Jaranson, 2005). Frequently, there will be no outward signs of the physical trauma, as many torturers want to inflict the maximum amount of physical pain without leaving visible physical scars (Berliner et al., 2004; Keller, Eisenman, & Saul, 1998; Shrestha & Sharma, 1995).

Cognitive symptoms stemming from their traumatic experiences are another major area of concern. Cognitive symptoms frequently reported include difficulty concentrating, memory difficulties, excessive rumination, and active attempts not to think about anything reminiscent of their traumatic experiences (Engdahl & Eberly, 1990). Clients have reported that they are no longer able to retain what they have just read or heard. Frequently, clients may be caught between conflicting extremes of avoidance and intrusion (Elsass, 1997; Haenel, 2001; Horowitz, 1976). They may be inundated by intrusive symptoms, such as rumination and nightmares, by which they cannot stop reliving their traumatic experiences. Simultaneously, they may avoid or deny their experience and suffer emotional numbing (Jaranson & Popkin, 1998). The etiology of the decrements in functioning must be assessed. Blunt trauma to the head, traumatic brain injury, and the associated neurological impairment may be the root cause of cognitive impairment, but other psychological causes must also be considered.

Emotional functioning is another important sphere affected by trauma. Research with Bosnian war survivors has shown that emotional difficulties and psychiatric diagnoses persist even after three years have elapsed since the fighting (Mollica et al., 2001). It has been noted that major depression and PTSD are the two most frequently utilized diagnoses for this population and that while PTSD seems to garner the most attention, major depression may be the most prevalent psychological stressor (Mollica, 2004). Depression is a common mental disorder that presents with depressed mood, loss of interest or pleasure, feelings of guilt or self-worth, disturbed sleep or appetite, low energy, and poor concentration (APA, 2013). Again, research data indicate that the emotional distress can become chronic for a majority of torture survivors living in exile (Carlsson et al., 2005).

Emotional responses may differ from survivor to survivor and may be manifested in their affective presentation. Some may present in a volatile, emotionally charged manner, particularly as they recount their trauma history. Some may even view relating their trauma history as a cathartic experience. In contrast, others may present with a flat affect. They may relate the most intimate and painful details of their trauma without changing the tone of their voice or their rate of speech. The cognitive and emotional aspects of the personality may appear disconnected from one another (Randall & Lutz, 1991). This disconnection is frequently an important issue in asylum proceedings with United States Citizenship and Immigration Service officers (USCIS) and United States Immigration and Customs Enforcement (ICE) judges. Immigration officials may ask how torture survivors will present emotionally or not be fully aware of the spectrum of "normal" presenting styles. Clinicians and service providers who engage in this forensic work must be prepared to explain and educate asylum adjudicators as to the complex and nuanced ways that traumatized immigrants may comport themselves emotionally and behaviorally (Smith, Lustig, & Gangsei, 2015).

Behavioral functioning is another area where resettlement workers, teachers, and job counselors often report that they observe signs that comprehensive mental health services may be needed for a particular survivor. This is particularly pertinent, as changes in one's perceived health status, patterns of thinking, and emotional functioning will have significant impact on one's behavior. There may be signs of behavioral withdrawal that mirror the attempts to avoid thoughts that pertain to the traumatic past (Randall & Lutz, 1991). Some clients may avoid individuals who come from their home countries or their region of the world. Some clients report avoiding any information such as news broadcasts, Internet reports, and so forth, about the situations in their home countries. Some have said that any new information, particularly negative news, can be overwhelming. In contrast, other clients may be very active in gathering as much information as possible. Clients have described this as an attempt to "stay connected" to the struggle and people they have left behind.

These dichotomous reactions reflect the precarious emotional balance that survivors are trying to maintain and demonstrates the different ways that survivors may react to similar stressors. Clients may have difficulty balancing their needs for assurance and connection, while maintaining vigilance against external threats and triggers that may activate painful memories (Elsass, 1997; Haenel, 2001; Silove et al., 1991). They may fluctuate from behaving as though they are anesthetized to experiencing intense surges of affect brought about by intrusive thoughts and dreams. Clients may also seek coping mechanisms that are not always positive or therapeutic. This may lead to detrimental changes in behavior, such as clients engaging in substance abuse. The substance dependence may have begun as an effort to self-medicate or reduce tension but grows beyond the survivor's control (Briere & Scott, 2006). The literature shows that substance abuse levels among trauma survivors who develop full-blown PTSD are elevated, relative to levels among survivors who do not develop PTSD (Chilcoat & Breslau, 1998). This is a potentially major issue to explore regarding survivors of refugee trauma who are searching for ways to cope with feelings of anxiety, depression, and marginalization.

MULTIPLE DOMAINS OF MARGINALIZATION

For those survivors who participate in the PSOT program, they are often confronted with the daunting task of living in New York City in circumstances that can be intimidating and disempowering on multiple levels. This is consistent with the reported experiences of displaced people around the world. There are numerous examples of the kinds of educational, vocational, linguistic, and cultural problems they face that make exile seem like a continuation of the torture experience (Carlsson, Mortensen, & Kastrup, 2006; van der Veer, 1998). Studies have shown that the additional stressors of refugee trauma serve to exacerbate psychological sequelae of torture and other human rights abuses (Quiroga & Jaranson, 2005). The literature states that it may not be migration itself that causes the increased symptomatology for refugees but the severe stress of the migration under harrowing circumstances and the multiple levels of disempowerment and insecurity faced in the new environments (Berliner et al., 2004; den Velde et al., 2000).

During training sessions and clinical consultations with refugee resettlement workers and affiliated service providers (a significant number of whom have their own personal immigration or refugee histories), PSOT presenters have remarked that the word "marginalization" is frequently utilized. These experts emphasize the deep impact that marginalization has on many domains of functioning for forced migrants. Here, we will briefly touch upon the domains of education, professional and vocational development, legal services, social services, and social adaptation that are impacted by complex and ongoing marginalization.

EDUCATIONAL CONTEXTS. There are many ways in which transnational migrants are marginalized in the educational domain. There may be linguistic challenges as they perhaps shift from being literate to semi or fully illiterate. Their access to education may be limited because of logistical or financial constraints. Years outside of the educational system may make for difficult to make appropriate educational placements; as refugee students may be forced to matriculate with students who are much younger than they are in order to be at the same educational level or perhaps be placed with their age-cohort, only to struggle and find that they are years behind them in educational exposure and experience. The modes of educating and teaching may be different from what a student experienced in his or her home country, and perhaps one's previous degrees and academic achievements may not be recognized.

PROFESSIONAL AND VOCATIONAL CONTEXTS. The professional and vocational realm is particularly problematic for forced migrants. Asylum seekers will often lack proper work authorization and be forced to remain unemployed or to work "off the books" or "under the table" jobs that can be exploitative and low paying. Many professionals lack a license or authorization in a field where they previously worked. Our clients have told us, "You never know who is driving your taxi or sweeping your floor." They may have been highly trained professionals who may have been forced to flee their homelands because of their professional activities, their economic status, or their service provision histories (Smith & Keller, 2007).

Many migrants experience relative disadvantage, as there may be differences in standards, resources, and technology in one's field between one's home country and here. Perhaps there are few employment opportunities in one's previous field, or one's profession is not respected like it was at home. Immigrants may find themselves working in jobs where they no longer have seniority and subsequently feel devalued. Dramatic shifts in how gender roles interplay with the vocational landscape can have significant impact not only in the workplace but also the ways in which migrants' familial and domestic contexts are navigated. Research shows that refugees and asylum seekers who have not been able to find gainful employment in their host countries or who have fewer social contacts manifest increased levels of social distress and that this continues many years after their initial victimization (Carlsson, Olsen, Mortensen, & Kastrup, 2006; Quiroga & Jaranson, 2005). In fact, recent data show that the emotional distress can be chronic for the majority of this marginalized population (Carlsson et al., 2005).

LEGAL CONTEXTS. There may be ways in which legal and forensic challenges also serve to marginalize transnational migrants, particularly asylum seekers. Many asylum seekers have never been in a formal courtroom setting before and may feel stigmatized that they have to "go in front of a judge." Not only is the context unfamiliar, it may seem intimidating (Smith, Lustig, & Gangsei, 2015). There may be different legal philosophies or differences in particular laws/expectations. This may have significant impact on how families function within the home, where "traditional" child rearing practices may run afoul of the child protection laws that exist in the United States. Some clients have quipped that the first word immigrant children learn in the United States is "9-1-1!" Conversely, even though transnational migrants may live in poor neighborhoods, occasionally in areas with high levels of crime and racial tension in which they may become victims of crime, some may avoid all contact with law enforcement or forensic personnel, based on negative or abusive experiences from their home countries. As such, some crimes, exploitation, and abuse in the community may not go reported, even though issues of safety and adaptation to life in this country are also very real concerns.

SOCIAL SERVICE CONTEXTS. In terms of social services, issues of loss, pride, and stigma may interfere with migrants' abilities to access resources that they merit and need. There may be fear that others in the community will know that they receive assistance, which can cause shameful feelings. It has been said that the only thing worse than a lack of information is misinformation, and there is a great deal of misinformation in expatriate communities. Our French speaking African clients warn each other to avoid "les conseilles de la rue" or "street advice" (Smith, Lustig, & Gangsei, 2015). So some people in need may not access appropriate and necessary assistance in terms of housing, food, or other basic needs, for the unfounded fear that it may have a negative impact upon their immigration status. Conversely, when migrants do attempt to access social services, they may become frustrated by bureaucratic processes or the inadequacy of the existing resources.

SOCIAL CONTEXTS. One way in which marginalization may be felt most profoundly is in the social context. Forced émigrés face linguistic challenges, as they may not speak the language of their host nation. There may be a plethora of ways in which cultural norms differ, like modes of dress, music, time orientation, hospitality, personal space, approaching/greeting strangers; group versus individual orientation; gender roles and sexuality; and issues linked to age. There may be significant feelings of being excluded by members of the host society, as manifested by teasing and bullying in school, enforced social isolation, and other exclusionary or assaultive behaviors. This may be compounded by divisions that exist within the expatriate communities. These challenges may exacerbate depressive and post-traumatic symptoms that some survivors may already be manifesting, which can feed into further socially isolative behaviors. Symptoms of avoidance and withdrawal linked to traumatic reactions may fuel distrust and social distancing. Anhedonia, lack of pleasure, and a lack of energy and initiative that may be linked to depressed moods can also feed into isolative behaviors that serve to reinforce the sense of social marginalization.

Such are some of the multifaceted emotional stressors that feed into the disempowerment, marginalization, and psychological distress that torture survivors and those who are living in exile are grappling with on a daily basis. These multiple losses, the social dislocation, the feelings of fear and inadequacy, as well as the cultural/linguistic barriers are all part of the psychological reality for those living in exile as refugees (Randall & Lutz, 1991). Clinicians may conceptualize these recurrent stressors as "sequential traumatizations" (Basoglu, Paker, Paker, Özmen, & Sahin, 1994; Quiroga & Jaranson, 2005) or chronic traumatic stress (Fondacaro & Mazzulla, 2015). Given the complex nature of the challenges that traumatized immigrants are facing, it is incumbent upon service providers to strive to provide holistic, nimble, culturally astute, interdisciplinary care. The fact that forced migrants are facing so many hurdles speaks to the many ways in which service providers may intervene to provide some relief and assistance as survivors move forward with their lives. In other words, the bad news is that there is so much to do, but the good news is that there are so many ways to be involved in the healing processes.

INTERDISCIPLINARY TREATMENT OF TORTURE SURVIVORS AND FORCED ÉMIGRÉS

The Bellevue/NYU Program for Survivors of Torture (PSOT) is devoted to helping to heal the bodies, minds, and spirits of people who have been tortured or persecuted, and I offer some of the program's processes and insights learned from its history of service to traumatized and uprooted survivors of torture. The program is located on the Lower East Side of Manhattan, one of the city's (and the nation's) most vibrant immigrant communities. Since its founding in 1995, the program has served over 5,000 men, women, and children from over 100 countries who are survivors of torture and refugee trauma. We are situated within two institutions of healing and training—the Bellevue Hospital Center (the nation's oldest existing public hospital) and the New York

University School of Medicine. This partnership provides significant clinical resources as we strive to bring coordinated, interdisciplinary care to our client population.

ESTABLISHING EMOTIONAL SAFETY. Across disciplines, one of the factors that have become evident in our work with torture survivors is that fostering a sense of emotional safety is of paramount importance. This finding is echoed throughout the psychological literature, where developing a relationship of confidence and trust with torture survivors has been described as being the first priority in treatment (Briere & Scott, 2006; Fabri, 2001; Fischman & Ross, 1990; Haenel, 2001; Herman, 1992; Keller et al., 1998; Pope & Garcia-Peltoniemi, 1991; Silove et al., 1991; Somnier & Genefke, 1986; van der Veer & van Waning, 2004; Vesti & Kastrup, 1991). This comes into play right away as prospective clients come into contact with our care coordination team—specifically our intake coordinators.

Initial contacts may take place telephonically or when prospective clients "walk-in," and our frontline staff members are trained in the value and importance of respectful, warm, human interactions. Their interactions with prospective clients will help set the tone for all further engagements with our program. Program staff members try to normalize the potentially confusing and intimidating hospital environment when greeting prospective clients or accompanying them for their initial medical assessment. This is consistent with psychological literature that describes normalizing a client's initial fears and anxieties as an important facet of creating a less threatening environment in which to begin treatment (Haenel, 2001). Prospective clients are screened to see if they live within New York State and whether or not the services they need and desire fit with the services we offer. If there is some mismatch in terms of parameters or needs, thoughtful referrals from our resource list are provided, along with full explanations of the rationale, to these survivors before they leave the hospital.

PSOT is a program within the Department of Emergency Medicine at Bellevue Hospital, with access to immediate assessment, triage, and intervention through the hospital's urgent care division. The reasoning is that in addition to the direct physical consequences of torture, there may be other public health imperatives that are exacerbated by a forced émigré's lack of access to proper medical care and screening (such as tuberculosis, untreated hypertension, etc.) that necessitate immediate intervention. As such, prospective clients for our program who have come into contact with the care coordination team are accompanied to the urgent care facilities and screened for any acute or emergent medical, emotional, or social service issues. Prospective clients are provided emergency care when needed, or they may be referred for mainstream Bellevue services—if deemed appropriate based on their presenting situation. This, in addition to basic screening for suicidality or other harmful ideation, help us to triage people who are navigating acutely dangerous situations, while providing a holding environment (and a sense of progress and being cared for) for clients who are awaiting their formal intake into our program.

Clients are also accompanied as they register and navigate other aspects of the hospital bureaucracy, with program staff and volunteers serving as interpreters and facilitators. Through this process, the client may sense that they have an ally, and a trusting relationship may begin to germinate as the staff helps to make the initial contacts more humane and manageable. Seemingly small actions can have more impact than words, especially at the outset of treatment (Fabri, 2001; Silove et al., 1991). Though we fully adhere to the notion of "It doesn't have to be therapy to be therapeutic," staff members from our social work and psychology departments are represented on the care coordination team, and our non-licensed intake administrative staff always have immediate access to clinicians should there be a question about safety or acute distress.

CLIENT-CENTERED PRACTICE BEGINNING AT INTAKE. Our intake process itself is a detailed and collaborative undertaking in which the client's voice is respected, and they have a good deal of influence in what the treatment priorities will be. This is consistent with the theory of human becoming, in which people are seen as the experts of their own lives and can be a crucial factor in developing effective medical and mental health interventions (Green, 2010; Smith & Akinsulure-Smith, 2011). When interviewing immigrants and refugees who may have suffered traumatic events, it is important to give them a sense of control over what they do or do not wish to share (Carrillo, Green, & Betancourt, 1999). In addition to our senior clinical staff, intake interviews are conducted by psychology interns and externs, social work interns, psychiatric residents, and medical residents—in conjunction with supervising staff. Each intake interview touches upon demographic information, including one's immigration status, housing situation, access to food, and educational and vocational needs as well as clinical indicators related to physical impairment and psychological stressors, such as post-traumatic, anxiety, and depressive symptoms. In addition to the semi-structured interview format, standardized measures are utilized to help bolster the initial diagnostic precision.

A central component to the intake interview is eliciting the trauma narrative to better understand a survivor's history and needs. Interviews in which a trauma victim recounts the events of his or her abuse can be extremely stressful and re-traumatizing for the individual (Iacopino, Allden, & Keller, 2001). It is also important to remember that many survivors have been tortured in conjunction with being interrogated for information by people in powerful positions. This is of crucial therapeutic importance, particularly during the initial interview, as there is a significant danger of re-traumatizing the client if the therapist strictly adheres to their usual information gathering techniques. It is counterproductive to insist on "uncovering the whole story," if the client is emotionally unprepared to do so (Gangsei, 2001; Silove et al., 1991). Discussing such events may result in exacerbation of physical and psychological symptoms for the individual. The psychological literature states that it is preferable to strike a balance between uncovering the story and validating the client's experiences (Elsass, 1997; Haenel, 2001). The role of the therapist at this stage has been described as both "witness and supportive human being" (Gurris, 2001, p. 51). Thus, it is essential that interviewers use judgment about how much information is needed about the traumatic events. Every effort should be made to accommodate any preference the client may have regarding the gender of the clinician and the interpreter. In certain cultures or situations, such as when an individual has experienced sexual assault, gender issues may be of even greater importance (Briere & Scott, 2006; Keller & Smith, 2007).

When the intake interview is completed, an intake narrative is composed by the clinician and supervisor. This narrative is then presented at our programmatic intake conferences that are interdisciplinary in nature and approach to decision-making. Students and senior staff from all concerned disciplines are represented and hear presentations regarding each intake.

The initial question to answer is whether or not the prospective client is someone who meets criteria for acceptance into our program. To that end, we consider the person's life experiences, their expressed and observed need for the services we provide, and whether or not our program is the "best fit" for that person and their current situation. If we feel that there are resources in the community that might be a better match for that person's presenting issues and needs, we will help to facilitate a direct linkage to the community resource.

INTERDISCIPLINARY TREATMENT PLANNING. For those who are accepted into our program, we engage in an interdisciplinary conversation about triage and initial treatment planning. All clients who are not already plugged in with medical services elsewhere in the hospital are given an appointment with a PSOT trained physician in our "Monday night clinic" (as mentioned, this service is currently being integrated further with the urgent care services in our hospital, which will expand the medical resources and appointment availability for our clients). "Monday night clinic" is a four-hour, weekly clinic where a panel of our program medical doctors, psychiatrists, and dental students provide care for PSOT clients. Our primary care physicians are trained to recognize and assess symptoms of PTSD and other acute psychiatric difficulties and are then able to make immediate referrals or consult with the mental health staff on site. This is consistent with practices that have proven effective in other clinical settings (Ko et al., 2008; Speer & Schneider, 2003). From Monday night clinic, referrals are made to specialized medical services when appropriate. This is especially frequent in terms of ob-gyn services, as we see an ever-increasing utilization of sexual violence against women and girls in conflict, in addition to the significant number of women who present to our clinic who have endured female genital cutting (Keller, Leviss, Levy, & Dyson, 2007).

INTEGRATED LEGAL AND SOCIAL SERVICES. Newly accepted clients will also be scheduled for more detailed legal and social service interviews—generally within a week of the intake conference. Our social and legal services team can delve deeper into the myriad of social, immigration, and educational issues that have been identified during the programmatic intake. These meetings are frequently among the first substantive service provision contacts with our team and go a long way in setting parameters for the interdisciplinary engagement with our clients (Mosenthal & Murphy, 2006). As stated earlier, many of the primary stressors that our clients are facing fall within the domain of legal and social issues (Kozaric-Kovacic, Kocijan-Hercigonja, & Jambrošic, 2002). Crucial areas of service provision include providing pertinent information, crisis intervention (for example, clients may come to our program very close to the 12-month filing deadline for asylum and will need immediate preparation of various forms, including the I-589 to officially apply for asylum), educational and housing referrals, as well as support in day-to-day matters, like getting appropriate winter clothing and adequate food. This support is not only important in and of itself but can be seen by clients as a sign that the program provides concrete services that can positively impact their lives. This may help to facilitate a client's engagement in other clinical services once they have internalized the notion that the program is actually there to assist them in tangible ways (Smith & Wilkinson, 2007).

ORIENTATION GROUPS. Another way in which clients are oriented into the program is through orientation (OR) groups. These groups have been developed as short-term, psychoeducational and supportive interventions by which clients learn about resources at the programmatic, hospital, and community levels. They also learn affect regulation skills, like deep breathing, grounding, and progressive muscle relaxation that largely come from a trauma-focused, cognitive, and behavioral perspective. Participants also learn about common psychological effects of trauma, the ins and outs of the asylum process, and speak with one of our psychiatrists about psychopharmacology and the "meaning of medication."

These groups are linguistically based, as we have run multinational groups for English, French, and Tibetan speakers. They are also staffed and conducted from an interdisciplinary framework. Frequently our group facilitators come from different disciplines, as social work interns may work with psychology externs, or psychology interns working with psychiatric residents, and so forth. There is frequently cross-discipline supervision, as our senior clinicians may work with trainees from outside of their department. Not only does this give us more flexibility in terms of scheduling and other logistics, but it helps to deepen the training experience as our trainees have hands-on experience working along with professionals from other disciplines and can broaden their perspectives on how to consider cases and intervene with specific clients. These groups also serve as an opportunity for further triage, and subsequent referrals for direct services are frequently made after clients have finished their orientation group participation.

MENTAL HEALTH SERVICE DELIVERY—INDIVIDUAL THERAPY. Our mental health services are varied, and also fall into the category of integrative and interdisciplinary interventions. Some clients will need psychopharmacological support as they cope with florid symptoms of PTSD and major depressive disorder, such as insomnia, anhedonia, exaggerated startle response, memory deficits, irritability, mood swings, and difficulty concentrating—among others. They may need to be stabilized psychiatrically before they engage in any sort of individual or group therapy (Aladjem, 2007). Conversely, some clients may need supportive interventions, such as four sessions of short-term individual stabilization, before they will engage in any sort of psychiatric treatment. The psycho-education and coping skills they receive in short-term therapy may reduce the stigma or misconceptions about psychotropic medications that a significant number of our clients harbor, based on what they had learned in their countries of origin.

For those clients who do engage in individual therapy, we follow an integrative model where aspects of trauma focused CBT, psychodynamic therapy, narrative exposure therapy, and interpersonal therapy may be used, depending upon the presenting issues being targeted and the sort of engagement and relationship that has developed with the client. At times, the therapeutic approach may be moderated by external stressors and realities. For example, a client may not be prepared to enter into his or her trauma narrative in any profound way, which would preclude engaging in any sort of exposure treatment at that particular time. But it may then be that the client must testify at his or her own immigration/asylum proceedings and needs to be able to delve into their trauma history in a detailed way. Treatment may then shift to a sort of non-annualized, supportive exposure that serves to help the client face their traumatic memories in a way they can tolerate through the use of affect regulation techniques and an overarching notion of "meaning making" and seeing the endeavor as part of their overcoming structural and legal barriers impeding them from beginning a new life on secure footing. These endeavors are usually done in conjunction with the client's legal team, where we may provide psycho-education to the lawyers about how to best approach eliciting the trauma history and how we can work collaboratively to best support the client (Wilkinson, 2007).

MENTAL HEALTH SERVICE DELIVERY—GROUP THERAPY. In addition to individual psychotherapy, PSOT has earned a reputation for being among the leaders in utilizing group modalities in culturally syntonic and adaptive ways. We have ongoing groups for traumatized individuals from many cultural and linguistic backgrounds; but the groups tend to be more supportive and are not trauma-focused groups per se. Group structure and norms vary among populations, as cultural norms are taken into consideration as group facilitators and participants cocreate the culture of each group (Smith & Impalli, 2007). For example, our support group for French-speaking African survivors (which has been existence for nearly 20 years) draws heavily from the West and Central African traditions of the extended family and the communal support and discussion necessary to confront individual challenges (Smith, 2003). Our group for people persecuted because of their sexual orientation tends to be more psychodynamic and process oriented. We also facilitate groups for Tibetan speaking survivors from Tibet and Nepal, English speaking African men, and a more geographically diverse group for English speaking clients. These groups are frequently facilitated by staff from differing disciplines, and the group supervision may also be provided across disciplines, for similar reasons as the orientation groups. Research shows that effective clinical collaboration happens when there is a sense of similarity of mission and mutual dependence among disciplines (Berg-Weger & Schneider, 1998).

ALTERNATIVE TREATMENT MODALITIES. The program also utilize modalities that are nonverbally based, such as art therapy and trauma-informed yoga. Not only are these interventions shown to be increasingly effective with highly traumatized populations who may have difficulty expressing their feelings verbally; but it helps with our program's extensive linguistic diversity—as clients who may not fit into one of our talk-oriented groups can still have meaningful client-to-client contact in a way that builds a sense of community and belonging.

COORDINATED SERVICE TEAMS. Beyond providing services across disciplines, it is important that ongoing communication among service providers and clinical stakeholders take place on a regular basis to ensure that we are working from the proverbial "same page" in terms of how to prioritize and implement targeted interventions for our clients. We regularly schedule such opportunities for cross-discipline discussion and case planning and strive to make the interactions more "horizontal" than hierarchical, so that all members of the team feel empowered to contribute and add their expertise to the team's conceptualizations (Atwal & Caldwell, 2005). To illustrate, each week the program staff have two intake conferences that were described earlier. We also have a "six-month follow-up" meeting every other week, in which clients have been interviewed by members of our social services team to assess their current functioning, service utilization, and to see where potential referrals may have fallen through the cracks (follow-up psychological measures are readministered during these interviews). The results of these interviews are then presented to an interdisciplinary team at the meeting so that updated triage, referrals, or crisis intervention can be implemented. In the intervening weeks, we have programmatic case conferences, which are dedicated to discussing particularly complex cases or those cases in some sort of acute distress. Again, all disciplines are represented around the table and participate in the discussion and planning of next steps.

At a programmatic level, the same focus on interdisciplinary support and communication is maintained. Our executive committee, which serves to guide the overall management and direction of the program, is comprised of directors of operations, clinical services, hospital/institutional relations, research, social services, and clinical training. These executive committee members are medical doctors, social workers, legal service providers, psychiatrists, psychologists, and administrative staff. Senior clinicians from all disciplines meet on a weekly basis for peer supervision, and the entire staff participates in our staff meetings and programmatic retreats. These meetings strive to make sure that standards of quality are maintained, that team cohesion is facilitated, and that the well-being of all staff members is prioritized (Vinokur-Kaplan, 1995). Research shows that such groups are most effective when relatively small teams are comprised of members from different occupations who have been engaged in the creation of the group's norms and functioning and who have the opportunity to exchange information in timely fashion (Xyrichis & Lowton, 2008).

CONCLUSION

We recognize the significant parallel processes that exist between our clients who are facing numerous and complex stressors and the service provision staff who are helping them to face these challenges. Again, there is so much to do that it can be overwhelming; but at the same time, the opportunities to intervene in some meaningful and tangible way are numerous and powerful. As particular interventions and approaches across populations are described in this volume, remember the constant emphases of a resilience-based, interdisciplinary approach that leads with humanity as its primary basis. As a woman who was displaced from Ethiopia once said to me,

"You know, we have nothing in common. We are different genders. We come from different continents and different countries. We speak different mother-tongues. We have different levels of education and social class. We worship differently and our immigration statuses are different. In fact, we have nothing in common—except for one thing. That is humanity. Let's begin there." Her words left an indelible mark on me for their clarity and profound nature. Our work is exactly what she said. It is based on the notion of shared humanity. It is really that simple—and also that complex.

REFLECTIVE QUESTIONS

1. Why is PTSD not an entirely accurate clinical description for the experiences of many traumatized migrants?

2. How would you describe the differences between multidisciplinary care and interdisciplinary care? How would these differences manifest themselves in your practice?

3. In what ways might you be best prepared or willing to intervene to provide tangible assistance for traumatized immigrants?

SUMMATIVE POINTS

- Forced émigrés are impacted by difficult and sometimes traumatic experiences that occur in their home countries and as they attempt to adapt to their challenging new circumstances in exile.

- These transitional challenges are frequently superimposed on the effects of the experiences of torture and other human rights abuses they have already endured.

- Resilience-based, culturally informed, interdisciplinary care is an evolving area of inquiry that is proving successful in providing effective and appropriate care for forced émigrés who have survived significant human rights abuses.

REFERENCES

Akukwe, C., Smith, H., & Wokocha, E. (2000). Enhancing the well-being of African refugees. In I. Berhane (Ed.), *Proceedings from the conference "African Refugees and the US response: Twenty years of resettlement"* (pp. 67–74). Arlington, VA: Ethiopian Community Development Council/African Resource Network.

Aladjem, A. (2007). The psychiatric care of survivors of torture, refugee trauma, and other human rights abuses. In H. Smith, A. Keller, & D. Lhewa (Eds.), *Like a refugee camp on First Avenue: Insights and experiences form the Bellevue/NYU Program for Survivors of Torture* (pp. 217–270). New York: Jacob and Valeria Langeloth Foundation.

American Psychiatric Association. (2013). *Diagnostic and statistical manual of mental disorders* (5th ed.). Washington, DC: Author.

Atwal, A., & Caldwell, K. (2005). Do all health and social care professionals interact equally: A study of interactions in multidisciplinary teams in the United Kingdom. *Scandinavian Journal of Caring Sciences*, 19, 268–273. doi: 10.1111/j.1471-6712.2005.00338.x

Baker, R. (1992). Psychological consequences for tortured refugees seeking asylum and refugee status in Europe. In M. Basoglu (Ed.), *Torture and its consequences: Current treatment approaches* (pp. 83–101). Cambridge: Cambridge University Press.

Basoglu, M., Paker, M., Paker, Ö., Özmen, E., & Sahin, D. (1994). Factors related to long-term traumatic stress responses in survivors of torture. *Journal of the American Medical Association*, 272, 357–63.

Berg-Weger, M., & Schneider, F. (1998). Interdisciplinary collaboration in social work education. *Journal of Social Work Education*, 34(1), 97–107.

Berliner, P., Mikkelson, E., Bovbjerg, A., & Wiking, M. (2004). Psychotherapy treatment of torture survivors. *International Journal of Psychosocial Rehabilitation*, 8, 85–96.

Bhui, K., Abdi, A., Abdi, M., Pereira, S., Dualeh, M., Robertson, D., . . . Ismail, H. (2003). Traumatic events, migration, characteristics and psychiatric symptoms among Somali refugees. *Social Psychiatry and Psychiatric Epidemiology*, 38, 35–43.

Briere, J. (2001, July). *Evaluation, measurement, and assessment approaches with severely traumatized populations.* Presentation to the Clinical Leadership Conference of the National Consortium of Torture Treatment Centers, Minneapolis, MN.

Briere, J., & Scott, C. (2006). *Principles of trauma therapy: A guide to symptoms, evaluation, and treatment.* Thousand Oaks, CA: Sage.

Carlsson, J. M., Mortensen, E. L., & Kastrup, M. (2005). A follow-up study of mental health and health-related quality of life in tortured refugees in multidisciplinary treatment. *Journal of Nervous and Mental Disease*, 193(10), 651–657.

Carlsson, J. M., Mortensen, E. L., & Kastrup, M. (2006). Predictors of mental health and quality of life in male tortured refugees. *Nordic Journal of Psychiatry*, 60(1), 51–57.

Carlsson, J. M., Olsen, D. R., Mortensen, E. L., & Kastrup, M. (2006). Mental health and health-related quality of life: A 10 year follow-up of tortured refugees. *Journal of Nervous and Mental Disease*, 194(10), 725–731.

Carrillo, J., Green, A., & Betancourt, J. (1999). Cross-cultural primary care: A patient based approach. *Annals of Internal Medicine*, 130, 829–834.

Chakraborty, A. (1991). Culture, colonialism, and psychiatry. *The Lancet*, 337, 1204–1207.

Chester, B., & Holtan, N. (1992). Working with refugee survivors of torture [Special issue, *Cross-Cultural Medicine: A Decade Later*]. *Western Journal of Medicine*, 157, 301–304.

Chilcoat, H., & Breslau, N. (1998). Investigation of causal pathways between PTSD and drug use disorders. *Addictive Behaviors*, 23, 827–840.

Crosby, S., Norredam, M., Paasche-Orlow, M. K., Piwowarczyk, L., Heeren, T., & Grodin, M. A. (2006). Prevalence of torture survivors among foreign-born patients presenting to an urban ambulatory care practice. *Journal of General Internal Medicine*, 21, 764–768.

de Jong, J. (2002). Public mental health, traumatic stress and human rights violations in low-income countries. In J. de Jong (Ed.), *Trauma, war, and violence: Public mental health in socio-cultural context* (pp. 1–92). New York: Kluwer Academic/Plenum Publishers.

den Velde, W. O., Hovens, J. E., Bramsen, I., McFarlane, A. C., Aarts, P. G. H., Falger, P. R. J., . . . van Duijn, H. (2000). A cross-national study of posttraumatic stress disorder in Dutch Australian immigrants. *Australia New Zealand Journal of Psychiatry, 39*, 919–928.

Eisenman, D. P., Gelberg, L., Liu, H., & Shapiro, M. F. (2003). Mental health and health-related quality of life among adult Latino primary care patients living in the United States with previous exposure to political violence. *Journal of American Medical Association, 290*, 627–634.

Eisenman, D. P., Keller, A. S., & Kim, G. (2000). Survivors of torture in a general medical setting: How often have patients been tortured, and how often is it missed? *Western Journal of Medicine, 172*, 301–304.

Elsass, P. (1997). *Treating victims of torture and violence: Theoretical, cross-cultural, and clinical implications.* New York and London: New York University Press.

Elsass, P. (1998). The existence of a torture syndrome. *Torture, 8*, 58–64.

Engdahl, B. E., & Eberly, R. E. (1990). The effects of torture and other maltreatment: Implications for psychology. In P. Suedfeld (Ed.), *Psychology and torture* (pp. 31–47). New York: Hemisphere Publishing.

Fabri, M. R. (2001). Reconstructing safety: Adjustments to the therapeutic frame in the treatment of survivors of political torture. *Professional Psychology: Research and Practice, 32*(5), 452–457.

Fischman, Y. (1998). Metaclinical issues in the treatment of psychopolitical trauma. *American Journal of Orthopsychiatry, 68*(1), 27–38.

Fischman, Y., & Ross, J. (1990). Group treatment of exiled survivors of torture. *American Journal of Orthopsychiatry, 60*(1), 135–142.

Fondacaro, K., & Mazzulla, E. (2015, September 18). *An introduction to the chronic traumatic stress framework and overview of the 10 module intervention for survivors of torture and trauma.* Seminar presented at the New England Survivors of Torture and Trauma: Psychology, Social Work and Law Conference, Burlington, VT.

Gangsei, D. (2001, October). *Developing a narrative in the psychological assessment of torture and refugee trauma. Paper* presented at the Clinical Symposium of the Torture Treatment Center Consortium, Chicago, IL.

Genefke, I., & Vesti, P. (1998). Diagnosis of governmental torture. In J. M. Jaranson & M. K. Popkin (Eds.), *Caring for victims of torture* (pp. 43–59). Washington, DC: American Psychiatric Press.

Green, B. L. (2010). Applying interdisciplinary theory in the care of Aboriginal women's mental health. *Journal of Psychiatric and Mental Health Nursing, 17*, 797–803. doi: 10.1111/j.1365-2850.2010.01593.x

Gurris, N. (2001). Psychic trauma through torture—Healing through psychotherapy? In S. Graesner & N. Gurris (Eds.), *Standing at the side of torture survivors: Treating a terrible assault on human dignity* (pp. 29–56). Baltimore, MD: Johns Hopkins University Press.

Haenel, F. (2001). Foreign bodies in the soul. In S. Graesner & N. Gurris (Eds.), *Standing at the side of torture survivors: Treating a terrible assault on human dignity* (pp. 1–28). Baltimore, MD: Johns Hopkins University Press.

Herman, J. L. (1992). *Trauma and recovery: The aftermath of violence—From domestic abuse to political terror*. New York: Basic Books.

Holtz, T. H. (1998). Refugee trauma versus torture trauma: A retrospective controlled cohort study of Tibetan refugees. *Journal of Nervous and Mental Disorders*, 186, 24–43.

Horowitz, M. J. (1976). *Stress response syndromes*. New York: Jason Aronsen.

Iacopino, V., Allden, K., & Keller, A. S. (2001). *Examining asylum seekers: A health professional's guide to medical and psychological evaluations*. Boston, MA: Physicians for Human Rights.

Jaranson, J. M. (1998). The science and politics of rehabilitating torture survivors: An overview. In J. M. Jaranson & M. K. Popkin (Eds.), *Caring for victims of torture* (pp. 15–40). Washington, DC: American Psychiatric Press.

Jaranson, J. M., Butcher, J., Halcon, L., Johnson, D.R., Robertson, C., Savik, K., . . . Westermeyer, J. (2004). Somali and Oromo refugees: Correlate of torture and trauma history. *American Journal of Public Health*, *94*, 591–598.

Jaranson, J. M., & Popkin, M. (Eds.). (1998). *Caring for victims of torture*. Washington, DC: American Psychiatric Press.

Keller, A., Eisenman, D., & Saul, J. (1998). Caring for survivors of torture in an urban, municipal hospital. *Journal of Ambulatory Care Management*, *21*(2), 20–29.

Keller, A., Ford, D., Sachs, E., Rosenfeld, B., Meserve, C., Trinh, C., . . . Cajee, M. (2003). *From persecution to prison: The health consequences of detention for asylum seekers.* Boston and New York: Physicians for Human Rights and The Bellevue/NYU Program for Survivors of Torture.

Keller, A., & Smith, H. (2007). The clinical interview and programmatic intake process. In H. Smith, A. Keller, & D. Lhewa (Eds.), Like a refugee camp on First Avenue: Insights and experiences form the Bellevue/NYU Program for Survivors of Torture (pp. 106–125). New York: Jacob and Valeria Langeloth Foundation.

Keller, A. S., Leviss, J., Levy, N., & Dyson, D. (2007). Medical evaluation and care for survivors of torture and refugee trauma. In Smith, H. E., Keller, A. S., & Lhewa, D. W. [Eds.] *Like a refugee camp on first avenue: Insights and experiences from the Bellevue/NYU Program for Survivors of Torture.* New York: Bellevue/NYU Program for Survivors of Torture.

Kinzie, J. D., Leung, P. K., & Boehnlein, J. K. (1997). Treatment of depressive disorders in refugees. In E. Lee (Ed.), *Working with Asian Americans: A guide for clinicians* (pp. 265–274). New York: The Guilford Press.

Ko, S. J., Ford, J. D., Kassam-Adams, N., Berkowitz, S. J., Wilson, C., & Wong, M. (2008). Creating trauma-informed systems: Child welfare, education, first responders, health care, juvenile justice. *Professional Psychology: Research and Practice*, *49*(4), 396–404. doi: 10.1037/0735-7028.39.4.396

Kozaric-Kovacic, D., Kocijan-Hercigonja, D., & Jambrošic, A. (2002). Psychiatric help to psychotraumatized persons during and after war in Croatia. *Croatian Medical Journal*, *43*(2), 221–228.

Mollica, R. F. (2004). Surviving torture. *New England Journal of Medicine, 351,* 5–7.

Mollica, R., Sarajlic, N., Chernoff, M., Lavelle, J., Vukovic, I., & Massagli, M. (2001). Longitudinal study of psychiatric symptoms, disability, mortality, and emigration among Bosnian refugees. *Journal of the American Medical Association, 286*(5), 546–554.

Montgomery, E., & Foldspang, A. (1994). Criterion-related validity of screening for exposure to torture. *Danish Medical Bulletin, 41,* 588–591.

Mosenthal, A. C., & Murphy, P. A. (2006). Interdisciplinary model for palliative care in the trauma and surgical intensive care unit: Robert Wood Johnson Foundation Demonstration Project for Improving Palliative Care in the Intensive Care Unit [Supplemental material]. *Critical Care Medicine, 34*(11), S399–S403.

Norwegian Refugee Council. (2015). Annual report for the Norwegian refugee council: Annual report 2015 from the board.

Pope, K., & Garcia-Peltoniemi, R. (1991). Responding to victims of torture: Clinical issues, professional responsibilities, and useful resources. *Professional Psychology: Research and Practice, 22*(4), 269–276.

Quiroga, J., & Jaranson, J. M. (2005). Politically-motivated torture and its survivors: A desk study review of the literature [Thematic Issue]. *Torture, 15*(2–3), 1–111.

Randall, G., & Lutz, E. (1991). *Serving survivors of torture.* Washington, DC: Association for the Advancement of Science.

Shrestha, N., & Sharma, B. (1995). *Torture and torture victims: A manual for medical professionals.* Kathmandu, Nepal: Center for Victims of Torture, Nepal.

Silove, D., Sinnerbrink, I., Field, A., Manicavasagar, V., & Steel, Z. (1997). Anxiety, depression and PTSD in asylum seekers: Associations with pre-migration trauma and post-migration stressors. *British Journal of Psychiatry, 170,* 352–357.

Silove, D., Tarn, R., Bowles, R., & Reid, J. (1991). Psychosocial needs of torture survivors. *Australian and New Zealand Journal of Psychiatry, 25,* 481–490.

Smith, H. (2003). Despair, resilience, and the meaning of family: Group therapy with French-speaking survivors of torture from Africa. In R. Carter & B. Wallace (Eds.), *Understanding and dealing with violence. Multicultural perspectives* (pp. 291–319). Thousand Oaks, CA: Sage.

Smith, H., & Akinsulure-Smith, A. (2011). Needed—not just needy: Empowerment as a therapeutic tool in the treatment of survivors of torture and refugee trauma. *African Journal of Traumatic Stress, 2,* 17–31.

Smith, H., & Impalli, E. (2007). Supportive group treatment with survivors of torture and refugee trauma. In H. Smith, A. Keller, & D. Lhewa (Eds.), *Like a refugee camp on First Avenue: Insights and experiences form the Bellevue/NYU Program for Survivors of Torture* (pp. 336–374). New York: Jacob and Valeria Langeloth Foundation.

Smith, H., & Keller, A. (2007). The context in which treatment takes place: The multi-faceted stressors facing survivors of torture and refugee trauma. In H. Smith, A. Keller, & D. Lhewa (Eds.), *Like a refugee camp on First Avenue: Insights and experiences form the Bellevue/*

NYU Program for Survivors of Torture (pp. 1–37). New York: Jacob and Valeria Langeloth Foundation.

Smith, H., Lustig, S., & Gangsei, D. (2015). Incredible until proven credible: Mental health expert testimony and the systemic and cultural challenges facing asylum applicants. In B. Lawrence & G. Ruffer (Eds.), *Adjudicating refugee and asylum status: The role of witness, expertise, and testimony* (pp. 180–201). London: Cambridge University Press.

Smith, H., & Wilkinson, J. (2007). Social service provision. In H. Smith, A. Keller, & D. Lhewa (Eds.), Like a refugee camp on First Avenue: Insights and experiences form the Bellevue/NYU Program for Survivors of Torture (pp. 271–298). New York: Jacob and Valeria Langeloth Foundation.

Somnier, F., & Genefke, I. (1986). Psychotherapy for victims of torture. *British Journal of Psychiatry, 149*, 323–329.

Speer, D. C., & Schneider, M. G. (2003). Mental health needs of older adults and primary care: Opportunity for interdisciplinary geriatric team practice. *Clinical Psychology: Science and Practice, 10*, 85–101. doi: 10.1093/clipsy.10.1.85

Straker, G. (1987). The continuous traumatic stress syndrome: The single therapeutic interview. *Psychology in Society, 8*, 48–78.

United Nations High Commissioner for Refugees. (2015, June 18). *World at war: UNHCR global trends. Forced displacement in 2014.* Geneva, Switzerland: Author. http://unhcr.org/556725e69 .html

van der Veer, G. (1998). *Counselling and therapy with refugees and victims of trauma: Psychological problems of victims of war, torture and repression* (2nd ed.). New York: John Wiley & Sons.

van der Veer, G., & van Waning, A. (2004). Creating a safe therapeutic sanctuary. In J. P. Wilson & B. Drozdek (Eds.), *Broken spirits: The treatment of traumatized asylum seekers, refugees, war and torture victims* (pp. 187–219). New York: Brunner-Routledge.

Vesti, P., & Kastrup, M. (1991). Psychotherapy for torture survivors. In M. Basoglu (Ed.), *Torture and its consequences: Current treatment approaches* (pp. 349–362). Cambridge, UK: Cambridge University Press.

Vinokur-Kaplan, D. (1995). Enhancing the effectiveness of interdisciplinary mental health treatment teams. *Administration and Policy in Mental Health, 22*(5), 521–530.

Volkan, V. D. (2004). From hope for a better life to broken spirits: An introduction. In J. P. Wilson & B. Drozdek (Eds.), *Broken spirits: The treatment of traumatized asylum seekers, refugees, war and torture victims* (pp. 7–12). New York: Brunner-Routledge.

Wilkinson, J. (2007). Immigration dynamics: Processes, challenges, and benefits. In H. Smith, A. Keller, & D. Lhewa (Eds.), *Like a refugee camp on First Avenue: Insights and experiences form the Bellevue/NYU Program for Survivors of Torture* (pp. 65–81). New York: Jacob and Valeria Langeloth Foundation.

Xyrichis, A., & Lowton, K. (2008). What fosters or prevents interprofessional teamworking in primary and community care? A literature review. *International Journal of Nursing Studies, 45*, 140–153. doi: 10.1016/j.ijnurstu.2007.01.015

Chapter 14

PRACTICE APPLICATIONS WITH WOMEN

ROWENA FONG, LAURIE COOK HEFFRON, AND KARIN WACHTER

KEY TERMS

migrant women, intimate partner/domestic violence, sexual violence, human trafficking, interventions

---

CHAPTER HIGHLIGHTS

- Discussion around the context of violence affecting immigrant and refugee women
- Examination of types of violence impacting women, including intimate partner/domestic violence, sexual violence, and human trafficking
- Implications for practice and intervention to address needs among migrant populations

---

INTRODUCTION

Many immigrants and refugees have strong transnational familial, economic, political, and emotional ties that transcend national states, and yet many remain socially and politically vulnerable populations (Furman, Negi, Schatz, & Jones, 2008). In developing social work practice with immigrant and refugee survivors of violence, it is important to consider the transnational context within which individuals and families operate. This chapter will consider transnational practice as it applies specifically to survivors of violence whose migration may be recognized as either forced or voluntary, including economic migrants, refugees and asylees, and victims of human trafficking.

We often consider migrants and immigrants as those who voluntarily migrate and refugees and asylees as forced migrants. However, differences between forced and voluntary migration exist along a continuum. In other words, migration is typically neither completely forced nor wholly voluntary (Snyder, 2012). Choices and agency are part of forced migration, and elements of coercion or force may exist for those who voluntarily choose to migrate (Nawyn et al., 2009). Both documented and undocumented immigrants face economic hardships and seek better economic opportunities (Dettlaff, 2012). While economic migrants are often considered to have migrated voluntarily, many experience violence and exploitation before, during, and/or after migrating. Refugees and asylees, on the other hand, are generally considered to be forced migrants, as they have escaped war or have fled persecution based on their race, religion, nationality, or political opinion (Fong, 2004; Snyder, 2012). Immigrant victims of human trafficking are a third category of migrants who have been made to work through force, fraud, or coercion, in a wide variety of industries, including the commercial sex industry.

While immigrants and refugees are often geographically separated from family and friends, many maintain strong social and emotional ties to their home countries. A transnational perspective implies the complex and flexible sense of belonging, identity, and responsibility that many individuals and families feel. Economic responsibilities, parenting roles, and communication often continue to exist across boundaries after an individual has migrated (Furman, Negi, Schatz, & Jones, 2008). Parenting from afar, in the context of migration, is a prime example of the ways that the transnational self spreads across both social and physical space (Soerens, 2015). Transnational mothers, in particular, struggle with the basic question of "how to be socially and emotionally present while physically absent" (Carling, Menjívar, & Schmalzbauer, 2012, p. 203).

Violence against women, in its many forms, is unfortunately interwoven throughout the migration experiences of immigrant and refugee women. **Intimate partner violence, sexual violence,** and **human trafficking** influence the transnational lived experiences of immigrant and refugee women and their families and must be considered in the development of therapeutic relationships and services. This chapter will focus on immigrant and refugee women who experience intimate partner violence, sexual violence, and/or human trafficking. We review two different case studies, which represent common and overlapping experiences of violence and exploitation. We also offer selected practice strategies for transnational practice.

WORKING WITH MIGRANT WOMEN EXPERIENCING INTIMATE PARTNER VIOLENCE

Sexual Violence and Human Trafficking

Case Description

Gloria[1] is a 31-year-old mother of three children ages 8, 11, and 13. She was born in a small town in Guatemala and fell in love with her husband Eduardo when she was

[1] This case example is a composite case developed from multiple research and practice interviews with immigrant survivors of domestic violence and human trafficking, in addition to human trafficking cases covered in the media.

(Continued)

(Continued)

17. Their relationship was romantic and positive in the beginning, but Eduardo soon became jealous and controlling of Gloria's activities and whereabouts. When Gloria became pregnant with their first child, Eduardo began to hit her periodically and force her to have sex with him when she didn't want to. Over the years, the violence and control grew, and Gloria tried to leave him several times. Each time, he would find her and convince her to come back to him, promising that the violence would stop and threatening her that she had no where else to go and no way to support the children on her own. Eventually, Gloria could no longer endure the abuse, and she decided to flee to the United States with a *coyote* (smuggler or guide). She placed her children in the care of her mother, planning to work hard and earn enough money in order to later bring them to the United States.

Gloria endured the difficult and long journey into Mexico and north toward the United States. The month-long journey included substantial walking, dangerous travels on the tops of trains known as *La Bestia* (the beast), and frequently going without adequate food, water, and shelter. Near the border between Mexico and the United States, Gloria and her travel partners were held hostage for three days by criminal gangs that control the border region and extorted for money in exchange for helping her cross the border into the United States. Since Gloria had already used her meager savings to pay the coyote, she was in a bind. Those who were holding her hostage introduced her to someone who offered her work in a restaurant in a large Texas city. Gloria was eager to work, repay this new debt, and begin saving money to bring her children, and she accepted.

When she arrived at the new work opportunity, Gloria discovered that it was not a restaurant after all. It was a *cantina* or bar, with hidden rooms in the back that operated as a brothel. Gloria, along with a dozen other Central American women, were forced to dance with cantina customers, flirt with them, and encourage them to buy drinks. On some occasions, she was also exploited in the behind-the-scenes commercial sex operation. Those in charge threatened her with deportation or physical harm to herself or her children if she escaped. Gloria was sometimes paid small amounts during this time, although her traffickers consistently inflated her debt arbitrarily. She was in a situation of debt bondage, in which her smuggling debt continued to rise without any way of fully paying it down.

After eight months of exploitation, local and federal law enforcement officers raided the operation, and Gloria and the other women were released. Currently, Gloria is in the process of adjusting her immigration status by applying for a T Visa.[2] Gloria struggles with finding and maintaining work and meeting her physical and mental health needs related to the trauma she experienced in Guatemala, during transit through Mexico, and in the United States. She

---

[2] The T Visa is designed for those who are or have been victims of human trafficking, allowing victims to remain in the United States to assist in an investigation or prosecution of human trafficking (www.uscis.gov).

generally feels down, on constant alert to possible danger in her surroundings, and worries about chronic pain and the possibility of having contracted a sexually transmitted illness. Furthermore, she has unmet dental and health needs that originated in childhood from lack of access to health care and has consistent difficulty meeting her own and her children's current financial needs. Gloria has difficulty accessing services in her community, given her erratic low-wage work schedule, language barriers, shame and social isolation, and depression/anxiety. Gloria's stated goal is to be reunited with her children. Her former husband continues to control her from Guatemala, in terms of children's care and money. She is concerned about her oldest daughter's safety and increased vulnerability to sexual violence at the hands of criminal gang networks and family members.

Background on Exposure to Violence

The types of trauma and abuse experienced by Gloria are neither uncommon to broader groups of migrant women nor to those who have been trafficked during or after migration to the United States. In fact, global estimates suggest that one third of the world's women experience some type of interpersonal violence, ranging from everyday experiences of domestic violence to femicide (Ellsberg, 2006; Menjívar, 2011). Emerging scholarship recognizes the role violence plays in motivations to migrate as a strategy to escape or resist violence (Haug, 2008; Salcido & Adelman, 2004; Wagner, 2009).

In fleeing violence, the migration process itself poses further risks of violence. Particularly because of undocumented status, Central American migrants, for example, are vulnerable to a wide range of violence—verbal and physical abuse, robbery, extortion, sexual assault, torture, human trafficking and smuggling, kidnapping, rape, and homicide—at the hands of fellow migrants, criminal gang networks, or municipal, state, and federal authorities in Mexico and the border regions to the north and to the south (INCIDE Social, 2012; Infante, Idrovo, Sánchez-Domínguez, Vinhas, & González-Vázquez, 2012). Women interviewed at migrant shelters in Arizona describe having experienced violence before and during their migration, and more than 70% reported having had an experience with violence before or after migrating to the United States (Conrad, 2013). Furthermore, many women face additional violence and exploitation, such as domestic violence and human trafficking, once resettled in the United States (Upegui-Hernández, 2012).

Human trafficking, sexual assault, and domestic violence can have severe physical and emotional health consequences, including depression, anxiety, suicidal behaviors, and sleep disturbances (Busch-Armendariz, Nsonwu, & Cook Heffron, 2011; Coker et al., 2002; Decker, Silverman, & Raj, 2007; Heise & Garcia-Moreno, 2002; Hodge, 2008; Macy & Johns, 2011; Raymond & Hughes, 2001). Sexual violence experienced by human trafficking victims is associated with higher levels of PTSD, depression, and anxiety (De Jong et al., 2001; Hossain, 2010; Shrestha et al., 1998). Research suggests that specific PTSD-related symptoms often include nightmares, difficulty

(Continued)

(Continued)

concentrating, becoming easily upset, difficulty relaxing, difficulty thinking, feelings of hopelessness, and sleep disorders (Clawson, Dutch, Solomon, & Grace, 2009). Trafficking victims often have histories of prior abuse (such as domestic and/or sexual violence) (Zimmerman et al., 2008).

Practices and Interventions

Survivors are resilient and strategic, and they actively seek safety and resources for themselves and their children (Fugate, Landis, Riordan, Naureckas, & Engel, 2005). However, the needs of this population frequently include complex and specialized physical, mental, and social health needs. Specialized and multidimensional services designed to meet the needs of immigrant/refugee survivors of domestic violence and human trafficking are not universally available. Unfortunately, mainstream Western mental health practices and interventions often fall short of adequately and appropriately meeting the needs of this population. The biculturalization of interventions (Fong, 2004), which combines indigenous and Western interventions, needs to be considered for these survivors. Furthermore, while evidence-informed practices are emerging, the research and knowledge base of effective interventions and responses are limited and need more attention.

Available mainstream services are often short term, narrowly focused, and rely on English language proficiency, legal immigration status, and a high level of familiarity with U.S. social service delivery systems. Western-style mental health services are often delivered in formal, professional settings, and the idea of divulging sensitive personal information to strangers may be unfamiliar and uncomfortable to many immigrant and refugee groups. In addition, mainstream information and referral services often involve providing clients with a list of the names and addresses of organizations for clients to contact.

Rather, working with immigrant and refugee survivors of trauma and violence demands a slower and more comprehensive and community-based approach. First, providers should be prepared for considerable rapport and trust building over time. Second, providers must balance immediate needs with longer-term needs. Immigrant and refugee survivors present a multiplicity of immediate needs—safety, housing, medical care, food, clothing, legal advocacy, crisis intervention, intensive case management, and trauma-informed mental health services, ideally delivered in the preferred language of the survivor (Busch-Armendariz, Nsonwu, & Cook Heffron, 2014). Beyond these immediate needs, immigrant and refugee survivors have long-term needs that may include employment assistance, legal services, independent and permanent housing, ongoing mental health care, English-language acquisition, family reunification, and children's education and healthcare.

A single point of contact model is useful in balancing the complex and multiple needs of survivors and in building trust between survivors and other providers. This involves building relationships with a collaborative network of community partners, such as domestic violence organizations, rape crisis centers, refugee resettlement agencies, faith communities, immigrant rights groups, and legal immigration providers. This model may better address the complex needs of survivors, more appropriately accommodate linguistic and cultural needs, and assist survivors in navigating complicated bureaucracies.

Finally, in working with immigrant and refugee survivors of violence, it is important to recognize the context of transnational families and resulting issues that relate to attachment, parenting, and grief and loss. In doing so, providers must also attend to the crucial role of social support and shared experience in reducing social isolation and increasing emotional well-being (Simich, Beiser, & Mawani, 2003). Included in the concept of social support are informational support and the need for reliable information—such as information about immigration status, expectations for reunification with children, eligibility for social services (for self and children), and rights as a victim of crime. Instrumental support is also important and may include comprehensive case management and navigation of social services that go beyond simple referrals and include a "warm transfer" and/or accompaniment to new providers. Networks other than professional helpers—family, friends, and ethnic communities—must be included in the facilitation of shared experience and social support.

While it has not been tested with immigrant survivors, multisystemic therapy (MST), which uses blended strategies from strategic and structural family therapy, problem-focused therapy, and cognitive behavioral therapy delivered in natural settings (such as home or work), shows promising evidence related to U.S.-born trafficked populations (Fong & Cardoso, 2010).

SUMMARY OF PROMISING PRACTICE PRINCIPLES

- Attend to both acute- and long-term service needs

- Expand knowledge of and response to pre-, peri-, and post-migration strengths and experiences of trauma

- Expand knowledge and recognition of the unique and complex needs of transnational families

- Recognize that immigrant survivors of violence are resilient and strategic

- Build relationships with community partners, including domestic violence organizations, rape crisis centers, refugee resettlement agencies, faith communities, immigrant rights groups, and legal immigration providers

- Consider community-based single-point of contact service models

Working With Women Experiencing Sexual Violence and Intimate Partner Violence

Case Description

Faith[3] is a 25-year-old woman who was born in a rural village in Northern Uganda and completed seven years of formal primary education. When she was 14 years old, she was abducted by the Lord's Resistance Army (LRA), a guerrilla group, and forced into captivity. Faith was forced to "marry" a LRA soldier and in the context of this "marriage," Faith was forced to submit to the soldier's sexual demands as well as to fulfill heavy domestic responsibilities.

Within the first year of her captivity, Faith gave birth to her son. The LRA frequently moved their location, and they eventually crossed into the Democratic Republic of the Congo (DRC) as the war ensued. After one and a half years in captivity and pregnant again, Faith took an unforeseen opportunity to escape with her son. Fleeing to a nearby village, Faith accepted refuge offered by an older man, Charles, who was widowed and had two young children. The village was later attacked and the population fled on foot to seek protection in the nearest town. Faith took flight with Charles and the three children to an internally displaced persons' camp, where they decided to officially marry before continuing. After a harrowing journey, they ultimately made their way over the border to Tanzania where they registered as refugees with the United Nations High Commissioner for Refugees (UNHCR).

The living conditions in the refugee camp were rudimentary, but the two older children could attend school. The food rations they received, however, were barely enough to sustain them, and Faith struggled to find ways to feed the five of them. She was desperate to get information about her family in Uganda and whether or not they had survived the attack on their village. Charles became increasingly short tempered and without any prospects to work, took to spending his time at the local bar. He would insult Faith and refer to her son and unborn child as "LRA." When he would come home after a day of drinking, he would become physically abusive if he perceived the food was inadequate or poorly prepared. Charles threatened to tell their neighbors that Faith had been "a LRA wife" and to divorce her so that he could find a wife who did not bring shame to him and his family. As her pregnancy advanced, Faith felt increasingly trapped and alone. Faith experienced complications during the delivery of her baby girl that she thinks may have contributed to her child's physical and intellectual disabilities.

Because of Charles's political affiliations in the DRC and status as a torture survivor, his case was selected for possible resettlement to the United States. At the prospect

---

[3]This case example is a composite case developed from interviews with refugee survivors of domestic and sexual violence.

of leaving to the United States, Charles stopped drinking and started focusing on the prospects of leaving, including learning as much English as he could. He continued to insult Faith and her two children, but the physical abuse and threats subsided. After several years in the Tanzanian refugee camp, the family of six departed for the United States and flew to Seattle, Washington, where they were met at the airport by a caseworker from the local refugee resettlement organization and taken to their apartment.

Faith has struggled to regain her footing since arriving to the United States. She has had very little contact with the resettlement agency that is responsible for assisting her family with settling in the United States. Charles is the one to go to the office to meet with their caseworker, and his name is on the electronic benefits transfer card that helps them to buy food as well as on the checks through which they receive short-term cash assistance. Her stepchildren learned American English quickly and are exerting a new level of independence in the United States, which makes Faith feel as if she has lost control. Faith struggles with the memories and feelings her two biological children can trigger about her time with the LRA. She is worried about her daughter's developmental disabilities, in particular. A teacher by training, Charles is frustrated at how little money he earns doing factory work and insists that Faith also go to work. She would like to be employed but does not feel like she can leave her daughter with strangers. Charles has started to drink again, and Faith is trying to find new ways of coping with the mounting tension in the household. Since coming to the United States, Faith has started to have regular nightmares about her time in captivity and is experiencing anxiety and a profound sense of loss. Faith feels alone and overwhelmed and desperately misses her family. Faith does not know whom she can trust.

Background on Exposure to Violence

Violence against women and girls is a global concern. Women and girls are at risk of physical, sexual, emotional, economic, and other forms of violence at all stages of the life cycle, and war and displacement increase women's vulnerability to various forms of violence (Hajdukowski-Ahmed, Khanlou, & Moussa, 2008). Sexual violence can be perpetrated en masse as a tool of war, colonization, and genocide (Nawyn, Reosti, & Gjokaj, 2009). The threat of violence and exploitation persists in flight, and forced migrant women may be forced to sell their bodies in exchange for basic necessities to sustain themselves and their families (Wachter, Cook Heffron, Snyder, Nsonwu, & Busch-Armendariz, 2016). Girls are particularly vulnerable to forced and early marriage and sex trafficking (García-Moreno et al., 2015). Contrary to popular belief, prevalence of intimate partner violence (IPV) in conflict settings can be higher than rates of wartime rape and sexual violence perpetrated by individuals outside the home (Stark & Ager, 2011).

Research on refugee women's experiences with IPV post-migration to Western countries is still nascent (Fisher, 2013), but emerging evidence highlights the extent to which women and girls' vulnerability to ongoing violence and abuse persists in settlement, impacted by their pre-resettlement experiences with violence (Bartolomei, Eckert, & Pittaway, 2014; Wachter et al., 2016). Immigration contributes to women's

(Continued)

(Continued)

isolation, economic dependence, inability to access social services, and for many, fear of deportation (Bhuyan & Velagapudi, 2013). Stressors in settlement may exacerbate women's longstanding vulnerability to being abused by male partners (Kasturirangan, Krishnan, & Riger, 2004). Men's pre-migration exposure to political violence (e.g., state-perpetrated armed conflict, repression, genocide, torture, forced disappearance of family members, and massacre) may be an important element to understanding men's perpetration of violence against their female intimate partners in post-migration (Gupta, Acevedo-Garcia, Hemenway, Decker, Raj, & Silverman, 2009).

The mental health consequences of IPV can include anxiety, depression, symptoms of post-traumatic stress disorder, antisocial behavior, suicidal behavior, low self-esteem, inability to trust others, sleep disturbances, and flashbacks (CDC, 2015a). Social consequences may include restricted access to services and isolation from social networks (Heise & Garcia-Moreno, 2002). The health consequences of sexual violence can include unwanted pregnancies, chronic pain, gynecological complications, frequent headaches, and sexually transmitted infections (CDC, 2015b), and in war zones, sexual violence may also result in profound physical injuries, disability, and maternal mortality (Kinyanda et al., 2010; Stark & Wessells, 2012). The mental health consequences of sexual violence in war zones may also include depression, anxiety, medically unexplained complaints, substance use, and suicidal ideation (Harvard Humanitarian Initiative, 2009; Johnson et al., 2008).

Lastly, the trauma of being forcibly separated from family and loved ones cannot be overstated. Women's membership in their pre-migration social networks often defined their status and position and afforded them varying degrees of social security. In forced migration, these entrenched social networks are disrupted and oftentimes permanently ruptured, leading to the immediate loss of resources and support embedded in those relational networks.

Practices and Interventions

"Research has found that immigrant women and racialized minorities may experience higher rates of violence but are less likely to seek support services" (Raj & Silverman, 2003).

Some immigrant/refugee service providers may not be well positioned to address the violence their female clients experience throughout their migration trajectories. Many resettlement agencies, for example, are limited in their ability to address violence against women because of a number of constraints, including the limited window of time during which they are typically mandated to provide case management services to refugees (e.g., 180 days); limited resources and competing priorities; and limited contact with female clientele who arrive to the United States with a husband or other male adults. Since the goal of the U.S. resettlement program is "self-sufficiency" in a matter of months post-arrival, the over-riding focus of service provision tends to focus on employment, housing, and securing public benefits, among other essentials. This "race to the finish line" approach to self-sufficiency, enforced by policy and funding, does not lend itself to a model of service provision that takes into account the complexities of people's pre- and post-migration experiences nor the specific factors that influence people's individual settlement journeys (Wachter et al., 2016).

Domestic and sexual assault providers have the potential to play an important role in enhancing local service provision available to refugee and immigrant women through their existing client advocacy and counseling services as well as through shelter and transitional housing programs (Busch-Armendariz, Wachter, Cook Heffron, Synder, & Nsonwu, 2014). Holistic service provision for immigrant and refugee clients would be enhanced through an exchange of training and expertise to build cultural competence in working with diverse refugee and immigrant groups as well as strategies for integrating the use of trained interpreters into their services. Gaps in services and unmet needs for immigrant and refugee survivors of IPV and sexual violence identified through a recent study include the following: language barriers and availability of culturally appropriate food at domestic violence shelters, transitional and long-term housing, legal assistance, health and mental health services, cultural competence of service providers, strategies for ensuring the safety of family members—children in particular—in the client's country of origin, and stronger collaborations and joint advocacy efforts between immigrant/refugee service providers and DV/SA advocates (Wachter & Donahue, 2015).

Screening for violence has been shown to be effective in helping service providers identify current or past violence or increased risk for abuse among clientele (Todahl & Walters, 2011). In 2014, the International Rescue Committee (IRC)[4] launched a pilot project "Bridge to Safety" in three resettlement offices as a step forward toward ensuring that refugee and immigrant women survivors of domestic and sexual violence have access to relevant support services. Preliminary findings indicate that screening adult refugee women for pre- and post-migration experiences of domestic and sexual violence soon after their arrival to the United States is an effective mechanism for communicating that IRC is a safe space for women to discuss their experiences, concerns, and needs related to violence (Wachter & Donahue, 2015). Findings indicate that a direct approach to screening that inquires about specific types of violence may be linked to increasing disclosures and thereby to increasing survivors' access to available services. After one year of implementation in which targeted training and mentoring were provided, non-specialized staff new to working on issues related to violence against women demonstrated not only the skills to respond effectively but also a high level of personal and professional commitment to the intervention and desire to see responses to violence against immigrant/refugee women prioritized as a core service (Wachter & Donahue, 2015). Screening is only as effective as the service options available to offer to women who chose to disclose. As discussed above, untapped potential for enhancing service provision to immigrant and refugee women persists and can be addressed, in part, through enhanced linkages between refugee resettlement and DV/SA organizations (Busch-Armendariz, Nsonwu, & Heffron, 2014).

---

[4]The International Rescue Committee (IRC) supports refugees in their resettlement processes to become self-sufficient in 22 cities across the United States.

- Determine the extent to which service providers have direct contact with immigrant/refugee clients.

- Assess the extent to which services for immigrant/refugee clients are provided in an environment conducive for women to talk about their experiences with violence.

- Explore the feasibility to screen immigrant/refugee clients for sexual violence and intimate partner violence.

- Evaluate the viability of local referral options for immigrant/refugee survivors. Anticipate and identify gaps.

- Forge partnerships to address gaps and to build capacity for immigrant/refugee service providers to respond effectively to disclosures and for DV/SA service providers to contextualize the past experiences and current needs of immigrant and refugee women.

CONCLUSION

Transnational practice with immigrant and refugee women, especially those who have experienced sexual violence, intimate partner violence, and/or human trafficking, needs to be reframed so that assessments, referral, and treatment services reflect the pre-, peri-, and post- migration experiences of trauma and attend to the realities of their transnational lives. A biculturalization of interventions (Fong, 2004) that combines Western and indigenous social services is an important framework for social service providers to know, understand, and follow in working with these clients. Hydle, Rvalshaugen, and Breunig (2014) also emphasize the importance of having communities that provide transnational services where workers, who might be social workers, community practitioners, or agency administrators, share and create knowledge by participating and living in the communities of the clients. This supports the community-based single-point of contact service model recommended in this chapter and promotes a better way of offering culturally competent services when the service provider and agency are located in the midst of transnational communities.

REFLECTIVE QUESTIONS

1. What role do members of a transnational family, sometimes separated by geographic distance, play in healing, treatment, or in therapeutic relationships?

2. How might immigrant and refugee women's parenting be impacted by both migration and by violence experienced before, during, or after migration?

3. What are some needs—medical, social, and psychological—you may encounter in working with transnational survivors of violence?

4. How might women's decision-making be influenced by transnational ties?

5. How might women's experiences with violence pre-, during, and post-migration influence their transnational ties and responsibilities?

6. How does taking into consideration women's transnational lives, ties, and responsibilities inform social work practice with immigrant and refugee clients?

SUMMATIVE POINTS

• Transnational practice working with immigrant and refugee women requires a reframing of assessment, referral, and treatment services to attend to the relevant pre-, peri-, and post-migration trauma experiences.

• Biculturalization of interventions integrates Western and indigenous social practices to be more culturally sensitive.

• Community-based service models based in the local community can be supportive of women who have survived violence in their migration while building valuable social support.

CRITICAL THINKING EXERCISES

Consider the two case studies presented in this chapter. How are Gloria and Faith's present day concerns influenced by their transnational ties and responsibilities, as per the reflective questions listed above? How do their stories, as told in the case studies, reveal aspects of their transnational lives, ties, and responsibilities? What questions, relevant to practice, remain unanswered?

Now consider the description of interventions and summaries of promising practice principles.

Reflect on how your current practice and practice context addresses immigrant and refugee women's experiences with violence and transnational lives. Taking into consideration your practice location and realities, envision how you may develop a practice with immigrant and refugee women that attends to their experiences with violence and their transnational lives, ties, and responsibilities. What modifications or additions might you make to enhance your practice to make it more sensitive and responsive to the complexities of their lives and intersecting experiences? What difference do you think these changes or additions will make to you as a practitioner and to meeting the needs of your clients? How will you evaluate the effectiveness of your transnational practice with immigrant and refugee women?

GLOSSARY

Human trafficking. Human trafficking was first defined at the international level and through federal law in the United States. The United Nations Protocol to Prevent, Suppress and Punish Trafficking in Persons, Especially Women and Children (2000)—or the Palermo Protocol—defines trafficking in persons as "the recruitment, transportation, transfer, harbouring or receipt of persons, by means of the threat or use of force or other forms of coercion, of abduction, of fraud, of deception, of the abuse of power or of a position of vulnerability or of the giving or receiving of payments or benefits to achieve the consent of a person having control over another person, for the purpose of exploitation" (Article 3). Similarly, the United States' Trafficking Victims Protection Act of 2000 (TVPA) defined human trafficking as "the recruitment, harboring, transporting, provision, or obtaining of a person for labor or services, through the use of force, fraud, or coercion for the purpose of subjection to involuntary servitude, peonage, debt bondage, slavery, or forced commercial sex acts" (TVPA, Section 103(8)). Human trafficking is often referred to as modern-day slavery, and it includes both labor trafficking and sex trafficking.

Sexual violence. The World Health Organization (WHO, 2014) defines sexual violence as any sexual act, attempt to obtain a sexual act, or other act directed against a person's sexuality using coercion, by any person regardless of their relationship to the victim, in any setting.

Intimate partner violence. The WHO defines IPV as the behavior by an intimate partner or ex-partner that causes physical, sexual, or psychological harm, including physical aggression, sexual coercion, psychological abuse, and controlling behaviors (World Health Organization, 2014).

REFERENCES

Bartolomei, L., Eckert, R., & Pittaway, E. (2014). "What happens there . . . follows us here": Resettled but still at risk: Refugee women and girls in Australia. *Refuge: Canada's Journal on Refugees*, *30*(2).

Bhuyan, R., & Velagapudi, K. (2013). From one "dragon sleigh" to another advocating for immigrant women facing violence in Kansas. *Affilia*, *28*(1), 65–78.

Busch-Armendariz, N. B., Nsonwu, M. B., & Cook Heffron, L. (2011). Human trafficking victims and their children: Assessing needs, vulnerabilities, strengths, and survivorship. *Journal of Applied Research on Children: Informing Policy for Children at Risk*, *2*(1), 3.

Busch-Armendariz, N., Nsonwu, M. B., & Cook Heffron, L. C. (2014). A kaleidoscope: The role of the social work practitioner and the strength of social work theories and practice in meeting the complex needs of people trafficked and the professionals that work with them. *International Social Work*, *57*(1), 7–18.

Busch-Armendariz, N., Wachter, K., Cook Heffron, L., Snyder, S., & Nsonwu, M. B. (2014). *The continuity of risk: A three city study of Congolese women-at-risk resettled in the US*. Austin, Texas: The Institute on Domestic Violence & Sexual Assault.

Carling, J., Menjívar, C., & Schmalzbauer, L. (2012). Central themes in the study of transnational parenthood. *Journal of Ethnic and Migration Studies*, *38*(2), 191–217. doi: 10.1080/1369183X .2012.646417

Center for Disease Control. (2015a, March 3). *Intimate partner violence: Consequences*. Retrieved from http://www.cdc.gov/violenceprevention/intimatepartnerviolence/consequences.html

Center for Disease Control. (2015b, February 19). *Sexual violence: Consequences*. Retrieved from http://www.cdc.gov/violenceprevention/sexualviolence/consequences.html

Clawson, H. J., Dutch, N., Solomon, A., & Grace, L. G. (2009). *Human trafficking into and within the United States: A review of the literature*. US Department of Health and Human Services, Office of the Assistant Secretary for Planning and Evaluation.

Coker, A. L., Davis, K. E., Arias, I., Desai, S., Sanderson, M., & Brandt, H. M. (2002). Physical and mental health effects of intimate partner violence for men and women. *American Journal of Preventive Medicine, 23*(4), 260–268.

Conrad, M. (2013). *Women's testimonios of life and migration in el cruce* (Doctoral dissertation). Arizona State University.

Decker, M. R., Silverman, J. G., & Raj, A. (2007). Sexual violence against adolescent girls: Influences of immigration and acculturation. *Violence Against Women, 13*, 498–513.

De Jong, J. T. V. M., Komproe, I. H., Van Ommeren, M., Masri, M. E., Araya, M., Khaled, N., . . . Somasundaram, D. (2001). Lifetime events and posttraumatic stress disorder in four post conflict settings. *Journal of the American Medical Association, 286*, 555–562.

Dettlaff, A. (2012). Immigrant children and families in child welfare. In A. Dettlaff & R. Fong (Eds.), *Child welfare practice with immigrant children and families* (pp. 1–12). New York: Routledge Press.

Ellsberg, M. C. (2006). "Violence against women: A global public health crisis." *Scandinavian Journal of Public Health, 34*(1), 1–4.

Faulkner, M., Mahapatra, N., Cook Heffron, L., Nsonwu, M., & Busch-Armendariz. (2013). Moving past victimization and trauma toward restoration: Mother survivors of sex trafficking share their inspiration. *International Perspectives in Victimology, 7*(2), 46–55.

Fisher, C. (2013). Changed and changing gender and family roles and domestic violence in African refugee background communities post-settlement in Perth, Australia. *Violence Against Women, 19*(7), 833–847.

Fong, R. (Ed.). (2004). *Culturally competent practice with immigrant and refugee children and families*. New York: Guilford Press.

Fong, R., & Cardoso, J. B. (2010). Child human trafficking victims: Challenges for the child welfare system. *Evaluation and Program Planning, 33*(3), 311–316. doi: 10.1016/j.evalprogplan .2009.06.018

Fugate, M., Landis, L., Riordan, K., Naureckas, S., & Engel, B. (2005). Barriers to domestic violence help seeking implications for intervention. *Violence Against Women, 11*(3), 290–310.

Furman, R., Negi, N., Schatz, M. C. S., & Jones, S. (2008). Transnational social work: Using a wraparound model. *Global Networks, 8*(4), 496–503. doi: 10.1111/j.1471- 0374.2008.00236.x

García-Moreno, C., Zimmerman, C., Morris-Gehring, A., Heise, L., Amin, A., Abrahams, N., . . . Watts, C. (2015). Addressing violence against women: A call to action. *The Lancet, 385*(9978), 1685–1695.

Gupta, J., Acevedo-Garcia, D., Hemenway, D., Decker, M. R., Raj, A., & Silverman, J. G. (2009). Premigration exposure to political violence and perpetration of intimate partner violence among immigrant men in Boston. *American Journal of Public Health, 99*(3), 462.

Hajdukowski-Ahmed, M., Khanlou, N., & Moussa, H. (Eds.). (2008). *Not born a refugee woman: Contesting identities, rethinking practices*. New York: Berghahn Books.

Harvard Humanitarian Initiative. (2009). *Characterizing sexual violence in the Democratic Republic of the Congo: Profiles of violence, community responses, and implications for the protection of women*. Cambridge, MA: Harvard Humanitarian Initiative and Open Society Institute.

Haug, D. S. (2008). Migration networks and migration decision-making. *Journal of Ethnic and Migration Studies, 34*(4), 585–605.

Heise, L., & Garcia-Moreno, C. (2002). Violence by intimate partners. In E. Krug, L. L. Dahlberg, & J. A. Mercy (Eds.), *World report on violence and health* (pp. 87–121). Geneva: World Health Organization.

Hodge, D. R. (2008). Sexual trafficking in the United States: A domestic problem with transnational dimensions. *Social Work, 52*, 143–152.

Hossain, M. C. M. (2010). The relationship of trauma to mental disorders among trafficked and sexually exploited girls and women. *American Journal of Public Health, 100*(12), 2442.

Hydle, K., Rvalshaugen, R., & Breunig, K. (2014). Transnational practices in communities of task and communities of learning. *Management Learning*, 609–629. New York: Sage.

INCIDE Social. (2012). Construyendo un model de atención para mujeres migrantes víctimas de violencia sexual en México. Mexico City, INCIDE Social. (Care model for migrant women victims of sexual violence).

Infante, C., Idrovo, A. J., Sanchez-Dominguez, M. S., Vinhas, S., & Gonzalez-Vazquez, T. (2012). Violence committed against migrants in transit: Experiences on the Northern Mexican border. *Journal of Immigrant and Minority Health, 14*(3), 449–459. doi: 10.1007/s10903-011-9489-y

Johnson, K., Asher, J., Rosborough, S., Raja, A., Panjabi, R., Beadling, C., & Lawry, L. (2008). Association of combatant status and sexual violence with health and mental health outcomes in postconflict Liberia. *Journal of the American Medical Association, 300*(6), 676–690.

Kasturirangan, A., Krishnan, S., & Riger, S. (2004). The impact of culture and minority status on women's experience of domestic violence. *Trauma Violence Abuse, 5*(4), 318–332.

Kinyanda, E., Musisi, S., Biryabarema, C., Ezati, I., Oboke, H., Ojiambo-Ochieng, R., . . . & Walugembe, J. (2010). War related sexual violence and its medical and psychological consequences as seen in Kitgum, Northern Uganda: A cross-sectional study. *BMC International Health and Human Rights, 10*(1), 28.

Macy, R. J., & Graham, L. M. (2012). Identifying domestic and international sex-trafficking victims during human service provision. *Trauma, Violence, & Abuse, 13*(2), 59–76. doi: 10.1177/1524838012440340

Macy, R. J., & Johns, N. (2011). Aftercare services for international sex trafficking survivors: Informing U.S. services and program development in an emerging practice area. *Trauma, Violence and Abuse, 12*, 87–98.

Menjívar, C. (2011). *Enduring violence: Ladina women's lives in Guatemala*. Berkeley: University of California Press.

Nawyn, S. J., Reosti, A., & Gjokaj, L. (2009). Gender in motion: How gender precipitates international migration. *Advances in Gender Research, 13*, 175–202.

Raj, A., & Silverman, J. (2003). Immigrant South Asian women at greater risk for injury from intimate partner violence. *American Journal of Public Health, 93*, 435–437.

Raymond, J. G., & Hughes, D. M. (2001). *Sex trafficking of women in the United States: International and domestic trends*. Washington, DC: U.S. Department of Justice.

Salcido, O., & Adelman, M. (2004). "He has me tied with the blessed and damned papers": Undocumented-immigrant battered women in Phoenix, Arizona. *Human Organization, 63*(2), 162–172.

Shrestha, N. M., Sharma, B., Van Ommeren, M., Regmi, S., Makaju, R., Kompro, I., . . . de Jong, J. T. (1998). Impact of torture on refugees displaced within the developing world: Symptomatology among Bhutanese refugees in Nepal. *Journal of the American Medical Association, 280*(5), 443–448.

Simich, L., Beiser, M., & Mawani, F. N. (2003). Social support and the significance of shared experience in refugee migration and resettlement. *Western Journal of Nursing Research, 25*(7), 872–891. doi: 10.1177/0193945903256705

Snyder, S. (2012). *Asylum-seeking, migration and church*. Burington, VT: Ashgate.

Soerens, M. (2015). Violence in the borderlands: A dialogical approach to intimate partner violence among migrant women. *Psychology & Society, 7*(1), 64–82.

Stark, L., & Ager, A. (2011). A systematic review of prevalence studies of gender-based violence in complex emergencies. *Trauma, Violence, & Abuse, 12*(3), 127–134.

Stark, L., & Wessells, M. (2012). Sexual violence as a weapon of war. *Journal of the American Medical Association, 308*(7), 677–678.

Todahl, J., & Walters, E. (2011). Universal screening for intimate partner violence: A systematic review. *Journal of Marital and Family Therapy, 37*(3), 355–369.

Upegui-Hernandez, D. (2012). What is missing in the transnational migration literature? A Latin American feminist psychological perspective [Special feature I]. *Feminism & Psychology, 22*(2), 228–239. doi: 10.1177/0959353511415831

Wachter, K., Cook Heffron, L., Snyder, S., Nsonwu, M., & Busch-Armendariz, N. (2016). Unsettled integration: Pre- and post-migration factors in Congolese refugee women's resettlement experiences in the United States. *International Social Work, 59*(6), 875–889. doi: 10.1177/0020872815580049

Wachter, K., & Donahue, K. (2015). *Bridge to safety: An evaluation of a pilot intervention to screen for and respond to domestic and sexual violence with refugee clients in the U.S.* New York, NY: International Rescue Committee. doi: 10.13140/RG.2.1.3643.3369

Wagner, H. (2009). Migration and violence against women: Very invisible. Basic migration and renegotiations in the migration process. *ANTHROPOS, 104*(1), 41–61.

World Health Organization. (2014). *Violence against women*. Retrieved from http://www.who.int/mediacentre/factsheets/fs239/en/

Zimmerman, C., Hossain, M., Yun, K., Gajdadziev, V., Guzun, N., Tchomarova, M., . . . Watts, C. (2008). The health of trafficked women: A survey of women entering posttrafficking services in Europe. *American Journal of Public Health, 98*(1), 55.

Chapter 15

PRACTICE APPLICATIONS WITH LGBTQ IMMIGRANTS AND REFUGEES

MILKA RAMIREZ

KEY TERMS

LGBTQ immigrant and refugees, sexual orientation, gender identity, identity formation among immigrants, cultural stigma, gay affirmative practice

---

CHAPTER HIGHLIGHTS

- Defining the relevant terms in the LGBTQ community
- Examining LGBTQ identity formation among immigrant and refugee populations
- Exploring cultural considerations, health and mental health needs, and stigma
- Discussing the gay affirmative practice framework
- Implications for delivering therapeutic practice and other resources to this community

---

"Today we are making U.N. history," U.S. Ambassador to the United Nations Samantha Power told the attendees during a briefing. "This is the first time in history that the council has held a meeting on the victimization of LGBT persons. It is the first time we are saying, in a single voice, that it is wrong to target people because of their sexual orientation and gender identity. It is a historic step. And it is, as we all know, long overdue."

Cassell (2015)

For the first time since World War II, the number of refugees, asylum seekers, and internally displaced people, worldwide, has exceeded 50 million people—including 16.7 million internally displaced, 16.7 million refugees, and 1.2 million individuals seeking asylum (UNHCR, 2013). Yet, because of global instability, by the time this goes to print, this figure is sure to rise. Recent to this discourse are lesbian, gay, bisexual, transgender, and queer (LGBTQ) people, due to no fewer than 76 countries currently criminalizing same-sex sexual acts or gender-variant behavior. Subsequently, our global dialogue about LGBTQ people has come to the forefront. Still an accurate number of LGBTQ people that are refugee or internally displaced or seek asylum is unknown: first, because some countries do not report this figure, and secondly and most relevant, because LGBTQ immigrant refugees fear disclosure because of imprisonment, physical/emotional abuse, sexual abuse, and even death (Hojem, 2009). A global perspective may be in order here. In 2013, the Pew Research Center surveyed 39 countries about their attitudes toward "homosexuality" and found that in North America, the European Union, and much of Latin America, there seemed to be acceptance of "homosexuality." However, they also found "widespread rejection in predominantly Muslim nations and in Africa, as well as in parts of Asia and in Russia. Opinion about the acceptability of homosexuality is divided in Israel, Poland and Bolivia" (Pew Research Center, 2013, p. 3). Additionally, in Africa and in predominantly Muslim countries there seemed to be the least acceptance of "homosexuality." For instance in sub-Saharan Africa, Nigeria, Ghana, Uganda, and Kenya, over 90% of people surveyed did not accept "homosexuality." In South Africa, where it is unconstitutional to discriminate against "homosexuality," 61% of those surveyed stated that "homosexuality" should not be accepted. In addition, the majority of Muslim countries rejected the acceptance of "homosexuality: 97% in Jordan, 95% in Egypt, 94% in Tunisia, 93% in the Palestinian territories, 93% in Indonesia, 87% in Pakistan, 86% in Malaysia, 80% in Lebanon, and 78% in Turkey. Other countries—59% South Korea, 57% China, 77% South Korea—did not accept "homosexuality."

Subsequently, these findings are germane to our times and pose significant practice implications and challenges in our attempt to address this growing segment of the population. Therefore, practice considerations with LGBTQ immigrant refugee populations are relevant and pressing. In this chapter, I present a practice framework for practitioners to consider when working with LGBTQ people. I begin by discussing the importance of language and terms for practitioners to take into account when working with LGBTQ people. In doing so, however, the importance of viewing language as ever changing and evolving must be underscored. Additionally, it is important to realize that the terms discussed in this chapter may not apply to all immigrant refugee populations, as many of these populations simply refer to terms such as MSM (men who have sex with men) or WSW (women who have sex with women). However, it is important that practitioners have an overview of different terms that may be used in the practice setting. Next, I provide an overview of Cass (1979) identity formation, in order to help practitioners think about factors that influence LGBTQ identity formation. With this said, it is important to note that this model falls short in considering transgender identity formation as well as the evolving concept of a queerness. However, this model is seminal, providing the foundation for how we have come to understand identity formation for LGBTQ people. In addition, it was the first model to consider a "normal" identity formation, underpinning current models. As such, it offers a firm base for practitioners to consider in their practice.

I then discuss how past and contemporary historical forces have influenced the lives of LGBTQ people, in hopes of connecting this to health-related disorders in LGBTQ populations. However, given that scant information is available about LGBTQ immigrant refugees, scant empirical evidence is available about this population. Notwithstanding, I contend that LGBTQ immigrant refugees are significantly impacted by a myriad of factors and in need of services. Subsequent, I present the case of Abdul, a 31-year-old gay identified man from Iraq, seeking asylum in the United States. This case is presented to illustrate theory to practice integration, using gay affirmative practice and a trauma-informed lens that takes into account cultural implications. Lastly, we discuss future implications for best practice with LGTBQ immigrant refugees and provide a list of useful websites as resources.

Before proceeding, it is important to note that this chapter is not meant to be an exhaustive discussion about all factors impacting LGBTQ immigrant refugees (as this would be impossible to achieve), given the complexities involved with this population. Rather, this chapter is written as a point of departure, in hopes of moving us toward a practice framework that understands multiple challenges faced by LGBTQ immigrant refugees and the importance of harnessing the insurmountable strengths inherent in us all (Saleeby, 2006). This chapter also hopes to raise awareness, in hopes of finding ways in which we can challenge systemic inequities that continue to disfranchise LGBTQ immigrant refugees (even if the challenge starts inward), creating a welcoming and affirming practice milieu for this growing population.

THE IMPORTANCE OF LANGUAGE

Language is fluid and cocreated through reciprocal processes between individuals and their environments. Thus, language is multidimensional, dynamic, and always adding to our world lexicon. As much, language should not be viewed as static, stoic, or absolute, but rather as a starting point or entry into the worldview of others. In so much, language has the ability to construct meaning and a shared identity. Language also has the ability to articulate differences yet transcend these differences in order to build a bridge toward understanding. In cross-cultural situations, where culturally competent social work practices take center stage, the use of language becomes especially relevant. Thus, knowing a population's particular use of language helps practitioners understand peoples' lived experiences, serving as a compass to better navigate our journey into uncharted waters. Although LGBTQ people include diverse communities, there exists a specific language in the LGBTQ culture that helps provide a starting point to discuss sexual orientation, gender identity, and gender expression. This is especially relevant with this population, because LGBTQ people have historically been marginalized by oppressive social structures, embedded in a long history of invisibility (D'Emilio, 1983; D'Emilio & Freedman, 1988). At the same time, it is imperative to use a stance of "not knowing" when working with LGBTQ people rather than imposing language that may be disempowering, restrictive, or oppressive.

For that reason, practitioners working with LGBTQ people are encouraged to engage in an ongoing process of self-reflection that honors an individual's self-determination.

DEFINING SEXUAL ORIENTATION, GENDER IDENTITY, GENDER EXPRESSION

In order to examine the diverse context surrounding language with LGBTQ populations, definitions for a number of key terms is discussed. Here, *sex* is understood as the biological construct, referring to the genetic/hormonal/anatomical/physiological characteristics (on whose basis) one is labeled with at birth—either male, female, or intersex. Whereas, *sexual orientation* refers to the type of erotic/love/affection/spiritual attraction one feels for others (often expressed based on romantic relationships between the person and the person(s) that one is attracted to). *Gender identity*, on the other hand, is understood as the sex that one identifies with, emotionally and psychologically. *Gender expression* denotes the cultural meanings of patterns of behaviors, experiences, and personality that are (typically labeled) masculine or feminine (Hock, 2016). (Note: unless otherwise indicated, the terms listed below are cited from Green & Peterson, 2003–2004.)

SEXUAL ORIENTATION. It is important that the term *Sexual orientation* not be mistakenly used for "*sexual preference*." *Sexual preference* is the types of sexual intercourse, stimulation, and gratification one likes to receive and participate in and may or may not be associated with an individual's "sexual orientation." Moreover, using the term sexual preference in place of the term sexual orientation creates an assumption that one has a choice (or "preference") of whom one is attracted. Yet there is no scientific evidence supporting this assumption (Rutter, 2006). Therefore, the appropriate term to use when referring to one's erotic/love/affection/spiritual attraction to others is "sexual orientation." Note, however, that sexual orientation is a diverse and fluid concept, meaning that people may identify in many different ways and/or identify with different sexual orientations throughout their lifespan. As a result, it is important that practitioners remain receptive to individuals whose sexual orientations fall "outside" mainstream society's views.

The term *lesbian* is usually used to describe women who have erotic/love/affection/ spiritual attraction to other women. The term *gay* usually describes men who have erotic/love/affection/spiritual attraction to other men. However, women may also embrace the term gay in order to describe their same-sex relationships with other women. On the other hand, a person that identifies *bisexual* usually experiences erotic/ love/affection/spiritual attraction to men and women and may also use the term gay. There are also individuals that identify as *pansexual*, who may experience erotic/love/ affection/spiritual attraction to all gender identities and gender expressions.

Of late, the term *queer* has begun to be used, in our society, often confusing people about its appropriateness. In the past the word *queer* was used as a derogatory slang term to identify lesbian, gay, bisexual, transgender people. However, in the 1980s it began to be embraced and reclaimed by members of this community as a symbol of resistance to stigmatizing language. Thus, the term queer began to be used by members of this community as a symbol of pride, representing all individuals who fall outside mainstream gender and sexual "norms" (Warner, 1991). Sometimes, LGBTQ people are referred to as *homosexual*, a medical definition for a person that is attracted to someone with the same biological sex. However, the term homosexual has often been rooted in stigma and may be considered offensive by LGBTQ people. Therefore, practitioners should exercise a great deal of caution when using the term homosexual. *Heterosexual* is also a medical definition for a person who is attracted to someone of the opposite biological sex (often referred to as *straight*).

GENDER IDENTITY AND EXPRESSION. *Cisgender* is a description for a person whose gender identity, gender expression, and biological sex all align (e.g., man, masculine, and male; woman, feminine, and female). For instance, a *cisman* is a person who identifies as a man, presents himself masculine, and has male biological sex, often referred to as simply a "heterosexual man." A *ciswoman* is a person who identifies as a woman, presents herself feminine, often referred to as simply a "heterosexual woman." *Transgender* is often used as a blanket term to describe all people who are outside traditional binary male/female roles. Occasionally "transgendered" is used, but the *ed* is misleading, as it implies something happened to the person to make them transgender, which is not the case. *Transitioning* is a term usually used to describe the process of moving from one biological sex/gender to another (or gender identity); sometimes this is done by hormone or surgical treatments. Whereas, *transsexual* is a term used for a person whose gender identity is the opposite of their biological sex. This individual usually undergoes some type of medical treatment to reassign their biological sex, aligning it with their gender identity. This individual may also choose to live in mainstream society (in the reassigned sex), identifying as straight. A *transman* or *transwoman*, however, was assigned a female sex at birth but identifies as a man (female to male or FTM) or was assigned a male at birth but identifies as a female (male to female or MTF). These individuals may or may not undergo hormone or surgical treatments to physically align themselves with how they internally identify. In addition, they may choose to continue to be part of the LGBTQ community, regardless of how they identify.

In short, gender expression is the external display of gender, through a combination of dress, demeanor, social behavior, and other factors, generally measured on a scale of masculinity and femininity. Whereas, gender identity is the internal perception of an individual's gender and how a person identifies. As much, gender expression and gender identity should not be confused with sexual orientation, as they are distinct concepts. Key findings from Gates' (2011) population-based survey of people in the United States found the following:

- "An estimated 3.5% of adults in the U.S. identify as lesbian, gay or bisexual and an estimated, 0.3% of adults are transgender. This implies that there are approximately nine million LGBT people in the United States,

- among adults who identify as LGB, bisexuals comprise a slight majority (1.8% compared to 1.7% who identify as lesbian or gay),

- women are substantially more likely than men to identify as bisexual. Bisexuals comprise more than half of the lesbian and bisexual population among women in eight of nine surveys considered in the brief,

- conversely, gay men comprise substantially more than half of gay and bisexual men in seven of the nine surveys." (p. 1)

Furthermore, of those who report any lifetime same-sex sexual behavior and any same-sex sexual attraction were substantially higher than estimates of those who identify as LGB. For instance, an estimated 19 million individuals (8.2%) report that they have engaged in same-sex sexual behavior, and nearly 25.6 million people (11%) acknowledge at least some same-sex sexual attraction. Consequently, it would seem that sexual orientation might be more fluid than widely believed. As such, it is important that practitioners remain open to various sexual orientations, gender identities, and gender expressions.

ADDITIONAL TERMS TO CONSIDER. The term *closeted* is used to describe a person who is keeping their sexuality or gender identity private from many (or any) people and has yet to "come out of the closet." *Coming out* of the closet is the process of revealing one's sexuality or gender identity to other people. Coming out of the closet is often incorrectly thought to be a one-time event, when in fact this is often a lifelong event that may take place multiple times throughout the lifespan, with various groups of people (i.e., various family members, friends, coworkers). A national probability sample revealed that gay men (n = 241) disclosed their gay orientation at a significantly earlier average age (age 15) than lesbians (age 18) (n = 152) or bisexual women (age 20) (n = 159), while the average age for bisexual men (n = 110) was between that of women and gay men (age 17.5). In addition, older adults were likely to "come out" later, when compared with younger adults. Yet gay and lesbian individuals were more likely to be out to their family members than bisexual individuals (Herek, Norton, Allen, & Sims, 2010). Subsequently, although a larger portion of the LGBTQ population identify as bisexual, it seems that this segment of the population may remain closeted to family members. This may be because of fear of acceptance or internalized stigma; unfortunately we do not have a national probability sample for transgender individuals. Therefore, we are limited in our ability to generalize to this population.

Outing someone is the act of disclosing another person's sexuality or gender identity to an individual or group, without the person's consent or approval. *Homophobia* is fear, anger, intolerance, resentment, or discomfort with people that do not identify as heterosexual. *Heterosexism* is the behavior that grants preferential treatment to heterosexual people and reinforces the idea that heterosexuality is somehow better or more "right" than being LGBTQ. *Internalized homophobia* refers to the personal acceptance and endorsement of stigma rooted in society's views about LGBTQ people. As stated earlier, language is ever changing and multidimensional; therefore before leaving this topic, it is important to understand that the terms described in this section are sure to change. Thus, it is also important to consider using these terms as adjectives rather than nouns. This perspective frees practitioners from constraining people to one facet of their lives. After all, one is not simply a lesbian, gay, or transgender person any more than one is simply a parent, child, student, or teacher. In fact, we are all complicated beings, so it would be prudent for practitioners to consider how language can be used in an inclusive way, as this will prevent myopic thinking and restrictive delivery of services.

IDENTITY FORMATION AND PRACTICE CONSIDERATIONS

Although there are various models that examine identity formation of LGBTQ people (e.g., D'Augelli, 1994; Lev, 2004; McCarn-Fassinger, 1996; Troiden, 1988), here we focus on Cass's (1979) six-stage model, grounded in interpersonal congruency, as it remains the most widely cited model on LGBTQ identity formation. Notwithstanding, evolving knowledge about identity formation has explored the complexities of race, ethnicity, gender identity, and gender expression with LGBTQ individuals, questioning whether Cass's model remains relevant in today's diverse and global society (Bilodeau & Ren, 2005; Lev, 2004).

Sexual Identity: The Cass Model

STAGE ONE, IDENTITY CONFUSION: "COULD I BE GAY?" In this stage of identity formation, individuals may begin to experience romantic and sexual attraction to same sex individuals, questioning if one is lesbian, gay, or bisexual. Cass contends that this is often met with a sense of inner conflict and personal feelings of alienation, with various possible responses: Individuals may avoid these feelings, deny that they exist, or reject them all together. Additionally, Cass contends that in this stage of identity development, it would be important that the person handle feelings of alienation that arise with the awareness of being different from others. Furthermore, she states that if individuals successfully repress or reject same-sex attraction, identity formation is foreclosed, leading to self-loathing and increased risk of self-harm. Therefore, in this stage of development, the practitioner's role is to help individuals explore any internal negative judgments that they may have about same-sex attraction and any uncertainties associated with being lesbian, gay, or bisexual. Furthermore, it is essential that practitioners have the skills necessary to explain the full spectrum of sexual identity and support explorations of same-sex attraction.

STAGE TWO, IDENTITY COMPARISON: "MAYBE THIS DOES APPLY TO ME." In this stage of identity formation, individuals may begin to accept the possibility of being lesbian or gay. Thus, people may begin to consider the implications of being lesbian, gay, or bisexual and what that implies for their own sense of being different. Individuals may experience a sense of loss for the things that may be absent from their lives by embracing their sexual orientation (i.e., family/friend support, mainstream acceptance). In this stage of development, individuals may attempt to negotiate these feelings by accepting the definition of lesbian, gay, or bisexual but continue to identify as heterosexual. Here, practitioners should help individuals develop their own understanding of what it means to be lesbian, gay, or bisexual. It is important that practitioners play the role of educator, continuing to provide information about identity formation, while providing information about the LGBTQ community. In addition, it is essential that practitioners validate feelings associated with loss, while helping to articulate new directions. Moreover, practitioners should be prepared to support the need to maintain a "heterosexual" identity. Lastly, it is also important that practitioners help individuals address feelings of isolation.

STAGE THREE, IDENTITY TOLERANCE: "I AM NOT THE ONLY ONE." In this stage of identity formation, social alienation is heightened, resulting in an increase "need" to connect with others that share a lesbian, gay, or bisexual identity. Self-disclosure is very selective, but there remains an emphasis on maintaining a public heterosexual identity. A crucial aspect of this stage is the quality of interactions with other lesbian, gay, or bisexual people, and its influence on identity development. An example may be in order here: If interactions with other lesbian, gay, or bisexual people is positive, then this will help individuals reevaluate negative self-images of identifying as lesbian, gay, or bisexual. However, if the quality of the interactions is negative, these experiences will reinforce a negative self-image and devaluation of the gay and lesbian culture. In this stage of identity formation, practitioners should help people find language to talk about important concerns related to their emerging identity, social discrimination, and fears. It is also important that practitioners help individuals understand that being lesbian, gay, or bisexual does not equate with a loss of future possibilities. Consequently, practitioners are tasked with helping people decrease social alienation by seeking support from other lesbian, gay, or bisexual people.

STAGE FOUR, IDENTITY ACCEPTANCE: "WHERE DO I BELONG?" In this stage of identity formation, there is an increased amount of contact with the "gay" subculture, along with a measured amount of inclusion of lesbian, gay, and bisexual friends. However, there is an effort to "pass" as straight. As such, there is a selective group of people that one may begin to come out to, feeling more comfortable around other lesbian, gay, or bisexual people. In addition, members of the lesbian, gay, and bisexual community are seen as positive and important figures. At this stage of development, it is important that practitioners support an exploration of shameful feelings derived from external and internalized homophobia and heterosexism. In addition, it will be important to assist individuals find positive connections to the LGBTQ community. Consequently, practitioners should be prepared to connect individuals to members/organizations that may serve as resources. Also, it will be important that practitioners help individuals resolve inner tensions often associated with not meeting expected social norms, whereby helping individuals find congruency between their private/public lives.

STAGE FIVE, IDENTITY PRIDE: "I'M OUT." In this stage of identity formation, there is nearly a complete acceptance of one's identity as a lesbian, gay, or bisexual individual. One may also be acutely aware of larger society's lack of acceptance for being lesbian, gay, or bisexual. Thus, people appear to be divided into two camps, bad heterosexual and good heterosexuals. Furthermore, there is a growing allegiance to the LGBTQ community, often leading to purposeful activism for other LGBTQ people and confrontation with establishments that act in discriminatory ways. According to Cass, in this stage of identity formation, one's identity as a lesbian, gay, or bisexual individual becomes the primary identity, individuals frequently disclose their identity with a great deal of pride.

As such, practitioners should continue to support exploration of feelings associated with anger, because of oppression and societal stigma. In addition, it will be essential that practitioners work with individuals to address negative reactions that they may encounter during the coming out process.

STAGE SIX, IDENTITY SYNTHESIS: "I AM WHO I AM." In this stage, individuals are aware of their sexual orientation (as an important part of their identity) but it is not the central part of their identity. People will begin to integrate multiple aspects of their identity, increasing their contact with supportive heterosexual individuals, and unifying their personal and public sexual identities. Consequently, individuals may begin to create personal and public spaces that are not solely defined by sexual orientation. Here, practitioners play an important role, supporting the integration process of individuals and the many roles that they play in society. In order to support the integration process it is important to communicate an authentic understanding and appreciation for the various roles that people play (e.g., partner, spouse, uncle, aunt, activist, etc.). Here, the key work to be accomplished is to assist individuals in integrating identity rather than merely defining themselves by sexual orientation.

In summary, Cass's (1979) model provides a foundation to help inform our understanding of identity formation with lesbian, gay, or bisexual people. Yet contextual influences are diverse and vary from one individual to the next. Cass's linear model of identity formation must be viewed with a critical eye, expecting variations in people's lives (Kaufman & Johnson, 2004). I will now turn our attention to historical context that impacts the lives of LGBTQ people.

A CONTEXT FOR LGBTQ HEALTH

Because of discriminatory and oppressive policies, most LGBTQ people have encountered stigma early in their lives. In addition, many practitioners and health systems that interface with LGBTQ people have been established within a society that historically stigmatized LGBTQ people. In order to contextualize LGBTQ health factors, this section presents some relevant key themes associated with stigma. However, this discussion is not intended to provide an extensive history of LGBTQ people but rather a background of historical forces that impact LGBTQ people.

CRIMINALIZATION, MENTAL ILLNESS, STIGMA. Throughout history, same-sex attraction has been viewed as deviant behavior and "homosexual," people categorized as sexual perverts, inverts, and pathological. Subsequently, LGBTQ people endured mass incarceration, sodomy laws that criminalized same-sex behavior, dishonorable military discharge, loss of employment, loss of custody of children, expulsion from academic institutions, forced sterilization, castration, and even death (D'Emilio, 1983; Katz, 1976; Miller, 2006). Furthermore, until 1972 homosexuality was considered a mental illness (American Psychological Association, 2009) believed to be treatable by various methods that included electric shock therapy, lobotomy, and until 2008, conversation/reparative therapy (American Psychological Association, 2008). Furthermore, the diagnosis of homosexuality was often used as a basis by which to deny employment and licensure in many occupations and encouraged states to confine people to psychiatric hospitals until they were deemed "cured" (Chauncey, 1982, 1993; D'Emilio, 1983; Silverstein, 1996). Adding to this discourse of stigma is the impact of the onset of AIDS in the 1980s. During this time, many hospitals, medical professionals, health insurance companies, and government institutions openly denied medical care to LGBTQ people impacted by AIDS. As such, many argue that these acts of institutionalized oppression enacted on LGBTQ people played a key role in the significant amount of gay men who died from AIDS (Curan & Jaffe, 2011). Subsequently, the AIDS crisis impacted the emotional well-being of thousands of LGBTQ people because of stigma associated with being LGBTQ, being outed because of having AIDS, losing friends because of AIDS, emotional and physical abuse because of homophobic rhetoric in mainstream society, and loss of friends and familial support (just to name a few).

In the 1960s with the rise of civil rights movements, the LGBTQ community began to address the oppression and discrimination founded in stigma and made concerted organized efforts to dispel the notion that same-sex attraction was a mental illness. One landmark battle that was won in this struggle was the overturning of the APA's decision that homosexuality was a mental illness (Conger, 1975). Also, because of the AIDS crisis, the LGBTQ community organized, forming self-help groups and community-based organizations (National Academy Press, 1993). As such, today we see military sanctions for LGTBQ people lifted, same-sex marriage legalized, and other advances in the human rights for LGBTQ people. Notwithstanding, transgender people continue to face widespread discrimination that includes losing custody of their children, housing discrimination, employment discrimination, lack of adequate health care, and being labeled with a mental disorder (gender dysphoria) by the American Psychological Association (Grant, Mottet, & Tanis, 2011). Therefore, the aforementioned historical and contemporary context, criminalization of LGBTQ people in at least 78 countries, and widespread disapproval of same-sex behavior (in significant parts of the world) emphasize the role that structural homophobia, depersonalization, and societal devaluation of LGBT people play in the prevalence of health-related diagnoses in LGBTQ populations.

HEALTH RELATED DIAGNOSES. First, King et al. (2008) found that risks for suicide and suicidal ideation for LGB individuals, and risk for depression for LGB individuals are two times higher (across the lifespan) than that of heterosexual individuals. What is more, risks of being diagnosed with a substance use disorder for lesbian and bisexual women are 1.5 times higher, when compared to heterosexual women. Also, deliberate self-harm was found to be a frequent cause of acute medical admissions for LGBT individuals (e.g., Bochenek & Brown, 2001; Case et al., 2004; Dilley et al., 2010; Meyer, Dietrich, & Schwartz, 2008; Morrow, 2004; Mustanski, Garofalo, & Emerson, 2010; Rivers & Cowie, 2006; van Wormer, Wells, & Boes, 2000; Wackerfuss, 2007; Walls, Freedenthal, & Wisneski, 2008). Second, in 2010, Black/African American men represented about 12% of the U.S. population yet accounted for approximately 44% on new HIV infections. Similarly (in 2010) Latinos comprised about 16% of the U.S. population, yet accounted for 21% of new HIV infections. However, men who have sex with men were heavily affected by HIV (63%), when compared to men who do not engage in same-sex behavior (25%). Furthermore, approximately 22% of HIV cases are among gay and bisexual youth ages 13 to 24. Yet over 50% of youth with HIV in the United States do not know that they are infected. Similarly, ethnic minority populations among the youth remain at higher risks of infection (CDC, 2015). Third, people of color are the largest group of people living with HIV/AIDS, globally. For instance, in 2013, 35 million people were living with HIV/AIDS, yet the vast majority of these individuals (24.7 million) were from sub-Saharan Africa (World Health Organization, 2016).

Although limited, empirical information specifically addresses LGBTQ immigrant refugee health related diagnosis. We know that because of the criminalization of LGBTQ people in at least 78 countries, millions of LGBTQ people risk imprisonment, persecution, and in five of these countries, death (e.g., in UNHCR, 2013). Recent reports (Westcott, 2015) indicate that at least 30 people have been killed for sodomy through stoning, shootings, beheadings, or being thrown from the top of buildings. Reports also indicated that many face physical and verbal abuse in detention camps, while awaiting their hearings (Chavez, 2011; Fialho, 2013). In addition, several LGBTQ refugee immigrants face domestic violence at home as well as community violence because of their sexual orientation, gender expression, or perceived sexual orientation and gender expression. Fried and Teixeira (2000) report that women as well as transgender women face discrimination at work, violence by the police, honor killings, and "corrective" rape from male family members.

We also know that overall, immigrant refugees face several challenges: fear for their lives, dislocation, physical and emotional abuse, and torture. As such, immigrant refugees are diagnosed with serious mental illnesses that include depression, post-traumatic stress disorder, and complex trauma (Akerman, 1997; Burnett & Peel, 2001; Tiong et al., 2006). Although limited information is available about LGBTQ immigrant refugees' health-related diagnoses, one may conclude that LGBTQ immigrant refugees face increased risks of being diagnosed with health-related diagnoses. With this said, it is important to understand that sexual orientation and gender identity in and of itself does not "cause" health-related diagnoses, disproportionally impacting LGBTQ people. On the contrary, empirical evidence suggest that factors such as institutional discrimination, internalized stigma, limited support and resources, accumulated stress, and victimization give rise to health-related diagnosis of LGBTQ people (Hatzenbuehler, Phil, McLaughlin, Keyes, & Hasin, 2010; Herek, 2004, 2007; Herek, Cogan, Gillis, & Glunt, 1998; Herek, Gillis, & Cogan, 1999, 2009; Herek, Norton, Allen, & Sims, 2010). As such, when working with LGBTQ immigrant refugees, it is important to integrate a practice framework that considers these factors. In order to apply the abovementioned ideas that have been discussed thus far, I turn our attention to the case of Abdul.

THEORY TO PRACTICE INTEGRATION

Practice with LGBTQ immigrant refugees must include an ecological perspective that affirms an individual's identity, understands the complexities associated with identity formation, infuses cultural influences, and examines the role of acculturation and trauma. While this framework is complex, it can maximize benefits for people who have experienced trauma and human rights violations because of their sexual orientation and gender expression, such as those from LGTBQ immigrant refugee backgrounds. Here we explore a practice approach through the case study of Abdul, a composite of many LGBTQ immigrant refugee experiences.

THE STORY OF ABDUL: HOPES FOR A BRIGHT FUTURE

Abdul is a 31-year-old Iraq male from Baghdad, Iraq. He grew up in a large, wealthy family, living a comfortable life with access to the best education. Abdul remembers having butlers, drivers, and maid staff and being surrounded constantly by people who catered to his needs. Abdul began to recognize his attraction to men during puberty and accepted his sexuality but feared his parent's reactions if they found out. His parents were both conservative Muslims, and he knew instinctively that heterosexual marriage was the only acceptable relationship in their eyes. Abdul also understood that being gay in his country was not only controversial but could also be dangerous. When he was around 16 years of age, he began feeling chronically depressed, often isolating himself from family. He felt constantly conflicted between his desire to be with his family and need to fully express himself.

Since he could not talk to his family, Abdul began searching for ways to connect with others who were in a similar situation. He made connections through online social platforms with men who understood the complexity of the situation and also lived in a culture that did not recognize or condone same-sex relationships. Abdul quickly realized the shared experiences of many of the men and felt the gravity of their unjust and dangerous situation. As he began making connections within the community, he began to feel a sense of urgency to make their suffering more visible and advocate for increased legal and social recognition in Iraq. Abdul began spending more time on his computer, and his family became increasingly suspicious of this behavior. One day, his father took his computer and discovered messages speaking about gay rights issues. When Abdul came home, his father quickly confronted him. His sadness turned to anger, and he began yelling obscenities at his son, ultimately threatening Abdul with a knife. His brother told Abdul that he would have no choice but to kill him if he continued to embarrass his family in this way. Abdul watched in horror as his entire family turned against him, and he now recognizes this as the most traumatic moment of his life.

Fearing for his safety, Abdul left his home. He turned to friends he had met online, and they opened up their home in Lebanon. He had hoped to connect with family living there, but they refused to speak to him after they learned he was gay. For the next four years, he worked in shops and restaurants, often working for long hours and receiving little money. Abdul remembers emotional abuse endured while working and his inability to combat the continued discrimination. He lived in constant poverty but was able to find a group of activists who were passionate about gay rights. Abdul was jailed multiple times for speaking out, occasionally experiencing physical abuse at the hands of the police. Abdul also suffered from depression connected to the loss of family and the life he had once known.

He felt that there were no options for him in the Middle East and applied for refugee status through the UNHCR on the grounds of homophobia. He was excited for the possibility of rebuilding his life after so much loss and arrived to the United States with hopes of a bright future. However, Abdul became frustrated when he learned he was still only qualified for a minimum wage job, and he saw his life as equivalent to what he experienced in Lebanon. Additionally, Abdul felt the loss of the community he had built and felt his closest relationships become strained because of the distance. Abdul attempted to connect to the LGBT community in Chicago but felt culturally different and alienated by the open sexuality within the community. Abdul began feeling more depressed than before and experienced frequent passive suicidal ideation. He found himself at bars alone at night hoping to connect with others and began engaging in risky sexual behaviors, because he saw this as his only way to get attention. He began avoiding work and was fired from his job after arriving late too many times. Abdul was referred to the mental health program after becoming emotional in ESL class and disclosing his feelings of depression to his teacher.

THE GAY AFFIRMATIVE PRACTICE FRAMEWORK

There is no one specific approach when working with LGBTQ individuals that has been proven to be more effective than others. However gay affirmative practice (GAP) has been supported as an essential, holistic framework to integrate when working with LGBTQ people (Crisp, 2002, 2005, 2006; Crisp & McCave, 2007; Hunter & Hickerson, 2003; Van Den Bergh & Crisp, 2004; van Wormer et al., 2000). Proponents of GAP call for practitioners to examine problems faced by LGBTQ people through a lens that recognizes the impact of oppressive systemic structures, not sexual pathology. In so much, practitioners are required to take an explicit stance against societal oppressive forces that serve to marginalize LGBTQ people (Tozer & McClanahan, 1999).

Clark (1987) proposed the following tasks for practitioners to adopt when practicing from an affirmative stance:

1. Help LGBTQ become aware of how oppression has affected them.

2. Desensitize the shame and guilt surrounding thoughts about same-sex attraction, behaviors, and feelings.

3. Encourage LGBTQ to express anger in response to being oppressed.

4. Encourage LGBTQ people to establish a support system with other LGBTQ people.

5. Challenge heterosexist practice and attitudes.

As such, practitioners that subscribe to GAP adopt a human rights framework that requires them to take into account sociopolitical factors that draw attention to issues of social justice and uphold people's rights. This is best accomplished by developing a knowledge base that emphasizes an ecological approach that pays attention to power differentials in the lives of LGBTQ people (1998, 2012). Appleby and Anastas (1998) contend that in order for social work to move toward a stance that is grounded in gay affirmative practice, social work must integrate cultural competency approaches that increase practice, assessment, and intervention skills. Crisp (2002) states that gay affirmative practices achieve this by integrating the person into environmental strengths perspective and cultural competency into its framework. Figure 15.1 is a visual representation of how Crisp views the integration of these concepts into GAP, followed by its application to the case of Abdul.

Aspects of person in environment in the gay affirmative practice framework are essential, calling upon practitioners to understand social political forces faced by Abdul as well as historical oppressive forces faced by LGBTQ people. As such, practitioners use this lens to understand power differential as well as power structures imposed in Abdul's life, as he immigrates to the United States. Although, one may argue,

Figure 15.1 Gay Affirmative and Social Work, Crisp, 2002

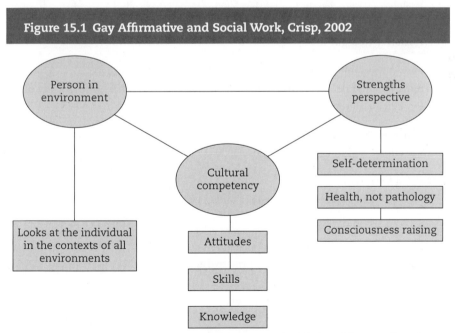

Source: Crisp, C. (2002). "Beyond homophobia: Development and validation of the Gay Affirmative Practice Scale (GAP)." *Dissertation Abstracts International* 64, 074 (2002). (UMI No. 3099441).

political systems in the United States (and other parts of the world) have changed to redress explicit marginalization of LGBTQ people. Abdul (and other LBTQ immigrant refugees) may not be aware of historical factors that have and continue to disenfranchise LGBTQ people. Therefore, practitioners must be able to articulate this historical context to Abdul, so he can understand its impact on his experiences in the United States. Moreover, it is important that practitioners not assume that Abdul is aware of this context, as he may have limited knowledge that may lead him to assume that he will be readily accepted and completely affirmed as a gay man in the United States. In short, practitioners must understand ecological factors that underpin the impact of LGBTQ immigrant refugees and be able to articulate this in order to shed light on environmental forces that shape their experiences.

Similarly, it is essential that the practitioner draw upon Abdul's strengths in order to help him access internal, interpersonal, and social-political resources. Hence, drawing on Saleeby's (2006) strengths perspective, the questions (listed below) help understand Abdul's worldview. In doing so, they serve as clinical interventions intended to help Abdul construct a counter narrative to that of sexual pathology. In addition, these questions are intended to help raise awareness of internal and external thoughts and feelings associated with being a gay man in Iraq and the United States and help Abdul move toward a vision grounded in self-determination.

1. How do you view yourself as a gay man? How do you think your family, people in your community, and the broader society back home view you and other gay men?

2. Back home, how do you think other gay men view themselves? Are there people back home that would disagree with how your family, community, and the broader society view gay men?

3. How do you think gay men in the United States view themselves? How do you think families, people in the community where you live, and broader society in the United States view gay men?

4. What similarities and differences do you see between how gay men are viewed back home and in the United States?

5. What aspects of being a gay man do you find to be in conflict with your upbringing? What supports would you need in order to resolve these conflicts?

Furthermore, in order to help Abdul move toward what Saleeby refers to as a "lexicon of strengths" (p. 10), the practitioner must also tap into Abdul's sense of empowerment. The questions listed below use a gay affirmative approach in this consideration:

• As a gay man in Iraq, how did you manage to thrive, given all the challenges that you had to contend with? What were you thinking as you faced these challenges? What helped sustain you?

- As you reflect on your experiences in Iraq, what have you learned about yourself? What have you learned about yourself, as a gay man?

- What are the special qualities that you believe you have that can help you deal with your current situation? As a gay man, what are the special qualities that you believe you have to deal with your current situation?

- Which moments in your life have given you special meaning? What parts of your world and culture would you like to recapture? How can I help you recover those parts of your world and culture?

I now turn to three central components that help highlight cultural competent practices with Abdul: (a) understanding lived experiences, (b) assessing identity formation, and (c) unique cultural factors. Recall, Abdul was "outed" by his father and forced to leave a home and country that provided him with financial security and male privilege. As such, it is important for practitioners to engage in a dialogical relationship with Abdul that places him in a position of expert in his own life. Thus, creating a safe space will allow Abdul to talk about what he experienced in his country of origin and feelings of lost privilege and societal status. Similarly, practitioners must help Abdul express feelings related to being "outed" by his father and physical threats that he endured by his family and political power structures, resulting in asylum status. The practitioners must help Abdul connect his experience of being outed to loss of home, family, and country in order to help him reconcile the array of losses that he has experienced.

Regarding Abdul's sexual orientation: When he lived in Baghdad, where was he in terms of his identity formation? Did that change? In order to provide clinical services that utilize a gay affirmative stance, practitioners should have the knowledge and skills to adequately assess this aspect of Abdul's life. Recall in Baghdad, during puberty, Abdul began to question his sexual orientation; he also articulated feelings of isolation because of his sexual orientation, and eventually sought other gay people, which led him to engage in political activism to challenge oppression of other gay people. Pursuant to Cass's (1979) theory of identity formation, Abdul, at the time of pre-immigration, would be assessed to have been in stage five—identity pride. For instance, Abdul had begun making positive connections with other gay people and participated in political action to address human rights violations of gay people in Iraq. Thus, he had submerged himself in the gay community, surrounded by other gay identified people that took pride in their identity.

Upon Abdul's arrival in the United States, he lost this social support system that affirmed a positive gay identity rooted in social action and advocacy. Although Abdul continued to identify as a gay man, he began to feel isolated from the gay community. This heightened his sense of alienation and increased his need to connect with others. Because of limited supports and resources that were put in place for Abdul to connect with the LGBTQ culture, he turned to the bar scene to connect with other gay men. However, Abdul's connections were superficial in nature and centered on sexual exchanges rather than meaningful interactions with others. Assessing all this information, practitioners should conclude that upon arrival in the United States, Abdul is likely to be in stage three—identity tolerance. Recall, in this stage, there is a need to increase contact with others that share a LGBTQ identity. One crucial factor in this stage is the quality of the interactions and how they help shape a person's sense of self. For Abdul, engaging in contact with other gay men, rooted in risky sexual behaviors, reaffirmed a gay identity embedded in sexual pathology.

It would be important not to place judgment on Abdul's behavior but rather to understand the importance of placing his behavior within larger social structures that led him to feel lonely, seeking connection with others. It would also be essential to connect Abdul to a formal support system with other LGBTQ people that understand his experience of forced immigration. Moreover, crucial to this work would be to help Abdul associate his participation with risky sexual behavior within the context of internalized stigma. In order words, how does risky sexual behavior reinforce internalized feelings of shame? Conversely, how have past positive experiences with others countered internalized feelings of shame, whereby, removing self-blame and shame in hopes of reintegrating a positive self-image. Also, acculturation plays a major role in Abdul's life. Here it is important to recognize that the field of acculturation is vast and quickly changing; therefore this section in purposefully selective. In this section, a definition of acculturation is provided, followed by a brief overview of Berry's (1997) fourfold model of acculturation and how it relates to continuing bound, underscoring the importance of gay affirmative practice.

Over time, various definitions of acculturation have been developed. However, here I draw on the work of Redfield, Linton, and Herskowits (1936): "Acculturation comprehends those phenomena which result when groups of individuals having different cultures come into continuous first-hand contact with subsequent changes in the original culture patterns of either or both groups" (p. 149). Thus, generally speaking, acculturation contends that people from different cultures are impacted, in some way, by interacting with other cultures. In so much, acculturation is multifaceted with far-reaching implications for individuals and societies. Berry's (1997) fourfold model is often discussed in order to understand the process of acculturation in the lives of people that immigrate to other parts of the world. Briefly this process is categorized as (1) total assimilation, which usually occurs when individuals adopt the cultural norms of a dominant or host culture, over their original culture; (2) separation, which usually occurs when individuals reject the dominant or host culture in favor of preserving their culture of origin; (3) integration, which usually occurs when individuals are able to adopt the cultural norms of the dominant or host culture while maintaining their culture of origin (also referred to as biculturalism); and (4) marginalization, which occurs when individuals reject both their culture of origin and the dominant host culture.

Henry (2012) contends that immigrant refugees that successfully reconcile pre-immigration trauma with cultural loss fair better in their ability to have a continual bound with their country of origin. Consequently, helping immigrant refugees navigate cultural expectations of their host country, while feeling connected to their country provides a practice framework that enhances cultural competency. In the case of

Abdul, this concept can be extended to include a gay affirmative stance. For instance, it would be important to help Abdul reconnect with his support systems in Iraq that he established on social media, when connecting to other gay men. This would establish a continual bound with his country of origin, whereby reinforcing positive mental representations of culture and alleviating his loss of country and culture. As such, establishing a continual bound with Abdul's country of origin will help him grapple with conflicting values, traditions, and cultural beliefs that can help move him toward an integrated acculturation process (as it is clear that Abdul longs for a connection to this host country). Similarly, it would be important to help Abdul connect globally with diverse members of the Muslim religion in order to establish relationships with global movement of LGBTQ Muslims.

APPLYING A TRAUMA-INFORMED LENS WHEN WORKING WITH LGBTQ IMMIGRANTS AND REFUGEES

Trauma theory dates back to the 19th century and is rooted in psychiatry and clinical psychology (Ringel & Brandell, 2012). However, for over three decades trauma-informed practice has expanded to other disciplines, informing our work with diverse populations and settings (e.g., Silove, Austin, & Steel, 2007). Because of extreme events experienced by most immigrant refugees, trauma frameworks have come to play a central role in the refugee literature (e.g., Hollifield et al., 2006; Mollica, Caspi-Yavin, & Bollini, 1992; Silove, Austin, & Steel, 2007). Therefore, it seems fitting to include a trauma-informed lens to the case of Abdul. Once again, it is important to understand that the field of trauma is vast, therefore this section in purposefully selective. Here, trauma is defined as an unexpected event that the person was unprepared to address and that is out of the person's control, which left the person feeling an intense sense of fear, helplessness, and horror (Vedat & Ozturk, 2006). There are several ways that people respond to trauma or the perception of a trauma that may help minimize damage (Carlson & Dalenberg, 2000). In the case of Abdul, note that he initially remained closeted about being gay, attempting to prevent the traumatic experience of being rejected by his family. However, after his father discovered Abdul's "secret," he outed Abdul. The act of Abdul being outed and physically threatened by his father and brother ultimately led to being ostracized from his family. Yet, Abdul attempted to correct and minimize the damage sustained by the traumatic event. For instance, Abdul sought a substitute support system and reached out to other gay men he had met on social platforms. In addition, he engaged in political activism to readdress issues of social injustice for gay men in Iraq and ultimately sought political asylum. Thus, in the face of trauma, Abdul demonstrated strong affect tolerance in his ability to modulate his affect, indicative of resiliency in the face of adversity. Subsequently, understanding psychological responses related to independent coping skills associated with Abdul's level of trauma offers insight into his initial response to trauma and indicates how to harness his strengths and capabilities.

However, upon Abdul's arrival to the United States, his ability to adjust was comprised. In order to offer some insight into Abdul's responses, it is important to use a trauma-informed lens to help us understand the impact of post-immigration stressors. Let us briefly turn our attention to the contribution of neuroscience and trauma to help frame this discussion. One of the most useful contributions of trauma theory is the understanding of how the brain responds to experiences of trauma. As such, we understand that the lower parts of the brain (e.g., limbic, brainstem) play a significant role in responding to perceived threat, triggering physiological reactions. Thus, responses to trauma may not operate at a deliberate cognitive level (Perry & Szalavitz, 2009). As such, at the time of trauma, these responses act as protective and adaptive functions. However, when the body's responses have become hypersensitive, they can be triggered in situations that are not (for all intents and purposes) threatening. Therefore, the person's ability to function on a day-to-day basis may be significantly impaired.

An example of how this relates to Abdul may be in order. Recall that Abdul successfully secured asylum status because of persecution on the grounds of sexual orientation, immigrating to the United States "in hopes of a bright future." However, he does not connect with any immigrant LGBTQ resources, which causes him to feel alienated and to engage in sexual behavior that he views as culturally inappropriate, experiencing significant difficulty in finding his place in gay culture and feeling culturally different from others. In turn, this resurfaces intense feelings of loss, associated with loss of family, home, friends, community, and country. Additionally, Abdul struggles to find financial security, associating his financial insecurity to his experiences in Iraq—when he was forced to live in poverty. Once again this resurfaces a deep sense of loss and distress linked to loss of possessions and social status. As a result, these feelings give way to a lost of controllability (or inhibited locus of control). Eventually, these experiences trigger a perceived threat to Abdul's sense of safety and impact his ability to function; whereby resulting in what is generally known to be secondary associations of trauma (Carlson & Dalenberg, 2000) that include suicidal ideation, guilt/shame, identity confusion, and difficulty in establishing interpersonal relationships.

Now, given that trauma treatment is complex, attempting to provide the same strategy at all times to everyone is sure to fail. So how should the practitioner proceed in the case of Abdul? One key point here is not to understate the importance of validating Abdul's post-immigration stressors. Also, it is important that practitioners understand that the therapeutic relationship serves as a proxy for attachment, providing Abdul with comfort and safety. Fundamentally, this requires an increase attention to attunement, intentionally eliciting Abdul's self-awareness about his thoughts and feelings, hence, asking how does Abdul feel right now, entering into a therapeutic relationship? Is this seen as a strength or weakness? In doing so, the practitioner should explore dynamics surrounding feelings of anger and sadness—such as how did Abdul feel about engaging in risky sex with other men? What about these feelings still persist? At the same time, it is essential to explore the underpinnings of what is going on inside Abdul's thought process and to carefully and safely uncover feelings related to trauma. For example, asking Abdul to share which past experiences made him more vulnerable, resulting in risky sexual behavior with other men. And what makes him more vulnerable now to feelings of distress? Similarly, it would be important to move Abdul toward a vision that overcomes and transforms adversity into opportunities.

Tedeschi and Calhoun (1995) have generally referred to this as post-traumatic growth, contending that there are five major domains: seeing new possibilities, changed relationships, the paradoxical view of being both stronger yet more vulnerable, a greater appreciation for life, and changes in the individual's spiritual and existential domain. In order to practice from this stance, it is imperative to expand Abdul's social network to include people and systems that can support aspects of his culture and gay identity. Practitioners should be self-reflective and ask themselves, how will this support system validate Abdul's articulation of trauma and alienation, while validating his cultural "differenceness?" Similarly, what will the practitioner do to continue to communicate a consistent and authentic positive self-regard for Abdul's lived experiences? How will the practitioner foster the onset of a narrative that helps accommodate trauma, while searching for meaning? Consequently, in order to practice from a trauma informed lens that harnesses both internal and external resources the practitioner must build capacities grounded in resiliency.

In summary, the case of Abdul was presented in hopes of offering ways to view Abdul from a multifaceted perspective—as such, calling upon practitioners to integrate knowledge about sexual orientation, identity formation, and culturally competent services with LGBTQ immigrant refugees. Notwithstanding, contextual influences are complex and diverse and vary from one individual to the next, so each individual has a unique set of needs and circumstances. Consequently, each practitioner must honor this uniqueness and implement a practice approach grounded within a framework that underscores the goodness of fit.

FINAL THOUGHTS

Practice approaches with LGBTQ immigrant refugees present a unique set of challenges and opportunities to redress social injustices for a segment of the population faced with human rights violations. Implementing best practice approaches described following may seem minimal at face value. However, they have the potential of shifting us toward action that challenges the milieu of practice, whereby moving us beyond a strategy that just helps LGBTQ immigrant refugees cope with their circumstances. Thus, one place to begin to change the climate of practice is ESL classes, as they present a unique opportunity to implement inclusive language about LGBTQ people and destigmatize LGBTQ identities. This would have a profound macro-effect, because most resettlement organizations offer ESL classes to help immigrant refugees integrate into their host country. Also, in many cases, this is the first place that immigrant refugees interface with formal services, offering an opportunity to create an affirming culture for LGBTQ immigrant refugees that accept their identity, setting the stage for a welcoming environment. Furthermore, we must advocate for gay affirmative practices to be included in all aspects of training, beginning with the application process to resettlement services. This will help address and prevent systemic heterosexist and homophobic cultures that continue to disenfranchise this population.

Additionally, it is important that practitioners and service providers use a trauma-informed lens that infuses concepts related to post-traumatic growth, ensuring a perspective that moves toward empowerment practices, founded in resiliency. Furthermore, in order to practice from a culturally competent perspective, practitioners must actively seek knowledge about local, international, and global same-sex affirming resources, thus connecting LGBTQ immigrant refugees to social networks that understand the unique challenges they face. As such, because of the stigma and fear faced by many LGBTQ immigrant refugees, it would be prudent for practitioners to infuse a gay affirmative stance that (minimally) include the following:

- Do not assume that the client is heterosexual.

- Assess the practice milieu to make sure that it is an inclusive space that welcomes diverse sexual orientations, gender identities, and expressions.

- Avoid gender specific language and heterosexist language in the practice setting.

- Reflect on one's heterosexual privilege and how this is communicated and perceived by others.

- Challenge heterosexist and homophobic practices (i.e., work climate, assessment tools, practice frameworks, theoretical underpinnings, just to name a few).

- Keep abreast of practice approaches, theory, and literature that address LGBTQ populations.

Furthermore, additional research must address intersex individuals, transgender people, and women, as scant information is available about these groups. Lastly, organizations working with immigrant refugee populations must make a concerted effort to raise awareness about the criminalization of LGBTQ immigrant refugees in order to advocate for this growing population, so they do not remain invisible.

SUMMATIVE POINTS

- This chapter highlighted the importance of understanding the complexity of language and diversity in human sexuality and presented Cass's (1979) identity formation as one model by which to understanding the emergence of sexual identity for LGBTQ people.

- There is a framework for working with the growing population of LGBTQ immigrant refugees that infuses an ecological perspective,

paying attention to individual as well as historical factors that have shaped our perspective on LGBTQ people.

- Using the case of Abdul, the chapter provides discussion of theory and practice integration illustrating the application of a gay affirmative practice framework as well as a trauma-informed lens applied in practice.

- There are valuable approaches that inform best practices with LGBTQ immigrant and refugee populations. Most importantly, those approaches need to be grounded in strength-based approaches that emphasize acceptance and resilience.

Websites Resources

Council on Social Work Education—Council on Sexual Orientation and Gender Identity and Expression: http://www.cswe.org/cms/15548.aspx

HumanRightsCampaign:http://www.hrc.org/topics/international?gclid=CM_L24-SjskCFQaTaQodag4OJw

The American Public Health Association: www.http://www.apha.org/

The International Association for Social Work Research: http://www.iaswg.org

The Society for Scientific Study of Sexuality: www.http://www.sexscience.org/

The World Association for Transgender Health: www.htpp://www.wpath.org/

REFERENCES

Akerman, L. K. (1997). Health problems in refugees. *Journal of the American Board of Family Medicine*, *10*(5), 337–348.

American Psychological Association. (2008). Resolution opposing discriminatory legislation and initiatives aimed at lesbian, gay, and bisexual persons. *American Psychologist*, *63*, 428–430.

American Psychological Association. (2009). *Report of the task force on appropriate therapeutic responses to sexual orientation*. Washington, DC: American Psychological Association.

Appleby, G. A., & Anastas, J. W. (1998). *Not just a passing phase*: *Social work with gay, lesbian and bisexual people*. New York, NY: Columbia University Press.

Berry, J. W. (1997). Immigration, acculturation and adaptation. *Applied Psychology*, *46*, 5–68.

Bilodeau, B. L., & Ren, K. A. (2005). A review of LGBT identity development models reveals fluidity, complexity, and contradictions. *New Directions for Student Services*, *111*, 25–39.

Bochenek, M., & Brown, W. A. (2001). *Hatred in the hallways: Violence and discrimination against lesbian, gay, bisexual and transgender students in U.S. schools*. New York: Human Rights Watch.

Burnett, A., & Peel, M. (2001). Asylum seekers and refugees in Britain: Health needs of asylum seekers refugees. *British Medical Journal*, (3), 322, 544–577.

Carlson, E. B., & Dalenberg, D. (2000). A conceptual framework for the impact of traumatic experiences. *Trauma, Violence, & Abuse*, *9*(1), 4–28.

Case, P., Austin, S. B., Hunter, D. J., Manson, J. E., Malspeis, S., Willett, W. C., & Spiegelman, D. (2004). Sexual orientation, health risk factors, and physical functioning in the nurses' health study II. *Journal of Women's Health*, *13*(9), 1033–1047.

Cass, V. (1979). Homosexual identity formation: A theoretical model. *Journal of Homosexuality, 4,* 219–235.

Cassell, H. (2015). *U.N. Security Council hears persecuted lgbts' stories.* Retrieved from htt://ebar.com/news/article.php? sec=news & article=70853

Center for Disease Control. (2015). *HIV basics.* Retrieved from http://www.cdc.gov/hiv/basics/

Chauncey, G., Jr. (1982). From sexual inversion to homosexuality: Medicine and the changing conceptualization of female deviance. *Salmagundi, 58–59,* 114–146.

Chauncey, G., Jr. (1993). The postwar sex crime panic. In W. Graebner (Ed.), *True stories for the American past* (pp. 160–178). New York: McGraw-Hill.

Chavez, K. (2011). Identifying the needs of LGBTQ immigrant and refugees in southern Arizona. *Journal of Homosexuality, 58*(2), 189–218.

Clark, D. (1987). *The new loving someone gay.* Berkeley, CA: Celestial Arts.

Conger, J. J. (1975). Proceedings of the American Psychological Association, incorporated, for the year 1974: Minutes of the annual meeting of the Council of Representatives. *American Psychologist, 30,* 620–651.

Crisp, C. (2002). Beyond homophobia: Development and validation of the Gay Affirmative Practice Scale (GAP). *Dissertation Abstracts International, 64,* 074. (UMI No. 3099441).

Crisp, C. (2005). Homophobia and use of gay affirmative practice in a sample of social workers and psychologists. *Journal of Gay & Lesbian Studies, 18*(1), 51–70.

Crisp, C. (2006). The gay affirmative practice scale (GAP): A new measure for assessing cultural competence with gay and lesbian clients. *Social Work, 51*(2), 115–126.

Crisp, C., & McCave, E. (2007). Gay affirmative practice: A model for social work practice with gay, lesbian and bisexual youth. *Child and Adolescent Social Work Journal, 24*(4), 403–421.

Curan, J. W., & Jaffe, H. W. (2011). *AIDS: The early years and CDC's response.* Retrieved from http://www.cdc.gov/mmwr/preview/mmwrhtml/su600a11.htm.

D'Augelli, A. R. (1994). Identity development and sexual orientation: Toward a model of lesbian, gay, and bisexual development. In E. J. Trickett, R. J. Watts, & D. Birman (Eds.), *Human diversity: Perspectives on people in context.* San Francisco: Jossey-Bass.

Dilley, J. A., Simmons, K. W., Boysun, M. J., Pizacani, B. A., & Stark, M. J. (2010). Demonstrating the importance and feasibility of including sexual orientation in public health surveys: Health disparities in the Pacific Northwest. *American Journal of Public Health, 100*(3), 460–467.

D'Emilio, J. (1983). *Sexual politics, sexual communities.* Chicago: The University of Chicago Press.

D'Emilio, J., & Freedman, E. B. (1988). *Intimate matters: A history of sexuality in America* (2nd ed.). Chicago, IL: The University of Chicago Press.

Fialho, C. (2013). A model immigration detention facility for LGBTI? *Forced Migration Review, 42,* 50–51.

Fried, S. T., & Teixeira, A. (2000). Input memo to the UN Security-General's study on violence against women. International Gay and Lesbian Human Rights Commission. Retrieved from http://www.un.org/womenwatch/daw/vaw/ngocontribute/International%20Gay%20and%20Lesbian%20Human%20Rights%20Commission.pdf.

Gates, G. J. (2011). *How many people are lesbian, gay, bisexual, and transgender?* Los Angeles: The Williams Institute on sexual orientation and gender identity lay and public policy at UCLA School of Law.

Grant, J. M., Mottet, L. A., & Tanis, J. (2011). *Injustice at every turn: A report of the national transgender discrimination survey*. Retrieved from http://www.thetaskforce.org/static_html/downloads/reports/reports/ntds_summary.pdf.

Green, E. R., & Peterson, E. N. (2003–2004). *LGBTI terminology*. Riverside, CA: UCLA Lesbian Gay Bisexual Transgender Resource Center. Retrieved from http://lgbt.ucla.edu/documents/LGBTTerminology.pdf.

Hatzenbuehler, M. L. M., Phil, M. S., McLaughlin, K. A., Keyes, K. A., & Hasin, D. S. (2010). *American Journal of Public Health*, *100*(3).

Henry, H. M. (2012). African refugees in Egypt: Trauma, loss and cultural adjustment. *Death Studies*, *36*, 583–604.

Herek, G. M. (2004). Beyond "homophobia": Thinking about sexual stigma and prejudice in the twenty-first century. *Sexuality Research and Social Policy*, *1*, 6–24.

Herek, G. M. (2007). Confronting sexual stigma and prejudice: Theory and practice. *Journal of Social Issues*, *63*, 905–925.

Herek, G. M., Cogan, J. C., Gillis, J. R., & Glunt, E. K. (1998). Correlates of internalized homophobia in a community sample of lesbians and gay men. *Journal of Gay and Lesbian Medical Association*, *2*, 17–25.

Herek, G. M., Gillis, J. R., & Cogan, J. C. (1999). Psychological sequelae of hate-crime victimization among lesbian, gay, and bisexual adults. *Journal of Consulting and Clinical Psychology*, *67*, 945–951.

Herek, G. M., Gillis, J. R., & Cogan, J. C. (2009). Internalized stigma among sexual minority adults: Insights from a social psychological perspective. *Journal of Counseling Psychology*, *56*, 32–43.

Herek, G. M., Norton, A., Allen, T., & Sims, C. (2010). Demographic, psychological, and social characteristics of self-identified lesbian, gay, and bisexual adults in a US probability sample. *Sexuality Research and Social Policy*, *7*(3), 176–200.

Hock, R. R. (2016). *Human sexuality*. Boston: Pearson.

Hojem, P. (2009). *New issues in refugee research: Fleeing for love: Asylum seekers and sexual orientation in Scandinavia*. United Nations High Commissioner for Refugees, Office for the Baltic and Nordic Count. Retrieved from http://www.unhcr.org/cgibin/texis/vtx/home/opendoc.PDF.pdf?docid=4b18e2fl19&quiery=Lesbian%20and%20gay.

Hollifield, M., Warner, T. D., Jenkins, J., Lian-Sinclair, N., Krakow, B., Eckert, V., Karadaghi, P., & Westermeyer, J. (2006). Assessing war trauma in refugees: Properties of the comprehensive trauma inventory. *Journal of Traumatic Stress-104*, *19*(4), 527–540.

Hunter, S., & Hickerson, J. C. (2003). *Affirmative practice: Understanding and working with lesbian, gay, bisexual and transgender persons.* Washington, DC: NASW Press.

Katz, J. N. (1976). *Gay American history: Lesbians and gay men in the U.S.A.* New York: Thomas Y. Crowell Company.

Kaufman, J., & Johnson, C. (2004). Stigmatized individuals and the process of identity. The Sociological Quarterly, 45(4), 807–833.

King, M., Semlyen, J., Tail, S. S., Killaspy, H., Osborn, D., Popelyuk, D., & Nazareth, I. (2008). A systematic review of mental disorder, suicide, and deliberate self harm in lesbian, gay and bisexual people. *BMC Psychiatry, 8*(70), 1–17.

Lev, A. I. (2004). *Transgender emergence: Theraputic guidelines for working with gender-variant people and their families.* New York: Routledge.

Levin, M. (1998). *Gay macho: The life and death of the homosexual clone.* New York: New York University Press.

Mallon, G. P. (1998). *Foundations of social work practice with lesbian and gay persons.* New York: The Haworth Press.

Mallon, G. P. (2013). *Foundation of social work practice with lesbian and gay persons.* New York: The Haworth Press.

McCarn, S. R., & Fassinger, R. E. (1996). Revisioning sexual minority identity formation: A minority identity formation: A new model of lesbian identity and its implications for counseling and research. *Counseling Psychology, 24,* 508–534.

Meyer, I. H., Dietrich, J., & Schwartz, S. (2008). Lifetime prevalence of mental disorders and suicide attempts in diverse lesbian, gay and bisexual populations. *American Journal of Public Health, 98*(6).

Miller, N. (2006). *Out of the past: Gay and lesbian history from 1869 to the present.* New York: Alyson Books.

Mollica, R. F., Caspi-Yavin, Y., & Bollini, P. (1992). The Harvard trauma questionnaiare: Validating a cross-cultural instrument for measuring torture, trauma, and posttraumatic stress disorder in Indochinese refugees. *The Journal of Nervous and Mental Disease, 180*(2), 111–116.

Morrow, D. F. (2004). Social work practice with gay, lesbian, bisexual, and transgender adolescents. *Families in Society, 85*(1), 91–99.

Mustanski, B. S., Garofalo, R., & Emerson, E. M. (2010). Mental health disorders, psychological distress, and suicidality in a diverse sample of lesbian, gay, bisexual, and transgender youths. *American Journal of Public Health, 100*(12), 2426–2432.

National Academy Press. (1993). *The social impact of AIDS in the United States.* Washington, DC: National Academy Press.

Perry, B., & Szalavitz, M. (2009). *The boy who was raised as a dog and other stories from a child psychiatrist's notebook: What traumatized children can teach us about loss, love and healing.* New York: Basic Books.

Pew Research Center. (2013). *The global divide on homosexuality: Greater acceptance in more secular and affluent countries.* Retrieved from http://www.pewglobal.org/files/2014/05/Pew-Global-Attitudes-Homosexuality-Report-REVISED-MAY-27-204.pdf.

Redfield, R., Linton, R., & Herskowits, M. (1936). Memorandum on the study of acculturation. *American Anthropologist, 38,* 149–152.

Ringel, S., & Brandell, J. (2012). Trauma: Contemporary directions in theory. *Practice and Research,* pp. 1–3.

Rivers, I., & Cowie, H. (2006). Bullying and homophobia in UK schools: A perspective on factors, afflicting resilience and recovery. *Journal of Gay and Lesbian Issues in Education, 5*(2), 115–126.

Rutter, M. (2006). *Genes and behavior.* Oxford, UK: Blackwell.

Saleeby, D. (2006). *The strengths perspective: In social work practice.* Boston: Pearson.

Silove, D., Austin, P., & Steel, Z. (2007). No refuge from terror: The impact of detention on the mental health of trauma-affected refugees seeking asylum in Australia. *Transcultural Psychiatry, 44*(3), 359–393.

Silverstein, D. (1996). History of treatment: The medical treatment of homosexuality. In R. P. Cabaj & T. S. Stein (Eds.), *Textbook of homosexuality and mental health.* American Psychiatric Association.

Tedeschi, R. G., & Calhoun, L. G. (1995). Trauma and transformations: Growing in the aftermath of suffering. Thousand Oaks, CA: Sage.

Tiong, A., Mahomed, S. P., Gardiner, J., Ryan, R., Linton, K. S., Walker, K. A., Scopel, J., & Biggs-Beverly, A. (2006). Health issues in newly arrived African refugees attending general practice clinics in Melbourne. Refugee Health Research, 185(11/12), 602–605.

Tozer, E. E., & McClanahan, M. K. (1999). Treating the purple menace: Ethical considerations of conversion therapy and affirmative alternatives. *Counseling Psychologist, 27*(5), 722–742.

Troiden, R. R. (1988). Homosexual identity development. Journal of Adolescent Health Care, 9, 105–113.

UNHCR. (2013). *War's human cost: UNHCR global trends.* Retrieved from http://www.unhcr.org/5399a14f9.html.

Van Den Bergh, N., & Crisp, C. (2004). Defining cultural practice with sexual minorities: Implications for social work education and practice. *Journal of Social Work Education, 40*(2), 222–238.

van Wormer, K., Wells, J., & Boes, M. (2000). *Social work with lesbians, gays, and bisexuals: A strengths perspective.* Boston, MA: Allyn and Bacon.

Vedat, S., & Ozturk, E. (2006). What is trauma and dissociation? *Journal of Trauma Practice, 4*(1–2), 7–20.

Wackerfuss, A. (2007). Homophobic bullying and same-sex desire in Anglo-American schools: An historical perspective. *Journal of Gay and Lesbian Social Services, 19*(3/4), 139–155.

Walls, N. E., Freedenthal, S. W., & Wisneski, H. (2008). Suicidal ideations and attempts among sexual minority youth receiving social services. *Social Work, 53*(1), 21–29.

Warner, M. (1991). *Fear of a queer planet*. Dike University Press.

Welsh, W. N., Green, J. R., & Jenkins, P. H. (1999). School disorder: The influence of individual, institutional, and community factors. *Criminology, 37*, 73–115.

Westcott, L. (2015). Gay refugees addresses U.N. Security Council in historic meeting on LGBT rights. Retrieved from http://www.Newsweek.com/gay-refugees-addresses-un-security-council-historic-meeting-lgbt-rights-365824.

World Health Organization. (2016). *The global HIV/AIDS epidemic*. Retrieved from http://www.aids .gov/hiv-aids-basic/hiv-aids-101/global-statistics/.

Chapter 16

PRACTICE APPLICATIONS WITH IMMIGRANT AND REFUGEE YOUTH

MOLLY A. BENSON, SAIDA M. ABDI, AND REBECCA E. FORD-PAZ

KEY TERMS

trauma, refugee and immigrant youth, resilience, trauma systems therapy for refugees, school and community-based interventions

---

CHAPTER HIGHLIGHTS

- Refugee and immigrant youth are at high risk for developing psychiatric symptoms because of high rates of traumatic exposure present not only pre-migration but also during their journey to the United States and post-resettlement.

- Treatment interventions for these youth must include a culturally and linguistically appropriate family engagement element to ensure accessibility and acceptability.

- School- and community-based interventions are ideal, because they make mental health services less stigmatizing and more accessible to an otherwise highly marginalized population.

- Trauma systems therapy for refugees (TST-R) is a promising practice for refugee populations that incorporates a cultural broker into a treatment team that offers a stepped-care model (universal prevention intervention as a gateway to individual trauma-focused therapy) and attends to practical barriers to treatment engagement as an integral part of therapeutic intervention.

As global conflicts and lack of economic opportunities drive populations in developing countries to seek safety and prosperity in the West, the United States (U.S.) is faced with how to help new arrivals on its shores, many of whom are vulnerable children. In 2014, there were 19.5 million refugees worldwide, and over 51% of those refugees were under the age of 18 (United Nations High Commissioner for Refugees, 2015 *Global Trends Report*). In 2014 the United States experienced an unaccompanied minor crisis, when over 50,000 youth, many with a history of trauma and without the care and support of parents and other caregivers, crossed the southern U.S. border (Child Trends, 2014; Office of Refugee Resettlement, 2015).

Refugee and immigrant children are in our neighborhoods and in our schools. They are part of our community. In fact, refugee and immigrant children are among the fastest growing populations in the United States. Across the globe, children account for 41% of refugees and displaced persons (United Nations on Global Issues, 2015), and in the United States they account for approximately 34% of refugees resettled since 2011 (Martin & Yankee, 2012). Similarly, between 1994 and 2014, the percentage of immigrant youth living in the United States increased from 18% to 25% (Child Trends Data Bank, 2014). The number of immigrant youth in the United States continues to grow. They are projected to represent 30% of the children in U.S. schools by 2015 (Morse, 2005). In addition, by 2040 it is projected that 50% of the youth in the United States will be children who were either born outside the United States and immigrated or whose parents are immigrants (Filindra, Blanding, & Coll, 2011). This chapter will focus on providing trauma-informed services with a social ecological framework to refugees and immigrants who have experienced violence and/or forced displacement as well as those who experience traumatic events (e.g., community violence) upon resettlement.

CHILDREN AND TRAUMA

Epidemiological studies of the prevalence of exposure to trauma in the general child and adolescent populations have demonstrated that childhood exposure to traumatic events is more common than once thought. According to Franks (2003) "from a psychological perspective, trauma occurs when a child experiences an intense event that threatens or causes harm to his or her emotional and physical well-being" (p. 5). Traumatic events can include direct exposure or the witnessing of harm or the threat of harm to others. Depending on what nation is studied, urban versus rural contexts, age, gender, and types of trauma studied, prevalence rates of exposure to traumatic events in the general child population range from about 20% to more than 80% (Fairbank & Fairbank, 2009). For example, Breslau, Wilcox, Storr, Lucia, and Anthony (2004) found that 82.5% of urban youth in the United States were exposed to at least one traumatic event in their lifetime, with boys (87.2%) reporting a higher rate than girls (78.4%). A sample of Somali refugee youth living in the United States reported exposure to 7.7 traumatic events on average (range of 0-22) throughout their lifetime (Kia-Keating & Ellis, 2007). There are two different types of trauma experienced by youth: discrete one-time events (e.g., car accident, assault) and chronic ongoing traumatic events (e.g., abuse, domestic violence exposure, community violence, prolonged separation from primary caregiver). As opposed to the former, the latter extreme traumatic or repetitive childhood stressors are common, often kept secret, and frequently go undetected by outsiders (Anda et al., 2006).

The impact of trauma on the children and adolescents has medical, educational, and psychiatric implications. Pediatric research demonstrates that during a traumatic event, children's hormonal stress response as well as central nervous system neurotransmitters involved in the "fight or flight" reaction, attention, and behavioral impulse control are affected (Perry & Pollard, 1998). Neural systems respond to prolonged, repetitive activation by altering their neurochemistry, eliminating neural pathways that are underutilized and nonessential in crises (but may be developmentally advantageous or protective) and by often taking longer to return to pre-event baseline state of equilibrium and regulation (Perry & Azad, 1999). Trauma exposure has demonstrated impact on structural brain growth as well as information processing (Ahmed, Spottiswoode, Carey, Stein, & Seedat, 2012; Moradi, Neshat Doost, Taghavi, Yule, & Dalgleish, 1999). Given the impact on brain development, it is no surprise that children's ability to learn in educational settings is influenced by exposure to trauma. Children exposed to violence have been shown to have decreased IQ and reading ability, lower grade point averages, increased absences, decreased high school graduation rates, and increased suspensions (Delaney-Black et al., 2003; Grogger, 1997; Hurt, Malmud, Brodsky, & Giannetta, 2001; Ramírez et al., 2012).

In the immediate aftermath of traumatic events, many may experience a range of symptoms associated with adjustment to trauma exposure, and some will develop longer-term psychological symptoms. Trauma exposure is considered a nonspecific risk factor for various mental conditions, with only about 30% of trauma-exposed children developing symptoms consistent with a diagnosis of post-traumatic stress disorder (PTSD) (Fletcher, 1996; Perry & Azad, 1999; Steinberg & Avenevoli, 2000). For those that do develop PTSD, the diagnostic criteria differs slightly depending on the age of the child, but symptoms cluster into four areas: (1) intrusive re-experiencing symptoms, (2) avoidance of trauma-related stimuli, (3) negative alterations in cognitions and mood, and (4) changes in arousal and reactivity level (with children younger than six only needing one of either the third or fourth criterion). Children manifest their PTSD symptoms in very different ways compared to adults. Children often demonstrate their symptoms through impulsive, distractible, inattentive behavior; dysphoria; emotional numbing; social avoidance; sleep disturbance; aggressive and repetitive play (sometimes reenacting the trauma); and delays or regressions in developmental milestones (Perry & Azad, 1999).

In the transnational context, there is also recognition that Western concepts and definitions of mental health disorders, such as PTSD, may not accurately reflect the true range of psychological, cultural, and community responses to traumatic events (e.g., Summerfield, 1999). Similarly, criticism has been expressed regarding the reliability and validity limitations of PTSD assessment measures for refugee groups (Hollifield et al., 2002), therefore raising concerns about how accurately these tools may reflect the complexity with which individuals in different cultures respond to trauma. Culture can influence the expression of symptoms as well as the meaning assigned to symptoms that may be associated with mental health (Kirmayer & Young, 1998). In many cultures, mental and physical health are inextricably linked, and symptom expression may more likely take the form of somatic symptoms (e.g., headaches, pain) than symptoms widely recognized as signs of depression in many Western cultures, such as sadness or hopelessness. For example, Hinton, Pich, Marques, Nickerson, and Pollack (2010) describe the somatic features of *khyal attacks* experienced by Cambodian refugees. Further critiques of the PTSD diagnostic criteria suggest concern that the "medicalization" of trauma both diminishes the capacity of those who experience it to respond with resilience as well as limits discussion of the psychosocial or social-environmental influences on adjustment (Almedom & Summerfield, 2004).

Childhood adjustment to traumatic stress is influenced by a wide range of factors in a child's social environment, which interacts with their internal experience and capacity to regulate. Factors affecting children's reactions to traumatic stress may include a child's age and coping repertoire, frequency and duration of exposure, proximity to the threat, genetic predisposition, gender, history of prior stress exposure, presence of supportive caregivers, and positive attachment relationships (Perry & Azad, 1999; Pine & Cohen, 2002). Additionally, a dose-response relationship has been found such that children exposed to four or more traumatic events are far more likely to meet criteria for psychiatric disorders than children exposed to fewer events (Copeland, Keeler, Angold, & Costello, 2007). These variables, including both child-focused (e.g., development, temperament) and external factors in the social ecology, such as ongoing exposure to trauma, trauma reminders, secondary stressors, and family adjustment that occur in the proximal and distal aftermath of exposure to trauma, may all interact in the developing child to influence adjustment and expression of symptoms over time (Pynoos, Steinberg, & Piacentini, 1999; Pynoos, Steinberg, & Wraith, 1995). The residual sequelae of childhood trauma can contribute to issues later in life, including a variety of attachment problems, neuropsychiatric problems, eating disorders, depression, suicidal behavior, anxiety, substance abuse, aggression, PTSD, and medical problems (Perry & Azad, 1999).

MIGRATION, TRAUMA, LOSS, DISPLACEMENT, AND RESILIENCE AMONG REFUGEE AND IMMIGRANT CHILDREN

While many children in our communities experience trauma and carry its scars, refugee and immigrant youth are even more likely to have experienced traumatic events than nonimmigrant youth.[1] Refugee children and adolescents are at particular

---

[1] It is important to clarify that refugees are a special subset of the immigrant population (see Chapter 1 of this text for a fuller discussion). According to the United Nations Charter, a refugee is an individual who "owing to a well-founded fear of being persecuted for reasons of race, religion, nationality, membership of a particular social group or political opinion, is outside the country of his nationality, and is unable to or, owing to such fear, is unwilling to avail himself of the protection of that country" (U.N. Charter art. 1, para. 2). An asylee is similar to a refugee in that they also meet these criteria of being in need of protection but they are already in the country in which they seek protection. Since they arrive in the United States through a federally managed program, refugees have access to many benefits, including health insurance, cash assistance, and housing. Asylees also gain access to these programs once they are granted asylum. An immigrant is someone who has left his/her country of origin voluntarily or sometimes involuntarily, but who has not proven to meet criteria (Valtonen, 2008). Some immigrants, such as those who arrive without documents, might be barred from receiving certain government assistance because of their status. Furthermore, even though many immigrants might leave their country of origin due "to a well-founded fear of being persecuted" (U.N. Charter art. 1, para. 2), they might be unable to prove it. Often it is humanitarian disasters, such as the war in Syria, that when whole populations are displaced that elicit granting the refugee status. Therefore, an individual might meet the criteria and yet be forced to flee and enter the United States as an immigrant rather than a refugee. Despite these differences in how forced immigrant and refugee children and their families arrive, many of their experiences and how these experiences impact their mental health are similar.

risk for trauma because of their risk of exposure to violence in their country of origin, during the process of displacement, and while living in refugee camps (Berthold, 2000; Pumariega, Rothe, & Pumariega, 2005; Schweitzer, Brough, Vromans, & Asic-Kobe, 2011). Studies of refugee youth consistently suggest that these children are exposed to a wide range of direct and indirect war-related violent events, such as being shot at or witnessing a shooting, watching a loved one be killed, suffering from a serious injury, and being tortured or being kidnapped (Berthold, 2000; Zarowsky, 2000). Many refugee children were also exposed to abuse, neglect, or community violence in their country of origin (Berthold, 2000; United Nations High Commissioner for Refugees, 2014; Zarowsky, 2000). Further, they report traumatic events directly related to the experience of being a refugee, including but not limited to loss and separation from family, displacement, loss of material possessions, and ongoing acculturation stressors (Berthold, 2000; Lustig et al., 2004). Others may have only known the experience of growing up in refugee camps and the chronic stressors and limited resources associated with that living environment, such as limited food and water supplies, violence in the camps, lack of sanitation, an increased risk for contracting illness, and overcrowded or inadequate housing (Bruijnl, 2009; Habib, Basma, & Yeretzian, 2006; Unite for Sight, 2015).

Some children and adolescents who arrive as immigrants without refugee status, particularly those who experience forced displacement, share many of the same traumatic and chronic stress experiences associated with migration. Minors who are forced to immigrate with their families or those that arrive unaccompanied (particularly those who come without legal documentation) are often fleeing abuse, gang/community violence, or persecution (Berthold, 2000; Berthold & Libal, 2016; Pumariega et al., 2005). Similar to refugee children, unaccompanied children immigrants cite their top reasons for migration as violence in their home country, violence/abuse in the home, and deprivation (UNHCR, 2014). Their process of migration (such as crossing dangerous borders by foot and traveling without a guardian and in the company of violent gangs or human traffickers) and possible detention also puts them at risk for further trauma (Berthold, 2000; Berthold & Libal, 2016; Pumariega et al., 2005). Youth that attempt border crossings to enter the United States, with or without a parent, as well as those legally seeking asylum, risk extreme exposure to the elements, hunger, sexual assault, trafficking, robbery, violence, and injury on their journeys (U.S. Customs and Border Protection, 2014).

Once resettled in the United States, refugee and immigrant youth remain at risk for ongoing exposure to trauma in their social environment. They are at risk for exposure to trauma such as community violence, prevalent in low-income communities, where they often reside (Berthold, 2000; Pumariega et al., 2005). For instance, Berthold (2000) found that adolescent Khmer refugees resettled in the United States reported exposure to community violence such as being threatened with a weapon, being jumped or beaten up, directly or indirectly witnessing someone else murdered, and being shot at, with boys reporting more violence exposure in the United States as compared to pre-migration. In another study of immigrant school children in Los Angeles, 80% of respondents reported witnessing violence, and 49% endorsed being victims of violence in the past year (Beehler, Birman, & Campbell, 2012; Jaycox et al., 2002). In addition, many immigrant youth live in constant fear of their parents being taken by immigration officials and deported (Valdez, Padilla, & Valentine, 2013). Parents' vulnerability to deportation may affect their emotional adjustment, ability to support their family financially, their relationships with their children, and their children's emotional well-being and school performance (Brabeck & Xu, 2010). Immigrant children experience compounded risks for the development of depression, anxiety, and PTSD from successive traumatic deportation-related experiences, including immigration raids and parental detention (Suárez-Orozco et al., 2012; Pérez Foster, 2001).

SOCIAL ECOLOGY FOR REFUGEE AND IMMIGRANT CHILDREN. The social-ecological model (Bronfenbrenner, 1979; see Figure 16.1) provides a helpful framework for understanding the experience of trauma and resettlement for refugee and immigrant children and adolescents. Not only are these children at risk for exposure to trauma, but they experience risk and resilience factors at all levels of their social ecology, including their interactions with family, peers, schools, community, and the greater culture. A range of risk and protective factors have been found to influence the trajectory of adjustment to trauma for refugees and displaced youth resettling in low- to high-income settings (Fazel, Reed, Panter-Brick, & Stein, 2012; Reed, Fazel, Jones, Panter-Brick, & Stein, 2012). Within families, trauma can impact parents' capacity to provide adequate care to their children (Almqvist & Broberg, 1999; McCloskey, Fernández-Esquer, Southwick, & Locke, 1995; Smith, Perrin, Yule, & Rabe-Hesketh, 2001). Refugee and trauma-exposed immigrant parents may struggle to provide the kind of protection and care that their children require at the very moment when the children are most vulnerable, because they are often struggling to cope with their own trauma experiences while adapting to a new culture and language. Refugee and immigrant children and families may also face a range of stressors in their social environment, including financial hardship, difficulty with family members finding employment, changes in social status and family roles, family disruptions and reunification, lack of resources, lack of adequate housing, difficulty accessing health and mental health care, loss of social support, food insecurity, discrimination, and academic/education system challenges (Beiser & Hou, 2001; Ellis, MacDonald, Lincoln, & Cabral, 2008; Sadavoy, Meier, & Ong, 2004; Suárez-Orozco, Yoshikawa, Teranishi, & Suárez-Orozco, 2011; Uba, 1992). In school, many of these children must adjust to class placement by age following a history of limited or disrupted education (Dryden-Peterson, 2011). They are also faced with the challenges associated with acculturating and navigating the complexities of child and adolescent development within the context of a new culture and language (Beiser & Hou, 2001).

Additional stress is often generated by differential acculturation rates between children and parents. This "acculturation gap" between parents and children can occur as youth attend school, socialize with peers, and learn language often faster than their parents or caregivers (Ho, 2010; Roysircar-Sodowsky & Maestas, 2000). This can lead to family conflict, whereby parents and children are no longer able to communicate or share experiences. Family roles can also become less stable as children gain competence in the new environment and parents become dependent on their children to translate and help them navigate the new culture (de las Fuentes & Vasquez, 1999; Ho, 2010;

Figure 16.1 Bronfenbrenner's Socio-Ecological Framework (1979)

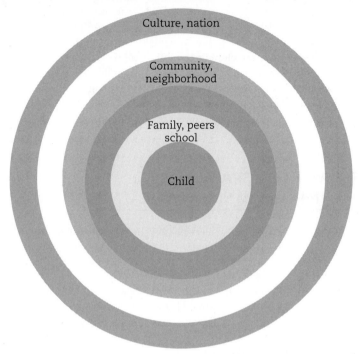

Culture, nation

Community,
neighborhood

Family, peers
school

Child

Source: Adapted from Bronfenbrenner, U. *The Ecology of Human Development: Experiments by Nature and Design.* (Cambridge, MA: Harvard University Press, 1979).

Kao, 1999). For both immigrant and refugee children, parental authority can be further undermined in families in which parents and children were separated for long periods of time and reunified upon resettlement (Mackey, 2013). In addition, research has shown some risk for increased symptoms of anxiety and depression for children reuniting with caregivers in the few years following migration (Suarez-Orozco, Bang, & Kim, 2011).

It is important to note that, despite the high rate of exposure to trauma, many refugee and immigrant youth are resilient and adapt well despite these experiences (American Psychological Association [APA], 2010; Collier, 2015). While trauma-exposed refugee and immigrant children face multiple stressors across multiple levels of their social ecology, we can also find resilience factors in these same levels and promote the capacity of the child's social ecology to sustain and support the child's well-being. Resilience is "defined as the ability to maintain a stable, healthy psychological and physical functioning despite exposure to trauma" (Measham et al., 2014, p. 209). While much research on resilience focuses on individual factors (Jacelon, 1997) there is also evidence that factors such the family (e.g., Rutter, 1985,

1999) and social support (Brooks, 1994; Werner, 1993) contribute to resilience in the face of adverse events. Among refugee children, Berthold (2000) found that greater family support was linked to positive outcomes among refugee youth and perceived social support from peers was linked to lower PTSD and depressive symptoms. In addition, stronger connections to either community of origin or the host community can be protective (Ellis et al., 2015). Kia-Keating and Ellis (2007) found that Somali adolescents who had greater attachment to school and higher sense of school belongingness showed lower levels of depression and higher levels of self-efficacy. Therefore, programs that promote these protective factors at the individual, family, and community level can act as a counterbalance to the negative effects of post-migration hassles and promote better mental health outcomes among refugee and immigrant youth.

REFUGEE AND IMMIGRANT MENTAL HEALTH SYMPTOMS AND SERVICE UTILIZATION

While many child refugees and immigrants demonstrate remarkable resilience, research has shown that they are at risk for a myriad of mental health problems, including PTSD, depression, anxiety disorders, educational challenges, and substance abuse (Beehler et al., 2012; Pumariega et al., 2005). And yet there is much evidence that points to limited utilization of mental health services upon resettlement in Western countries (Canadian Task Force on Mental Health Issues Affecting Immigrants and Refugees, 1988; Chen & Kazanjian, 2005; Cooper-Patrick et al., 1999; Ellis et al., 2010; Gallo, Marino, Ford, & Anthony, 1995; Vega et al., 1999). In general, minority groups in the United States are among the least likely to seek or receive mental health services (McMiller & Weisz, 1996). Furthermore, research shows that immigrant children struggle to access mental health services (United States Department of Health and Human Services, 2001). Among a sample of Somali youth, only 7.7% of those who met the clinical criteria for PTSD were seeking formal mental health services (Ellis et al., 2010). Among immigrants, research has shown a similar lower utilization of mental health services. For example, Latino children, a group who account for much of the growth of the immigrant population in the United States (Filindra et al., 2011; Hernandez et al., 2011), have been identified as having greater unmet mental health needs compared to other groups (Dettlaff & Cardoso, 2010; Hough et al., 2002; Kataoka, Zhang, & Wells, 2002).

BARRIERS TO MENTAL HEALTH CARE ACCESS

Multiple factors have been identified to contribute to the lack of access to mental health services for refugee and immigrant youth. Factors impacting this often include practical barriers—such as lack of transportation or access to health insurance, limited availability of culturally sensitive services and/or multilingual providers or interpreters, lack of trust of Western medical health services, and incongruence between beliefs about physical/mental health and help-seeking (Leong & Lau, 2001; Sadavoy et al., 2004; Wong et al., 2006). Below, we will focus on three key factors to access mental health care for this population.

LINGUISTIC AND CULTURAL ACCESSIBILITY. One of the major obstacles to access to mental health services for refugee and immigrant youth is the lack of linguistically and culturally accessible care (APA, 2010; Ellis, Miller, Baldwin, & Abdi, 2011). Cultural and linguistic accessibility is not just about having interpreters but rather about a having a care system that understands the cultural background of the child and family and that integrates their understanding and experiences into any intervention. In immigrant communities in which social relations and connections are keys to help seeking behaviors, services that do not provide cultural and linguistic support cannot engage children and their families successfully (APA, 2010).

STIGMA. Seeking mental health services can be perceived as stigmatizing and therefore is a significant barrier to seeking care (Leong & Lau, 2001; Uba, 1994 as cited in Wong et al., 2006). Immigrant and refugee families, whose experience with mental health systems is limited and often daunting, may view mental health as a taboo subject (Delgado, Jones, & Rohani, 2005; Ellis et al., 2011; Scuglik, Alarcon, Lapeyre, Williams, & Logan, 2007). Caregivers may also fear breaches of confidentiality and the long-term consequences of labeling a child as "mentally ill." Thus any service that seeks to engage this population must start with an understanding of the impact of stigma and strategies to reduce it.

PRIMACY OF RESETTLEMENT STRESSORS. Some researchers have identified the primacy of resettlement stressors as one of the key barriers to mental health access (APA, 2010; Berry, Kim, Minde, & Mok, 1987; Gil & Vega, 1996; Mena, Padilla, & Maldonado, 1987; Williams & Berry, 1991). Refugee and immigrant families are often engaged in a major struggle to rebuild their lives in a new country and culture. They are seeking jobs and trying to pay housing costs and support their children while also learning new language and adapting to a new culture themselves. As well, many might face discrimination and other stressors associated with being a minority, becoming a minority in a foreign land while also dealing with the loss of position and social connections because of migration. These multiple stressors can take priority over mental health needs—often not perceived by families as urgent or misattributed to more culturally available causes. Any program seeking to engage refugee and immigrant children and their families into care must address these barriers and seek to focus on helping refugee families with issues such as housing, schools, stressors, and intergenerational conflict. By addressing these resettlement stressors, programs can reduce the stress in a child's social environment, therefore impacting their mental health and simultaneously building trust and engagement with refugee families.

STRATEGIES FOR IMPROVING SERVICES FOR REFUGEE AND IMMIGRANT CHILDREN

As discussed above, research shows that a high percentage of refugee children need psychosocial/mental health support, and yet only a minority of those in need utilize mental health services. Therefore, there is a need to adapt mental health services to the needs of refugee children and their caregivers in order to make these services more accessible. Given the broad social ecological impact on mental health, development, and service delivery to children and adolescents, interventions must seek to address both barriers to care and stressors that may be contributing to their overall adjustment (Ellis et al., 2011). This requires services that are not only trauma informed but seek to understand, recognize, and address the broader social ecological context in which these children live (Miller & Rasmussen, 2010; UNHCR, 2013). As such, movement away from a Western medical model that is narrowly focused on psychological symptoms toward a psychosocial approach that attends to other factors in the child's life is crucial to both engagement in services and a child's recovery from exposure to trauma. Services must "address a range of needs, including basic daily living, education, and physical and mental health, across the numerous contexts in which these children function" (APA, 2010, p. 68). Key concepts in addressing these needs include offering accessible services that focus on the child's social environment—beyond office-based individual treatment—to address stressors in their family, school, and community. For example, if a family's key stressor is finding stable and safe housing, a mental health program that addresses this key issue can engage the family by working on what the family identifies as the most pressing need while at the same time building trust and gaining access and opportunity to provide mental health support.

These services must also address practical barriers and stigma. This can be achieved through engaging communities, caregivers, and embedding services in more acceptable environments (e.g., schools, primary care). For example, research by Ellis and colleagues (2010) found that Somali youth were much more likely to see schools as acceptable sources of support as opposed to traditional office or clinic-based mental health services. Children and adolescents are typically dependent on caregivers to seek or consent to treatment; therefore, services must also engage parents and other adults in the community.

In addition, services should be culturally responsive and sensitive to meet the needs of children, adolescents, and their caregivers, from diverse communities. Ideally, services can be offered in a client's native language by someone familiar with the cultural norms, values, and perceptions of mental health. Yet given the immense diversity within refugee and immigrant populations and the contrasting lack of diversity among medical and mental health providers in the United States (American Medical Student Association, 2015; Migration Policy Institute, 2015a, 2015b), this is often not possible or realistic. Programs must therefore make an effort to integrate interpreter and other language services, cross-cultural training, and cultural humility (Chang, Simon, & Dong, 2012) into their service delivery.

One optimal way to increase language and cultural sensitivity is through the use of cultural brokers. Cultural brokering is the "act of bridging, linking, or mediating between groups or persons of different cultural backgrounds for the purpose of reducing conflict or producing change" (Jezewski, 1990, p. vii as cited in National Center for Cultural Competence [NCCC], 2004). Cultural brokering combines two key elements that can enhance access to mental health care: (1) provision of a well-trained linguistic and cultural support (NCCC, 2004) and (2) the gateway model (Stiffman, Pescosolido, & Cabassa, 2004) to connect youth to services. Building on the Network-Episode Model (NEM; Pescosolido & Boyer, 1999), the Gateway Provider model emphasizes the importance of engaging and educating those who have contact and influence over youth who are in need of mental health services. For example, parents, school staff, and community members act as "gateway providers"(Stiffman et al., 2004). The gateway provider can be an effective approach to increase mental health services for refugee and immigrant children (Ellis et al., 2011). Cultural brokers are often trusted members of a refugee or immigrant community who speak both the native language of the population being served and that of the host community. Cultural brokers may be formally trained interpreters or community health workers or community members identified with a skill set suited to this work who can be trained to work in this capacity. Because of their access and knowledge about the community, they act as "gateway providers" themselves. They are also able to engage and educate other gateway providers, such as community members, school personnel, and other providers. Cultural brokers are knowledgeable about their own culture's understanding of illness and help-seeking behavior but also familiar with the health/mental health service system (National Center for Cultural Competence [NCCC], 2004). Acting as a bridge between the community and the service system, cultural brokers can help reduce stigma, overcome cultural and linguistic barriers, and help address both mental health symptoms and social environment stressors. Partnerships with community leaders and community agencies can also increase a program's cultural knowledge and integration into the local community.

EXAMPLE OF A CULTURALLY RESPONSIVE TRAUMA-FOCUSED TREATMENT PROGRAM FOR REFUGEE YOUTH

One model of intervention that seeks to integrate these key elements of care for refugee and immigrant children and adolescents is trauma systems therapy for refugees (Baldwin & Ellis, 2012; Ellis et al., 2011; Ellis et al., 2013). TST-R is an adaptation of trauma systems therapy (TST), which is an evidence-based organizational and clinical model that addresses both a child's social environment and their capacity to self-regulate following a history of trauma (Saxe, Ellis, & Kaplow, 2006). TST was developed to address the needs of traumatized children who experience chronic or repeated trauma and live in social ecologies characterized by ongoing stress and/ or threat (Saxe et al., 2006). This "trauma system," targeted by TST, involves a traumatized child who may be having difficulty regulating their emotional states and a social environment and/or system of care that is not sufficiently able to help the child contain this dysregulation (Saxe et al., 2006). TST is a phase-based trauma-informed approach to intervention that is responsive to the needs, both internal and external, in a child's trauma system.

The adaptation of TST for refugees (TST-R) specifically addresses the needs of refugee and immigrant children and adolescents, including the barriers to seeking traditional mental health care within this population (Ellis et al., 2013). In 2010 and 2012, respectively, the American Psychological Association (APA) published two specialized task force reports on refugee and war-affected youth (APA, 2010) and immigration (Suárez-Orozco et al., 2012). Both recommend that essential components of interventions for these populations include the use of comprehensive, community-based services (e.g., incorporating the social ecological perspective, flexibility, embedding services in schools, forming community partnerships), culturally competent services, and the integration of evidence-based practice with practice-based evidence (APA, 2010; Suárez-Orozco et al., 2012). Consistent with APA's (2010) recommendations, TST-R is a comprehensive, multi-tiered, community- and school-based model (Figure 16.2). Throughout the TST-R intervention model, cultural brokers play an important role in engaging the community, child/family, and providers to facilitate culturally competent care.

The first tier of intervention in TST-R is focused on developing community-based partnerships, engagement of community members, education, and stigma reduction (Ellis et al., 2013). These efforts are typically accomplished with collaborations

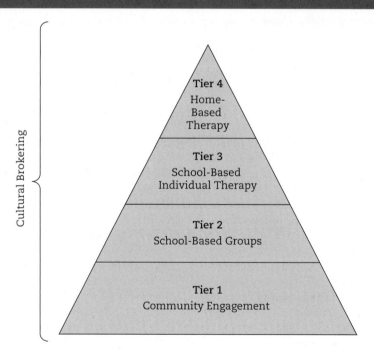

Figure 16.2 Trauma Systems Therapy for Refugees (TST-R) Multi-Tiered Prevention and Intervention Model

Cultural Brokering

Tier 4
Home-Based Therapy

Tier 3
School-Based Individual Therapy

Tier 2
School-Based Groups

Tier 1
Community Engagement

between providers, community leaders, and cultural brokers. Cultural brokers play a key role in raising awareness within refugee resettlement communities and developing partnerships with community stakeholders. This work often involves engaging multigenerational members of the community. The next level of TST-R involves school-based groups that are offered to refugee youth to support their acculturation, adjustment to school, and their development of self-regulation skills (Ellis et al., 2013). The groups are offered to youth with and without identified psychological symptoms and therefore, they serve as prevention, intervention, and as a gateway for identifying and facilitating referrals for students in need of additional mental health support. Cultural brokers co-facilitate groups with clinicians and play an essential role in engaging families to participate in groups, providing cultural information, and brokering during the groups, and in demonstrating cross-cultural communication with the co-facilitator. Clinicians within this model typically have graduate level training in social work or psychology and universally attend to social ecological factors that have an impact on a child's functioning.

The top two tiers of TST-R treatment build upon the community engagement and group-based work. They are based on the TST model (Saxe et al., 2006) of intervention with the incorporation of cultural brokering. Children and adolescents are assessed within their "trauma system"—priority problems are identified that incorporate the intersection of the child's social environmental stressors and their capacity to self-regulate. Interventions, therefore, address directly the stressors in a refugee child's social ecology that may be contributing to their ongoing struggles with adjustment and trauma. At the highest levels of need, home-based services are provided by a cultural broker and clinician working together to address the child's community-, family-, or school-level needs with the goal of stabilizing the child's social environment and/or a caregiver's capacity to support their child (Ellis et al., 2013). This intervention, therefore, directly targets stressors primary to the refugee experience, such as community violence, resettlement stressors/basic needs, family acculturation differences, and educational challenges. Through close collaboration with cultural brokers, clinicians and treatment teams are able to facilitate cross-cultural communication and engagement in culturally competent services. As a child's environment stabilizes or for those already living in more stable environments, intervention consists of individual trauma-focused treatment. However clinicians continue to collaborate with cultural brokers as needed and to identify social environmental stressors and triggers as part of the treatment process.

TST-R was initially developed for Somali refugee youth. In an initial study of 30 Somali middle-school students, Ellis and colleagues (2013) reported 100% engagement in services and a reduction in PTSD, depression, and resource hardships across all tiers of intervention over time. For children with higher PTSD symptoms, decreasing their daily social environmental stressors had significant impact on their symptoms (Ellis et al., 2013). These promising results suggest that TST-R is a model that facilitates engagement, symptom reduction, and alleviation of social environmental hardships among refugee youth. This program has subsequently been disseminated to Somali refugee children and adolescents living in other resettlement communities as well as to Bhutanese refugee children and families as a pilot project. The following case study describes TST-R.

REFLECTIVE QUESTIONS

- How are immigrant and refugee children impacted by trauma?

- Often refugee/immigrant children do not self-identify as such. There also may be fear of deportation if they talk about their migration experience. How would you go about identifying a refugee/immigrant child in your community?

- Why is it important to address barriers to care that are unique to this community?

- Who would serve as a good cultural broker in your community? What resources could be made available to support such a position on a mental health care team?

CASE STUDY

Ali, a 12-year-old refugee male, originally from Somalia, was struggling at school. Ali often appeared sad, was getting into fights with his peers, and was unable to sit still in class or follow directions. His teachers and school counselors were very concerned about him falling behind his peers academically. They wrote multiple letters to Ali's parents, explaining their concerns and suggesting that they sign consent for Ali to receive counseling in school or find alternative mental health care outside school. They never got a response. The school counselor called Ali's home and found that the mother did not speak any English. She was not able to get hold of the father. Ali's symptoms seemed to be getting worse but he was not getting any support. The teachers were frustrated, and Ali was feeling hopeless.

The principal at Ali's school invited school-based clinicians trained in the trauma systems therapy for refugees model/approach to provide services to students in the school because of the concern about a large number of struggling refugee students who were not engaging in services. Ali was one of the first students referred for services. A cultural broker who spoke Somali called the mother and was able to explain to the mother why the school was calling the house. She asked the mother permission to visit the home and was able to conduct a home visit. She spoke to the mother in her native language and not only presented concerns about Ali but framed it in a way that was de-stigmatizing. She discussed her role as a cultural broker and the importance of supporting Ali in his education and in his resettlement process. Stressing her shared understanding of how Somali community deals with issues such as Ali's helped de-stigmatize her involvement and put the parents at ease. Once the mother became receptive to the idea of providing support for Ali in school, the cultural broker asked if Ali could participate in a non-clinical group that was designed to support all refugee youth and not just those experiencing difficulties. The mother consented to group participation and shared her belief that Ali's issues were because of his brother's behavior at home. Ali's older sibling was having violent outbursts, making the whole family afraid but unsure what to do. The family had not taken the older brother to a clinician, because they felt that his behavior was because of "Jinn" (i.e., spirits possessing him), and they have been seeing a traditional healer to rid him of the spirit. The cultural broker supported the family's decision to seek traditional help, while also explaining that when children arrive to the United States, they often have different experiences than their parents did back home and that there are ways in which the U.S. healthcare system might be able to help. She talked about how when people from their culture have back pain in the United States, they still seek traditional medicine but also use pain killers or other medicine prescribed by a physician. She offered to connect the mother and her child to a program that will support them both in school and at home. She told the mother that she worked with a team that can do home visits and work with the whole family. She explained again that helping the children overcome these difficulties was crucial to school success.

Over a period of six months, a home-based therapy team (the cultural broker and a clinician from a partner agency) worked with the family. A clinician from the home visiting team was able to see Ali individually and the cultural broker co-led the groups in school. They helped the older brother connect to services; they provided support around other stressors, such as helping the family find adequate housing, ensuring appropriate school placement, and ensuring the father's job was protected during the times he needed to be out of work to deal with his sons' needs. All of these issues, typically barriers to traditional mental health care, were identified because of the trust built with the family by the cultural broker and addressed by the TST-R team as concerns directly related to their children's mental health and important factors to treatment engagement.

This case illustrates the importance of creating care systems that are suited to the needs and reflect the worldview of refugee and immigrant children and their families. Ali had identified mental health needs that were not being met and which were affecting his school functioning. TST-R was an appropriate program for him because it was **school-based program,** thus allowing for **early identification** of need and provision of services in **non-stigmatizing** space. Also, having nonclinical groups in the school allowed for initial engagement into service without the stigma attached to mental health. The presence of the cultural broker removed **linguistic and cultural** barriers. It also led to a **successful engagement** by reducing stigma, framing services in a culturally and linguistically appropriate manner, and bridging relationships with systems, family, and providers. The **home-based therapy model,** which pairs **cultural brokers and clinicians,** brought services to the whole family. Also, service resembles a culturally familiar support system, because the family received support with not just mental health issues but also other **resettlement stressors,** such as housing and employment. This **holistic** approach to care was key to success, since it created a relationship with the family that went beyond the stigma-laden mental healthcare. Throughout the process, the cultural broker serves as a **bridge,** educating and informing providers and family and creating a shared understanding of the issues that are being addressed and the solutions proposed and helping the family become partners in the process rather than feeling as though a foreign cultural practice is being imposed on them.

SUMMATIVE POINTS

- While many demonstrate remarkable resilience, refugee and immigrant youth are at high risk for developing psychiatric symptoms because of high rates of traumatic exposure present not only pre-migration but also during their journey to the United States and post-resettlement.

- Treatment interventions for these youth must include a culturally and linguistically appropriate family engagement element to ensure accessibility and acceptability. They must address stressors in the social environment that are key to both engagement and reduction of symptoms.

- School- and community-based interventions are ideal, because they make mental health services less stigmatizing and more accessible to an otherwise highly marginalized population.

- Trauma systems therapy for refugees (TST-R) is a promising practice for refugee populations that incorporates a cultural broker into a treatment team that offers a stepped-care model (universal prevention intervention as a gateway to individual trauma-focused therapy) and attends to practical barriers to treatment engagement as an integral part of therapeutic intervention.

REFERENCES

Ahmed, F., Spottiswoode, B. S., Carey, P. D., Stein, D. J., & Seedat, S. (2012). Relationship between neurocognition and regional brain volumes in traumatized adolescents with and without posttraumatic stress disorder. *Neuropsychobiology*, *66*(3), 174–184.

Almedom, A. M., & Summerfield, D. (2004). Mental well-being in settings of "complex emergency": An overview. *Journal of Biosocial Science*, *36*(04), 381–388.

Almqvist, K., & Broberg, A. G. (1999). Mental health and social adjustment in young refugee children 31/2 years after their arrival in Sweden. *Journal of the American Academy of Child & Adolescent Psychiatry*, *38*(6), 723–730.

American Medical Student Association. (2015). *Enriching medicine through diversity*. Retrieved from http://www.amsa.org/about/mission-aspirations/diversity/

American Psychological Association. (2010). *Resilience and recovery after war: Refugee children and families in the United States*. Retrieved from https://www.apa.org/pubs/info/reports/refugees-full-report.pdf

Anda, R. F., Felitti, V. J., Bremner, J. D., Walker, J. D., Whitfield, C. H., Perry, B. D., . . . & Giles, W. H. (2006). The enduring effects of abuse and related adverse experiences in childhood. *European Archives of Psychiatry and Clinical Neuroscience*, *256*(3), 174–186.

Baldwin, H. E., & Ellis, H. B. (2012). Prevention and early intervention programs for special populations. In J. G. Beck & D. M. Sloan (Eds.), *The Oxford handbook of traumatic stress disorders* (pp. 403–412). New York: Oxford University Press.

Beehler, S., Birman, D., & Campbell, R. (2012). The effectiveness of cultural adjustment and trauma services (CATS): Generating practice-based evidence on a comprehensive, school-based mental health intervention for immigrant youth. *American Journal of Community Psychology*, *50*(1–2), 155–168.

Beiser, M., & Hou, F. (2001). Language acquisition, unemployment and depressive disorder among Southeast Asian refugees: A 10-year study. *Social Science & Medicine*, *53*(10), 1321–1334.

Berry, J. W., Kim, U., Minde, T., & Mok, D. (1987). Comparative studies of acculturative stress. *International Migration Review*, *21*, 491–511.

Berthold, S. M. (2000). War traumas and community violence: Psychological, behavioral, and academic outcomes among Khmer refugee adolescents. *Journal of Multicultural Social Work*, *8*(1–2), 15–46.

Berthold, S. M., & Libal, K. (2016). Migrant children's rights to health and rehabilitation: A primer for US social workers. *Journal of Human Rights and Social Work*, *1*, 85–95.

Brabeck, K., & Xu, Q. (2010). The impact of detention and deportation on Latino immigrant children and families: A quantitative exploration. *Hispanic Journal of Behavioral Sciences*, *32*(3), 341–361.

Breslau, N., Wilcox, H. C., Storr, C., Lucia, V. C., & Anthony, J. C. (2004). Trauma exposure and posttraumatic stress disorder: A study of youths in urban America. *Journal of Urban Health*, *81*, 530–544.

Bronfenbrenner, U. (1979). *The ecology of human development: Experiments by nature and design.* Cambridge, MA: Harvard University Press.

Brooks, R. B. (1994). Children at risk: Fostering resilience and hope. *American Journal of Orthopsychiatry*, *64*(4), 545.

Bruijnl, D. (2009). *Living conditions and well-being of refugees.* (Human Development Research Paper 2009/25). United Nations Development Programme Human Development Reports. Available at: http://www.rrojasdatabank.info/HDRP_2009_25.pdf

Canadian Task Force on Mental Health Issues Affecting Immigrants and Refugees. (1988). *After the door has been opened: Mental health issues affecting immigrants and refugees in Canada.* Ottawa: Multiculturalism and Citizenship Canada.

Chang, E. S., Simon, M., & Dong, X. (2012). Integrating cultural humility into health care professional education and training. *Advances in Health Sciences Education*, *17*(2), 269–278.

Chen, A. W., & Kazanjian, A. (2005). Rate of mental health service utilization by Chinese immigrants in British Columbia. *Canadian Journal of Public Health/Revue Canadienne de Sante'e Publique*, pp. 49–51.

Child Trends. (2014). *Understanding the risks to the children crossing the border.* Retrieved from http://www.childtrends.org/understanding-the-risks-to-the-children-crossing-the-border/

Child Trends Data Bank. (2014). *Immigrant children.* Retrieved from http://www.childtrends.org/?indicators=immigrant-children

Collier, L. (2015). Helping immigrant children heal: Psychologists are working to help undocumented immigrant children recover from trauma and deal with the uncertainties of their lives. *Monitor on Psychology*, *46*(3). Retrieved from http://www.apa.org/monitor/2015/03/immigrant-children.aspx

Cooper-Patrick, L., Gallo, J. J., Gonzales, J. J., Vu, H. T., Powe, N. R., Nelson, C., & Ford, D. E. (1999). Race, gender, and partnership in the patient-physician relationship. *Journal of the American Medical Association*, *282*(6), 583–589.

Copeland, W. E., Keeler, G., Angold, A., & Costello, E. J. (2007). Traumatic events and posttraumatic stress in childhood. *Archives of General Psychiatry*, *64*(5), 577–584.

Delaney-Black, V., Covington, C., Ondersma, S. J., Nordstrom-Klee, B., Templin, T., Ager, J., . . . Sokol, R. J. (2003). Violence exposure, trauma and IQ and/or reading deficits among urban children. *Journal of the American Academy of Child and Adolescent Psychiatry*, *42*(1), 48.

de las Fuentes, C., & Vásquez, M. J. T. (1999). Immigrant adolescent girls of color: Facing American challenges. In N. B. Johnson, M. C. Roberts, & J. Worell (Eds.), *Beyond appearance: A new look at adolescent girls* (pp. 131–150). Washington, DC: American Psychological Association.

Delgado, M., Jones, K., & Rohani, M. (2005). *Social work practice with refugee and immigrant youth.* Boston, MA: Pearson.

Dettlaff, A. J., & Cardoso, J. B. (2010). Mental health need and service use among Latino children of immigrants in the child welfare system. *Children and Youth Services Review*, *32*(10), 1373–1379.

Dryden-Peterson, S. (2011). *Refugee education: A global review*. United Nations High Commissioner for Refugees. Retrieved from http://www.unhcr.org/4fe317589.pdf

Ellis, B., Abdi, S., Lazarevic, V., White, M., Lincoln, A., Stern, J., & Horgan, J. (2015). Relation of psychosocial factors to diverse behaviors and attitudes among Somali refugees. *American Journal of Orthopsychiatry*, *86*(4), 393–408.

Ellis, B. H., Lincoln, A. K., Charney, M. E., Ford-Paz, R., Benson, M., & Strunin, L. (2010). Mental health service utilization of Somali adolescents: Religion, community, and school as gateways to healing. *Transcultural Psychiatry*, *47*(5), 789–811.

Ellis, B. H., MacDonald, H. Z., Lincoln, A. K., & Cabral, H. J. (2008). Mental health of Somali adolescent refugees: The role of trauma, stress, and perceived discrimination. *Journal of Consulting and Clinical Psychology*, *76*(2), 184.

Ellis, B. H., Miller, A. B., Abdi, S., Barrett, C., Blood, E. A., & Betancourt, T. S. (2013). Multi-tier mental health program for refugee youth. *Journal of Consulting and Clinical Psychology*, *81*(1), 129–140.

Ellis, B. H., Miller, A. B., Baldwin, H., & Abdi, S. (2011). New directions in refugee youth mental health services: Overcoming barriers to engagement. *Journal of Child & Adolescent Trauma*, *4*(1), 69–85.

Fairbank, J. A., & Fairbank, D. W. (2009). *Current Psychiatry Reports*, *11*(4), 289–295.

Fazel, M., Reed, R. V., Panter-Brick, C., & Stein, A. (2012). Mental health of displaced and refugee children resettled in high-income countries: Risk and protective factors. *The Lancet*, *379*(9812), 266–282.

Filindra, A., Blanding, D., & Coll, C. G. (2011). The power of context: State-level policies and politics and the educational performance of the children of immigrants in the United States. *Harvard Educational Review*, *81*(3), 407–437.

Fletcher, K. E. (1996). Childhood posttraumatic stress disorder. *Child psychopathology*, 242–276.

Franks, R. (2003, Fall). What is child traumatic stress? Claiming children. *Newsletter of the Federation of Families for Children's Mental Health*, pp. 5–6.

Gallo, J. J., Marino, S., Ford, D., & Anthony, J. C. (1995). Filters on the pathway to mental health care, II. Sociodemographic factors. *Psychological Medicine*, *25*(06), 1149–1160.

Gil, A. G., & Vega, W. A. (1996). Two different worlds: Acculturation stress and adaptation among Cuban and Nicaraguan families. *Journal of Social and Personal Relationships*, *13*(3), 435–456.

Grogger, J. (1997). Local violence and educational attainment. *Journal of Human Resources*, *32*, 659–682.

Habib, R. R., Basma, S. H., & Yeretzian, J. S. (2006). Harboring illnesses: On the association between disease and living conditions in a Palestinian refugee camp in Lebanon. *International Journal of Environmental Health Research*, *16*(2), 99–111.

Hernandez, D. J., Denton, N. A., & Blanchard, V. L. (2011). Children in the United States of America: A statistical portrait by race-ethnicity, immigrant origins, and language. *Annals Of The American Academy Of Political And Social Science, 633*(1), 102–127.

Hinton, D. E., Pich, V., Marques, L., Nickerson, A., & Pollack, M. H. (2010). Khyâl attacks: A key idiom of distress among traumatized Cambodia refugees. *Culture, Medicine And Psychiatry, 34*(2), 244–278.

Ho, J. (2010). Acculturation gaps in Vietnamese immigrant families: Impact on family relationships. *International Journal of Intercultural Relations, 34*(1), 22–33.

Hollifield, M., Warner, T. D., Lian, N., Krakow, B., Jenkins, J. H., Kesler, J., . . . Westermeyer, J. (2002). Measuring trauma and health status in refugees: A critical review. *Journal of the American Medical Association, 288*(5), 611–621.

Hough, R. L., Hazen, A. L., Soriano, F. I., Wood, P. A., McCabe, K., & Yeh, M. (2002). Mental health services for Latino adolescents with psychiatric disorders. *Psychiatric Services, 53*, 1556–1562.

Hurt, H., Malmud, E., Brodsky, N. L., & Giannetta, J. (2001). Exposure to violence: Psychological and academic correlates in child witnesses. *Archives of pediatrics & adolescent medicine, 155*(12), 1351–1356.

Jacelon, C. (1997). The trait and process of resilience. *Journal of Advanced Nursing, 25*(1), 123–129.

Jaycox, L. H., Stein, B. D., Kataoka, S. H., Wong, M., Fink, A., Escudero, P., & Zaragoza, C. (2002). Violence exposure, posttraumatic stress disorder, and depressive symptoms among recent immigrant schoolchildren. *Journal of the American Academy of Adolescent Psychiatry, 41*, 1104–1110.

Kao, G. (1999). Psychological well-being and educational achievement among immigrant youth. In D. J. Hernández (Ed.), *Children of immigrants: Health, adjustment, and public assistance* (pp. 410–477). Washington, DC: National Academy Press.

Kataoka, S. H., Zhang, L., & Wells, K. B. (2002). Unmet need for mental health care among U.S. children: Variation by ethnicity and insurance status. *American Journal of Psychiatry, 159*, 1548–1555.

Kia-Keating, M., & Ellis, B. H. (2007). Belonging and connection to school in resettlement: Young refugees, school belonging, and psychosocial adjustment. *Clinical Child Psychology and Psychiatry, 12*(1), 29–43.

Kirmayer, L. J., & Young, A. (1998). Culture and somatization: Clinical, epidemiological, and ethnographic perspectives. *Psychosomatic Medicine, 60*(4), 420–430.

Leong, F. T., & Lau, A. S. (2001). Barriers to providing effective mental health services to Asian Americans. *Mental Health Services Research, 3*(4), 201–214.

Lustig, S. L., Kia-Keating, M., Knight, W. G., Geltman, P., Ellis, H., Kinzie, J. D., . . . Saxe, G. N. (2004). Review of child and adolescent refugee mental health. *Journal of the American Academy of Child & Adolescent Psychiatry, 43*(1), 24–36.

Mackey, S. (2013). Rebuilding family life: An exploration of female refugees' experiences of family reunification and integration in Ireland. *Critical Social Thinking, 6*, 162–183.

Martin, D. C., & Yankee, J. E. (2012). *Refugees and asylees: 2011* (Annual Flow Report). Department of Homeland Security. Retrieved from http://www.dhs.gov/xlibrary/assets/statistics/publications/ois_rfa_fr_2011.pdf

McCloskey, L. A., Fernández-Esquer, M. E., Southwick, K., & Locke, C. (1995). The psychological effects of political and domestic violence on Central American and Mexican immigrant mothers and children. *Journal of Community Psychology*, *23*(2), 95–115.

McMiller, W. P., & Weisz, J. R. (1996). Help-seeking preceding mental health clinic intake among African-American, Latino, and Caucasian youths. *Journal of the American Academy of Child & Adolescent Psychiatry*, *35*(8), 1086–1094.

Measham, T., Guzder, J., Rousseau, C., Pacione, L., Blais-McPherson, M., & Nadeau, L. (2014). Refugee children and their families: Supporting psychological well-being and positive adaptation following migration. *Current Problems in Pediatric and Adolescent Health Care*, *44*(7), 208–215.

Mena, F. J., Padilla, A. M., & Maldonado, M. (1987). Acculturative stress and specific coping strategies among immigrant and later generation college students. *Hispanic Journal of Behavioral Sciences*, *9*, 207–225.

Migration Policy Institute. (2015a, February 26). *Frequently requested statistics on immigrants and immigration in the United States*. Retrieved from http://www.migrationpolicy.org/article/frequently-requested-statistics-immigrants-and-immigration-united-states

Migration Policy Institute. (2015b, June 26). *Resettling increasingly diverse refugee populations in the United States: Integration challenges and successes*. Retrieved from http://www.migrationpolicy.org/events/resettling-increasingly-diverse-refugee-populations-united-states-integration-challenges-and

Miller, K. E., & Rasmussen, A. (2010). War exposure, daily stressors, and mental health in conflict and post-conflict settings: Bridging the divide between trauma-focused and psychosocial frameworks. *Social Science & Medicine*, *70*(1), 7–16.

Moradi, A. R., Neshat Doost, H. T., Taghavi, M. R., Yule, W., & Dalgleish, T. (1999). Everyday memory deficits in children and adolescents with PTSD: Performance on the Rivermead Behavioural Memory Test. *Journal of Child Psychology and Psychiatry*, *40*(03), 357–361.

Morse, A. (2005). A look at immigrant youth: Prospects and promising practices. In *National Conference of State Legislatures, Children's Policy Initiative*. Retrieved from http://www.ncsl.org/research/immigration/a-look-at-immigrant-youth-prospects-and-promisin.aspx

National Center for Cultural Competence. (2004). *Bridging the cultural divide in health care settings: The essential role of cultural broker programs*. Retrieved from http://culturalbroker.info/Cultural_Broker_EN.pdf

Office of Refugee Resettlement. (2015, September 10). Facts and data. Retrieved from http://www.acf.hhs.gov/programs/orr/about/ucs/facts-and-data

Pérez Foster, R. (2001). When immigration is trauma: Guidelines for the individual and family clinician. *American Journal of Orthopsychiatry*, *71*(2), 153.

Perry, B. D., & Azad, I. (1999). Posttraumatic stress disorders in children and adolescents. *Current Opinion in Pediatrics*, *11*(4), 310–316.

Perry, B. D., & Pollard, R. (1998). Homeostasis, stress, trauma, and adaptation: A neurodevelopmental view of childhood trauma. *Child and Adolescent Psychiatric Clinics of North America, 7*, 33–51.

Pescosolido, B. A., & Boyer, C. A. (1999). How do people come to use mental health services? Current knowledge and changing perspectives. In A. V. Horwitz & T. L. Scheid (Eds.), *A handbook for the study of mental health: Social contexts, theories, and systems* (pp. 392–411). New York: Cambridge University Press.

Pine, D. S., & Cohen, J. A. (2002). Trauma in children and adolescents: Risk and treatment of psychiatric sequelae. *Biological Psychiatry, 51*(7), 519–531.

Pumariega, A. J., Rothe, E., & Pumariega, J. B. (2005). Mental health of immigrants and refugees. *Community Mental Health Journal, 41*, 581–597.

Pynoos, R. S., Steinberg, A. M., & Piacentini, J. C. (1999). A developmental psychopathology model of childhood traumatic stress and intersection with anxiety disorders. *Biological Psychiatry, 46*(11), 1542–1554.

Pynoos, R., Steinberg, A., & Wraith, R. (1995). A developmental model of childhood traumatic stress. In D. Cicchetti & D. Cohen (Eds.), *Developmental psychopathology: Vol. 2. Risk, disorder, and adaptation* (pp. 72–95). New York: Wiley.

Ramírez, M., Wu, Y., Kataoka, S., Wong, M., Yang, J., Peek-Asa, C., & Stein, B. (2012). Youth violence across multiple dimensions: A study of violence, absenteeism, and suspensions among middle school children. *Journal of Pediatrics, 161*(3), 542–546.

Reed, R. V., Fazel, M., Jones, L., Panter-Brick, C., & Stein, A. (2012). Mental health of displaced and refugee children resettled in low-income and middle-income countries: Risk and protective factors. *The Lancet, 379*(9812), 250–265.

Roysircar-Sodowsky, G., & Maestas, M. V. (2000). Acculturation, ethnic identity, and acculturative stress: Evidence and measurement. In D. R. Henry (Ed.), *Handbook of cross-cultural and multicultural personality assessment* (pp. 131–172). Mahwah, NJ: Lawrence Erlbaum Associates.

Rutter, M. (1985). Resilience in the face of adversity. Protective factors and resistance to psychiatric disorder. *The British Journal of Psychiatry, 147*(6), 598–611.

Rutter, M. (1999). Resilience concepts and findings: Implications for family therapy. *Journal of Family Therapy, 21*(2), 119–144.

Sadavoy, J., Meier, R., & Ong, A. Y. M. (2004). Barriers to access to mental health services for ethnic seniors: The Toronto study. *Canadian Journal of Psychiatry, 49*(3), 192–199.

Saxe, G. N., Ellis, H. B., & Kaplow, J. B. (2006). *Collaborative treatment of traumatized children and teens: The trauma systems therapy approach.* New York: The Guilford Press.

Schweitzer, R. D., Brough, M., Vromans, L., & Asic-Kobe, M. (2011). Mental health of newly arrived Burmese refugees in Australia: Contributions of pre-migration and post-migration experience. *Australian and New Zealand Journal of Psychiatry, 45*(4), 299–307.

Scuglik, D. L., Alarcon, R. D., Lapeyre, A. C., III, Williams, M. D., & Logan, K. M. (2007). When the poetry no longer rhymes: Mental health issues among Somali immigrants in the USA. *Transcultural Psychiatry, 44*, 581–595.

Smith, P., Perrin, S., Yule, W., & Rabe-Hesketh, S. (2001). War exposure and maternal reactions in the psychological adjustment of children from Bosnia-Hercegovina. *Journal of Child Psychology and Psychiatry*, *42*(03), 395–404.

Steinberg, L., & Avenevoli, S. (2000). The role of context in the development of psychopathology: A conceptual framework and some speculative propositions. *Child Development*, *71*(1), 66–74.

Stiffman, A. R., Pescosolido, B., & Cabassa, L. J. (2004). Building a model to understand youth service access: The gateway provider model. *Mental Health Services Research*, *6*, 189–198.

Suárez-Orozco, C., Bang, H. J., & Kim, H. Y. (2011). I felt like my heart was staying behind: Psychological implications of family separations & reunifications for immigrant youth. *Journal Of Adolescent Research*, *26*(2), 222–257.

Suárez-Orozco, C., Birman, D., Manuel Casas, J., Nakamura, N., Tummala-Narra, P., Zárate, M., & Vasquez, M. (2012). *Crossroads: The psychology of immigration in the new century.* American Psychological Association. Presidential Task Force on Immigration. Available at http://www.apa.org/topics/ immigration/immigration-report.pdf.

Suárez-Orozco, C., Yoshikawa, H., Teranishi, R., & Suárez-Orozco, M. (2011). Growing up in the shadows: The developmental implications of unauthorized status. *Harvard Educational Review*, *81*(3), 438–472, 619–620.

Summerfield, D. (1999). A critique of seven assumptions behind psychological trauma programmes in war-affected areas. *Social Science & Medicine*, *48*(10), 1449–1462.

Tugade, M. M., & Fredrickson, B. L. (2004). Resilient individuals use positive emotions to bounce back from negative emotional experiences. *Journal of Personality and Social Psychology*, *86*(2), 320.

Uba, L. (1992). Cultural barriers to health care for southeast Asian refugees. *Public Health Reports*, *107*(5), 544–548.

Unite for Sight. (2015). *Module 2: Food, water, sanitation and housing in refugee camps.* Retrieved from http://www.uniteforsight.org/refugee-health/module3

United Nations Global Issues. (2015). Refugees: The numbers. Retrieved from http://www.un.org/en/globalissues/briefingpapers/refugees/

United Nations High Commissioner for Refugees. (2013). *UNHCR's mental health and psychosocial support: For persons of concern.* Retrieved from http://www.unhcr.org/research/evalreports/51bec3359/unhcrs-mental-health-psychosocial-support-persons-concern.html

United Nations High Commissioner for Refugees. (2014). *Children on the run: Unaccompanied children leaving Central America and Mexico and in need for international protection.* Retrieved from http://www.unhcr.org/56fc26d27.html

United Nations High Commission for Refugees. (2015). *Global trends report 2014.* http://www.unhcr.org/en-us/statistics/country/556725e69/unhcr-global-trends-2014.html

United States Department of Health and Human Services. (2001). *Mental health: Culture, race, and ethnicity* (A supplement to mental health: A report of the Surgeon General. US Department of Health and Human Services, Substance Abuse and Mental Health Services Administration, Center for Mental Health Services). Rockville, MD.

U.S. Customs and Border Protection. (2014). *CBP commissioner discusses dangers of crossing U.S. border, awareness, campaign*. Retrieved from http://www.cbp.gov/newsroom/national-media-release/2014-07-02-000000/cbp-commissioner-discusses-dangers-crossing-us

Valdez, C. R., Padilla, G., & Valentine, J. L. (2013). Consequences of Arizona's immigration policy on social capital among Mexican mothers with unauthorized immigration status. *Hispanic Journal of Behavioral Sciences, 35*(3). doi: 10.1177/0739986313488312.

Valtonen, K. (2008). *Social work and migration: Immigrant and refugee settlement and integration*. Farnham, England: Ashgate Publishing.

Vega, W. A., Kolody, B., Aguilar-Gaxiola, S., & Catalano, R. (1999). Gaps in service utilization by Mexican Americans with mental health problems. *American Journal of Psychiatry, 156*, 928–934.

Werner, E. E. (1993). Risk, resilience, and recovery: Perspectives from the Kauai Longitudinal Study. *Development and Psychopathology, 5*(04), 503–515.

Williams, C. L., & Berry, J. W. (1991). Primary prevention of acculturative stress among refugees: Application of psychological theory and practice. *American Psychologist, 46*(6), 632–641.

Wong, E. C., Marshall, G. N., Schell, T. L., Elliott, M. N., Hambarsoomians, K., Chun, C. A., & Berthold, S. M. (2006). Barriers to mental health care utilization for US Cambodian refugees. *Journal of Consulting and Clinical Psychology, 74*(6), 1116–1120.

Zarowsky, C. (2000). Trauma stories: Violence, emotion and politics in Somali Ethiopia. *Transcultural Psychiatry, 37*(3), 383–402.

CONSOLIDATION

> **"The land flourished because it was fed from so many sources—because it was nourished by so many cultures and traditions and peoples."**
>
> **~ Lyndon B. Johnson**

Learning Objectives

Summarize the strengths and challenges of using an integrative model in direct practice with non-Western populations.

Cultivate critical thinking and awareness in order to enhance cultural humility and competence when working with immigrant populations.

Discuss ethical practice with transnational populations.

Examine global migration trends and its implications for transnational practice worldwide.

INTRODUCTION

The final component of the book is appropriately titled *Unit V: "Consolidation."* This section discusses the connection between theory, practice, and the future in global social work with transnational populations. The co-editors contribute the first chapter in this section (Chapter 17), discussing the common denominator needed in working with all transnational populations irrespective of setting; specifically, the need to maintain both critical thinking and self-awareness skills in order to be most effective in the field. And the final chapter (Chapter 18) provides a discussion around professional accountability, a discussion of ethical standards, the future of global social work, and the implications for transnational practice and international social justice. Again, the role of culture across all practice modalities and target groups cannot be understated. Culture informs how we understand practice dynamics with individuals, groups, communities, and organizations. Culture informs what theories are applicable and should be used based on need and client qualities—for example, practice with women, youth, or LGBTQ immigrants and refugees. This final section stresses the importance of critical thinking and critical awareness around the unique nature of immigration for each individual and subgroup, recognizing that certain migration experiences are more challenging than others. The spectrum of vulnerable and trauma experience related to individual coping, resilience, and circumstance is broad, yet this book presents strategies to identify relevant needs that can be addressed in a compassionate and culturally respectful manner.

As global migration patterns steadily increase and we encounter more trauma-exposed, ethnically diverse immigrants in our communities, we professionals need effective tools to guide our work. This text does not explicitly discuss the role of policy analysis, advocacy, and research in explicit chapters, but these areas of learning and study are salient. Policy analysis should be informed by the discussions presented in the text, and research evaluating the effectiveness of treatment modalities described will both inform policy and direction toward the most impactful approaches to working with trauma-exposed populations. While this book provides a starting point for our discussion of transnational practice, we hope future editions will integrate content on specific needs and relevant subgroups to transnational practice as well as discussion around policy and research. For now, we present relevant theoretical frameworks, models, case examples (if applicable), and discussions intended to inform and begin preparing the next generation of professionals to meet the diverse needs of transnational populations wherever we encounter them.

Chapter 17

MAINTAINING CRITICAL CONSCIOUSNESS, COLLABORATIVE ACCOMPANIMENT, AND CULTURAL HUMILITY

The Common Denominators of Transnational Practice

AIMEE HILADO AND MARTA LUNDY

KEY TERMS

critical consciousness, cultural humility, collaborative practice, ecological responsiveness, cultural relevance

---

CHAPTER HIGHLIGHTS

- Overview of the book's purpose and the relevance of transnational practice
- Discussion of lessons learned across the various chapters for professionals working with immigrant and refugee populations
- Discussion of key considerations for working with vulnerable, trauma-experienced immigrants and refugees who have mental health needs
- Examination of common denominators for culturally sensitive transnational practice

---

INTRODUCTION

The text examines the nature of transnational practice with immigrant and refugee populations. It elucidates the relevance of migration experiences, culture, and the application of modalities of practice in addressing mental health problems and adjustment to life in a new country. Against the background of the global migration crises occurring across the Middle East, Africa, Central and South America, and Southeast Asia, this book is also a call to prepare providers—broadly, mental health, and community health—to respond to the changing make-up of immigrants and refugees arriving in destination countries on a daily basis. Many of the discussions around health and mental health needs, adjustment factors, and the relevance of migration experiences equally apply across these diverse health care settings. Moreover, our aim is to direct this content to mental health providers who are uniquely positioned to address the adverse effects of oppression, exploitation, stress, and trauma and the resultant cumulative impact on general well-being and the adjustment process for new immigrants and refugees worldwide.

The five units of this book organize what we believe are essential definitions, theories, and conceptual and applied frameworks for collaborating with immigrant and refugee populations in a culturally respectful and sensitive manner. Unit 1 begins by outlining labels used to understand immigrant and refugee populations based on migration status and reason for migration, the context and relevance of migration experiences, and the importance of health and well-being as it relates to acculturation. Unit 2 defines the conceptualization and utility of transnational practice across service settings worldwide and the theoretical orientations that are necessary when adapting and integrating Westerns models of practice with non-Western populations. Unit 3 examines six different intervention modalities—practice with individuals, families, groups, communities, organizations, and local workforces—that employ culturally relevant and sensitive integrative practice approaches with strategies currently in the field. Unit 4 builds on the conceptual frameworks presented in Unit 3, with specific applications to trauma-exposed immigrants and refugees, women, LGBTQ immigrants and refugees, and immigrant/refugee youth. We wrap up the book with this final unit, Unit 5, examining common themes across theory application, modalities, and subgroups when applied to vulnerable, trauma-experienced immigrants and refugees. It is the final unit where we explore all the best practices and considerations necessary to provide the utmost respectful, collaborative, and responsive care to this group. And we discuss the implications for providers worldwide with a call for social justice across all disciplines and service settings.

The migration factors that push or pull individuals, families, and even entire communities to move to new countries will continue to change based on prolonged wars/conflicts, sociopolitical forces, climate change, and individual dreams for a different (and perhaps better) future. As such, culturally responsive service providers must be aware of the relevant experiences, belief systems, and opportunities for professional growth that are relevant in becoming effective partners in the service of immigrant and refugee clients. To support the development of the culturally responsive provider, the following sections examine what we know are critical dimensions of effective transnational practice with immigrants and refugees.

RELEVANCE OF PRE-MIGRATION AND POST-MIGRATION EXPERIENCES

The Unit 1 Introduction (Hilado & Lundy), Chapter 2 (Allweiss & Hilado), and Chapter 3 (Hilado & Allweiss) each provide context on current migration trends globally and the experience for immigrants and refugees pre-migration, in transit, and upon entry into their destination country. Forces such as war/regional conflict, economic insecurity and housing instability, climate change, and the pursuit of new opportunities all continue to be catalysts for movement across borders. The nature and causes of movement—forced or survival migration (see introduction)—are equally valuable in shaping how an immigrant or refugee responds to the natural transitions and stresses of the migration journey.

Pre-arrival experiences are meaningful in shaping the outlook of a client during transition from one's home/host[1] country and upon arrival in a new country. Considering one's resilience, temperament, and other inherent qualities, forced or survival migration will be understood and the reactions to the transition will be varied across different cultural communities. Individuals and communities who live in violence-laden areas and who are fleeing for safety could potentially see the migration experience as liberating and opportunities for a better future. These same individuals, however, can equally mourn the loss of country, culture, and norms that comes with their departure. The cumulative process of these experiences can impact a person at different levels (e.g., physical, psychological, social, spiritual, financial), and the outcomes can impact how one functions at present and moving forward.

Upon arrival in a destination country, adjustment to a new culture and new environment depends on many factors, including not only how one is initially greeted but also individual and sociocultural factors such as health, social support systems (relatives, friends, social service agencies), and social capital (language skills, vocational skills, employment contacts, etc.). As discussed by Hilado and Allweiss (Chapter 3), many immigrants and refugees are coming from countries and circumstances that have compromised both physical and mental health; both are necessary for general functioning and adaptation to novel environments. New arrivals will face the demands of learning new systems—for example, education, medical, banking, and employment systems—as successful adjustment requires a level of health stability in order for people to thrive. To illustrate, it is difficult to concentrate in school or on the job if you have a chronic untreated illness or adverse mental health symptoms that keep you from concentrating, sleeping, or being able to make logical decisions in daily life.

These discussions reflect one of the core purposes of this book—that is, to prepare professionals for the realities of supporting transnational immigrant and refugee populations worldwide. Effective transnational practice involves full acknowledgment of the breadth of positive and traumatic experiences that shape a person or family, the depth of individual and collective strength and courage, and the impact of current contextual factors on the individual, family, and community before they even enter their destination country. It also involves applying that knowledge and awareness in a manner that informs the need for specific concrete resources and supports (health, mental health, social-emotional) relevant to each individual and family that must be acquired to stabilize their arrival. In addition, considering the circumstances of

---

[1] Host country applies to those with refugee or undocumented status who are displaced from their country of origin.

the process of either forced or survival migration, human beings require facilitating environments in which to rebuild their lives in order to thrive and become productive participants in their new home country. Informative, welcoming providers can establish an empowering environment by acknowledging the hardships and difficulties, affirming individual and familial strengths and resilience, and by being sensitive to their cultural heritage. In turn, providers offer a pathway for newest members of society to truly thrive, not simply survive, in their new community.

THE ROLE OF CULTURE

The role of culture is a critically relevant dimension of the transnational migration experience for immigrants and refugees and is a component that deeply shapes belief systems and acculturation levels in one's destination country. Culture encompasses beliefs, traditions, values, possessions, knowledge, and attitudes that are distinct from one group to another. It is transmitted, maintained, and evolves through rituals, language, objects, and social institutions, with each passing generation. And there is such rich diversity of cultural belief systems that exist in modern society, reflecting an evolution of thinking and being influenced by the intersection of historical doctrine and rituals with new age context. As it relates to direct practice with immigrants and refugees, culture takes center stage in shaping the degree to which a professional can build a supportive relationship to address needs. For example and as referenced in Hilado (Chapter 7), culture influences the nonverbal and verbal communication strategies that engage immigrant and refugee clients, the buy-in for health and mental health interventions, and even how health problems are understood. Culture shapes family norms and expectations (Lundy, Chapter 8), and it is the bind that ties and shapes a community with tangible and social-emotional support networks for immigrants and refugees in a new country (Goodman et al., Chapter 10).

The idea of developing cultural competence has been a longstanding goal for any professional working with diverse populations (Tervalon & Murray-Garcia, 1998). Training programs have offered singular courses in cultural diversity, exposing students to concentrated race- and/or ethnic-based materials, but more and more scholars and practitioners have cited the possible connotations of this type of training or idea of competence (Hook, Davis, Own, Worthington, & Utsey, 2013). The reality is that culture is an immeasurably complex and ever-changing facet of life, and no one person could ever become entirely proficient in understanding the full nature of culture for all people at all times. Strikingly, the term cultural competence and the training programs to build it feel misguided. No one course or a lifetime of practice could make any person fully competent to address every nuanced behavior, reaction, or belief that may present itself among different groups. While professionals should seek competence in cultural understanding and sensitivity, it should come with a spirit of knowing that attainment of competence requires an ongoing learning process rather than a final endpoint that can be gained with simple studies in a silo and/or through observation. The ideas of culture should undergird all courses in a training program aimed at supporting work with immigrants and refugees, and competence should never be marketed as attained upon completion of a program.

Cultural humility (Chang, Simon, & Dong, 2010; Foster, 2009), to be discussed later in this chapter, has become a more acceptable stance in the discussion of understanding cultural relevance when working with diverse populations. It suggests an approach to practice wherein the professional comes from a place of unknowing and curiosity about culture. There are no preconceived judgments but instead a collaborative process with the client (individual, family, community) as teacher in understanding the meaning of culture in her[2] life and how to integrate that into meaningful work that will bring a person to her full potential. Cultural humility does not mean there is no knowledge or understanding of culture. Instead, it is recognizing that culture manifests and influences in varied ways and learning those unique facets of a person at each encounter. Such a stance can support effective engagement, balancing the power dynamic away from the professional by providing resources to the client and to a collaborative relationship in which both parties benefit; the professional grows while the client's needs are met in a culturally sensitive manner. Ultimately, culture is the lens through which all human beings understand their respective "world"—the client's world, the professional's world—and this reality needs to be integrated into practice.

TRANSNATIONAL PRACTICE: A CULTURALLY RELEVANT APPROACH TO SUPPORTING IMMIGRANT AND REFUGEE CLIENTS

Defined in Chapter 4, transnational practice is an approach to practice that integrates a variety of generalist and clinical approaches that can and have been used to support the diverse needs of ethnically, culturally, religiously, and linguistically diverse individuals and communities. We have used the term transnational rather than international practice, because of the presence of many family units across national boundaries that still constitute an intact and communicative family unit, and the multidirectional nature of connections we have with communities throughout the world. And we see transnational practice as both a conceptual and applied framework that requires a multicultural, multilevel approach to serving immigrants and refugees that is collaborative, holistic, and honors culture and personal experiences. Interventions require advocacy at the systems and community level alongside concrete resources and empowerment at the community and individual level. Furthermore, it is a call to practice that applies to diverse disciplines but is particularly useful for mental health and community health providers working with vulnerable and often trauma-exposed new immigrants.

The units and respective chapters illustrate applications across practice modalities and subgroups within the immigrant and refugee population and in some cases, with examples to further highlight its utility in the field. Irrespective of practice setting (i.e., individuals, families, groups, communities) or unique need (e.g., survivors of torture, LGBTQ populations, or youth), the transnational ideas remain relevant, flexible, and

---

[2] We use the pronoun *her* to represent immigrants and refugees in the singular but fully recognize that the discussions can involve those who identify as men, intersex, or transgender.

applicable to each modality and group. The focus on the client process makes it equally powerful, given client-focused strategies show more promise in increasing engagement and retention in services. But more than that, the focus on the client process in this approach places the variables that shape one's identity and worldview at center stage. It is the client's worldview—not the professional's nor that of mainstream society— that matters most in helping her find her voice and path in a new country. And when professionals put the client at the center of the intervention, the nature of the work will organically account for the client's culture, migration experiences, and adjustment needs, because these factors define the client's current functioning and outlook for the future. As a result, the networks of support that will be mobilized in response should be comprehensive and holistic, because the reality of the client will be better realized within this framework. The Western theories used to conceptualize need and formulate intervention plans will be adapted to honor cultural traditions and present-day circumstances. Simultaneously, the relationship becomes paramount with the client as teacher and the professional as part of an integrated collaborative support system. As client systems struggle to adapt and adjust to the host country or a new environment, with all that entails, both the client system and the professional helping system melds and evolves to become ever more useful to the client. Often discussions around best practices for working with immigrants and refugees emphasize the importance of cultural sensitivity and responsiveness, and we believe our framework achieves this end.

TREATMENT MODALITIES: LESSONS LEARNED

Each of the chapters in Unit 3 provides a conceptual and applied integrative framework for practice that follows the same principles as our transnational practice framework. Across different modalities—individuals, couples and families, groups, communities, organizations, and within international communities—there are lessons to be gained for professionals with goals outlined for client and professional alike. Moreover, the chapters discuss the relevance of cultural context, the impact of trauma and client vulnerability, and the migration experience as it applies to each mode of practice. Lessons for professionals permeate the various chapters and can be categorized within the following themes: cultural relevance and client/professional collaboration, the role of language, critical self-reflection, ecological/contextual responsiveness, and integrative theoretical frameworks.

CULTURAL RELEVANCE. The relevance of culture and the resultant affirming collaboration of the professional with the client system was evident across multiple chapters, and its value cannot be understated when working with newly arrived immigrants, refugees, and asylees. Professionals who take a client-centered approach to practice should directly address culture, ensuring the practice is culturally aligned and culturally sensitive (Goodman et al., Chapter 10) while recognizing that culture informs interpersonal skills and interactions between professional-client and client within the community with active collaboration and accompaniment facilitating this process (Hilado, Chapter 7; Lundy et al., Chapter 9; Lundy, Chapter 8). Furthermore, professionals should seek experiential opportunities to immerse themselves in the culture of those they intend to serve as it will broaden their understanding of a given group and could be an opportunity to truly reflect on the role of the professional in supporting an ethnic community different from one's own (Sokhem et al., Chapter 12). The cultural beliefs of the professional are also a consideration, and awareness of any biases is necessary to ensure that ethical practice ensues.

THE ROLE OF LANGUAGE. Language, both verbal and nonverbal communication, is a vehicle for building partnerships, conveying one's worldview, and a critical element of adjusting to life in a new country. In the area of language, various chapters focused on the importance of education around terms that may have multiple or divergent meanings in the client's country of origin. Authors called for awareness around the use of idioms that may not translate well and attending to body language that may reflect affect and discomfort more readily than words (Hilado & Allweiss, Chapter 3). And the role of the interpreter or cultural broker remains salient in creating a trusting relationship when confidential information is shared but also helps the professional and participant navigate any cultural differences that can keep both parties from understanding one another, when professionals and clients are just beginning to build a partnership and learning about one another. All being said, language is an element of culture that remains relevant in transnational work.

ECOLOGICAL/CONTEXTUAL RESPONSIVENESS. Newly arrived immigrants and refugees arriving in any country are walking into a sociopolitical environment with a long-standing historical context of leadership patterns, social hierarchies, systems of power and oppressions, diverse perception of foreigners, and patterns of discrimination and exclusion. Immigrants and refugees are also stepping into novel environments in which they need to learn the language, culture, expectations, and rules and regulations while building new social support networks. Several chapters discussed the importance of understanding the context of the receiving country and being explicit in providing education to newcomers that will allow them to navigate and thrive (Brettell, Chapter 5; Deepak, Chapter 6). According to Goodman et al. (Chapter 10), communities can be natural vehicles of support and preserve culture, therefore local ecologies do matter when trying to design and deliver culturally sensitive services. Hilado (Chapter 7) further highlighted the relevance of building supports (social, financial, health, etc.) within the community at-large, so that new arrivals feel comfortable and competent in accessing resources in their respective neighborhoods independently in the future. Moreover and according to Sokhem et al. (Chapter 12), the sustainability of any program and the engagement of any audience requires a belief in and commitment from the people, the organizations, and the surrounding community engaged in the process. Thus new immigrant arrivals and professionals seeking to support new arrivals must be knowledgeable of the social environment, the supportive practices, and the adverse stereotypes/belief systems that will directly influence the adjustment of newcomers.

SPECIFIC NEEDS AMONG IMMIGRANT AND REFUGEE COMMUNITIES: LESSONS LEARNED

The text specifically discusses the needs of different subgroups with immigrant, refugee, and asylee populations, including survivors of torture, violence-afflicted women, LGBTQ, and youth in Unit 4. The authors for each chapter provided specific examples, engagement strategies, and perspectives that were particularly useful for working with the respective groups in the field. Collectively, four themes emerged.

AREAS OF FUNCTIONING. Broadly, the negative effects of trauma and exposure to violence led to varying degrees of impairment across the dimensions of physical, cognitive, and emotional functioning. Migration itself has been understood to predispose immigrants and refugees to a degree of physical and psychological vulnerability as a result of the pre-migration stressors that resulted in the move and the acculturative stress that comes during transit and relocation to a host country. The vulnerability that comes with adjustment to a new country can further complicate functioning when compounded with other adverse experiences. Survivors of torture (Smith, Chapter 13) are reconciling what the author termed the 4Ds—disintegration of psyche, dispossession through multiple and recurrent losses, dislocation from home and country, and disempowerment to deal with one's internal and external world. Women who have been trafficked or survived domestic violence equally experience physical and psychological consequences that impair their ability to function (Fong et al., Chapter 14). And for LGBTQ immigrants, refugees, and asylees who were persecuted for their sexual orientation or remained hidden for fear of the repercussions, the process of coming out and identity formation also may present challenges to cognitive and psychological/affective well-being.

IDENTITY DEVELOPMENT. All new immigrants have an opportunity to redefine themselves in a new country. This theme was particularly relevant across the Unit 4 chapters, as each author discussed identity development as a process of redefining oneself in terms that were more strength based and hopeful. Rather than being labeled a victim, the focus was defining oneself as a survivor who was resilient, strategic, and an architect of one's future. For immigrant and refugee youth, one priority was reconciling cultural norms surrounding youth identity from the country of origin with the opportunities and expectations of the destination country's culture. Across the different subgroups, divergent belief systems may cause conflict; thus interventions could be supportive of that process—reconciling personal beliefs and cultures and developing a new sense of self in a new country.

PRACTICE STRATEGIES. The authors consistently called for slower paced interventions that would allow a trusting relationship to be built between client and providers; mental health providers were noted specifically in these chapters. There was also a consistent call for comprehensive culture-centered supports that looked at all needs—adjustment, health, mental health—that impact a person's level of functioning in a new environment and the use of a coordinated network of support that could address tangible as well as social-emotional needs that may be present. From an ecological systems perspective, the physical and social environment matters for implementing culturally responsive interventions with both community-based programs and school-based programs (for youth), as both were cited as salient settings that increase access and acceptability of supportive services. Indeed, they may be seen as less stigmatized and more natural for new immigrants and refugees who typically thrive in community settings in their own countries. Finally, it was suggested that trauma-based approaches could be very useful given the shared narrative among immigrants and refugees who are forced to leave their countries for varying reasons.

ADDITIONAL AREAS OF LEARNING. There are more topics of discussion that are necessary but not included in this text. The unique experiences of asylum seekers, undocumented immigrants and minors, the experiences of men, the impact of family migration on youth, and internally displaced persons also deserve equal consideration. And there is diversity of experiences based on region: for instance, asylum seekers from North Korea versus children trafficked from Pakistan versus internally displaced persons in South Sudan. Future editions of the text will explore these areas, but for now, there are common themes around trauma, cultural relevance, and mental health needs that can equally apply to these respective groups.

Together, these four themes highlighted that the adjustment and healing (if applicable) process is one that is not linear. Multiple and recurrent stressors (pre-migration, migration, and post-migration/resettlement stressors) will remain pertinent to how a new immigrant adapts to change throughout her life. Professionals engaged in transnational practice are thus required to create meaningful relationships that then serve as a vehicle for changing one's narrative from victim and hopeless to survivor and empowered. There is a parallel process in the helping relationship between professional and client as well. The professional develops a critical understanding of the client's needs, and simultaneously, the client grows in understanding of her own needs and the world around her. Irrespective of the country of origin or the circumstances surrounding each migration story, these common lessons can provide insight and guide the practice that should be useful to providers. The hope is that provider and client will be profoundly changed and become advocates for maintaining responsive and culturally relevant resources for new immigrants widely.

THE COMMON DENOMINATORS OF TRANSNATIONAL PRACTICE

The comprehensive discussions around practice considerations and lessons learned provide the backdrop for the main purpose of this chapter and the book. When professionals have a vested interest in providing the most relevant and culturally responsive interventions, what are the common denominators of sound transnational practice? Yes, there is diversity among immigrant and refugee experiences, biological predispositions for health and mental health, and individual and collective resilience.

Yes, we can account for culture, language, and concrete resources for new immigrants. And yes, we can even inform ourselves of the unique circumstances that could directly influence health and adjustment outcomes. Despite the diversity that can be encountered in the field and the knowledge that we can gain through learning and observation, what ties effective practice together? We believe it comes down to three components: *critical consciousness, collaborative accompaniment*, and *cultural humility*.

These components are not new to the discussion of direct practice, but they often are not explicitly included in the discussions of services with immigrant and refugee populations. We highlight these common elements, because they are so critical in the process of reorienting our understanding of transnational practice for populations migrating *now*. We believe critical consciousness, cultural humility, and collaborative accompaniment practice should not simply be a consideration when working with immigrants and refugees. Instead, these elements should be at the center of the therapeutic[3] relationship and remain at the forefront of the professional's identity and approach to practice. This is particularly critical for mental health and community health providers whose work focuses on healing and stabilization that requires mutual trust, consistency, and honest engagement in order to be effective. For those migrating to new countries now, the level of trauma and migration stressors are different and arguably higher than those who immigrated to new countries even two decades prior. We are in a time of the most extensive global migration crisis in history, thus our responses must be adapted to meet a new level of need encountered in the field.

CRITICAL CONSCIOUSNESS. Critical consciousness is a concept that became widely popular with the work of Paulo Freire (1921–1997) and his philosophy of education for critical consciousness. Over the years, his ideas around critical consciousness have been adapted and applied across diverse professions beyond education (Gay & Kirkland, 2003) to include the health fields (Campbell & MacPhail, 2002; Kumagai & Lypson, 2009) and social work (Sakamoto & Pitner, 2005). It is the capacity for deep self-reflection and an in-depth understanding of the world with its perceptions, sociopolitical incongruence, and contradictions. Critical consciousness calls for an awakening of one's way of thinking and a call to take action on the elements that oppress and marginalize segments of society. Thus, we discuss critical consciousness as both an internal and external process—to become self-aware and acquire an understanding of the needs of immigrant and refugee populations and then use that knowledge to take action at varying levels with the individual (micro), the community (meso), and within the larger society (macro) to broadly impact the lives of new immigrants and refugees.

The true effectiveness of transnational practice and its integrative approach to serving immigrants and refugees is best realized when professionals working with these groups prioritize critical consciousness in their practice approach. By doing so, personal biases

---

[3] We recognize that not all providers using this text will be trained to provide clinical or health services; however, we believe that culturally sensitive engagement in all settings—case management settings, public aid offices, other human resource services—can be experienced as therapeutic for new immigrants and refugees when the engagement is respectful to the client's experiences and culture.

will be accounted for and the strengths of a client- and culture-centered practice framework can be realized. It allows professionals to see the reality of the client, not simply the personal circumstances but the larger sociopolitical structures that directly influence her ability to rebuild her life and thrive in a new country. Critical consciousness will allow professionals a vehicle to more deeply connect with clients because of a great understanding of self and other, but it also should galvanize the professional to look at ways of creating systematic change that can impact larger swaths of society. It will allow professionals to critically challenge power dynamics in the provider-user relationship and demonstrate how even within helping relationships, the power differential can be oppressive, thereby mimicking difficult circumstances experienced pre-arrival. All of this knowledge can help forge strong provider-client relationships and support positive outcomes generally. For these reasons, critical consciousness must be a cornerstone of transnational practice and not simply an afterthought when one has time to reflect on a session. It should guide engagement, inform interventions, and direct community and social advocacy movements (and the inter-group dialogue that must happen) that go beyond the individual encounters with immigrant and refugee clients.

Specific strategies in practice include the following:

- Self-reflect (prior and after meeting with a client), examine personal biases, emotions, and thought patterns that were informed by the encounter.

- Learn about a client's culture of origin with available resources (online, print) in tandem with learning from the client's depiction of her culture.

- Investigate larger sociopolitical systems in the client's country of origin and the experiences within that country.

- Investigate sociopolitical forces in the destination country and how they may influence the client's adaptation and acculturation to a new country.

- Empower clients and strengthen the working relationships by acknowledging and affirming the clients' experience and ideas as well as sharing knowledge gained from the investigative process.

- Devise advocacy efforts with the client, her community, organizations, and other partners to combat systemic barriers while adjusting client's narrative to include these activities that facilitate her as an agent of change in her own life.

COLLABORATIVE ACCOMPANIMENT. Applied in the following segment, this component of practice truly establishes the tone of the relationship and the interaction between client and provider systems. Collaboration is a long held principal of social work; social worker/client collaboration are hallmarks of the social work profession and including inter- and intraprofessional collaboration as a practice skill. "What distinguishes collaboration is the enduring quality, i.e., significant to all levels and types of practice, all stages of any helping process, and its requirement for common objectives to facilitate change and common objectives to carry out tasks by sharing resources, power, and authority" (Germain, 1984; Lawson & Anderson, 1996; Specht, 1969, 1975, as cited in Graham & Barter, 1999, p. 7). Accompaniment is a concept derived from the Society of Jesus religious order, as a method of being with others. Accompaniment is a healing partnership that emerges through the mutual recognition of the inherent human dignity between a helping person and those who suffer; it arises when space is given to talk, share, and simply be (O'Neill & Sophn, 1998). "In accompaniment work, we move beyond a mere delivery of services through offering companionship, active listening and solidarity, focusing on individual's personal needs and concerns" (Hampson, Crea, Calvo, & Alvarez, 2014, p. 7). When combined, these two concepts establish a purposeful, empathic, egalitarian, and respectful relationship that becomes a guide for all of the work that is required to secure the necessary resources, explore any difficulties, select methods of problem solving, and work together toward the adjustment and adaptation in a host environment.

Specific strategies in practice include the following:

- Reflect on any power dynamics that may exist in the helping relationship and focus on empowering clients so that their "voice" is heard in the treatment space.

- Use silence as an instrument of reflection and respect the client's experience in session rather than fill the void with suggestions. Silence communicates being present without an agenda.

- Demonstrate active listening skills that validate the client's reality and use strength-based language to summarize their life narrative, acknowledging and accepting the experiences that have shaped her.

CULTURAL HUMILITY. Historically, professionals across diverse disciplines have been trained to work with multicultural populations with curriculum that sought cultural competence as an outcome. In more recent years, we are seeing a paradigm shift in which there is a now a critical distinction between cultural competence and cultural humility, with the latter gaining greater attention and endorsement. It is an interpersonal stance that focuses on the "other" rather than self, characterized by a deep respect of the client, a curiosity and genuine desire to learn about the other person, and an expressed effort to ensure balance in the power dynamics so that the individual or family remains the focus and priority of the working relationship. Cultural humility is also committing to lifelong self-evaluation and critique and a commitment to creating clinical advocacy partnerships in the community to redress the imbalances that impact individuals and underserved populations (Tervalon & Murray-Garcia, 1998). Medical training programs for residents (Cruess, Cruess, & Steinert, 2010; Juarez et al., 2006), healthcare professionals (Chang et al., 2010), mental health programs (Hook et al., 2013), child welfare programs (Ortega & Faller, 2011), and even global approaches and partnerships (Foster, 2009; Miller, 2009) are integrating concepts of cultural humility as best practice for engaging multicultural populations.

An outgrowth of employing a culturally humble approach to transnational practice is collaborative practice. By virtue of what cultural humility means, engaging populations (in the case of our discussions, immigrants and refugees) using a nonpaternalistic position lends itself to building partnerships. The professional needs to deeply learn about the client—her culture, her worldview, her needs—making the client the teacher in this regard. The approach honors the client's culture and experiences while creating a safe space for disclosing needs to someone outside her community and accessing social and tangible resources to move forward. In this role, the provider is simply a vehicle for information sharing, and the client should be affirmed and thereby empowered to make decisions to better her life. Naturally, the professional can provide guidance, but ultimately placing the decision-making power in the hands of the client is more powerful in sustaining outcomes for her. Research looking at the efficacy of cultural humility is promising, suggesting that it is positively associated with developing strong working alliances and self-improvements for the client (Hook et al., 2013).

Specific strategies in practice include the following:

- Begin new encounters with clients without any preconceived ideas about the client and her needs.

- Enter the working alliance as a learner and the client as teacher.

- Allow the client to articulate her worldview and her understanding of needs, and then use that information as the center of your work.

- Empower the client and articulate the collaborative process to ensure power dynamics in the therapeutic relationships do not impede progress.

- Commit to ongoing self-reflection (individually or with another professional) to control for bias and ensure "self"-focused work (versus "other"-focused) to enter the working alliance with the client.

- Create partnerships to advocate for practices that honor the client's culture and worldview, which in turn can strengthen the working alliance and the sustainability of outcomes that embody the client (not professionals) voice.

Taken together, critical consciousness, collaborative accompaniment, and cultural humility are invaluable components of contextual, thoughtful, impactful transnational practice with immigrant and refugee populations. Both concepts encompass many of the lessons suggested throughout this book, emphasizing the importance of placing the client and her culture at the center of any intervention, while controlling for power dynamics that could inhibit her from changing her narrative from victim to empowered survivor of change. Both concepts also focus on the role of the professional as a critical component of her new social support network and advocate who has the capacity to address systemic barriers that may keep new immigrants vulnerable and marginalized broadly. Similar to other discussions, the gains of critical consciousness and cultural humility are not for the client alone. The professional, through the parallel process, should also experience gains by becoming more self-aware of personal and systemic bias that can continue to oppress others. The professional should also feel more empowered to effect change, because she understands the reality of her clients more deeply as a result of being more conscious and humble. Gains for both parties can be realized with active and consistent application of these common denominators in practice.

COLLABORATING AND CONNECTING: BUILDING A TRANSNATIONAL WORKFORCE

The global migration crisis and trends in migration patterns have been documented with increasing numbers worldwide. Health and mental health needs continue to increase for those in prolonged displacement and conflict zones (see Chapter 3). Many of our authors competently articulate the complex stressors that face new immigrants and refugees in their destination countries along with suggestions for supporting interventions at varying levels to meet the unique needs of this target group. Be it mobilizing services for individuals, families, and communities or capacity building in organizations, there is a call to develop a competent transnational workforce that embodies an understanding of culture and the role of critical consciousness and cultural humility in the field.

No one profession could meet the breadth of need presented among vulnerable, trauma-experienced immigrants (documented and undocumented) and refugees worldwide. There is a need for collaboration between health, public health, mental health, education, and other human service fields to capture all the resources necessary to stabilize the lives of new immigrants, develop communities of support, and promote engaged citizens who will be productive and contribute to society in their own way. We have seen and heard of the terror and violence that can be bred when populations are underserved, isolated, discriminated, and ignored. Countries continue to responsibly try to avoid tragedies such as 9/11 in the United States, the bombings in Paris and London, and the growth of extremist groups like ISIL.

Given the collective responsibility we have as human beings to ensure others have a chance for a life of dignity, freedom, and opportunity, the workforce must be varied and broad. All the disciplines mentioned can benefit from multicultural curriculum oriented with cultural humility and collaborative accompaniment along with critical consciousness as integral engagement vehicles. Training programs must also be relevant to the ethnic populations migrating today. Related to this is the call for more research on best practices in working with immigrants and refugees across service settings and using that research to inform policies. Currently, immigration, health, and public benefit policies (particularly those in the United States) do not accurately reflect the circumstances and needs of vulnerable and trauma-exposed immigrants and refugees. As suggested by some authors, newly arrived immigrants may not have the financial resources to adjust well to a new country (see Chapter 2), they may remain uninsured/under-insured (see Chapter 3) and not seek adequate services to stabilize health, and families remain separated because of slow or narrow family reunification policies and lack of funding.

We present micro level and meso-level interventions (Bronfenbrenner), with a focus on mental health, but there are larger macro systems—policy, research, governance, and public health—that are equally relevant to this discussion of transnational practice. Our book provides just one perspective in thinking about culturally responsive transnational practice, and the discussion must continue as populations change and lessons are gained in the field. As the field of transnational practice evolves with the ever-changing migration patterns, the mandate remains that professionals must have access to resources that will prepare them to become competent and compassionate in their engagement of the newest members of our communities worldwide. Our efforts to welcome and to facilitate others to rebuild their lives will contribute to building a better global society and world.

REFLECTIVE QUESTIONS

1. Micro practice: What specific strategies have you employed in your practice that embody critical consciousness, collaborative accompaniment, and/or cultural humility?

2. Macro practice: How can the concepts of critical consciousness and/or cultural humility be applied to macro settings, such as governance and policy development?

SUMMATIVE POINTS

- Critical consciousness and cultural humility are common denominators in all settings of transnational practice.

- Transnational practice embodies a parallel process between professionals and clients, and the quality of this alliance directly influences outcomes for both parties.

- The role of culture cannot be understated in transnational work with immigrants and refugees across settings.

- The concepts presented in this chapter can apply to diverse human service disciplines and service settings that encounter immigrant (documented and undocumented) and refugee clients.

REFERENCES

Campbell, C., & MacPhail, C. (2002). Peer education, gender and the development of critical consciousness: Participatory HIV prevention by South African youth. *Social Science & Medicine, 55*(2), 331–345. doi: 10.1016/S0277-9536(01)00289-1

Chang, E., Simon, M., & Dong, X. (2010). Integrating cultural humility into health care professional education and training. *Advancements in Health Science Education, 19*(2), 269–278. doi: 10.1007/s10459-010-9264-1

Cruess, S. R., Cruess, R. L., & Steinert, Y. (2010). Linking the teaching of professionalism to the social contract: A call for cultural humility. *Medical Teacher, 32*(5), 357–359. doi: 10.3109/01421591003692722

Foster, J. (2009). Cultural humility and the importance of long-term relationships in international partnerships. *Journal of Obstetric, Gynecologic, & Neonatal Nursing, 38*(1), 100–107. doi: 10.1111/j.1552-6909.2008.00313.x

Gay, G., & Kirkland, K. (2003). Developing cultural critical consciousness and self-reflection in preserving teacher education. *Theory into Practice: Special Edition: Teacher Reflection and Race in Cultural Contexts, 42*(3), 181–187. doi: 10.1207/s15430421tip4203_3

Graham, J. R., & Barter, K. (1999, January–February). Collaboration: A social work practice method. *Families in Society.*

Hampson, J., Crea, T. M., Calvo, R., & Alvarez, F. (2014). The value of accompaniment: Faith and responses to displacement. *Forced Migration Review, 48,* 7–8.

Hook, J. N., Davis, D. W., Own, J., Worthington, E. L., & Utsey, S. O. (2013). Cultural humility: Measuring openness to culturally diverse clients. *Journal of Counseling Psychology, 60*(3), 353–366. doi: 10.1037/a0032595

Juarez, J. A., Marvel, K., Brezinski, K. L., Glazner, C., Towbin, M. M., & Lawton, S. (2006). Bridging the gap: A curriculum to teach residents cultural humility. *Residency Education, 38*(2), 97–102.

Kumagai, A., & Lypson, M. (2009). Beyond cultural competence: Critical consciousness, social justice, and multicultural education. *Academic Medicine, 84*(6), 782–787. doi: 10.1097/ACM.0b013e3181a42398

Miller, S. (2009). Cultural humility is the first step to becoming global care providers. *Journal of Obstetric, Gynecologic, & Neonatal Nursing, 38*(1), 92–93. doi: 10.1111/j.1552-6909.2008.00311.x

O'Neill, W. R., S. J., & Sophn, W. C. (1998). Rights of passage: The ethics of immigration and refugee policy. *Theological Studies, 59,* 84–106.

Ortega, R. M., & Faller, K. C. (2011). Training child welfare workers from an intersectional cultural humility perspective: A paradigm shift. *Child Welfare, 90*(5), 27–49.

Sakamoto, I., & Pitner, R. O. (2005). Use of critical consciousness in anti-oppressive social work practice: Disentangling power dynamics at personal and structural levels. British Journal of Social Work, 35(4), 435–452. doi: 10.1093/bjsw/bch190

Tervalon, M., & Murray-Garcia, J. (1998). Cultural humility versus cultural competence: A critical distinction in defining physician training outcomes in multicultural education. *Journal of Health Care for the Poor and Underserved, 9*(2), 117–125. doi: 10.1353/hpu.2010.0233

Chapter 18

SOCIAL JUSTICE AND IMPLICATIONS FOR THE FIELD

COLLEEN LUNDY AND KATHERINE VAN WORMER

KEY TERMS

humanitarian crisis, migration crisis, social justice, human rights, trauma informed, settlement houses, Jane Addams

---

> The inhumanity shown to people escaping war and poverty is a direct result of political failures in many global, regional, and national political bodies, which lack the will to do what is needed. This lack of will is an abdication of responsibility and the main obstacle to alleviating the trauma of the people trying to find safety and security. These political bodies have proven they can, when they have the will, find large sums of money to bail out banks and other financial institutions—but they seem reluctant to help people in need.
>
> ~ IFSW Statement on the Refugee Crisis,
> September 5, 2015

Given the current migration and humanitarian crisis, attention to the role of social workers in immigrant and refugee settlement is most timely and needed. This chapter summarizes the current migration crisis, situates social work as a global profession, draws on social work's international presence and human rights, and focuses on the initiatives, both historical and current, of the social work profession in Canada and the United States. Central to the discussion is social work's long commitment to social justice, human rights, and peace, and the importance of understanding the social, political, and environmental context that is impacting on so many lives.

THE CURRENT MIGRATION CRISIS

Wars, armed conflict, and persecution in Iraq, Syria, and North Africa and parts of sub-Saharan Africa have resulted in the mass movement of people (UNHCR, 2014). There are now a record 65.3 million displaced people worldwide; of these, 21.3 million are refugees. There are currently 10 million stateless people who are denied their basic human rights. This humanitarian crisis will become more acute, since 34,000 people flee persecution and conflict every day (UNHCR, 2015).

We are now witnessing an unprecedented exodus of people as they make their way by land or across the Mediterranean to Europe, frequently finding closed borders or perishing in the sea. Of these 51% are children under 18 years of age; many are separated from families and traveling alone (UNHRC, 2016). The September 2, 2015, photo of the lifeless toddler, Alan Kurdi, found on a Turkish beach as his family risked a sea crossing, captured the attention of the dire situation facing so many. At least 3,800 adults and children have died in the Mediterranean Sea so far in 2016 as they tried to reach Europe (Ottawa Citizen, 2016).

What receives little attention is the impact of climate change (which 97% of scientists agree is human-made, NASA, 2016) on the current migration crisis. Scientists report that a severe drought and warming climate caused farmers to abandon their farms and flee to the cities, thereby contributing to instability and the start of the Syrian war (Kelley et al., 2015). The situation was compounded when the United Nations World Food Programme (WFP) faced a severe lack of funding and was forced to implement deep cuts to food assistance for vulnerable Syrian refugees in Jordan and Lebanon.

Children are among the most vulnerable during these crises. As reported by the United Children's Fund (UNICEF, 2014) concerning the refugees from the civil war in Syria:

1. After years of a brutal civil war, it [Syria] is now the largest producer of refugees: more than four million people have fled the country, according to United Nations estimates, about half of them children. Witnesses have reported children and infants killed by snipers, victims of summary executions or torture. Based on global averages relating to armed conflict, tens of thousands of Syrian children could now be living with life-altering injuries due to the conflict. Doctors on Syria's frontlines have reported treating significant numbers of amputations, spinal cord injuries, whole-body burns from incendiary weapons, as well as internal injuries from blasts and bullets, which will result in permanent disabilities. (p. 4)

2. There are currently 1,300 unaccompanied children in a temporary camp close to Vienna (Truell, 2015). In the United States, as we discuss later in this chapter, thousands of children have fled from street gangs, extortion, and sexual assault in El Salvador and later mistreatment at the hands of smugglers. Having survived this harrowing journey across Mexico, they have run into bureaucratic hold-ups as they

wait to join their relatives who are already settled (Shear, 2015). Terror that such children have experienced can only be imagined.

3. The current humanitarian crisis and dramatic increase in the displacement of people can be attributed to the neoliberal and imperialist practices that results in war, state repression, natural disasters, and environmental changes (Vickers, 2015). As the social work profession engages in humanitarian intervention, Tom Vickers reminds us that "It is this highly political and contested field that social workers intervene, often driven by a mission of human rights and a commitment to listen to local voices and needs but nevertheless embedded in the huge inequalities of wealth and power, within and between countries, which arise from imperialist capitalism" (Vickers, 2015, p. 4).

SOCIAL WORK'S RICH HISTORY

Social work historically has been at the forefront of providing settlement services to refugees and immigrants and a profession committed to peace, social justice, and human rights. In the early 1900s, in both Canada and the United States, socially minded individuals responded to the conditions of poverty through either the charity organization movement or the settlement movement. Many of those they served were immigrants and refugees. The settlement workers were socially minded and established settlement houses in the inner cities and often lived alongside of the destitute and provided needed services to those they considered "neighbours in need" (Lundblad, 1995).

Jane Addams (1860–1935), a renowned leader of the settlement movement, was deeply committed to social justice and peace. In 1889, she established Hull House in Chicago, a settlement house that covered two city blocks and included twenty-six apartments and twenty-seven rooms (Trolander, 1975). Hull House was located in a neighborhood of "an extraordinary mix of immigrants—Italian, Greek, Irish, Russian Jews, Germans, and others," and the settlement house activities focused on "improving the quality of life for immigrants by offering them art, drama, and music as well as public baths, baby care, job training, and classes in English and citizenship" (Elshtain, 2002, p. xxiv). Among those who visited Hull House for inspiration and strategies for responding to the poor were Canadian child welfare advocate J. J. Kelso, William Lyon Mackenzie King—future prime minister of Canada (Jennissen & Lundy, 2011)—and Sidney and Beatrice Webb, leaders of British Fabian socialism (Elshtain, 2002, p. xxvii). Hundreds of settlement houses in both Canada and the United States responded to the influx of European immigrants and provided essential services for successful integration into the country.

Jane Addams was also a peace activist and founded the Women's International League for Peace and Freedom. Addams' active opposition to the First World War was considered subversive, and she was harshly criticized in the media and placed under surveillance by the Department of Justice (Klosterman & Stratton, 2006). In

1931, her efforts to build peace were duly recognized when she was the first woman to be awarded the Nobel Peace Prize. As today, historically newcomers encountered discrimination based on their country of origin, and quotas were established to restrict entry of people from selected countries, such as the U.S 1921 Quota Act (Leighninger, 2007).

SOCIAL WORK IS A GLOBAL, HUMAN RIGHTS PROFESSION

Community social work practice evolved from the settlement movement, and currently social workers offer settlement services in community centers and specific settlement agencies. In response to the current refugee crisis, social workers are at the forefront of responding to the tragic migration and providing services to thousands of refugees—both adults and children—seeking shelter, safety, and food. Social work is considered to be "a singular vehicle for carrying out critical human service interventions for the well-being and welfare of this client constituency of 'newcomers' or 'newer citizens'" (Valtonen, 2008, p. 15). At the same time, social workers are aware of the impact of neoliberalism, economic globalization, war, and poverty and how these conditions undermine human rights.

The International Federation of Social Workers (IFSW) position is to advocate "through its UN accreditation, for global governance to bring an end to the conflicts that drive the crisis and for better coordination to support for the refugees access to host countries" (IFSW, October 26, 2015). IFSW also facilitates the gathering of social workers in affected countries (IFSW, October 26, 2015). Social work is the only profession with formal connections to the United Nations. The IFSW, a world-wide organization established in 1928, has 116 country members and advocates for social justice, human rights, and social development. The profession is unique in that IFSW has been granted Special Consultative Status by the Economic and Social Council (ECOSOC) of the United Nations and the United Nations Children's Fund (UNICEF). Also IFSW works with the World Health Organization (WHO), the Office of the United Nations High Commissioner for Refugees (UNHCR), and the Office of the United Nations High Commissioner for Human Rights (OHCHR) (Lundy, 2011).

The global definition of the social work profession states that "Principles of social justice, human rights, collective responsibility and respect for diversities are central to social work" (IFSW, 2014). Social work is the only helping profession with human rights embedded in the code of ethics (in Canada), and in the United States, although not mentioned directly in the code of ethics, human rights are acknowledged by the National Association of Social Workers (NASW) (2015b), which includes a chapter, "International Policy on Human Rights" in the NASW book on policy statements. Regarding immigrants and refugees, the NASW (2015a) policy statement supports policies that "ensure fair treatment and due process in accordance with international human rights for all asylum seekers" (p. 179). In addition, the statement supports policies that "provide resettlement programs to include trauma and mental health counseling" (p. 180).

IFSW is using its United Nations connection to advocate for a global response to end the conflict that is creating the current migration crisis. Social workers across Europe are on the frontlines, providing needed assistance to arriving refugees. For example, Austrian social workers are set up in Vienna's main railway station with tables of food, clothing, and hygiene products. As they meet packed trains, they are also prepared to provide vital information, such as where to wash, sleep, and register lost family members (Truell, 2015). Their committed and coordinated actions have set an example for politicians to follow.

HUMAN NEEDS AND HUMAN RIGHTS

Refugee protection is viewed as a human rights concern since "the violation of human rights occurring and perpetrated during periods of repression, internal conflicts and wars give rise to forced migration and refugee situations" (Valtonen, 2008, p. 23). Often those who come to social workers for help are experiencing difficulties related to their basic human needs. However, we argue that attention to human needs without attention to human rights is inadequate—both are closely interconnected. Both Stanley Witkin (1998) and Davis Gil (1999) refer to the 1948 UNDHR, which includes social, political, and economic rights. We argue that a discussion of human rights places human needs within a political framework.

Ecological and structural approaches acknowledge that the problems facing people are rooted in broad economic, social, and political conditions. Similarly, individual behavior is in part shaped and affected by these conditions. It is important for social workers to understand this context that shapes both the lives of individuals and frames social work practice. The IFSW (2000) identifies five contexts of social work practice in the publication *Human Rights and Social Work*:

> *Geographical.* Practice is located within a set of boundaries such as agency, nation-state, and region; *Political.* Every country has a political system that sets the context for practice; *Socio-economic.* Basic human aspirations are adequate work, health, education and access to social security and social services. The social cohesion of any group or nation depends to a large extent on the equitable sharing of resources; *Cultural.* The beliefs, practices, and culture of individuals, families, groups, communities and nations ought to be respected (as long as the rights of another are not violated); *Spiritual.* Central to social work practice is attention to values, philosophies, and ideals of those who social workers attempt to help and at the same time to social workers own values.

Immigration and refugee policies structurally impact the opportunities of those entering the country. Those entering illegally have a precarious status and often are denied social services and health care and thereby, their basic human rights (Madore, 2010). They are often employed as undocumented workers and face exploitation and fear of deportation.

A STRUCTURAL FRAMEWORK FOR SETTLEMENT PRACTICE

The goal of settlement practice if successful is to foster the conditions "in which the settling persons can participate fully in the economic, social, cultural and political life of a society" (Valtonen, 2008, p. 62). There is a direct connection between a person's economic and social position in society and their emotional and physical health. Political uncertainty, poverty, and gender and racial discrimination all create stress and contribute to ill health. The challenge for social workers is to be aware of the ever changing context facing people in need and how their issues and problems are rooted in broad social, political, and economic conditions (Lundy, 2011). Using an ecosystems/structural framework, we place a special emphasis on the importance of a societal context and structural factors that provides a sense of safety for children and their families when dealing with trauma and loss. Ecological approaches bring our attention to how cultural and psychological experiences shape human behavior. Refugees and immigrants arrive with unique factors, characteristics, and hardships.

Mary Nash (2005) believes that social workers involved in settlements benefit from a grounding in community practice and cultural competence. Effective social workers will have a critical analysis of the social structures and the political pressures, international as well as local, which lead to both voluntary and forced migration and eventual settlement. This, together with knowledge of human rights and social justice issues, provides a foundation on which to build the necessary community work skills for appropriate intervention in a complex field (p. 140).

It is also important that social workers "familiarize themselves with the structural nature of the struggles associated with the immigration and refugee determination process as well as the indirect consequences that accompany transnational migration, including family breakdown, separation trauma, depression, integration difficulties, social isolation, psychological ramifications and financial struggle" (Madore, 2010, p. 49).

Currently, in the wake of the Syrian conflict and terrorist attacks, Muslim citizens and newcomers to Canada and the United States are facing Islamophobia and racist attitudes. Clearly, "political Islam" and the brutal actions of Daesh[1] do not represent the majority of Muslims. Muslims, according to David Hodge, are among the most misunderstood populations in the United States (and we might add Canada), and he

---

[1]Daesh is the preferred term to replace reference to the Islamic State since the extremists do not represent Muslims nor are they a sovereign state. When spoken it sounds like an Arabic word meaning "one who sows discord."

provides social workers a summary of the beliefs, practices, and values of those practicing Islam and the diversity within the religion. Community is a fundamental value of Islam, and Hodge points out that "Muslims tend to emphasize benevolence, care for others, cooperation between individuals, empathy, equality and justice between people, the importance of social support and positive human relatedness" (Hodge, 2005, p. 165).

Unique to this chapter is the tailoring of trauma-informed theory for work with refugee populations, with a sensitivity to the suffering they have so recently endured. Situated within a structural approach, addressing trauma takes into consideration the historical, cultural, and environmental factors in the lives of refugees. For mental health professionals, including social workers, a familiarity with the source of behavior that may seem pathological or irrational but that may stem from traits that aided the survival of refugees from war and persecution is essential. Refugee workers and their social service organizations can play a crucial role in helping reduce the stress of the new arrivals and fostering their healing and resilience. This is the essence of trauma-informed care, an approach with a special meaning to social workers involved in international practice.

WAR REFUGEES: TRAUMA RELATED TO TERROR AND PERSECUTION

People entering the United States, Canada, or other countries who are recognized as refugees have suffered three traumas: persecution in the country of origin, the dangers of the migration journey to escape, and challenges in the host country because of discriminatory treatment and cultural clash (Michultka, 2009). Ideally, refugees will be admitted to a country that will provide the care that these war survivors will need. The challenge to social workers and others in the context of such trauma is to help provide humanizing conditions to ensure a sense of safety for these children and their families. The acknowledgment of trauma affecting all refugees from war is an important first step in meeting the psychological needs of refugee populations. Fortunately, the United Nations Center for Human Rights (UNCHR) recognizes the impact of trauma; this realization is reflected in the humanitarian relief programming (Cox & Pawar, 2013). UNICEF workers, similarly, understand that behavior that might seem abnormal is a normal response to an abnormal and brutalizing situation.

In the refugee camps, workers understand that families' coping mechanisms may have broken down, that family violence can be a common result of the constant tension and powerlessness that many refugees experience (UNICEF, 2014). A survey of children in one refugee camp found that a third of all children displayed aggressive behavior and self-harm. A large majority of the girls admitted to having difficulty with their emotions compared to just under half of the boys. The lucky few get to resettle in a country where they and their families can receive services geared toward their assimilation into the culture, where they can become citizens. The following narrative is provided by a young woman who became a student of social work at the University of Northern Iowa (correspondence with van Wormer, May 4, 2012; the narrator wished to be anonymous).

I was born in Sudan, but was raised in Ethiopia. It was difficult to live in such a harsh environment in Ethiopia. The reason my family and I lived in an Ethiopian refugee camp was the civil war that was going on in Sudan and still going on right now. As we settled in refugee camp, people were moving from place to a place because there were also other tribal members who were attacking us from where we stayed. It made it too hard to get around everything including going to school, looking for food, water, clothing and so on. People were dying from starvation including children, sickness, and shortage of food. Basically everything was so far away from where we lived. In order to get food whether you bought it or went hunting, it was always dangerous. Either there were animals chasing people and killing them or other tribal members would stop you under the bushes and do whatever they pleased. If you are a woman, they rape you or kidnap you, and if you are man or a young man they kill you. People were not allowed to leave the camp or get out of the village.

During the 10 years I lived in Ethiopia, these were the major difficulties that I faced, including taking care of my brother and sister, dealing with sickness and shortage of food. As a ten-year-old who started taking on the role of woman, it wasn't just hard, but sad at the same time. Watching my parents go their separate ways to look for food was killing me so I had to do something. I found it very hard as a ten-year-old looking after my seven-year-old brother and my three-year-old sister when I had no idea what I was doing. While my parents were gone, I learned how to be a caretaker for them. Sometimes when either my brother or sister got sick it frustrated me because I was not able to do anything about it and there was no doctor in the village that could help. Walking to the hospital three hours from where we lived was frightening to me because sometime couldn't get help right away or for the whole day.

Shortage of food was another major problem I faced while I was in Ethiopia. This was the main reason why my parents were not home with us all the time because they had to find a way to take care of their children. When dealing with this kind of situation, I learned how to extend food for at least one day because whatever food my mom or dad brought with them it did not last for long and we had to keep some for the next day since we didn't know what was going to happen or what are we going to eat.

When coming to America it wasn't an easy process to do. My dad had to do a lot of paper work with the UN people and sometime people get denied after filling out the application for coming to America. My family and I waited for good three years just to process the application.

Social workers who work with refugees need an understanding of what languishing for years in a refugee camp does to people and how difficult adjustment is in a foreign country after that. At the same time, survival skills such as we could see from the student's narrative above, will help sustain them in the strange world to which they come.

ENVIRONMENTAL REFUGEES: TRAUMA RELATED TO NATURAL DISASTERS

War is not the only cause of the mass migrations of people who have narrowly survived catastrophic experiences. Natural disasters—storms, tsunamis, floods, drought, fires—and more distinctly human-made disasters—such as nuclear explosions and radioactive incidents—also are conducive of personal trauma as well as grief and loss. What we are talking about are environmental refugees. Social workers are often involved in humanitarian relief efforts in such circumstances, generally through an organization such as the Red Cross or the U.S. Federal Emergency Management Agency (FEMA) in direct response teams (Dominelli, 2013).

The concept of *environmental justice* relates to the fact that all people should have access to safe and healthy environments. It is a well-known fact that the extent of damage caused by natural disasters falls most heavily upon groups of people who are socially and economically marginalized. Extreme weather and environmental disasters are shaped, in part, by climate change. The current drought and lack of water and fires in California and Alberta are a direct result.

Human-made disasters include pollution of the earth's soil, water, air, and deforestation, and the disposal of toxic wastes. Much of this can be attributed to capitalism and the exploitation of natural resources for a profit. Armed conflicts over finite resources involving land, water, minerals, and oil are increasing globally (Dominelli, 2013). The conflicts themselves further contribute to the pollution and damage to resources.

Acute land hunger has pushed people onto uninhabitable regions, such as flood plains and drought-prone areas; then when inevitable natural disaster strikes, these people are forced to evacuate for safety. Environmental degradation, such as soil erosion and deforestation, has caused mass population shifts, often from rural to urban areas. Similarly, millions have been forced to migrate as technological feats, such as dam construction and urban and highway development, have claimed the land. And yet, environmental refugees do not get the international help from nongovernmental or governmental organizations that are accorded to political refugees. However, these people are every bit as needy in their often urgent flights from their homelands. As political scientist Susan George (2010) informs us, millions of environmental refugees are "already virtually on our doorsteps" (p. 182).

Social workers will find themselves on the front lines and need to be prepared to work with people in crisis, serious health problems as a result of exposure to the harsh elements, drought and food insecurity, and loss of life of family members. Forced to migrate into foreign lands where they often are unwanted, environmental refugees are subject to trauma as well as an overriding sense of grief and loss.

THE PLIGHT OF IMMIGRANT CHILDREN IN THE UNITED STATES

Throughout Central America, huge numbers of children are escaping situations of horror, sometimes with their parents, sometimes alone. They are on the run from gangs. In El Salvador, Honduras, and Guatemala, boys are threatened to be killed if they don't join; girls are at risk of being sold into sexual slavery. In 2014, almost 70,000 kids from El Salvador, Guatemala, and Honduras arrived at the U.S. Mexico border (Wiltz, 2015). They had endured unimaginable obstacles on this dangerous flight. Many of these children are still in the United States today, most in a state of legal limbo. There are far fewer new arrivals today, as the Mexican authorities are either detaining them or deporting them back to their countries (Stillman, 2016).

Other children are greatly affected through their family's status, especially if one or more of their family members are undocumented. Because of The Illegal Immigration Reform and Immigrant Responsibility Act (IIRIRA), signed by President Clinton in 1996, key defenses against deportation were eliminated and many more immigrants, including legal permanent residents, were subjected to detention and deportation. IIRIRA defined a greatly expanded range of criminal convictions—including relatively minor, nonviolent ones—for which legal permanent residents could be automatically deported. IIRIRA also made it much more difficult for people fleeing persecution to apply for asylum. Whole families languished in detention centers because of this law. According to Human Rights Watch (2016), international law prohibits the detention of children except as a last resort. Human Rights Watch calls for repeal of the 1996 law that is tearing apart families and instilling fear in children.

A FRAMEWORK FOR TRAUMA-INFORMED CARE

From this perspective, the social worker views each person as an individual with unique characteristics that, in interaction with the environment, may place him or her at risk for the development of trauma related symptoms or conversely, may insulate him or her from unpleasant experiences. The CSWE (2013) has issued guidelines for graduate programs of social work that have a trauma-informed concentration. Social work educators are urged to take into account disproportionate exposure to trauma on the basis of culture, race, and national origin, and to "incorporate an understanding of the influence of historical trauma on various cultures into assessment activities" (p. 15).

Health management experts Bloom and Farragher (2013) in their book, *Restoring Sanctuary: A New Operating System for Trauma-Informed Systems of Care*, offer insights to enhance our understanding of social organizations as living systems. Their focus is on human service organizations, most of which serve people with mental health issues. The starting point for change, they contend, is for education of management and staff in how the organizational system works and how the moral/social environment of the agency filters through the system. When workplace stress is pronounced, for example, the whole atmosphere can become toxic to the extent that destructive processes parallel the very trauma-related processes that brought the clients to the agency to get help. A perceived lack of safety erodes trust at every level of the organization.

Refugee centers and camps today are overwhelmed with the influx of hundreds of thousands of families fleeing the war zones in the Middle East. Meeting the survivors' physical needs takes precedence over addressing their psychological needs. The risk of secondary trauma by staff is a high risk in a situation of continual exposure to narratives of horror and grief. At the organizational level, many leaders and their staff have lost sight of the mission of their work and have become cynical and demoralized. Moreover, the people operating such facilities often run them in a military fashion and in ways that are counterproductive to the needs of psychologically vulnerable people (Cox & Pawar, 2013). The end result in such situations is heightened authoritarianism by the managers and burnout for the staff. The result for providers is "a collective kind of trauma" (Bloom & Farragher, 2013, p. 21).

In *Restoring Sanctuary*, Bloom and Farragher (2013) tell us how a dysfunctional organization can be transformed into one that is trauma informed. Staff members must be reeducated into a whole new way of thinking to get beyond the negative labeling, overreliance on medication to control clients, and other forms of behavioral "management."

So what is trauma-informed care? According to the National Center for Trauma-Informed Care (2013), which is under the auspices of SAMHSA, when a human service program takes the step to become trauma informed, every part of its organization must be assessed and modified based on an awareness of the centrality of trauma in the mental health field. The focus of trauma-informed care is ecological and therefore can be understood within an ecosystems framework in that it is focused on interventions directed toward the organization or environment. Because immigrants often have been forced to migrate to escape situations of war or natural disasters, they are likely to be trauma survivors. The physical environment, therefore, must generate a sense of safety, and the social atmosphere should evoke a sense of peace and warmth. To achieve this end, service providers and the entire staff first require an understanding of the way in which trauma experiences shape survivors' responses to the services offered. Traumatized individuals, for example, might approach agency personnel with an aloof or sarcastic manner; his or her defenses are up. To establish trust with uprooted people under these circumstances, staff members need to learn to avoid behaviors and practices that inadvertently might trigger a flashback to a traumatic event. Detention centers, where many asylum seekers end up as their cases are processed, are the worst possible places for refugees to begin their resettlement. Such systems, as in the United States, operate outside the standards of international or constitutional law and utilize practices of control that exacerbate fear and anxiety and often lead to re-traumatization.

Brian Sims (2013), senior medical advisor for the National Association of State Mental Health Program Directors, in his presentation on the neurobiology of trauma, emphasized the importance of establishing a safe space for victims of severe trauma. Treatment centers and institutions that are trauma informed, he said, do not ask "What's wrong with you?" but rather ask "What happened to you?" The following are facts that he provided in his talk:

- Trauma-informed care, first and foremost, appreciates the high prevalence of trauma in survivors of victimization.

- The worst place to treat trauma is in any jail-like facility.

- The use of seclusion and restraints of survivors is a trigger for re-traumatization.

- Restraint produces a strong emotional response and further outbursts or a complete shutting down of feeling.

In his discussion of triggers for re-traumatization, Sims listed loud noises, yelling, a light suddenly coming on, touching, grabbing, and isolation as behaviors to avoid. The person who has experienced severe trauma experiences neurological changes that interfere with his or her reasoning ability. The symptoms can be improved with medication, but this is only a temporary solution. Treatment needs to get at the cause, which is the trauma itself. Non–trauma-informed care, as Sims further indicates, relies on behavior seen as deliberately provocative. Calming strategies are needed instead. Examples are going for a walk, quiet talking, working out, and lying down.

IMPLICATIONS FOR SOCIAL WORKERS

Social workers, regardless of their place of employment, will be responding to the needs of refugees and immigrants. However, it has been noted that social work programs often do not offer course offerings that concentrate in the area of refugee and immigrant settlement. A small study of social workers in British Columbia concluded that they may not be well prepared to effectively work with newcomers (Yan & Chan, 2010). One exemplary course was offered in 2008 by Laura Praglin, associate professor of social work at the University of Northern Iowa titled "Working with Immigrant and Refugee Populations," the course was described as follows:

> This seminar introduces students to various perspectives (historical, sociological, psychological, political, economic) related to social work intervention with immigrant and refugee populations in the United States, with particular attention to the Midwest. The format requires extensive student participation through assigned readings, presentations, guest speakers, and class discussions. The seminar welcomes the perspectives of other academic disciplines and helping professions, as well as cross-cultural analyses of this timely topic.

Indeed, the topic was very timely, because during finals week in nearby Postville, Iowa, the U.S. Immigration and Customs Enforcement (ICE) conducted the largest single raid of a workplace in U.S. history until that time and arrested, imprisoned, and later deported around 400 immigrant workers who had false identity papers. These workers had lived with their families as an active part of the community, so the mass raid and breakup of families was a serious blow to the town of Postville.

Social workers who work with immigrant families need to recognize the anxiety that undocumented immigrants face, never knowing if they will be subject to deportation themselves or if they will lose a family member to deportation. Children in such families are especially fearful.

As social workers assist immigrants and refugees in the settlement of their new country, they should note that they face many new challenges, including trauma and loss of family, language barriers, unfamiliar customs and climate, and often discrimination. Then there is the pressure to secure a job, the lack of a social and community connection, and poverty. These stressors can impact their spiritual, physical, emotional, and mental well-being. Alongside these challenges, undocumented immigrants face deportation risks.

Because children are more prone to the impact of trauma long-term than adults, social workers should strive for early intervention when possible (Clervil, Guarino, DeCandia, & Beach, 2013). Because family members have also been exposed to events, such as violence or an urgent escape and loss of home and loved ones, their fear responses can be frightening to children and interfere with their sense of trust and safety.

The children of escaping refugees are apt to have nightmares, fear, anxiety, and depression. In teens, fear responses may be expressed through acting-out behavior and aggression (Clervil et al., 2013). Their sense of trust has been violated.

Children need to understand the impact of the situation on their parents so, if the parents become noncommunicative in some way, the children can recognize it is not their fault or not that the parents no longer love them. Counseling from an outsider who is aware of their situation can be extremely helpful under these circumstances.

For immigrants and refugees of all ages, lack of trust and a constant need to be vigilant for danger make it difficult for survivors to ask for help when they need it. Bureaucratic requirements for settlement, including extensive questioning and paperwork, may act as triggers for a trauma response. Agency rules and regulations may be perceived as disrespectful and not dissimilar to prior acts of victimization (Clervil et al., 2013). Also it is important to recognize the resilience in newcomers and the strength that they have to adapt and thrive.

Recommendations from the National Center on Family Homelessness, based on their intensive, two-year pilot project designed to offer trauma-informed services to recently displaced families and children, are relevant for social workers responding to the needs of refugees (Clervil et al., 2013). Using a trauma-informed approach at the agency with engaged staff at every level is vital for understanding and responding to the needs to survivors. This includes

- Understanding and assessing displacements

- Integrating consumer voices in a response

- Designing environments that are safe, welcoming, flexible, and responsive to individual needs, including those of culturally and linguistically diverse populations. (p. 13)

The challenges of responding to newcomers who have experienced trauma and loss and have language and cultural differences are immense. Social workers are equipped with the knowledge and skills to welcome them to the country, connect, and assist in the settlement process.

Micro Issues

- How would you describe the influence of principals for human rights and social justice on your professional clinical practice? How might these translate into your professional collaborative relationship with the female child in the case study above?

- What concepts of social justice and human rights might resonate with and work well for the child from Ethiopia in the case study? With your own clients?

Macro Issues

- What agency policies and structures would you describe as relevant and necessary to maintain an inclusive, safe agency environment for both staff and clients, particularly in relation to the case study? Do they exist at your current agency?

- What methods would you suggest for your agency to include more community partnerships and facilitate greater community engagement with the agency?

REFLECTIVE QUESTIONS

1. What methods of information would you use to stay informed and aware of the migration and environmental disasters that are currently a global crisis?

2. How would you describe the historical focus on human rights and social justice in clinical practice, and in what ways does it impact your practice with immigrants and refugees?

3. How does your own personal family history influence your clinical practice with immigrants and refugees?

REFERENCES

Bloom, S. L., & Farragher, B. (2013). *Restoring sanctuary: A new operating system for trauma-informed systems of care.* New York: Oxford University Press.

Clervil, R., Guarino, K., DeCandia, C. J., & Beach, C. A. (2013). *Trauma informed care for displaced populations: A guide for community-based service providers.* Waltham, MA: The National Center on Family Homelessness, a practice area of American Institutes for Research.

Council on Social Work Education. (2013). *Guidelines for advanced social work practice in trauma.* Alexandria, VA: Author.

Cox, D., & Pawar, M. (2013). *International social work: Issues, strategies, and programs.* Thousand Oaks, CA: Sage.

Dominelli, L. (2013). Social work education for disaster relief work. In M. Gray, J. Coates, & T. Hetherington (Eds.), *Environmental social work* (pp. 280–297). New York: Routledge.

Elshtain, J. B. (2002). A return to Hull House. In J. B. Elshtain (Ed.), *The Jane Addams reader* (pp. xxxi–xxxiv). New York, NY: Basic Books.

George, S. (2010). *Whose crisis, whose future: Towards a greener, fairer, richer world.* Cambridge, England: Polity Press.

Gil, D. (1999). *Confronting injustice and oppression: Concepts and strategies for social workers.* New York: Columbia University Press.

Hodge, D. R. (2005, April). Social work and the house of Islam: Orienting practitioners to the beliefs and values of Muslims in the United States. *Social Work, 50*(2), 162–170.

Human Rights Watch. (2016, April 25). U.S.: 20 years of immigrant abuses. Retrieved from www.hrw.org

International Federation of Social Work. (2014). *Global definition of social work.* http://ifsw.org/get-involved/global-definition-of-social-work/

International Federation of Social Work. (2015, September 5). *Statement on the refugee crisis.* http://ifsw.org/news/statement-on-the-refugee-crisis/

International Federation of Social Work. (2015, October 26). *The refugee crisis: Social workers at the forefront of finding solutions.* http://ifsw.org/news/the-refugee-crisi-social-workers-at-the-forefront-of-finding-solution

International Federation of Social Work, Centre for Human Rights. (2000). *Human rights and social work: A manual for schools of social work and the social work profession.* New York/Geneva: International Federation of Social Workers, United Nations.

Jennissen, T., & Lundy, C. (2011). *One hundred years of social work: A history of the profession in English Canada 1900–2000.* Waterloo: Wilfrid Laurier University Press.

Kelley, C. P., Mohatadi, S., Cane, M. A., Seager, R., & Yochanan K. (2015). Climate change in the fertile crescent and the implications of the Syrian drought. *Proceedings of the National Academy of Sciences*, *112*(11), 3241–3246. doi: 10.1073/pnas.1421533112

Klosterman, E. M., & Stratton, D. C. (2006). Speaking truth to power: Jane Addams's values base for peacemaking. *Affilia: Journal of Women in Social Work*, *21*(2), 158–168.

Leighninger, L. (2007). Jane Addams' reponses to quotas on immigration. *Journal of Progressive Human Services*, *1*(2), 77–81.

Lundblad, K. (1995). Jane Addams and social reform: A role model for the 1990's. *Social Work*, *40*(5), 661–669.

Lundy, C. (2011). *Social work, social justice and human rights: A structural approach to practice* (2nd ed.). Toronto: University of Toronto Press.

Madore, S. (2010). Citizenship and access: Precarious experiences within Canada. *Canadian Social Work*, *12*(2), 45–50.

Michultka, D. (2009). Mental health issues in new immigrant communities. In F. Chang-Muy & E. Congress (Eds.), *Social work with immigrants and refugees* (pp. 135–172). New York: Springer Publishing Company.

NASA. (2016, July 21). Scientific consensus: Earth's climate is warming. Global climate change: Vital signs of the planet. National Aeronautics and Space Administration (NASA). Retrieved from www.climate.nasa.gov

Nash, M. (2005). Responding to settlement needs: Migrants and refugees and community development. In M. Nash, R. Munford, & K. O'Donoghue (Eds.), *Social work theories in action* (pp. 140–154). London: Jessica Kingsley.

National Association of Social Workers (NASW). (2015a). *Immigrants and refugees. Social work speaks: Policy statements* (10th ed., pp. 176–181). Washington, DC: NASW Press.

National Association of Social Workers (NASW). (2015b). *International policy on human rights. Social work speaks: Policy statements* (10th ed., pp. 182–186). Washington, DC: NASW Press.

National Center for Trauma-Informed Care. (2013). *Trauma-informed care and treatment services*. Rockville, MD: Substance Abuse and Mental Health Services Administration.

Ottawa Citizen. (2016, October 27). At least 3,800 migrants have died in the Mediterranean in 2016. *Ottawa Citizen*, p. NP5.

Shear, M. (2015). Child migrants waiting for U.S. to honor vow. *New York Times*, p. A1.

Sims, B. (2013, September 26). *The neurobiology of trauma*. Presentation at a conference on trauma-informed care, Cedar Falls, University of Northern Iowa.

Stillman, A. (2016, February). All you can do is run: Central American children fleeing violence head for Mexico. *The Guardian.* Retrieved from www.theguardian.com

Trolander, J. A. (1975). Settlement houses and the great depression. Detroit: Wayne State University Press.

Truell, R. (2015, November 23). Social workers response to Europe's refugee crisis a testament to human hope. *The Guardian.* http://www.theguardian.com/social-care-network/

UNHCR. (2014). *Statistical yearbook.* http://www.unhcr.org/566584fc9.html

UNHCR. (2015). *Figures at a glance.* http://www.unhcr.org/figures-at-a-glance.html

UNHCR. (2016). *Global displacement hits record high.* http://www.unhcr.org/news/latest/2016/6/5763b65a4/global-forced-displacement-hits-record-high.html

United Nations Children's Fund (UNICEF). (2014, March). *Under siege: The devastating impact on children of three years of conflict in Syria.* Regional Office for the Middle East and North Africa. Amman, Jordan: Author. Retrieved from www.unicef.org

Valtonen, K. (2008). *Social work and migration: Immigrant and refugee settlement and integration.* Burlington, VT: Ashgate Publishing.

Vickers, T. (2015). Grappling with power and inequality in humanitarian interventions [Editorial]. *International Social Work, 58*(5), 625–627.

Wiltz, T. (2015, August 24). Unaccompanied children from Central America, one year later. *Huffington Post.* Retrieved from www.huffingtonpost.com

Witkin, S. (1998, May). Human rights and social work. *Social Work, 43*(3), 197–201.

Yan, M. C., & Chan, S. (2010). Are social workers ready to work with newcomers? *Canadian Social Work, 12*(2), 16–23.

RESOURCE LIST
Working With Immigrants, Refugees, and Asylees

Deportation and Detention	
Corrections Corporation of America	www.cca.org
Detention Watch Network	www.detentionwatchnetwork.org
Know Your Rights! Protect Yourself Against Immigration Raids	http://unitedwedream.org/thank-deportation-defense-card-handy-phone

Domestic Violence/Interpersonal Violence	
Battered Women's Justice Project	www.bwjp.org
Between Friends, Chicago	www.betweenfriendschicago.org
Cycle of Violence Chart	www.icadv.org
Domestic Violence (Population-Specific Approaches) and Human Trafficking	www.VAWnet.org
Forced Migration Review	www.fmr.org
Illinois Coalition Against Domestic Violence • Provides education & information to providers and survivors of DV/IPV • Personal safety plan • How to use a computer and ensure safety • Orders of protection • How to determine if you are a victim of domestic violence	www.ilcadv.org
International & Global: Female Genital Mutilation	www.VAWnet.org
International & Global: Violence Against Women Globally	www.VAWnet.org
Mujeres Latinas En Accion	www.mujereslatinasenaccion.org
National Center DV Trauma & Mental Health	http://www.nationalcenterdvtraumamh.org

Source: United Nations General Assembly, 1948

National Coalition Against Domestic Violence	www.ncadv.org
National Immigrant Family Violence Institute	http://www.nifvi.org
National Sexual Violence Resource Center	www.nsvrc.org
University of Minnesota Coalition Against Violence	www.mincava.edu

Human Rights

Know Your Rights! Protect Yourself Against Immigration Raids	http://unitedwedream.org/thank-deportation-defense-card-handy-phone
Freedom House	www.freedomhouse.org
Human Rights Watch	www.humanrightswatch.org www.hrw.org
Amnesty International	www.amnestyinternational.org
ethnomed	http://ethnomed.org/culture

Immigrants

Asian American Institute	www.aaichicago.org
Catholic Campaign for Immigration Reform	www.justicefor immigrants.org
Catholic Charities Latino Affairs Chicago	www.latinoaffairs@catholiccharities.net
Catholic Legal Immigration Center	https://www.cliniclegal.org
Chicago New Sanctuary Coalition	www.crln.org/Chicago-new-sanctuary
Coalition of African, Arab, Asian, Europe and Latino Immigrants of Illinois	www.caaaelii.org
Cair-Chicago Council on American-Islamic Relations	www.cairchicago.org
CoreCivic	http://www.cca.com
Council of Islamic Organizations of Greater Chicago	www.ciogc.org
Fair Immigration Reform Movement	http://www.fairimmigration.wordpress.com
Heartland Alliance Chicago	www.heartalliance.org
Illinois Coalition for Immigrant and Refugee Rights	www.icirr.org
Immigrant Legal Resource Center	http://www.ilrc.org/about-the-ilrc

Interfaith Immigration Coalition	http://www.interfaithimmigrationcoalition.org
Latino Policy Forum	www.latinopolicyforum.org
Lutheran Immigration & Refugee Services	www.lirs.org
Migration Policy Institute	www.migrationpolicy.org
National Immigrant Justice Center	www.immigrantjustice.org
National Immigrant Family Violence Institute	http://www.nifvi.org
No More Deaths	www.nomoredeaths.org
Pew Hispanic Research	www.pewhispanic.org
The United Nations High Commissioner	http://www.unhcr.org/en-us/the-high-commissioner.html
United Nations	www.un.org
United States Immigration & Customs	www.ice.gov
Women Thrive: Because When Women Thrive, the Whole World Thrives	http://womenthrive.org
The Young Center for Immigrant Children's Rights	http://www.theYoungCenter.org

LGBTQIA

Lesbian, Gay, Bi-sexual, Transgender, & Transexual, Queer: Questioning, Intersex, Asexual, & Ally

| Heartland Alliance: Rainbow Welcome Initiative | http://www.rainbowwelcome.org |

Medical Resources

Global Efforts

Doctors Without Borders	www.doctorswithoutborders.org
Office of Coordination of Humanitarian Affairs	www.unocha.org
United Nations High Commissioner for Refugees (Health Initiatives)	www.unhcr.org

National Professional Associations (United States)

| National Association of Community Health | www.nachc.com |
| National Association for Home Care and Hospice | www.nahc.org |

General Health Provider Networks	www.nahpusa.com
National Association of Advisors for the Health Professions	www.naahp.org
American Health Care Association	www.ahca.org
Health Provider Professional Development	www.nahq.org
National Association of Social Workers	www.nasw.org
U.S. Center for Disease Control	www.cdc.gov

Mental Health Resources

Global Efforts

Office of Coordination of Humanitarian Affairs	www.unocha.org
United Nations High Commissioner for Refugees (Mental Health Initiatives)	www.unhcr.org
World Health Organization	www.who.org

National Organizations & Professional Associations (United States)

American Counseling Association	www.counseling.org
Association for Psychological Sciences	www.psychologicalscience.org
National Alliance on Mental Illness	www.nami.org
National Association of Social Workers	www.nasw.org
National Council for Behavioral Health	www.thenationalcouncil.org
National Institute for Mental Health	www.nimh.nih.gov
Substance Abuse and Mental Health Services Administration	www.SAMHSA.gov
U.S. Department of Health and Human Services	www.HHS.gov
World Association on Infant Mental Health	www.waimh.org

Local Programs (Illinois)

Illinois Association for Infant Mental Health	www.ilaimh.org
Illinois Refugee Mental Health Task Force	www.ilrmh.org
Illinois Children's Trauma Coalition	www.ictc.org

Refugees and Asylum Seekers	
Embrace Refugees	www.embracerefugees.org
Illinois Coalition for Immigrant and Refugee Rights	www.icirr.org
Jesuit Refugee Services	http://www.jrusa.org
Lutheran Immigration & Refugee Services	www.lirs.org
Migration Policy Institute	www.migrationpolicy.org
Refugee Council USA	www.refugeecouncil.org
Reform Immigration for America	www.reformimmigrationforamerica.org
Refugee International	www.refugeeinternational.org
RefugeeOne, Refugee Resettlement Agency (Chicago, Illinois)	www.refugeeone.org
The Refugee Center Online	www.refugeecenter.org
The Refugee Project	www.therefugeeproject.org
U.S. Office of Health & Human Services, Administration of Children & Families, Office of Refugee Resettlement	http://www.acf.hhs.gov/programs/orr

Youth	
Find Youth Information	http://www.findyouthinfo.gov
Immigrant Youth Justice League	http://www.iyjl.org
Immigrant Youth Coalition	http://theiyc.org

Women's Issues	
Association for Women's Rights Associated	www.awid.org
Women Thrive: Because When Women Thrive, the Whole World Thrives	http://womenthrive.org
Association for Women's Rights in Development	www.awid.org
OECD Development Centre's Social Institutions and Gender Index (SIGI)	http://www.genderindex.org
Women for Women International	http://www.womenforwomen.org

UNIVERSAL DECLARATION OF HUMAN RIGHTS

PREAMBLE

Whereas recognition of the inherent dignity and of the equal and inalienable rights of all members of the human family is the foundation of freedom, justice and peace in the world,

Whereas disregard and contempt for human rights have resulted in barbarous acts which have outraged the conscience of mankind, and the advent of a world in which human beings shall enjoy freedom of speech and belief and freedom from fear and want has been proclaimed as the highest aspiration of the common people,

Whereas it is essential, if man is not to be compelled to have recourse, as a last resort, to rebellion against tyranny and oppression, that human rights should be protected by the rule of law,

Whereas it is essential to promote the development of friendly relations between nations,

Whereas the peoples of the United Nations have in the Charter reaffirmed their faith in fundamental human rights, in the dignity and worth of the human person and in the equal rights of men and women and have determined to promote social progress and better standards of life in larger freedom,

Whereas Member States have pledged themselves to achieve, in cooperation with the United Nations, the promotion of universal respect for and observance of human rights and fundamental freedoms,

Whereas a common understanding of these rights and freedoms is of the greatest importance for the full realization of this pledge,

Now, therefore the General Assembly proclaims this Universal Declaration of Human Rights as a common standard of achievement for all peoples and all nations, to the end that every individual and every organ of society, keeping this Declaration constantly in mind, shall strive by teaching and education to promote respect for these rights and freedoms and by progressive measures, national and international, to secure their universal and effective recognition and observance, both among the peoples of Member States themselves and among the peoples of territories under their jurisdiction.

Source: United Nations General Assembly, *The Universal Declaration of Human Rights* (Paris: United Nations General Assembly, 1948).

Article 1

All human beings are born free and equal in dignity and rights. They are endowed with reason and conscience and should act towards one another in a spirit of brotherhood.

Article 2

Everyone is entitled to all the rights and freedoms set forth in this Declaration, without distinction of any kind, such as race, colour, sex, language, religion, political or other opinion, national or social origin, property, birth or other status.

Furthermore, no distinction shall be made on the basis of the political, jurisdictional or international status of the country or territory to which a person belongs, whether it be independent, trust, non-self-governing or under any other limitation of sovereignty.

Article 3

Everyone has the right to life, liberty and security of person.

Article 4

No one shall be held in slavery or servitude; slavery and the slave trade shall be prohibited in all their forms.

Article 5

No one shall be subjected to torture or to cruel, inhuman or degrading treatment or punishment.

Article 6

Everyone has the right to recognition everywhere as a person before the law.

Article 7

All are equal before the law and are entitled without any discrimination to equal protection of the law. All are entitled to equal protection against any discrimination in violation of this Declaration and against any incitement to such discrimination.

Article 8

Everyone has the right to an effective remedy by the competent national tribunals for acts violating the fundamental rights granted him by the constitution or by law.

Article 9

No one shall be subjected to arbitrary arrest, detention or exile.

Article 10

Everyone is entitled in full equality to a fair and public hearing by an independent and impartial tribunal, in the determination of his rights and obligations and of any criminal charge against him.

Article 11

1. Everyone charged with a penal offence has the right to be presumed innocent until proved guilty according to law in a public trial at which he has had all the guarantees necessary for his defence.

2. No one shall be held guilty of any penal offence on account of any act or omission which did not constitute a penal offence, under national or international law, at the time when it was committed. Nor shall a heavier penalty be imposed than the one that was applicable at the time the penal offence was committed.

Article 12

No one shall be subjected to arbitrary interference with his privacy, family, home or correspondence, nor to attacks upon his honour and reputation. Everyone has the right to the protection of the law against such interference or attacks.

Article 13

1. Everyone has the right to freedom of movement and residence within the borders of each State.

2. Everyone has the right to leave any country, including his own, and to return to his country.

Article 14

1. Everyone has the right to seek and to enjoy in other countries asylum from persecution.

2. This right may not be invoked in the case of prosecutions genuinely arising from non-political crimes or from acts contrary to the purposes and principles of the United Nations.

Article 15

1. Everyone has the right to a nationality.

2. No one shall be arbitrarily deprived of his nationality nor denied the right to change his nationality.

Article 16

1. Men and women of full age, without any limitation due to race, nationality or religion, have the right to marry and to found a family. They are entitled to equal rights as to marriage, during marriage and at its dissolution.

2. Marriage shall be entered into only with the free and full consent of the intending spouses.

3. The family is the natural and fundamental group unit of society and is entitled to protection by society and the State.

Article 17

1. Everyone has the right to own property alone as well as in association with others.

2. No one shall be arbitrarily deprived of his property.

Article 18

Everyone has the right to freedom of thought, conscience and religion; this right includes freedom to change his religion or belief, and freedom, either alone or in community with others and in public or private, to manifest his religion or belief in teaching, practice, worship and observance.

Article 19

Everyone has the right to freedom of opinion and expression; this right includes freedom to hold opinions without interference and to seek, receive and impart information and ideas through any media and regardless of frontiers.

Article 20

1. Everyone has the right to freedom of peaceful assembly and association.

2. No one may be compelled to belong to an association.

Article 21

1. Everyone has the right to take part in the government of his country, directly or through freely chosen representatives.

2. Everyone has the right to equal access to public service in his country.

3. The will of the people shall be the basis of the authority of government; this will shall be expressed in periodic and genuine elections which shall be by universal and equal suffrage and shall be held by secret vote or by equivalent free voting procedures.

Article 22

Everyone, as a member of society, has the right to social security and is entitled to realization, through national effort and international co-operation and in accordance with the organization and resources of each State, of the economic, social and cultural rights indispensable for his dignity and the free development of his personality.

Article 23

1. Everyone has the right to work, to free choice of employment, to just and favourable conditions of work and to protection against unemployment.

2. Everyone, without any discrimination, has the right to equal pay for equal work.

3. Everyone who works has the right to just and favourable remuneration ensuring for himself and his family an existence worthy of human dignity, and supplemented, if necessary, by other means of social protection.

4. Everyone has the right to form and to join trade unions for the protection of his interests.

Article 24

Everyone has the right to rest and leisure, including reasonable limitation of working hours and periodic holidays with pay.

Article 25

1. Everyone has the right to a standard of living adequate for the health and well-being of himself and of his family, including food, clothing, housing and medical care and necessary social services, and the right to security in the event of unemployment, sickness, disability, widowhood, old age or other lack of livelihood in circumstances beyond his control.

2. Motherhood and childhood are entitled to special care and assistance. All children, whether born in or out of wedlock, shall enjoy the same social protection.

Article 26

1. Everyone has the right to education. Education shall be free, at least in the elementary and fundamental stages. Elementary education shall be compulsory. Technical and professional education shall be made generally available and higher education shall be equally accessible to all on the basis of merit.

2. Education shall be directed to the full development of the human personality and to the strengthening of respect for human rights and fundamental freedoms. It shall promote understanding, tolerance and friendship among all nations, racial or religious groups, and shall further the activities of the United Nations for the maintenance of peace.

3. Parents have a prior right to choose the kind of education that shall be given to their children.

Article 27

1. Everyone has the right freely to participate in the cultural life of the community, to enjoy the arts and to share in scientific advancement and its benefits.

2. Everyone has the right to the protection of the moral and material interests resulting from any scientific, literary or artistic production of which he is the author.

Article 28

Everyone is entitled to a social and international order in which the rights and freedoms set forth in this Declaration can be fully realized.

Article 29

1. Everyone has duties to the community in which alone the free and full development of his personality is possible.

2. In the exercise of his rights and freedoms, everyone shall be subject only to such limitations as are determined by law solely for the purpose of securing due recognition and respect for the rights and freedoms of others and of meeting the just requirements of morality, public order and the general welfare in a democratic society.

3. These rights and freedoms may in no case be exercised contrary to the purposes and principles of the United Nations.

Article 30

Nothing in this Declaration may be interpreted as implying for any State, group or person any right to engage in any activity or to perform any act aimed at the destruction of any of the rights and freedoms set forth herein.

SAMPLE ASSESSMENT OUTLINE

This assessment outline is intended to identify and facilitate client description of the environment and experiences and seeks to learn about the culture and personal identity of the client system with the purpose of becoming useful and a positive resource for the client system.

IDENTIFY ALL CLIENT SYSTEMS AND LOCATION TO THE CLIENT SYSTEM

Relationships, names, descriptions (genogram and ecological map with as complete information as possible), mother, father, son/brother, daughter/sister, aunts, uncles, godparents, grandparents, stepparents, and so forth

Non-related but relevant others: neighbors, friends, school, work, sponsoring family or organization, church, mosque, temple, and so forth

Topics	
Influential circumstances—for example, culture, ethnicity, race, sexual orientation, education, and so forth	1. Specific information related to the identified client difficulties. 2. Country of origin, length of time in United States, plan to relocate in future to be with family, and so forth. 3. Resettlement and/or refugee camps, detention, other holding environments in client's life. 4. Family system from individualistic or collectivist culture.
Reasons left country of origin. Who accompanied or are you alone? Languages?	1. Determine languages spoken, ability to hear, understand, and so forth. 2. Reasons for leaving/experiences of oppression—for example, political persecution, gangs and violence, sexual harassment, economic hardships, lack of education, family illness, medical needs, and so forth. 3. Determine if can ask specifically about trauma, discrimination, poverty, and so forth.
Migration experiences	Ask about their narrative, life story. Listen! Ask about stages of migration: pre, in transit, post, resettlement
Referral source	1. Does the referral source help you identify the client system difficulty? 2. How will you collaborate with the referral source, and is it possible? 3. Is your agency relevant or equipped to handle the client's needs and/or concerns?
Client system problems/ difficulties	1. Determine undocumented status, e.g., importance of activism for Dreamers as one example. 2. Does client understand what a clinician/counselor/social worker is? Does client know why she is at the agency? 3. What does the client want to have happen now in her life?

Client system strengths	1. Evaluate if group work would be beneficial to client—decrease isolation and loneliness? 2. Is client able to participate in groups? Support groups? Community change groups? Survivor groups? Psychoeducational groups?
Ask the client to describe how s/he came to be in the current situation	If possible, facilitate for the client a thorough description of his/her/their current situation, including how s/he/they came to be in that situation.
How does client describe the problems and how does client identify solutions?	Working with the client on his/her recommendations for resolution of problems can be empowering. It also provides information about what the client may be first able to accomplish and/or what the client is aware of at this point in time.
Short-term goals	Identify the short-term goals that you and the client system establish as well as goals you identify as potentially helpful from professional experience and perspective.
Long-term goals	Identify the long-term goals that you and the client system establish as well as goals you identify as potentially helpful from professional experience and perspective.
Significant environment influences	1. Describe family relationship patterns. 2. Identify employment history, current level of support from the community, extended and family systems, friendships, and so forth.
Significant historical material	1. History of mental illness; substance abuse; physical, emotional, and/or sexual abuse; domestic violence; illness; deaths; suicides; and so forth. 2. Inquire about personal experience but also observation as helpless bystander to brutality to others, and so forth.
Individual personality structure and functioning	1. Functioning of the client system. 2. Client exhibit specific defense mechanisms? 3. Interpersonal interaction patterns & long-term relational patterns. 4. How does this information help you to better understand and provide potential insight for how to become useful to the client?
Therapeutic relationship	Affective and working state of the therapeutic relationship. Consider your own process. Remain critically self-aware.
Guiding theories	1. Always begin with concrete services—for example, water, food, and shelter, medical exam, psychiatric evaluation and medication, and so forth. 2. Identify specific theories and relevance to client system. 3. Document studies that support using theory and/or models.

Intervention plans	1. Describe your relationship with the client. 2. Facts presented in assessment. Have client's situation, circumstances, problems changed since initial assessment? 3. Your understanding of the problem(s) based on client's ongoing description of difficulty. 4. Identify client's strengths, resilience, hardiness, abilities, and skills. 5. Identify community resources, systems, and challenges. 6. How is the client functioning? Is she functioning well in life despite the presence of the presenting concern? What is the degree of disruption and to what areas of life? What is going well? What is going less well? 7. What is doable? (recognize the limitations of time, resources, language skills, etc.) 8. Link a practice model or theories to your decisions. What theoretical models most closely explain the client's circumstances, difficulties? Is your intervention plan linked to the assessment and needs of the client? Can you provide evidence from literature that your chosen model "works" with the identified situation, environmental challenges and problem(s)?
Practice evaluation	How will the goals, assessment, and evaluation of practice combine to give you information about the needs of client and process of the work?
Termination	Describe when discussions about termination are to begin. Describe the process of termination for client(s) and for social work provider/practitioner. Discuss how you think endings may be experienced by each—for example, the client(s) and the provider/practitioner.

WARNING!
PROTECT YOURSELF FROM IMMIGRATION RAIDS!

Some people who are not United States citizens have been arrested or detained by the U.S. government. Learn how to protect yourself if this happens to you!

Source: Reprinted with permission from the American Friends Service Committee, *Protect Yourself from Immigration Raids* (Takoma Park, MD: CASA of Maryland, n.d.)

PROTECT YOUR IMMIGRATION STATUS!

THE RIGHT TO REMAIN SILENT:

If you are arrested it is your right to refuse to answer any question. Don't lie! Don't say anything or say only: "I need to speak to my lawyer."

IMPORTANT!

Please, be aware that in some states, it is a minor crime not to provide your name when asked by a police officer. It is a good idea to check with a criminal or immigration lawyer to determine the law in your state. At the same time, remember that providing your name has risks. If you do provide your name, provide your real name.

IF YOU ARE UNDOCUMENTED...

✔ Don't provide government officials information about your immigration status.

✔ Do not lie.

✔ Do not give false documents.

✔ Do not carry papers from another country. If you do, the government can use this information in a deportation proceeding.

✔ Show them the Know Your Rights Card attached.

Source: Reprinted with permission from the American Friends Service Committee, *Protect Yourself from Immigration Raids* (Takoma Park, MD: CASA of Maryland, n.d.)

IF POLICE OR IMMIGRATION COMES TO YOUR HOME:

You have the right to see a warrant if the Police Department, FBI, Immigration or other government official tries to enter your home. A warrant is a paper signed by a judge giving the officer to enter permission your home. The warrant will specify the areas that the official has the right to search.

Do not open the door. Ask the officer to slip the warrant underneath the door. If you open the door and allow the official to come into the house, this may be considered giving him/her "consent" to enter. If s/he enters without a warrant, request the names and badge numbers of the officers and say that you did not "consent" to a search. Also, write down the names, addresses and phone numbers of anyone who witnessed the incident.

If the officer has a warrant, observe whether the official searches any other areas that are not listed in the warrant. Get a receipt for any property taken by the official.

IF IMMIGRATION COMES TO YOUR HOME ...

IF POLICE OR IMMIGRATION COMES TO YOUR WORKPLACE:

Immigration must have a warrant signed by a judge or the employer's permission to enter your workplace. If it is a public place, they do not need a warrant.

Stay calm. Do not run. This may be viewed as an admission that you have something to hide.

IF POLICE OR IMMIGRATION STOPS YOU ON THE STREET OR IN A PUBLIC PLACE :

If an immigration officer stops you on the street and does not have a warrant, s/he may not arrest you unless s/he has evidence that you are a non-citizen. Do not tell immigration your immigration status or where you were born. Also, do not carry with you any documents from your country of origin or false documents.

Source: Reprinted with permission from the American Friends Service Committee, *Protect Yourself from Immigration Raids* (Takoma Park, MD: CASA of Maryland, n.d.)

IF YOU ARE ARRESTED YOU SHOULD...

1. FIND OUT WHO HAS ARRESTED YOU

Write down the name of the officers and their agency (Police Dept., FBI, Immigration), along with their identification numbers and license plate numbers. You can find this information on their uniform or their cars.

2. DON'T SIGN ANY DOCUMENTS BEFORE SPEAKING WITH A LAWYER.

Government officials may try to intimidate you or trick you into signing. Don't let yourself be tricked! You may be signing away your right to a hearing before an immigration judge.

3. CONTACT YOUR ATTORNEY OR A FAMILY MEMBER

You have the right to make a telephone call after you are arrested. Memorize the telephone number of your attorney, family member, friend or union spokesperson, and contact him/her immediately.

4. CONTACT YOUR CONSULATE

If you are a foreign national arrested in the U.S., you have the right to call your consulate or to have the deportation officer inform the consulate of your arrest. Ask the deportation officer to see a list of embassies and write down the phone number. The consul may assist you in finding a lawyer or offer to contact your family.

5. ASK FOR BOND

Once you are in immigration custody, ask for bond (even if immigration says you are not eligible). You have to show that you are not a flight risk or a danger to the community. Also, get a copy of the "Notice to Appear," a document that contains the immigration charges against you.

Source: Reprinted with permission from the American Friends Service Committee, *Protect Yourself from Immigration Raids* (Takoma Park, MD: CASA of Maryland, n.d.)

IF YOU ARE ACCUSED OF A CRIME...

ASK YOUR ATTORNEY TO HELP YOU GET RELEASED FROM POLICE CUSTODY

If you are arrested by local police, they must charge you with a crime in court within 48 hours (not counting weekends and holidays), or else release you. If police do file criminal charges, then you must still be released if (1) the charges are dropped, (2) you are granted and post bail, (3) you win your criminal case, or (4) you complete your sentence.

The police may contact Immigration to learn more about your immigration status. For example, if you have an outstanding deportation order, the police may inform Immigration that you are in police custody.

Immigration may then place a "detainer" on you, which gives Immigration an additional 48 hours to pick you up. If Immigration fails to pick you up within this time, the police must release you.

If the police don't file criminal charges AND if immigration does not file a detainer, call an attorney or community organization to help you get released from police custody. They can write a demand letter to the jail or the sheriff.

WHAT SHOULD YOU DO IF YOU HAVE BEEN ACCUSED OF A CRIME?

Consult with an immigration attorney to make sure that the crime will not affect your immigration status. If you want to apply for citizenship or a permanent residency card (green card), talk to your lawyer.

WHAT SHOULD YOU DO IF YOU ARE FACING DEPORTATION AND YOU NEED AN ATTORNEY?

Find an attorney who specializes in deportation defense. Always keep with you the complete name and contact information of your attorney. Request a written contract from your attorney before paying him/her. Make sure your attorney looks at the NTA or your immigration papers before making promises. Don't be tricked by people who are only after your money!

Source: Reprinted with permission from the American Friends Service Committee, *Protect Yourself from Immigration Raids* (Takoma Park, MD: CASA of Maryland, n.d.)

DEVELOP
A SAFETY
PLAN

1. MAKE A PLAN OF ACTION WITH YOUR CO-WORKERS

✔ Talk with your co-workers to see if they are willing to make a collective decision that everyone - regardless of their immigration status - will remain silent and ask to speak with an attorney in the event of a workplace raid.

✔ Tell co-workers not to run and to remain calm if there is a raid.

✔ If there is a union at your workplace, contact your union spokesperson to find out more about preparing for a raid.

2. KNOW WHAT DOCUMENTS YOU SHOULD CARRY WITH YOU

✔ Carry a card with the contact information of your immigration attorney and/or union representative.

✔ Carry a card, indicating that you wish to remain silent. A sample card is attached.

3. MAKE A PLAN TO CARE FOR YOUR FAMILY:

✔ If you have children or elderly relatives, make arrangements in advance for a family member or friend to care for them if you are detained. Have the telephone numbers of this relative or friend with you at all times and make sure other people know of these plans.

✔ Make sure you designate individuals you trust to make decisions for you if you are detained. They can help you withdraw money for deportation expenses or pay a mortgage. You can sign a power of attorney agreement to give this power to someone if you are arrested.

Source: Reprinted with permission from the American Friends Service Committee, *Protect Yourself from Immigration Raids* (Takoma Park, MD: CASA of Maryland, n.d.)

✔ Make sure your family has your immigration number (if you have one) and your full name and your date of birth. You will find this number on your work permission or your residency card. The number begins with an "A."

✔ Make sure your family knows how to contact you if you are detained. Family members should contact the local office of Immigration and Customs Enforcement's Detention and Removal Branch if they do not know where you are detained. Ask to speak with the supervisory deportation officer, and give the full name and A# of the detainee. If you do not have the contact information for your local field office, contact the Washington DC Headquarters at 202-305-2734.

4. FIND AN IMMIGRATION ATTORNEY:

✔ Find an attorney who specializes in deportation defense who may be able to represent you if you are detained. Memorize the name and phone number of your immigration attorney.

✔ Have the names and phone numbers of several good immigration attorneys posted near the telephone at home so family members can call an attorney if you are detained.

5. HAVE A COPY OF ALL IMMIGRATION DOCUMENTS:

✔ Keep a copy of all immigration documents that have been filed with immigration with a friend or family member who you trust. Also, collect important papers, such as birth certificates, marriage certificates and passports. Place these documents in a secure, easy to find location so that your family can get access to these materials easily.

✔ Make a list of the names and contact information of any lawyer who has ever represented you.

Source: Reprinted with permission from the American Friends Service Committee, *Protect Yourself from Immigration Raids* (Takoma Park, MD: CASA of Maryland, n.d.).

RIGHT TO REMAIN SILENT CARD:

Present the following card to immigration or the police if you are arrested to exercise your right to remain silent and to request an attorney.

> **KNOW YOUR RIGHTS!**
> If you are detained by immigration or the police:
>
> ✔ Hand the card to the official, and remain silent.
>
> ✔ The card explains that you are exercising your right to refuse to answer any questions until you have consulted with a lawyer.
>
> **TO WHOM IT MAY CONCERN:**
>
> Please be informed that I am choosing to exercise my right to remain silent and the right to refuse to answer your questions. If I am detained, I request to contact an attorney immediately. I am also exercising my right to refuse to sign anything until I consult with my attorney.
>
> Thank you.

THESE MATERIALS WERE PREPARED THROUGH THE COLLABORATION OF:

CASA of Maryland
Detention Watch Network
National Immigration Project of the National Lawyer's Guild

Special thanks to Julie Dahlstrom of the National Immigration Project and Juan Carlos Ruiz of National Community Capacity Consultants for their work in developing the contents of these materials.

Layout and Popular Methodology
CASA of Maryland Education and Leadership Department

Illustrations
CASA of Maryland

Silver Spring, MD
March 2007

Source: Reprinted with permission from the American Friends Service Committee, *Protect Yourself from Immigration Raids* (Takoma Park, MD: CASA of Maryland, n.d.)

MY ACTION PLAN IN CASE OF AN ICE RAID

Keep this Action Plan in a location that is safe but easy to access by you and your family. Fill in the blanks with the pertinent information and mark Yes or No to the questions suggested here to help you plan what you would do in a particular situation.

I entered the country: _____ with inspection; _____ without inspection.

Yes ☐ No ☐ I have assets and personal items that can be converted into cash.

Yes ☐ No ☐ I have relatives in this community.

I charge Mr/Mrs/Ms _____ with a power of
(name of individual)
attorney or notarized statement to manage my assets and personal items in accordance with my instructions.

Yes ☐ No ☐ I want legal assistance from an attorney or paralegal in case of being held by ICE on immigration matters.

Yes ☐ No ☐ I have children at my home or who reside in my community.

☐ In case of my having to leave the country, I leave my children in the custody of my partner/spouse:

_____
(write the complete name of the individual above)

☐ In case of my having to leave the country, I wish to leave my children under the custody of a family member or another trusted person. Toward that end, I leave a power of attorney or notarized letter in his/her possession:

_____
(write the complete name of the individual above)

Yes ☐ No ☐ Immigration and Customs Enforcement (ICE) should be notified that I want my children to accompany me in case of repatriation to my country. I have already prepared travel documents authorizing my spouse or family member to take my children to wherever is necessary.

Yes ☐ No ☐ I have Form G-28 signed by me and/or for each member of my family that would need such document in case of being detained by ICE.

Yes ☐ No ☐ I have a retainer agreement with an attorney to represent me on immigration

matters. His/her name is: _____.

His/her phone is _____.

Source: Reprinted with permission from the American Friends Service Committee, *Protect Yourself from Immigration Raids* (Takoma Park, MD: CASA of Maryland, n.d.)

Yes ☐ **No** ☐ There is a copy of My Action Plan on file at my church, community organization or trade union. This institution already has instructions on how to help me:

_____

(name of institution with a copy of My Action Plan)

_____

(name of the individual responsible)

Yes ☐ **No** ☐ I want to leave all those assets and personal items that could not be converted into cash in the hands of a community organization for the use of other individuals in need:

_____

(name of organization)

_____

(name of the individual responsible)

Additional Information (optional)

Yes ☐ **No** ☐ I wish to report any and all problems that could be construed as a violation of my work rights, constitutional rights, or human rights. Toward that end I enclose information where I could be contacted outside the country, or to get in touch with two of my relatives and/or friends who could locate me after repatriation:

Name: _____

Phone: _____

Address: _____

_____

Name: _____

Phone: _____

Address: _____

_____

Prepared by Sandra Sanchez, director, AFSC Immigrant Voices Program, Des Moines, IA. This document may be used by any church, trade union, educational or community organization as long as you credit us in your events. Thanks!

Source: Reprinted with permission from the American Friends Service Committee, *Protect Yourself from Immigration Raids* (Takoma Park, MD: CASA of Maryland, n.d.)

SAFETY PLANNING FOR SURVIVORS OF VIOLENCE

ABOUT SAFETY PLANNING . . .

A safety plan can help you stay safer even when you think you won't leave and even if your abuser doesn't live with you. If you are concerned about your safety, develop a safety plan. Do it for yourself. Do it for the safer life that you and your children deserve.

A safety plan is a tool to help you think about what you can do to protect yourself from abuse. This information can get you started. To speak to someone about a personal plan that suits your situation, call your local domestic violence program.

The information here comes from the collective experience of domestic violence shelters, police, prosecutors, and other battered women. A safety plan is a tool that has worked for others, and it can help you think about ways in which you can stay safer. After you've reviewed this information, you may want more help. Confidential, free service is available to you when you call a domestic violence program.

THINGS I CAN DO BEFORE A VIOLENT INCIDENT . . .

- Identify a neighbor I can tell about the violence and ask them to call the police if they hear a disturbance at my house.

- Devise a code word or signal to use with family, friends, or neighbors when I need them to call the police.

- Open my own savings account to increase my independence.

- Leave money, an extra set of keys, copies of important documents, and extra clothes with someone I trust.

- Decide where I'll go if I leave my home, even if right now I don't think it will come to that.

- Identify a domestic-violence shelter to call. Find out if a friend or relative will let me stay with them or lend me money.

- Keep the shelter hotline close at hand and keep change or a calling card on me at all times.

- Identify which door, window, stairwell, or elevator offers the quickest way out of my home, and practice my escape route.

- Teach my children to dial 911.

Source: Reprinted with permission from Illinois Coalition Against Domestic Violence

- Pack a bag and have it ready to go in case I must leave home. Keep the bag in a private but accessible place where I can grab it quickly. I'll need to take the following items:

  - Money—cash, my checkbook, credit cards, ATM cards, and so forth

  - Identification—driver's license and registration, Social Security card, passport, green card, public assistance ID, work permit, and so forth

  - Important papers—such as divorce papers; school and vaccination records; and birth certificates for me and my children

  - Clothing

  - Keys—house, car, or work

  - Medications

- If I already have an order of protection, I need to keep it with me at all times.

- Review my safety plan as often as possible.

THINGS I CAN DO DURING A VIOLENT INCIDENT . . .

- If an argument starts, stay close to a room or area with easy access to an exit. Stay away from the bathroom, kitchen, or anywhere near weapons.

- Get away. Try to get my packed bag on the way out, but if it's too dangerous, just leave. Go to a relative, friend, or shelter.

- Call 911 or my local police. The police must try to protect you from future abuse. They are required to provide or arrange transportation to a hospital or other safe place for you. The police should also arrest the abuser if they have enough evidence of a crime. They must give you a paper that explains your rights and lists a social service agency that can help.

- Use my judgement and intuition. If the situation is very dangerous, I can give the abuser what he wants to calm him down. I have to protect myself and the kids until we are out of danger.

THINGS I CAN DO AFTER A VIOLENT INCIDENT . . .

Get medical attention immediately. Ask the clinic to take pictures of my injuries.

- Make a police report, even if I don't want the abuser arrested. The report will become evidence of past abuse, which might prove helpful to me in the future. The abuser will not be notified that you made the report. . . . Make the report as soon as possible after the abuse.

Source: Reprinted with permission from Illinois Coalition Against Domestic Violence

- Save evidence, in case I decide to take legal action now or later. Evidence includes medical records and police reports, dated photos of my injuries or the house in disarray, torn clothing, any weapons used, and statements from anyone who saw the attack.

- Go to court to get an order of protection from domestic abuse. I can call the local domestic violence program to learn more about this option and to get help with court action.

- Seek out people who want to help me. Decide who I can talk openly with to receive the support I need. Plan to attend a victim's support group for at least two weeks to learn more about myself and the relationship.

- During an emergency, call 911 or local police.

- I can increase my safety and prepare in advance for the possibility of further violence. I have choices about how to best get myself and my children to safety.

Source: Reprinted with permission from Illinois Coalition Against Domestic Violence

INDEX

Delara, M., 184
Department of State. *See* U.S. Department of State
Deportations
    fear of, 343–344, 393
    resisting, 118–119
    from United States, 30, 117, 390, 393
Depression
    of human trafficking survivors, 299
    of LGBTQ people, 322
    of refugees, 65
    screening tools, 236
    social isolation and, 283
    of trauma survivors, 29, 279, 283
    See also Mental health
Detention
    of asylum seekers, 278, 391
    of children, 116–117, 390
    conditions at centers, 391
    resisting, 118–119
    U.S. policies, 116–117, 158, 390, 391, 392–393
    of women, 116–117
Development-induced displacement, 11, 12
Diagnostic and Statistical Manual of Mental
        Disorders (DSM), 135, 136
Direct practice, 127
    See also Individuals, practice with
Disaster-induced displacement, 11, 12, 35, 37, 389
Discrimination
    in communities, 104–106, 107–108
    contexts, 103–106
    coping strategies, 100, 106–108, 109–110
    data collection, 100–101
    ethnic, 46
    group versus personal, 100, 101–103
    against LGBTQ individuals, 321, 322
    perceived, 99–100, 101–103
    racial, 104–105, 106, 109–110, 132
    against stateless persons, 38
    as stressor, 132
    in workplace, 103–104, 106–107
Displacement, 11, 12
    See also Internally displaced persons; Migration;
        Refugees
Domestic employment, 115–116
Domestic violence. *See* Intimate partner violence
Domestic Violence Safety Plan (NCADV), 198
Dow, H. D., 127, 133
Drachman, D., 183

DSM. *See* Diagnostic and Statistical Manual of
    Mental Disorders
Duran, B., 205

Ecological responsiveness, 371
Ecological systems perspective
    benefits and challenges, 88 (table)
    children and youth, 344–345,
        345 (figure), 348
    in community practice, 206–208, 210
    concepts, 86
    contexts, 244, 385, 386
    in practice with families, 161, 166 (table)
    in practice with LGBTQ immigrants and
        refugees, 322–323
    training local workforce, 257
Economic contributions of immigrants, 15, 20
    See also Employment; Local workforce, culturally
        appropriate training for
Economic empowerment, 118
Education
    challenges for migrants, 281
    in cultural competence, 368
    of professionals working with migrants, 378
    of social workers, 390, 392–393
    See also Schools
Eilertson, D. E., 247
Eisenman, D. P., 278
Ellis, B. H., 346, 348, 351–352
El Salvador
    asylum seekers from, 9
    immigrants from, 101–102, 104–105
    unaccompanied minors from, 35–36, 390
    undocumented migrants from, 9, 10 (figure)
    See also Central America
Elsass, P., 137
*Emotional Health Manual. See Manual of
    Emotional Health*
Emotional safety, 284
Employment
    assistance services, 49
    availability in host countries, 49–50, 132,
        281–282
    discrimination in, 103–104, 106–107
    training, 50
    of women, 115–116
Empowerment
    of clients, 375, 376

idioms, 268–269, 371

importance, 371

nonverbal communication and, 139, 142, 143, 371

See also Interpreters

Latin America. *See* Central America

Latinas, community-based practices, 212–217

See also Mexican immigrants; Women; Women's support groups

Latino cultures, importance of family, 186

Latvia, stateless persons in, 38

Learning and training needs assessment (LTNA), 259–264, 265 (figure)

Learning theories, 130

Lebanon, refugees in, 2

Legal issues, 282

Lesbian, gay, bisexual, transgender, and queer (LGBTQ) immigrants and refugees

asylum seekers, 28

English-language training, 331

estimated number of, 313

fear of disclosure, 313

fear of persecution, 28, 322

gay affirmative practice, 324–329, 325 (figure), 331–332

health, 322

intimate partner violence, 322

language and terminology, 314–318, 331

mental health needs, 322

practice with, 322–332

risks, 322

trauma-informed practice, 329–332

Lesbian, gay, bisexual, transgender, and queer (LGBTQ) people

criminalized behaviors, 313, 320, 322

discrimination against, 321, 322

health, 321, 322–323

identity formation, 313–314, 318–320, 327–328

language and terminology, 314–318

mental health needs, 322

stigmatization, 313, 317, 320–321

in United States, 316–317

Lesbians, 315

Letiecq, B., 206

Lev-Wiesel, R., 167

LGBTQ immigrants. *See* Lesbian, gay, bisexual, transgender, and queer immigrants and refugees

Liberatory psychological perspective, 207

Lie, B., 247

Life model, 86, 88 (table)

Linton, R., 328

Local workforce

capacity building, 257–258, 270

power dynamics, 260

Local workforce, culturally appropriate training for

delivery, 266–269

developing programs, 264–266

evaluation and follow-up, 269–270

integrative approach, 257

interpreters, 266, 269

language issues, 264–265, 266, 268–269

needs assessment, 259–264, 265 (figure)

participation, 269

preparations, 257–258

roles of professionals, 266–267

sensitive topics, 261–262, 267–268

terminology use, 268

Lord, G., 185–186

Loyola University Chicago, School of Social Work, 183, 189–190

LTNA. *See* Learning and training needs assessment

Lucia, V. C., 340

Lundeberg, K., 167

Lundy, Marta, 189–190

Lysgaard, S., 43

MAAs. *See* Mutual aid associations

Manual of Emotional Health (*El Manual de Salud Emocional*)

future use, 197–200

history in Mexico, 180

leadership training, 181

methodology, 182

principles, 182

revisions for use in United States, 181–183

themes, 180, 182, 187, 187–188 (table), 193–194, 198

use in rural Mexican communities, 180–181

See also Women's support groups

Marginalization

collective action, 207

of cultural groups, 45

multiple domains, 281–283

Marques, L., 341

Medicaid, 61–62

Self-help groups, 182
Self-sufficiency, 49
Settlement houses, 383
Sex, biological construct, 315
Sexual orientation
    definition, 315
    fluidity, 315, 317
    See also Lesbian, gay, bisexual, transgender, and
        queer immigrants and refugees
Sexual preference, 315
Sexual violence
    in Cambodia, 255
    cultural sensitivities in discussing, 261–262
    health consequences, 299, 304
    mental health needs of survivors, 299–301, 304
    mental health services for survivors, 304–306
    in migration journeys, 299
    prevalence, 299, 303
    in refugee camps, 388
    screening for, 305
    victims, 46, 286
    See also Intimate partner violence
Shannon, P., 63
Shields, S. A., 81
Shulman, H., 207
Sikhs, 105
Sims, Brian, 391–392
Skinner, B. F., 130
Social ecology. *See* Ecological systems perspective
Social justice, 160, 161, 166 (table), 383, 384
Social networks, 164, 186, 304
Social services
    access to, 282
    in Mexico, 117
    for migrants, 205
    for resettlement, 44, 46–51, 368, 384, 385,
        386–387, 393–394
    for torture survivors, 286–287
Social services organizations. *See* Organizations
Social supports
    for children and youth, 346
    definition, 48
    effects of migration, 34, 67
    familial, 48–49, 164, 205, 217, 301, 346
    importance, 48, 206, 217, 371
Social work profession
    contexts of practice, 385
    credentials, 67–68

education, 390, 392–393
ethics codes, x, 384
history, x–xi, 82–83, 383–384
human rights and, 384
settlement services, 384, 385, 386–387, 393–394
training, 255
United Nations and, 384, 385
See also Local workforce
Socioeconomic systems, transitions to new, 34
Solidarity
    with client, 92
    with refugees, 83
    unbounded or inclusive, 171
    in women's groups, 180, 181, 182, 186
Solidarity movements, 83
Solution-focused family therapy, 162, 166 (table)
Solutions-focused problem-based theory,
        87, 91 (table)
Somalia, refugees from, 2, 60–61, 340, 346, 348,
        351–352
Spirituality. *See* Religion and spirituality
Stacey, M., 14
Stages of migration. *See* Migration stages
Stakeholders, community, 218, 351
State Department. *See* U.S. Department of State
Stateless persons, 8 (figure), 9, 38, 382
Stigma, 137, 313, 317, 320–321, 347
Stirratt, M. J., 81
Stith, S. M., 167
Storr, C., 340
Strengths perspective
    in community practice, 210
    cultural mergence model, 232–233, 244
    with families, 163–165, 171
    gay affirmative practice, 326–327
    with refugees, 50
    See also Resilience
Stressors
    intimate partner violence and, 45–46
    in migration process, 40, 132–133, 163, 179,
        216–217, 387
    pre-migration, 132–133, 216, 372
    in resettlement process, 50, 65, 115, 132–133,
        216–217, 229, 281–283, 343–344
    for trauma-exposed immigrants and refugees,
        276–278
    for undocumented migrants, 41–42, 216
    for women, 184–185